MARKETING RESEARCH
IN CANADA

MARKETING RESEARCH IN CANADA

René Y. Darmon   McGill University
Michel Laroche   Concordia University
K. Lee McGown   Concordia University

Canadian Cataloguing in Publication Data

Darmon, René Y.
    Marketing research in Canada

Bibliography: p.
Includes index.
ISBN 0-7715-5609-8

1. Marketing research – Canada.   2. Marketing
research.   I. Laroche, Michel.   II. McGown, K. L.
III. Title.

HF5415.2.D37 1989   658.8′3971   C89-093293-X

Design/Michael van Elsen

ISBN 0-7715-**5609-8**

1 2 3 4 5   JD   93 92 91 90 89

Written, Printed, and Bound in Canada

CONTENTS

Foreword *vii*
Preface *ix*

■ Foreword

My review of *Marketing Research in Canada* was from the perspective of a practitioner of marketing research for more than fifteen years and a former university professor for eight years. My conclusion is that this book is truly different from competing textbooks. Its distinctively Canadian content and practical and conceptual frameworks will undoubtedly be of immense benefit to its intended audiences—students, instructors, and practitioners of marketing research.

The book's Canadian content is unique, including an up-to-date and revealing history of marketing research in Canada, an in-depth review of the problems and research issues particular to Canada, the numerous Canadian examples presented, and the Canadian mini-cases.

The authors also advance some interesting propositions such as, for example, that marketing research is the cornerstone for the implementation of the marketing concept, and that a marketing management decision problem is an action-oriented issue whereas a marketing research problem is an information-seeking issue. In addition, pseudo-research is defined and discussed in a frank and forthright manner.

For the marketing research student, *Marketing Research in Canada* provides numerous well-explained and well-presented examples and applications to further clarify discussions. Careers and compensation levels are discussed, and the subject of ethics in marketing research is explored. In addition, readers are cautioned against taking for granted the advanced technology available for marketing research activities.

Marketing research instructors will find that this textbook is best suited for a first-year course in the subject. Its varied content and structure permits its use in community colleges, universities, and CEGEPs. Again, the numerous examples and applications provided (including details of the contents of a business-world marketing research proposal) will be invaluable, facilitating the communication of many concepts in this field. In addition, the questions at the end of each chapter will aid in class discussion of the relevant issues, and the mini-cases provide an opportunity to highlight the subject matter covered in the relevant chapter.

Marketing Research in Canada will also prove very useful for practitioners of marketing research. Several informative aspects of the field are covered, such as organization and compensation, and sources of information and data are identified, including sample data reports from such organizations as PMB, BBM, and the A.C. Nielsen Company. "Must" reading for this group are the applications chapters, Chapters 14 to 16, and Appendix 2, which reviews the ethical issues in marketing research.

Of prime importance is the fact that *Marketing Research in Canada* is *not* an adapted U.S. textbook, as is the case with many introductory marketing textbooks. It is uniquely Canadian, as evidenced by the numerous Canadian examples, applications, and references to many Canadian authors, including, for example, Barnes, Brisoux, Cooper, Day, Forbes, Greeno, Haines, Jones, McTavish, Turner, Wyckham, and yours truly, just to name a few.

In summary, this straightforward book is a valuable asset to those exposed to and involved with marketing research in Canada. Perhaps it will be adapted for the U.S. market!

Jacques C. Bourgeois, PhD.
National Partner
Marketing Strategy and Research
The Coopers & Lybrand Consulting Group

Preface

Marketing managers of Canadian companies operate in an increasingly competitive and complex environment. Traditional markets are being eroded by foreign competitors. Consumer needs are constantly evolving, forcing companies to further segment their markets into "niche strategies" and to modify their products to satisfy these new needs. To achieve economies of scale, companies are forced to seek new international markets, and the cycle begins again.

To respond to these challenges in an effective and efficient manner, marketing managers in Canadian companies must have sound, accurate, and relevant information on all of their markets—current and potential, domestic and international. This type of information is often not easy to find or to obtain, which highlights the necessity for marketing research.

Many marketing research methods and techniques are dependent on a number of factors unique to Canada, including its geography; its patterns of population distribution and other demographic factors; its multicultural make-up and strong regional cultures; and its bilingual, and in some areas, multilingual nature. Therefore, a textbook such as *Marketing Research in Canada*, developed by Canadian writers and researchers, is essential to students, instructors, and practitioners.

The main objectives of *Marketing Research in Canada* are

- to provide the reader with a basic understanding of the marketing research process within the environment faced by Canadian managers, through an applications-oriented approach. The use of numerous practical examples and realistic cases provides a sound framework for learning.

- to provide marketing managers and researchers with the proper means to obtain sound, accurate information on Canadian markets, and to help them to assess the managerial significance of this information.

- to develop an understanding of the role of marketing research as a managerial function within the firm, and to assess the relevance and limitations of marketing research to the decision-making process. This objective applies to small, medium, and large Canadian firms, in the consumer, industrial, and service areas.

- to analyse the various steps involved in the process of obtaining information relevant to decision making, to describe theoretical and practical frameworks for each step of the process, and to assess the usefulness of alternative approaches.

Marketing Research in Canada will be of great interest and assistance to three particular groups of people:

- marketing students in Canadian universities, community colleges, and CEGEPs taking electives in marketing research or working toward a certificate in marketing research

- instructors of marketing research courses

- marketing managers and researchers in Canadian firms, directors in government agencies, and private consultants doing marketing research in Canada

Marketing Research in Canada has distinctive characteristics that will appeal to many readers and users:

- All examples, illustrations, exercises, and problems are relevant to the Canadian student's frame of reference. The text endeavours to answer all questions relating to marketing research in the Canadian environment, from problem formulation, research design, and secondary sources of data, to measurement and questionnaire design issues in a multicultural society.

- *Marketing Research in Canada* is written in clear and simple language, using a minimum of quantitative techniques. The only prerequisite for comprehension of this text is one semester of marketing. *Marketing Research in Canada* is complete, concise, and very easy to read, making it ideal for a one-semester course.

- The textbook has a strong managerial orientation throughout, with examples, questions, problems, mini-cases, and three "applications" chapters. It makes extensive use of charts, explicative diagrams, and relevant Canadian examples, as well as statistical information from appropriate sources (e.g., Statistics Canada, trade publications).

- At the end of each chapter are a summary of the chapter's contents, a set of related questions and problems, and a complete reference list of information sources. The mini-cases challenge students to apply the principles learned to realistic situations, and promote class discussion of the material.

- A comprehensive *Instructor's Manual* accompanies *Marketing Research in Canada*.

The organization of *Marketing Research in Canada* follows the same logic as the development of a marketing research project. The text is divided into four major parts.

The first part, *Decision Making and Marketing Research*, introduces the reader to the marketing research process (Chapter 1), the role of marketing research in the firm's marketing information system (Chapter 2), determination of the research problems to be tackled (Chapter 3), and the nature of research designs (Chapter 4).

The second part, *The Data-collection Process*, provides a step-by-step approach for collecting the information to answer the problem at hand, from internal and external secondary sources in Canada (Chapter 5), collecting primary data (Chapter 6), designing and conducting a survey (Chapter 7), constructing an effective questionnaire (Chapter 8), determining the proper measurement of the variables of the problem (Chapter 9), and defining the proper sample (Chapter 10).

The third part, *Data Analysis and Report Preparation*, introduces the reader in a non-technical, progressive fashion to elementary statistics (Chapter 11) and advanced statistics (Chapter 12), and explains how to write a good research report (Chapter 13).

The fourth part, *Selected Applications*, contains chapters on the applications of all of the previous chapters to product research in Canada (Chapter 14), advertising research in Canada (Chapter 15), and sales and distribution location research (Chapter 16).

Finally, two important issues are treated in the appendixes. Appendix 1 deals with the contemporary use of computers, and Appendix 2 with the ethical issues in marketing research in Canada.

Many people have worked very hard to make this book possible, and we are extremely grateful to all of them. First of all, we are most grateful to Gage Educational Publishing for having the foresight to publish the first Canadian marketing research textbook, and particularly to Robert M. McElman, former president of Gage, for his leadership of an energetic and committed editorial, sales, and marketing group; Janet Turner for her encouragement, assistance, and effective managing of this project; and June Trusty and Darleen Rotozinski for their editorial assistance.

Secondly, we owe a great debt of gratitude to all of the reviewers who spent long hours reading the earlier drafts of the manuscript, and provided us with very useful feedback, comments, and suggestions. Having acted as reviewers ourselves, we know that this is an act of dedication to the discipline. Thus, many thanks to Stan Reid (formerly at the University of New Brunswick, now at the University of West Indies); John Knapp (Northern Alberta Institute of Technology); Mari-Lou MacDonald-Wright (Fanshawe College), and a fourth reviewer who wishes to remain anonymous.

Thirdly, we thank our colleague Jerry A. Rosenblatt (Concordia) for his generous contribution of Appendix 1. Also, many thanks to Michel Bergier, Chankon Kim, B. Z. Gidengil, and Kemal Buyukkurt (Concordia) for their useful suggestions and encouragement during the development of this manuscript.

In addition, this project has benefited from the assistance and strong encouragement of some of the best professional marketing researchers in Canada: Frank S. Lyman (Canadian Facts), Chris Commins, A.B. Blankenship, Chuck Chakrapani, Hugh Thom and Ken Deal (Professional Marketing Research Society), Marilyn E. Sandler (Canadian Association of Marketing Research Organizations), and Jacques Bourgeois (The Coopers & Lybrand Consulting Group). Also, our secretaries, Pina Vicario, Susan Altimas, Carol Anselmi, Nancy Theriault, and Margaret Nickel deserve our sincere thanks for their patience, attention to detail, and competent typing of a long and complicated manuscript.

Finally, we are thankful to our families for their support and understanding during the extensive process of developing the manuscript. And to all of you interested in marketing research in Canada, we sincerely hope that this book will help you to stay ahead in the information age.

René Y. Darmon
Michel Laroche
K. Lee McGown

PART 1

DECISION MAKING AND MARKETING RESEARCH

CHAPTER 1

THE MARKETING RESEARCH PROCESS

Consider the following situations:

- A Canadian manufacturer wants to bring out a new, economy, low-horse power, high-gasoline-mileage automobile. Such a car might satisfy demands for vehicles that produce a minimum amount of pollution, but the manufacturer wonders if a Canadian-made car will satisfy Canadian motorists.

- The dean of the School of Business at a new and rapidly growing urban university, knowing that many undergraduate students work full-time, is considering offering more evening courses. However, the dean does not know if the demand for these extra courses will justify hiring more faculty.

- A recent college graduate with a major in Marketing wants to remain in the small town near the campus and pursue her interest in stereos by opening a hi-fi shop catering to college students. She knows that students are interested in buying stereo equipment and parts but wonders if, considering students' limited resources, such a business could generate the sales needed to survive.

- Friends and acquaintances of the owner of a professional football team urge him to move his team to a new and larger home stadium on the outskirts of the city. Although the new stadium rental will be substantially higher and it will thus be necessary to raise ticket prices 25%, profits will be much greater if the new stadium averages attendance of at least 75% of seating capacity during each home game.

All of the business people just described face a common problem, one faced every day by planners in our society: how to make the right decision under conditions of uncertainty. Each situation presents the marketing problem of determining consumer preferences and then satisfying these preferences within the context of the organization and the environment in which it operates. Obviously, the task of determining and satisfying consumer preferences is an enormously complex one, especially if such a task is to be successfully and profitably accomplished by a firm in a competitive, capitalistic environment. However, one fundamental and increasingly important method by which uncertainty can be reduced in dealing with marketing problems is **marketing research**.

What Is Marketing Research?

The American Marketing Association has developed the most universally accepted definition of marketing research as "the systematic gathering, recording and analyzing of data about problems relating to the marketing of goods and services."[1] This definition has two important aspects. First, it is sufficiently broad to include all problems, including those of the non-profit sector, encountered in the marketing of goods and services. Second, it explicitly recognizes the systematic nature of the research process in which data are gathered, recorded, and analysed.

Although this definition does not say so directly, it should be noted that the data must always be gathered, recorded, and analysed in an objective and accurate fashion. All too often, objectivity and accuracy are missing from research investigations, and the research is designed only to support or "prove" what management wants to see. A common example of this type of research can be seen almost every day on television commercials in which research studies are cited to prove that "doctors recommend" the sponsor's particular product. Left unsaid by the sponsor is that only two medical doctors need to have recommended the product to make this statement technically correct, although the product might have left hundreds of other physicians unimpressed.

Properly conducted marketing research—unlike much research used to sell consumer goods or to justify top management decisions and ideas—is a means of acquiring needed information to aid management in making marketing decisions and in identifying and solving marketing problems. As the importance of the marketing function and the cost of business decisions have increased steadily and dramatically over the years, so has the need for accurate and objective information obtained through the marketing research process.

In this chapter, the marketing process and the role of research in the firm's marketing efforts will be examined. Also, the location of the research department in the organizational structure, the organization of the research department, and the duties and responsibilities usually assigned to research will be discussed.

The fast-changing, dynamic nature of Canadian business today has dramatically increased the necessity for accurate, up-to-date information, so that executives can act immediately on profit threats and opportunities.

Marketing Research and Marketing

Twentieth-century Canadians live in an era of increasing specialization where individual self-sufficiency has become a rarity. Thus, each of us is highly dependent on the actions of others, and we must trade with each other to survive.

Using money as a medium of exchange, we acquire desired goods and services brought to us by a complex marketing system and enjoy a standard of living undreamed of in earlier times.

The Development of Marketing

Marketing activities are essential to the level of affluence and the high consumption patterns enjoyed by Canadians. A modern marketing system cannot exist without efficient producers and affluent consumers. Without a modern, highly industrialized manufacturing sector, the marketing sector languishes, because it is in this commercial environment that exchange flourishes, with the accompanying specialization and division of labour.

Marketing, to the American Marketing Association, is "the process of planning and executing the conception, pricing, promotion and distribution of ideas, goods, and services to create exchanges that satisfy individual and organizational objectives."[2] This definition recognizes that marketing constitutes the exchange process by which human needs and wants are satisfied through the acquisition of products. Goods and services that the consumer accepts as satisfying some needs and wants should be developed with the customer in mind. This definition encompasses the activities of non-profit institutions as well as the marketing of an idea (e.g., "stop smoking") or a service (e.g., insurance).

Firms whose activities begin with the customer, not with the production process, are said to be **marketing oriented**. In the past, many business firms in our society were strictly **production oriented**. That is, especially in times when goods and services were scarce, it was considered important to produce goods first and then worry about selling them. Subsequently, many firms moved toward sales orientation, where the marketing function was viewed simply as a sales function: the firms produced goods, and it was the marketing departments' duty to sell these goods. Other functions of advertising or research were basically ignored or unknown. In recent years, though, a marketing orientation has become more predominant. Firms having a marketing orientation recognize that they must identify customer needs and then fulfil them. Such a marketing orientation implies adoption of the marketing concept.

One firm that has passed through all of these stages is Pillsbury, the manufacturer of flour, baking mixes, and animal feeds. Founded in 1869, Pillsbuy was a production-oriented firm until about 1930. The company then moved to a sales orientation, which continued basically unchanged for almost thirty years, until in 1958 the firm became a total "marketing company."[3]

The Marketing Concept and the Marketing Mix

The marketing concept, first implemented at General Electric, is a philosophy or a way of thinking that permeates an entire organization. This marketing concept incorporates three key criteria:

1. *Customer orientation*: The objectives of the firm are stated in eternal human needs.

2. *Profitable sales*: The key objective is long-run, not short-run, profit.

3. *Integrated marketing*: Top marketing management reports directly to the firm's top management.

Figure 1.1 graphically illustrates the task of marketing management in incorporating the marketing concept. The central focus of the marketing concept is the customer, shown here in the centre of the diagram as *Market Segments*, surrounded by the **marketing mix**—product, price, place (otherwise known as distribution), and promotion. These four factors are considered generally control-

FIGURE 1.1
Decision Framework of the Marketing Manager

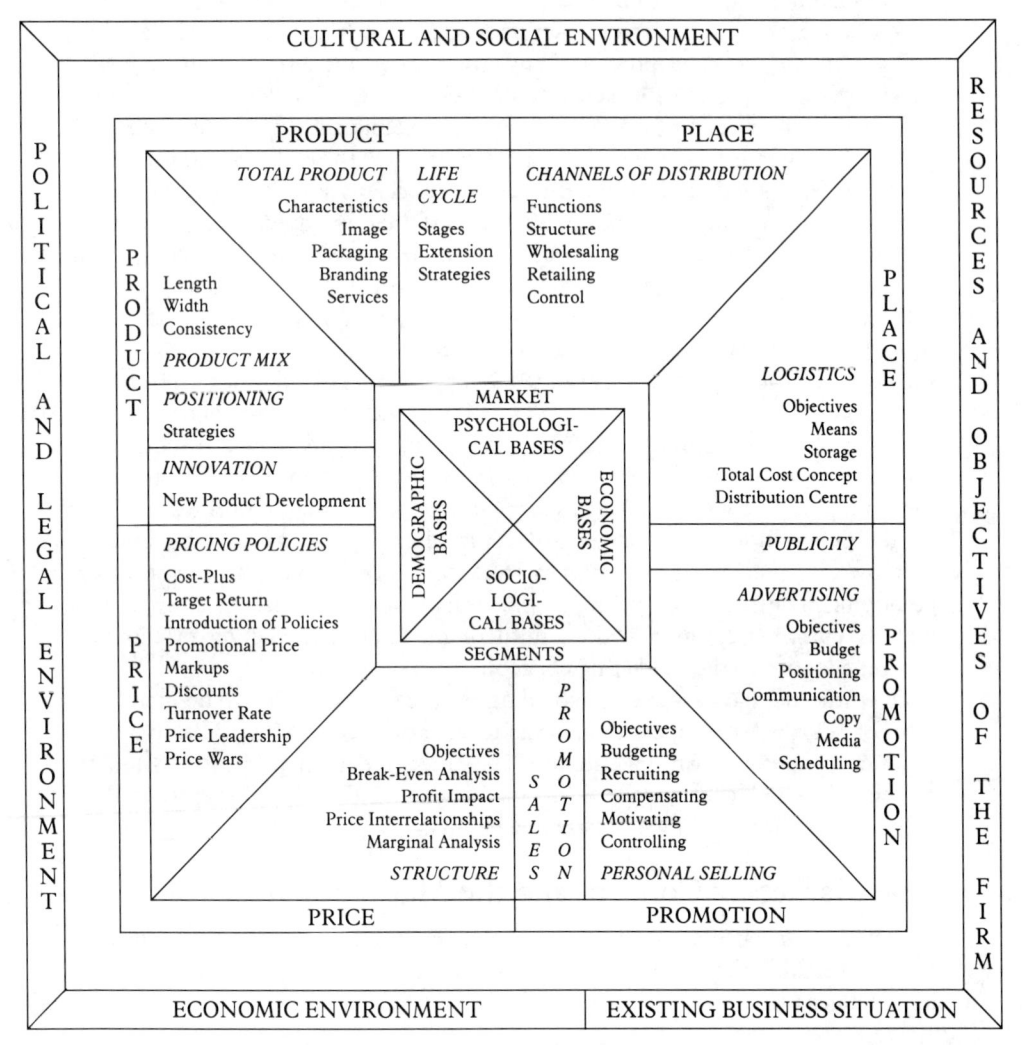

Source: René Y. Darmon, Michel Laroche, and John V. Petrof, *Marketing in Canada: A Management Perspective.* Toronto: McGraw-Hill Ryerson, 1985, p. 46.

lable by the firm. Factors that are less controllable by the firm include the political and legal environment, the resources and objectives of the firm, the existing business situation, the economic environment, and lastly, the cultural and social environment.

The key activity that makes the marketing concept work is marketing research. If the central focus of the firm is the consumer and if the objective of the firm is consumer orientation with profitable sales, then it is only through marketing research that the firm can ascertain what consumers desire and then determine how to satisfy these wants.

Central to the task of marketing research is research of the four basic factors of the marketing mix that are generally controllable by the firm: product policies, pricing policies, distribution policies, and promotion policies. Research into the external and generally uncontrollable factors, shown in the outside border of Figure 1.1, is also necessary for firms that want to maintain a competitive market position. For example, most large firms engage in economic forecasting, and an anticipated downturn in the economy will cause such firms to forego new capital spending.

Thus, we can see that modern marketing goes hand in hand with twentieth-century industrialized society in North America. Our industrial society functions on the bases of exchange and specialization. In moving away from the production orientation of earlier times, more and more firms have adopted a marketing orientation and the marketing concept. The cornerstone of this foundation is marketing research—only through modern marketing research techniques can the marketing concept be fully implemented.

■ Marketing Research in Canada

A Brief History of Marketing Research in Canada

Just as modern marketing and the marketing concept are relatively recent developments, marketing research, as an organized business activity, is not only relatively recent but is still in its infancy. The birth of modern marketing research can be traced back to 1911, when the first formal marketing research department was established. In that year Charles Parlin was appointed manager of the Commercial Research and Advertising Department of the Curtis Publishing Company. However, there were virtually no organized marketing research activities before World War I. Research techniques were then relatively unsophisticated and consisted of first-hand observation, a few elementary surveys, and some sales and operating cost analyses.

The years between the two world wars saw the gradual development of more advanced marketing research techniques. That the users of these techniques had a long way to go, however, was well demonstrated by the 1936 *Literary Digest* election disaster: in that year, on the basis of some rather crude sampling, the now-defunct *Literary Digest* predicted that Alf Landon would defeat Franklin Roosevelt in the presidential election. The reverse actually happened. In 1923 the

A.C. Nielsen Company, now the world's largest marketing research firm, was established in the United States. Subsequently, under the influence of the U.S. research firms and a few manufacturing companies, marketing research was introduced in Canada.

In their history of marketing research in Canada, Blankenship *et al.* identified five important periods, as detailed below.[4]

The Beginning (1929-38)

The first Canadian marketing research department was established in 1929 by Warren Brown, president of National Publicity, which later became Cockfield Brown. As told by Henry King, who on January 2, 1929, became the first full-time Canadian marketing researcher:

> Warren Brown, then President of National Publicity, had heard and read about this new development, "Marketing Research", in the United States, recognized that it was the coming thing, and had the vision to see that its adoption in Canada by what was then one of Canada's top advertising agencies, and still is, would be extremely advantageous.
>
> Before 1928, market research data had been obtained only from local publications, a source that Warren Brown knew was both inadequate and in many instances unreliable or biased.
>
> In January, 1929, a merger of Warren Brown's National Publicity and Harry Cockfield's Advertising Service took effect, and arrangements were made that Goforth would be the full-time Director of Research at Cockfield Brown when the McGill academic year ended.[5]

In its first few years, the department worked on projects for both agency clients and Canadian organizations such as the Department of Fisheries and British Properties of Vancouver.[6]

The first *independent* Canadian research agency, Ethel Fulford and Associates, was established in Toronto in 1932 with the encouragement of Brown. Frank Ryan, who was employed by Cockfield Brown, suggested in 1932 that there was a need for some dependable information on the number of homes listening to radio stations.[7] The purpose of this new type of agency was to go beyond collecting compiled information to the direct gathering of data, to provide independent information to the advertising agency. The latter would use this information to sell advertising time on radio. This company grew rapidly and in 1943 changed its name to Canadian Facts Ltd. Among its first clients were Procter & Gamble and Lever Brothers.

During this period, there is some evidence of the existence of three other independent research firms: Canadian Business Research Bureau (1929-35); the Harold S. Edgar District Market Surveys (1933-?), and on October 1, 1936, Walker Elliott and Paul Haynes established in Montreal a research firm called Elliott-Haynes (which was renamed Elliott Research in 1965). Paul Haynes was also a professional hockey player with the Canadiens.

To summarize, this early period was characterized by a strong U.S. influence, an emphasis on survey research and on media and copy research. In the beginning, marketing research was very unsophisticated, very peripheral to decision making, and almost all of the firms were located in Toronto.[8]

The War Interlude (1939–45)

Responding to the research need of U.S. firms operating in Canada, the A.C. Nielsen Company of Canada started an office in Toronto on April 1, 1944.

Opinion polls came into being during this period and in 1941 Dr. George Gallup, responding to requests by *The Toronto Star* and Southam Newspapers, helped form the Canadian Institute of Public Opinion, which in 1955 became the Gallup Poll of Canada.

To help advance the discipline, practice, and professional standards of advertising research, several organizations were created. The Bureau of Broadcast Measurement (BBM) was created in 1944 to provide broadcast media services (see Chapter 15). One of the earliest Canadian consumer panels was established in 1939 by Walter Smith, who worked in the Catalogue Division of Eaton's.

To summarize, this period was characterized by a continuing stronger U.S. influence, and the main emphasis of research was on the war effort and on media studies. Research firms performed well and grew.[9]

The Early Post-war Years (1946–59)

During the years following World War II, marketing research made rapid strides. In these years, probability sampling (introduced in 1948 by Canadian Facts), regression methods, store panels, omnibus studies, motivation research, regression and correlations (terms that will be explained later), and other more sophisticated research techniques came into widespread use. Since that time, marketing research departments have been established at a rapid rate and few large firms today are without at least one person assigned full-time to research.

As shown in Figure 1.2, approximately 97% of all existing Canadian marketing research departments were started since 1948, 87% since 1958, 69% since 1968, and 38% since 1978.[10] These figures are comparable to those for the United States, with the difference being that 8% of the U.S. marketing research departments were started before 1948, compared with 3% in Canada.

After resigning from Elliott-Haynes, Paul Haynes and three other partners established International Surveys Limited (ISL) in 1946, with the assistance of, and patterned after, Industrial Surveys (a U.S. firm that later changed its name to Market Research Corporation of America). Haynes put together a national consumer panel diary service, which provided longitudinal data for both purchases and media exposure.

David Starch (Canada) Limited was established in 1958 as a joint partnership between the U.S. company, Daniel Starch and Staff, and Gruneon Research Limited, a large Canadian research firm of the time.

Created in 1949 the Canadian Advertising Research Foundation is a non-profit organization supported by advertisers, advertising agencies, and media. Its objectives are to develop new research methods and techniques, analyse and evaluate existing methods and techniques, and establish research standards. For example, the Foundation distributes a booklet entitled *Media Research Standards and Full Consultation Procedures and Requirements*.[11]

The period of 1946 to 1959 was the golden age for the creation of research firms. There was a high growth in the number of marketing research departments in

FIGURE 1.2
Number of New Marketing Research Departments
Formed in Successive 5-Year Periods
(not cumulative)

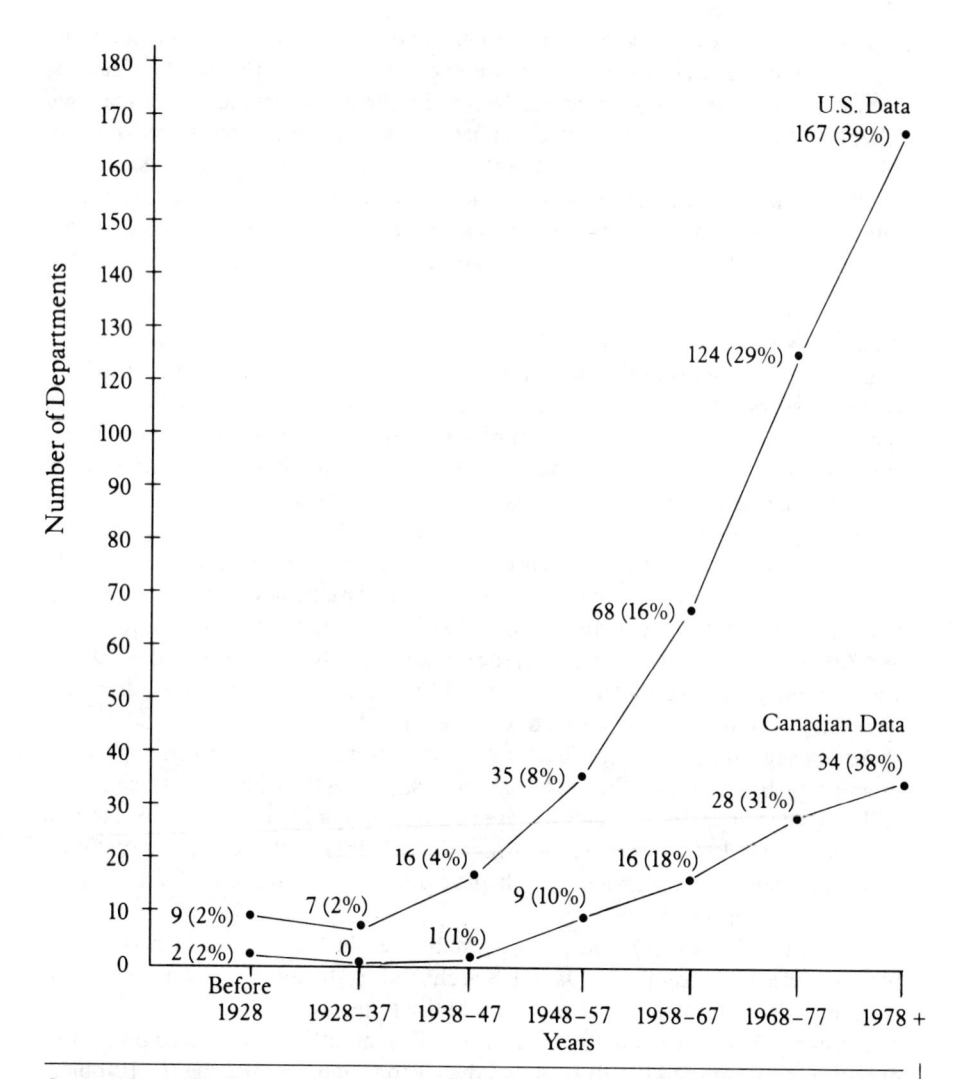

Source: Joyce Chang, David Conway, and George H. Haines, Jr., "A Comparison of Business Use of Marketing Research in Canada and the United States," *Marketing,* 7. Ed. Thomas E. Muller, Administrative Sciences Association of Canada (ASAC), p. 282.

advertising agencies (one in five had a research department in 1959), advertising research departments, and retailer research. Media research continued to develop and other institutions also were discovering marketing research. Methods and techniques were changing rapidly, particularly sampling and motivation research.[12]

The Middle Post-war Years (1960–69)

In 1961 another major firm, Market Facts of Canada, was established as a joint venture of John Robertson, a Canadian, and the U.S. firm Market Facts Inc. In 1964 it built its consumer mail panels with 12 000 families, provided tracking studies, and introduced market segmentation to the Canadian market.

The sixties saw the creation of many university-based survey centres, in particular at the University of Alberta, York University, and the University of Montréal. Also in 1960, the Professional Marketing and Research Society (PMRS) was founded to provide a forum for the development and advancement of marketing research in Canada.

The years 1960 to 1969 were characterized by three major types of changes:[13]

1. *Institutional changes*: Moves to the brand management system, creation of tabulating firms and academic centres, political polling, and growth in media research

2. *Technical changes*: Virtual disappearance of motivation research, increased use of computers, and growth in mall research

3. *Changes in application areas*: The demise of automobile research and a lesser amount of research input from the United States

More Recent Years (1970–88)

In the seventies, Canada saw an influx of researchers from the United Kingdom, the creation of specialized agencies and boutiques, and the more widespread use of sophisticated research techniques. This period witnessed a proliferation of marketing research houses due to an increase in demand for such services and a better appreciation of the need for marketing information. Marketing research truly became a profession, requiring proper training and continuing education.

By 1985 the membership of PMRS had grown to more than 800, compared with 150 in 1970. In 1975 the Canadian Association of Marketing Research Organizations (CAMRO) was created, with its main objective being to foster high standards of quality and professionalism among marketing research companies.

The accomplishments of the years 1970 to 1988 will be highlighted in the rest of this chapter and also throughout this text.

Use of Marketing Research in Canada

One survey looked at Canadian companies that have at least one full-time employee in charge of marketing research.[14] However, many small or medium-sized firms that rely on market studies often cannot justify hiring an employee on a full-time basis to do research or the hiring of specialized agencies for such services. Thus, the following findings of this survey should be considered as conservative. Approximately, 39% of the companies surveyed had at least one full-time employee in charge of marketing research. This percentage varied according to the size of the company: 64% of large firms had a marketing research department, against 41% for medium-sized firms and 27% for small firms.

The trends revealed by this survey are quite interesting. The number of Canadian firms with a marketing research department more than doubled in every decade from 1950. This rate of increase was greatest for small firms.

These results and trends are similar to those found in other industrialized countries, indicating that marketing research plays a formal role in a large number of companies, and that it has become the rule rather than an exception. This tendency to rely on marketing research can be illustrated by two product introductions—*Pressdent*, and the launching of the Manic soccer team in Montreal.

The inventors of *Pressdent*, an aerosol-can toothpaste, asked an independent agency to conduct some research. It was found that

> *Crest* and *Colgate* dominate the market with 47% and 18% of sales, respectively, but that loyalty to more recent brands is far from rock-solid. More importantly, 70% of the people surveyed said they would be ready to purchase a toothpaste in an aerosol can. Another important point that was established is that 60% of women surveyed declared taste as the most important criterion in their choice.[15]

After this survey and before introduction, the product was tested by 250 men and women. These consumers found the package to be more clean and convenient and they liked the taste of the toothpaste, which they compared to that of *Crest*.

Before launching the Manic Soccer Club, a survey was done of the composition of soccer game audiences. It was found that attendees went to the stadium accompanied by two or more family members, and that women represented more than 35% of the spectators. Thus, the organizers decided to target the family market with a low-price strategy and family subscriptions that provided a 25% rebate.[16]

Considerations Specific to Canadian Marketing Research

Due to a number of factors relevant to the Canadian environment, several problems can be identified, as discussed below.

Costs Relative to Market Size

Canada is a relatively small country, approximately one-tenth the size of the United States. To obtain the same degree of precision as the United States in survey results, the cost of marketing research would be the same, everything else being equal, since precision is a function of the sample size (as will be explained in Chapter 10, "Sampling"). Thus, in comparison to the revenues, the cost of marketing research in Canada is much higher than it is in the United States.[17]

Patterns of Population Distribution

The mosaic nature of the Canadian population creates additional constraints for researchers, which contribute to increased research costs.[18] In addition to language problems, which will be discussed next, the uneven concentration of various groups in the population require more complicated sampling techniques as well as a larger sample size to properly cover the various subsamples. For example, in conducting a market test in Canada, it is often not possible to use one single market as representative of Canada as a whole. Instead one must use a combination of markets. Incidentally, the United States *does* have a single market that is held to represent the entire population of the United States Peoria, Illinois.

Multilingualism

Canada has two official languages, French and English, as well as sizable concentrations of other ethnic groups such as Italian, Ukrainian, Native peoples, Dutch, Scandinavian, Polish, German, and Chinese. Surveys have to be conducted using at least French and English versions, which adds to the cost of research in a number of ways:[19] translation can be done only by experts with proper pre-tests, field interviews have to be bilingual, and coding of open-ended questions has to be performed by experts. These same problems exist when the survey questionnaire must be in yet another language.

Some examples of the problems encountered when planning a study in English and then carrying it into French Canada are given by Jacques Ferron:

> ...because the study [plan] is finalized before translations come as an after-thought, clients are usually stuck with a methodology that works for only part of the total sample...attempting to measure a brand image by getting the respondents to personify a brand (in terms usually associated with real people) works well among anglophones, but hardly at all among francophones [who] cannot...respond in such "illogical" terms....[20]

Also, actual wording can become a real challenge. Literal translations often do not work, sometimes resulting in misleading wording. To ensure that questions mean the same thing to both audiences, Ferron feels that it requires "real French thinking" or a French researcher to unite the questions from the start. A poor translation might produce different findings between the English- and French-Canadian audiences, since the questions are perceived differently.

■ Role of Research in the Firm

Increasing Importance of Research

Administrators are becoming increasingly dependent on marketing research to supply them with the quick and accurate flow of information needed to make business decisions. The increasing importance of marketing research is based on three trends:

1. *The shift from local to national and international marketing*: Executives are located farther and farther away from their markets and therefore are more than ever dependent on accurate information flow for the decision-making

process. By being so far away from the place where sales occur, the executives can lose touch with the market and be unable to act on intuition. They must have reliable market information.

2. *The transition from consumer needs to consumer wants*: As consumers' **real income** (purchasing power) has risen, **discretionary income** (income that can be spent for non-essential goods and services) has become increasingly significant. Also, consumers are able to choose among competing products. Because discretionary income is used for non-essentials, marketing executives will require more information about the products on which buyers *want* to spend their income. Not only must the shopper decide whether to spend discretionary income for a colour television, a sailboat, a stereo system, or a vacation, but also a further decision must be made concerning the style, make, and model of colour television, sailboat, or stereo, or vacation destination. Measuring the strength and direction of consumer preferences is far more complex with discretionary than with essential expenditures, so marketing executives require more information on consumer preferences.

3. *The shift from price to non-price competition*: Marketers require extensive information on the effectiveness of such marketing tools as branding, product differentiation, advertising, and sales promotion, since it is these tools that create real or imagined differences in the minds of consumers about competing products. Firms lacking this essential information are at a competitive disadvantage in relation to other firms in the same industry. It could be expected that, all other things being equal, the firm with inadequate information flow (marketing research) will pay a severe penalty in the form of reduced sales and profits.

Types of Marketing Research Units

The structure of marketing research units in Canadian companies changed slowly from 1967 to 1984, as indicated in Table 1.1. The percentage of companies with a formal Canadian marketing research department has increased from 12% to 21.5%, and those with at least one person assigned to the marketing research function from 37% to 50.5%.[21] In addition, it was found that in 1984, 54% of existing advertising agencies had marketing research units.[22]

Corporate Location of the Marketing Research Department

Since the main purpose of marketing research is the provision of accurate and objective data about problems facing marketing management, it logically follows that the research unit should be located within the marketing department. Firms with marketing research departments are usually organized as illustrated in Figure 1.3. This diagram shows a somewhat simplified, but the most logical and typical, location of the marketing research department in large organizations. According to this arrangement the marketing research manager reports directly to the marketing vice-president and is on the same level as sales and advertising managers.

TABLE 1.1
Types of Marketing Research Units in Canada

Type of Unit	1967 %	1984 %	Change (1967–84)
Research departments in Canada doing work for entire company	8	14	6
Separate departments	2	6	4
Foreign departments, Canadian subsidiary	2	1.5	(.5)
Total having formal Canadian research department	12	21.5	9.5
No formal department; at least one person assigned to functions	25	29	4
Total delegating marketing research to specific staff personnel	37	50.5	13.5
Foreign departments only	8	4.5	(3.5)
Total with access to company research data	45	55	10
No employees formally engaged in market research	55	37	(10)
Other	–	8	–
Total	100	100	0

Source: Chang, et al., "Comparison of Business Use," p. 293.

However, in some types of businesses the marketing research manager reports directly to top management—the president and executive vice-president of the organization. For example, the American Marketing Association reported in 1978 that more than two-thirds of marketing research managers in advertising agencies reported directly to top management.[23] However, the majority of marketing research managers still report directly to marketing management. Although in 1967 more than 50% of marketing research managers reported to the president, vice-president, or general manager, in 1984 only 17.5% did so. About two-thirds of marketing research managers reported to sales or marketing management.[24] This perhaps indicates that marketing research is generally accepted as a normal function and is becoming better integrated into the decision-making process, which is a change of attitude from earlier times.[25]

Organization and Responsibilities of the Marketing Research Department

Like the location of the marketing research department within the firm, the internal structure also varies, particularly in degree of centralization. Highly centralized firms usually have just one marketing research department, while

FIGURE 1.3

Corporate Location of the Marketing Research Department

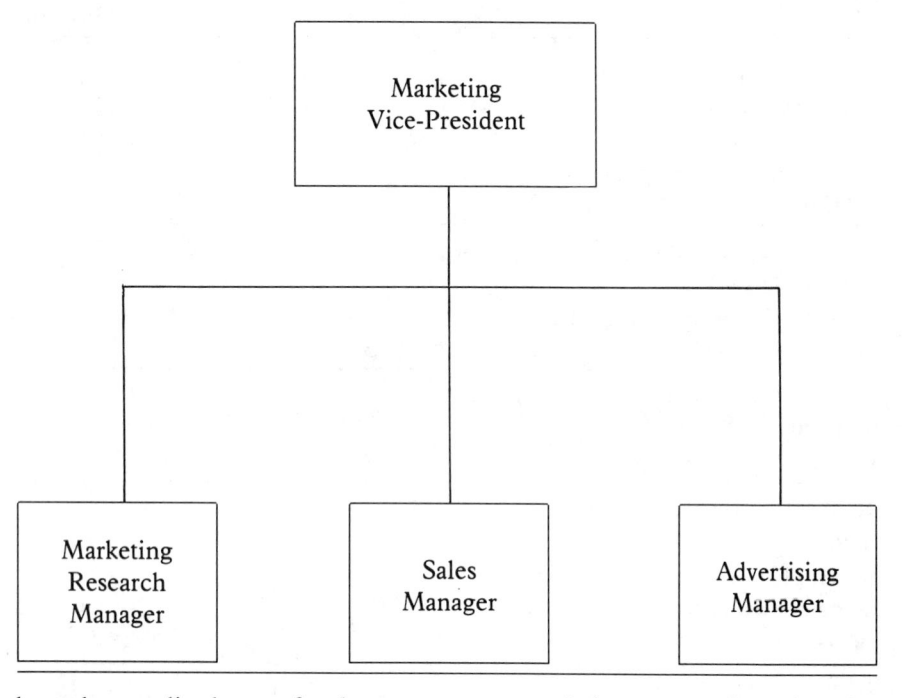

large decentralized ones often have separate research departments for each major operating division.

The broad definition of marketing research presented at the beginning of this chapter recognizes that the duties and responsibilities assigned to research departments are seldom the same in any two organizations, especially considering that some departments have only one person assigned full-time, whereas others have many full-time personnel. The duties of the research department might be limited by a lack of financial and human resources. In firms where marketing functions are given limited attention, the responsibilities of the research department might be confined to simple surveys and sales forecasts.

Why is there so much variation of the corporate position and function of research departments among organizations? The role of marketing research in the firm is determined essentially by three characteristics of the organization: the nature of the business, the size of the firm's annual sales, and top-management attitudes toward the marketing function.

Nature of the Business

The term "nature of the business" refers to the type of activities in which the enterprise is involved—whether the firm is engaged in the selling of consumer or industrial products, is the manufacturer or the middleman, is the advertising agency or the advertising medium, and so on. For example, firms that sell consumer products are more likely to be engaged in marketing research than those that sell in the industrial market, which usually involves a limited number of large customers. A firm like Catelli, with a multiplicity of consumer goods sold to the mass market, is in a much different position relevant to marketing research than is Atlas Copco, which sells equipment for mining, construction, and manufacturing. A large consumer goods firm is much more likely than an industrial firm of the same size to engage in such research activities as panel operations, studies of premiums and coupons, test markets, store audits, copy research, packaging research, and studies of advertising effectiveness, all of which are discussed later in this textbook.

Size of the Firm

Size, based on annual sales, is the second major variable that determines the role of research in the firm. In looking at the annual sales of corporations, the Conference Board of Canada found that among corporations with annual sales of more than $500 million, 64% had marketing research departments, with a high of 92% for industrial firms and a low of 44% for trade-related firms. At the opposite end of the spectrum, of those corporations with annual sales of less than $100 million, only 27% had marketing research departments, with a high of 41% for service firms and a low of 0% for financial firms.[26] Results of the survey are presented in Table 1.2.

This does not mean that a small company has less need for marketing research than does a large company but rather that small firms often cannot afford in-house research. Therefore, small companies either do without marketing research (one of the causes contributing to the high mortality rate among small businesses) or decide to contract with a professional marketing research firm.

Top-Management Attitudes

Top-management attitudes toward the marketing function are critical in determining the role of research within the organization. Firms that can be characterized as marketing oriented include Imasco, Molson, and virtually all the large

TABLE 1.2
Prevalence of Marketing Research Departments by Industry and Size

Company Size by Sales (million)	All (%)	Manufacturing Industrial (%)	Manufacturing Consumer (%)	Manufacturing Total (%)	Non-manufacturing Trade (%)	Non-manufacturing Financial (%)	Non-manufacturing Service (%)	Non-manufacturing Other (%)	Non-manufacturing Total (%)
Small (up to $100)	27	24	35	30	25	0	41	14	24
Medium ($100 to $500)	41	48	57	52	13	57	60	14	30
Large (more than $500)	64	92	56	77	44	80	70	44	58
Total	39	44	44	44	28	64	53	17	34

Source: Kenneth B. Wong and Randall G. Chapman, *Marketing Research in Canada: A Status Report.* Ottawa: The Conference Board in Canada, 1978, p. 4.

consumer goods companies selling to the mass market. Other large organizations, even though their goods or services might be directed at the mass market, might still not be market oriented. For example, is Canada Post market oriented?

Even today, many large firms still retain an attitude best described as production oriented, not market oriented. These firms, whether through ignorance or through deliberate policy, do not fully incorporate the marketing function and therefore marketing research is not given prominence. In such organizations, top management often views marketing simply as sales or as a very low-level function existing to service production or engineering departments. Top management in these organizations might be hostile to, or ignorant of, the role of marketing, and thus marketing research suffers.[27]

■ Research Activities

The activities of marketing research departments can be grouped under five major headings: advertising research, business economics and corporate research, corporate responsibility research, product research, and sales and market research. Table 1.3 lists thirty-three different marketing research activities under these five headings. The most common activities are determination of market characteristics, measurement of market potential, market-share analysis, determination of market characteristics, sales analysis, competitive product studies, new product acceptance and potential short-range forecasting, long-range forecasting, and studies of business trends. In general, fewer than half of the firms do their own advertising research; such research is often done by the client's advertising agency. Also a high percentage of business economics and corporate research is done by a department other than the research department. The statistics in Table 1.3 also show that U.S. firms tend to do more marketing research than their Canadian counterparts, for each main category of research and each type of research activity. This might be due to the fact that fewer Canadian firms have formal marketing research departments than do U.S. firms.[28]

There are some differences between industrial and consumer companies. Consumer companies are more likely to undertake studies involving consumer panel operations; premium, coupons, and deals; test markets and store audits; advertising copy; packaging; and advertising effectiveness. Inasmuch as all of these activities are traditionally of much greater importance to consumer companies, it is logical that consumer companies are more likely to be involved than are industrial firms.

Advertising, product research, and marketing analysis are the research activities in which advertising agencies are more likely to be engaged. Publishers' and broadcasters' research activities are focussed on media research, market-share analysis, determination of market characteristics, sales analyses, and measurement of market potential. Companies are also involved in corporate responsibility research, an area that has received considerable attention in recent years because of pressure from consumer groups and government agencies.

TABLE 1.3
Marketing Research Activities of Canadian and U.S. Firms

Activity	% Doing	Done by Marketing Research Dept. (%)	Done by Another Dept (%)	Done by Outside Firm (%)
Advertising Research				
Motivation research	25 (47)*	9 (30)	3 (2)	14 (15)
Copy research	33 (61)	9 (30)	3 (6)	21 (25)
Studies of effectiveness	42 (68)	11 (22)	4 (14)	27 (32)
Studies of competitive advertising	39 (76)	15 (42)	6 (5)	17 (21)
Media research	36 (67)	6 (36)	4 (11)	25 (20)
Business Economics and Corporate Research				
Short-range forecasting	51 (89)	25 (51)	25 (36)	1 (2)
Long-range forecasting	50 (87)	26 (49)	23 (34)	1 (4)
Studies of business trends	49 (91)	31 (68)	14 (20)	4 (3)
Pricing, profit, and/or value analysis	50 (83)	17 (34)	32 (47)	1 (2)
Location studies	35 (68)	9 (29)	23 (35)	3 (4)
Acquisition/diversification studies	41 (73)	13 (33)	27 (38)	2 (2)
Export and international studies	33 (49)	12 (22)	20 (25)	1 (2)
Marketing information systems	41 (80)	6 (25)	34 (53)	1 (2)
Operations research	34 (65)	4 (14)	30 (50)	1 (1)
Internal employee studies	39 (76)	7 (25)	29 (45)	3 (6)
Corporate Responsibility Research				
Consumers' "right to know" studies	16 (18)	5 (7)	9 (9)	1 (2)
Ecological impact studies	16 (23)	3 (2)	11 (17)	2 (4)
Studies of legal constraints	29 (46)	6 (10)	17 (31)	5 (5)
Social values and policies studies	18 (39)	7 (18)	10 (13)	1 (7)
Product Research				
New product modelling/optimization	48 (76)	24 (59)	20 (10)	4 (6)
Competitive product studies	54 (87)	30 (71)	20 (10)	4 (6)
Product testing (existing products)	52 (80)	20 (55)	24 (19)	8 (6)
Packaging research design characteristics	41 (65)	15 (44)	17 (12)	8 (9)
Sales and Market Research				
Measurement of market potential	59 (97)	39 (88)	12 (4)	8 (5)
Market-share analysis	61 (97)	39 (85)	13 (6)	9 (6)
Determination of market characteristics	60 (97)	36 (88)	16 (3)	7 (6)
Sales analysis	58 (92)	26 (67)	29 (23)	4 (2)
Establishment of sales quotas, etc.	54 (78)	16 (23)	37 (54)	1 (1)
Distribution channels and costs	49 (71)	15 (32)	33 (38)	2 (1)
Test markets, store audits	35 (59)	16 (43)	15 (7)	4 (9)
Consumer panel studies	33 (63)	9 (46)	11 (43)	13 (4)
Sales compensation studies	37 (60)	5 (13)	26 (43)	7 (4)
Studies of premiums, coupons, etc.	28 (58)	11 (38)	11 (14)	5 (6)

***Note**: Bracketed figures are U.S. percentages

Source: Chang et al., "Comparison of Business Use," p. 284.

Scope of Present-day Research Activities

Marketing research activities should be regarded as essential information-gathering and -processing activities that help top management to make critical decisions, and should not be limited merely to analyses of the marketing mix. Well-balanced marketing research should take into consideration all of the activities listed in Table 1.3. To carry out these activities, increasingly sophisticated techniques are required. Since competent, modern marketing research assists top management in implementing successful marketing concepts, the techniques used must go well beyond elementary surveys and analyses of internal data. In recent years, far more advanced techniques have been developed that incorporate test-marketing, laboratory studies, multi-attribute attitude models, and Bayesian statistical analysis, which are discussed later in this text. The historical evolution of these techniques clearly shows the increasing complexity of the marketing research process and indicates why research analysts must be able to use quantitative techniques. Many college and university students question the relevancy of quantitative courses, but marketing research is a field where the practical application of statistical techniques can readily be demonstrated in a meaningful and utilitarian context.

Research Budgets[29]

The amount spent on marketing research in Canada has risen dramatically during the last twenty years. Whereas the median budget in 1966 was $15 000, the amount in 1984 was $100 000. The total marketing research budget was estimated at $2.6 billion in 1984, and the actual total expenditures at $1.7 billion. As a percentage of sales, marketing research budgets rose from 0.1% in 1966 to 0.6% in 1984. Similarly, actual marketing research expenditures increased from 0.1% in 1966 to 0.4% in 1984. By comparison, advertising expenditures as a percentage of gross national product (GNP) were 1.3% in 1984, down from 1.5% in 1966.

Approximately half of the companies surveyed reported that they had a marketing research budget, and among these, 69% indicated that they used outside services. The increase in research budgets and expenditures reflects the rising importance of marketing research in Canada and more growth is expected in the future.

■ Careers and Compensations[30]

Career opportunities in marketing research have increased dramatically in recent years for both men and women. Many college and university graduates go directly into the employ of corporate marketing research departments. The continuing expansion of the marketing research function provides career avenues at the entrance level for graduates with majors in statistics, economics, marketing, psychology, and mathematics.

Figure 1.4 presents the results of a comparative survey to determine compensation levels for marketing research positions in Canada and the United States. Six

FIGURE 1.4

Mean Compensation for Some Marketing Research Positions

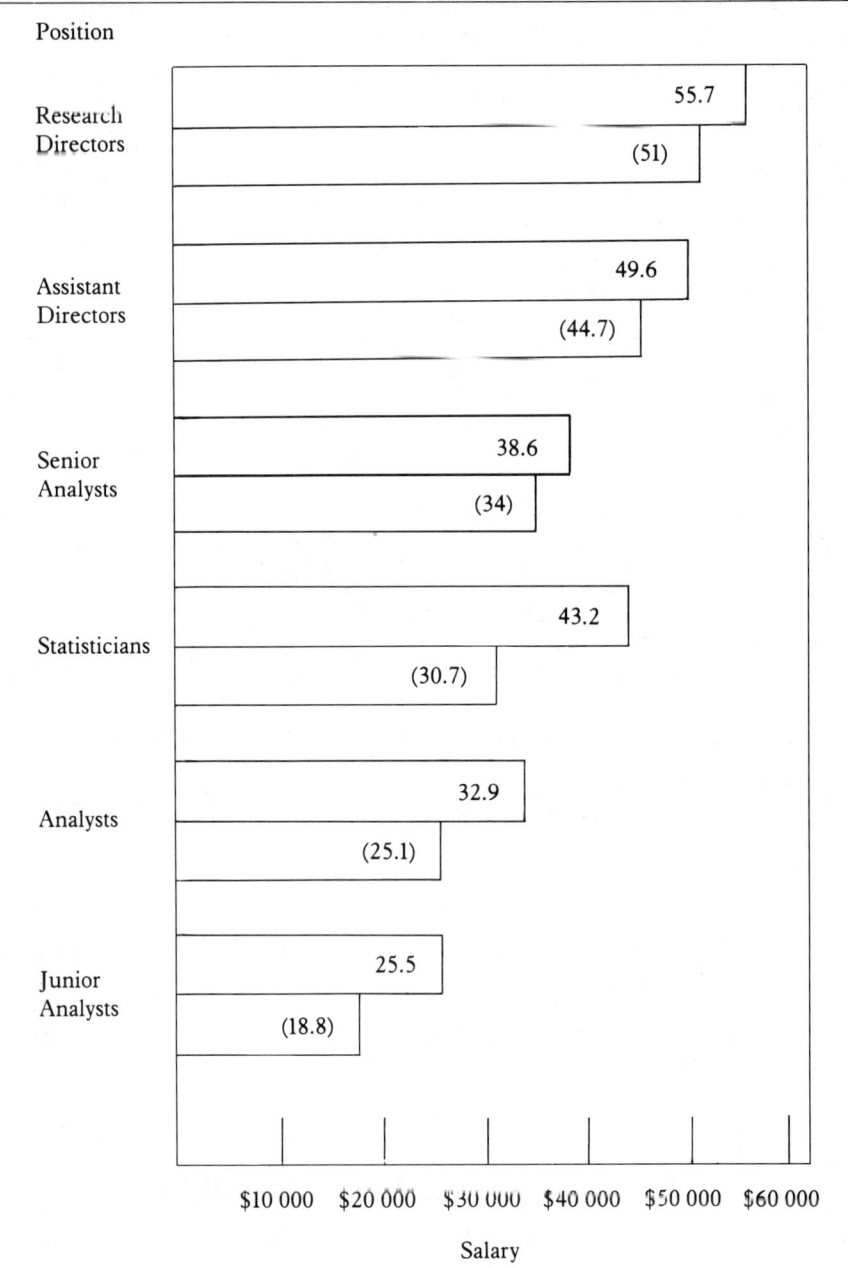

Position

Research Directors — 55.7 (51)

Assistant Directors — 49.6 (44.7)

Senior Analysts — 38.6 (34)

Statisticians — 43.2 (30.7)

Analysts — 32.9 (25.1)

Junior Analysts — 25.5 (18.8)

$10 000 $20 000 $30 000 $40 000 $50 000 $60 000

Salary

Note: 1983 U.S. figures in brackets

Source: Chang et al., "Comparison of Business Use," p. 287.

job positions are shown, although in actual practice there are considerably more positions available in the marketing research field. Illustrated in the figure are the mean compensation levels for these six positions in 1984 for Canada and in 1983 for the United States. Annual salary levels in 1984 ranged from approximately $55 700 a year for Canadian research directors to a low of approximately $25 500 for junior analysts. Mean compensation levels in the United States are in general higher when corrected by the current exchange rate. In the past, women were employed primarily only in junior professional research positions, and salary levels for women were considerably lower than those for men. Today, however, at the professional level, these differences have narrowed, although men still outnumber women in upper levels and vice versa.

In corporate research departments there are three principal job categories: research directors, analysts, and clerical staff. The research director holds the senior position and has responsibility for the entire research program. The various levels of analysts constitute the largest professional responsibility for completing projects. The majority of employees in a research department fall into the category of clerical staff, who usually perform routine tasks, such as tabulating data.

Professional marketing researchers often have graduate degrees in one or more of the five fields previously mentioned, and many research directors hold doctorates in psychology, marketing, or related fields. A master's or doctoral degree can be of significant benefit if research methodology and problem solving have been stressed in the graduate program.

Career opportunities in marketing research have grown at a rapid rate and should continue to grow in the foreseeable future. The viability of marketing research as a professional field is favourably affected by four factors:

- increased competition and new product introduction, which require better information to assist in decision making

- growing sophistication of planning procedures and the need to justify recommendations

- the increasing availability of data and software, making research more accessible physically and financially

- Better-educated management that understands the value and rewards of good research

Agencies Performing and Utilizing Marketing Research

Some organizations both perform and utilize their own marketing research. Other firms, called **buyers**, might use research but contract with outside agencies, called **suppliers**, to have the research performed. Other organizations might not utilize research themselves but specialize in performing research for clients. Organizations supplying and buying marketing research can be grouped into the following nine major categories.

1. *Manufacturers* are the principal users of marketing research, and large manufacturers usually do their own research in-house. Firms most likely to be engaged in both conducting and utilizing research are the large consumer goods manufacturers, such as Johnson & Johnson and General Motors. Nearly all of large manufacturers have their own research departments, with one or more full-time research professionals, and they usually do not need to rely on independent research firms for data.

2. *Advertising agencies* have long been leading suppliers and users of marketing research. Much of the research done by advertising agencies is done on behalf of their clients. Traditionally, the cost of advertising research performed by agencies for their clients is included in their fees, although for large projects this cost might be billed separately. All but the smallest advertising agencies usually have their own separate research departments. The work of these departments might involve measuring both the efficiency and the effectiveness of advertising for the agency and its clients. Some advertising agencies have research departments that are involved in more than the measuring of advertising impact. In these cases, the activities of the departments are similar to those of full-time marketing research agencies, and they perform a wide range of typical marketing research functions.

3. *Advertising media* are both suppliers and users of marketing research. Such advertising media as radio, television, newspapers, and magazines are typically quite interested in both the size and the demographic composition of their audiences. They need accurate and reliable audience measurement data to provide to their clients. Since advertising media are directly dependent on advertisers for a large portion of their income, and since media advertising rates are directly proportional to audience size, there has been a tendency in the past for some media to inflate audience size. Today, with the help of such organizations as the Audit Bureau of Circulation, most media research done by the media themselves is performed in an objective and accurate manner. However, it is still advisable to have outside research agencies, rather than the media themselves, do media research, in order to convince media buyers that the figures are unbiassed. Otherwise, an unethical magazine could report a 50% increase in circulation and raise advertising rates accordingly. That this increase might have come from an increase just in press run (with the extra copies of the magazine gathering mildew in a warehouse), and not in actual circulation, might not be mentioned.

4. *Retailers and wholesalers* as a group have traditionally been neither major suppliers nor major users of marketing research. However, a change is underway, and some of the large retail chains, such as Eaton's and The Bay, are using more and more research and now have their own research departments. Retail chains are particularly interested in store location research and the effectiveness of their promotion programs. Had the Great Atlantic and Pacific Tea Company (better known as A & P) relied more heavily on marketing

research, it might well have retained its position as the number-one supermarket retailer in the United States. Certainly, competent marketing research should have enabled A & P to avoid its disastrous post-war marketing mistake of ignoring large shopping centres and retaining small neighbourhood stores. Some wholesalers conduct limited research studies, but most are too small to use extensive marketing research effectively.

5. *Independent marketing research firms* represent a tremendously diverse contribution to the field. Some of these agencies are one-person specialized consulting firms and contract to define or solve individual marketing problems. Other independent marketing research firms, such as the A.C. Nielsen Company, are quite large and employ thousands of people, with offices all over the world. These research firms conduct research on a continuing basis, selling their survey results to subscribers. Syndicated data services, such as the Print Measurement Bureau and Starch Canada, specialize in gathering and selling certain types of data to clients on a subscription basis. The data might include advertising readership or recognition, brand image studies, store audits, and consumer panel reports. Although independent marketing research firms are major performers of marketing research, they seldom conduct studies for their own internal purposes.

6. *Government agencies* at the federal level conduct a tremendous amount of marketing research for internal purposes and for the general public. Marketing research conducted by such federal government agencies as Statistics Canada provide a wealth of data, indispensable for many firms. For example, data gathered by Statistics Canada on population characteristics are vital to developers looking for population trends, to ensure wise location of retail shopping centres and stores. Data gathered by these government research agencies are widely available, either free or at a nominal cost. Many firms have wasted a great deal of time and money seeking data already available from government research agencies.

7. *Trade and professional associations* collect much valuable market data from their members. Associations such as the Canadian Manufacturers' Association or the Television Bureau of Canada collect invaluable data not only on the characteristics of their members but also on industry practices. The American Marketing Association's *Survey of Marketing Research*, conducted every five years, is one example. Data gathered by these associations can be particularly important to small member firms that do not have the resources to undertake their own research activities.

8. *Universities and foundations* have long been engaged in marketing research, although little of it is of a commercial nature. Much university research is done by professors through business research bureaus and is for public benefit. In many of these research studies the federal government is the client. Large private foundations also fund a great deal of research. However, these studies tend to deal with broad economic or business problems and are not always directly applicable to individual firms.

9. *Other agencies* include financial institutions and financial reporting services. *Marketing* magazine, the Canadian Media Directors' Council, and *Canadian Advertising Rates and Data* provide statistical information on a continuous basis that is of particular value to media and advertising agencies.

■ Summary

Marketing research is "the systematic gathering, recording and analyzing of data about problems relating to the marketing of goods and services." We have used the American Marketing Association's definition because it is sufficiently broad to include all marketing problems, even those of the non-profit sector. This definition implicitly recognizes that research data must always be gathered and processed in an objective and accurate manner.

Today, more and more firms have shifted from a production orientation to a marketing orientation. This shift involves adoption of the marketing concept, a way of thinking that permeates the entire organization and incorporates three basic criteria: customer orientation, profitable sales, and integrated marketing. The key factor that holds the marketing concept together and makes it work is marketing research. Without such research, a firm cannot possibly be customer oriented. Marketing research is needed to help the firm find the markets and then sell to satisfy them. The marketing mix, which is a combination of the four key elements—product, price, place, and promotion—that constitute the core of any firm's marketing program, is built directly around the customer under the marketing concept.

The history of marketing research in Canada comprises five distinct periods: the beginning (1929–38), the war interlude (1939–45), the early post-war years (1946–59), the middle post-war years (1960–69), and more recent years (1970–88).

As an organized business activity, marketing research is primarily a post-World War II phenomenon, although the earliest commercial marketing research is considered to date from the beginning of the twentieth century. The rapidly increasing importance of marketing research information to business people is a result of three major changes: the shift from local to national and international marketing, the transition from consumer needs to consumer wants, and the shift from price to non-price competition.

In a large firm, the manager of the marketing research department is usually on the same level as the sales manager and the advertising manager. The marketing research manager in such a firm usually reports to the vice-president of marketing but sometimes to top management. The research department might be organized on a centralized or decentralized basis, depending on the organization of the company itself. Research department responsibilities vary among firms; for example, sales research might be done by the accounting department. Three factors determine the role of marketing research in the firm: the nature of the business, the size in annual sales of the organization, and top-management attitudes toward the marketing function.

As the field of marketing research has grown dramatically, so have its career opportunities. College and university graduates with advanced degrees in statistics, economics, marketing, psychology, and mathematics can look forward to rewarding professional careers as marketing research professionals. Within the corporate research department there are three principal job categories: research director, analyst, and clerical worker. Increasingly intense competition, greater reliance on marketing plans and decisions, more sophisticated technology, and the extremely low level of present-day expenditures on marketing research are all factors that should cause this field to continue to grow at a rapid rate for the foreseeable future.

For Discussion

1. "You cannot have an affluent, industrialized society without modern marketing." Discuss the full meaning and implication of this statement. Do you agree or disagree? Why?

2. Modern marketing research is said to be the cornerstone of the marketing concept. What is meant by this statement? Is it possible to implement a marketing concept without marketing research?

3. How is marketing research defined in this chapter? Explain in your own words what this definition means.

4. What is the role of marketing research in the firm? Should the marketing research manager report to the vice-president of marketing or to top management. Explain.

5. Should the marketing function be centralized or decentralized? When might it be best to centralize and when best to decentralize it? Give examples.

6. If modern marketing research is essential to the financial well-being of the organization, why does not everyone use marketing research?

7. In your opinion, why is organized marketing research of such recent origin?

8. Can you think of any possible trends that would cause a curtailment of research activities by Canadian firms?

9. State your opinion of why corporate responsibility research has been such a fast-growing marketing research activity. What conditions have caused this recent growth?

10. Why might a client firm prefer an independent marketing research agency, rather than the advertising media's own research department, to conduct research into the effectiveness of that advertising media's message?

Problems

Mini-Case: Kimura Hardware Corporation (Part A)

Kimura Hardware Corporation is a regional chain of hardware stores operating in Ontario and Quebec. Toshio Kimura, founder and largest shareholder of the chain, has always followed an intuitive "seat of the pants" approach to running the operation, which currently grosses $7.5 million annually and produces a net after-tax profit of $50 000. Kimura operates ten stores and employs approximately fifty employees. The chain has never established a marketing research department, nor does Toshio have any intention of doing so.

Recently, Toshio's daughter, Keiko, joined the firm after graduating in marketing from Hillgreen University. A quick examination of the firm's operating strategies revealed to her that marketing decisions are being made on the basis of Toshio's intuition and experience. Furthermore, careful analysis showed that the company's growth rate is tapering off and that profit margins have been narrowing for the past three years.

Keiko is convinced that some basic marketing research is necessary to pinpoint the causes of the slow-down, but she is not sure what to do. She wonders if perhaps the company should establish its own marketing research department, although she is sure that Toshio will oppose the idea.

Questions

1. a) Should the company establish a marketing research department? Defend your answer.
   b) What kind of research program would you recommend to identify the problem? Why?

2. Select an independent marketing firm in your area and arrange interviews with some key people in the firm.
   a) Prepare a profile of the firm, its services, and its clients.
   b) Describe in detail the functions of each position within the firm.
   c) Compare career opportunities and compensation in marketing research with other career areas in marketing such as sales and advertising.

Endnotes

1. *Report of the Definitions Committee of the American Marketing Association.* Chicago: American Marketing Association, 1961, p. 15.
2. "AMA Board Approves New Marketing Definition." *Marketing Education*, vol. 4, no. 2 (Spring 1985), p. 1.
3. Robert J. Keith, "The Marketing Revolution." *Journal of Marketing*, 24 (January 1960), pp. 35–38.
4. A.B. Blankenship, Chuck Chakrapani, and W. Harold Poole, *A History of Marketing Research in Canada*. Toronto: Professional Marketing Research Society, 1985.
5. Henry King, "The Beginnings of Marketing Research in Canada." *The Marketer*, vol. II, no. 1 (Spring/Summer 1966), pp. 4–5.
6. Ibid, p. 5.
7. Ibid, p. 4.
8. Blankenship et al., *History of Marketing Research*, pp. 28–29.
9. Ibid, pp. 90–92.
10. Joyce Chang, David Conway, and George H. Haines, Jr., "A Comparison of Business Use of Marketing Research in Canada and the United States." *Marketing*, 7. Ed. Thomas E. Muller. Administrative Sciences Association of Canada (ASAC), 1986, pp. 280–88.
11. Canadian Advertising Research Foundation.
12. Blankenship et al., *History of Marketing Research*, pp. 66–68.
13. Ibid, pp. 90–92.
14. Kenneth B. Wong and Randall G. Chapman, *Marketing Research in Canada: A Status Report*. Ottawa: The Conference Board of Canada, 1978, p. 5.
15. "Trois Québecois lancent un nouveau type de dentifrice." *Les Affaires*, October 3, 1981, p. 13.
16. "Le Manic vise le marché familial avec des prix très bas." *Les Affaires*, March 14, 1981, p. 22.
17. B.E. Mallen, V.H. Kirpalani, and R. Savitt, *Principles of Marketing in Canada*. Scarborough, ON: Prentice-Hall, 1980, p. 223.
18. R.Y. Darmon, M. Laroche, and J.V. Petrof, *Marketing in Canada: A Management Perspective*. Toronto: McGraw-Hill Ryerson, 1985.
19. Mallen et al., *Principles of Marketing*, p. 223.

20. Blankenship, et al, *History of Marketing Research*, p. 154.
21. Winston H. Mahatoo, ed., *Marketing Research in Canada*. Toronto: Thomas Nelson, 1968; Joyce Chang, David Conway, and George H. Haines, Jr., "Marketing Research in Canada: A 1985 Update." *Marketing*, 7. ASAC, 1986, pp. 289–98.
22. Chang et al., "Comparison of Business Use," p. 294.
23. Dik Warren Twedt, ed., *1978 Survey of Marketing Research*. Chicago: American Marketing Association, 1978, pp. 24–25.
24. Chang et al., "Comparison of Business Use," p. 295.

25. Kenneth G. Hardy and Joseph N. Fry, "Marketing Research in Canada: What's Going On?" *Canadian Marketing Problems and Prospects*. Eds. Donald W. Thompson and David S. Leighton. Toronto: John Wiley, 1973, pp. 252–68.

26. Wong and Chapman, *Marketing Research in Canada*, pp. 4–5.

27. Michael P. Heffring, "Expectations of Marketing Research: the Manager-Researcher Gap." *Marketing*, 1. Ed. V.J. Jones. ASAC, 1980, pp. 191–201.

28. Chang et al., "Comparison of Business Use, p. 281.

29. Ibid., pp. 294-95.

30. Ibid.

CHAPTER 2

MARKETING RESEARCH WITHIN THE MARKETING INFORMATION SYSTEM

The growing importance of marketing research to the marketing decision-making process was discussed in the first chapter. As the marketing process became consumer oriented, marketers began to feel the need to find and process a large amount of market information. Marketing managers felt the need for this information because they had to ensure that their products and services would be wanted and accepted by consumers. To collect information and to obtain intelligence about environmental market forces that affect market demand, the marketing manager has had to develop information systems that are based on increasingly sophisticated and complex techniques. This need for information has sometimes given rise to formal organizational units that are called **marketing information systems.**

A marketing information system includes four types of information research and processing that generally are essential to efficient marketing decision making:

- the systematic collection and analysis of a firm's internal data, such as sales and profit data or accounting information

- the systematic collection and processing of market information from external sources, such as the intelligence collected by the company's salespeople or the acquisition of reports from syndicated sources of market data

- in-house marketing research

- the development and use of marketing decision support systems, generally based on operational research and management science techniques.

Obviously, in any marketing organization that has adopted the modern marketing concept, all of these activities take place at various levels of sophistication. Typically, they have grown independently of each other in the marketing organization, but with the recent trend toward integrated management information systems, these activities have sometimes been grouped into homogenous and centrally managed information centres.

This chapter is devoted to a description of marketing information systems. First, the role of information research in the marketing decision-making process is discussed from the information provider's point of view. Second, the different parts of the marketing information system are briefly reviewed, including data collection procedures. Then the nature of data and primary data sources available in marketing are examined. Finally, data analysis activities are briefly outlined.

The Need for Marketing Information

The first question that a student of marketing might ask is, "Why do marketing research at all?" One might argue against marketing research projects by pointing out their high cost and the delay they entail in decision making. In addition, no research project can totally eliminate risk and uncertainty, and there is always some probability that the research will produce an inaccurate answer to the question asked. It is also fairly easy to find examples of products that were successfully launched with no prior research. One such example is the typewriter correction fluid *Liquid Paper*, which was invented in 1951 by a secretary, Bette Graham. Liquid Paper Corporation, established with a loan of $500, was sold to Gillette for $4.75 million in 1979.[1]

However, the extraordinary success of Liquid Paper Corporation and of other similar companies is unusual. A lot of publicity is given to such unusual success stories but you rarely hear about the incredible number of market failures of bright and promising product ideas! The fact is that businesses cannot rely on a hit-or-miss decision process for such crucial questions as those pertaining to the introduction of new products.

To better understand the need for marketing research in a modern economy, let us first contrast a product-oriented marketing organization and one using the marketing concept. Figure 2.1 shows the process followed by a product-oriented sales organization. A product is typically conceived and designed by the research and development department, and produced according to the specifications of that department. The sales department is then asked to sell the product, designing the marketing program that will direct the flow of goods to the market—if possible, at a profit. However, this process, which was prevalent a few decades ago, does not seem to be able to generate profits in today's marketplace. It has been superseded by the market-oriented approach and the marketing concept.

The market-oriented organization shown in Figure 2.2 is essentially different from the product-oriented firm in the sense that the product or service is designed

FIGURE 2.1
The Sales Process of the Product-Oriented Organization

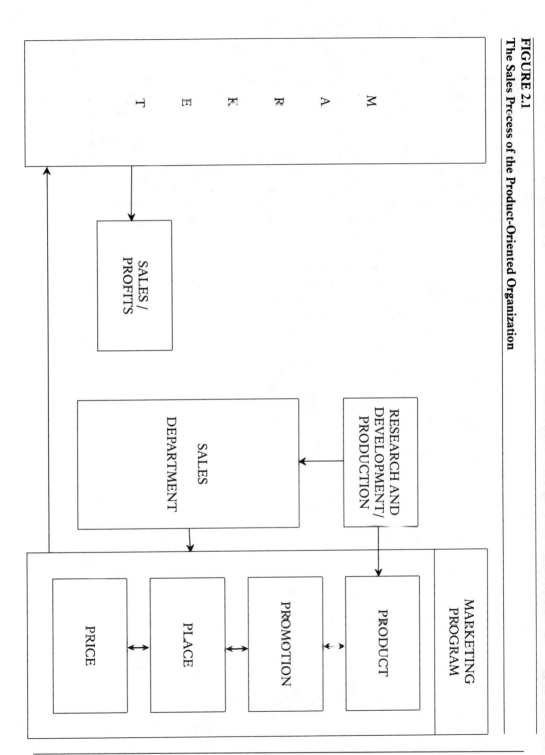

according to the specifications of the market. Today, no wise manufacturer would contemplate launching a product unless it is known to answer specific market segments' needs and to be acceptable to a sufficient number of consumers. In other words, not only will the new product or service be designed according to the needs and wants of the market, but the marketing program itself will be tailored to best reach, inform, and convince consumers that the product constitutes the best means for answering those needs.[2]

Applying the marketing concept might seem to be easy at first glance. In order to be successful, however, the implementation of the market-orientation philosophy requires that marketers thoroughly understand the various consumers' needs and wants, and how these needs are presently satisfied by competing product classes or other brands. Consequently, no firm can efficiently apply the marketing concept unless it has up-to-date, accurate, and reasonably complete information about the following market/consumer dimensions.

1. *Market characteristics*: What is the size of the market? What is its potential? What evolution trends is it likely to follow?

2. *Consumer behaviour*: Why do people buy this type of product? What benefits do they anticipate when they purchase the product? How homogeneous are they in terms of those benefits? How do consumers perceive the different brands/companies in the marketplace? What are consumers' attitudes toward them? How satisfied are they with the present product offerings? How much time are they willing to spend to shop for the product/brand? How price-sensitive are they? These are only a few of the questions that marketers often ask themselves about consumer behaviour.

3. *Market environment*: How might environmental forces affect the market? What are the present and future economic conditions that will affect demand for the product or service? How fast is technology likely to affect future demand and competitive products? What legislation (as well as trends in this legislation) is likely to affect the firm's future operations in relation to its markets? Who are the major competitors? What are their present offerings? What are their strengths? Their weaknesses? Their strategies? What are the main organizations that can be efficiently used to distribute the product to various market segments (distribution channels, advertising agencies, research firms, etc.)? This set of questions is by no means limitative and only provides a sample of the questions typically asked by managers who try to implement the marketing concept.[3]

Finding the information to answer such questions is by no means an easy task for a marketing manager. Although some answers are easier to obtain than others, answering most of these questions requires a formal procedure. Obviously marketing research plays a significant role in this process, but one fact should be clear: marketing information-acquisition activities are a consequence of the marketing concept. No firm can implement the marketing concept unless it is substantially involved in extensive marketing information-search activities.[4]

FIGURE 2.2
The Marketing Process of the Market-Oriented Organization

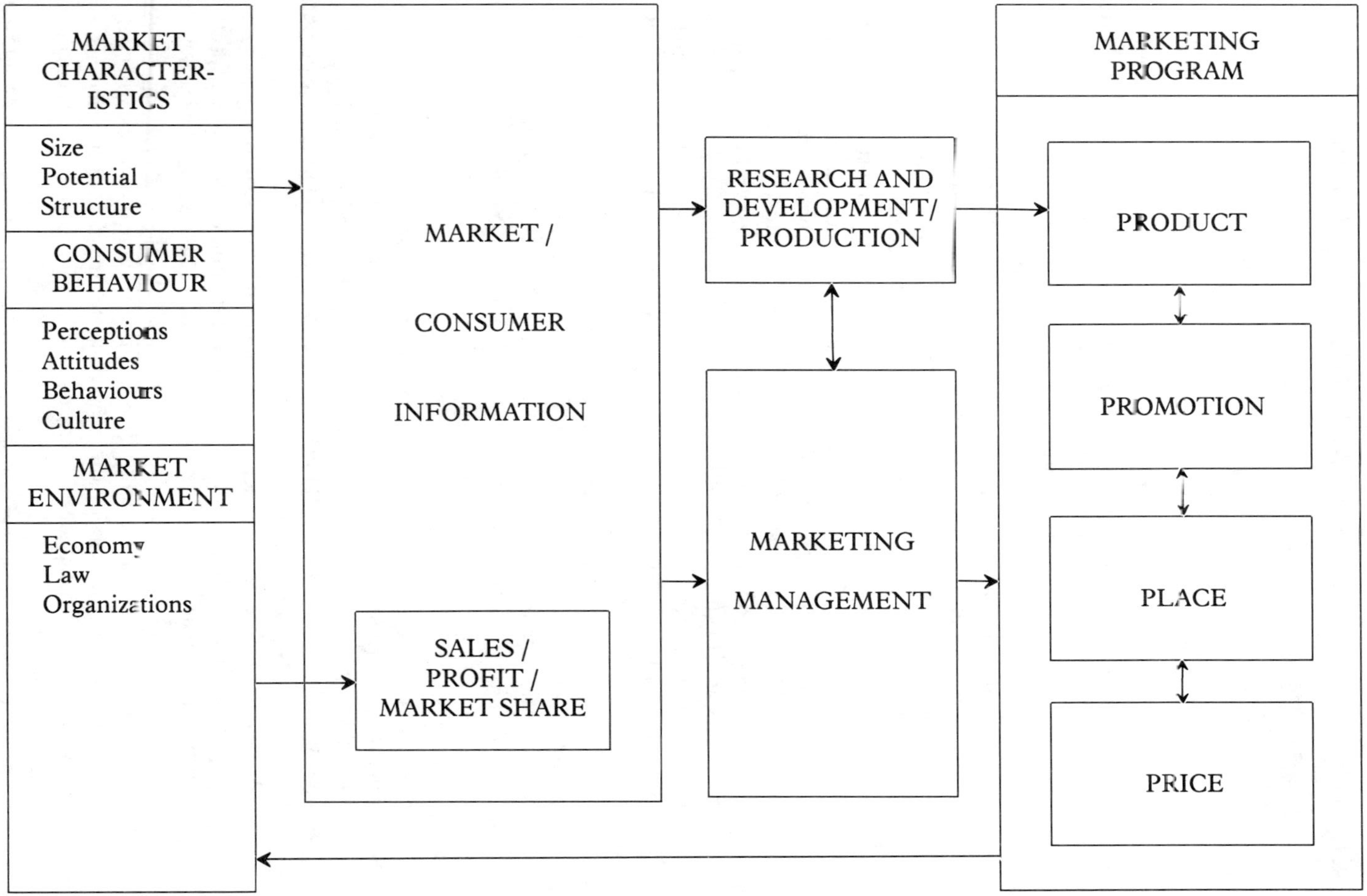

MARKET CHARACTER-ISTICS	
Size	
Potential	
Structure	
CONSUMER BEHAVIOUR	
Perceptions	
Attitudes	
Behaviours	
Culture	
MARKET ENVIRONMENT	
Economy	
Law	
Organizieations	

MARKET / CONSUMER INFORMATION

SALES / PROFIT / MARKET SHARE

RESEARCH AND DEVELOPMENT/ PRODUCTION

MARKETING MANAGEMENT

MARKETING PROGRAM

PRODUCT

PROMOTION

PLACE

PRICE

■ *Major Types of Marketing Information Required*

Market Situation Information

Some information about the market environment is readily available to a marketing manager. For instance, it is often fairly easy for a firm to find out the prices of the main competitive products and brands on the market. Also, it usually is easy to find out about the government regulations that affect its activities. In contrast, it is often difficult to forecast the future economic situation of a specific market, to ascertain potential of a given market segment, or to have a good understanding of the marketing strategy currently followed by each competitor. Therefore, when marketers want to obtain such information, they generally need to carry out systematic research, often using more or less formal procedures.

An important Toronto-based company manufacturing industrial filters must decide which types of filters should be manufactured for successfully entering the Quebec market. Which firms in which industries are likely to be its best potential customers? What are the specific needs of the Quebec potential customers?

A shoe retailer operating in the Maritime provinces wants to expand its operations and open several outlets in smaller localities. To identify the best possible locations for the new stores, she wants to know the different market potentials, customer needs, and the competitive situation in several candidate localities.

To find new product ideas, a national candy bar producer wants to know the present consumers better. Who are they (age, family income, socio-economic characteristics, etc.)? Why do they buy the product? In which situations?

All of these illustrative cases have one element in common: they require descriptive information about specific markets. The first type of marketing information that is important to a marketer could be called **market situation information**. This data permits a marketing manager to understand the market, its structures, environment, and the position held by the firm in the market. This information will help to define the marketing objectives and a marketing strategy. It is essential to understand all of the basic facts about a market in order to properly identify market opportunities.

As was seen before, in a product-oriented organization, research is synonymous with research and development. It involves research on the technical aspects of the product or research on methods to develop new products at the lowest possible cost. In contrast, in the market-oriented organization, the research and development department, although pursuing essentially the same objectives, will operate from the data supplied about the market in terms of consumer needs and acceptance of new product ideas. Today, consumer orientation is a prerequisite for successful marketing.

The development of successful new ideas is becoming increasingly difficult. The process of screening, analysing the business elements, developing, test-marketing, and finally launching a product or service is extremely costly, and at each stage, information about the consumer, the market, and the marketing environment is crucial to the long-run profitability of the firm. Consider, for example, one step in the new product development process—the step between test-marketing and market introduction. If success is defined as the decision to launch the product nationally after test marketing then, according to one five-year Nielson study, only some 39% of new products were successful.[5] The study also showed that only 35% of new brands were successful, while the figure for line extensions was 49%. Thus, through test-marketing, 61% of all new products were eliminated. This does not mean that the remaining products were *successfully* launched, but only that they *were* launched.

For all of these reasons, when marketing analysts identify consumer needs that are not being fully satisfied with existing products and services, they ask the research and development department to try to find a product that can fulfil the consumers' expectations. Of course, this product must be technically and economically feasible. This is represented by the upper part of Figure 2.3.

Market Response Information

Of course, questions about the product itself are not the only issue; other problems might surface. For example, what advertising or promotional campaign should be used? In what media and how often should the product be advertised? At what price should a new product be sold? What effect will changes in price have on sales and/or competitors' prices? Where should the product be sold? Should substantial discounts be given to dealers for volume purchases? This list of questions about product, promotion, price, and place is by no means complete. It gives, however, an indication of the type of question that marketing managers must answer when they decide on a marketing strategy.

This is the reason why a second type of marketing research is currently undertaken by a marketing manager—**market response information** research. Unlike market situation information research, which is concerned with the present state of the market, market response research aims at predicting how the market will be in some future period of time. These studies are likely to generate short-, medium-, or long-range forecasts. For instance, in order to predict the market demand in a few years, the forecaster should specify a set of conditions that is likely to prevail during this period of time. For instance, market demand can be forecasted under the scenario of strong economic growth or, alternatively, under the scenario of economic recession. In other words, the analyst is trying to find out how the market will *respond* to the various conditions specified in the scenario.

In other instances, a marketing manager often needs answers to questions such as: What would happen to sales and profits if the promotion budget for next year were cut by 50%? What would happen to sales if ten salespeople were added to the sales team next year? And so on. Obviously, in such cases the marketer would like to learn something about the way in which the market would respond to such marketing actions. These relationships play an extremely important role in marketing. If, for instance, a manager knows the relationship that links sales and profits to such marketing variables as the advertising appropriation, the promotion budget, or the sales force size, this is sufficient (and necessary) knowledge to determine the optimal level of the marketing variable that should enter the

FIGURE 2.3
Types of Marketing Research

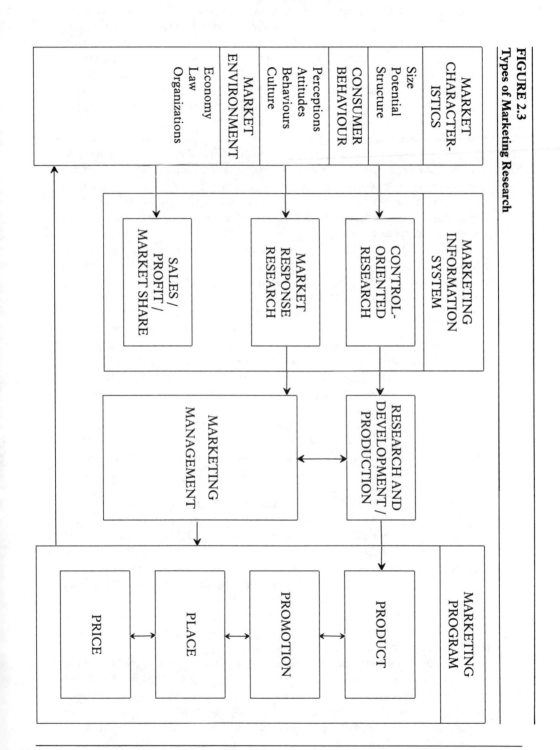

marketing program. This is essentially what is described in Figure 2.3, contrasting the different uses that usually are made of market situation research and market response research.

Estimating market responses to marketing variables is typically a difficult and time-consuming research problem that involves substantial resources. However, such estimates are often warranted by the benefits they produce in the development of adequate strategic and tactical marketing programs.

Actual and Forecasted Information

Another way to look at the type of marketing information needed by a manager is according to the time aspect of the data: whether it is actual or forecasted information. Very often, marketing managers must know the present characteristics of a market (for instance, the consumers' age or income patterns). This is **actual information**. In other instances, they might want to know what the situation of the market will be in the future, or what evolutionary trend will prevail for the main environmental variables, or what next year's most likely market response will be to an anticipated price increase, perhaps following an expected increase in energy cost. This is **forecasted information**. Of course, forecasted information could be needed for the near future (short-range forecasts) or for the more distant future (medium- or long-range forecasts).

Types of Market Studies

When the two preceding dichotomous classifications of marketing information (i.e., according to their content and their timing), are considered simultaneously, four types of marketing information can be defined. These four categories of information lead to a classification of research studies currently carried out in marketing. These studies are research projects conducted to find the information defined in each cell of Table 2.1: *descriptive, predictive, causal-descriptive, causal-predictive*.

Descriptive Studies

As their name implies, these studies are essentially designed to *describe* the present state of the market and the present marketing environment. Descriptive marketing studies are concerned about the current state of the marketing environmental variables.

TABLE 2.1
Classifications of Marketing Information,
According to Their Nature, Scope, and Content

	Present	Future	
		Short-run	Long-run
Market Situation Information	Descriptive Research	Predictive Research	
Market Response Information	Causal-Descriptive Research	Causal-Predictive Research	

Predictive Studies

These studies attempt to *predict* the value of some environmental variables in the more or less distant future.

Causal-Descriptive Studies

Causal-descriptive studies are carried out to describe the present relationships that exist between marketing performance measures and marketing and environmental variables. Any attempt to specifiy all or part of the response functions is a causal-descriptive study.

Causal-Predictive Studies

More frequently, a marketing manager is concerned with the future response of the market to the future value of a marketing or an environmental variable. To provide such information, causal as well as predictive studies are needed.

As could be surmised, the difficulties encountered in collecting and analysing marketing information increase as the focus of the research moves from the present to the future, and from market situation research to market response research. Consequently, in terms of research difficulty and sophistication of the research methodology implied, the different types of information research comply with the following hierarchy, in order of increasing difficulty:

1. descriptive research

2. predictive research

3. causal-descriptive research

4. causal-predictive research

■ Examples of Typical Marketing Information Research

Market Situation Research

Although the type of information collected varies with the specific company's needs, two broad categories can be identified: information related to consumers (micro-environment) and information related to the macro-environment.

In the first category, family structure, education, religion, and social customs are important considerations, especially for the international marketer. For example, if after-sales service for such products as tractors is an important part of the marketing effort, a company must know how many people in a particular country have at least some technical training.

Another example is the marketing of birth control devices in underdeveloped countries. Although these devices are generally financed by the government, serious familial, educational, religious, and social obstacles have been encountered. One important obstacle is that large segments of the market are illiterate.

Companies operating within one nation or one geographical area of a nation must also take these elements into consideration. In Canada, for example, the trend toward small nuclear families and the increasing number of working wives has many implications. For example, demand for baby food and diapers is decreasing. Even the demand for cottage cheese is related to race, religion, family size, age, and area demographics.[6]

In addition to general information about consumers, companies usually need more specific details. In the radio broadcasting business, for example, advertising rates are directly related to the number of people listening to a particular station. It is important therefore for the programmer to know the type of music that the target audience wants to hear and the desirability of such services as frequent weather and/or news reports, traffic reports, and consumer affairs programs. In the toothpaste industry, it is crucial to know the relative importance to consumers of decay prevention and of breath freshening and whitening agents.[7]

Car manufacturers need to know why consumers buy particular makes. Brand loyalty might be far less important than it was in the past for the average car buyer, while factors such as quality of workmanship, value per dollar, and low gas mileage are increasingly important.[8]

The second broad category of information needed by firms is related to the marketing environment. Such elements as the nature of the competition, the political and legal environment, and economic conditions can be of critical importance. These factors can determine whether it is at all possible to enter a particular market or market segment, and whether a product might be very successful, moderately successful, or a total failure.

Competition

The competition must be analysed to determine the number of competitors or potential competitors, the relative strength of each competitor, the resources at their disposal, how their actions affect the company in question, and how the company's actions can be expected to affect the competitors. For example, in an industry where total market demand is fairly stagnant, such as the sewing pattern industry, any one company can grow at the expense of the others. However, the sewing pattern market is dominated by Simplicity, McCall, Butterick, and Vogue. Any move by another company to gain market share is likely to be met by strong resistance, due to the competitive structure and the nature of the distribution system.[9]

The toothpaste industry is also highly concentrated. The competitive balance was severely disturbed when a relatively new brand, *Aqua-fresh*, gained 15% market share within one year. *Aqua-fresh* was the number-three brand, behind *Crest* and *Colgate*, in a market where a 1% market share was worth $6.59 million in revenues. Beecham, the producers, spent $19 million to promote *Aqua-fresh*, forcing the competitors to react with increased advertising and new advertising campaigns.[10]

Political/Legal Environment

The political/legal environment includes the laws and restrictions governing all facets of economic life, as well as the nature of the government, its stability, and the influence of various lobbies. For example, the overthrow of the Shah of Iran in 1979 meant an end to the marketing of alcoholic beverages in that country and created many difficulties for all western firms.

Another example is the restriction of marketing through official government agencies, which sometimes means that traditional advertising and promotional tools cannot be used. Also, tariff barriers can effectively close a market. However, firms that are not multinational might be severely restricted in their activities by political/legal factors. Laws concerning energy efficiency have grave consequences for car and appliance manufacturers. For example, an antitrust suit by the U.S. Justice Department against IBM led to the policy of decentralization of marketing strategy.[11]

Government action also can affect such things as advertising content. Consider the advertising of Warner-Lambert's *Listerine*, a mouthwash, which claimed that *Listerine* aided in preventing and curing colds. A legal precedent was set when the Federal Trade Commission (FTC) won a case against the company on the basis of unsubstantiated advertising.[12] Interestingly enough, the FTC hired a research firm to conduct consumer surveys to determine whether consumers perceived and recalled the medicinal claims. It was found that consumers did indeed recall these claims, and Warner-Lambert was forced to run corrective advertising. One study shows that although the corrective advertising significantly changed consumers' belief in the medicinal properties of the product, there was no significant change in the perception of the company's honesty or in the intention of consumers to buy *Listerine*.[13]

Economic Conditions

Economic conditions are of crucial importance because they are related to the ability to buy. Level of income is one factor, its distribution is another. The market for washing machines, for example, is likely to be small in a country where someone can be hired to do the wash by hand at a few dollars per day.

The rate of change of buying power is another important variable in long-term strategy. Rates and availability of consumer financing and other economic statistics can be very valuable. For example, lack of electricity in certain countries means that Singer has a market for foot-operated sewing machines and NCR has a market for hand-operated cash registers.

In industrial nations, inflation and cyclical downturns have important effects on many industries. The appliance industry, for example, is closely related to economic cycles. The Canadian market is 70% saturated in laundry equipment and 90% saturated in refrigeration equipment; as a result, replacement sales account for a large proportion of sales. Replacement sales for durables are sensitive to changes in economic conditions because consumers have the option of postponing their purchases in bad times. Indeed, any product bought with discretionary income is very sensitive to economic cycles.[14]

Combination of Factors

A combination of competitive, political/legal, and/or economic factors can force a firm to change its marketing strategy. For example, the British wool textile industry had been steadily declining since World War II. High inflation and interest rates made British fabrics less competitive on world markets, while European imports threatened British markets. The largest British wool manufacturer, Illingworth Morris, facing a loss of $3.2 million on sales of $238 million in the fiscal year ending March 31, 1980, decided to enter the U.S. market. The U.S. market was virtually closed, however, protected by a 50% tariff. The company's marketing strategy—its plans for market segmentation, marketing positioning, market entry, marketing mix, and timing—therefore had to be made under competitive, economic, and legal constraints.[15]

Examples of typical questions being asked by marketing managers and leading to descriptive market studies are shown in Table 2.2, and to predictive market studies in Table 2.3.

Market Response Research

The second type of marketing research is market response research. Typical examples are research into the relationship between changes in price and sales, and between changes in advertising (amount or content) and sales. The response of sales to advertising is generally thought to be strictly increasing at a decreasing rate. For example, based on the results of market research that concluded consumers would respond favourably to new *Trac II* blades, Gillette gave away some ten million free sample razors over a five-year period. Gillette Canada had previously lost about 10% of the market, mostly to Wilkinson Sword.[16]

TABLE 2.2
Examples of Questions Leading to Descriptive Market Research Studies

Environmental Variables	Example of Typical Marketing Information Research
Market Situation Analysis	
Micro-environment (consumer behaviour)	
Motivations	Why do people buy this type of product?
Perceptions of brand image	How do consumers perceive our brand?
Perceptions of products	How do consumers perceive this type of product?
Attitudes	What are people's attitudes toward our products?
Purchasing habits	How do people buy and consume our products?
Loyalty/switching	Are people loyal or do they switch brands? How often? Why?
Macro-environment	
Socio-economic profile	What is the socio-economic profile of our customers?
Competitive environment	What is the marketing strategy followed by our main competitors?
Legal environment	What laws and regulations affect selling a product in a given market?
Institutional environment	What are the institutions through which our product could be sold?
Economic environment	Are the economic conditions favourable to selling our products in a new market?
Cultural environment	Do cultural conditions warrant a change of product/ marketing program to enter a new foreign market?

TABLE 2.3

Examples of Questions Leading to Predictive Market Research Studies

Environmental Variables	Example of Typical Marketing Information Research
Market Situation Analysis	
Micro-environment (consumer behaviour)	
Motivations	How are buyers' motivations likely to change in the next few years?
Perceptions of brand image	Other things being equal, is our brand image likely to improve or deteriorate?
Perceptions of products	Is this product category's future bright or bleak over the next 5 or 20 years?
Attitudes	Are consumer attitudes toward use of this product likely to change?
Purchasing habits	Will purchasing habits in supermarkets be the same 20 years from now?
Loyalty/switching	Is the trend in the industry toward more or less brand loyalty?
Macro-environment	
Socio-economic profile	Is the typical consumer profile of our product likely to change rapidly?
Competitive environment	Is there a trend toward concentration in this industry?
Legal environment	What is the most likely piece of legislation regarding packaging to be passed in the next 5 years?
Institutional environment	What is the most likely evolution of our retailers in the next 10 years?
Economic environment	How long will interest rates remain above 15%?
Cultural environment	Will the product be accepted in underdeveloped countries within the foreseeable future?

In the toothpaste market, Procter & Gamble (*Crest, Gleem*), Colgate-Palmolive (*Colgate, Ultra-brite*), and Lever Brothers (*Aim, Close-up*) increased advertising expenditures in the face of the onslaught of *Aqua-fresh*. Overall industry advertising expenditures were estimated to have increased by 30% over the year before. Procter & Gamble also reacted by test-marketing a new toothpaste, a gel called *Pace*. All three companies produced new advertising campaigns.[17]

Test-marketing and testing consumer response to various advertising campaigns are types of market response research. Consider, for example, the test-marketing of the liquid hand soap *Softsoap* by Minnetonka. The product was launched nationally in January 1980, backed by a $6-million advertising campaign. Since total company sales in 1979 were $24 million, and since the product was up against such competitive giants as Procter & Gamble, the launch strategy entailed a considerable risk. The product was test-marketed in three stages over a period of a year and a half. The first stage involved three cities and was designed to determine the sales response function to gross television rating points. Stage two of the test-marketing involved three additional cities. The final stage involved ten cities that represented 14% of the population. Only after this extensive test-marketing was the product launched and the $6-million budget established.[18]

Examples of typical questions being asked by marketing managers and leading to causal-descriptive marketing research studies are given in Table 2.4, and to causal-predictive studies in Table 2.5.

TABLE 2.4
Examples of Questions Leading to Causal-descriptive Market Research Studies

Variables	Example of Typical Marketing Information Research
Marketing Variables	
Product	Does our line offer of several similar models affect sales negatively in a certain market?
Price	Does a price discount hurt our relations with certain small retailers?
Place	Would we sell more if we used a different distribution channel?
Advertising	Has our advertising campaign been effective in this market?
Personal selling	Can salespeople be more efficient through specialization?
Environmental Variables	
Consumer behaviour	Is the state of the economy an important cause of our sales decrease?
Socio-economic profile	Is revenue class an important factor in the purchase of this type of product
Legal environment	Are sales strongly affected by regulations on advertising?
Institutional environment	Is selling in a given market highly dependent on the type of dealers who distribute the products?
Economic environment	Is activity in this industry strongly dependent on interest rates?
Competitive environment	Are sales of our brand highly dependent on competitive advertising?

■ Elements of a Marketing Information System

Most firms use some more or less formal system for obtaining marketing information. Some of these systems are extremely simple and unstructured. Others are complex and highly structured, and have been designed to achieve the highest possible level of efficiency.[19] In this section the various elements that comprise a complete marketing information system are described. In the following sections more attention will be devoted to those parts of the marketing information system

TABLE 2.5
Examples of Questions Leading to Causal-predictive Research Studies

Variables	Example of Typical Marketing Information Research
Marketing Variables	
Product	What long-run effect on sales will our new product design have?
Price	Is the market going to positively react to our small price decrease?
Place	Will extending our distribution have a positive effect on our profit margin?
Advertising	Which of the two proposed advertising themes would be the more effective in the short run?
Personal selling	Would sales increase if we set higher quotas for our sales force?
Environmental Variables	
Consumer behaviour	How is the changing motivation pattern in the market going to affect future sales?
Socio-economic profile	Is the decreasing purchasing power in the market going to affect our profits?
Legal environment	Would a new piece of legislation on advertising to a specific audience (e.g., children) prevent us from selling in a market?
Institutional environment	How would sales change if we decided to switch distribution channels?
Economic environment	How will the new economic trends affect our industry and our firm in the near future?
Competitive environment	Will a new competitor hurt our sales? By how much?

that are more common. The more sophisticated and less widely used parts of such systems will be discussed in less detail.

Figure 2.4 describes the structure of a marketing system, and shows the place and role of such a system in the overall marketing planning process. A marketing information system is a complex set of interactions among data, statistical tools, management science-based decision support systems, and computing facilities.

The Data

The central part of such a system is the data bank, which should contain only data that have some relevance to the marketing operations of the firm. These data should relate in some way to aspects of the market environment, market characteristics, consumer behaviour, or market performance of the firm.

The data can come from many different sources. A useful classification of marketing data is the dichotomy between secondary and primary data. **Secondary data** include data that have already been collected for some purpose other than answering the specific needs of the marketing organization. Consequently, when such data are needed, they do not need to be collected again. **Primary data** are data that have not been collected, and that will be collected for answering the specific needs of a company.

FIGURE 2.4
The Marketing Information System

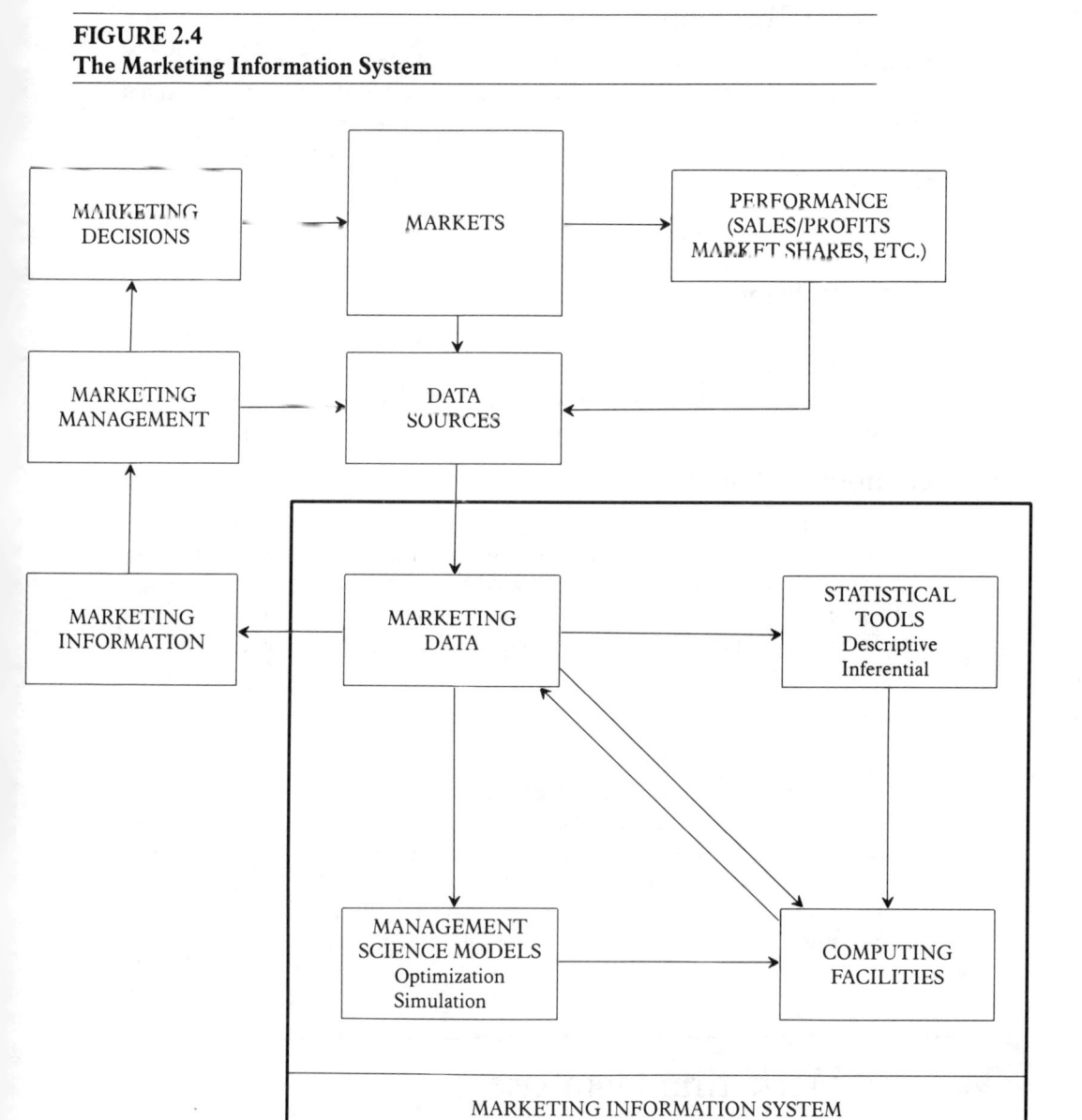

Generally, marketing raw data are numerous but are not readily usable by management. Frequently, they first need to be checked for accuracy, properly tabulated, summarized, and put into a usable format. This processing of raw data into information that is relevant to the needs of marketing managers is the essential function of the marketing information system. This task, however, would be next to impossible without the help of the three other parts of the marketing information system that are briefly outlined below.

Statistical Techniques

Statistical packages such as the Statistical Analysis System, the Statistical Package for the Social Sciences (Version X), and the Biomedical Computer Program include a large number of statistical techniques that are routinely used for analysing marketing data. Through statistical techniques, raw data are processed and yield additional data, but at a superior level of quality to, and much more meaningful than, the input raw data. This is why a data bank is enriched by the output data of statistical analyses.

Decision Support Systems

In the same way, decision support systems are a means of integrating raw data and market intelligence to produce decisions. They are essentially based on management science techniques, and typically imply simulation or optimization techniques.

Computing Facilities

Given the large amount of data involved, the magnitude of the problems, and the number of operations required for processing these data, modern marketing information systems have benefited greatly from recent computer technology. High-speed modern computers, with their almost unlimited capacity to store data, have made possible the development of very sophisticated marketing information systems.

As Figure 2.4 suggests, once the marketing information system has collected and processed the raw marketing data into usable form, marketing management can use the information to make better decisions and to design more effective marketing programs. This results in higher performance in terms of sales and/or profits, and/or market share, or any other management objective. These performance data are then used by the marketing information system for control purposes. In the following section, the data base, statistical techniques, and marketing decision support system components of the information system will be discussed in greater detail.

■ The Marketing Database

Figure 2.5 shows that marketing data can be classified according to their purpose and their source. Control-oriented data are continuously and regularly collected and are part of an ongoing flow of information received by marketing management. Decision-oriented data are collected only when the need arises. In the latter case, special procedures must be set up for the data collection.

Control- and decision-oriented data answer very different marketing information needs. Using control-oriented data, a marketing manager can check that everything in the marketplace has happened more or less as predicted. When

FIGURE 2.5
The Marketing Data Bank

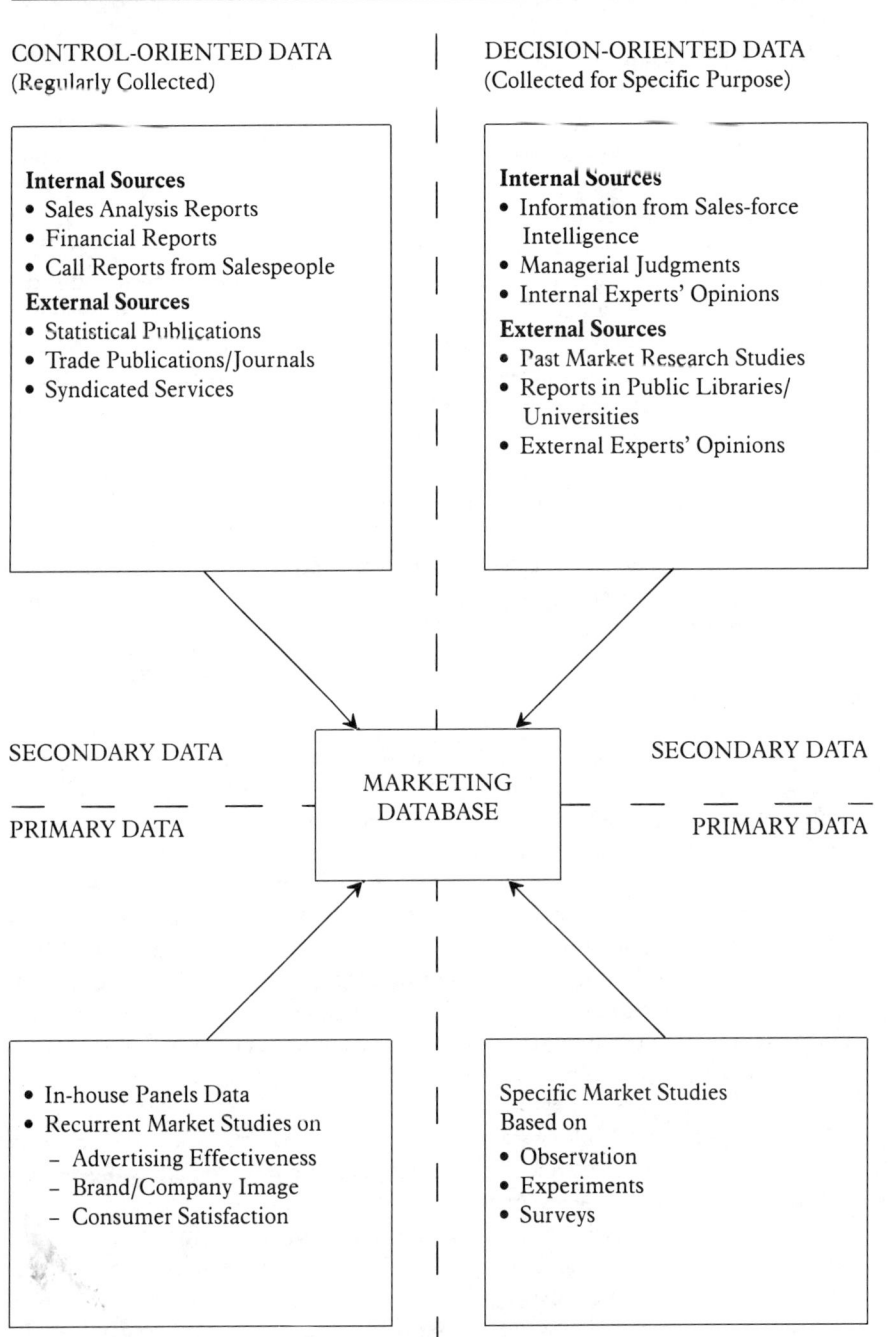

CONTROL-ORIENTED DATA
(Regularly Collected)

DECISION-ORIENTED DATA
(Collected for Specific Purpose)

Internal Sources
- Sales Analysis Reports
- Financial Reports
- Call Reports from Salespeople

External Sources
- Statistical Publications
- Trade Publications/Journals
- Syndicated Services

Internal Sources
- Information from Sales-force
  Intelligence
- Managerial Judgments
- Internal Experts' Opinions

External Sources
- Past Market Research Studies
- Reports in Public Libraries/
  Universities
- External Experts' Opinions

SECONDARY DATA

MARKETING
DATABASE

SECONDARY DATA

PRIMARY DATA

PRIMARY DATA

- In-house Panels Data
- Recurrent Market Studies on
  - Advertising Effectiveness
  - Brand/Company Image
  - Consumer Satisfaction

Specific Market Studies
Based on
- Observation
- Experiments
- Surveys

these analyses yield unexpected results, they generally unveil symptoms of a marketing problem. As an example, the marketing manager of an electrical appliance manufacturing firm receives a monthly report of the company sales that is broken down by product lines and geographical areas. The manager uses this data for comparing the actual sales volume of each product in each region with the forecasted sales as specified in the marketing plan.

Assume that in a certain month the marketing manager notices that, in the Calgary area, sales are 40% below their forecasted level. The control information pinpoints the symptoms of a marketing problem. For example, sales might have dropped as a result of declining economic conditions in this market and might have equally affected all of the Calgary electrical appliance manufacturers. The marketing information system signals a potential problem area. To identify the specific problem, the marketing manager might want to know what the sales of the major competitors in Calgary were during the same month. With this information, the marketing manager could assess whether the firm's own market share has been stable (i.e., all manufacturers were equally affected) or has decreased (i.e., only the firm's sales were affected).

In this case, if competitors' sales are not collected on an ongoing basis by the firm's information system, a special marketing study could be designed to solve a specific problem, as defined by the marketing manager. This would then be an example of decision-oriented data collection. In contrast to control-oriented data collection, these data are collected to solve a precise marketing decision problem, through ad hoc research studies.

Marketing Data Sources

Secondary data might come from internal or external sources, which will be discussed in greater detail in Chapter 5, "The Data-Collection Process." It is worth noting here, however, that a more recently recognized and important source of marketing data is managerial judgments, as well as the opinions of internal or external experts. This source is very useful because of the impossibility of finding certain types of information (especially historical data that have not been formally collected) or because of the high cost of collecting such data. Since marketing managers can draw on the knowledge that they have acquired from experience, their opinions often can be used when objective data are not available. Managerial judgments are typically used in decision models, as will be discussed in the next section. Certain methods have been devised to collect such data as accurately and precisely as possible.

Primary data collection is generally more expensive, since a marketing researcher must undertake a specific research study in order to collect the desired data. Of course, sometimes a firm has its own in-house panel. Also, certain marketing research studies are often carried out at regular time intervals, perhaps, to ascertain the effects of various advertising campaigns, or to monitor how the company or a brand image is evolving over time, or to measure the current level of consumer satisfaction. However, the trend is for primary data research to be carried out on an ad hoc basis, according to the specific requirements of the marketing problem to be solved. In these cases, an original research design and a particular research strategy are generally required.

Primary Sources of Marketing Data

There are at least three broad types of primary data sources: observation, experimentation, and marketing surveys. The survey technique has reached such a
stage of development and is so widely used that sometimes it is (unduly) thought
of as the only method for carrying out marketing research, at least in the eyes of
the general public.

Observation. This is the most basic data collection procedure. It consists essentially of observing, for example, sales representatives, sales clerks, or some aspect
of consumer behaviour. Obviously, what can be observed is only the overt
behaviour of individuals (or the results of behaviour), or some material facts, such
as the prices charged by various stores for a given item. No information can be
obtained about the thoughts, opinions, and deeper feelings of the observed
subjects. However, even when information on consumer behaviour is all that a
marketing manager needs, this information can be questionable because it can be
affected by two important sources of error: the observer's bias and errors that result
when the subjects know they are being observed.

However, this method of collecting data can sometimes be refined. Some
marketing researchers now use objective recording devices such as cameras or
tape recorders, particularly for advertising pre-test studies. Another possible
improvement consists of concealing the observer(s) or recording devices from
view. For example, some supermarkets have hidden cameras in the ceiling of
some stores to record the shoppers' movements along the aisles. In other cases,
cameras are concealed behind the shelves in a supermarket to record the eyelid
movements of consumers when they look at certain products and brands. In any
case, however, data collected through observational methods are essentially
descriptive and hardly explanatory in nature. They often need to be supplemented
by other data collection techniques.

Experimentation. When researchers attempt to establish a causal relationship
between two variables, experimentation is the most appropriate research method
to use.[20] For instance, if they want to find out which advertising appeal results in
the highest sales level, or which of three possible compensation schemes best
motivates salespeople, a causal relationship is implied between advertising appeal
and sales and between the incentive compensation plan and motivation. An
experiment will give indications about the nature of the relationship (i.e., its
direction, shape, and amplitude). In practice, however, sales probably will vary as
the result of a large number of factors other than (or in addition to) the variable
under investigation.

Consequently, the principle of experimentation consists of measuring how a
phenomenon (the dependent variable) varies as another variable (the causal or
independent variable) is manipulated and submitted to some systematic variation.
The objective is to keep all other factors constant or, if possible, to control and/or
measure the variations of other factors. This principle is simple enough, but is
very difficult to implement in many situations. Numerous experimental designs
or methods are used to ensure that only the effect of the experimental variable is
measured. However, because of the complex issues involved, each experimental
design has advantages as well as the potential for certain types of error.[21]
Experimental designs will be discussed in Chapter 4.

Because of the serious difficulties involved in setting up experimental designs where marketing variables can be manipulated by the researcher, it is not surprising that this method of investigation has to date had only limited applications in marketing. As was previously emphasized, the environment in which marketing decisions are made is very complex. Also, the costs of experimentation in marketing are substantial: in addition to the direct costs of research, the opportunity costs involved are often very high. For instance, assessment of the effect of various promotional deals on sales requires that less effective deals be purposely tried out in some markets. This certainly results in opportunity losses that might be more or less substantial and lasting. For all of these reasons, therefore, although experimentation as well as observation are often useful techniques in certain specific instances, they are not always the best approaches for collecting primary marketing data.

Market Survey. Because many marketing problems involve some aspect of consumer behaviour, it is not surprising that market surveys have been one of the most widely used techniques to collect marketing data. The principle of a market survey is to interview current or potential consumers who have, and are willing to provide, the information that a marketing researcher wants to obtain, using a questionnaire. In most cases, a marketer wants to obtain information about socio-demographic profiles, lifestyles, personalities, past or present behaviour, buying intentions or intended buying behaviour, as well as perceptions, preferences, attitudes, and opinions. Because the sizes of the populations involved are generally very large, interviewing all of the consumers in a market segment would be too costly and time-consuming. Consequently, only a sample of the whole population is chosen and interviewed. If the sample of respondents has been chosen according to certain probabilistic procedures, the sample is likely to have the same general characteristics as the whole population. Using statistical theory, sampling errors as well as the confidence intervals around the computed statistics can be estimated through simple formulas. Thus, by accepting calculated risks or errors, a marketing researcher can save the time, effort, and money that would be necessary to interview the whole population.

Several steps are typically involved in a market survey. Unfortunately, each step involves some risk of error. Some types of errors can be controlled to a certain extent; other types can be avoided only through the extensive expertise and know-how of the marketing researcher. In any marketing survey there is room for judgment, and generally a researcher's experience cannot be superseded by a set of "recipes." This is why sometimes two surveys, even with the same general objectives, have yielded different results.

■ The Marketing Research Process

In designing and implementing the research study, a designated series of steps must be followed carefully, in chronological order. This series of steps, known as the **research process**, is shown in Figure 2.6; the large numbers indicate the chapters that cover these topics in more depth.

FIGURE 2.6
The Marketing Research Process

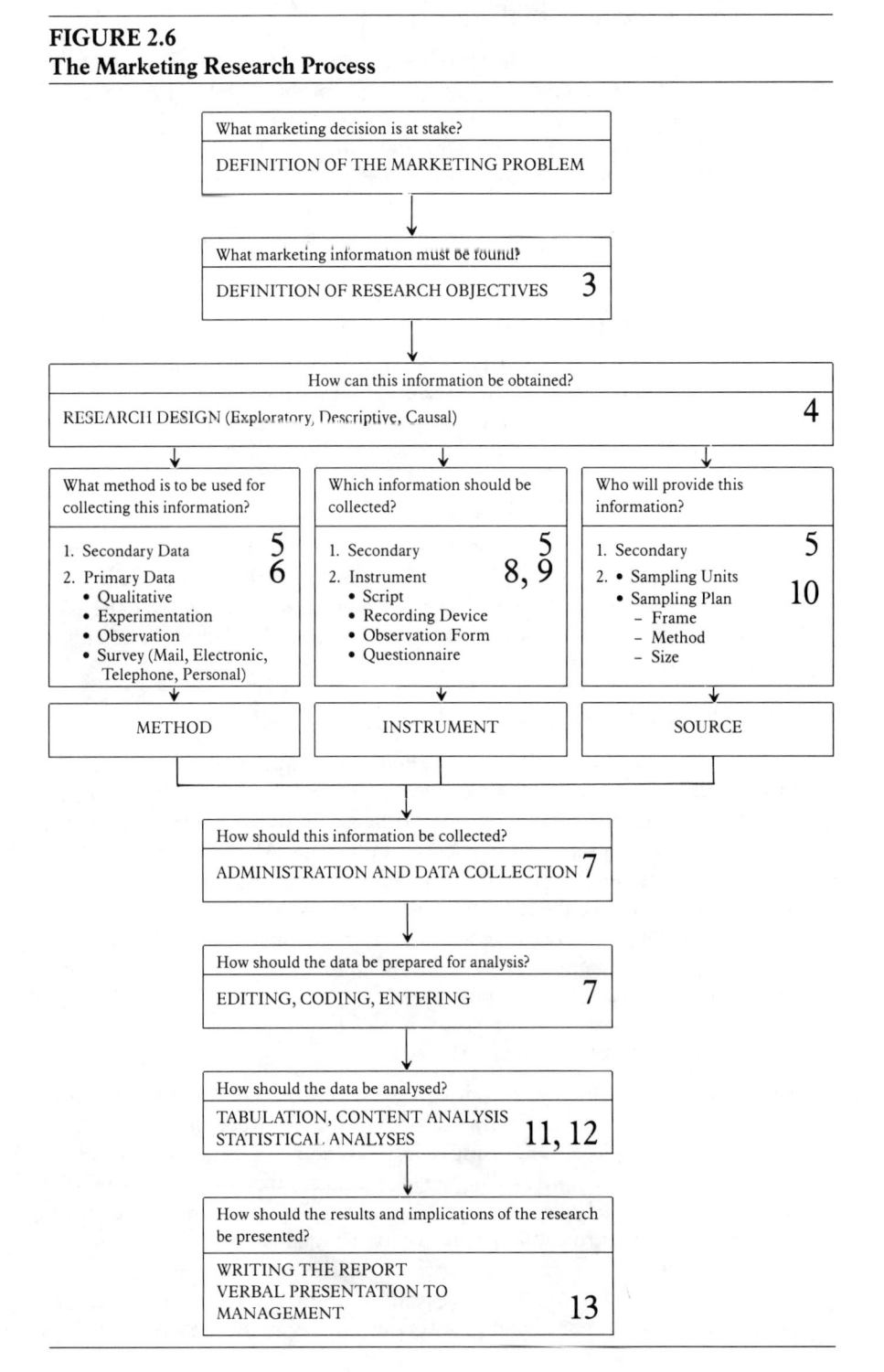

Marketing Problem Definition

Marketing problem definition, the first step in the research process, is considered the most critical to the success of the project. If the problem is stated vaguely, or if the wrong problem is defined, then the rest of the research is completely useless. For example, is the problem faced by the company one of declining sales, or are declining sales merely a symptom of the real problem, which could be poor product development or inadequate advertising and sales promotion? The marketing problem is not properly defined unless the researcher understands *what marketing decision is at stake*.

Research Objectives Definition

The second step of the research process consists of translating the marketing decision problem into a very precise research problem. As will be seen in the next chapter, this is a very important and difficult task. The purpose of this step is to answer the question: *What marketing information must be found?*

Research Design Specification

A clear definition of the research objectives makes possible the third step, research design. The research design serves as a framework for the study, guiding the collection and analysis of the data. The research design focusses on the data collection methods, the measuring instruments to be utilized, and the sampling plan to be followed.

Choice of Data Collection Method(s)

In choosing the proper data collection method(s), cost and time considerations, as well as the quality of the data collected, are of prime importance. For example, the researcher can save considerable time and expense by always going to secondary data sources before attempting to collect primary data. All too often firms have wasted immense amounts of time and money gathering primary data when the same data were already available from secondary sources. If satisfactory secondary data are not available, the researcher must rely on primary data gathered from observation, experimentation, or personal, telephone, or mail surveys, or from managerial judgments.

Selecting the Research Instruments

The instruments used in research design for measuring and/or collecting the information might be mechanical, such as a tape recorder or a camera. In situations where the researcher is using the survey method, the instrument will be the questionnaire. Although in Chapter 8 questionnaire construction will be discussed in some detail, it is worth noting here that this research instrument must be utilized with great caution. Construction of good questionnaires is a skill that takes considerable time for a professional marketing researcher to develop. Care must be exercised in the types of questions asked, the form and wording of questions, the choice of words, and the order in which certain sensitive questions are asked.

Sampling Plan Specification

In the sampling plan, the basic question concerns who is to be part of the study. Since it might not be possible to question everyone in the relevant universe (the whole collection of items studied by the researcher), especially in the case of consumer convenience-goods manufacturers, a sample or subsection of people in that universe must be used. We must determine what the sampling unit will be, how large our sample should be, and what our sampling procedure will be.

Data Collection

Data collection, the third major step in the marketing process, is also known as field work. Research design must have been completed before data collection can begin. The gathering of primary data is usually considered to be the most expensive and the most error-prone step in the research process, so great caution must be exercised at this point. Problems arise when respondents refuse to co-operate or are not at home, and when there is bias on the part of either respondent or interviewer. These field work problems can be reduced by carefully selecting, training, controlling, and evaluating the field force.

Data Analysis

Data analysis, the fourth step, is the statistical analysis of the data that have been edited, coded, and tabulated. This step is particularly important in cases where the researcher has amassed large amounts of information from many respondents. The purpose is to determine if anything meaningful can be gathered from this mass of data, and it is to the data analysis step that the researcher must bring the kind of quantitative skills that will be discussed in the next section.

Report Preparation

The purpose of the research report, the fifth step, is presentation to the audience of the essential findings of the study in a clear and concise manner. The written research report follows a carefully designed format that allows the reader to ascertain the key elements immediately, so that action can be taken.

An effective research report is prepared with the level of the audience in mind. Technical sections and computer print-outs usually are reserved for the appendix.

■ Data Analysis

The preceding section discussed the procedures used to collect relevant marketing data. Very frequently, however, the raw data that are the output of the data collection process do not by themselves permit a marketing manager to make better decisions. In fact, a market survey or an experiment typically results in an extremely large amount of computer output, analyses, and statistical tables. Unfortunately, a very long series of numbers cannot be interpreted and digested right away because of the inability of the human mind to readily integrate a large number of facts. Generally, meaningful results can be achieved only through careful data processing and analysis.

A researcher might have several objectives when analysing marketing data to be used by a marketing manager. The primary goal might be to reduce large amounts of data to only a few key numbers, or into a visual display that will reveal the meaning of the data at a glance. Descriptive statistics can be used in order to achieve this most elementary objective. More and more sophisticated descriptive statistical tools can also be used to portray large quantities of data.

Inferential statistics can be used when a researcher needs to infer to the population as a whole the conclusions derived from the sample observations. This technique meets with the requirements of market surveys in that it measures some consumer characteristics of a representative sample of consumers and allows inference of the conclusions for the entire market segment.

At a still higher level of analysis, a researcher might attempt to link the data themselves to marketing decisions. Frequently, although the data have been properly summarized and the conclusions are deemed to be applicable to the whole population, the results of various analyses do not readily point to specific marketing decisions. An additional step is necessary to bridge the gap between marketing data and marketing decisions. This step is made possible by marketing decision support systems.

Statistical Techniques

Multivariate statistical techniques are increasingly applied in analysing marketing data.[22] These techniques, which are suitable for the analysis of phenomena when a very large number of variables are involved, have found an obvious field of application in marketing research. Such techniques are called multidimensional scaling,[23] multiple regression analysis, multiple discriminant analysis, canonical correlation, factor analysis,[24] correspondence analysis,[25] and clustering techniques. These techniques are discussed further in Chapter 12, "Introduction to Advanced Statistics."

As was already discussed, data reduction is a frequent objective of marketing data analysis. For example, let us assume that a researcher wants to estimate the consumption of breakfast cereals in Halifax. The researcher could, for instance, list all of the households in the Halifax area, and note yearly breakfast cereal consumption of each household. Obviously, this long list would not be very informative or useful to a marketing manager. It would definitely be more appropriate to compute the mean consumption across all of the households and to estimate, for example, the average household consumption of breakfast cereals in Halifax at three boxes per month. By doing this, the researcher has summarized all of the information that has been collected by one single number: the mean. (In practice, however, a measure of dispersion or a distribution of the consumption levels of households would also be very informative.) Thus, other statistics could yield summary measures of different aspects of the data.

To illustrate a multivariate technique as a data reduction tool, consider the example of a marketing researcher who was interested in learning about the perceptions of certain brands of beer in a given market segment of the province of Quebec.[26] He could have started by listing all of the attributes that he knew consumers use to evaluate brands of beer. Let us assume that the researcher identified fifty such attributes, and that he was interested in knowing how six leading brands (*Labatt's 50, O'Keefe, Brador, Molson, Laurentide, Carlsberg*) were perceived. Assuming that he selected a representative sample of 1000 beer drinkers in the relevant market segment, the market researcher could have asked each of the 1000 respondents to rate each brand on the basis of the fifty attributes on a nine-point scale. This simple research exercise would have resulted in 300 000 pieces of information (i.e., 6 brands × 50 attributes × 1000 respondents). Obviously, if the analysis had stopped here, the marketing manager would learn very little about consumers' brand perceptions

First, it is likely that a few of the fifty attributes are very closely correlated—that they are essentially measuring the same thing. Second, it is probable that some attributes are very important and others are less important to the consumers. Using a multivariate statistical technique (in this case, multiple discriminant analysis), the results are shown in Figure 2.7, which is summarized by the following.

> The diagram shows quite clearly that in this case, consumers essentially use two sets of attributes to differentiate among the brands. The horizontal axis is a high price-high quality versus lower price-lower quality dimension. The vertical axis is a light-heavy dimension. The attributes which are essentially used by consumers to differentiate among the brands are shown on the diagram and are as close to an axis as they are correlated with this dimension. In addition, the mean perceptions for each brand by the consumers are also positioned on the graph. Thus, Carlsberg is perceived by this segment of Quebec consumers as a high-quality beer, low in alcohol, with a snobbish, feminine, occasional drinker connotation. In contrast, Molson is perceived as a rather heavy, strong, darker and more popular beer.[27]

This example shows how the analysis and the resulting diagram extracted meaning from 300 000 raw scaling numbers, yielding a simple, easy-to-interpret visual display. Of course, this is only a limited example of what multivariate statistical techniques can do for marketing researchers. Other applications could emphasize statistical inferences—probability statements about the true characteristics of a population, given the observations that a researcher has made on a sample. The application of such techniques to marketing problems has been constantly increasing over the last twenty years, and is being extended to new marketing problem areas. Percepetual maps like that shown in Figure 2.7, can also be used for new product positioning, or for the specification of market segmentation strategies.

Marketing Decision Support Systems

Even after marketing data have been analysed and their meaning extracted, the problem remains that the marketing manager must make decisions based on them. To provide assistance for this major step, some firms use marketing decision support systems[28] that generally are based on management science- or operations research-based models.

A model is a simplified replication of the real world. Thus, a marketing model represents some marketing phenomenon. When management scientists build models they delete some less important or irrelevant variables. Thus, the model is a much simpler system but retains the most relevant aspects of the real world for the purpose of the marketing manager. A model can be a logical flow chart or even a verbal description of a marketing phenomenon. More often, a model is highly structured and includes mathematical relationships that formally link the various variables of the system. Over the last few years a number of such marketing decision support systems have been successfully implemented.[29]

FIGURE 2.7
Perceptual Map of Selected Brands of Beer
in a Given Quebec Market Segment

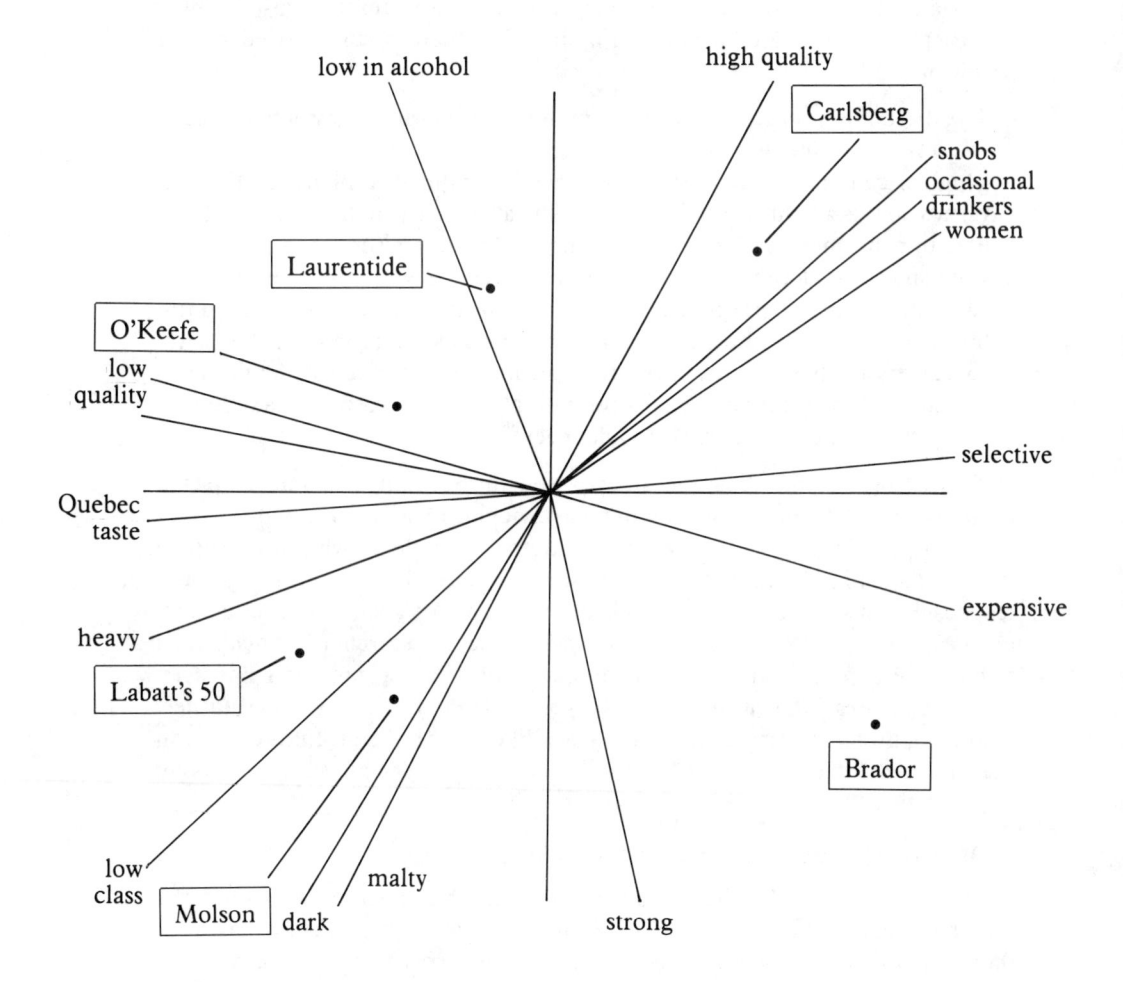

Source: René Y. Darmon, "Multiple Joint Space Analysis for Improved Advertising Strategy." *The Canadian Marketer*, vol. 10, 1979, p. 14.

■ Summary

This chapter was devoted to a description of the marketing information systems that marketers use to define their strategies and tactics. Research was shown to be a logical consequence of the modern marketing concept. To design a product that satisfies consumer needs and wants, a marketer requires information about consumer preferences, buying behaviours, tastes, media exposure habits, and the market environment.

Marketing research is a management tool that a marketing manager can use to gain differential advantages over competitors. However, marketing research is also a costly activity that must be viewed from a cost/benefit perspective. It is a complicated process that cannot be carried out effectively without professional capabilities.

Marketing information systems fulfil two major roles: data collection and data analysis. Marketing data might come from internal or external secondary sources or from primary sources, depending on cost. Market surveys are the main method of primary marketing data collection. The marketing research process comprises a designated series of steps that must be followed carefully and in chronological order.

Finally, data can be analysed through simple or elaborate statistical techniques, such as multivariate statistical methods. Sophisticated marketing information systems also include a number of decision models that permit a marketing manager to analyse marketing data to facilitate decision making. Some firms have decision support systems to assist in this process.

For Discussion

1. Contrast the role of marketing research in a consumer-oriented versus a product-oriented organization.

2. Explain why, in your opinion, some firms have felt the need to develop large marketing information systems. What problem might arise when using such systems?

3. Why do you think marketing research might not yet be common practice among small and medium-sized Canadian firms? Is this situation likely to change in the next few years? If so, how?

4. What is the difference between primary and secondary marketing data? Give examples of both.

5. Explain market situation research and market response research.

6. List and describe the major steps of a marketing research study.

7. Is the use of managerial judgment as a source of marketing data compatible with the scientific approach? Explain.

8. What are the main marketing data sources? Give specific examples.

9. Explain the difference between descriptive, predictive, and causal research.

10. Show how a research study can combine causal and predictive aspects, or causal and descriptive aspects.

Problems

1. **Mini-Case: Masutti Inc.**

   Masutti Inc. is a franchised distributor of automative parts throughout the eastern regions of Canada. The dealership purchases its stock from the parent company, Masutti Manufacturing, which makes spark plugs, batteries, gaskets, fan belts, headlights, and other car parts. In addition, the outlets carry other brands of the same items, as well as tires, car paint, tools, and related products. The franchises sell to small industries that do auto repairs, such as gas stations, truck companies, taxi companies, factories, and body repair shops. Most of the customers are businesses that are located close to the franchises. The public also can purchase automotive parts over the counter.

   Masutti Inc. wants to carry out marketing research to determine where it should locate new franchises.

   Questions
   1. In order to carry out this market study, to what extent should a researcher rely on secondary data? On primary data?

   2. List information that the researcher would need to know to answer this research question.

2. The marketing manager of a leading canned-vegetable manufacturer wants to assess the impact on sales of the shelf space given to products in the super-markets. Nine supermarkets in the Saskatoon area decided to co-operate in the following experiment. In the first three supermarkets, one metre of shelf space is allocated to the firm's brand. In the next three supermarkets, two metres; in the last three supermarkets, three metres. For one week, the sales are recorded in each supermarket at the end of each day. Evaluate this research design. What problems could be encountered that could affect the results of this study? How could such a research design be improved? What are the costs involved in this design? How could a marketer use the results of the study?

3. The marketing researcher for a company that manufactures a major brand of instant coffee wants to learn about the attitudes of British Columbia house-wives toward regular and instant coffee. Outline a research proposal that could be used by this marketing researcher. What are the limitations of using a survey for this type of research?

Endnotes

1. "Liquid Gold." *Fortune*, November 5, 1979.
2. Neil H. Borden, "The Concept of the Marketing Mix," *Journal of Advertising Research*, 4 (June 1964), pp. 2–7.
3. S.B. Ash and J.W. Hanson, "The Use of Research Techniques by Professional Marketing Researchers." *Proceedings*. Ed. Robert G. Wyckham. Administrative Sciences Association of Canada (ASAC), 1981, pp. 11–20.
4. R. Deshpande, "The Organizational Context of Market Research Use." *Journal of Marketing*, 4 (Fall 1982), pp. 90–101.
5. "New or Me Too: Which Type of Product is More Successful?" *The Nielsen Reporter*, 2, 1980.
6. *Progressive Grocer*, September 1980.
7. "The Big Squeeze on Toothpaste." *The New York Times*, September 20, 1980.
8. "Chrysler and Autoweek." *Popular Science*, November 1980.
9. "What's in a Pattern?" *The New York Times*, February 29, 1976.
10. *The New York Times*, September 21, 1980.
11. *Sales and Marketing Management*, September 15, 1980.
12. Dorothy Cohen, "The FTC's Advertising Substantiation Program." *Journal of Marketing*, 44 (Winter 1980).
13. R. Mizerski, Neil Allison, and Stephen Calvert, "A Controlled Field Study of Corrective Advertising Using Multiple Exposures and Commercial Medium." *Journal of Marketing Research*, 17 (August 1980).
14. "Whirlpool: Battling an Ebb Tide of Consumer Spending." *The New York Times*, August 10, 1980.
15. "How Pamela Mason Is Rattling British Wool." *The New York Times*, August 10, 1980.
16. "The Blitz that Kept Gillette on Top." *Financial Times*, September 24, 1979.
17. "The Big Squeeze in Toothpaste." *The New York Times*, September 21, 1980.
18. "Taking on the Soap Giants." *Marketing and Media Decisions*, October 1980.
19. See, for example, David B. Montgomery and Glen L. Urban, "Marketing Information Systems: An Emerging View." *Journal of Marketing Research*, 8 (May 1970), pp. 226–34.
20. For a discussion of experimental designs, see Donald T. Campbell and Julian C. Stanley, *Experimental and Quasi-Experimental Designs for Research*. Chicago: Rand McNally and Co., 1963.
21. See, for example, Seymour Banks, *Experimentation in Marketing*. New York: McGraw-Hill, 1965.
22. A good treatment of statistical multivariate techniques applied to marketing is given in Paul E. Green and Donald S. Tull, *Research for Marketing Decisions*. 3rd ed. Englewood Cliffs, NJ: Prentice-Hall, 1975.
23. Paul E. Green, and Frank M. Carmone, *Multidimensional Scaling and Related Techniques in Marketing Analysis*. Boston: Allyn and Bacon.

24. Examples of applications of techniques to marketing problems can be found in David A. Aaker, *Multivariate Analysis in Marketing: Theory and Applications*. Belmont, CA: Wadsworth Publishing Co., 1971; Jagdish N. Sheth, ed., *Multivariate Methods for Market and Survey Research*. Chicago: American Marketing Association, 1977.

25. See, for example, Ludovic Lebart and Jean-Pierre Fenelon, *Statistiques et Informatique Appliquées*. 3rd ed. Paris: Dunod, 1975.

26. René Y. Darmon, "Multiple Joint Space Analysis for Improved Advertising Strategy." *The Canadian Marketer*, 10 (1979), pp. 10–14.

27. Ibid., p. 14.

28. More information on this subject can be found in David B. Montgomery and Glen L. Urban, *Management Science in Marketing*. Englewood Cliffs, NJ: Prentice-Hall, 1969; Philip Kotler, *Marketing Decision Making: A Model Building Approach*. New York: Holt, Rinehart and Winston, 1971.

29. See, for instance, John D.C. Little, "Models and Managers: The Concept of a Decision Calculus." *Management Science*. (April 1970); Leonard M. Lodish, "Callplan: An Interactive Sales Call Planning System." *Management Science*, 2 (December 1970); John D. C. Little and Leonard M. Lodish, "A Media Planning Calculus." *Operations Research*, vol. XVII (January–February 1969); Dennis H. Gensch, *Advertising Planning*, New York: Elsevier Scientific Publishing Co., 1973; *Simulatics Media Mix: Technical Description*. New York: The Simulatics Corporation, October, 1962; Glen L. Urban, "Perceptor: A Model for Product Positioning." *Management Science*, 21 (April 1975), pp. 858–71; Glen L. Urban, "Sprinter Mod. I: A Basic New Product Analysis Model," paper presented at the 1969 AMA Businessmen's Meeting in Atlanta, June 17, 1969; and Glen L. Urban, "Sprinter Mod. III: A Model for the Analysis of New Frequently Purchased Consumer Products." *Operations Research* (September 1970); Henry Claycamp and Lucien T. Liddy, "Prediction of New Product Performance: An Analytical Approach." *Journal of Marketing Research*, 6 (November 1969), pp. 414–20; Alvin J. Silk and Glen L. Urban, "Pre-test Market Evaluation of New Packaged Goods." *Journal of Marketing Research*, 15 (May 1978), pp. 171–91; John D.C. Little, "Brandaid: An On-line Marketing Mix Model," Part 1 and Part 2. *Operations Research*, 23 (July–August 1975), pp. 628–73.

3 TRANSLATING MARKETING PROBLEMS INTO RESEARCH PROJECTS

Despite the growing acceptance of marketing research by Canadian firms, several obstacles still lie in the way of optimal use of this function and of a more systematic approach to marketing research. First and foremost among these is the frequent lack of effective communication between the manager and the researcher.

Of course, conducting marketing research is rarely a simple task. A researcher typically faces a host of problems. One of the main problems, manager-researcher interface, is examined at length in this chapter. For illustrative purposes, a case study is used that focusses on the complex set of interactions between manager and researcher that are involved throughout the decision process. This chapter also provides some examples of pseudo-marketing research.

Intuition vs. Scientific Method in Marketing Research

The Intuitive Approach

Most marketers know that when marketing decisions are made without the benefit of formal marketing research, the result is often disaster. For example, the decision to bypass a test market in the haste to get a new product directly to the mass market cost one major food processor millions of dollars and a loss of the goodwill of both customers and distributors. It was discovered—too late—that the packages leaked while on retail store shelves and that the product, a snack for kids, was too sweet for many customers.

All too often, business and marketing decisions are made on the basis of "gut feelings" or intuition. One dictionary defines intuition as "the power of knowing or the knowledge obtained without recourse to inference or reasoning." Thus, a marketing manager might say, "I don't think we should introduce this new product line; my intuition tells me that it won't succeed." The manager might be right, but if so, it is only by chance. Valuable past experience might have played a part in this intuitive feeling, but to make important decisions strictly by intuition is a course of action that is highly prone to error and totally non-scientific.

Several conditions might cause managers to rely on intuition instead of more objective methods in decision making. For example, often answers are called for immediately, action must be taken at once, and there simply is not enough time— so these managers feel—to conduct a proper research study. Lack of money is another reason; there may not be sufficient funds in the budget to conduct a research study into the problem. A lack of marketing research expertise is still another reason for relying on intuition, and a final reason is ignorance. Some managers are unaware of the potential benefits that are derived from a properly conducted research study and therefore rely on their intuition in making decisions. For example, being unaware of *Sales Management*'s "Annual Survey of Buying Power" could cause a manager to rely on guesswork in estimating the purchasing power of consumers in a given area, when this information has already been compiled and is currently available.

The Scientific Approach

Even the area of marketing research is sometimes subject to such questions as: Are marketing and business activities so hopelessly complex that they cannot be understood by scientific thinking? Should scientific thinking be reserved for scientists in their laboratories? Are years of actual practice rather than scientific techniques the only valid aid for executives faced with making decisions? Research professionals know that scientific progress has been rapid in business and that scientific thinking is invaluable in analysing business problems, although some doubters remain.

The question of whether marketing is a science or an art is also sometimes raised. The answer is that marketing activities involve both science and art. Marketing research represents a relatively new area of scientific inquiry and as a behavioural science it has not yet reached maturity. Many marketing research studies are not shared throughout the profession, because most research is done in secrecy and firms do not want competitors to know the results. The extent of scientific progress in marketing has been described by Theodore Beckman:

> Whether marketing is more of a science or more of an art is debatable, but it is certainly an area in which considerable scientific progress is being made, both in the sense of the expansion of a body of classified and systematized knowledge and also with respect to increasing application of scientific methods to basic research and in decision-making processes within firms.[1]

In spite of the difficulties encountered in bringing scientific principles to such a complex area as marketing, success is gradually being achieved. The evolving sophistication of marketing research techniques and methodologies is an important contribution to the use of scientific methods in marketing. As the marketing process becomes more scientific, marketing research becomes an increasingly valuable aid and a competitive weapon in decision making. On the other hand, poorly conducted or misused marketing research represents a waste of the organization's time, personnel, and resources, and offers no improvement over reliance solely on intuition. It is the responsibility of management to sponsor cost-effective research efforts.

■ Applying the Scientific Method

The scientific method is an impartial, consistent, and systematic process that can be used to solve business problems. It consists of four steps: observation, formulation of hypotheses, prediction of the future, and testing of the hypotheses.

Whereas the feasibility of applying the scientific method is taken for granted in the natural sciences, in the social sciences doubts are sometimes expressed. To the question whether the scientific method can be applied in business and in marketing, the answer is an emphatic *yes*. The scientific method is universally applicable:

> The scientific method of investigation and analysis is used by all scientists. . . .
> It makes no difference whether the investigation is in the fields traditionally
> held to be sciences, such as chemistry and physics, or as in the various areas of
> human relations, including business and the other social sciences.[2]

In other words, a research project is scientific when the scientific way of carrying out an investigation is used correctly and when the search for information is systematic, objective, and as thorough as possible. Thus, the four steps of the scientific method are applicable to any area of scientific inquiry. The following is an example of the application of the four steps.

A marketing manager for a large manufacturer of wooden tennis rackets sees that sales are stable but wants to improve the long-term sales outlook for the firm. Therefore, the manager takes the following steps:

1. *Observation*: She observes that competitors who manufacture aluminum rackets have increasing sales.

2. *Formulation of hypothesis*. She assumes that her firm's flat growth rate is due solely to the fact that it manufacturers only wooden tennis rackets.

3. *Prediction of the future*. She predicts that sales will increase if her firm starts to manufacture aluminum tennis rackets of comparable quality.

4. *Testing the hypothesis*. The firm produces some aluminum tennis rackets and test-markets them.

In this example, the market test proved the prediction to be correct—sales did increase with the firm's introduction of aluminum tennis rackets. If sales had not increased, the marketing manager would at least have known that the problem had nothing to do with the type of tennis racket that the firm was manufacturing. She might then have hypothesized that other firms were spending more on advertising than her firm was, or perhaps that there were differences in the price structure, quality, or channels of distribution used by her firm. Further application of the steps in the scientific method would have allowed her to isolate the problem and then develop a sound strategy to overcome it.

Limitations of the Scientific Method

The scientific method is not without its limitations. For example, all steps might be followed faithfully, but if the researcher is not objective, the process is invalid. If the measurement techniques are not accurate, the results will not be useful to management. The scientific method also implies that the researcher must continue to investigate the problem exhaustively, doing replication studies when necessary. Thus, in looking at research data and determining whether the scientific method has been properly followed, we must not only examine the steps that have been taken but also we must determine whether the researcher was objective, whether the measurement was accurate, and whether the investigation was thorough.

Difficulties are inherent in applying the scientific method in marketing—difficulties that stem from the wide gulf between controllable laboratory conditions and uncontrollable conditions in the marketplace. For example, if we want to know the effect of increased advertising expenditures on sales, we need a tightly controlled marketplace situation where only one element, advertising expenditures, can be allowed to vary, with all other variables, such as competitor reaction, held constant. This situation is virtually impossible in a marketing environment.

The difficulties encountered in using the scientific method in marketing revolve around several factors. Although these difficulties are being reduced as more comprehensive marketing studies are developed and as research techniques improve, they still are present.[3] Designing a research project to supply information that is relevant to a given marketing problem is very difficult. Perhaps this is why certain firms, particularly small- and medium-sized firms, are often reluctant to use marketing research to back up their marketing decisions. Some of the difficulties inherent in collecting relevant marketing information are outlined in the following section.

Complex Marketing Phenomena

As was already discussed, marketing phenomena are complex. Consumers are human beings—they change, evolve with time, and are often unpredictable. Typically, marketing research has to deal with human behaviour. Social science research that aims at explaining human behaviour is still in its infancy and can provide only scant help to a marketing researcher. The fact that any marketing system is constantly evolving adds to this complexity. Thus, any study done at a specific point in time can give only a static and already outdated picture of the market as it was when the research was done. Yet marketing managers must base their decisions on what a market will be like in the future. If a marketing researcher can be sure about one thing, it is that tomorrow's market will be different from today's. This is why even the best marketing research leaves ample room for marketing managers to form their own vision of how the market will evolve in the next few years.

Another element that contributes to the complexity of marketing systems is that it is very difficult to assess the effects of a single marketing action on the whole system. For example, what is the effect on sales of a temporary promotional action (for example, a coupon worth ten-cents-off on a jar of instant coffee)? This relationship is difficult to assess because sales might have varied during the promotional period due to a host of other uncontrollable factors that might also have varied and sometimes cannot even be measured. For example, increased sales of instant coffee might also be caused by the action of a competitor, or by an unexpected expansion of the global market demand for this type of product. Other factors, such as changes in an advertising campaign, can interact with the price variation. In other words, the two varying elements (price and advertising) can yield larger (or smaller) sales variations than the variation of any one marketing factor. To complete this picture, it should be added that a marketing action (an increase of the advertising budget, for example) generally has lagged effects. Money spent on advertising one month will have sales effects (although increasingly less important) over subsequent months and possibly over subsequent years. For all of these reasons, a marketing researcher often has a difficult time understanding and accounting for occurrences in the marketplace, not to mention predicting what will happen in the future.

Imperfect Marketing Research Techniques and Methods

A second factor that makes a marketing researcher's task difficult is the inaccuracy of most marketing research techniques. Substantial progress to improve research methods and measurement techniques used in marketing and related disciplines has been achieved in the last few years. However, in spite of these improvements, a great deal still remains to be done before marketing researchers can be provided with sufficiently valid and reliable techniques.

The Difficulty of Obtaining Accurate Measurements

The scientific method is characterized by valid measurement, something that is often quite difficult in marketing. The question arises of how we actually can measure human attitudes and opinions or values. Researchers are faced with the difficulty of trying to determine the real meaning of such words as *like* or *dislike*. Does *like* translate into *will buy*? The answer might be yes, but what if the product is an expensive sports car and the respondent is a university undergraduate with a total income of $3000 per year? The uninvolved observer might say, "I agree with you there, but would anyone willingly buy a product that he actually disliked?" The answer is yes and no. For example, consider the sales of *Listerine*, a product that specifically advertises the fact that it has an unpleasant taste. Consumers purchase *Listerine* because of its other (including psychological) attributes—its reputed ability to kill germs and improve bad breath.

A problem faced by interviewers is determining whether interviewees are responding accurately. In other words, are they actually telling the truth? Many relatively sophisticated techniques have been developed to enhance the accuracy of the researcher's attempts to measure human responses. As will be seen in

Chapter 9, researchers might use Stapel or Likert-type scales to measure the relative strengths of respondents' preferences, but the process of accurately measuring consumer attitudes is full of pitfalls for unwary researchers. No legitimate research techniques can guarantee that respondents will tell the truth.

The Influence of the Measurement Process on Results

Measuring human activities and attitudes is far more difficult and complex than measuring the behaviour of white rats in a cage. Humans, when they know that they are being observed and measured, often tend to react other than normally. A classic example of the process of measurement influencing the results is the case that gave the "Hawthorne Effect" its name. Studies were conducted by Elton Mayo at the Hawthorne Plant of the Western Electric Company to determine the effect of lighting on the output of a group of workers involved in assembling electrical components. First, the lighting was increased substantially in intensity, and worker productivity increased. Later the intensity of the light was reduced, and output increased still more.[4] Although the results of this study caused some observers to claim that the findings confirmed that production level was greater in the dark, other social factors were present. The real issue was that the process of measurement had influenced the results. People, knowing that they were being measured, responded by working harder when the intensity of light was reduced, contrary to what might have been predicted.

In marketing research the Hawthorne Effect occurs when, for example, interviewees answer questions in a manner that they think will please the researcher. This leads to a question often raised in conjunction with the Nielsen or Bureau of Broadcast Measurement (BBM) ratings: Does the act of recording television programs watched cause a change in viewing habits? If so, this effect would cause error to be built into these television ratings, a charge that producers of programs with low ratings sometimes level at Nielsen or BBM.

Difficulty of Using Experiments to Test Hypotheses

A key component in the scientific method is the establishing and testing of hypotheses. In the pure sciences it is possible to establish laboratory conditions in which the researcher can first control all of the variables, then allow one to fluctuate, and then measure the results. However, the business world is not a laboratory and the researcher faces the virtually impossible task of establishing a controlled environment in which to conduct measurements. Replication—reproducing the same experiment again and again—cannot be carried out completely in marketing research. If, for example, researchers want to duplicate the media mix in several test markets, they will find it impossible to control all variables that might affect the sales of the product. Activities of competitors, human values, the weather, and business conditions are all factors that typically are beyond the control of the marketing researcher in such cases, making it difficult to test hypotheses developed for research purposes.

Difficulty in Making Accurate Predictions

Accurate prediction in marketing research also can be extremely difficult. In a laboratory experiment the scientist can predict with a great deal of precision the behaviour of a rat in a maze. However, predicting the behaviour of consumers in the marketplace is not nearly so exact a science. Researchers face almost insurmountable obstacles in accurately predicting future economic conditions, market demand, and consumer buying behaviour. Too many things can happen between the prediction and the actual behaviour for predictions to be made with a high degree of accuracy. However, although researchers face major obstacles in accurate prediction, research can reduce the degree of uncertainty and the margin of error, thereby providing businesses with much-needed forecasts that are reasonably reliable. Just as meteorologists predict future weather events and are sometimes wrong, researchers who predict future market conditions are not always correct. However, just as the general public relies on weather predictions, business people must rely on market predictions.

Lack of Communication

Another problem is the lack of communication between the researchers who are responsible for analysing the market and the marketing managers who must make decisions based on the outcome of such analyses. First, there is generally a basic difference in the personality profile of an individual who has chosen to make a career of trying to understand and predict human behaviour and that of an individual who is by nature a decision maker and a person of action.

Unfortunately, the failure of some marketing research departments or the disillusionment of some executives with marketing research can be traced back to this lack of communication. For instance, a marketing researcher should realize that he or she is not supposed to acquire a complete understanding of a particular marketing phenomenon. Rather, the task is to provide only the infomation that a particular decision maker needs to solve a decision problem. Too often, there is a fundamental difference between what management expects from research and what it gets.

Typically, to assist in making a decision, a manager needs a simple, clear-cut set of facts that will unambiguously indicate the course that should be followed. The researcher, on the other hand, might provide a report that is reflective of the complexity of the market and that sometimes is overloaded with subtleties that are irrelevant to the marketing decision. In addition, marketing researchers are well aware of the uncertainty that pervades the real state of nature, and their research findings reflect this inherent uncertainty. This tends to frustrate any managers who expect research to perform miracles and maybe do not realize that research can only *reduce* their uncertainty, not eliminate it.

Finally, research reports are often written in abstract terms and the manager must translate them into concrete language that is more in line with his or her own experience and education. If the manager has not been able to communicate clearly the decision problem involved and the researcher does not provide only understandable relevant information, a communications gap exists. Meaningful dialogue between a marketing manager and a marketing researcher often is difficult because of the lack of a common language, which is generally aggravated by the essentially different personalities of the two people.

Author John G. Keane has outlined seven possible areas of top management-marketing research conflict, which are shown in Table 3.1. According to Keane, improving the efficiency of marketing researchers in assisting management in decision making "calls for tightening the interrelationship between the two groups."[5]

Fortunately, the gap is beginning to shrink. Marketing researchers with a marketing background are becoming increasingly aware of the problems and needs of the decision maker. Also, today's marketing managers are better informed and trained and are more aware of marketing research problems and constraints and of the benefits to be gained from careful, relevant research. However, here again, a great deal still remains to be accomplished.

TABLE 3.1
Probable Areas of Top Management-Marketing Research Conflict

Top-Management Position	*Area*	*Marketing Research Position*
MR lacks sense of accountability. Sole MR function is as an information provider.	Research Responsibility	Responsibility should be explicitly defined and consistently followed. Desire decision making involvement with TM.
Generally poor communicators. Lack enthusiasm, salesmanship, and imagination.	Research Personnel	TM is anti-intellectual. Researchers should be hired, judged and compensated on research capabilities.
Research costs too much. Since MR contribution is difficult to measure, budget cuts are relatively defensible.	Budget	"You get what you pay for" defense. Needs to be continuing, long-range TM commitment.
Tend to be over-engineered. Not executed with proper sense of urgency. Exhibit ritualized, staid approach.	Assignments	Too many non-researchable requests. Too many "fire-fighting" requests. Insufficient time and money allocated.
MR best equipped to do this. General direction sufficient... MR must appreciate and respond. Can't help changing circumstances.	Problem Definition	TM generally unsympathetic to this widespread problem. Not given all the relevant facts. Changed after research is under way.
Characterized as dull with too much researchese and qualifiers. Not decision-oriented. Too often reported after the fact.	Research Reporting	TM treats superficially. Good research demands thorough reporting and documentation. Insufficient lead-time given.
Free to use as it pleases... MR shouldn't question. Changes in need and timing of research are sometimes unavoidable. MR deceived by not knowing all the facts.	Use of Research	TM use to support a predetermined position represents misuse. Isn't used after requested and conducted...wasteful. Uses to confirm or excuse past actions.

Source: John G. Keane, "Some Observations in Marketing Research in Top Management Decision Making." *Journal of Marketing*, 33 (October 1969).

■ Translating Decision Problems into Research Problems

Marketing executives must fully understand the problem before considering possible courses of action. In addition, to make the best decision concerning which course of action should be taken, they must assess the probable outcome of the contemplated course of action

One way in which marketing managers can reduce uncertainty is to conduct formal and structured marketing research. However, the marketing decision maker is always faced with making the choice either to delay action in order to collect more information and reduce uncertainty or to accept the current level of uncertainty and act immediately. In any case, some form of research is often used throughout every step of the problem-solving process, from problem detection to the actual decision making.

The following is a simple fictitious, but quite typical case study that illustrates the usefulness, but also the difficulty and complexity, of the dialogue that must take place between a decision maker and a researcher, using different types of research. We will start with exploratory research.

Use of Exploratory Research

Case Study: The Peasoup Company (Part A)

On August 5, 1988, Marc Briand, the marketing manager of the Peasoup Company, a leading canned-soup manufacturer, received the sales report for the month of July 1988, showing sales broken down by sales district. He was concerned to see that for the third consecutive month, Montreal sales had fallen 15% below their level for the same period in 1987. In fact, sales forecasts for this area had predicted a 20% increase over last year, and it became clear that sales objectives would not be met this year in the Montreal district.

When sales started decreasing in May 1988, Briand first believed that a new accounting procedure in the Montreal office might explain the difference. Orders had been recorded differently, and the sales figures were not strictly comparable with those of the previous year. Briand asked Keetah Pimi, the company's accountant, to give him sales figures for both periods, computed with the same accounting procedure, for comparison purposes. On August 7, Pimi came up with these figures, which showed a still sharper sales decrease in the Montreal district.

After looking at these figures, Briand called the district sales manager, Midori Amano, and asked her to give her view of the situation in the Montreal district. Amano replied that sales were dropping in Montreal for several reasons. First, business generally had been decreasing faster in Montreal than in other parts of Canada; second, two large supermarket chains had started successfully introducing lower-priced, private brands. Other national brands had reacted by cutting their prices, but she had not been allowed to do so when she had asked for authorization from Briand several months previously. In addition, the Peasoup campaign in French has not been very successful. The ads were poorly done and. . . .

After this assessment of the situation, Briand decided that something had to be done, because he could not let the company's position deteriorate in the very important Montreal market.

He called Moira Buchanan, the market research director, explained the situation to her, and asked if she could provide more precise information about what was happening in the Montreal district. He explained that the situation was urgent and that he required her report within two weeks.

Situation Analysis

At the beginning of this case study, Briand observed the *symptoms* of a problem: Symptoms are a superficial manifestation of a problem, in the same way that a person notices that he has a fever or a stomachache and realizes that he is ill. However, the symptoms do not necessarily identify the illness. So Briand needed a diagnosis of the situation to explain why there was a gap between the actual and expected sales figures.

At this stage, very little about why the sales drop occurred could be stated with any degree of certainty. Briand could not even be sure that there really *was* a marketing problem. However, the observed discrepancy between expected and actual sales was sufficiently intriguing to warrant some kind of investigation.

The logical first step, therefore, was to determine whether there really was a marketing problem. All possible sources of ambiguity or error had to be eliminated, starting with the change in accounting procedures. By having the sales figures for 1987 and 1988 computed in exactly the same way, Briand made sure that 1988's sales really did fall short of sales forecasts, and that the symptoms did reflect a marketing problem. In doing this, he accomplished the first stage of a diagnostic process.

Next it was necessary to identify other possible causes, to find out in which direction research efforts should be oriented. Therefore, he sought the relevant market information by interviewing a knowledgeable source, in this case the district sales manager, Amano. The latter gave several possible reasons for the declining sales:

- a general business slow-down in the Montreal area

- new competition in the canned-soup market, with competitive pricing policies

- a resulting price war, in which the Peasoup Company had not participated

- the ineffectiveness of the Peasoup advertising campaign in French

However, this information was only qualitative, and had not been obtained in a scientific, structured manner. It merely reflected the intuition and experience of one individual. Therefore, this information would be used only as a basis for further research.

To narrow down the list of possibilities and further the process of diagnosis, Briand called on the research director, Buchanan, to conduct an informal market analysis that was to be completed within a relatively short period of time. This is the typical situation in which exploratory research is needed.

Objectives and Methods of Exploratory Research
Exploratory research is generally used in the early stages of a problem-solving process, to define the problem and detect its roots. To conduct formal, structured research at a stage when the marketer has only a vague idea of the problem would be costly and probably ineffective. Therefore, researchers start by undertaking less expensive, fast, qualitative research. In the case of the Peasoup Company the objective of the research was to pinpoint or at least narrow down the list of possible causes of a sales decline in the Montreal area, in order to identify the company's problem.

Being essentially informal, exploratory research is characterized by qualitative methods, unstructured interviews, the lack of formal and structured hypotheses, and the heavy use of secondary data sources and of managerial judgments. The exploratory research process is typically carried out until enough evidence has been collected to answer a basic question (in the case of the Peasoup Company, the reason for the sales decline) or until nothing more precise can be learned using this method.

Application of Exploratory Research in the Peasoup Company Case
Two weeks later, Briand held a meeting with Buchanan and Amano. Buchanan reported that she had investigated two sets of hypotheses that were not mutually exclusive:
• Sales were normal, given the conditions in the Montreal area, but sales forecasts were overestimated.
• Sales forecasts were accurate, but some unforeseen event occured in the Montreal market.

Buchanan had carried out her investigation by informally interviewing important company customers and company salespeople. She had also analysed Nielsen reports to compare market shares in several areas, and had read trade journals that discussed the business trends in various markets.

Finally, Buchanan reported that as a result of her fast, informal investigation, two possible causes of company's sales decline in Montreal had been identified:
• the introduction of the private brands of good-quality canned soup at a substantially lower price
• the inadequate Peasoup advertising campaign in French, which was unable to effectively convey the quality appeal to this market segment

Of course, she pointed out, any combination of the two causes could also be a possible explanation of the sales decline.

Buchanan felt that at this stage she could not be more precise, and that if Briand needed a more accurate assessment of the situation, a more formal market research study would be needed.

Note that although Buchanan carried out only exploratory research, she still attempted to be as systematic as possible and tried to apply the scientific method to the extent that this was feasible.

Two main hypotheses were investigated: that the sales forecasts were overestimated, which implied that the marketer's view of the market might have been faulty or, if this was not the case, that some unforeseen event had occurred in the Montreal market. Of course, it also was possible that the sales forecast was

FIGURE 3.1
Role of Exploratory Research for Problem Diagnosis

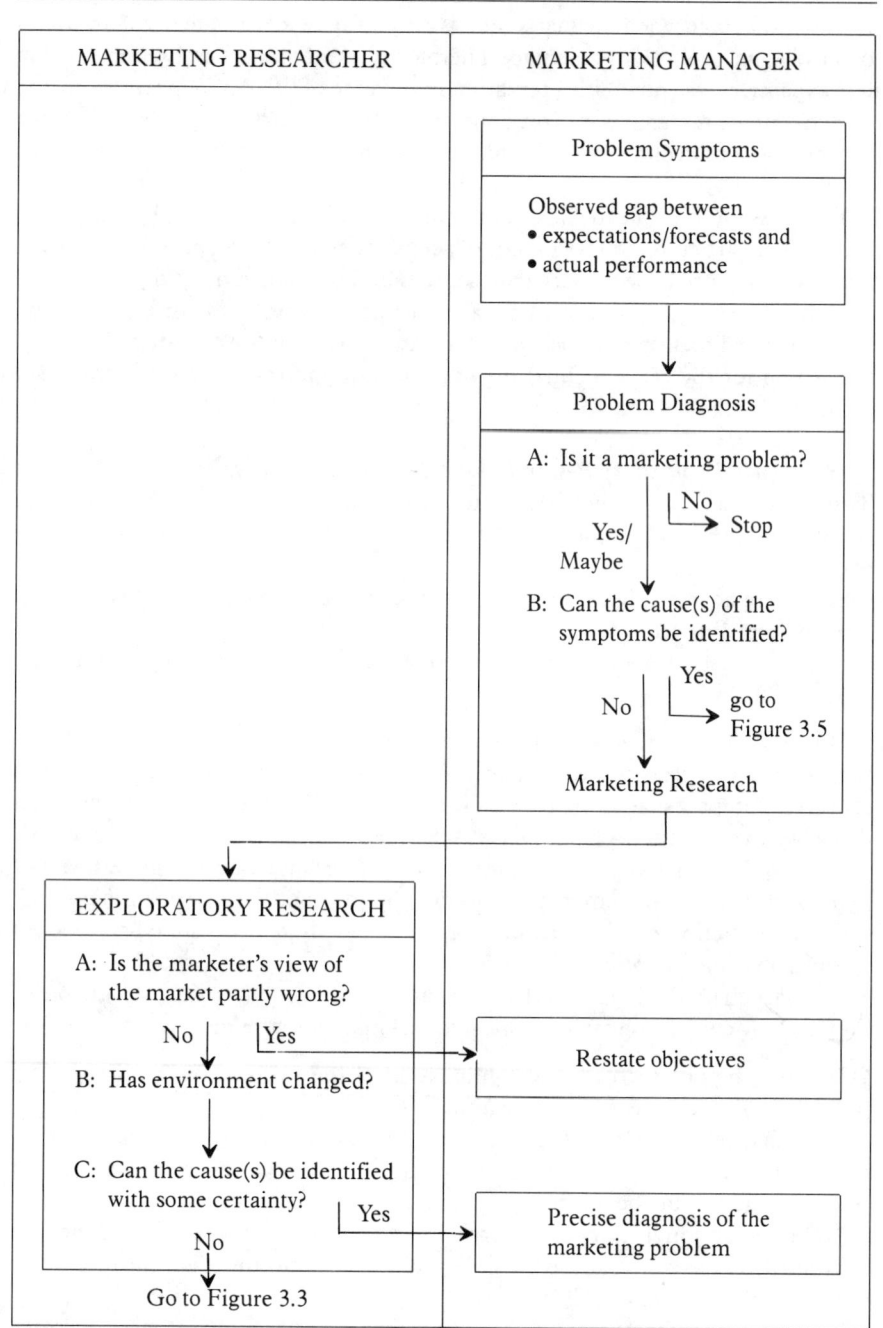

incorrect *and* that some unforeseen event had occurred. In any case, as a result of her informal and unstructured investigation, Buchanan managed to obtain a clearer view of the marketing situation and problem. To learn its causes, she now knew which questions to ask and therefore knew where to direct her research effort. She was now ready to engage in a process of more formal and systematic information seeking. The exploratory research process is summarized in the flow chart in Figure 3.1.

Use of Descriptive Research

Cast Study: The Peasoup Company (Part B)

Briand thought that the problem was serious enough to warrant the expenditure of some time and money to pinpoint the real cause of the problem. Consequently, he asked Buchanan to prepare a research proposal that would spell out the objectives of the study, the methodology to be followed, and time and cost estimates for the project. Two days later, Buchanan submitted the research proposal shown in Figure 3.2. After a short discussion, Briand approved the proposal.

FIGURE 3.2
Research Proposal for the Peasoup Company

RESEARCH PROPOSAL

Objectives
The proposed research will test the following hypotheses:
1. The sales decline in the Montreal area has been caused by a switch of Peasoup Company customers to the newly introduced private brand.
2. The sales decline in the Montreal area has been caused by the lack of effectiveness of the French advertising campaign.

Information to Be Collected
1. Who are the consumers who switched to the private brands and from which brands did they switch?
2. Who are the Peasoup Company customers who switched to the private brands (especially brand awareness, brand loyalty, price sensitivity, etc.)?
3. Among French-speaking customers who have seen Peasoup Company ads, what are their opinions of these ads and what do they recall about them?
4. Have the purchasing patterns among French-speaking and English-speaking Peasoup Company customers changed significantly?

Methodology
A survey of a random sample of 300 customers in the Montreal area will be carried out through personal interviews.

Time
The study will take approximately four weeks

Cost
The estimated cost of the study is $2000.

Situation Analysis
Because the exploratory research could not yield a precise diagnosis of the marketing problem, a formal research project was warranted. In this case, the objective was to identify precisely the cause of the sales decline. Note that because the set of possible causes had been reduced to a manageable set of two causes, a structured research project could be designed to address precise hypotheses about the market.

Objectives and Methods of Descriptive Research
As its name implies, descriptive research aims at describing the state of the market or how the market works. Descriptive studies must address precise objectives and/or hypotheses, as in the case of the Peasoup Company. Descriptive research essentially uses secondary and primary data sources, and typically uses the observation and the survey methods.

Application of Descriptive Research in the Peasoup Company Case
At the end of four weeks, Buchanan held a meeting with the executives of the Peasoup Company to present the results of her investigation. Her main conclusion was that the introduction of the private brands offering good-equality products at a substantially lower price was responsible for the company's sales decline in the Montreal market. The French advertising campaign was found to have had no significant negative effect on sales during the period under consideration.

As a result of this formal research study, Briand was quite confident (although still not entirely sure) that he had traced the roots of the problem. The diagnostic stage had been completed and he now had to translate the information into a specific marketing decision problem, complete with objectives and the different options that were available to him. The second stage of the research/decision maker interaction is summarized in Figure 3.3.

Use of Predictive Research

Case Study: The Peasoup Company (Part C)
After receiving Buchanan's report, Briand considered possible ways in which he might solve his problem, and had a series of meetings with various sales and advertising people in his company. Finally, he decided that he had to react, but he hesitated between two possible courses of action:

• The company could cut its retail price to almost the private brand level.

• The company could launch a new line of soup under a different brand name. These soups would be of a lower quality than the present line, but they could sell at less than the private brands' prices.

Since he could not figure out which action (if any) might succeed in changing the sales trend, he called Buchanan again and asked her to set up a research study that would help him to make a sound choice.

Buchanan had a lengthy meeting with Briand and the district sales manager, Amano, during which she asked them what type of information they were

FIGURE 3.3
Role of Descriptive Marketing Research for Problem Diagnosis

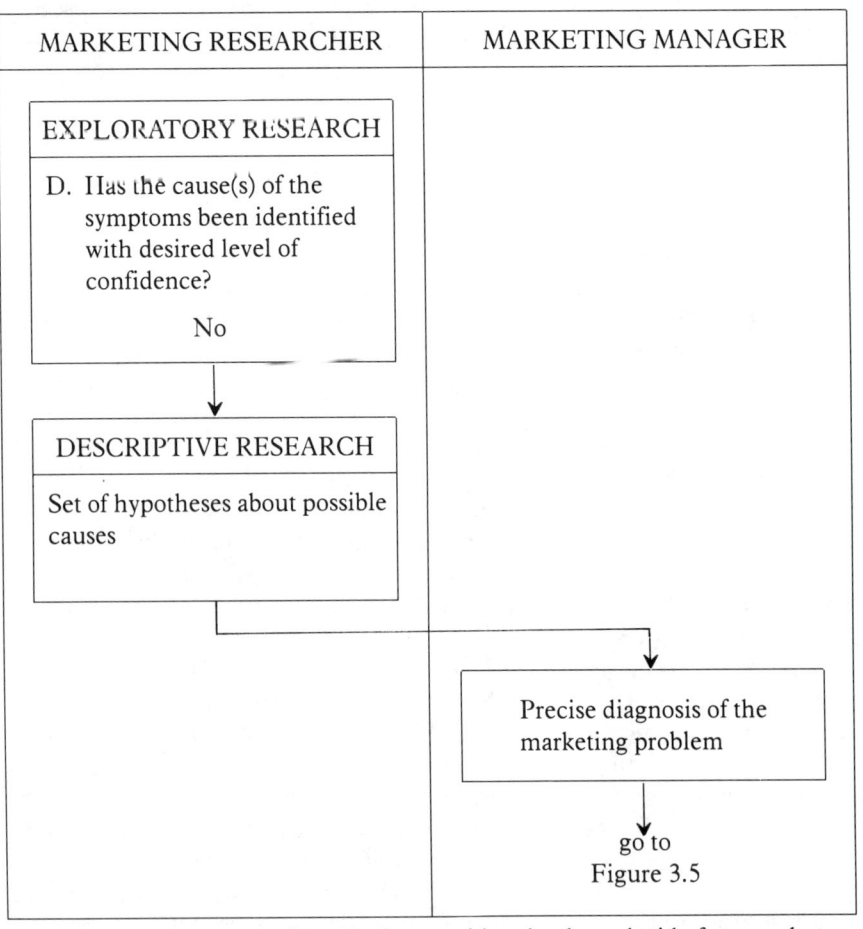

expecting from the research, and what would make them decide for one alternative or the other. Amano favoured the alternative that could generate more sales. Briand, who was the final decision maker, was less definite. At the end of the one-day meeting, Buchanan was able to summarize Briand's point of view as follows:

- He would definitely choose the price-cutting alternative if he could be reasonably sure that sales would get back to the forecasted level within a six-month period *and* if this gain would be at the expense of the private brands, in an attempt to push them out of the market.

- If that was not likely, he would favour the second alternative, provided that total company sales would reach the forecasted level over a one-year period *and* if the new brand would be in a break-even situation after one year.

- If the research indicated that neither the first nor the second possibility was likely to result, the situation would have to be reassessed and new alternative actions would have to be devised and investigated.

Back in her office, Buchanan drew up a list of the information that was needed to give an appropriate answer to Briand. Then she outlined the main steps of a research study, along with a schedule. She estimated that a $12 000 research budget would be necessary to carry out a six-month research study. Finally Buchanan called another meeting, this time with Briand and the company's accountant, Pimi, to get final approval of the research project.

Situation Analysis

By now, Briand faced a precisely defined marketing decision problem. Such a problem implies that the decision maker is contemplating two or more courses of action in order to reach precise objectives, and that there is some doubt as to which course of action will best contribute to those objectives. Obviously, Briand could specify the marketing decision problem in precise terms only because he knew (or thought he knew) the real cause of the problem. If the diagnosis was wrong, as in a medical situation, the possible remedies would have little or no effect.

Because the private brand introduction was identified as the only major cause of sales decline, Briand was contemplating two possible courses of action to counter-act the effects of this cause. Obviously, because there was still a great deal of uncertainty as to which of the alternatives would best contribute to the objectives of the company (in this case, sales recovery), Briand called on Buchanan to provide relevant information on the probable market reactions to the two contem-plated moves.

At this point, Buchanan had reached a critical point in the researcher/manager interaction, and one of the most difficult and delicate tasks in marketing research: she must translate Briand's decision problem into an information-seeking prob-lem. The major difficulty of this task results from the fact that this translation is affected by the decision style of the decision maker, and by the decision rules or criteria that the marketing decision maker uses for selecting one of the options.

That is the reason why Buchanan had to hold a typically lengthy meeting with Briand and Amano. Unless she properly understood the decisions at stake and the precise decision rules that would be used to select the proper action, she would not be able to specify properly what information the decision maker needed to make his decision.

One particular fact in the Peasoup Company case illustrates the sensitive position in which researchers often find themselves. Buchanan was presented with two different sets of criteria. The district sales manager favoured the decision that she felt would generate the most sales. Briand's reasoning was a lot more complicated. Depending on whether Buchanan did the research for Amano or for Briand, two substantially different research problems had to be specified.

Research Study for Midori Amano. Although Amano is not the decision maker in this case, let us pretend that the research study should be designed to help her to make a decision in the Peasoup Company case. Amano's decision rules could be stated as follows:

1. If sales after a price cut would increase, then cut prices.

2. If sales after a price cut would decrease, then launch the new brand.

Consequently, to help Amano in her decision, Buchanan should provide her with the following information:

1. sales level after cutting prices (time horizon should be specified)

2. sales level of new brand

3. sales level of existing product lines after new brand introduction

Research Study for Marc Briand. Briand's decision rules were somewhat more complex and could be summarized as follows:

1. If price cutting would return sales to forecasted levels within six months, decreasing the sales of the competitors' brands, then cut prices.

2. If total sales of a new product could reach forecasted levels after twelve months and if new brand sales could reach a break-even level within that period, launch the new brand.

Otherwise the situation would have to be reassessed.

Obviously, to help Briand make his decision a different set of information was needed (and probably a different research design) from that needed by Amano. This information could be summarized as follows:

1. sales level after cutting prices, over a six-month period

2. variation of competitors' sales levels after the price cut, over a six-month period

3. sales level of new brand, over a one-year period

4. sales levels of existing lines after new brand introduction, over a one-year period

5. break-even analysis of new brand

Obviously, the information gathered for Amano would be irrelevant for Briand's purposes, and vice versa. Because Briand was the decision maker, Buchanan should provide the information needed by Briand and select her research design accordingly.

To summarize, translating a marketing decision problem into a marketing research problem is a difficult and often lengthy process, because the two problems have fundamentally different natures. The marketing decision problem is always defined in terms of *action*, while the marketing research problem is an *information-seeking* problem. The manager's view of the world and his or her decision criteria are seldom explicit, but the researcher must take them into consideration when defining the research problem. It is *not* up to the researcher to decide what the manager needs, but rather to determine the definition of the decision problem and the context of this problem by working closely with the marketing manager. This can be achieved only through close collaboration and mutual understanding. To have a complete understanding of a manager's decision rules, the researcher should be able to predict, under a set of exhaustive and mutually exclusive unknown market conditions, which action should be taken by the marketer. This process is summarized in Figure 3.4.

FIGURE 3.4
The Interaction Between Research and Marketing Management

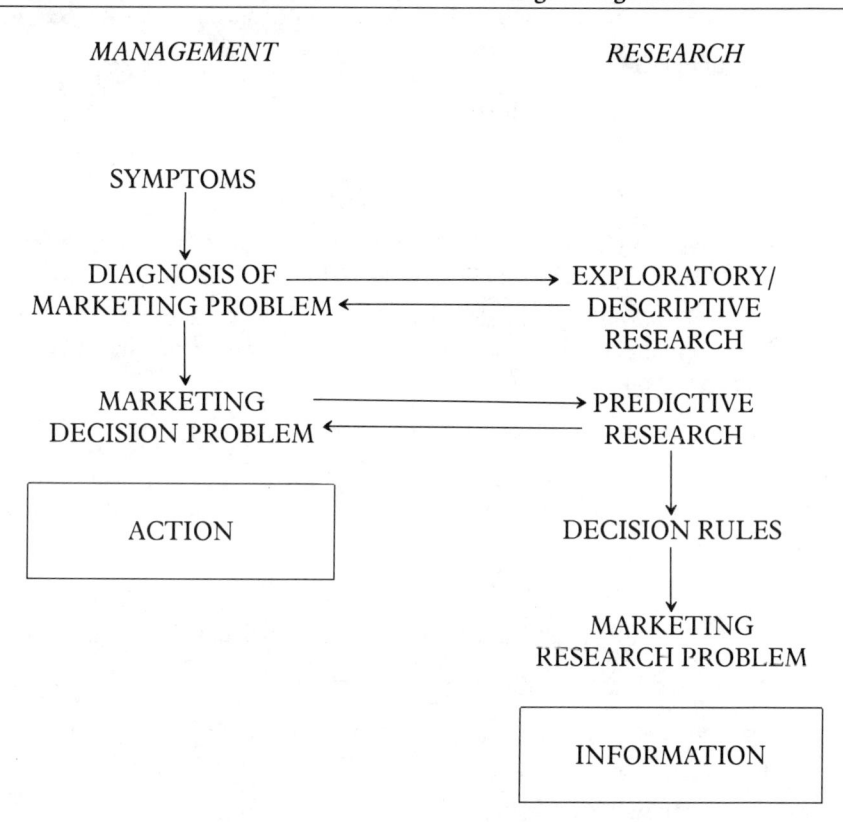

Objectives and Methods of Predictive Research
As its name implies, predictive research aims at predicting the market's reactions to a number of possible courses of action defined by a marketing manager. The methods of predictive research are similar to those of descriptive research. In addition, however, experimentation can be a valuable method to predict how the market might react to manipulated sets of conditions.

Application of Predictive Research in the Peasoup Company Case
In this case, the precise research design was not specified. However, it should be clear that at this stage, Buchanan needed to have defined the major characteristics of the research design (such as data collection method, sample sizes) because, before giving the green light to the research project, Briand would need at least three types of information:

• the time required for the research project

• the cost of the research project

• the level of accuracy that could be expected from the results

This process is summarized in Figure 3.5.

FIGURE 3.5
Role of Predictive Marketing Research in Marketing Decision Making

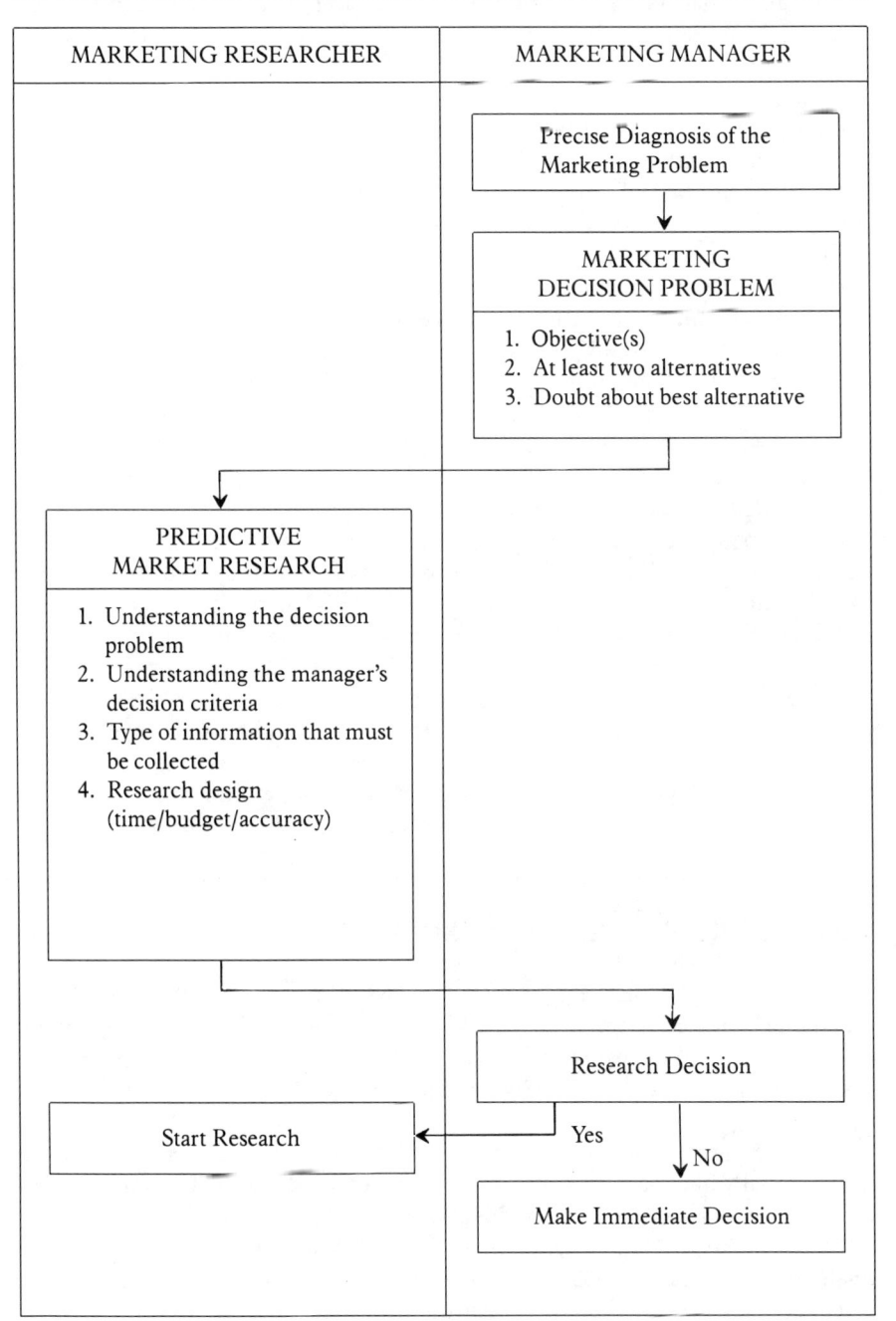

■ The Research Decision

Marketing managers will approve a specific research proposal only if they expect that the benefits from the marketing information collected in the study will warrant the costs of research. This is the reason why it is important to understand how the three critical elements of research cost, research time, and the expected accuracy of the study's results can be taken into account for assessing the value of a specific research project.

Consider the case of a manufacturer who contemplates penetration of a new market. The manufacturer could make this important decision simply by relying on her own experience and on her own assessment of the situation. We have seen that managerial judgments and experience are often an important source of valuable marketing data, within limits. However, few managers would take this course because the risk of making a mistake would be substantial and the costs attached to such a marketing mistake would typically be prohibitive.

Therefore, most manufacturers would commission a marketing research study to assess the chances of success before penetrating a new market. Note, however, that marketing research is not able to yield results with absolute certainty. At best, it can reduce the risks of a wrong decision by the manufacturer.

Although marketing research helps marketers to make better decisions, its usage is obviously limited. It is a costly process in terms of direct research expenditures as well as in time and, consequently, in the opportunity cost of indecision. Therefore, too much research might adversely affect the firm's profit in the same way that too little research might be costly to the firm in terms of wrong decisions. Between these two extremes of too much and too little research, there must be an optimal amount of research that in the long run yields the maximum profit level to the company. Decision theorists have devised formal ways to identify the optimal level of information that a decision maker should have in a given situation. This procedure is called the **Bayesian decision theory**.[6]

■ Pseudo-marketing Research

After absorbing the material presented so far in this chapter, the prospective marketing researcher might well ask, "By carefully following the scientific method, will I produce research reports that can be used by management in making marketing decisions?" Unfortunately, the answer to this question might be negative.

Much research undertaken today, no matter how scientifically conducted, might actually have very little influence on marketing decisions. This is true even though conventional wisdom holds that the central function of marketing research is to provide information to aid in making decisions. It is impossible to quantify the amount of research conducted for reasons other than legitimate aid to actual decision making because executives are understandably reluctant to admit that this happens.

This illegitimate use of marketing research could be called **pseudo-research**. Pseudo-research is research that has no influence on the decision-making process; it is window dressing, undertaken for such purposes as boosting executive egos, selling advertising, and empire building. Pseudo-research activities can be grouped into four categories:

1. *Organizational politics*: Research becomes pseudo-research when it is used solely or primarily to gain power, justify decisions, or serve as a scapegoat.

2. *Service promotion*: Pseudo-research is often undertaken to impress on clients and prospects the fact that the sponsor is sophisticated, modern, or sincere. In other words, the act of gathering information, not the information itself, is the important thing.

3. *Personal satisfaction*: This is a broad category that includes ego-bolstering efforts and attempts to keep up with business fads and fashions, assuage anxiety, and make use of acquired skills.[7].

4. *Lack of investigative objectivity*.

Organizational Politics

Marketing research can become pseudo-research when it falls victim to organizational politics. Pseudo-research sometimes is used for the acquisition of power in the organization through empire building and increased visibility. Management might abuse the research function by having marketing research personnel conduct useless studies in an effort to enhance the power and visibility of executives.

Pseudo-research is also used to justify decisions made before the information has been gathered. Advertising media selection is one example of this practice. All too often in the case of research conducted by advertising agencies, the researcher's goal is to sell advertising and the buyer's goal is to justify the purchase of media space or time. Research becomes pseudo when researchers deliberately make sure that their findings are what clients want to hear. It takes a courageous or foolhardy research manager to report that the chief executive's pet marketing project is doomed to failure. What if, in 1957, Ford Motor Company's marketing research manager had solid data indicating the likelihood of failure for the Edsel automobile, which was named after a member of the Ford family?

Organizational politics can cause research to become pseudo when it is used as a scapegoat for marketing plans and projects that fail. Extensive research might go into a marketing plan but then be ignored, regardless of its findings. In these cases, if the plan is successful, the marketing manager gets the credit. If the plan fails, marketing research is often held responsible, even though the research manager might have warned against its implementation.

Service Promotion

Pseudo-research enters into service promotion when service organizations, such as advertising agencies, use research in an attempt to attract new business. Pseudo-research undertaken for promotional purposes often leads to heavy, highly technical research reports that are virtually unreadable. Unfortunately, it is this type of research that fosters the notion of the typical researcher as an impractical egghead; in the long run, it is damaging to the research profession.

Personal Satisfaction

Research becomes pseudo when it is undertaken primarily to provide personal satisfaction for executives by boosting egos, enhancing self-esteem, and assuring anxious executives that something is being done. An example of pseudo-research undertaken for personal satisfaction is provided by Stewart Smith of Lee Creative Research in St. Louis, Missouri:

> A product manager once demanded that I run a market test for a new product. I had reason to suspect that he was really interested in a nationwide introduction of the product but needed a confidence-booster to take this step. The exchange between us went something like this:
> **Researcher:** "What if the test results are favorable?"
> **Product Manager:** "Why, we'll launch the product nationally, of course."
> **Researcher:** "And if the results are unfavorable?"
> **Product Manager:** "They won't be. I'm sure of that."
> **Researcher:** "But just suppose they are."
> **Product Manager:** "I don't think we should throw out a good product just because of one little market test."
> **Researcher:** "Then why test?"
> **Product Manager:** "Listen, Smith, this is a major product introduction. It's got to have some research behind it."[8]

By carefully following the scientific method, many problems that inhibit the development of quality research can be avoided. However, adhering to the scientific method, even though it might lead to the highest quality of research, is no guarantee that marketing research will be properly utilized by management. The danger lies in the fact that research, regardless of quality and utility, is still subject to abuse.

Is it possible, then, to eliminate pseudo-research in marketing? It probably is not possible, but if marketing researchers are aware that it exists, they could demand to know what use will be made of research findings. However, it seems reasonable to assume that researchers might not want to become involved in the pitfalls and dangers of corporate politics. For this reason, it is likely that, despite the best efforts of marketing researchers, much research will continue to be pseudo in nature.

Lack of Investigative Objectivity

A final obstacle in applying the scientific method to marketing lies in the difficulty of securing researcher objectivity. One of the basic requirements of the scientific method is that the investigator always be objective and report data in an impartial manner. In the pure sciences, there are cases of bias, particularly in instances where investigators are seeking additional research money or are attempting to establish their professional reputations. However, such cases are rare.

Unfortunately, in marketing research, the investigator often is not impartial. Many times research is conducted merely to substantiate what management wants to hear. Using research to find desired answers is not unknown in scientific investigations, but it is a particular problem in marketing research, where the research department is vulnerable to management pressure to come up with the "right" answers.

Lack of investigative objectivity is not always deliberate; it can be subconscious. For example, during the interviewing process, researchers might cause bias through the wording of questions or the use of leading questions. This problem can become particularly acute when investigators are relatively untrained and therefore ignorant of the bias that they might be subconsciously introducing during the interviewing process. The answer to this problem lies in better selection and training procedures for the field force. However, time and budgetary constraints often make it difficult to prepare interviewers properly.

These problems encountered in applying the scientific method in marketing research are presented not to discourage use of this method, but rather to familiarize the student with the difficulties. Awareness of these problems should enable the researcher to take advance corrective action to avoid some of the pitfalls.

■ Summary

Most marketing decisions are made without reliance on formal research. A high percentage of these decisions are made on the basis of intuition—a gut feeling about something. Lack of time, money, or expertise, and ignorance of the marketing research process in general are all reasons why executives might rely on intuition instead of research in making decisions. Whether marketing is an art or a science is a subject for endless debate. It is, however, definitely an area in which increased scientific progress is being made.

The scientific method is being used increasingly in marketing research. The steps involved in the scientific method are observation, formulation of hypotheses, prediction of the future, and testing the hypotheses. These steps are followed by all scientists in both the natural and social sciences, including marketing and marketing research. There are, unfortunately, certain difficulties in applying the scientific method in marketing research. These difficulties stem from the complexity of the subject, the difficulty of obtaining accurate measurements, the influence of the measurement process on results, the difficulty of using experiments to test hypotheses, and the difficulty of making accurate predictions.

As was illustrated by a case study, the necessary interaction between a marketing manager and the researcher is a complex and difficult process. This process is essential for translating marketing decision problems into research problems.

Assessing the value of a marketing research proposal can be done in the frame-work of the Bayesian decision theory, which formally accounts for research costs, time, and the level of accuracy obtained.

Much marketing research, no matter how scientific, is pseudo-research—research undertaken for reasons other than to aid in the making of business decisions. Pseudo-research might be the result of organizational politics, when it is used to gain power, justify decisions, or serve as a scapegoat. It might result from service promotion undertaken to impress clients and prospective clients, where the act of gathering information becomes the most important matter, not the information itself. It also might be used to foster personal satisfaction—boosting egos, reducing anxiety, and assuring executives that something in being done. Organizational politics will almost certainly guarantee the continuation of pseudo-research. However, marketing research managers should be on their guard. Also, in some cases, they can try to reduce the amount of pseudo-research by asking in advance what the purpose of the research is and how it will be applied in the process of making marketing decisions.

For Discussion

1. If the scientific method is the best technique for reducing uncertainty in making decisions, why would any other method be used? Why, for example, might a manager rely on intuition instead of scientific research in making marketing decisions?

2. Is marketing research a science or an art? Explain your answer. Although there are certain difficulties in applying the scientific method in marketing research, what are some of the developments that might make this easier in the future?

3. Define and describe the scientific approach to marketing research.

4. Describe the steps that are typically followed in using the scientific method.

5. What are the major difficulties in applying the scientific method to marketing situation?

6. Describe the communication problems between researchers and marketing managers that often exist.

7. How can a researcher translate a decision problem into a marketing research problem?

8. What is the difference between the symptoms of a marketing problem and the problem itself?

9. Explain the diagnostic stage of a marketing study.

10. What are the major types of pseudo-research in marketing?

Problems

1. **Mini-case: The Merchants' and Consumers' Bank** (Part A)

   At the beginning of October every year the senior and regional executives of the Merchants' and Consumers' Bank meet to define policy and plan the bank's direction for the future. The meeting is usually a four-day workshop, organized months in advance, during which the major issues for the short- and long-term future are addressed. This year, Emil Melnick, the senior vice-president of finance and investments, presented a brief in which the revenue and costs generated by the bank's operations were trended over the past ten years and results projected for the next ten years. The most revealing projection, although not a surprising one, was that the bank's spread (profit margin) will become narrower.

   Dollars deposited in the bank's coffer by businesses and individuals, Melnick noted, have been becoming more costly to obtain and loans are less profitable because of tight competition in the market. Therefore, the profit made by lending out the money deposited by customers is decreasing significantly. Melnick's recommendation was that the main emphasis for the next few years should be on attracting a greater volume of low-cost deposits—savings accounts that offer relatively low interest rates.

   The Merchants' and Consumers' Bank is one of the oldest and largest banks in Canada, with approximately three hundred branches located strategically across the country. For administrative purposes, it is divided into five regions, with each regional office managing between twenty-five and forty branches. Because it is a large and rather conservative bank, it has a reputation as a solid and reliable trustee of the public's money. The public, however, gives it higher ratings than other banks as a bank "for rich people and corporations." Only four other banks, smaller ones, are as frequently associated with these images in consumer surveys.

   The marketing approach at the Merchants' and Consumers' Bank has always been a very conservative one. In the past, the marketing department has usually reacted to changes in the marketplace, rather than anticipating them through proper planning. Its marketing strategy has been to appeal to the total market rather than to use a target-market approach. This has been true, in particular, of some of the larger advertising campaigns. However, in recent years, the research department has conducted surveys among the banking population in order to provide much-needed input into marketing decision making. Profiles of users of different banking services have been obtained, which provide some insight into financial attitudes, banking behaviour, and demographics of the banking population.

   The marketing department is divided into the advertising and promotion department, the branch location department, the marketing research department, and the various service departments—deposit services, automated services, and the new services development department (see Exhibit 3.1). When the new goal of generating low-cost deposits was announced, the deposit

EXHIBIT 3.1
Organization of the Marketing Department of the
Merchants' and Consumers' Bank

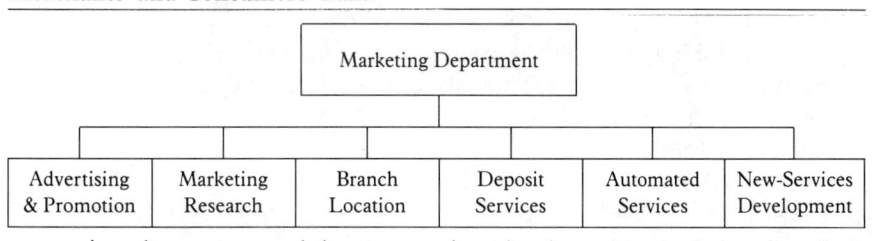

services department and the new-services development people began actively reviewing past research results, trying to uncover target segments or undeveloped needs in the marketplace.

Colleen Doyle, the manager of the new-services development department, was particularly eager to come up with new ideas and opportunities to meet this latest request from top management. She came across a memo referred to her a few months previously by the marketing director. The memo had come from Silvia Lind, the regional manager of the wealthier Ontario region. Lind mentioned that a local one-branch bank in her region had come out with a special type of deposit account for senior citizens, offering a higher rate of interest than most other banks. The banks also offered free bill-paying privileges to this group of customers. This had resulted in a significant loss of low-cost funds from the Merchants' and Consumers' Bank in that region, because some older customers had taken their money out and deposited it into the competitor's bank.

In essence, Lind was asking head office to consider providing senior citizens with a comparable service, so that she could regain or at least retain her share of this age group. In fact, only four customers had left the one branch in Lind's region to switch to the other bank. However, these four customers had deposits large enough to make her notice the difference.

When this matter was originally brought to her attention, Doyle had notified Lind that her office was looking into the matter but that it was not expected to be resolved in the near future. The Merchants' and Consumers' Bank never introduces a service in only one branch or region; it usually introduces it in all three hundred branches at the same time. In addition, Doyle had other priorities at the time. As she read through the memo this time, however, a possibility began to take shape in her mind—maybe now the timing was just right for a special service for senior citizens.

Doyle tracked down all of the information that she could get on this group of customers. Government statistics provided a population distribution by various age groups based on the most recent census, which indicated that

- of the total population, 11% was sixty-five years of age and older

- approximately 14% of the population aged sixty to sixty-four was disabled to some extent, and this figure increased to 21% among the sixty-five to seventy-year-olds and to 42% of people over seventy years of age.

- the number of Canadians aged sixty to sixty-five was equally distributed between the two sexes; however, the proportion of women increased and that of men decreased after the age of sixty-five so that, among people aged seventy-five or over, 66% were women.

- of the population aged sixty-five and over, 74% lived in the cities; the remaining 26% lived in smaller towns and rural areas.

The marketing research department of the bank had conducted a national financial service study the previous year and had the information broken down by different age groups. The last two subgroups were people aged between sixty and sixty-four and those aged sixty-five or more. These two last groupings were of greatest interest to Doyle. Her first observation was of the demographic distributions:

Education: People aged sixty and older were less likely to have completed college or university than younger population segments.

Marital status: 55% were married and 33% were widowed.

Income: Average family yearly income was very low, since few senior citizens were working and earning income.

Residence: A majority (77%) owned their own homes.

Banking service profile: They made greater use than other age groups of savings accounts, term deposits, and safe deposit boxes and safekeeping services. However, they wrote fewer cheques per month and paid fewer bills at the bank than other age groups.

Balances in accounts: Although they represented a relatively small percentage of the total population, they controlled a disproportionately large percentage of personal savings deposit business.

Doyle suspected that these older customers would not switch banks very often, so that whatever her bank offered them had to have a strong drawing power to succeed in increasing the bank's market share and volume of deposits. Consequently, she decided that the bank should not only give these people a better rate on savings accounts but also should consider developing a package of services specially designed to meet their needs.

The timing for this type of service would also be appropriate, in that it would improve the bank's lagging public image: recent criticism from pressure groups and social agencies charged that the big Merchants' and Consumers' Bank was so intent on reaping profits that it neglected the small saver and charged unfair prices for some of its services.

However, the bank's primary consideration would be to make the service for senior citizens profitable. For this to happen, the service had to appeal above all to the wealthier among them. If this subgroup did not apply for the service, the program would fail, since they had the largest deposits of low-cost funds in bank savings accounts.

Doyle's idea was to combine a number of services, many of which involved service-charge payments by customers, and offer them to this market either at no cost or at a very nominal fee. The features under consideration were

- Chequing accounts for which customers would not have to pay service charges. Previous research indicated that they wrote few checks, so that the bank's income loss on this feature would be minimal.

- Special cheques with extra-large print, easy to read and easy to fill out. Each cheque and deposit slip would have its own duplicate copy, providing customers with duplicate records of all transactions.

- No service charges on payments of utility bills (such as telephone and electricity) at the bank

- No bank commission on traveller's cheques

- Five-year term deposits that would pay interest at the end of the term

- A no-charge direct deposit to savings accounts of pension cheques, dividends, etc.

- A special subscription to a monthly periodical on retirement living

- A free financial calendar and diary for the convenient recording of investments, interest payment dates, and dividends

The only requirement was to be that the customer be sixty-five years of age or older and have some type of savings account at the bank.

Doyle then went over each item with the bank's cost analyst and projected the total cost of the package to the bank's customer base of people over sixty-five. The projection was based on this group's current level of use of individual services. Surprisingly, because of the low usage of some of the features by senior citizens, the total cost was reasonable and even insignificant, compared with the total benefit derived from the use of their low-cost funds.

The initial costs, as well as the promotion and staff training, would be substantial but, if amortized over the next few years, also fairly reasonable. The service would begin to pay for itself after the third year of operation.

The ideas for this package of services were all Colleen Doyle's, with no input from the potential customers. She realized that this was a missing link and consulted David Meyer of the marketing research department. She provided him with the background, the marketing problem, and her proposed solution.

Questions

1. According to the problem definition stated above, what were Doyle's marketing objectives?

2. What research objectives would Doyle define for Meyer, the marketing researcher?

3. What topics should be covered in any consumer research on this subject?

4. Propose a research study to secure the information requirements developed in question 3.

2. Zen's Service Centre is a modern gasoline station located at a major intersection in a suburban city. For the past five years, Zen has been operating a profitable business, characterized by a steadily increasing monthly sales volume. However, during the previous six months, the sales volume levelled off and a modest downturn began. Zen has asked you, the researcher, to suggest some hypotheses that might explain this downturn in sales. What would you suggest, and how might you test each of your hypotheses? Should anything be done before any hypotheses are formulated?

3. You are the marketing research manager for a medium-sized company. The vice-president of marketing has requested that you conduct a research study on consumer preferences for a new product that he says the company might introduce. You know for a fact that the company intends to introduce this new product whether or not the research indicates that it should be introduced. What do you do?

Endnotes

1. Theodore N. Beckman, Williams R. Davidson, and W. Wayne Talarzyk, *Marketing*. 9th ed. New York: Ronald Press, 1973, p. 611.
2. Vernon Clover and Howard Balsey, *Business Research Methods*. Columbus, OH: Grid, 1974, p. 23.
3. Harper Boyd and Ralph Westfall, *Marketing Research: Text and Cases*. 4th ed Homewood, IL: Richard D. Irwin, 1972, pp. 37–40.
4. Henry L. Sisk, *Principles of Management*. Cincinnati, OH: Southwestern Publishing Co., 1969, pp. 29–30.
5. John G. Keane, "Some Observations on Marketing Research in Top Management Decision Making." *Journal of Marketing*, 33 (October 1969), pp. 10–15.
6. For more details on the Bayesian approach to marketing decision problems, see, for example, Paul E. Green, "Bayesian Statistics and Product Decision." *Business Horizons* (Fall 1962), pp. 101–109.
7. Stewart A. Smith, "Research and Pseudo-research in Marketing." *Harvard Business Review* (March-April 1974), pp. 73–76.
8. Ibid., p. 76.

CHAPTER 4   THE RESEARCH DESIGN

As discussed in the preceding chapter, one fundamental aspect of marketing research is that it is an activity that is oriented completely toward the needs of the marketing decision maker. Once agreement has been reached on the type of information that should be sought, what dollar cost, within what time frame, and with what level of accuracy, the marketing researcher must take the next step— detailed specification of the **research design**.

In Chapter 2 research design was defined as the strategy that the marketing researcher intends to follow to obtain the marketing information that management needs for solving a specific problem. It is the blueprint of the research activities, which focusses on the data collection methods, the measuring instruments to be utilized, and the sampling plan to be followed. Of course, basic decisions on the research design must be made while developing the research proposal, to provide a time/cost/accuracy estimate. Once the proposal has been accepted, the research design must be specified in detail.

This chapter outlines the main types of research design typically used in marketing research studies. Two of these designs—qualitative and experimental designs—will be highlighted.

■ Selecting a Marketing Research Design

Main Types of Marketing Research Designs

Marketing research designs can be conveniently classified into four main types: qualitative, observational, experimental, and survey designs. As shown in Figure 4.1, the qualitative design has a special status, because it will either be used entirely for the research project, or it will typically be the first stage of most research projects that use any of the three other types of designs. Frequently

FIGURE 4.1
Main Types of Research Designs

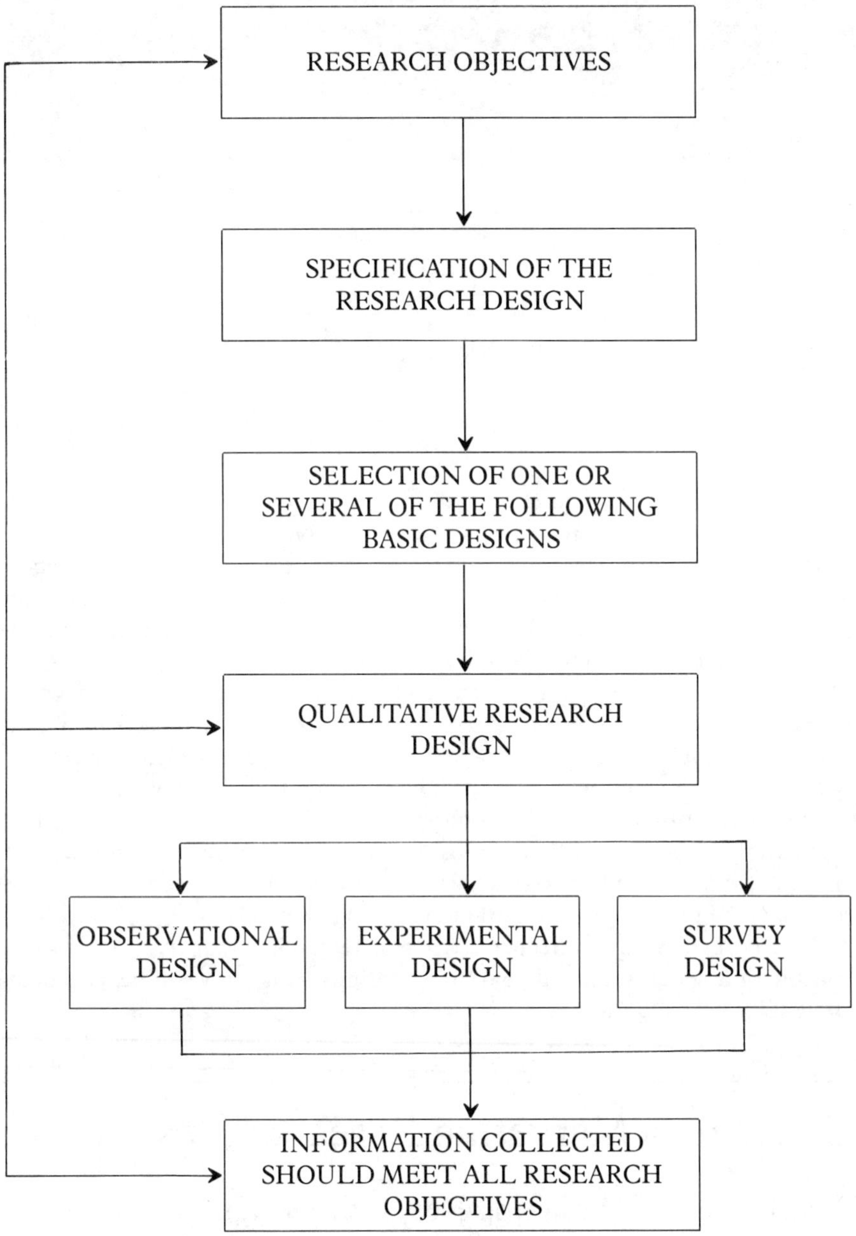

```
                    ┌──────────────────────────────┐
            ┌──────▶│     RESEARCH OBJECTIVES       │
            │       └──────────────────────────────┘
            │                      │
            │                      ▼
            │       ┌──────────────────────────────┐
            │       │     SPECIFICATION OF THE      │
            │       │       RESEARCH DESIGN         │
            │       └──────────────────────────────┘
            │                      │
            │                      ▼
            │       ┌──────────────────────────────┐
            │       │     SELECTION OF ONE OR       │
            │       │   SEVERAL OF THE FOLLOWING    │
            │       │        BASIC DESIGNS          │
            │       └──────────────────────────────┘
            │                      │
            │                      ▼
            │       ┌──────────────────────────────┐
            ├──────▶│    QUALITATIVE RESEARCH       │
            │       │          DESIGN               │
            │       └──────────────────────────────┘
            │                      │
            │          ┌───────────┼───────────┐
            │          ▼           ▼           ▼
            │   ┌────────────┐ ┌──────────┐ ┌──────────┐
            │   │OBSERVATIONAL│ │EXPERIMENTAL│ │ SURVEY │
            │   │   DESIGN    │ │  DESIGN   │ │ DESIGN │
            │   └────────────┘ └──────────┘ └──────────┘
            │          │           │           │
            │          └───────────┼───────────┘
            │                      ▼
            │       ┌──────────────────────────────┐
            │       │   INFORMATION COLLECTED       │
            └──────▶│ SHOULD MEET ALL RESEARCH      │
                    │         OBJECTIVES            │
                    └──────────────────────────────┘
```

a complete research project might use several types of the basic designs. For instance, to collect marketing information needed, a marketing researcher might have to do some qualitative research, followed by a consumer survey and an experiment in selected retail stores.

Criteria for Selecting the Research Design

Figure 4.2 shows that three major criteria can be used to select the proper marketing research design. The first criterion is the nature of the information that is required. The classification of this information as exploratory, descriptive, or causal decides the type(s) of design to be used. For example, exploratory research typically requires a qualitative design. Descriptive research generally leads to the selection of a survey or observational design, often preceded by some qualitative research. Causal research typically requires an experimental design, although observational and survey designs can be used in cases where experimentation is not possible or practical.

The second criterion that shapes the research design is the source of the information. If all of the data can be obtained from secondary sources, it would not be time- and cost-efficient to collect it from primary sources. Finally, the third important criterion is choice of the most efficient way to collect the information. The phrase "most efficient way" implies the best time/cost/accuracy compromise that each method can provide. As we mentioned before, although an experiment might be the most accurate way to study a causal relationship, this may not always be the most practical way from a cost perspective.

Because of the importance of each type of design in marketing research, each design will be described in some detail. The qualitative and the experimental designs will be discussed in the balance of this chapter. The observational design is discussed in Chapter 6 and the survey design is discussed in Chapter 7.

Qualitative Research Designs

Qualitative Techniques for Exploratory Research

All marketing research projects of any significant scope must begin with exploratory research. This preliminary phase is absolutely essential to obtain a proper definition of the problem at hand. For example, in the Peasoup Company case presented in Chapter 3, management was faced with declining market share. However, the specific problem causing this decline was unknown and could have been a continuation of many different factors: changes in competitors' promotion or pricing policies or some completely unsuspected problem or problems. It is the job of the investigator in this exploratory phase to define the problem and to develop hypotheses to be tested conclusively through more formal research designs.

Exactly *how*, then, does the research investigator go about the process of establishing and conducting exploratory research design? First and foremost, it

FIGURE 4.2
Selection of a Research Design

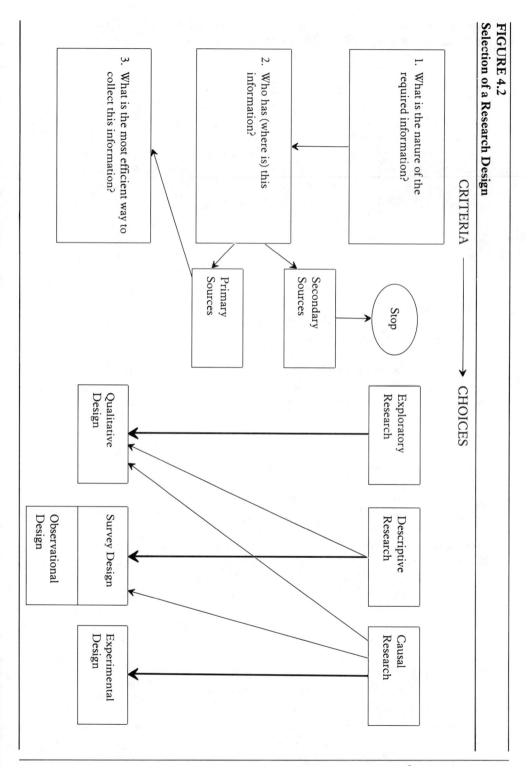

CRITERIA ⟶ CHOICES

1. What is the nature of the required information?

2. Who has (where is) this information?

Primary Sources

Secondary Sources

Stop

3. What is the most efficient way to collect this information?

Exploratory Research

Descriptive Research

Causal Research

Qualitative Design

Survey Design
Observational Design

Experimental Design

must be kept in mind that there is no set way of conducting exploratory research. Key requirements for the investigator are imagination and flexibility. Exploratory research studies are not characterized by formal research design, nor are they basically very scientific in nature. Since the purpose of exploratory research is to bring the central problem into focus, the researcher might utilize any number of informal approaches in an attempt to define the problem.

Although the exploratory study is characterized by its informal approach, it is nevertheless of critical importance to the overall study. The investigator establishes exploratory research design primarily through one or more of three approaches: examining existing literature, questioning people with particular expertise in the area, and carefully examining a few selected cases.

Examining Existing Literature

Logically, the first place the researcher should check is existing literature on the subject, such relevant secondary data as trade publications, learned journals, government reports, and even newspapers. It might be desirable to examine the internal records of the firm, which would include sales records and other similar material. How could the marketing research manager for the Peasoup Company utilize this survey of literature in her exploratory research? A quick analysis of the firm's internal sales records might reveal sharply declining sales in certain geographical regions of the country; analysis of company financial records might indicate sharply escalating costs resulting from rising costs of labour and materials, causing rapidly escalating prices. Examination of journal articles and government reports might reveal that consumer tastes are turning away from the very thick, high-calorie soups that the Peasoup Company produces. Thus, after a brief study of existing data, the research manager could begin to formulate some ideas about the principal problem at hand.

Questioning People with Expertise

The questioning of people with particular knowledge or expertise in the subject area does not constitute a scientifically conducted statistical survey. Rather, it represents an attempt to obtain additional input from people who might have some particular knowledge of the subject under investigation. Such people would include executives, sales personnel, and other relevant people within the firm, as well as others from outside the organization. The category certainly could be logically expanded to include middlemen and perhaps a few consumers. Middlemen are of particular importance, in that wholesalers and especially retailers are often much closer to the market and its problems than is the manufacturer. These middlemen, therefore, are in a position to provide vital information about the manfacturer's products and those of the competitors.

Ultimately, the investigator might want to question a limited number of consumers or industrial users who are familiar with the issue or the product. In this context, the Peasoup Company's marketing research department might begin an informal survey of knowledgeable people in the firm, including not only those in the marketing department but also some in the production and financial departments. Local retailers who carry Peasoup's products on their supermarket store shelves might be questioned for their opinions on the cause of Peasoup's decline in market share. Additionally, the research department might survey on a very informal basis some particularly heavy consumers of soup, in an attempt to gain greater insight into Peasoup's marketing problems.

Intensive Analysis of Selected Cases

Analysis of selected cases is another form that exploratory research design might take. The usual pattern for exploratory research is arbitrary selection of a few extreme examples and thorough analysis of these cases. For example, if the research goal is to determine the reason for varying salesperson productivity, the firm might want to examine case histories of several of its best and worst salespeople. The research goal in this case would be to determine if, for example, there were significant educational or age variations between highly productive and highly unproductive sales personnel. Peasoup's approach in this particular instance might be to take selected retail outlets where sales have varied widely and subject these outlets to analysis, to determine whether there are significant differences between retail establishments where sales are high and ones where sales are low.

Exploratory research, then, is particularly important to the pattern of investigation. Exploratory research provides a relatively low-cost, low-risk form of research that can pay very high dividends. The main benefit is a much clearer picture of the problem. Unfortunately, the exploratory phase of marketing research is often skipped:

> One of the most serious defects in the current research practice of many firms is the failure to give adequate consideration to the exploratory phase of research. In many instances this step is skipped entirely or conducted in a very superficial manner.[1]

Many reasons could account for this fact. Sometimes, management feels that exploratory research is too time-consuming, or that it is not worth the additional expense required, or that it will not add sufficiently to the understanding of the situation that managers already have. When this important phase of the research process is skipped, however, undesirable consequences might follow. For example, this might result in unnecessary or duplicated research effort, or in research that does not address the actual problem faced by management.

In other instances, management waits too long before resorting to research. This could result in research being carried out under severe time constraints and management pressures. Under such circumstances, it is not unusual for the exploratory phase of research to suffer. Take, for example, the case of a large food products manufacturer who, in October of a given year, prepared five new television commercials to be used in May of the following year. Instead of planning for the test research immediately, the company waited until April before deciding on a research agency and a specific research proposal. Obviously, there was no time left for carrying out exploratory research or for questionnaire pre-testing. Consequently the study could not be of the best possible quality.

Qualitative Techniques for Motivation Research

The purpose of motivation research in marketing is to answer the question *why* — to discover the reasons why people favour one brand over another. Motivation research is a very difficult process, mainly because of the tremendous number of factors that can influence a consumer decision. Unfortunately, the direct approach generally does not work in motivation research: the researcher cannot simply go up to a consumer and ask why that person prefers one product over another and expect to get the correct answer. The fact is that either the consumer does not know why or that the person knows but is unwilling to tell you.

The Consumer Does Not Know

Most people, especially those without exposure to the methods and findings of motivation research, are surprised to learn that consumers are generally unaware of their own "true" reasons for specific brand and product selections. For instance, beer drinkers are often extremely brand-loyal and if you ask them why they prefer specific brands they will answer, without hesitation, "Taste!" Unfortunately, this answer does not square with the well-documented fact that the average consumer is unable to distinguish among various bottles of unlabelled beer. If you do not believe it, try the following. Select several brands of beer, including your favourite, and have someone pour them into unmarked glasses for you to taste-test. The odds are that you will identify your favourite brand no more often than if you were guessing at random. The beer drinker is brand-loyal, but only to a specific beer image, not to a specific beer taste. Thus, if you want to discover why someone is brand-loyal to a particular beer or almost any similar product, you must investigate his or her attitudes toward the various brands and thereby determine the various images represented by the different brands and the various personality profiles of the consumers of those brands.

Another reason that consumers do not know their true reasons for purchasing (and thereby fail to give accurate answers to direct questioning) is that, regardless of the specifics of the purchase situation, they tend to parrot the answers that have been conditioned by advertising. Thus, if you ask someone what he likes about the taste of his favourite beer, he probably will reply in terms of his brand's advertising theme or slogan. Consumers can also become confused about what brand they actually bought, because of the influence of heavy product identification with a single brand: hence, all facial tissue is *Kleenex*, all soup is *Campbell*, all cola soft drinks are *Coke*, all photocopiers are *Xerox*, and so forth. From the standpoint of the major manufacturer, this heavy brand-product identification can be viewed as either a blessing or a curse, depending on the management's objectives. However, from the standpoint of the marketing researcher, it is a total disaster. In response to direct questioning concerning purchase behaviour, all that the researchers obtain are major brand names—even when the consumer is buying off brands.

The Consumer Will Not Tell

Another reason for incorrect answers lies in the choice, made by many consumers, not to tell the correct answer even if they know it. Generally speaking, it can be assumed that a significant amount of deliberate misrepresentation will occur any time the subject area is either morally sensitive or status-related. Thus, people tend to overestimate their income, their charitable giving, and their purchases of name-brand items, and they tend to underestimate their drinking, their smoking, and their purchases of house-brand items. Respondents will also modify their answers in an attempt to appear logical and intelligent. For instance, purchasers of a new *Cadillac* might know that the reason they bought such an expensive car was to show it off to friends and relatives, but it is doubtful that they will say so to the interviewer. Rather, they will talk of the outstanding safety and good resale value of the car. The true reasons can be discerned only through the use of the relatively indirect methods of motivation research.

The reasons for consumer preferences are seldom logical. The researcher who approaches the question in a direct, logical, straightforward manner will often obtain very misleading results. Whereas some motivation research *can* be conducted in a relatively direct fashion, in other cases valid results can be obtained only from very indirect and seemingly roundabout methods. Furthermore, since the nature of such an investigation is subjective, the conclusions produced are often highly speculative and might vary greatly on the basis of the person performing the research.

Motivation Research Techniques

In this section we will present a variety of motivation research techniques under three basic headings: individual in-depth interviews, focus groups, and projective techniques. In this order of presentation, the various techniques move from fairly direct to extremely indirect, from the relatively objective to the totally subjective.

Individual In-depth Interviews

Individual in-depth interviews can produce valuable results even when the respondent is unwilling or unable to respond meaningfully to a direct question.

The idea, taken from the Freudian psychoanalyst's couch, is to get consumers to talk at length about all their feelings concerning a product and the "pleasures, joys, enthusiasms, agonies, nightmares, deceptions and apprehensions" that the use of that product brings to mind.[2] The rationale behind this technique is that consumers will be able to express their true (hidden) feelings regarding the product if the discussion lasts long enough. So the consumer and the analyst (most motivation researchers who perform this technique are trained in psychology, not marketing) sit down together and begin talking. Although the analyst tries to keep the discussion pointed roughly toward the product and its use, a rambling conversation ensues, which might last several hours or more for each consumer.

Several things about this method should be immediately apparent. First of all, the entire process is extremely subjective. The direction that the conversation takes is subjective, and highly dependent on the interviewer-respondent relationship. Likewise, the conclusions that the interviewer draws from these ramblings are also highly subjective. Different interviewers might come to vastly different conclusions about the significance (if any) of a given statement and about what should be done in response.

Finally, it should be noted that this process has a very high per-unit cost ratio. Each interview is extremely expensive because highly trained analysts must spend great lengths of time interviewing and then analysing the results of each interview. For this reason, sample sizes in in-depth interview studies tend to be frighteningly small, perhaps as few as eight or ten people. Therefore, conclusions about the perceptions and feelings of an entire nation are based on the ramblings of a mere handful of people. Because of the uncertainities brought on by the small sample size and the highly subjective nature of the process, in-depth interviews are used primarily as an exploratory technique. Research directions obtained from the in-depth interviews can be explored more fully by more exhaustive and exacting quantitative surveys.

The Focus Group

This discussion of in-depth interviewing has assumed that one consumer is interviewed by one analyst. In the focus group, however, several consumers participate in the discussion at the same time. There are various reasons why the focus group is gaining in popularity over the single-person, in-depth interview. Most importantly, focus groups provide cost savings, in that a larger sample size can be interviewed for the same cost. An additional advantage is that the larger number of people interviewed tends to make the research less dependent on the interaction of a single interviewer-respondent pair; hence, it is not quite as subjective a process. And finally, the group setting encourages some respondents to talk more freely, because they find that other people share many of their problems and feelings. In fact, sometimes the research team will plant one of its own members in the group to act as a catalyst—to be the first to broach taboo topics and so forth.

Usually, the focus group meets in a comfortable, homelike room and the conversation is recorded on hidden tape recorders and often on hidden cameras as well. When these tapes are played for a group of creative thinkers, many good ideas for product design, new product usage, and advertising campaign strategy often emerge. Therefore, the use of focus groups has become a very important tool of marketing and advertising strategists.

Projective Techniques

Projective techniques are a still more indirect group of motivation research methods: they can provide insight into the thinking of consumers even when consumers are deliberately trying to misrepresent their feelings. For attitude research and in-depth interviewing, it is assumed that the consumers' true feelings will immediately or eventually emerge. However, what can be done to discover these true feelings when the respondent is intentionally giving answers that are intended to impress, not inform?

The answer to that question lies in the use of projective techniques, which employ a stimulus that is usually quite vague. Because of this vagueness, the respondents are forced to use their imagination to make their responses truly meaningful. In doing so, they project themselves and their personalities into the situation.

Probably the most famous use of this technique in marketing is Mason Haire's Nescafé study.[3] The problem prompting this research was that instant coffee, at the time of its introduction, was very unpopular. The reason given by housewives was that they or their husbands did not like the taste, yet blind taste tests consistently revealed that there was no discernible difference. In an effort to get at the true reason for the dislike of instant coffee, Haire formulated two grocery shopping lists that were identical except that one showed instant coffee and the other showed ground coffee. Housewives were then asked to describe the shopper who would buy each basket of groceries. Evaluations of the housewife who bought the regular ground coffee were consistently good: the woman was seen as thoughtful, efficient, and loving. On the other hand, the shopping list with the instant coffee produced many negative descriptions. The Nescafé instant coffee housewife was seen by many as lazy, wasteful, a poor planner, and a bad wife. The problem here was not the taste, it was the image. The ritual of preparing coffee was an integral part of the way in which many wives showed their affection for their husbands, and the claim of "bad taste" was just an excuse, given by both husbands and wives, for insisting on the maintenance of this ritual. (Note that this research took place in the early 1950s; attitudes toward instant coffee and the institution of marriage and love obviously have changed markedly since then.) With this information in hand, the instant coffee industry took a different advertising tack. No longer did the ads stress ease and convenience, which are obvious. Instead, the quality and taste were emphasized, and to assuage any lingering guilt, some ads featured the solicitous wife hovering affectionately around the family members at the dining table, while the voice-over cooed, "Gives you more time to be with your family."

Projective techniques can range from quite objective and structured to quite subjective and unstructured. The projective techniques presented here are given in order of increasing subjectivity.

Word Association. In word association, which has been used by analysts for more than a century, the interviewer calls out a series of words and the respondent quickly replies with the first word that comes to mind. For instance, what is the first word that pops into *your* mind for each of these products: oatmeal, coal, prunes, beer, crystal, wool? If your answers were dull, strike, laxative, belch, break, and itch, then those products are facing some image problems that need to be addressed in their advertising!

Sentence Completion. Sentence completion is similar to word association, except that the respondent completes an unfinished sentence; for example, I don't like to eat bananas because...., People who go to Palm Beach are...., Some people don't like to fly because.... Notice that the last two examples involve double projection, in that the respondents must project themselves not only into an unfinished sentence but also into the persona of someone else. By answering for someone else, respondents can say things that they would be embarrassed to say if the situation was directly concerned with themselves. For instance, if asked about who goes to Palm Beach, respondents might reply, "The rich and famous," whereas if asked why they did not go to Palm Beach, they might say, "Because there are too many pushy snobs." In other words, what is going on in the respondents' minds is that they really would like to go to Palm Beach but are too poor. So rather than admit that they are poor and unknown, they give other reasons.

To the question about flying, the respondent might reply that many people are afraid of flying, whereas if asked directly about a fear of flying, the respondent would most often deny such fear.

Story Completion. In story completion the respondent supplies the end of a story; for example: John and Mary recently bought a new Ford. After about two months and 1400 miles, the transmission began knocking violently. The mechanic at the local filling station said that it sounded like the whole transmission was about to give out. John and Mary took the car back to the dealer from whom they had bought it and. . . . As you can imagine, the respondents' attitudes toward both that specific make of car and car warranties in general will be vigorously expressed as respondents complete the story.

The Rosenweig Picture Frustration Test. In the Rosenweig Picture Frustration Test, the respondent is shown a cartoon-type drawing, usually involving two characters. One of the caption balloons is completed but the other is blank and the respondent must fill it in. Consider the situation in Figure 4.3. It seems probable that many women and more than a few men would guess that the woman is making a negative comment, such as, "Ugh, who wants to look at an old boat?" or, "Yeah, you want a boat so that you and your cronies can go drinking and 'fishing.'" This type of response would indicate that boating advertisers need to address some effort to the cultivation of enthusiasm among women, in addition to their regular advertising in male-oriented magazines. For example, the advertiser might place ads in women's or general interest magazines showing a happy family out on a fishing or camping trip, with the wife beaming, "Our family hasn't had this much fun in years. . .and our new Waterking motorboat made it all possible."

FIGURE 4.3
Rosenweig Picture Frustration Test

The Thematic Apperception Test. The Thematic Apperception Test is a picture frustration cartoon-type test with none of the balloons supplied. The respondent is asked to tell what is happening in the picture. For example, the picture frustration test in Figure 4.4 could be used to determine true attitudes of racial prejudice. In the picture, a white policeman is facing a black man; nothing else is known about the situation. Maybe the black man is asking for directions; maybe they are two friends who have run into each other; maybe the black man is an

FIGURE 4.4
Thematic Apperception Test

Figure 4.5
Rorschach Ink-blot Test

undercover or off-duty policeman. However, if white respondents immediately jump to the conclusion that the policemen is arresting a lawbreaker, or if black respondents jump to the conclusion that a brother is being hassled by a "pig," they are giving strong evidence of deep-seated racial prejudice, prejudice that could easily have been hidden had the question been of a direct nature.

Rorschach Tests. Although their use in marketing is limited, no discussion of projective techniques is complete without at least a mention of the famous Rorschach or ink-blot tests. Most of us have seen examples of these tests (see Figure 4.5). The Rorschach test expresses in a classic way the rationale behind all projective tests: filling in the missing parts of a vague and incomplete stimulus, the respondents project themselves and their personalities into the picture.

Experimental Research Designs

Experimentation and Causation

Experimental research is concerned with determining conclusively whether a causal relationship exists between two variables. For example, the researcher might want to know the exact effect of a package change on sales of a product. Exploratory research might be used to define the issue and to develop some tentative hypotheses for testing. Descriptive research, including surveys and panels, could be used to analyse where sales have taken place or to describe the characteristics of consumers purchasing the product, the characteristics of retailers handling the product, and the attitudes of consumers toward the advertising programs. Cross-classification of data gathered in survey research might provide additional information that would lead the investigator to suspect certain cause-and-effect relationships. However, only through careful experimental design can the researcher build a conclusive case for the existence of particular causal relationships. Inferential relationships among variables can be meaningfully determined only through experimentation.

Difficulties of Experimentation

Experimentation in marketing research was a rare phenomenon before 1960, despite its long-standing acceptance in the sciences. Since 1960 experimentation has gradually become much more widespread in marketing research. Experimentation can be regarded as one of the key aspects in the implementation of the scientific method. It is a process of manipulating one variable in a controlled environment while holding all other variables constant, in order to establish a causal relationship. A marketing research example would be an experiment in which the investigator varies one experimental variable (e.g., package size) in order to use the effect the change will have on the dependent variable (e.g., sales). Test markets might incorporate this experimental approach.

Because of the requirement of a highly controlled situation, it is often difficult to use experiments in marketing research practically. In a laboratory environment, scientists might successfully experiment with white rats by feeding only one of two groups of white rats a certain drug. The business world, though, does not offer a laboratory situation, nor can all variables be held constant while only one is manipulated. This limitation often results in less than completely satisfactory experimental research designs. Researchers are forced to accept artificial situations when building models, or they are forced to accept less than completely controlled situations. Therefore, less confidence can be placed in data generated from marketing experiments than in that derived from scientific experiments.

Consider an example. The marketing research manager for a soap manufacturer might decide to test advertising effectiveness in an experimental research design. Suppose it was decided to show a series of hard-hitting, revolutionary television commercials advertising *Cleano* soap in a test-market city and compare results (sales) between this city and another comparable city where conventional advertising had been used. At the end of a two-month trial period, the sales figures from the two cities were evaluated and it was found that *Cleano's* sales in the area where the new advertising campaign had been conducted showed a 10% increase over those in the other city. Could the *Cleano* researchers then infer that the increase in sales was a direct result of the advertising program? Perhaps, but a conclusive causal relationship could be established only if the conditions in the two cities were virtually identical. If, for example, one of the competitors introduced a new product in only one of the two cities, the experiment would have been invalid. A strike of supermarket employees in one of the two cities also would have invalidated the experiment. It is necessary for investigators to exercise extreme caution in using this research design to infer causal relationships.

Types of Experimental Designs

Marketing researchers might use any number of designs for controlling the collection of data in experimental research. Table 4.1 presents an overview of three of the most significant types of experimental designs used in marketing research to establish causal relationships. While only three experimental designs are being discussed here, there are numerous others, most of which are far more complex in nature and scope and are best reserved for more advanced courses in marketing research.

Simple Before/After Design

The least complex of these three experimental research designs is the simple before/after design. The before/after design does not conform absolutely to the definition of an experimental design used here, because there is no control group. The dependent variable is measured before and then again after subjects have been exposed to the experimental variable. Figure 4.6 graphically depicts usage of the experimental design involving before/after without control group. This figure shows the effect on sales measured by the Cleano Corporation after the new advertising format was adopted. Sales showed a modest increase, but the research manager wonders if the sales increase can be directly attributed to the new advertising campaign. Changes in competitors' marketing strategies, consumer attitudes, the weather, and consumer income are factors other than the advertising program that could have had an influence on *Cleano* sales.

TABLE 4.1
Types of Experimental Research Group Designs

	Simple Before/After		Before/After with Control Group		After-Only with Control Group	
	Experimental Group	Control Group	Experimental Group	Control Group	Experimental Group	Control Group
Measure Before Exposure?	Yes	N.A.*	Yes	Yes	No	No
Variable Exposure?	Yes	N.A.	Yes	No	Yes	No
Measure After Exposure?	Yes	N.A.	Yes	Yes	Yes	Yes

*Not applicable

This simple before/after design is better than the after-only design, which measures the dependent variable only after the subjects have been exposed to the experimental variable. Since in an after-only design no measurement is made before introduction of the experimental variable, there is no measurement of the process of change. Before/after designs do give the investigator some opportunity to measure experimental variables. The principal weakness in before/after designs, represented by the arrow in Figure 4.6, is one of time or history. The longer the time period between the before measurement and the after measurement, the greater the danger that factors other than the experimental variable will have affected the second measurement. To yield realistic results, these research designs should be conducted in the marketplace by a field study rather than in the

FIGURE 4.6
Before/after-without-control-group Design

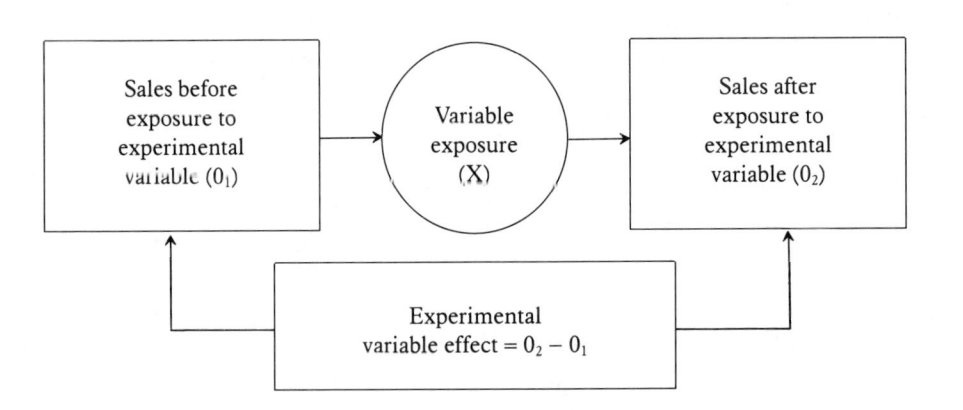

$$\text{Experimental variable effect} = 0_2 - 0_1$$

laboratory with a laboratory experiment, and over a period of time respondents in the field will be exposed to influences other than the experimental variable. Some technique is needed that will allow the investigator to analyse the process of change, and this technique involves the use of a control group.

Before/After with Control Group

The before/after-with-control-group design is basically the same as the before/after design except that a control group is added. This control group is measured at the same time as the experimental group, both before and after the experiment has been conducted. The only difference between the two groups is that the control group is not exposed to the experimental variable. Figure 4.7 illustrates the before/after-with-control-group design.

The design used in Figure 4.7 allows researchers to determine the effect on an experimental variable—advertising—on the dependent variable—sales—in City A.

FIGURE 4.7
Before/after-with-control-group Design

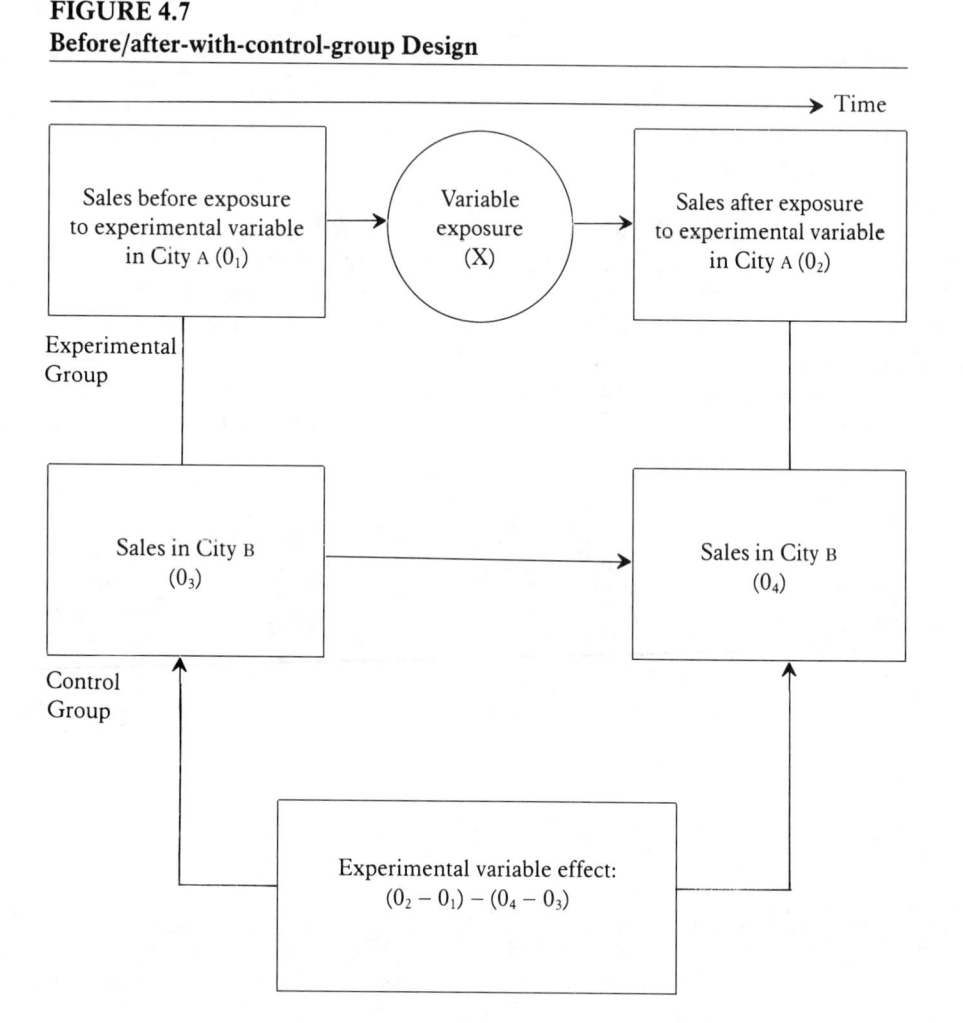

$\longrightarrow$ Time

Sales before exposure to experimental variable in City A (0_1)

Variable exposure (X)

Sales after exposure to experimental variable in City A (0_2)

Experimental Group

Sales in City B (0_3)

Sales in City B (0_4)

Control Group

Experimental variable effect:
$(0_2 - 0_1) - (0_4 - 0_3)$

An independent control group, City B, is used to see if any changes in sales would have taken place without the introduction of the experimental variable. The time between measurements is the same for both groups. This design is sounder than the simple before/after-without-control-group design and in theory it closes the major loopholes in the before/after design by permitting analysis of the process of change over time.

However, implementation of the before/after-with-control-group design involves several problems. First is the problem of selecting identical experimental and control groups. In our example, we used two cities. In reality, no two cities are exactly alike; there are always variations in size, ethnic group composition, employment characteristics, geography, and personal attitudes between any two cities that the researcher may select. Nor can the researcher control the actions of competitors. There is no way, for example, to prevent a major competitor from introducing a new advertising campaign in City B and not in City A.

Another problem with this design arises when interaction occurs between members of the experimental group and members of the control group: some residents of City B might be exposed to the advertising message intended only for those in City A. For example, they might visit City A, read its newspapers, or watch its television by a cable hookup. In some cases where firms have introduced new products in test-market cities, the products have proved so popular that people have come from outlying regions to purchase them, thus increasing their sales to unrealistically high levels (Coors beer is an example of a product that has attracted buyers from considerable distances). Where panel groups are used to measure effectiveness of experimental variables, there is no guarantee that members of the experimental group and the control group will not communicate with one another and therefore bias the results. It should be recognized, therefore, that introduction of a control group does not eliminate the problem of the dependent variable being affected by things other than the experimental variable, a factor that causes much despair among marketing research professionals.

After-Only-with-Control-Group Design

Numerous problems arise in using the two research designs previously presented. Both can be somewhat cumbersome, and neither can overcome the problem of time and possible respondent interaction. The presence of a control group does not in itself adequately prevent bias in the results of the study caused by factors beyond the control of the researcher. However, the after-only-with-control-group design, illustrated in Figure 4.8, can be used to measure the effect of the experimental variable without a before measurement. This design is relatively simple to implement. In addition to simplicity, time and measurement effects are avoided, and for these reasons the after-only-with-control-group design is the most widely used marketing research experimental design.

The main challenge facing the investigator who uses this research design is ensuring that the experimental and control groups have the same fundamental characteristics and are physically separated during the questioning process, to avoid any interaction.

As mentioned by Boyd, Westfall, and Stasch, the after-only-with-control-group design can fit "many marketing problems and is easy to use. Many promotional

FIGURE 4.8
After-only-with-control-group Design

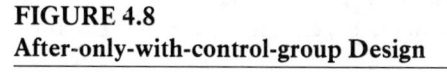

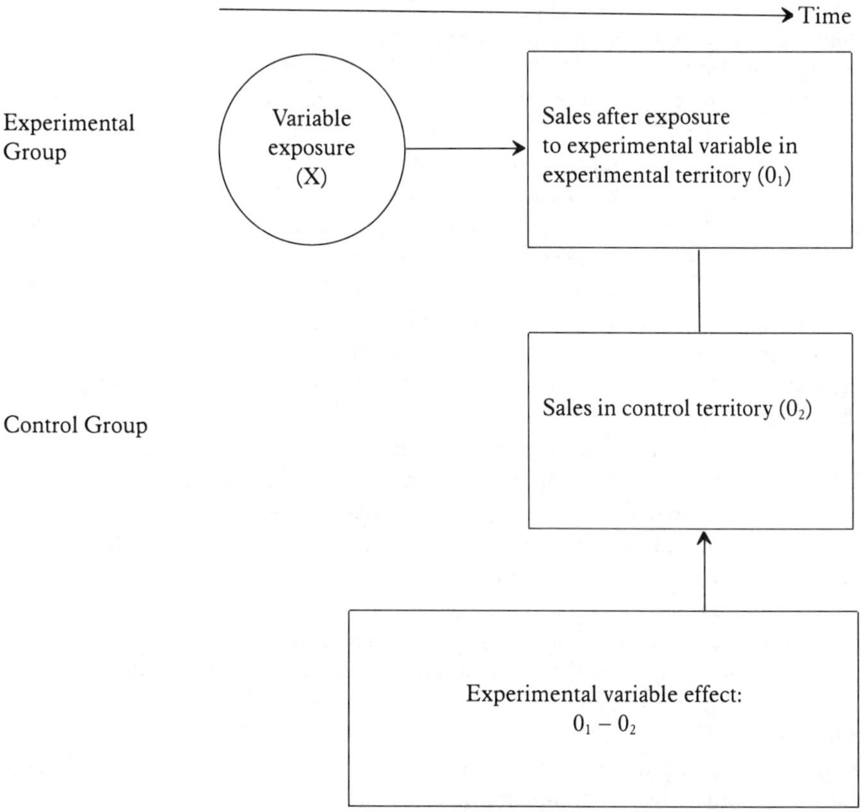

Experimental
Group

Variable
exposure
(X)

Sales after exposure
to experimental variable in
experimental territory (0_1)

Control Group

Sales in control territory (0_2)

Experimental variable effect:
$0_1 - 0_2$

devices can be tested this way...."[4] and product tests often require this type of design. These authors report the case of a dried milk company that believed that consumers were not aware of its products. Consequently, they set up a sampling campaign, but could not assess the impact of the promotional program. In an after-only experiment, a sample group of consumers was given samples of dried milk. This group and a control group were subsequently sent coupons for discount purchase of the product at some grocery stores. Because the coupons sent to both groups were differentiated, the manufacturer could compare the number of coupons redeemed in each group, and thereby assess the effect of the sampling promotional campaign.

In another instance, General Motors used this experimental research design to determine the level of consumer acceptance of, and satisfaction with, nylon-cord tires versus the traditional rayon-cord tires. Nylon-cord tires were more expensive and were suspected of wearing out before traditional rayon-cord tires did. To assess the importance of the problem, the company equipped 40 000 *Chevrolets* with the nylon-cord tires and kept track of the serial numbers of these cars. Eventually, a survey was carried out in which these car owners were interviewed and the results were compared to those of car owners with rayon-cord tires.

Laboratory and Field Experiments

Experimental research designs can be conducted in the laboratory or in the field. A laboratory experiment is an artificially created situation in which the researcher controls one or more variables while manipulating other variables at will. A field experiment occurs in a real-world environment, the field, where the investigator attempts to control all other variables while manipulating the one that is the experimental variable. Thus, although the field experiment is more realistic, the laboratory experiment offers greater control. Before deciding whether to use laboratory or field experiments, marketing managers should evaluate three aspects of experimentation: the type of information necessary, the validity requirements of the information, and the time and cost necessary to obtain the required information.

Type of Information Necessary

Before deciding whether to undertake a laboratory or a field experiment, the investigator must first assess the type of information necessary for the study. If the study is attitudinal in nature (e.g., measuring consumer attitudes toward an advertisement or a product concept), a laboratory experiment might be perfectly satisfactory. However, if information is needed on the effect of a factor (e.g., that of a change of promotion techniques on sales), a laboratory experiment would probably be unsatisfactory and an experiment in the field would be necessary.

Validity Requirements

It is at this point that the researcher must weigh the alternatives of internal and external validity for the experiment.[5] Internal validity refers to the amount of control built into the experiment, whereas external validity refers to its realism: laboratory experiments are strong on internal and weak on external validity, and the opposite is true for field experiments (see Table 4.2).

TABLE 4.2
Comparison of Laboratory and Field Experiments

Experimental Aspect	Experimental Setting	
	Laboratory	Field
Data generated		
Basic theory	Strong	Moderate
Specific information	Weak	Strong
Validity of data		
Internal	Strong	Weak
External	Weak	Strong
Cost		
Resources	Strong	Weak
Time	Strong	Weak

Source: Keith Cox and Ben Enis, *Experimentation for Marketing Decisions*. Scranton, PA: International Textbook, Co., 1969, p. 107.

Time and Cost Factors

Laboratory experiments usually take less time and cost less than field experiments. A laboratory experiment that takes a few days might take several weeks if conducted in the field. Since both time and money are usually at a premium in organizations, these factors might dictate laboratory experiments even when field experiments might be more desirable. Table 4.2 presents a brief comparison of the major characteristics of the laboratory and the field experiment.

◼ Summary

The focus of this chapter has been on research design, the overall framework or plan used for the collection and analysis of data in the marketing research project. Incorporated in any good research design should be problem definition, a plan for the gathering and analysis of data, a time framework, and a budget estimate. The research design presents an organized, systematic approach to the formulation, implementation, and control of the research project.

Four basic types of research designs are presented in this chapter: qualitative, observational, experimental, and survey. Qualitative research is often used for exploratory purposes.

Exploratory research is a preliminary step in which the main focus is on achieving a clear definition of the problem. Exploratory research designs are unstructured, rather than formal, and can be accomplished by one or more of three approaches: examining existing literature, questioning knowledgeable individuals, and examining a few selected cases.

Qualitative research is also used for motivation research. This chapter has considered some of the methods by which researchers investigate the psychology of consumers to discover not only what, but also why, they buy. The study of consumer motivation is vastly different from the traditional "nose-counting" type of research discussed in other sections of this book. Motivation research is much more subjective and much less direct than traditional research. Often, the researcher will be trying to find the reasons for consumers' behaviour when they themselves do not know the reasons. In other situations, the researcher will be trying to obtain valid, accurate information when respondents are deliberately misrepresenting their feelings.

This chapter has also examined a variety of motivation research techniques. The in-depth interview employs a rambling, in-depth conversation between a respondent and a trained analyst or, in the case of a focus group, between a group of respondents and a trained analyst. This method is highly subjective and is used primarily for exploratory studies.

Whereas in-depth interview research assumes that respondents can and will give truthful answers to direct questions, projective techniques assume that the respondents either cannot or will not be able to provide correct answers. Accordingly, indirect questioning is used: the respondent is given a vague stimulus and must fill in missing elements to create a meaningful situation. In filling in these missing elements, respondents project themselves and their personalities into the situations. Projective techniques include word association, sentence and story completion, the Rosenweig Picture Frustration Test, the Thematic Apperception Test, and Rorschach Tests.

Experimental research design can be used to measure cause-and-effect relationships. Central to this design is the experiment, a highly controlled situation in which the investigator manipulates one or more experimental variables while holding all other variables constant. Marketing research experiments can be conducted in the field or in the laboratory. Whereas the field experiment is more realistic, the laboratory experiment offers greater control—a trade-off situation.

Numerous highly complex experimental research designs are used by some professional marketing researchers and by many academics. In this chapter, three relatively simple designs were presented: the simple before/after design, the before/after-with-control-group design, and the after-only-with-control-group design. Each has its advantages and disadvantages, but the after-only-with-control-group design is the one most commonly used by professional marketing researchers.

Marketing researchers must decide whether to use laboratory or field experiments, although sometimes a combination of the two is possible. In determining which to use, researchers must evaluate the type of information required, the validity requirements of this information, and the time and cost necessary to obtain the required information. The choice of using a laboratory or a field experiment represents a trade-off among the three factors. The greatest problem facing researchers using experimental design is one of creating a realistic and controlled environment in which to conduct the experiment and effectively measure its effects.

For Discussion

1. What is meant by research design? Is it possible to conduct a market research study without a formal research design? If so, how?

2. Of the four principal research designs mentioned in this chapter, which do you think is the most important? Why? Could a marketing research study be conducted using all four of these designs? Give an example.

3. Compare and contrast traditional (quantitative) research and motivation research.

4. Why is it difficult to obtain answers through direct questioning concerning respondents' reasons for various purchases?

5. What is in-depth interviewing? What are the advantages of focus groups over individual in-depth interviews? Why are focus groups popular with marketing and advertising strategists?

6. What is the rationale behind projective tests? How do they work? Why are they needed?

7. In your opinion, why was experimentation in marketing research a rare phenomenon before 1960? Why has it become much more popular since that time?

8. Which of the three experimental designs presented in the chapter seems to you to be most meaningful? Why?

9. Under what conditions might a laboratory experiment be better than a field experiment?

10. Which do you think is more important in experimental design, internal or external validity? Why?

Problems

1. **Mini-case: Jaison Corporation**

   The Jaison Corporation, established in 1967, is a Canadian manufacturer of men's toiletries. Originally the company manufactured only shaving cream and soap, but soon it began to introduce some new products to the market, such as shampoo and aftershave lotion.

   The annual sales of the Jaison Corporation averaged approximately $2 500 000 in the period 1985–88 (see Exhibit 4.1 for a record of sales). Of this amount, approximately 40% was represented by sales of shaving cream, 10% by soap, 15% by shampoo, and 35% by aftershave lotion.

   EXHIBIT 4.1
   Breakdown of the Jaison
   Corporation Annual Sales

Year	Sales Volume ($)
1985	2 100 000
1986	2 400 000
1987	2 900 000
1988	2 600 000

   The growth policy of the company was implemented by introducing new products to the market, and toward the end of 1988 Charles Mendez, the company's president, was planning to introduce deodorants.

   On January 26, 1989, Mendez received a report from the marketing research department that stated, "According to the results of the survey conducted by our department, the strong antiperspirant effect is the most important attribute the consumer looks for in a deodorant."

   With this information, Mendez advised Roberta Naldini, product research director for the company, to make up some samples of antiperspirant deodorants.

In May, Naldini walked into Mendez's office with two containers and said, "Here are the results of our extensive research, and both have the same desired effect sought by the market. The experimental deodorant in container A has a better fragrance than B, but the latter is drier than the former."

Mendez then requested that the marketing research department perform a product test.

Questions

1. Propose a research design for the product test.

2. Why is the design you have proposed the best one, given the circumstances?

2. A marketing researcher wants to find out the effect of various possible price levels on the sales of a particular brand. Outline a research design that could answer this question. Be as precise as possible. You may make any reasonable assumptions.

3. As the marketing researcher for an airline company, you are required to study the extent to which people are afraid of flying. Devise a questionnaire and tests based on the projective techniques discussed in the text, and administer it to a convenience sample of potential consumers. Interpret the results.

Endnotes

1. James N. Myers and Richard R. Mead, *The Management of Marketing Research*. Scranton, PA: International Textbook Co., 1969, pp. 66–67.
2. Vance Packard, *The Hidden Persuaders*. New York: Pocket Books, 1957, p. 31.
3. Mason Haire, "Projective Techniques in Marketing Research." *Journal of Marketing*, 14 (April 1950), pp. 649–56.
4. Harper W. Boyd, Ralph Westfall, and Stanley F. Stasch. *Marketing Research*. Homewood, IL: Irwin, p. 82.
5. Keith K. Cox and Ben M. Enis, *Experimentation for Marketing Decisions*. Scranton, PA: International Textbook Co., 1969, p. 106.

PART 2

THE DATA-COLLECTION PROCESS

5 INTERNAL AND EXTERNAL SECONDARY DATA

In the previous chapter we discussed the issue of research design, which was defined as an overall framework or plan for the collection and analysis of data in the marketing research project. Whether the research design is exploratory, descriptive, inferential, or a combination, it will have as its purpose the generation of useful data that can then be analysed for the solving of business problems. Data analysis, the subject of Chapters 11 and 12, converts a mass of data into useful information presented in a concise and orderly format to facilitate decision making.

Modern business in Canada can be characterized as becoming increasingly information-dependent, by which we mean that, in the fast-changing, complex business world of today, managers are more than ever in need of up-to-date information on which to base decisions. Since the task of gathering and disseminating this information falls to the marketing research department, researchers must have substantial familiarity with the sources and types of information. The researcher must know when and how to use the library or to go into the field for needed information, because the cost and time trade-offs between the two can be of critical importance. To obtain information efficiently, marketing researchers must have considerable knowledge about both primary and secondary data-collection techniques, as well as an understanding of the appropriate times to gather and use one or the other, or both.

■ Primary and Secondary Data

Information can be characterized as being either primary or secondary in nature, depending on the purpose for which the data were originally gathered. The terms *primary* and *secondary* are somewhat confusing, because they in no way describe the priority of importance. Primary data, the subject of the following chapter, are original data gathered by the researcher for the project at hand. Secondary data are data already existing in printed or electronic form, having been previously gathered for some project other than the current one. Neither type of data is more important than the other, although they have relative advantages and disadvantages.

An example will illustrate the use of primary and secondary data. If a large food retailing chain wanted to know what percentage of consumer family income was spent for grocery products, this information could be secured from either primary or secondary research. Primary research might involve conducting a survey among consumers to gather the information; a thorough survey might take weeks to complete and cost well over $100 000. On the other hand, the researcher could go to external secondary resources, such as published government reports, and secure the same information. This case illustrates two benefits of secondary over primary data—economy and speed. By using secondary data, the information would have been gathered much faster and more cheaply than by the lengthy, costly, and often cumbersome process of surveying consumers in a primary data-gathering field research project.

One cardinal rule must be followed in beginning a marketing research study:

Always begin by exhaustively searching through all secondary data before attempting to gather primary data.

Many students, as well as some professionals who should know better, invariably reverse the procedure. When presented with a research problem to be solved, they make the mistake of rushing to gather primary data through survey research, when adequate and full information to solve the problem already exists in published secondary form. The end result is that, by failing to search exhaustively through secondary information, the researchers waste much time and money in collecting primary data.

This bypassing of secondary information often results from the aspiring researcher's ignorance about the existence and location of this information in a gloomy and unfamiliar place—the library. It also results from the assumption that primary data is more impressive than is secondary data. Some researchers have a bias against using secondary material, holding the mistaken belief that primary, or survey, research is what marketing research is all about. Unfortunately, this attitude has caused firms to lose much time and money in research projects.

Primary and Secondary Data Sources

It is sometimes easy to confuse primary and secondary data with primary and secondary sources; therefore, it is important to be aware of the distinction between the two.

Secondary data can be gathered from either primary or secondary sources. A primary source is the source that originated the data, whereas a secondary source is a source that secured the data from the original source. The government's *Census of Canada*, conducted every five years, is an example of a primary source. A local newspaper that published certain census population characteristics would be regarded as a secondary source, since the newspaper would be quoting a primary source, the *Census of Canada*.

Are both primary and secondary sources equally acceptable? The answer is *definitely not*. In using secondary data, researchers always should go first to the primary source, not the secondary source, of the secondary information. The two main reasons for using primary sources before secondary sources are that primary sources are more complete and more accurate than secondary sources. The primary source is more complete because it is the source that contains the full amount of information in an unabridged form. Also, the primary source will usually describe the process by which the data were gathered, thus allowing the researcher to make an assessment of the quality of the information.

Primary sources are considered more accurate than secondary sources because of the likelihood that secondary sources might have misinterpreted the original sources. The possibility of typographical errors is increased in using secondary sources, just as in the case of passing information by word of mouth: the more people who repeat a given message, the more apt the message is to become distorted. Secondary sources might omit significant footnotes or key textual elements and therefore change the meaning of the primary source. The danger of overreliance on secondary sources can be illustrated by examining the field of history, where secondary sources are used and reused in the rewriting and updating of history books. This process often allows and perpetuates distortions or inaccuracies. However, it is not always possible to use primary source material; in these cases the investigator must rely on secondary source information.

■ Sources of Secondary Data

When beginning a secondary data search, the researcher could become confused in looking at the vast array of secondary data source material available, including from trade associations, government publications, trade publications, research foundations, commercial sources, other business firms, one's own organization, and last but not least, libraries. Simplicity and logic permit the division of sources of secondary data into two groups: internal and external data sources. This classification is represented in Table 5.1.

For example, a recent study of the clothing industry in southern Ontario, more specifically dress and sportswear manufacturers, found the pattern of information sources indicated in Table 5.2, with the percentage of firms using each type of information sources.[1]

According to the table, the most frequently used internal sources are past sales figures and sales projections. Informally, employee feedback is used by 42% of companies. Among external sources, trade journals, magazines, and shows are the most commonly used. Informally, information gleaned from competitors, industry sources, suppliers, and retailers and fabric suppliers are often used. This is due to the very competitive nature of the fashion industry.

TABLE 5.1
Classification of Secondary Data Sources

Sources of Data	Data Collected	
	Regularly	On Ad Hoc Basis
Internal	Sales reports Accounting reports Reports from salespeople	Information provided by • sales force • employees • internal experts
External	Statistical reports Syndicated services (e.g., panels, omnibus studies) Trade publications Trade shows	Previously conducted market surveys Statisti- cal and other docu- ments (e.g., in libraries, universities)

TABLE 5.2
Commonly Used Information Sources in the Clothing Industry

Sources of Data	Data Collected			
	Formally	%	Informally	%
Internal	Previous season's sales	96	Employee feedback	42
	Sales projections	66	Intuitive attitude/	
	Analysis of sales		gut reaction	46
	data/market trends	38		
External	Fabric shows	21	Casual observation	58
	Trade shows	71	Retailers	71
	Trade journals and		Fabric suppliers	71
	magazines	75	Industry personnel,	
	Fashion/colour		sales agents,	
	services	33	advertisers	75
			Monitoring/observing	
			competitors	88

Source: Adapted from Judy Farlow and Majorie Wall, "Marketing Information Sources and Product Planning: The Case of the Clothing Industry," *Marketing*, 8. Ed. Ronald E. Turner. Administrative Sciences Association of Canada (ASAC) 1987, p. 15.

Internal Secondary Data Sources

Internal secondary data are found within the organization where the research is being conducted. Internal secondary data have been gathered for some purpose other than the project at hand. Sources of such data include sales and accounting data, verbal or written reports from the sales force, and internally generated research reports.

Internal Accounting System

This information system includes sales from the time an order is signed until the customer's account is cleared—all of the steps in processing the order, such as order shipments, billings, and collections. This is the basic component of a marketing information system since it provides essential marketing data and does not necessitate extra expenditure. However, the quality of the internal accounting reporting system varies from one firm to another. In some firms, sales reports are not available to management until several weeks after the end of a given period, and very little in the way of sales analyses and break-downs are provided. Other companies have accounting systems that provide up-to-date sales reports for the year, month, week, or even day, by territory, salesperson, type of customer, and product line. In addition, special analyses such as sales as a percentage of predicted sales or quotas by region, product line, or salesperson, are provided.

Between these two extremes, there is a wide range of internal accounting systems. In designing the best internal accounting system, at least three factors should be considered: the urgency of the information—often a marketing manager does not need an instantaneous reporting system, since a lapse of time might be necessary before reacting to change, just as a precaution that it has occurred as a result of random factors; the total costs of the reporting system; and all of the benefits provided by a sophisticated internal accounting system. A marketing information system based on internal accounting data constitutes one of the least costly managerial tools for marketers.

The Sales Force as a Marketing Intelligence System

Another relatively inexpensive type of internal information system is the intelligence system based on a firm's field sales force.[2] Unfortunately, such systematic and well-organized systems are often underutilized by many firms, even though the salespeople are in a unique position to recognize and collect relevant information concerning the marketplace.[3] Salespeople are in regular contact with their customers; they are often the first ones to learn about price changes made by competitors, new competitive products or brands, or the evolving needs of certain customers. Unfortunately, such information often is not reported to top marketing mangement[4] because there is no formal system for transmitting and processing such information, which often gets lost before it can reach top management. Without the existence of a formal, well-structured information-reporting system, salespeople are not aware that some information is of critical value to the firm or that the marketing manager is not aware of those facts. Even when they know that this information is valuable, there is no established procedure to indicate to whom in the organization it should be transmitted. Finally, salespeople often lack the motivation to fulfil this intelligence-reporting role, or even resent having to do it. This is the case when sales personnel are paid exclusively on a commission basis and they feel that they are not remunerated for any activity that is not directly related to sales.

For all of these reasons, a sales force intelligence-reporting system should be formally set up and sales representatives should be given the means and motivation to accomplish this task. The means should consist of providing them with all of the facilities to easily, accurately, and promptly report relevant market information. Sales representatives should be given instructions concerning which types of information should be reported and to whom in the organization they should transmit this information. Simple devices, such as preprinted forms, would minimize the effort and time spent by each salesperson on this task. In order to motivate them into doing a proper intelligence-reporting job, salespeople should be evaluated on their performance in this area and be rewarded when they report useful information.

Internal Research Reports

Previously conducted research studies and published reports constitute the third principal source of internal secondary data. These are a significant source of data, especially in large firms where the research function and report writing are well established. Giant, monolithic organizations, such as Bell Canada, have a well-established research and report writing system that results in the publication of numerous detailed reports and studies, which can be used as secondary data sources for future studies and reports. For example, the Bell Business Planning Group of Canada has produced a series of internal research reports dealing with such diverse areas as the *Impact of Communication Services in the Eastern Arctic, Exploration in the Future of Educational Technology, Cross-Impact Matrix Applications in Technology and Policy Assessment, Cross-Impact Analysis in Bell Canada, Exploration of the Future in Medical Technology, Group Judgemental Data in Cross-Impact Analysis and Technology Assessment*, and numerous others. Obviously, not every firm, especially not smaller ones, will have access to such a wealth of internal secondary data. However, even in medium-sized firms a substantial amount of internal cost and accounting data exist that are often overlooked.

Although internal secondary data might be somewhat limited, they do provide the most logical place for the researcher to begin the investigation. Research projects should begin with a careful review of internal secondary data, because these data are the least expensive to gather of any type in marketing research. Also, since these are data that have been generated within the organization, they are the most easily accessible of all types of information.

External Secondary Data Sources

External secondary data are those obtained from outside the organization. External secondary sources provide data that can be used in two basic ways: as general references in helping firms to be in contact with their outside environments, and as an aid in solving specific problems. Although external data sources might not be the originating sources for secondary information, they are of such importance that no intelligent information system can afford to overlook them. An almost unlimited amount of secondary information is available to the marketing researcher, making proper use of external data sources a formidable task. This vast amount of available secondary information presents to research professionals the major problem of determining which sources are useful and where they are located. Lack of knowledge of external secondary sources causes decision makers to act without complete information in attempting to solve marketing problems. The end result can be lost sales and lower profits.

Secondary source data can be collected in a systematic fashion. Many firms subscribe regularly to official government documents or carefully screen trade publications. The various reports published by Statistics Canada are often used. Many firms also receive reports from other organizations. In addition, a firm might subscribe to one or several syndicated services that provide information on industry sales, market shares, and so on. A marketing researcher might also have access to other data sources providing other types of information, such as libraries and trade associations. This is why it is useful for a marketing researcher to know which sources of secondary data are available and to be able to access readily the information relevant to the problem at hand.

Classifications of External Secondary Data Sources[5]

Although no clearly defined classification system exists because of the large number of different sources, for simplicity external sources can be put into four categories: publications of government agencies, syndicated commercial information, trade and professional association publications, and other miscellaneous published sources. However, the sources classified here might also contain internal secondary information. Each of these four general categories of external secondary information is described below.

Government Agencies

The continually expanding role of government, especially at the federal level, into virtually all phases of business and consumer activity generates enormous amounts of secondary data that is available to the public. One important by-product of this constant government expansion is that, in its efforts to oversee the activities of individuals and organizations, the federal government has compiled a wealth of statistical data. Nearly all federal government agencies collect and disseminate statistical data of interest to marketing research professionals. Accordingly, a complete listing of all federal government information-collecting activities would be well beyond the page constraints of this text; indeed, it could fill at least a complete textbook itself.

The information-collection and -dissemination activities of the federal government are well known to people outside the research profession. For example, Statistics Canada is the single most important source of marketing information within the federal government and the single largest gatherer of statistical data in the country. Established by *The Statistics Act of 1918* as the Dominion Bureau of Statistics and renamed in 1971, this agency is a vital source of published statistical information. By definition, a census is a complete enumeration of each and every item in a given universe. Typically, marketing researchers find it impractical to try to conduct a census of large populations, preferring instead to take a sample from the population, for two reasons. First, in a large universe such as the total population of Canada, only the federal government has the resources to undertake enumeration of every item in the universe. Second, the federal government has the authority to require respondents to reply to census questions, which private industry does not have.

The federal government conducts surveys at periodic intervals on population, housing, business, manufacturing, agriculture, transportation, governments, and mineral industries. The oldest, best-known, and most important of these is the *Census of Canada*. Conducted every five years, the *Census of Canada* has been modified many times over the years. Not only does this census give the total number of people living in Canada and within each province, census metropolitan area, federal electoral district, city, subdivision of five thousand and over, and census tract, but also it makes available detailed breakdowns of the demographic traits of the population. Ethnic, social, educational, and occupational characteristics are all presented in detail by the census.

The *Census of Canada* even includes a detailed breakdown of occupational characteristics of population in a given geographical area. Putting together information on occupations and information on income characteristics, the marketing researcher is in a position to make educated guesses about the purchasing power of residents in a geographical area, a factor that is very important in locating specialty shops and shopping centres.

For example, in 1981 and 1986,[6] a short questionnaire was sent out to all households in Canada, asking six questions: name, relationship, birthdate, gender, marital status, and first language of each household member. A long questionnaire was sent out to a random sample of 20% of all households to collect information on forty additional subjects, as shown in Table 5.3.

This information can be used at various levels of aggregation, as shown in Table 5.4. The number of census tracts that can be used for the data in Table 5.3 is 5059, and they can be aggregated according to the needs of the researcher. A final disaggregation can be obtained using the 38 233 enumeration areas. The advantage of enumeration areas is that they include both rural areas and small towns and villages and represent a neighbourhood-type, small unit of analysis.

For marketing purposes, it is convenient to organize the data according to enumeration area files, as indicated in Table 5.5. Some examples of the type of marketing applications of the census data are

- selling-effort allocation, using percentage distribution of income, population, and retail sales among territories

TABLE 5.3
Topics of Census Questions

Household Members	Origins	Schooling	Occupation	Income	Marital Status	Housing
name	birth date	years	employment	type	status	ownership
of each	birth place	qualifi-	employer	amount	children	mortage
relation-	citizenship	cations	industry			rent
ships	immigration	attendance	occupation			taxes
sex	ethnicity					heating
	first					repairs
	language					structure
	religion					rooms
						value

Source: Ronald E. Turner, "Marketing Applications of the 1981 Census Data." *Marketing*, 6. Ed. Jean Charles Chebat. ASAC, 1985, p. 336.

TABLE 5.4
Geographic Records in User Summary Tapes

Geographic Breakdowns	Number of Geographic Records	
	100% Data	20% Data*
Census Tracts		
Canada	1	1
Provinces	12	12
CMA/CA**	37	37
Census Tracts	5 088	5 059
Enumeration Areas		
Canada	1	1
Provinces	12	12
Federal Electoral Districts	282	282
Enumeration District	41 197	38 233
Census Subdivisions		
Canada	1	1
Provinces	12	12
Census Divisions	266	266
Census Subdivisions	5 710	5 372

*Data from some of the small units are suppressed to preserve anonymity.
**CMA: Census Metropolitan Area; CA: Census Agglomeration

Source: Turner, "Marketing Applications," p. 337.

TABLE 5.5
Variables and Categories in Each Enumeration Area Record

Age	Five-year intervals from 0 to 75+
Sex and marital status	Never married; spouse present or absent; widowed
Mother tongue	English; French; German; Italian; Ukranian; other
Ethnic origin	British; French; German; Italian; Ukranian; other
Years of schooling	Grade; college; university; diploma; certificate; degree
Employment status by age	Employed; unemployed, by five age categories
Occupation type	Thirteen occupation categories
Income from employment	Average income; without income
Ownership and tenancy	Dwellings occupied by owner; by tenant
Occupancy per room	Persons per room owned, rented
Owner monthly payments	Five categories and average payment
Tenant monthly payments	Five categories and average payment
Dwelling structural type	Detached; multiple; apartment; movable
Value of dwelling	Four categories for private dwellings
Location	Enumeration area; postal code; universal transverse mercator

Source: Turner, "Marketing Applications," p. 341.

- direct-mail enhancements, using the Statistics Canada cross-referencing system between postal codes and enumeration areas

- survey research to augment a questionnaire by not asking questions already included in the census data

- neighbourhood store location, using the universal transverse mercator (UTM) system developed by Statistics Canada, which provides geographical co-ordinates of the centre of an enumeration area

The 1986 census, which took place in June 1986, contains very similar characteristics and the data obtained found the same type of marketing applications. This information is available through Statistics Canada's computerized data bank and retrieval service, called CANSIM. In addition, Telichart links this database with a Telidon terminal, allowing the business manager to obtain colour graphic representation of the data.

In addition to census data, Statistics Canada provides basic statistical information, collected mostly through surveys, which covers the following areas:[7]

1. *primary industries*, including farm crops, livestock and animal products, forestry, and mining

2. *manufacturing*, providing detailed information such as the number of employees, cost of fuel and electricity, and value of shipment of goods, covering most Canadian manufacturing industries

3. *transportation, communications, and utilities*, including air, rail, road, water and pipeline transport, telephone, telecommunications, radio and television broadcasting, cable television, and utilities

4. *commerce, construction, finance, and prices*, including reports on business conditions (e.g., retail trade), construction and housing, external trade, international travel, balance of payments, and international investments and government finance

5. *employment, unemployment, and labour income*

6. *education, culture, health, and welfare*

Finally, Statistics Canada annually publishes the *Market Research Handbook*, which contains in condensed form the most useful data on demographics, economic indicators, sectorial information, and household facilities and equipment.

In 1971 the Statistics Act allowed the distribution of microdata files from the *Household Survey*, and in 1986 some from the *Labour Force Survey* were made available at prices ranging between $400 and $1000.[8] From the *Household Survey*, the *Family Expenditures Survey* (FAMEX) has been extensively used by researchers in Canada, both in the commercial[9] and academic fields.[10]

In addition, Statistics Canada provides data derived from income tax by forward sortation area (FSA), which are the first three characters of the postal codes and indicate a residential or rural area.[11]

Although Statistics Canada is considered to be the most important of the government agencies in providing useful information for marketing research, numerous others also publish significant information. For example, Consumer and Corporate Affairs Canada regularly conducts studies on consumer problems and regulations related to, for example, banking, energy, or the elderly, as well as truth in advertising. In particular, it publishes a quarterly *Misleading Advertising Bulletin* that reports on cases of unethical uses of advertising by businesses.

The Economic Council of Canada publishes an annual report as well as ad hoc studies on national and international topics related to the Canadian economy. In addition, the Public Archives Canada branch has collected information in machine readable format, covering most federal government institutions, some non-profit institutions, provincial governments, universities, and miscellaneous sources in the private sector.[12] Also, federal and provincial royal commissions conduct studies on topical economic and business problems, and often publish very useful and detailed reports.

Finally, provincial governments have developed a variety of sources of information on economic sectors of interest to the province, such as education, cultural factors, and patterns of international trade. Provincial publications and reports are referenced in the *ProFile Index*.

Syndicated Commercial Information

The second major external source of secondary data is syndicated commercial information. Syndicated commercial information is marketing research data sold on a continuing subscription basis by private firms for a profit. Syndicated commercial information, unlike special reports prepared solely for one firm, can be purchased by a number of buyers, since such syndicated information is not tailored for any one firm. Because it is not collected for any particular project, syndicated commercial information is not considered primary data but is included in secondary data sources. Suppliers of syndicated commercial information can be divided into two groups: those who supply financial data and those who supply market data.

Suppliers of Financial Data

The best-known syndicated sources of financial data are *The Financial Post*, Moody's Investors Service Inc., and Standard and Poor's Corporation. These firms supply up-to-date financial information about large, publicly held corporations. For example, Moody's publishes the *Stock Survey*, *Bond Survey*, *Handbook of Common Stocks*, *Industrial Manual*, OTC *Industrial Manual*, *Bank and Finance Manual*, *Transportation Manual*, *Public Utility Manual*, and *Municipal and Government Manual*. Standard and Poor's Corporation publishes the *Industry Survey* and *Standard Corporation Records*. The latter provides detailed financial and operating data about medium-sized and large firms trading on the major stock exchanges in North America. Poor's *Register of Corporations, Directors and Executives* is an annual publication that lists the products, sales, officers, and employees of approximately thirty thousand U.S. and Canadian firms. Both Moody's and Standard and Poor's syndicated services constantly send updated information to subscribers.

Numerous other sources of financial data are also available to marketing managers, depending on the type of information required. For example, if the firm needs an estimate of the credit worthiness of potential customers, a common method is to employ the services of Dun & Bradstreet, the international credit-reporting firm. While Moody's and Standard and Poor's services are reported and available in university libraries, other firms, such as Dun & Bradstreet or Retail Credit, do not publish their information, but rather, sell it on an individual basis.

Suppliers of Market Data

A second group of commercial information firms supply market data: professional research firms collect channel information and then sell it on a syndicated basis. Manufacturers of consumer products are particularly interested in securing additional information on sales activities of middlemen, wholesalers, and retailers in their channels of distribution. Among the syndicated services to which a firm can subscribe are store audit panels, consumer panels, and media surveys.

Store audit panels are a representative sample of retailers. Periodically (e.g., every month) a panel auditor surveys each retailer and records the inventory level for each product and each brand, by size, model, etc. For each item, records are kept of the shipments received by the retailer during a pre-specified period of time. Thus, retail sales between two store audits can be estimated. For example, the March sales for an item can be estimated by using the following formula:

Retail sales in March = inventory at the beginning of March
  + shipment received in March
  − inventory at the end of March

A.C. Nielsen of Canada specializes in gathering channel information and making it available to subscribers, particularly manufacturers. It provides a variety of syndicated services of interest to marketing researchers. Nielsen's *Retail Index Survey* is conducted every two months in a sample of approximately two thousand food and drug stores, where Nielsen representatives audit complete sales and inventory levels of each store in the sample during that time period. As an incentive, each store is given a copy of the report plus some small monetary reward. Information derived from the *Retail Index Survey* is available to subscribers, who receive bimonthly reports on total sales by product class, brand, price, and stockturn (merchandise turnover). A series of such *Retail Index Survey* reports might be expensive, but manufacturers receive valuable data not only about their own sales but about sales of competitors. Thus, although a firm such as Catelli would know its own sales into the channels, it could learn what General Foods' sales were in a given product class.

Consumer panels comprise a representative sample of consumers in a given market. Each panel member agrees to keep a diary in which he or she records the products and brands purchased, their sizes, the price paid for each item, and the retail outlet patronized. By aggregating data over all consumers, retail sales of a brand as well as competitors' sales can be estimated. Consumer panels can give reasonably accurate estimates of a brand market share, especially for high-volume items. One example of this is the Consumers Mail Panel developed by Market

Facts of Canada and based on a sample of one thousand families. Other consumer panels are operated by International Surveys Limited and Dialogue Canada.

Radio and television audience panels are similar to consumer panels, except that members are required to record in their diaries their television-viewing and/or their radio-listening habits. By aggregating this information, the audience size of programs and stations can be estimated. With these estimates, an advertiser can elect to advertise on the programs when the audience profile best matches that of the targeted market segments. A.C. Nielsen of Canada and the Bureau of Broadcast Measurement provide such services. These are described in more detail in Chapter 15.

Estimates of **advertising spending** by brand and major media are provided on a regular basis by Elliott Research Corporation. These are obtained by monitoring use of advertising in the media, estimating the time and space costs, and tabulating these by brand, industry, and medium.

Trade and Professional Associations

Trade and professional associations provide an excellent but often overlooked external secondary data source. A main objective of trade and professional associations is to provide information about the industry and its environment to members. To accomplish this objective, these associations publish books, magazines, journals, and newspapers that are sent to members and libraries. For example, publications of the American Marketing Association include the *Journal of Marketing*, the *Journal of Marketing Research*, *Marketing News*, and many others. The Administrative Sciences Association of Canada publishes the *Canadian Journal of Administrative Sciences*. In the advertising field, there is *Marketing*, a weekly publication of McLean-Hunter, *Advertising Age*, a weekly publication of Crain Communications, Inc., and the *Journal of Advertising Research*, published by the Advertising Research Foundation.

Other important publications are the magazines *Supermarketing* and *Progressive Grocer*, trade publications in the retail grocery field. Still others are *Sales Management* and the *Journal of Retailing*.

These are only a few of the many publications prepared by trade, professional, and learned organizations. Many of these publications are quite specialized, such as *Supermarketing*, whereas others, such as the *Journal of Marketing*, are of much more general interest. Virtually all of these periodicals should be available in any good university library, and these, as well as others, would be cross-referenced in an index called the *Business Periodicals Index* (BPI).

Miscellaneous Published Sources

By no means do government agencies, syndicated commercial sources, and trade and professional associations constitute the only sources for published external data. There is an almost unlimited number of other published sources of various types that are of relevance to marketing researchers. Of this enormous array of periodicals, newspapers, special published reports, dissertations, books, and monographs, it would be impossible to list or otherwise describe more than a few.

One particularly useful external source is *The Financial Post Canadian Markets* published by McLean-Hunter. This annual issue contains statistical information, arranged in geographical categories, on effective buying income, population, and retail sales for various types of retail outlets. It also contains information on industrial parks, transportation, and contacts for more than five hundred areas.

These miscellaneous published sources are referenced in library card catalogues and in published collections of abstracts and indexes. The card catalogues provide references to all books in the library by author, title, and subject heading. Collections of abstracts include, among the most useful, *Dissertation Abstracts*, *Psychological Abstracts*, and *Sociological Abstracts*. Indexes provide a comprehensive cross-classification of newspaper articles and published articles. Some of the most important are the *Business Periodicals Index*, *The Wall Street Journal Index* (WSJI), the *Social Science Citation Index*, the *Readers' Guide to Periodical Literature*, and *The New York Times Index*. No review of external published secondary data is complete without having consulted these major indexes. The following is a guide to some of these miscellaneous published sources.

1. *Dissertation Abstracts* (Ann Arbor, MI: University Microfilms). Published monthly by subject field and author. All doctoral dissertations accepted by American and Canadian institutions of higher learning are listed.

2. *Canadian Periodical Index* (Ottawa: Canadian Library Association). Published monthly; indexes by subject all of the articles appearing in approximately 75 periodicals, covering all aspects of business.

3. *Business Periodicals Index* (New York: N.W. Wilson Co.). Indexes by subject all of the articles appearing in approximately 160 U.S. periodicals, covering all aspects of business.

4. *Readers' Guide to Periodical Literature* (New York: N.W. Wilson Co.). Indexes by subject more than 100 popular U.S. periodicals. These periodicals tend to be less useful than those listed in BPI for most marketing research projects.

5. *The New York Times Index* (New York: The New York Times Company). Indexes by subject all articles appearing in *The New York Times*.

6. *The Wall Street Journal Index* (New York: Dow Jones and Co.). Arranged in two sections: corporate news and general news. Corporate news is indexed by firm and general news by subject, alphabetically.

7. *Public Affairs Information Service Index* (PAISI) (New York: Public Affairs Information Service). Organized by subject area. Various types of English-language publications on economics and public affairs are indexed.

8. *Canadian Trade Index* (Canadian Association of Manufacturers). Organized by manufacturer's income and economic sector. Very useful for exporters.

9. *Fraser's Canadian Trade Directory* (McLean-Hunter). Organized by industrial sectors.

Other sources are non-profit research foundations such as the Institute for Research in Public Policy, the Conference Board of Canada (which publishes a *Handbook of Canadian Consumer Markets*), the C.D. Howe Institute, the Fraser Institute, and the Hudson Institute.

Finally, one might note that there are a great number of documents said to belong to the underground literature, such as reports and research papers. To provide access to this secondary data, a team of French researchers created the DOGE database, which covers parts of Europe and North America and is available from Grenoble (Institute d'Administration des Enterprises) or Laval University (Faculté des sciences de l'administration).

Value of Secondary Data

Organizations find external secondary information very useful in making long term strategic plans. Changes in the demographic characteristics of the population, retail sales, and disposable personal income of consumers are examples of the types of external secondary data that firms often require. For this type of data, the primary source would be Statistics Canada and the secondary source would be a periodical that reported census statistics, such as *Canadian Business* or *The Financial Post*.

Specific problems also can be solved with the aid of external secondary information. In research projects, such information is most often used as an aid in developing hypotheses in exploratory research, although it is also used in solving problems through conclusive research. For example, a retail firm that wants to know the demographic and income characteristics of consumers living in a certain geographic area needs only to consult external secondary information, in this case published government census reports, to be able to find the information and avoid costly primary data-gathering surveys. The manager of a newly created marketing research department wanting to know the salary level at which employees in that department should be paid could, by examining the American Marketing Association's *Survey of Marketing Research*, determine the average salaries for research employees in a number of different categories by size of the organization.

The preceding examples illustrate the wide range of relatively inexpensive information sources that researchers can utilize. Before trying to gather information from primary sources, the marketing researcher should make sure that this information is not already available in a secondary source. This could result in significant savings in time and money.

■ Using the Library

By now it should have become obvious that there is no lack of external sources of secondary published information. The sources noted above provide a mass of data on virtually any subject. However, knowing about the existence of these sources and knowing how to locate and use them are two fundamentally different matters. The answer to the question of locating these external sources of marketing information is the library. Most college and university students, as well as many marketing research professionals, have only the vaguest idea of proper utilization of library facilities in secondary research. Libraries are often perceived as musty, dim, forbidding places, to be avoided at all costs. Despite this perception, the ability to use library facilities successfully is an absolute necessity for marketing researchers.

Although many large firms maintain in-house library facilities, the most up-to-date and complete collection of external secondary information will be found in good college, university, or large city libraries. University libraries are especially useful, since most of them have been designated official depositories for federal government statistical data, which means that all census and other similar information is automatically sent to them.

The thorough search through secondary data that should initiate any research study means a comprehensive library search. In Figure 5.1 a library search flow diagram is presented, to show the researcher how to proceed systematically in locating secondary material on an unfamiliar topic.

If the researcher has selected or been assigned a research project on a totally unfamiliar topic, a good place to begin is with a search through appropriate textbooks, encyclopedias, and reference works. These sources should provide basic familiarity with the subject.

Then a comprehensive bibliography on the subject should be located: a bibliography facilitates the quick acquisition of a complete inventory that encompasses all materials on the research topic.[13] It is recommended that the researcher go first to the *Bibliographic Index: A Cumulative Bibliography of Bibliographies*[14] Organized by subject, the *Bibliographic Index* indexes books, magazine articles, and other printed materials containing bibliographies. This index therefore makes it easier to locate publications in which authors have listed their own reference sources on a particular subject. Another valuable bibliography has been published by the AMA: *A Basic Bibliography on Marketing Research*.[15]

The library search procedure outlined in Figure 5.1 indicates that the next step is to examine books, periodicals, government documents, and then other miscellaneous or special sources. When searching for books in a particular area, the researcher should begin by going to the card catalogue. Books are referenced in card catalogues under author, title, or subject. Often problems arise in looking for a particular topic in the subject catalogues. For example, if one looks under the subject heading *Marketing*, there will be such an endless array of titles that it might prove more time-consuming than worthwhile.

Periodicals are usually a more fruitful source of material for most marketing research projects. In this case, the proper procedure is first to consult the appropriate indexes: the *Business Periodicals Index*, the *Canadian Periodical Index*, *The Wall Street Journal Index*, the *Public Affairs Information Service Index*, and the *Readers' Guide*. These indexes cross-reference hundreds of magazines and newspapers that can be utilized by marketing researchers.

Government documents, especially at the federal level, represent an excellent source of secondary data found in the library. The best place to begin in a search for the appropriate government document is the *Statistics Canada Catalogue* or the *Machine Readable Archives Catalogue* published by the Public Archives of Canada. The latter is a constantly updated comprehensive listing of public documents issued by all branches of the government. A complete description of each government document is given, including author name, title of the report, a

FIGURE 5.1
Library Search Flow Diagram

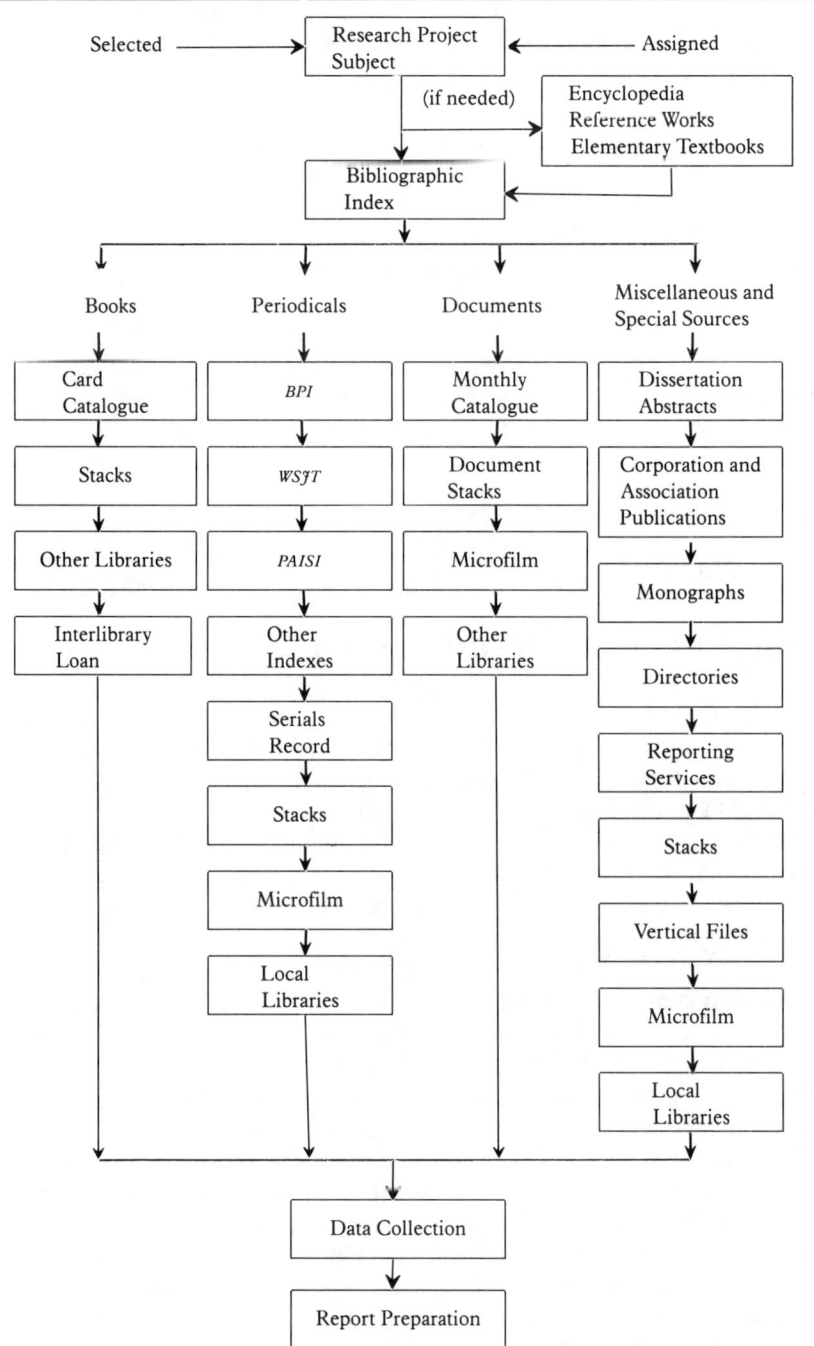

Source: Adapted from C. William Emory, *Business Research Methods*, Homewood, IL: Richard D. Irwin, 1976, p. 183.

brief discussion, length of the report, cost, and where the publication can be obtained.

Numerous miscellaneous and special sources of information also are available. These include *Dissertation Abstracts*, various publications of corporations and trade associations, monographs, directories, and such reporting services as Standard and Poor's or Moody's.

If at this point the researcher is still unable to locate all of the secondary information considered necessary, the reference librarian should be consulted and asked for additional suggestions. The required information might be on microfilm or in some other form in a university or public library. In the case of books unavailable at a particular library, it might be necessary to use interlibrary loan services, whereby the needed publication can be borrowed by one library from another.

On completion of the library search, the next task is to determine how much of the information collected can be used in preparation of the research report. As a general rule, only a very small proportion of the total amount of data collected in a library search will be incorporated directly into the report. This problem presents the researcher with one of the major tasks in report writing: synthesizing the mass of data into a useful and readable format. This process will be covered in some detail in Chapter 13, "The Research Report."

■ Evaluation of Secondary Data

At the beginning of this chapter secondary data was identified as data already existing in printed or electronic form. Since secondary data have been gathered for some project other than the one presently being considered, there are unique advantages and disadvantages associated with their use in lieu of primary data. Marketing researchers must be aware of the merits, as well as the drawbacks, of using secondary sources, so that the best combination of secondary and primary data can be incorporated into the research project.

Advantages of Secondary Data

In comparing primary data and secondary data, three major advantages of secondary data emerge. First, secondary data can be gathered much more quickly than can primary data. For example, a library search of a few hours, if conducted properly, will often reveal information that would have taken the researcher months to collect using survey research to gather primary data.

A second advantage of secondary data is their relatively low cost: most secondary data are available at little or no cost. Data found in libraries, such as journal articles, can be secured at the cost of photocopying the required pages. Even in cases where secondary information is gathered by commercial firms and syndicated services for a fee to subscribers, such as Nielsen's *Retail Index*, the cost is still appreciably lower than if the individual firm had gone out to collect the same primary information. All of the subscribers help to bear the cost, thus reducing the expense for each firm.

A final reason dictating use of secondary data is that certain types of information might be available *only* from secondary data sources. That is, some types of information might be impractical or virtually impossible to gather through primary research, no matter how thoroughly conducted. One example is census information.

Disadvantages of Secondary Data

When comparing secondary data with primary data we must recognize that secondary data have limitations. The two main problems associated with their use are that the data might not be appropriate for the needs of the project, and that the data might not be accurate.

Data Appropriateness

By *data appropriateness* we mean the degree to which the data conform to the information requirements of the problem. Secondary data might not be appropriate for use in solving a particular research problem for various reasons. First, the information might be out of date. Often, it has been so long since the secondary data were originally gathered and published that they are no longer useful. Rapidly changing attitudes, values, and demographic characteristics of the population quickly make secondary marketing data obsolete and no longer appropriate as a source of reliable information.

Another reason that secondary data might not be appropriate is a lack of standard classifications. Despite attempts to establish uniform classifications in marketing research by such groups as the American Marketing Association, there are still substantial variations in defining classes of, for example, demographic data. One research study might classify respondents in the age brackets of 20–29, 30–39, 40–49, and so on, whereas another study might break down consumer age groupings into the brackets 15–25, 26–35, 36–45, and so forth. It becomes difficult to do a meaningful comparison of distinctions and similarities between responses of data gathered in the two studies.

Finally, all too often there is a significant difference in units of measurement in secondary data. For example, many different measurements of consumer income are reported in different studies. Is consumer income measured on the basis of median income, individual income, family income, reported income, or some other unit? Obviously, there are some differences among these units. To take another example, consider a retail store whose customers come from a certain trading area (the geographical territory from which the firm's customers are drawn). The firm's management, in attempting to make marketing decisions based on available population statistics, might find that these data are available only by census tract or city—units that will be of little use to the firm if they do not match the trading area from which customers are drawn.[16]

Data Accuracy

The second major disadvantage often encountered in attempting to utilize secondary data is its lack of accuracy. Unfortunately, much secondary information suffers from this limitation. There is a particular problem, as indicated earlier in this chapter, when using secondary instead of original sources. Even in original sources, data might be inaccurate because of simple errors made by the researcher who collected and published the information. Worse still, data might have been made inaccurate by deliberate attempts to manipulate them to suit the needs of the original research project. Thus, the issue often becomes one of credibility. If one is attempting to assess the cost involved in producing and marketing prescription drugs, does one believe *Consumer Reports* or the Pharmaceutical Manufacturers' Association of Canada? Another example involves gasoline mileage of automobiles. Again, the question is which source, if either, is to be believed: claims made by Detroit automobile manufacturers based on their research studies or claims by Transport Canada based on its research studies?

The bottom line is that researchers must exercise caution in accepting the accuracy of secondary data. Professional researchers should always be sceptical when evaluating such data and should be looking for simple or deliberate errors in published reports. Researchers should always try to ascertain the identity of the person or persons who published the information and to uncover possible motives for publishing it. It is also desirable to evaluate data for evidence of careful research, the method of data collection utilized, and the purpose of the research. The question that should always be asked is: Why was this published? Failure to be critical might compound original errors and extend them over time.

■ Summary

The subject of this chapter is secondary data—data that already exist in published form, having been previously gathered for some project other than the one presently under consideration. Primary data are original data gathered by the researcher for the project at hand. In no way do the terms *primary* and *secondary* infer any hierarchy of importance of the two types.

Some researchers have an unfortunate tendency to begin a data search with primary data. A cardinal rule to be followed in any marketing research study is always to begin by exhaustively searching through all relevant secondary data before attempting to gather primary data. The reason for this procedure is that secondary data can be secured much more cheaply and quickly than primary data.

Secondary data can be gathered from either primary or secondary sources. A primary source is the source that originated the data, whereas a secondary source is one that secured the data from the original publication. Primary sources are distinctly preferable for research use because they tend to be more complete and more accurate than secondary sources.

Useful secondary data can be found both internally and externally. Internal secondary data are located within the organization where the research is being conducted but have been gathered for some project other than the one at hand. Internal secondary data include sales and accounting data, reports from the sales force, and internally generated research reports. The researcher should research internal secondary data thoroughly before going to external data.

External data are those obtained outside the organization. They can be used as general references in maintaining contact with the outside environment and as an aid in solving specific problems. Four principal external sources for secondary data exist: publications of government agencies, syndicated commercial information, trade and professional association publications, and other miscellaneous published sources. The single most important source of secondary information is the federal government; within the government, the most valuable source is Statistics Canada.

Virtually all sources of external secondary information mentioned in this chapter can be found in any good college or university library, although relatively few people know how to use library facilities. A library search flow diagram is presented in the chapter to aid the student in using library facilities in preparation of research reports. One of the first things to do in the library in beginning a research project is to check the indexes, particularly the *Business Periodicals Index*, which gives references to all major business periodicals. The card catalogue provides a starting place in the search for appropriate books, and the *Machine Readable Archives Catalogue* provides references to government documents.

Secondary data have both strengths and weaknesses when compared with primary data. Advantages of secondary data are speed, economy, and the difficulty or impossibility of obtaining the information through primary research. The disadvantages of secondary data are that they might not be appropriate for the needs of the project and they might not be accurate.

In conclusion, in the opinion of some authors,

> The positions for which social science students are likely to be preparing themselves—teaching, administration in government or business, community consultation, social work—increasingly call for the ability to evaluate and to use research results: to judge whether a study has been carried out in such a way that one can have reasonable confidence in its findings and whether its findings are applicable to the specific situation at hand."[17]

For Discussion

1. A new brand of beer that will appeal mainly to women and upper-income consumers is being planned for introduction by a major brewer. Your client, the brewer, wants to estimate the sales potential for this new product. Your task is to identify at least five specific sources of external secondary information (not indexes) that could be consulted to estimate sales potential for the new beer.

2. Go to the library and, using census data, locate the most recent figures for total wholesale trade and percentage of total sales by type of wholesale operation. Specifically, you are to find out (a) the number of wholesale establishments and their most recent gross sales and (b) sales for all of the following: merchant wholesalers, manufacturers' sales branches and offices, merchandise agents and brokers, petroleum bulk plants and terminals, and assemblers of farm products.

3. Can you identify a research problem where *only* secondary information would be available? Explain why or why not.

4. What is the best single source for locating government documents? What information does it contain?

5. As a researcher, how might you overcome some of the limitations or disadvantages associated with using secondary data?

6. Go the library and find the following: (a) the name of the chief marketing executive in Canada for the Ford Motor Company, (b) the title of a recent Canadian doctoral dissertation on marketing, (c) the median number of years of school completed for male adults in Regina, and (d) the most recent total food retailing sales for British Columbia.

7. Explain the difference between primary sources and secondary sources of secondary information. Which is better? Why?

8. What are the factors at which you should be looking when examining the reliability of secondary information?

9. A local department store manager has asked you to use census data in estimating the average income of consumers living in the store's trading area. What problems might you encounter in fulfilling this request?

10. What is the difference between internal secondary data and external secondary data? Which of the two would you examine first in a research project? Why?

Problems

1. **Mini-case: Kimura Hardware Corporation** (Part B)
   Keiko Kimura, a recent marketing graduate of Hillgreen University, has just joined the management team of her father's business, the Kimura Hardware Corporation. Annual gross sales are approximately 7.5 million. Net profits after taxes are $50 000. The chain has ten stores with a total of fifty employees.

   A careful review of the operating data has revealed that the growth rate has been tapering off and profit margins have been narrowing over the past three years. Three problems particularly bother Keiko:

   1. One store in a remotely located area has experienced a deficit every month for the past two and a half years. Keiko suspects there has been a shift in the population of the town, a rise in unemployment, or a drop in average income. Alternatively, the problem might lie with store management. Therefore, Keiko would also like to know which departments in the store have been hardest hit and which products consumers are buying.

   2. After reviewing the inventory listings, Keiko has become concerned about stock turnover and how it compares to that of competitors. She wonders where she can obtain this information.

3. To better acquaint herself with the industry, Keiko would like to draw an industry profile of several large publicly owned competitors. She needs to obtain the following information: gross margin on sales, net profit after taxes, earnings per share, and stock prices over the last three years. She hopes to find individual articles on some of the larger stores, industry marketing trends, and management innovations.

Questions

1. What specific data sources would you suggest that Keiko consult?

2. Where is the best place for Keiko to locate these sources?

2. A manufacturer of home safety equipment has invented a new electronic lock and is thinking of introducing the product first in your province.
   a) Research has identified the major potential market as homeowners. Using the latest information available from Statistics Canada, estimate the size of that market.
   b) If the product is to be distributed through hardware, discount, and department stores, is the figure obtained from (a) reasonable? Explain.
   c) If a direct-mail campaign is to be developed, how can the census data be used to enhance the effectiveness of the campaign?

Endnotes

1. Judy Farlow and Majorie Wall, "Marketing Information Sources and Product Planning: The Case of the Clothing Industry." *Marketing*, 8. Ed. Ronald E. Turner. Administratives Sciences Association of Canada (ASAC) 1987, pp. 11–20.

2. For a discussion of the sales force as an intelligence system, see Charles S. Goodman, *Management of the Personal Selling Function*. New York: Holt, Rinehart and Winston, 1971, Chapter 8.

3. J.E. Klompmaker, "Incorporating Information from Salespeople into the Marketing Planning Process." *The Journal of Personal Selling and Sales Management*, 1 (1980), pp. 76–82.

4. Dan M. Robertson, "Sales Force Feedback on Competitors' Activities." *Journal of Marketing* (April 1974), pp. 69–71.

5. For a more detailed inventory of secondary sources of marketing information in Canada, see Ronald Rotenberg and Beth Hatton, "Sources of Marketing Information in Canada." *The Canadian Marketer* (Autumn 1974), pp. 35–41.

6. For more details, see Ronald E. Turner, "Marketing Applications of the 1981 Census Data." *Marketing*, 6. Ed. Jean Charles Chebat. Montreal: ASAC, 1985, pp. 335–42.

7. Statistics Canada, *Catalogue 1984*. Ottawa: Supply and Services Canada.

8. U. Nevraumont, "Public Use Microdata Tapes from Household Surveys—Data Considerations." *Marketing*, 6. Ed. Jean Charles Chabet. ASAC, 1985, p. 103.

9. William Goldstein, "The Use of the FAMEX Survey in the Private Sector." Ibid., p. 104.

10. E. Anne Hope and Nathan D. Kling, "The FAMEX Microdata Tape—Frustrations of a First Time User." Ibid., pp. 105–106.

11. Statistics Canada, *Urban FSA and Rural Postal Code Summary Data 1984*. Cat. 17-602, 1986, Ottawa: Supply and Services Canada.

12. Public Archives Canada, *Machine Readable Archives Division*. General Guide Series 1983. Ottawa: Supply and Services, Canada, 1984.

13. C. William Emory, *Business Research Methods*. Homewood, IL: Richard D. Irwin, 1976, p. 182.

14. Laurel Cooley, ed., *Bibliographic Index: A Cumulative Bibliography of Bibliographies*. New York: N.W. Wilson Co., 1937–.

15. Robert Ferber, Alain Cousineau, Millard Crask, and Hugh G. Wales, comps., *A Basic Bibliography on Marketing Research*. 3rd ed. Chicago: American Marketing Association, 1974.

16. For some examples and proposed solutions, see Turner, "Marketing Applications of the 1981 Census Data."

17. Claire Selltiz, Mary Jahoda, Morton Deutsch, and Stuart W. Cook, *Research Methods in Social Relations*. Rev. ed. New York: Holt, Rinehart and Winston, 1959, p. 6.

6

PRIMARY DATA

By now it should be evident that not only are the information requirements of marketing managers extremely complex but also that marketing researchers must develop substantial expertise in securing the required information. The need for expertise becomes particularly obvious when one considers that information requirements and data-collection conditions vary substantially from one problem to the next. For example, locating a retail site and determining probable consumer acceptance of a new soft drink will necessitate radically different research designs and types of data.

In the previous chapter it was noted that the proper way to begin the process of collecting needed marketing information is by a thorough review of secondary data. Many marketing research questions can be answered and problems solved merely by going to existing data sources. However, in other cases, the required material might not be available, or the material that *is* available might be inadequate. In cases where information requirements cannot be satisfied from secondary sources, the researcher must gather primary data.

■ What Are Primary Data?

Primary data are original data gathered by the researcher expressly to solve the problem under consideration at that time. These data have not been previously collected or assembled for any other known project and therefore cannot have been already published in any form. In short, they are data that did not previously exist in any organized fashion.

■ Sources of Primary Data

A classification of primary sources is provided in Table 6.1. Since this information has not already been collected or is not available to the marketing researcher, the marketing researcher must design a specific research project to gather the data. This type of research is often expensive, so the data is not normally collected on a regular basis. However, a firm might organize its own "home panel" to use for a variety of products or projects. Some studies are carried out at various time intervals to track market shares or to measure the effects of an advertising campaign, for example. However, primary data research tends to be carried out on an ad hoc basis, to answer a specific marketing problem with an original research design and strategy.

TABLE 6.1
Classification of Primary Sources

Regularly Collected Data	Data Collected on Ad Hoc Basis
Panels of consumers	Qualitative research
Recurrent surveys	Ad hoc market surveys
Tracking studies	Experimentation studies
Focus groups	Observation studies

Where can researchers go to collect primary data? The four major sources are one's own organization, middlemen, customers and potential customers, and the competition.

The Organization

One's own organization is an important source of both primary and secondary data. For example, to obtain primary data, Procter & Gamble uses its own employees when testing new products and product concepts, and reports that these employees are some of the most objective and critical evaluators that the company has.[1] Salespeople and executives often provide valuable input toward decisions on marketing forecasting, particularly in industrial goods firms where salespeople have close contact with industrial customers and their needs.

Middlemen

Members of the manufacturer's channel of distribution are often very good sources of primary data. Wholesalers and retailers, because of their proximity to the market, are often much more knowledgeable about current market trends and customer preferences than is the manufacturer. For example, the major breweries have their wholesalers provide market information on sales to retailers. This procedure allows a firm like Labatt to have a good record of the retail beer sales in any area of the country.

Customers and Potential Customers

Customers are the most important of the four major sources of primary data identified in this chapter. From the marketing concept of attempting to assess customer wants and needs it logically follows that marketing managers must be directly concerned with what consumers think of existing products and what they would like in new products. In their attempts to attract and hold customers, firms seek information about consumer attitudes, knowledge, behaviour, and purchase intentions. A firm like Carling O'Keefe might conduct a survey among potential customers (beer drinkers) to find out what their purchase intentions might be if Carling O'Keefe were to introduce a new brand of super premium beer to compete with Labatt *Classic*. Information gathered from such a survey would be important, although it would not guarantee market success for the new Carling O'Keefe brand.

The Competition

In a market with pure competition, competitors might be a very poor source of any kind of marketing information. However, most market competition in our economic system is not "pure"—in most markets, competitors are usually large enough to influence each other. Particularly in industries dominated by a few large competitors, firms tend to exchange market information. The information most commonly available concerns pricing policies. It is not unusual to find competing firms exchanging information about prices and pricing policies, including planned price increases—although these practices, which may be viewed by the federal Bureau of Competition Policy of Consumer and Corporate Affairs as acting in restraint of competition, are best avoided. To expect a competitor to reveal much marketing information would, however, be unrealistic. Some friendly exchange of non-sensitive information might occur, but as a practical and ethical matter, competitors are not usually reliable sources of primary data.

Other, more devious, approaches hold attractions for some market rivals bent on securing market information from competitors by less-than-ethical means. Industrial espionage (the theft of trade secrets from competitors) is an illegal method of obtaining market information. However, the folly in this method of securing primary data from competitors was well demonstrated by the Watergate misadventure in the United States during the early 1970s.

■ Types of Primary Data

A question common to marketing researchers attempting to secure primary data from respondents relates to the types of primary data that is required. For instance, if a firm such as McDonald's, the international hamburger chain, wanted to conduct a marketing research study to gain better in-depth analysis of customers and their buying habits, what types of primary data would be wanted? The firm might be interested in getting a detailed profile of the average customer of a

McDonald's retail outlet, or it might want information concerning *why* people patronize McDonald's instead of Burger King or Harvey's. In the first instance, the needed information could be secured from brief questionnaires filled out on location by the respondents; in the second case, a complete and accurate answer to the question *why* would probably involve personal interviews and possibly the usage of motivation research techniques, such as in-depth interviewing. The needs of each particular data-collection survey dictate the types of primary data that the researcher will collect.

Although specific primary data requirements will vary substantially with almost every survey conducted, certain general types of primary information are widely available and might be required in almost any major survey. Four main types of primary data can be secured from respondents: purchase intentions, attitudes and opinions, activities or behaviour, and demographic characteristics.

Purchasing Intentions

Marketing managers are keenly interested in measuring consumers' purchase intentions. A specific research survey might be commissioned, for example, to find out what consumer purchasing intentions would be toward a new type of dog food, in which case potential customers would be asked if they would be willing to buy this product. A broader type of survey of purchasing intentions is conducted by the Survey Research Center at the University of Michigan.[2] Consumers are asked about their purchasing intentions for such consumer durables as automobiles, major appliances, and even housing. The Survey Research Center then reports four responses: a definite intention to buy, a probable intention to buy, undecided, and a definite intention not to buy. This type of data not only indicates consumer willingness to purchase big-ticket items but also is regarded as a general measure of consumer confidence in the economy and as a key variable in forecasting future economic up- or downturns.

A word of caution against overreliance on surveys of consumer purchasing intentions should be included at this point. It is true that a great deal of time and effort is expended in marketing research in attempting to predict probable purchasing behaviour. However, no matter how scientifically obtained, survey results must be treated with a measure of caution. There is no guarantee that purchase intentions will be translated into purchase actions. In other words, a consumer reporting a definite intention to purchase a new automobile when the new models come out could change this intention for any number of reasons: changes in general economic conditions (a rise in interest rates, for example), the consumer's own economic conditions (such as the loss of a job), or some change in buyer preferences (perhaps the decision to buy a camper trailer instead of a new car).

Attitudes and Opinions

Marketing managers want to know the level of consumer awareness of the firm and its products and the attitudes or opinions held about them. Attitude-research issues and measurement techniques are more fully discussed in subsequent chapters of this textbook. At this point it is important to note that firms often conduct studies of such issues as brand awareness and corporate image, not only to learn what consumers think about the firm and its products, but also to locate any need for a campaign to change consumer attitudes and opinions. For example, studies conducted after the 1986 collapse of world oil prices revealed that most consumers had a totally unrealistic conception of oil company profits, thinking that profits were much larger than they really were. In an attempt to change this misconception, petroleum companies undertook a massive advertising and public relations campaign directed at improving industry image and consumer perception of petroleum industry profit margins.

Activities or Behaviour

Many primary data-gathering studies are concerned with finding out what consumers are doing. For example, how long does the average shopper spend in the retail supermarket? Who usually does the family grocery shopping? How often does your family take holidays? How much do you usually spend for an evening's entertainment? What brand of tea do you drink? The answers to these types of questions provide primary data on the *who*, *what*, *when*, and *where* of consumer behaviour and attitudes. Research into consumer motivation is conducted to answer the *why* aspect of buyer behaviour.

Demographic Characteristics

The types of primary data discussed thus far provide the researcher with useful information concerning consumer intentions to purchase a particular product and consumer attitudes toward the product or the firm, and perhaps also with a good indication of overall shopping activities or habits. However, the picture obtained so far would not identify, for example, the category of consumers most likely to shop in the early morning as opposed to in the evening, or the consumers most likely to purchase a *Cadillac Seville*. This is why almost every major primary data-gathering survey of consumers includes collection of demographic data about the respondents.

Demographic characteristics include the respondent's educational level, income, ethnic group, age, gender, occupation, marital status, and other related variables. These types of primary data are gathered for purposes of cross-classification, so that marketers can determine, for example, the profile of the consumer most likely to read *Chatelaine* or *Canadian Business* or to watch television from 1:00 p.m. to 3:00 p.m. on weekdays. The research results would then indicate the types of articles or programs that could be developed to appeal to this individual's interests.

Primary data gathered in this fashion can be used in segmenting consumer markets. Table 6.2 illustrates the major demographic segmentation variables used by researchers. Regarding the use of demographic variables in market segmentation, it has been written that

> Segments defined in terms of needs and/or behaviour generally do not coincide with socioeconomic classifications, so that the choice of segmentation bases is crucial in the design of a segmentation strategy. When marketers use a definition based on consumer needs and behaviour, they can make better decisions about the product or service mix that best suits the needs of a seg-

TABLE 6.2
Demographic Segmentation Variables

Variables	Categories
Age	Children (2-11), Teens (12-17) Adults: 18–34, 35–49, 50–64, 65+
Gender	Male, female
Income	Under $5000, $5000–$9999, $10 000–$14 999, $15 000–$19 999, $20 000–$29 999, $30 000–$39 999, $40 000–$40 999, $50 000+
Family size	1–2, 3–4, 5+
Education	Grade school or less, some high school, high school graduate, some college, college graduate, some university, university graduate
Occupation	Professional and white-collar, including managers, officials, proprietors, clerical personnel, salespeople; technical and blue-collar, including supervisors, operators, maintenance people; retired people; farmers; students; homemakers; unemployed
Social class	Lower-lower, upper-lower, lower-middle, middle-middle, upper-middle, lower-upper, upper-upper
Religion	Catholic, Protestant, Jewish, other, none
Mother tongue	English, French, German, Italian, Ukranian, Chinese, other
Ethnic origin	British, French, German, Italian, Ukranian, Chinese, Native, other
Geographic location	Postal codes (first three characters)

ment and can develop more effective elements of the marketing program, especially the distribution and media plans. If socioeconomic variables are used as segmentation bases, they may define segments that are easier to reach but are less homogeneous in needs and behaviour. With this dilemma in mind, marketing managers can rely on their judgement and on formal market research in selecting the best possible segmentation bases.[3]

The use of demographics in market segmentation confronts researchers with certain risks. Often psychological variables are more important in influencing consumer purchases than are actual demographic variables. Consider the following example:

The Ford Motor Company utilized buyers' age in developing its target market for its Mustang automobile; the car was designed to appeal to young people who wanted an inexpensive sporty automobile. Ford found, to its surprise, that the car was being purchased by all age groups. It then realized that its target market was not the chronologically young but the psychologically young.[4]

Nor is level of income totally reliable as a predictor of buyer behaviour, although in many instances it is considered an acceptable indicator of *ability*, if not willingness, to buy. Income is a demographic variable that can be deceptive. One would think that low-income families would buy lottery tickets and upper-income families would buy sailboats. Yet many lottery tickets are bought by upper-income people and some sailboats are bought by lower-income families. This suggests that the marketing researcher should use both income *and* social class when researching bases for segmenting consumer markets.[5]

After this introduction to the sources and types of primary data, we are now ready to examine the basic methods used in gathering these data.

■ Basic Methods of Gathering Primary Data

Five basic primary data-gathering methods exist: qualitative research, experimentation, opinions of knowledgeable sources, market surveys, and observation. These five methods are not mutually exclusive; a research design for a project could incorporate several of these methods. Since qualitative research, experimentation, and opinions of knowledgeable sources were covered in Chapter 4, our discussion here of these primary data-gathering methods will be limited to a brief review of the main features of these methods.

Qualitative Research

Qualitative research includes various techniques used in marketing research in the early stages of problem definition, to enable a manager to understand a problem or to formulate a problem more precisely. Often, for a new product and/or a new brand, a number of *why* questions are raised. These questions require a qualitative answer, and those answers are in turn used either to make decisions or to develop precise questions that will be used in quantitative research; for example, a larger-scale consumer survey. The following is a brief discussion of the most commonly used qualitative techniques.

In-Depth Interview
Using the individual in-depth interviewing technique, interviewers attempt to elicit as much information as possible about a new product, a new package, or a new advertisement from a small sample of respondents. These interviews tend to be lengthy and expensive.

Focus Groups
Instead of interviewing just one person at a time, a moderator attempts to generate some discussion among a group of eight to twelve people about a new product, package, or advertisement. The entire focus group exchange is taped and content-analysed later on.

Projective Techniques

Projective techniques require respondents to describe the reactions of a third party, such as a neighbour, a colleague, or a cartoon character, to some sensitive or ego-involving stimulus, such as life insurance, fear of flying, or the use of contraceptives. Examples of such techniques are word-association tests, sentence-completion tests, and Thematic Apperception Tests, which use a drawing that is to be analysed by the respondent.

Experimentation

The experimental method is comparatively new to the marketing field and is extremely difficult to apply. Briefly, it is a tightly controlled situation in which the researcher holds all other variables constant while systematically manipulating one variable. In a crude sense, this manipulation might involve experimenting with the advertising budget, while attempting to keep constant all other factors of the marketing mix.

Opinions of Knowledgeable Sources

This method has found its greatest application in forecasting sales, but could also be used to collect other types of primary data, such as evaluation of new product ideas on market potential. A detailed description of this method is provided in Chapter 16.

A variant of the method in the international fields uses the tools of teleconferencing and the technique of focus group interviewing.[6] This method has been found to be most effective and to allow communications with time-pressured business managers in diverse geographic areas.

The remainder of this chapter is focussed on an examination of the two principal methods of collecting primary data: surveys and observation. Not all aspects of these two methods are covered in this chapter; more details will be provided later.

Market Survey Method

The marketing manager of a large hotel chain, such as CP Hotels, wants to know which features of the hotel chain that guests find most attractive. A manufacturer of stereo equipment wants to know if customers would buy a more expensive model if it was added to the product line. The manager of a large department chain would like to know whether extending operating hours into the evening would efficiently accommodate customers who have to work during the day. Although partial answers to these questions can be obtained from secondary data, the best way to secure answers is through survey research.

Survey research is the systematic gathering of data from respondents through questionnaires. The purpose of survey research is to facilitate understanding or enable prediction of some aspect of behaviour of the population being surveyed. The major steps to be completed in a typical market survey are detailed in Figure 6.1, with the large numbers indicating the chapters that cover these topics in depth.

FIGURE 6.1
Major Steps Involved in Completing a Typical Market Survey

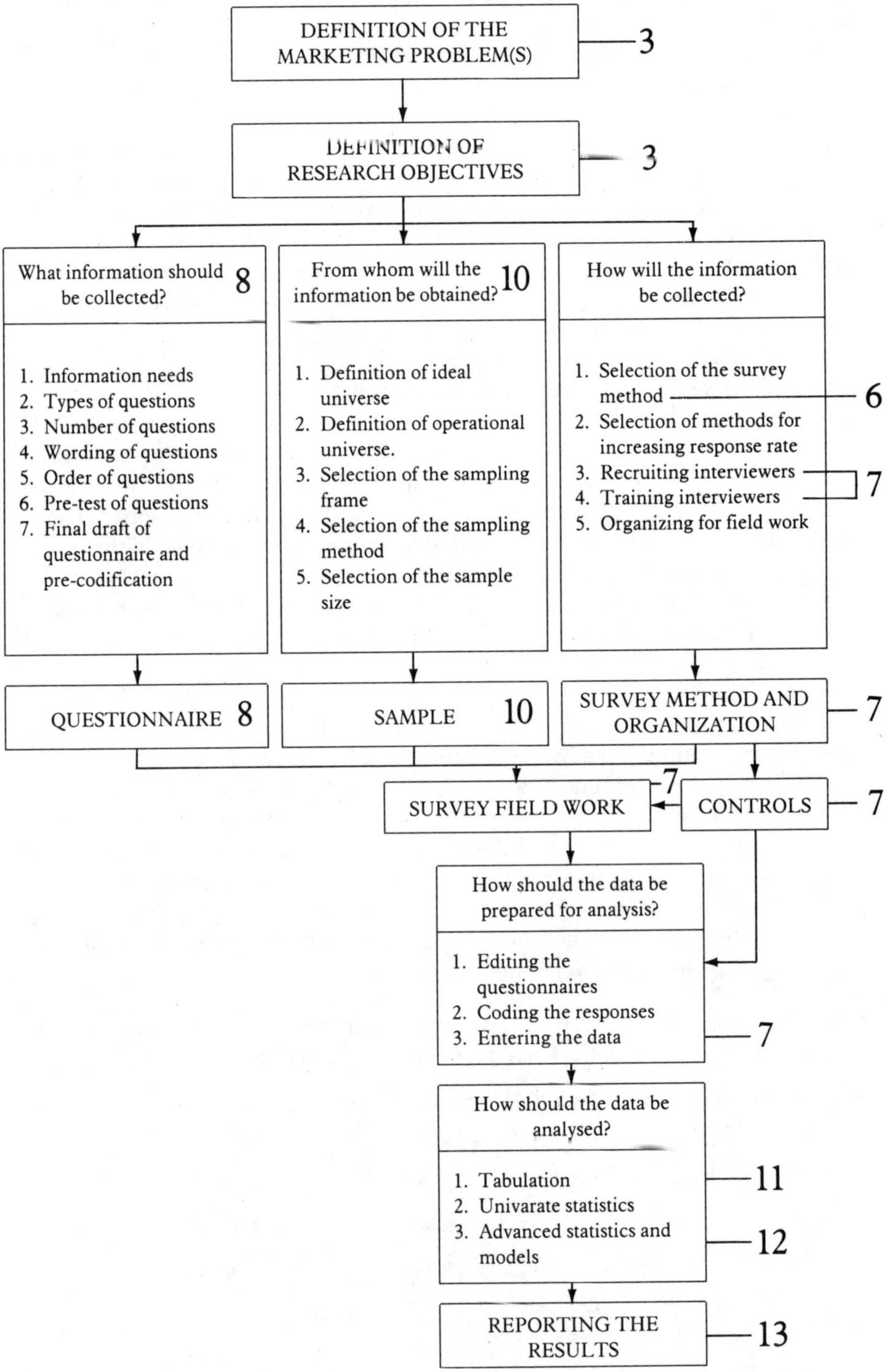

```
        ┌─────────────────────────────┐
        │   DEFINITION OF THE         │── 3
        │   MARKETING PROBLEM(S)      │
        └─────────────────────────────┘
                     │
        ┌─────────────────────────────┐
        │   DEFINITION OF             │── 3
        │   RESEARCH OBJECTIVES       │
        └─────────────────────────────┘
```

What information should be collected? 8	From whom will the information be obtained? 10	How will the information be collected?
1. Information needs 2. Types of questions 3. Number of questions 4. Wording of questions 5. Order of questions 6. Pre-test of questions 7. Final draft of questionnaire and pre-codification	1. Definition of ideal universe 2. Definition of operational universe. 3. Selection of the sampling frame 4. Selection of the sampling method 5. Selection of the sample size	1. Selection of the survey method —— 6 2. Selection of methods for increasing response rate 3. Recruiting interviewers ┐ 4. Training interviewers ┘ 7 5. Organizing for field work

| QUESTIONNAIRE 8 | SAMPLE 10 | SURVEY METHOD AND ORGANIZATION —— 7 |

```
        ┌──────────────────────┐  ┌───────────────┐
        │ SURVEY FIELD WORK    │◄─│  CONTROLS     │── 7
        └──────────────────────┘  └───────────────┘
                          7
```

How should the data be prepared for analysis?

1. Editing the questionnaires
2. Coding the responses
3. Entering the data —— 7

How should the data be analysed?

1. Tabulation —— 11
2. Univarate statistics
3. Advanced statistics and models —— 12

```
        ┌─────────────────────┐
        │  REPORTING THE      │── 13
        │  RESULTS            │
        └─────────────────────┘
```

A **questionnaire** is a formal list of questions to be answered as part of the survey. Telephone or face-to-face contacts enable respondents to complete the questionnaire with the assistance of an interviewer. Survey research can take place without any personal contact between researcher and respondents, by the use of a mail questionnaire.

Involved in survey research are survey administration, questionnaire construction, data analysis, and sampling—topics covered in the next six chapters.

Once the investigator has decided to use the survey approach in securing primary data from respondents, the next decision to be made is on the method of communication that will be used for the interview. Will the personal interview, the telephone interview, or the mail questionnaire be most appropriate for the survey? Unfortunately, no clear-cut answer to this question exists; if any one method was always the best, all researchers would undoubtedly be using that one alone, and not all three. A study found that faulty segmentation inferences can be drawn when data is gathered by more than one survey method.[7]

When collecting information from respondents, marketing researchers strive to utilize methods that will secure accurate information in the shortest period of time at the least cost. The ideal survey would be characterized by flexibility, allowing the maximum amount of data to be gathered; providing accuracy, control, a high response rate, and speed; and requiring a minimum amount of supervision and cost. All of these characteristics, however, do not apply to any single method of communication. Each method is appropriate some of the time, depending on the nature of the survey and the requirements of the investigator. Before discussing the relative strengths and weaknesses of each of these methods, let us briefly describe them.

Personal Interview

In the personal interview, the investigator asks questions of the respondents in a face-to-face meeting. Personal interviews can be conducted on a door-to-door basis or in public places such as shopping centres. The usual approach is for the interviewers to identify themselves to potential respondents and attempt to secure the respondents' co-operation in answering a list of predetermined questions. These answers may be tape-recorded or written down by the interviewer.

In terms of the *quality* of information gathered, the personal interview is always the best method to use, and it is the only one to use with projective techniques. In addition, personal interviews are indicated where

- the data collection procedure requires that a great deal of instruction or explanation be given to the respondent prior to asking the questions

- it is critically important that the respondent properly understand the questions to be answered

- the questionnaire is very long and complex

The major drawback of personal interviewing is that it is a very expensive method of data collection. The costs include

- selecting and training interviewers

- many time-consuming factors, e.g., planning the interview route, travelling to the respondents' location, waiting, calling back if respondents not available on the first call, interviewing, and reporting to the researcher

Telephone Survey

In a telephone survey, prospective respondents are telephoned, usually at home, and asked to answer a series of questions over the telephone.[8] This form of survey communication has become more common in recent years, as home telephone ownership has become almost universal and costs of personal interviewing have rapidly escalated. In addition, the personal contact by telephone allows some control over the interview; for example, to correct miscomprehension of a question or to make sure that all questions are properly answered. Another advantage of telephone interviewing is that several calls can be made to the same number at a very low marginal cost if the respondent is not at home when first called. However, telephone interviews are indicated only for relatively short questionnaires that do not touch on personal or sensitive subjects. Other drawbacks of telephone interviewing are

- respondents might be annoyed at being disturbed at home, in particular during dinner or in the middle of a television program

- they might not be willing to give personal data (e.g., income, age, education) or opinions to a stranger on the phone

- only very simple questions can be asked by telephone, not a ten-choice multiple question or a nine-point scale

- refusals tend to be very high, as well as non-completion if the questionnaire is too long

Mail Survey

The usual procedure followed in mail surveys is to mail to each potential respondent a questionnaire, complete with instructions and a self-addressed, stamped envelope. No personal interaction occurs between respondent and interviewer. Respondents fill out questionnaires and return them at their convenience. Sometimes mail questionnaires are distributed to respondents by personal delivery or newspaper and magazine inserts, but in most instances the entire process relies on the mail system.

Mail surveys are indicated when the research budget is limited, the questionnaire is too long or complex for a telephone interview, and it is essential that a random sample be used.

The main drawback of mail surveys is that there is very little motivation for the respondent to fill out the questionnaire. Mail surveys have had a historically very low response rate. However, to increase the response rate, several methods can be used. For instance, response rates have improved after the researcher has sent respondents a premium or a reminder. Also, the respondent might be better motivated to answer a questionnaire if it comes with a carefully written covering letter that explains the objectives of the survey, or if the questionnaire comes from a non-commercial source such as a college or university professor or a student writing a thesis.

Electronic Interactive Surveys

This procedure covers several new developments, all based on improving interaction with the respondents and lowering the cost of research. These methods combine some of the benefits of personal and mail interviews. The two major electronic interactive survey methods are

1. *Computer interactive survey method*: This procedure uses a microcomputer to administer a fairly complex questionnaire.[9] The computer is programmed to be fully interactive with the respondent in the same way that a personal interview is adjusted to suit the respondent's situation. However, respondents have to go to the location where the microcomputer is situated.

2. *Two-way cable systems*: With this procedure, the questionnaire is sent through cable to the home of the respondent. With a keyboard and a decoder attached to a television set, the respondent provides simple answers to the questions as they appear on the television screen.

Determining Which Survey Technique to Use

Seven specific factors should be examined before a decision is made as to which survey technique should be used: cost, speed, accuracy, amount of data generated, response rate, flexibility, and control. It should be noted that these factors do not constitute a completely exhaustive list of all criteria that might be used in selecting a proper survey method, nor are they mutually exclusive. Recognize, too, that there might be cases where specific conditions of the research projects under consideration entail an exception to the general rules.

Cost

Cost is a major consideration in any research undertaking and is usually the most important reason why telephone or mail interviews are used instead of personal interviews. Costs will vary, depending on the necessary response rate, the length of the questionnaire, the quality and quantity of information desired, and the location of the interviews. Still, the personal or face-to-face interview is nearly always much more expensive than the other methods. If the questionnaire is administered on a door-to-door basis, cost considerations include the total time of the interviewer, the amount of time devoted to each completed interview, and transportation expenses. Because of these problems, electronic interaction might replace personal interviewing in many applications. Rapidly escalating postal rates have driven up the cost of the mail questionnaire substantially, but this form of communication still remains the least expensive where a large sample on a national basis is required.

Speed

The speediest method is the one that allows the survey to be completed in the shortest period of time, which in this case is generally considered to be the telephone interview. Typically, professional telephone surveys are conducted by dividing a room into cubicles, each equipped with a telephone that can be monitored by a supervisor sitting in a central control room. In each cubicle a telephone interviewer sits and calls the numbers on a given list. The ensuing interview seldom takes more than ten minutes, because it is difficult to sustain respondent interest much longer than that. A supervisor on a central control board can listen in on any conversation to verify that the interview is taking place in the prescribed manner. Conducted in this manner, a complete telephone survey could easily take two weeks or longer to complete. As it becomes fully operational, electronic interaction will become almost as fast as telephone interviewing. Interviews conducted on a door-to-door basis are usually considered the slowest of the three methods. The mail interview occupies an intermediate position in speed, although in recent years Canadian mail efficiency and speed have been questioned.

Accuracy
Accuracy refers to freedom from mistakes in the data. Inaccurate information might be the fault of either the interviewer or the respondent, or both. Inaccuracies result from simple errors in misinterpreting questions and from deliberate attempts by respondents to provide incorrect replies. The accuracy of the information obtained is also a function of the interviewer: inaccuracies can result from interviewer bias, cheating, or misinterpretation of responses.

Inaccurate responses from consumers might stem from unwillingness to provide information, inability to remember answers to questions asked, or misinterpretation of the questions. The anonymous nature of the mail questionnaire makes this survey method best for information of a sensitive nature, such as questions about usage of deodorants, drinking habits, and use of credit. Note the difference in answers to the same questions from personal interviews and mail questionnaires in Table 6.3. Inaccuracies caused by a respondent's misunderstanding or misinterpreting of a question can best be minimized by personal

TABLE 6.3
Responses to the Same Questions via Personal Interview and Mail Panel

Question	Personal Interview % Yes	Mail Panel % Yes
Have you ever used a hair rinse?	37	51
Have you ever used eye shadow?	46	59
Have you ever purchased margarine?	75	82
Has anyone in your family ever borrowed money from a regular bank?	17	42
Has anyone in your family ever borrowed money from a credit union?	16	22
Has anyone in your family ever borrowed money from a small loan company?	11	13

Source: William D. O'Dell, "Personal Interviews or Mail Panels." *Journal of Marketing,* 26 (October 1962) p. 36.

interview. In this case, interviewers can explain questions, provide additional interpretation, and make certain that respondents do indeed understand what is wanted. The mail questionnaire has proved to be the least effective method of securing accurate responses, since there is no interaction between interviewer and respondent.

The interviewer also might be responsible for inaccurate data in survey research. Interviewer bias, which occurs when the interviewer consciously or unconsciously distorts or otherwise influences responses to questions, is a major source of inaccuracy in survey data. Poorly trained or motivated interviewers might make errors in asking questions or in interpreting or recording responses, or they might deliberately falsify interview results. A simple variation in tone of voice in asking certain questions among certain respondents will produce different answers. This problem, as well as ways to overcome it, will be covered in greater detail in Chapter 7, "Survey Administration." Since there is no direct interviewer-interviewee interaction, the mail questionnaire reduces problems associated with poorly trained or unmotivated interviewers. Also, electronic interaction will not have this problem of interviewer bias. The personal interview has the greatest likelihood of interviewer error, a factor that necessitates careful selection and training of, and control over, interviewers in field operations.

Amount of Data Generated

Which of the survey approaches is capable of collecting the most information from respondents? Although mail questionnaires often are long and personal interviews usually are short, personal interviews and electronic interaction usually elicit the greatest amount of respondent data. Whereas the respondents' commitment to complete a mail questionnaire or telephone interview is limited, respondents usually feel obligated to answer all of the questions in a personal interview because of the presence of the interviewer. Also, the face-to-face nature of the personal interview permits at-home interviews of forty-five minutes in many instances, and interviews of one hour are not unknown.

The telephone is not a good approach if lengthy interviews are required. The telephone interview competes with other interviewee home activities, making it difficult to hold an interview for longer than five or ten minutes. Each question in a telephone interview must be read to the respondent and then often reread or explained. Therefore, the very process of asking questions consumes an enormous part of the telephone interview, leaving relatively little time for responses; this approach is best used, therefore, when only limited amounts of information are required.

Response Rate

Response rate refers to the percentage of planned interviews that are successfully completed. In other words, it is sample size divided by completed interviews. Non-response is the result of two basic situations: refusals and not-at-homes.

Survey response rates can vary tremendously, from close to 0% to almost 100%. Characteristics of the population from which the sample was drawn, interviewer skill, and respondents' interest in the subject, as well as the survey instrument used, are all factors affecting response rate.[10] Response rate is also influenced by increased public concern about privacy and security, the increasing participation in the labour force by married women[11] and the gradual shift in housing patterns (such as to high-rise apartments) that discourage door-to-door interviewing.

Which survey method yields the highest response rate? The answer to this question is not an easy one because marketing research literature yields conflicting answers and most marketing research textbooks neatly avoid even attempting to give an answer. The issue is complex in that there are different types of telephone surveys, mail questionnaires, electronic interactive procedures, and personal interviews that, in turn, yield different response rates.

Still, it appears that the highest response rates can be achieved through personal interviews, using ongoing panels as interviewees. Even though some mail questionnaires have had extremely high response rates, the fact remains that "the major disadvantage of mail surveys...is generally believed to be their low response rates."[12] In general, response rates from mail surveys are the lower of the three methods, mainly because callbacks can be made with personal and telephone interviews.

Flexibility
Of the three methods, the personal interview and the electronic interview are the most easily adjusted to changing conditions. Skilled interviewers can rephrase questions when necessary, to ensure that respondents understand. The length of the personal interview can be varied at the discretion of the interviewer. Also, the personal interview allows the interviewer to use both sight and hearing, whereas the other methods permit only one sense. The rigid nature of fixed written questions makes a mail interview the least flexible approach.

Control
Three aspects of control are useful in evaluating these three methods of communication. The first, **sample control**, or sample validity, refers to control over sample membership—the degree to which the sample reflects the universe. Although nearly all households have telephones, an increasing percentage have unlisted telephone numbers, especially single women. Lower-income families are also underrepresented among telephone owners, because many cannot afford the monthly charges. Since everyone has a mail box, mail surveys are considered the best source of sample control. However, one caution should be exercised: an incomplete or out-of-date mailing list will severely hamper the effectiveness of a mail questionnaire. Thus, a good mailing list is a prerequisite for sample control. Similarly, electronic interactive methods might suffer from a low initial penetration of two-way cable systems.

The second aspect of control is **interview control**, or the researcher's degree of control over the interview. The absence of personal contact causes the mail questionnaire to be subject to the least amount of interview control; the personal interview is characterized by the greatest amount of interview control. Interview control is important because it assures the researcher that the respondent is responding accurately to the questions asked. The face-to-face interview allows the interviewer to explain questions, making sure that respondents understand them, and to determine if flagrantly inaccurate replies are being given. For example, if a respondent in a tar-paper shack claimed an income of more than $50 000 per year, the interviewer might be suspicious, but the claim might go unquestioned with a mail questionnaire. Another reason why the interviewer has the least control over mail questionnaires is that the person who filled out the questionnaire might not have been the one for whom the questionnaire was intended. For example, a questionnaire sent to the head of the household might conceivably be filled out by the head of the household's eleven-year-old son, yielding inaccurate or misleading data as a result.

The third aspect of control, **administrative control**, refers to the degree of control of the research manager over the interviewer. The least amount of administrative control is provided with the personal interview conducted in the field. The research manager often does not know whether the interviews were conducted properly or, in some cases, conducted at all. Good administrative control can be maintained over telephone interviewing, but the best control is afforded by the mail questionnaire, which eliminates the middleman—the non-professional interviewer—between the research professional and the respondent. The research manager knows that the mail questionnaire has definitely been sent out and also knows that the questions have been asked in a uniform and consistent manner, something that is not possible when questions are being asked orally by various people.

Choosing the Right Survey Method

Which of these four survey methods, then, is the best one to use: personal interview, telephone, mail, or electronic interaction? The answer to this question depends on the needs of the particular research project. The requirements of, and constraints placed on, the research will dictate which method will be chosen. The selection can be made only after careful evaluation of the strengths and weaknesses of each of these techniques in each of the seven categories just discussed (see Table 6.4 for a summary). Recognize that no one technique is always superior and that the criteria or goals may conflict.

Observational Method

Often information requirements of the research project are such that survey data acquired by questioning are not satisfactory. In other cases, even though the survey method is used, it might be supplemented by observation techniques. The observational method involves the gathering of primary data by physically or mechanically recording some designated aspect of consumer behaviour.

In some instances, observational research might be the only way in which information can be collected. In one study, where the problem was to analyse information content in television advertising, the researchers were obliged to rely solely on observation.[13] A sample of 378 commercials, randomly selected from all times during the week and on three networks, was colour-videotaped then later played back so that each advertisement's content could be carefully reviewed. This mechanical observational approach, videotaping, permitted the researchers

TABLE 6.4
Determining Which Survey Technique to Use

Criteria	Technique			
	Personal Interview	Telephone Survey	Mail Survey	Electronic Interaction
Cost*	Most	Intermediate	Least	Intermediate
Speed	Slowest	Fastest	Intermediate	Very Fast
Accuracy	Most	Intermediate	Least	Very
Amount of data generated	Most	Least	Intermediate	Most
Response rate	Highest	Intermediate	Lowest	Second-highest
Flexibility	Most	Intermediate	Least	Very
Control				
Sample**	Intermediate	Worst	Best	Low
Interview	Best	Intermediate	Worst	Second-worst
Administrative	Worst	Intermediate	Best	Best

* Where the sample is scattered on a nationwide basis
** Assumes an accurate mailing list and low penetration of electronic interactive instruments

to evaluate the informational content of the commercials carefully and accurately, something that would not have been possible using any other method.

The observational method might at times be the most practical for gathering needed market information. Traffic counts are commonly employed in site-location analysis for fast-food retailers. In this process, traffic patterns are recorded visually or mechanically, as in the case of a mechanical automobile counter used on highways to count the number of cars passing a certain location, perhaps a billboard.

Observation vs. Survey

The two most basic ways in which primary data can be collected are by *questioning* and by *observing*. These two approaches lend themselves to two basic methods of collecting data: the survey method and the observational method. The observational method has both advantages and limitations.

First among the advantages is the fact that the need for respondent co-operation can be eliminated. Unlike the survey approach, subjects are not asked to reply to oral or written questions. Consequently, refusals, not-at-homes, and incorrect responses from consumers are all avoided. Observation is used quite commonly instead of questioning when suburban shopping centre or supermarket owners want to measure the trading area—the geographical territory from which customers are drawn. This measurement can be made easily by observing and recording licence plate numbers of automobiles in the parking lot. Provincial automobile registration data permit researchers to secure quickly the desired information—consumer home addresses—from which they can determine the distances shoppers have travelled. Subjects are unaware that a research study has been conducted and there is no need to ask for their co-operation.

The second advantage is that the observational method is more objective: it avoids interviewer-interviewee bias, thus permitting more accurate information collection. Also, questioning is impractical if a study of the behaviour of infants, companies, or animals is required. In the previously discussed case in which the information content in television advertising was analysed, researchers could have conducted a survey of television viewers' attitudes toward the subject, but it was thought that more objective results could be obtained by the researchers' own observations.

Consumer unwillingness to divulge purchases of off-brand or non-prestige items makes questioning an unreliable approach to collecting objective information on private brand merchandise and cut-rate gasoline. In fact, one research study in which automobile licence numbers had been recorded at an independent gasoline service station revealed a reluctance by owners of prestige cars—*Cadillacs* and *Lincolns*—to admit purchasing such gasoline.

At least two limitations emerge in an evaluation of the observational method. First, the method is limited to measuring overt behaviour or external factors. It cannot measure motives or such internal factors as attitudes, beliefs, and values. Therefore, this method misses one of the most important aspects of consumer action—the *why* of human behaviour. By observing consumers in a supermarket check-out line, the researcher is able to determine *what* consumers bought, but it is impossible to determine *why* these items were purchased.

The second limitation of the observational method is that subjects cannot be observed or otherwise measured at all times. While the trained observer can faithfully record what is purchased in the supermarket, it is impossible to observe when and how the items are consumed in homes. Or, to present another example, it could be observed that women over fifty years of age are much more likely to purchase cold cream than women under age thirty; however, usage patterns or application techniques cannot be observed: no researcher is likely to be permitted into private bedrooms or bathrooms.

Types of Observational Methods
There are three major types of observational methods: direct, contrived, and mechanical. A discussion of each follows.

Direct Observation
The most frequently employed method is direct observation, in which respondents' actions are observed and recorded by a trained observer. Direct observation takes place in a real, not contrived or artificially created, setting, and no mechanical recording devices are used. It is a method of data collection that is particularly useful in cases where survey techniques might yield inaccurate responses. For example, a manufacturer of milk cartons might want to know if shoppers would actually use labelling information, such as unit pricing or open code dating, before purchasing the product. By asking shoppers whether they would actually use such a service, the researcher is posing a motherhood-type question—few, if any respondents would admit purchasing a product without utilizing all of the information available. By stationing a trained observer in the local supermarket near the milk counter, however, the researcher is able to record by observation

how many subjects actually read the labelling information before selecting the product.

This example illustrates two problems associated with using direct observation. First, misinterpretation of respondent actions is a problem. The researcher is unable to determine for certain if the consumer actually *reads* the labelling information. Second, direct observation could result in wasted time—the researcher might have to wait a long time between shoppers. This second limitation is among the major reasons for the use of contrived observation.

Contrived Observation

Contrived observation involves the creation of an artificial situation to allow more efficient and effective observation of the action being measured. In some cases it might be necessary to create an artificial situation to reduce the lengthy waiting time associated with direct observation. In other cases, contrived observation might be necessary because direct observation is impractical or impossible. For example, the manager of a large department store has received reports that sales personnel have been ignoring poorly dressed prospective customers. Directly observing or questioning salesclerks would be impractical. Therefore, both shabbily dressed and well-dressed researchers, posing as customers, are sent in to record salespeople's reactions. In this manner, measurements can be quickly and accurately obtained, thus answering the research question although not solving the problem. Many companies commonly use contrived observation to measure employee courtesy by having trained interviewers, pretending to be customers, confront sales personnel with complaints or difficult questions.

Mechanical Observation

In some cases, mechanical devices, such as cameras or other recording instruments, can be used with greater efficiency and precision than can personal observers. Data secured in this fashion are generally considered to be more objective than data obtained using personal observation. In particular, four mechanical devices have been found to be most useful—the people meter, the perceptoscope, the eye camera, and the psychogalvanometer.

1. *The people meter*: This is an innovation that is presently under study by the Bureau of Broadcast Measurement. This device is a computer attached to television sets that records when the television set is on and to what channel and program the set is tuned. With additional equipment, the meter can correlate commercial viewing with purchases of certain brands of products.[14] The people meter is discussed in greater detail in Chapter 15, "Advertising Research in Canada."

2. *The perceptoscope*: The perceptoscope is a camera that measures pupil dilation. It is used in advertising research in a laboratory setting. The use of this instrument is based on the premise that pupil dilation is an indication of interest and might help in evaluating advertising copy—the more the consumer's pupil dilates, the greater the interest. Presumably, such an instrument would be most interesting in evaluating respondents' reactions as they read the latest edition of *Playboy* or *Playgirl* magazine.

3. *The eye camera*: This instrument, first developed in 1890, was not actually utilized in a research situation until almost fifty years later, when *Look*, magazine made a practical application of it in 1938. The eye camera measures movement of the eye and is considered useful in measuring which parts of advertising copy are most attractive or appealing to readers.

4. *The psychogalvanometer*: This device measures galvanic skin responses and perspiration in determining emotional reactions of respondents exposed to products or product concepts. Researchers then ascertain whether respondents react emotionally to various advertisements or brands. Unfortunately, the device provides little other information to researchers.

It should be noted that of the four mechanical methods, none is without a substantial body of critics. The perceptoscope, the eye camera, and the psychogalvanometer are instruments sometimes used in advertising research in a laboratory setting. Their practical value is questioned by many researchers but, primarily because of the inexact and uncertain nature of advertising research, they continue to be used.

Regarding pupil size and eye direction, the following observations are illustrative of current knowledge:

Enlarged pupil size is indicative of favorable attitudes toward the communicator.

Message communication appears to be influenced by the direction of the eyes, and whether their angle is consistent with appeal of the message and the receiver's attitude toward the message.

When eye direction is to the right, rational and objective thoughts are reinforced: eyes directed toward the left reinforce emotional and subjective expressions.

How an advertiser treats eye size and eye direction in his advertisements may enhance the effectiveness of the advertising appeal.[15]

Since it cannot measure whether a television program or commercial is actually being viewed, or by whom, the people meter is also subject to criticism.

In general, then, mechanical observational devices are inferior to personal observation, although there are specific situations in which they might be used appropriately.

■ Evaluation of Primary Data

Nearly all professional marketing research reports contain both primary and secondary data. Although the two types of data are of equal importance, researchers should always first go to secondary data.

Because primary data are generated by original research to answer specific questions that cannot be answered by secondary data, primary data have two advantages: they are specific and they are relevant. *Specificity* means that the information is collected specifically for the project at hand; data tailored to the particular problem under consideration are more desirable. *Relevance* refers to the data's appropriateness for the problem under consideration. Primary data are more relevant than secondary data because they are more up to date; primary data are also more likely to provide specific solutions to the research problem.

The two principal limitations of primary data are cost and time requirements. Regardless of which method is used to collect primary data, first-hand information is almost always expensive. No matter how desirable primary data might be, if the firm's research budget will not allow for this expense, then it cannot be undertaken. Since many marketing decisions must be made extremely quickly, collecting primary data might not be possible. The length of time required to collect, tabulate, code, and analyse first-hand information might make it impractical to obtain such data, if the firm is to keep ahead of competitors.

■ Summary

Basically, two types of information are used by market researchers: primary data and secondary data. Secondary data, the subject of Chapter 5, are data that already exist, having been previously collected for some purpose other than the one under consideration. Primary data are original data collected or developed by the researcher. Typically, the solution to a given research problem will call for both primary and secondary data. Primary data should be collected only after secondary data sources have been thoroughly researched.

Four major sources of primary data exist: the organization, middlemen, customers and prospective customers, and competitors. Of these four sources, customers and potential customers represent the most important source of information. Four major types of primary data can be obtained from consumers: purchase intentions, attitudes and opinions, activities or behaviour, and demographic characteristics. Demographic characteristics provide a rich source of information useful in market segmentation.

Qualitative research, experimentation, opinions of knowledgeable sources, market surveys, and observation constitute the five basic methods of gathering primary data. The survey method is the most common of these five. Four survey techniques exist: personal interview, telephone survey, mail survey and electronic interaction. Before attempting to decide which of the four should be used, the researcher should consider the following factors: cost, speed, accuracy, amount of data generated, response rate, flexibility, and control. Observational techniques include direct observation, contrived observation, and mechanical observation, of which direct observation is by far the most popular. Many of the methods used in mechanical observation, such as the eye camera and the perceptoscope, are useful primarily in a laboratory setting and currently have limited practical applicability.

Researchers must carefully evaluate both the strengths and weaknesses associated with using primary data. The two principal strengths are specificity and relevance, and the major limitations are cost and time requirements.

For Discussion

1. In your own words, distinguish between primary and secondary data. Give an example of a research problem that could be solved by using both primary and secondary data.

2. There are at least two major reasons for not using competitors as a source of primary information. What are they?

3. Four main types of primary data can be secured from respondents. Design a research project that utilizes all four types.

4. Design the part of a mail questionnaire that will secure the necessary demographic information from consumers for a manufacturer planning to introduce a new organic cereal priced above the market.

5. What is the problem associated with using conventional demographic variables as a basis for segmenting consumer markets?

6. Compare the relative efficiency of the survey and observational methods in (a) cost, (b) accuracy, and (c) time requirements.

7. Design four simple research problems, each of which could best be solved by a different one of the four types of survey: personal, telephone, mail, and electronic.

8. Assuming time and cost considerations were of relatively minor importance, which type of survey would you recommend? Why?

9. Which method of communication is best if the primary consideration in the survey is control? Be sure to cover all aspects of control.

10. Some people assert that contrived observation is an unethical practice. Do you agree or disagree with that statement? Why or why not?

Problems

1. **Mini-Case: The Merchants' and Consumers' Bank** (Part B)
   The Merchants' and Consumers' Bank is one of the oldest and largest chartered banks in Canada, with three hundred branches across the country. Recently it began investigating the possibility of offering low-cost banking services to senior citizens. The bulk of the research is presently being handled by David Meyer of the marketing research department.
   The bank has never been interested in actively promoting banking services for senior citizens but has, instead, always taken these consumers for granted. Realizing that little banking information was available about senior citizens, except for some demographic statistics collected in previous surveys, Meyer decided first to collect some primary data on this potential target market.

His first step was to call Theresa Falcone, manager of a small branch on the outskirts of Victoria. Falcone's bank is located near a prominent upper-income citizens' residence, and consequently she is familiar with this consumer segment.

From her experience as a branch manager, Falcone produced the following observations about the banking patterns and attitudes of senior citizens:

- Senior citizens purchase more money orders than the average population because they like to have the copy that proves that payments have been made.

- Many senior citizens are holders of Canada Savings Bonds. They store their coupons in safekeeping or in safety deposit boxes, and often they forget to clip coupons. For this reason, a coupon-clipping service offered at a reasonable price would probably be appreciated.

- Many senior citizens, desiring security and liquidity above all, keep money in high-interest savings accounts rather than investing it more profitably.

- Retired people want to have money coming in on a regular basis, the way it did when they were working. If their savings are invested, they live off the yearly dividends, so they must budget the lump sums on a monthly basis. Therefore, the bank might offer senior citizens a deposit account that would pay interest on a monthly basis.

Meyer found Falcone's comments relevant and recommended that the bank include some of them in the final package.

Next, Meyer spoke to the president of the Golden Age Association and to other people involved in social agencies dealing with senior citizens. The consensus was that retired people would be very interested in such services and would even switch banks to obtain them.

During this preliminary investigation, four people have become involved in a debate on primary data-collection methods: Meyer; the manager of the new-services development department; the marketing director; and an outside consultant.

Meyer is a strong believer in testing new services. He has proposed that a questionnaire be mailed directly to seniors selected randomly from lists of various social organizations, on the assumption that active members of these clubs will be more likely than other seniors to make use of the new banking services.

Colleen Doyle, the manager of the new-services development department, thinks that individual door-to-door interviews would provide better insight into the specific needs of seniors. These interviews would give feedback on the usefulness of the package and would uncover new ideas that could be promoted. She is sure that seniors will readily accept such a package, because it offer them useful specialized services at a very low cost. Knowing that older people tire easily and often have hearing problems, she opposes group interviews. Furthermore, she fears that wealthy seniors might monopolize financial discussions, inhibiting their less-well-off peers.

Ernst Kubos, director of marketing, has also become involved. Prior to taking his current job at the bank, he was president of his own marketing consulting firm. Kubos contends that door-to-door interviewing would be too time-consuming and expensive. He expects the competition to introduce similar plans within six months of the launching of the new program at Merchants' Bank. Kubos favours telephone surveys: he wants to formulate the plan, test it, and implement it within as short a time as possible.

Jacqueline Gauthier, a consultant who has done extensive research for the bank in the past five years, has also been contacted. She proposes electronic interaction, using two-way cable systems. The interviews could be held across the country to allow for regional differences. Gauthier rejects door-to-door interviewing as too costly and too slow. Senior citizens comprise a relatively small proportion of the population, and many of them are disabled and would be unwilling to open their doors to strangers to discuss financial matters. Gauthier estimates that more than two thousand contacts would have to be made to obtain two hundred completed interviews.

The director of marketing research wants Meyer to submit a report by the end of the week, outlining the method of primary data collection to be used.

Questions

1. Evaluate each of the four proposed primary data-collection methods. Which methods would you recommend if you were David Meyer?

2. What specific information should be gathered in the study?

2. You have been asked to do a survey of consumers' attitudes toward fast-food chains in your area. You have determined that you need 300 completed questionnaires, that the questionnaire contains 20 questions, and that response rates usually are 50% for telephone, 20% for mail, and 70% for personal interviews. To decide on the best method to use, you need a comparative analysis of all three techniques, covering costs, speed, and accuracy. After this analysis, what method would you recommend?

Endnotes

1. Peter Vanderwicken, "P & G's Secret Ingredient." *Fortune* (July 1974), p. 79.
2. Gilbert A. Churchill, *Marketing Research: Methodological Foundations*. 2nd ed. Hinsdale, IL: Dryden Press, 1979, p. 160.
3. René Y. Darmon, Michel Laroche, and John V. Petrof, *Marketing in Canada: A Management Perspective*. Toronto: McGraw Hill-Ryerson, 1985, pp. 170–71
4. Philip Kotler and Ronald E. Turner, *Marketing Management: Analysis, Planning and Control*. Canadian 5th ed.. Scarborough, ON: Prentice-Hall Canada Inc., 1985, p. 261
5. D.W. Greeno and W.F. Bennett, "Social Class and Income as Complementary Segmentation Bases: A Canadian Perspective." *Marketing*, 4. Ed. J.D. Forbes. Administrative Sciences Association of Canada (ASAC), 1983, pp. 113–22.
6. Donald Shiner, "International Focus Group Conduct Using Teleconferencing: A Methodology." *Marketing, 8*. Ed. Ronald E. Turner. ASAC, 1987, pp. 236–40.
7. D.A. Schellinck and T.K. Clarke, "When Segment Characteristics Are Not Segment Characteristics: Combining Survey Methods." *Marketing*, 4. Ed. James D. Forbes. ASAC, 1983, pp. 328–33.
8. D.J. Tigert, J.C. Barnes, and J.C. Bourgeois, "Research on Research: Mail Panel vs. Telephone Survey in Retail Image Analysis." *The Canadian Marketer* (Winter 1978), pp. 22–27.
9. Nancy J. Church, "Computer Interactive Data Collection Methodology: A Review and Preliminary Observations." *Marketing*, 6. Ed. J.C. Chebat. ASAC, 1985, pp. 73–82.
10. Ronald E. Turner, "The Package Questionnaire and Nonresponse Bias." *Marketing*, 3. Ed. Michel Laroche. ASAC, 1982, pp. 304–22.
11. Richard Sparkman and Meryl Cook, "An Experimental Investigation of the Relationship Between Response Rate and Non-response Bias on Telephone Surveys of Women." *Marketing*, 7. Ed. T.E. Muller. ASAC, 1986, pp. 387–95.
12. Leslie Kanuk and Conrad Berenson, "Mail Survey and Response Rates: A Literature Review." *Journal of Marketing Research*, 12 (November 1975), p. 440–53.
13. Alan Resnick and Bruce L. Stern, "An Analysis of Information Content in Television Advertising." *Journal of Marketing*, 41 (January 1977), pp. 50–54.
14. Colin Wright, "People Meters: Numbers Crunched While You Wait." *Marketing* (October 28, 1985), pp. 11–14.
15. Albert S. King, "Pupil Size, Eye Direction, and Message Appeal: Some Preliminary Findings." *Journal of Marketing*, 36, (July 1972), p. 57.

CHAPTER

7

SURVEY ADMINISTRATION

In the previous chapter the various sources and types of primary data were examined. This chapter reviews the process by which primary data are gathered, coded, and edited before data analysis. We will call this process **survey administration.**

No matter how well designed it might be, the research questionnaire itself is incapable of securing the needed information for a study. In a field survey the questionnaire is merely one part of a triangle; the other two are the *interviewer* and the *respondent*. When a survey is carried out by personal or telephone interview, the interview can be viewed as a social process: social interaction and communication occur between interviewer and respondent. This process directly influences the three components of survey administration, the relationship among which is shown in Figure 7.1.

FIGURE 7.1
Components of Survey Administration

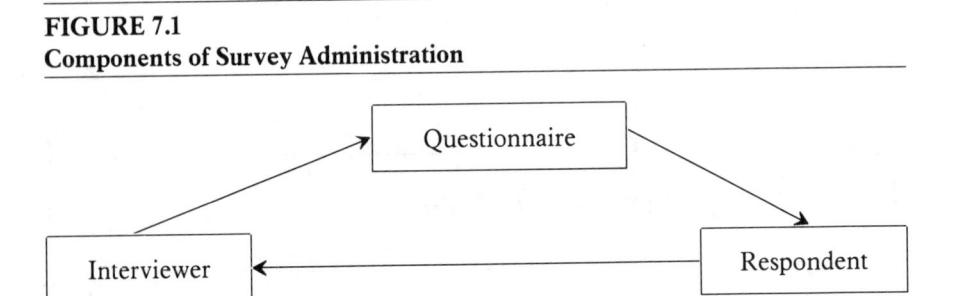

■ Administration of Mail Surveys

Although this chapter focusses primarily on the personal interview, some unique problems are presented by administration of the mail questionnaire. Basically these problems revolve around sample control and response. **Sample control** refers to obtaining representative samples to be used for the mail questionnaire, whereas **response** refers to the response rate, or percentage of usable questionnaires returned by respondents. Since a discussion of methods for dealing with response rates is included later in this chapter, the discussion here is confined to the issue of sample control.

The biggest problem in sample control for mail surveys is obtaining a satisfactory **sampling frame** (the complete list from which the sample will be selected). Unfortunately, satisfactory sampling frames might not be readily obtainable. Telephone books and city directories are often used to secure samples from the general population, but these sources might not be representative: some people do not have telephones, others have unlisted telephone numbers, and the lists themselves are quickly outdated in our highly mobile society.

Quite often researchers purchase mailing lists, particularly for sales solicitation purposes. For example, at one time or another you might have taken out a subscription to a magazine and then noticed an increase in the junk mail arriving at your address over the next several months. This increase occurs because most publications regularly sell their subscription lists.

Another option available to researchers wanting to secure representative mail survey sampling frames is mail panels. A **mail panel** is a commercial firm's listing of people who have agreed to answer mail questionnaires. Market Facts of Canada, International Survey Limited, and Dialogue Canada are three of these. At any one time, several thousand Canadian families are members of these firms' panels. Usually they serve without significant compensation but with the assurance that their panel membership will not be divulged to sales solicitors. For a fee, the mail panel firm will send out mail questionnaires and sometimes new consumer products to members of its panel. Advantages of using this approach are its simplicity and high response rate. The major disadvantage is the impossibility of knowing whether the mail panel is truly representative of the consumers that the researcher is trying to contact.

When a survey is not administered by mail, the research manager must be aware of, and able to anticipate, potential problems with the people involved—the interviewers and the respondents.

■ Interview Personnel Problems

Marketing research managers often encounter problems in attracting, holding, and motivating competent interview personnel. Since most field interviewers are relatively unskilled, poorly paid non-professionals, it is the responsibility of the marketing research professional to see that they do a competent job, and here problems often occur. Even if a very good questionnaire has been constructed and sound sampling techniques have been followed, poor questionnaire administration, stemming directly from interviewer problems, will severely limit the validity of the study. Problems of this sort centre around recruiting good interviewers, training interviewers, interviewer error, and cheating.

Recruiting Good Interviewers

Who are the people typically involved in personal interviewing? Interviewers have traditionally tended to be university students and homemakers, two categories of people who are often willing to work on a part-time basis at the minimum wage level. Where skilled interviewing techniques are required, as for in-depth interviews or motivation research, interviewers are usually paid much more than minimum wages. However, most interviewing in the field does not require highly skilled personnel, since the structured format permits questionnaires to be administered by people without extensive training or education in the social sciences.

Obtaining personnel for field interviews is usually not too difficult a task. Most large research firms have an ongoing list of people used in previous field surveys who can be called on to participate in the next project. Additional interviewers can be obtained by newspaper advertising or by contacting university placement offices for part-time student help. As with most jobs, there is little difficulty in securing personnel; the difficulty is in securing personnel with the characteristics necessary for successful job performance.

The ideal interviewer is one with whom the respondent can readily identify. Interviewers should have an agreeable personal appearance and be somewhat extroverted. Homemakers are very suitable because they are often available for part-time work during the day. Also, it is common procedure to use female instead of male interviewers, especially in door-to-door interviewing, because male interviewers are more apt to encounter refusals if only women are at home. It is absolutely necessary that interviewers be able to speak with total strangers and have no qualms about approaching strangers. In summarizing the native characteristics essential for good interviewers, one author wrote:

> Good health is essential! Field interviewing is a tiring job, and an interviewer is likely to be on her feet much of the day, walking from house to house or office to office. The incessant repetition of battling resistance and establishing rapport is exhausting in itself. Sometimes there are cumbersome or heavy displays to carry, tape recorders to haul from car to respondent and other such impediments. Strong feet, steady nerves, and sensitivities as invulnerable as possible are interviewer essentials. Interviewers should be of prime age, that is, over 18 if they are to be taken seriously and under 55 for health stamina.[1]

Finally, interviewers must be able to communicate with, and relate to, the various cultural groups in Canada. Some surveys must be conducted in both French and English. Therefore, interviewers must be fluent in one of these languages. Sometimes interviewing must be conducted in German, Ukrainian, or Chinese, and selected interviewers must be fluent in these languages and preferably hired from among these cultural groups.

Training Interviewers

Once the interviewers possessing the basic required characteristics have been selected, the next step is to train them. Interviewing has become a highly professional activity that requires extensive training and experience. Interviewers must know how to select respondents to be interviewed, how to approach them and gain their confidence, and how to ask questions without introducing bias. A poorly trained interviewer can give wrong signals to respondents through non-verbal communication (e.g., a smile, a nod, a frown, or any other type of gesture that might be misinterpreted). The respondent might then give the answers perceived to be those expected by the interviewer.

A poorly trained or motivated field force can ruin any research study. It is the responsibility of the marketing research professional to ensure that field inter-viewers are properly trained in procedures to be used in the project and to see that interviewers are properly motivated to do a good job. Training, as opposed to education, is job-specific and is designed to enable the worker to perform the job at hand successfully. Interviewer training can be accomplished by three methods: written instructions, training in person, or on-the-job training. Any good training program should give prospective interviewers exposure to both written and oral training instructions, along with the opportunity to ask questions and engage in practice interviewing or role-playing.

Written instructions include textbooks, manuals, or other materials that can be sent to the interviewer through the mail. Written instructions are best used as the primary phase of interviewer training, followed by personal or on-the-job training (on the principle that the best way to learn how to do something is by actually doing it, not reading about it).

Personal training is considered to be superior to the study of written instruc-tions at home. Training classes in both official languages (when necessary) held on the premises of the research house are the usual means of conducting personal training. Such classes might last only a few hours or, in some cases, a week or more. Although personal training classes are conducted by most large research companies, they vary a great deal in both form and content.

Field training, or on-the-job training, is probably the best of the three methods, but it should not be undertaken unless the interviewer has had some previous training. In this method the interviewer accompanies a more experienced super-visor on the first assignment in the field. The supervisor might conduct the first interview while the trainee watches. During the second interview the trainee interviews while the supervisor watches; after the interview, the instructor gives feedback to the trainee. This procedure might be repeated for subsequent interviews until the supervisor is assured that the trainee is competent to proceed alone. This method of training is the best of the three but is much more expensive than the others.

Many items are covered in a good training program. Interviewers are taught, among other things, to

- recognize the type of respondents to be interviewed, how to establish proper rapport with them, and how to schedule interviews, to minimize refusals

- determine the number of calls to be made on respondents before eliminating them from the list, and if refused, how to accept it graciously

- know how to phrase questions properly, how to react when asked questions by respondents, how to record answers properly, and what to do when the interview is completed

FIGURE 7.2
A Few Do's and Don't's Given to Interviewers

Do's

1. Always carry proper identification.
2. Interview strangers, not friends, unless specifically told to interview people you know.
3. Sell yourself to the respondent—make her like you!
4. Conduct the interview in a relaxed, friendly way. Remember that you set the tempo and, in a way, are your respondent's hostess even though you are in her home.
5. Read the questions, word for word, exactly as written.
6. Follow the order of questions on the questionnaire.
7. Give the respondent plenty of time to think each question through.
8. Record replies verbatim except when otherwise instructed, or when the length of the reply prevents doing so.
9. Make your entries accurate and legible.
10. Unless otherwise instructed, record unsolicited comments that pertain to the subject matter.
11. While on the premises, check your interviews for completeness and legibility.
12. Start early in the day while people are still at home.
13. Meet your deadline...beat it if possible.

Don'ts

1. Don't ever compromise with quality. If you can't complete an assignment, notify your supervisor, but don't rush interviews.
2. Don't let personal problems interfere with your work.
3. Don't deviate from a business attitude while calling on your respondents. Don't accept alcoholic drinks.
4. Don't do anything but the survey at hand. Don't try to combine one survey with another, or with sales or other activities.
5. Don't take anyone with you when you interview.
6. Don't deviate from prescribed sampling in order to seek "good" respondents. Don't reuse the same respondents.
7. Don't interpret questions. If they are not understood, reread them, and ask the respondent to interpret them herself.
8. Don't concentrate your interviews in one or two neighbourhoods unless told to do so. Don't work near your own home.
9. Don't allow the respondent to read over your shoulder. Don't ever let her read the questionnaire or the responses you have recorded unless specifically instructed to do so.
10. Don't ever begin work unless fully equipped.

Source: Robert Ferber, ed., *Handbook of Marketing Research* p. 2-128. Copyright 1974, McGraw-Hill Book Co. Used with permission of McGraw-Hill Book Co.

Figure 7.2 presents a list of do's and don't's often given to interviewers in a training program. This list is by no means exhaustive, but it should give you a sense of the general content of a training program. These do's and don't's might sound simplistic, but they are the keys to successful interviewing.

In conclusion, it is clear that field work requires careful planning that involves trained interviewers, precise work schedules, contingency plans, and field work controls. Contingency plans include having replacements ready to go into the field to replace missing interviewers, who might be sick, injured, or get discouraged and quit. Control procedures should make sure that instructions and rules are followed by interviewers, and that no cheating is taking place.

Interviewer Error

Despite careful selection and training procedures, there will usually be some interviewer error present in the research study. Such error is a sadly neglected area in marketing research. Great effort might be expended in questionnaire construction, proper sampling, data analyses, problem formulation, and other related areas, but all of this effort can be wasted by errors in field work. Professional researchers must be aware of interviewer errors and take corrective action to keep these errors to a minimum. Without this control, interviewing becomes the weak link in the research process. Too many errors can destroy the usefulness of the survey; in fact, it has been estimated that "one out of every four surveys may contain serious errors."[2]

What types of errors do interviewers make? Two major types are errors in asking questions and errors in recording responses.

Errors in asking questions occur when interviewers do not ask questions exactly as they are worded, when they omit certain questions, when they change the question sequence, or when they fail to ask all questions in exactly the same manner. An example of this last error would be the use of a disdainful manner in asking respondents whether they had watched an X-rated movie: the interviewer's tone would reduce the likelihood of affirmative answers. This is an example of interviewer bias—an interviewer's distortion of, or influence on, respondent answers.

Multiple-choice questions are particularly susceptible to interviewer bias if the interviewer places too much emphasis on one alternative when stating the question. Interviewer bias can be detected and sometimes reduced by using a tape recorder to record both questions and answers given in interviews. One difficulty encountered here is getting both interviewer and respondent to accept the presence of this control without the recorder itself introducing bias (the bias in this instance would be a Hawthorne Effect caused by the presence of the tape recorder).

Errors in recording answers result from simple computational mistakes made by the interviewer, from misinterpretation or misunderstanding of respondents' answers, or from failure to demonstrate that a suspect response is not correct. For this final reason, one of the ingredients of the interviewer training program should be instructions to press for additional comments when incomplete or questionable answers are given.

Interviewer errors can also be caused by social distance between interviewer and respondent, especially in view of Canada's increasingly varied cultural mosaic. When the two come from radically different socio-economic backgrounds, the chance of the interviewer making an error is substantially increased. Cultural differences can compound this problem. For example, a French-Canadian respondent might easily be misunderstood by a unilingual Anglophone interviewer. This type of interviewer error can be reduced by providing interviewers from the same social and cultural background as respondents, something that is particularly desirable in door to-door, neighbourhood interviewing. Using this approach not only will increase accuracy but also will help to increase response rate by reducing the number of refusals.

The Advertising Research Foundation has developed the Field Audit and Completion Test (FACT), an interview verification service to catch interviewer errors. About 10% of respondents are re-interviewed, usually by sending a postcard or by random telephone calls, in which questions are asked to verify whether interviews took place under proper conditions:

1. Did the interviewer actually interview the person she claims to have interviewed? Even when probed, an occasional respondent will deny ever having been visited by an interviewer.

2. Was the person interviewed a qualified respondent as designated by the study? Interviewing a teenage daughter when the study calls for housewives would constitute an error on this item.

3. Does the respondent reside at the address reported? Substituting neighbors or friends for designated respondents can distort the sample.

4. Was the interview conducted according to study specifications? If the study specifies personal interviews, those conducted by telephone are not accepted.

5. Was the interview conducted at the place indicated? Interviews conducted on street corners or at parties are not accepted if the study calls for at-home interviews.[3]

The answer must be affirmative for all of these questions in order for the interview to be verified. An additional four questions, tailored to each interview, might then be asked to determine how well the interviewer performed. Questions are asked to find out whether the interviewer asked all of the questions, recorded answers correctly, and followed directions. FACT has been shown to be an important verification service for catching interviewer errors. (For verification checks to be made, of course, the questionnaire must include spaces for the respondent's name, address, and telephone number.)

Cheating

Cheating is deliberate falsification of data by the interviewer. It is a major interviewer problem, not an interviewer "error." The full extent to which cheating occurs is generally unknown, probably because no one involved in cheating is likely to report it and because cheating is most likely to occur when no controls are present and there is therefore little likelihood of detection.

Cheating can take several forms. The most glaring example of cheating is the "street corner method," in which interviewers, rather than conducting actual door-to-door interviews, fill out a stack of questionnaires themselves, or have friends or relatives, instead of the intended respondents, fill out the questionnaires. A milder form of cheating occurs when interviewers fail to ask all of the questions on the questionnaire. Cheating is much more apt to occur when adequate controls of supervision are not present.

Cheating can probably never be eliminated completely. However, it can be controlled. Proper control will minimize the amount of cheating by discouraging it in the first place and detecting it when it does occur. Controls include good training, proper field supervision, and verification checks, such as the FACT method. Where interviewer cheating is detected, a more intensive verification audit must be taken to determine the full extent of cheating in the survey. If extensive cheating is found to have taken place, the cheater should be fired and the survey redone. Otherwise, cheating will continue, and the reputation of the research firm will be damaged.

■ Problems with Respondents

Two major types of respondent problems, known collectively as **non-sampling errors**, can be identified: **response error** and **non-response error**. The first is a communications problem in which inaccurate responses are given to the researcher; the second stems from not-at-homes and refusals to co-operate. These problems are of critical importance to researchers, because such non-sampling errors can bias results and distort a study.

Response Error

Of the non-sampling errors covered in this chapter, response error, which occurs when a respondent gives an incorrect answer to a question, is the most difficult to detect. The difficulty of detecting response error is increased if neither interviewer nor respondent is aware that error has occurred. For example, the respondent might misinterpret the question and, accordingly, give a misleading response. See Figure 7.3 for an overview of respondent problems.

Causes of Response Error

Causes of response errors have been covered briefly in previous chapters. Two major causes can be identified as semantics and deliberate falsification.

Semantics, which refers here to the misinterpretation of questions by respondents, is probably the greatest cause of response error. Semantic errors might be caused by poor wording of questions, interviewer error in reading or explaining the questions to the respondent, or a lack of understanding resulting from differing educational or cultural backgrounds.

FIGURE 7.3
Sources of Respondent Problems

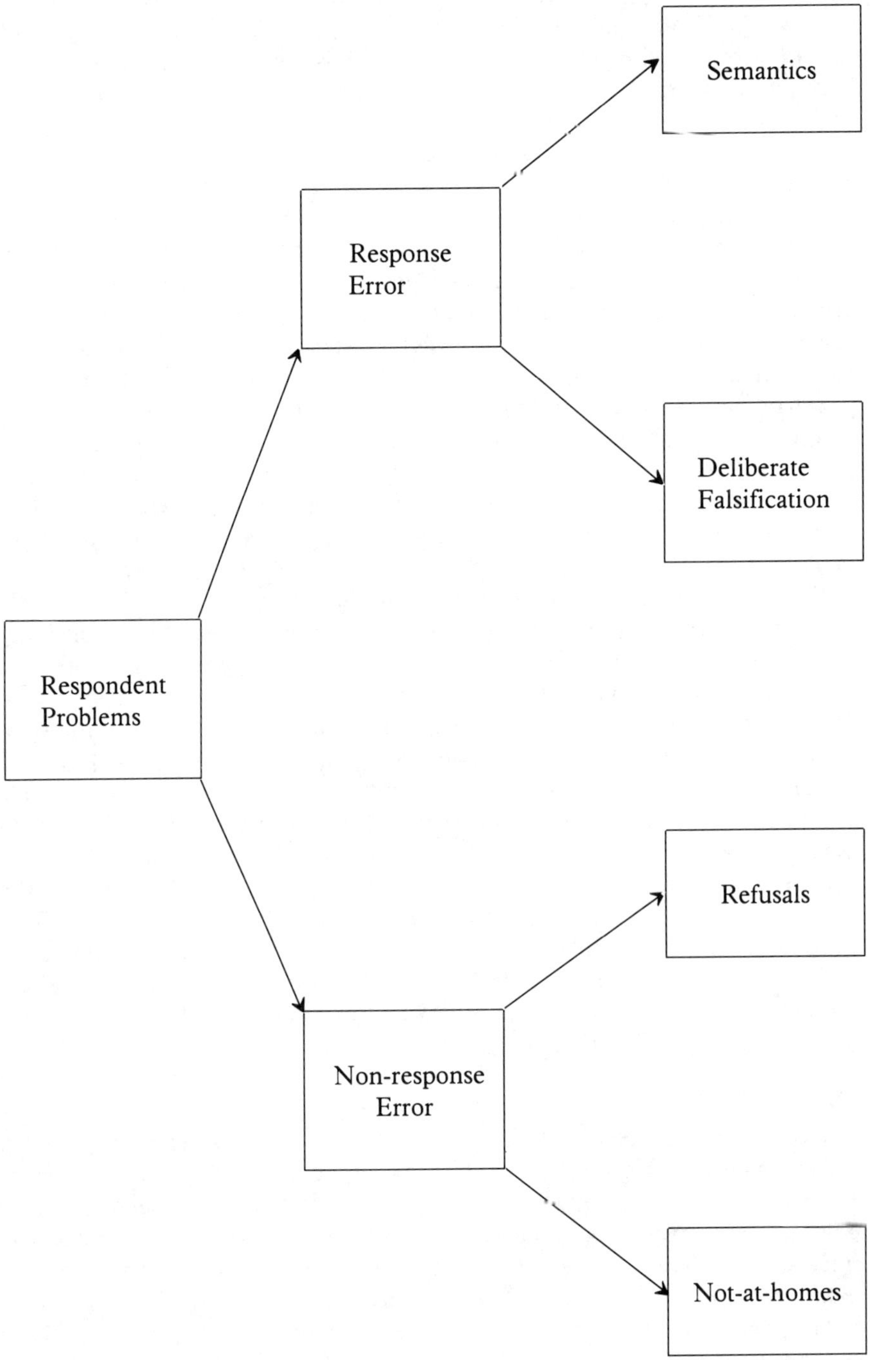

Consider the question "Do you often drink coffee?" What does "often" mean? Daily? Weekly? "Often" might be interpreted differently by each respondent. Errors in semantics or question misunderstandings can be controlled by proper interviewer training and extensive questionnaire pre-testing to ensure that questions will be clearly understood by respondents. And, as mentioned previously, where personal interviews are to be conducted, it is desirable to have interviewers from the same ethnic or cultural background as the respondents, especially in cases where respondents might not be fluent in either English or French.

Deliberate falsification of responses is believed to be less of a problem than question misinterpretation. People are usually honest, and if they have consented to respond to a questionnaire, it is unlikely that they will falsify their answers.

Three conditions under which respondents will knowingly give incorrect answers to interviewers can be identified, however. First, some respondents might deliberately attempt to mislead the interviewer, out of a conscious desire to "play games" in answering questionnaires. This is most likely to happen when someone other than the intended respondent is replying to the questionnaire—for example, a twelve-year-old child rather than the head of the household.

A second reason why a respondent will knowingly provide incorrect answers is a desire to "help" the interviewer. This problem can occur if respondents know the purpose or the sponsor of the study. In this instance they will identify themselves as users of that sponsor's products in a disproportionate number of cases.

Thirdly, inaccurate replies are likely to result when interviewers ask potentially embarrassing questions. For example, consumers typically report beer consumption patterns considerably lower than the sales that are reported by brewers. Asking questions about beer *purchases* instead of beer *consumption* is one way to get around this problem, because consumers are likely to be more truthful when responding to a less direct or less incriminating question.

Although it can never be completely avoided, response error can be held to a minimum by establishing certain procedures. Interviewers should be carefully trained so that they can detect inconsistent answers. Questionnaires should be constructed to minimize embarrassing questions and to avoid identifying the purpose of the survey or the name of its sponsor. Survey control should be exercised to ensure that only the intended respondent replies to the questionnaire, not a child or a neighbour. In general, the influence of the questioning process itself must be carefully controlled; otherwise, respondents might supply answers that are contrary to the facts.

Non-response Error

The second major type of non-sampling error, non-response error, occurs when consumers do not respond to a study. Non-response error, also known as non-response bias, is error caused by a difference in characteristics between those who do and those who do not respond to a survey. Non-response error is an extremely important problem in marketing research, although it is often unrecognized and extremely difficult to measure. How, for example, do you know if people who do not respond are different from those who do, when no information is available on the non-respondents?

Importance of Non-response Error to Research Data

Why is non-response error considered so important by marketing researchers? What is wrong with a 50% response rate in a survey, provided that the sample size obtained is large enough to be statistically significant? The answer to this question is response bias. Although great pains might be taken to ensure that a sample is selected in a random manner to be representative of the universe being surveyed, non-response bias can ruin this careful planning. (See Chapter 10 for a discussion of probability sampling.)

How do respondents differ from non-respondents in a typical survey? In general, the response rate tends to be higher among older people than among young people; the lowest response rate is from young males. Older people, especially retired people, have more time to fill out questionnaires and are more likely to be at home than are younger, working-aged people. In the case of questionnaires sent through the mail, response rate is higher among the better-educated segments; people with little education might not have the literary skills necessary to interpret and fill out written questionnaires properly. Women are more likely to respond to telephone and door-to-door surveys than are men, because more women than men are found at home during the day. Non-response bias in telephone surveys is found among people in the highest and lowest income brackets: the former might have unlisted telephone numbers and the latter often cannot afford telephones. Researchers need to plan studies carefully to minimize non-response bias. Ways of reducing this type of error will be covered later in this chapter.

Causes of Non-response Error

Refusals and *not-at-homes* constitute the two main sources of non-response error. Not only are both of these sources of error serious, but also they are on the increase. Today, more people than ever before are refusing to co-operate with researchers or are otherwise unavailable to participate in survey research. Regardless of methods used, whether telephone, mail, or personal interview, non-response is on the upswing for many reasons.

Refusals

A refusal occurs when a respondent declines to participate in a survey. Refusal rates vary widely from survey to survey. The number of refusals is influenced by such things as the personality of the interviewer, the type of survey being conducted, respondent interest in the survey material, the personality of the respondent, and the circumstances surrounding the interview itself.

The refusal rate is in general increasing. Figure 7.4 illustrates one reason for the increasing refusal rate in personal interviews—crime. Many people, especially women alone at home during the day, will refuse to allow a stranger into their homes. Given the crime rate in North America, this reluctance to open doors to strangers is understandable. Obscene telephone callers masquerading as legitimate marketing researchers have compounded the difficulties of getting people to respond to telephone interviews. Another reason for the increasing refusal rate has been the abuse of marketing research by sales and solicitation agents.

FIGURE 7.4
An Example of a Refusal

"Sorry, sir, I'm not going to open up seven locks and disconnect the burglar alarm just to tell you what shampoos I favor."

Sometimes respondents are called and asked to participate in marketing research studies when, in fact, they are being asked to purchase some item, such as encyclopedias. This type of abuse has naturally made many people reluctant to participate in studies. If respondents suspect that a study is not legitimate, refusals will soar. Consumer confidence can be gained by giving interviewers proper identification and by notifying respondents in advance.

Interest in the survey has a positive effect on response rate. A survey conducted by the Canadian Medical Association among member doctors regarding attitudes toward extra billing would almost certainly achieve a much higher response rate than would a general consumer survey designed to find out which type of soap powder or bleach is used in the home. In the latter case many respondents would claim that they were too busy, too tired, or just not interested in filling out the questionnaire.

A good covering letter is invaluable in creating interest in mail surveys. Figure 7.5 shows an example of a covering letter that accompanied a questionnaire relating to consumption of several products. The response was excellent.

Lastly, both the method of survey communication and the characteristics of the respondent interviewed have an effect on the response rate. Generally speaking, personal interviews have the highest response rate and mail questionnaires the

FIGURE 7.5
An Example of a Covering Letter

CONCORDIA UNIVERSITY

Dear Sir/Madam,

As part of a program of academic research at Concordia University, we are interested in finding out how Canadians of various backgrounds live and the types of products that they normally consume.

We would very much appreciate your participation in completing this questionnaire. This should take approximately thirty minutes of your time, and your participation is totally anonymous and voluntary. You will not be approached to buy anything as a result of your participation in this survey. You are free to discontinue your participation at any time.

As this type of academic research is important to the advancement of knowledge, we sincerely hope that you will agree to participate in this research and that you enjoy filling out this questionnaire.

Yours very truly,

Michel Laroche
Professor of Marketing

Telephone: (514) 848-2942

FACULTY OF COMMERCE AND ADMINISTRATION
MAILING ADDRESS:
1455 DE MAISONNEUVE BLVD. WEST
MONTREAL, QUEBEC   H3G 1M8

lowest. Respondents differ from non-respondents in age, marital status, occupation, geographic region, income, and education. Of these characteristics, education is the most significant, especially in mail surveys: the better-educated consumer is more likely to respond.[4] In personal interviews and telephone surveys, refusals tend to be concentrated at both extremes of the population—the highest and the lowest socio-economic groups.

Not-at-homes

As a cause of non-response error, not-at-homes are on the increase. This type of non-response occurs when the respondent either is not at home when the interviewer calls or cannot otherwise be located. This definition also includes, then, those who have moved recently—a particularly acute problem in today's mobile society.

The problem with not-at-homes is that they quite likely have characteristics that differentiate them from those who are at home. It has been demonstrated that not-at-home respondents are often younger, better educated, more likely to live in urban areas, and have higher incomes than those who are at home.[5] The not-at-home problem is further aggravated by the increasing rate at which women participate in the labour force. Today, there are many more families in which both husband and wife work than there were only a generation ago, it is therefore increasingly difficult for researchers to find anyone at home during the day. Such two-career families might also be reluctant to grant an interviewer time to conduct a survey during the evening, as their at-home time is limited.

Should the researcher fail to consider not-at-homes, survey results might be biassed. Since some segments of the population are less likely than others to be at home at certain times, underrepresentation of these respondents can invalidate survey results: the results might be distorted by having too many retired people in the sample and too few young, employed males or too few high-income families.

Methods of Reducing Non-Response Error

Fortunately, there are techniques and methods that can increase response rates. Although even the best survey is extremely unlikely to gain a 100% response rate, non-response error can be reduced substantially in personal interviews and telephone and mail surveys. In all cases, careful planning and execution are necessary to increase response rate and hold non-response bias to a minimum.

Increasing Response in Telephone and Personal Interviews

Non-response error can be reduced in both telephone and personal interviews by using advance notification and callbacks. Advance notification means informing the chosen respondents in advance of the survey. This preliminary notification could be by letter or, in the case of personal interviews, an advance telephone call.

If the first attempt to contact a respondent is not successful, callbacks must be made. Usually at least three callbacks are recommended, at different times of the day and week, to contact respondents missed in the first round. Researchers have found that a second callback can double the response rate.[6] Since homemakers and retired people are the groups most likely to be home on weekdays, it might be necessary for the researcher to use evenings and weekends to contact working couples or people otherwise absent from home during the day. Care must be taken, however, to avoid calling too early in the morning, too late in the evening, or on religious holidays. Generally speaking, the single best time for telephone interviewing is between 6:00 p.m. and 9:00 p.m. on Mondays; never call on Saturday night.

Increasing Response in Mail Surveys

A major cause of poor response rates from mail surveys is lack of respondent interest in the research problem. Who, for example, can be highly motivated to fill out a lengthy questionnaire describing supermarket buying behaviour? Respondent interest and motivation can be increased in the following three ways: advance notification, follow-ups, and selective concurrent techniques. All of these can be used at the same time: respondents can be notified in advance that they will be receiving questionnaires and callbacks and repeat mailings can be used to remind respondents that they have not yet replied. Such concurrent techniques as identifying the survey sponsor, guaranteeing anonymity, and using monetary incentives also can be used.

Advance notification, particularly by telephone, is effective in increasing response rates; it also serves to accelerate the rate of return. However, follow-ups appear to be a better investment than preliminary notification.

Follow-ups, or reminders, are almost universally successful in increasing response rates. Since each successive follow-up results in added returns, the very persistent (and well-financed) researcher usually can achieve an extremely high total response rate. As with all marketing research, however, the value of additional information obtained must be weighed against the cost of successive contact. In other words, is the additional time, effort, and expense worth it?

Concurrent techniques that can be employed include

1. *Adjusting questionnaire length*: Although common sense suggests that short questionnaires should obtain higher response rates than longer questionnaires, research evidence does not support this view.

2. *Stating survey sponsorship*: Official or "respected" sponsorship tends to increase response.

3. *Including return envelopes*: Inclusion of a stamped return envelope encourages response because it facilitates questionnaire return.

4. *Including postage*: Special delivery is very effective in increasing response rates. However, findings do not show a significant advantage for first class over third class, for commemorative stamps over ordinary postage, for stamped mail over metered mail, or for multiple-denomination stamps over single, large-denomination stamps.

5. *Personalization*: Personalization of the mailing has no clear-cut advantage in improved response rates. For example, neither personal inside addresses nor

individually signed covering letters significantly increase response rates; personally typed covering letters have proved somewhat effective in most cases cited, but not in all. One study testing the use of a titled signature versus one without a title did show a significant advantage for the titled signature.

6. *Using covering letters*: The covering letter appears to be the most logical vehicle for persuading individuals to respond, yet the very few reported studies offer no insights about its formulation.

7. *Guaranteeing anonymity*: The promise of anonymity to respondents—either explicit or implied—has no significant effect on response rates.

8. *Varying questionnaire size, reproduction, and colour*: Questionnaire size, method of reproduction, and colour have no significant effect on response rates.

9. *Using money incentives*: A fifty-cent or one-dollar incentive sent with the questionnaire is very effective in increasing response rate. Larger sums tend to bring in more responses but at a cost that might exceed the value of the added information.

10. *Stating deadline dates*: Deadlines do not increase the response rate; however, they do serve to accelerate the rate of questionnaire return.[7]

11. *Offering non-monetary premiums*: Using non-cash incentives might increase the response rate, although some non-monetary premiums might be more efficient than others, depending on their symbolic value to respondents. For example, a study found that both ballpoint pens and lottery tickets increased the response rate, and that the lottery ticket was a great deal more effective than the ballpoint pen, because in addition to its symbolic value it offers a monetary value.[8]

Although response rates might "range from below 20% to 100%, there is still no reliable evidence identifying the factors responsible for this enormous variation".[9] Advance notification, follow-ups, and the concurrent techniques noted previously are all used to improve response rates in mail surveys, but with varying degrees of success. The best results have been attributed to the use of follow-ups and monetary incentives. Still, careful usage of all of these techniques will increase the efficiency of mail surveys by reducing costs and improving predictive validity. Unfortunately, higher response rates do not necessarily result in reduced bias.[10]

How to Treat Non-Response Bias
So far we have identified what non-response error is, how it is caused, and some ways of reducing it. Since non-response error can almost never be completely eliminated in any survey, however, the problem facing the professional marketing researcher is how to treat the remaining non-response error in each survey. Several methods, varying in sophistication and validity, are used by researchers. They include substitution, weighting, callbacks, and ignoring the problem.

Substitution

A common way of treating non-response bias is substitution of someone other than the intended respondent. In the telephone survey, substitution might take the form of calling the next number in the phone book if there is no answer at the first. In personal interviews, substitution might be accomplished by having another member of the household complete the questionnaire or by going to a neighbour. However, although substitution might facilitate the completion of the survey, it does not reduce non-response error, which can still be present because the units substituted might differ from those originally selected in the sample. Substitution is only valid if non-random sampling techniques, which involve no attempt to obtain a representative sample, are being used. In some cases questioning other members of the household has been reported as being successful in cases where "the questions are relatively objective, when informants have a high degree of observability with respect to respondents, when the population is homogeneous, and when the setting of the interview provides no clearcut motivation to distort responses...."[11]

Weighting

A second approach to treating non-response bias is weighting of the non-responses. Segments of the sample that the researcher considers under-represented, such as inner-city new Canadians, can be adjusted by weighting "the results of the central city interviews that are secured in order to give them full representation in the results".[12] The weakness of this approach is that weighted returns often differ from those that would be secured if callbacks were made.

Callbacks

Otherwise known as follows-ups or reminders, callbacks are the best approach to the problem of non-response. If the first attempt to contact the respondent fails, then at least three callbacks should be made at different times of the day and week. Callbacks can take the form of postcard reminders, telephone calls, or personal visits; all have been shown to be reliable in increasing the response rate.

The main drawback of callbacks is that, although they might increase response rate and thus reduce non-response bias, they do not solve the non-response problem. Still, they are perhaps the most effective way to deal with non-response bias, and when effectively used, can decrease it substantially.

Ignoring the Problem

By far the most common way of dealing with non-response bias is to ignore the problem completely. In most instances, researchers assume that there is no difference between respondents and non-respondents, and there is some qualified support that such differences might indeed by minimal.[13]

While ignoring non-response bias is certainly the easiest method, this can lead to invalidation of the survey results, although the researcher might not be aware that this has occurred. Therefore, ignoring the problem is the worst possible course to follow.

Probably non-response bias can never be completely avoided. Callbacks or reminders are the most effective way of holding it to a minimum, but lack of time and research funds might make callbacks problematic. Still, if the non-response problem is ignored, marketing researchers must be prepared to accept the consequences—consequences that have been described as "the very weak foundations upon which so many research reports and subsequent management decisions are based".[14]

■ Data Preparation

Once the actual field work has been properly planned and executed, the next step in the survey is the preparation of the data. This procedure involves three major steps. The first step is **editing**, which is the verification of the questionnaires as they come back from the field. This involves checking for possible recording errors, identifying questionnaires that have been poorly filled out or those that are of questionable accuracy. The second step is **coding**, which is the allocation of a predetermined code to each answer. If the question is close-ended, this is a rather mechanical procedure; however, open-ended questions require a more careful and comprehensive treatment. The final step is **data entry**, which is the entry of these codes into a computer, as well as verification of the accuracy of the files created. Data are then prepared and readied for analysis, which is discussed in Chapters 11 and 12.

Editing

Inexperienced researchers often have the impression that once a set of responses is collected, the job of tabulating and analysing those responses should be very straightforward. Experienced researchers know that, in most cases, the job will be anything but simple; they realize that the coding of questionnaires is far from mechanical and that much subjective editing and interpretation are necessary before the analysis can be completed. No mere description of the process will suffice; only after one has waded through several hundred survey forms, each with a variety of errors, omissions, and inconsistencies, does one realize the magnitude of the task that coding, and editing in preparation for coding, can present. Some researchers estimate that approximately 25% (and possibly more) of the time and resources of a survey project is spent on the process of coding the questionnaires into a format suitable for numerical tabulation. Therefore the coding of the data, which is usually viewed as a quick, automatic process of inconsequential cost, must be seen in its true perspective as one of the most expensive and most crucial parts of the entire research project.

Thus, one of the researcher's considerations must be to prepare a survey instrument that will produce results that can readily be coded. Too many open-ended or ambiguous questions can result in prohibitively expensive coding costs. In addition, there is more chance of coding error, which could distort or even negate the results of the entire project. Even when the editing and coding process is carefully monitored and supervised, because of the large amount of detail work, countless little errors can enter into the calculations. Quality-control studies indicate that for every one hundred human calculations, five are incorrect, and studies of data coding and editing often reveal that to up 10% of all material has been misprocessed in some manner. Marketing researchers deal with this problem by trying to provide intensive supervision and support to eliminate as many of the errors as possible. However, then they often must simply assume that the undetected errors that are bound to get through will be self-cancelling—that the errors made in one direction will be offset by those made in the other. Although this is a reasonable enough assumption, this is yet another possible source of non-sampling error.

Problems Caused by Respondents

Even when the researcher has taken pains to produce what should be a very codable questionnaire and has closely supervised the work of trained coders, the respondents themselves can create a large number of unavoidable problems.

Many times while working on a set of questionnaires, a researcher gets the distinct impression that the answers are just not making sense. For example, a respondent might say that he prefers hamburgers from Harvey's over hamburgers from McDonald's, only to say later in the questionnaire that he has never tried a Harvey's hamburger. Or perhaps the respondent has written down a number of replies but they are illegible. Or perhaps, in a dichotomous question, the respondent has checked both *yes* and *no* and written a series of qualifiers. In cases such as these, what is the researcher to do?

Perhaps the respondent has left a number of the questions blank, or certain questions are producing a large number of *don't know* responses, or the respondent gives other, similar responses, indicating that the respondent really does not know what he or she is talking about. Again, what is the researcher to do? What value does the researcher assign in these situations?

Missing Data

All of the situations just described fall into the basic category of missing data. Missing data represents the single most severe problem for the researcher trying to edit, code, and tabulate numerical data. The researcher can attempt to deal with this problem in several ways, although none of them is entirely satisfactory as a replacement for the actual data that has been omitted. Four approaches that can be tried are predicting the individual respondent's probable response, substituting the overall group average or distribution, randomly inserting a replacement value, or leaving that question blank in the coding.

Predicting Response

In some cases, it might be possible to predict the respondent's probable response. For instance, if a respondent said that she was retired and living on social security, but did not put down her age, we could assume with reasonable safety that she was at least sixty-five years old. Also, in the case of personal interviews, the interviewer might have obtained a strong impression of the respondent during the conversation and might feel qualified to predict the respondent's answers for some questions.

Group Average

In cases where information is lacking on the individual respondent, the group average of those respondents who did answer the question might be substituted for the missing item. In the case of a frequency distribution, the blanks might be distributed among the classes in the ratio observed in the completed items.

Replacement Value

When the number of missing items is small, the difficulty of computing group averages, making individual predictions, and so on can be avoided by substituting arbitrarily assigned values in place of the missing items. Although there is very little in this technique to recommend it statistically, it does fill in the blanks in an efficient and economical manner.

Leaving the Question Blank

It might seem strange to the reader that so much effort is being made to fill in missing responses. After all, if the respondent left the question blank, why not simply record that answer as a non-response? Of course, this is exactly what is done in many situations. However, the researcher is anxious to have as few blanks as possible in the final set of numbers because in some types of numerical calculations, including virtually all computer analyses, blanks are treated as zeros. Thus, if someone was embarrassed about his age and left that question blank, then his age would become zero by default. You can see that if the data contained a sizable number of these zeros, the results would soon become worthless. Correlations between age and income, between age and buying patterns—even the average age of the group—would be greatly distorted by the presence of such zeros.

A related problem is that because of the computer's inability to differentiate between zeros and blanks, it is inadvisable to use zero as a valid code: a coding format such as *yes = 1* and *no = 0* will not differentiate the *no* responses from the non-respondents.

Coding

All numbers are not alike. In other words, on a questionnaire, the symbol that looks like the number 5 might not actually represent what we consider to be the quantity five. Therefore, much of the data you encounter, especially in marketing, might not be numeric at all, but simply symbolic.

As a matter of fact, several different types of data exist, each of a different strength. It is important that you realize the differences between the various types of data, because not all are appropriate for all types of analysis.

Types of Data

Most marketing researchers note four types of data:

- *Nominal*: From *nominate*—to name, to classify. The numbers in nominal data have no intrinsic value; they are used only for classification. For example, football jerseys might be coded *male = 1*, *female = 2*.

- *Ordinal*: To order. The numbers indicate position or order but not distance.

Simply knowing, for example, that the finish order was first, second, and third, one still does not know whether it was a close race or a lopsided victory.

- *Interval*: Similar to *ordinal*, but with constant intervals. The numbers tell both position and distance. The distance between positions is assumed to be equal in most interval scales and there is no fixed zero point. Temperature is an example.

- *Ratio*: Can form meaningful ratios. The most powerful kind of data, ratio data have a fixed zero point. Examples are money and length.

These types of data are presented in order of their strength, starting with the weakest and proceeding to the strongest. The type of data is very important to the marketing researcher, because the type of statistical analysis that can be performed on the data is theoretically dependent on the type of data that was collected. The dependence is theoretical because, in actuality, once the numbers have been entered, the computer will perform any type of analysis desired. However, unless the data are of the proper strength, the results might be as meaningless as an average of the numerals on a football team's shirts or, at best, misleading in that they might overstate or understate the true differences between groups of numbers.

It is also important to note that, by changing the format of the question, the researcher can ask essentially the same question but obtain different types of data. For instance, consider a question regarding income, as illustrated by the following.

Ordinal	Interval	Ratio
What is your income?	**What is your income?**	**What is your income?**
_____ very low	_____ less than $5000	
_____ low	_____ $5000 to $9999	
_____ average	_____ $10 000 to $14 999	
_____ high	_____ $15 000 to $20 000	My annual income is
_____ very high	_____ more than $20 000	$ _____.

Note, also, that data can always be broken down from the higher forms into the weaker forms. Thus, a researcher could form interval data from ratio data, and ordinal data from interval data. The reverse does not hold; strong data can be downgraded into weak data, but weak data cannot be upgraded into strong. For this reason, the survey instrument should be designed to obtain the highest level of data possible.

Coding Nominal Data

When coding, it is necessary to guard against accidentally coding nominal data into the form of some higher data. Consider the following coding of a question regarding marital status:

Single 1
Married 2
Separated 3
Divorced 4
Widowed 5

Notice that the nominal data has been inadvertently converted into ordinal data. Although it is true that steps 4 or 5 would have to follow steps 1 and 2, and that 1 must precede 2, the scale as a whole breaks down as ordinal data. Being now improperly coded as ordinal data, the answers to this question cannot be statistically related to answers to any other questions in any meaningful way. Any analysis (correlation, regression, even averages and dispersions) using such a batch of data will be useless.

In order to code such a question so that it will be significant in conjunction with other questions, each category of the question must be coded as a separate question, turning one question into five:

Single . . . . Yes = 1, No = 2
Married . . . . Yes = 1, No = 2
Separated . . . . Yes = 1, No = 2
Divorced . . . . Yes = 1, No = 2
Widowed . . . . Yes = 1, No = 2

Although this might seem like a lot of extra work, it represents the only way of handling nominal data in a valid fashion, and the technique should be used whenever nominal data are encountered.

Maintaining Logical Consistency

It is quite common to see *yes =1* and *no = 2*, but a better coding would be *yes = 2* and *no = 1*. In this way the more positive reply will be associated with the higher number. In the example above, therefore, the coding should be

Single . . . . Yes = 2, No = 1
Married . . . . Yes = 2, No = 1
Separated . . . . Yes = 2, No = 1
Divorced . . . . Yes = 2, No = 1
Widowed . . . . Yes = 2, No = 1

A researcher should always try to arrange the coding so that an increasing amount of the quantity gets a higher value in the code. Consider the original coding in the example on marital status (*yes = 1, no = 2*). If the respondents were divided into two groups and the researcher averaged the replies to the *single* question, that coding would indicate that the group with the *higher* average had the *lower* number of singles. Such logical flips can become quite confusing, particularly when there are many variables to consider. Therefore, it is important to keep the intuitive meanings of the answers consistent with the coding.

Coding Open-Ended Questions

When a questionnaire uses some open-ended questions, the researcher must develop a coding scheme that will allow entry of these answers into the computer.

Typically, a coding scheme of open-ended questions relies on some form of content analysis of *all* returned questionnaires. First, the researcher reads all of the answers to the open-ended questions and establishes a detailed list of all of the types of answers given. Second, these types of answers are given a specific code by the researcher, either using the detailed list or using a list reduced by combining similar categories. Finally, all of the questionnaires are coded using the previous scheme.

For example, let us assume that the question asked of respondents who had just taken a winter vacation was "What was your destination? _____" This question might generate a long list of winter vacation destinations, from Banff to Florida and from Greece to Hawaii. The researcher might decide to keep separate all of these destinations and give each one of them a code, perhaps from 01 to 25, if 25 destinations were mentioned. However, a simpler coding procedure could be used if such detailed information is not necessary, and destinations could be regrouped into general areas such as the Caribbean, southern United States, northern United States, eastern Canada, western Canada, Pacific Islands, southern Europe, and northern Europe.

Data Entry Methods

Most research projects involve a large amount of data that has to be analysed by computers, so the next step is to enter the data into a computer. There are basically three methods of data entry:

1. The old method consists in keypunching the coded answers into predetermined fields in a computer card; e.g., age is always punched into columns 31 and 32. Cards are then used by a card reader and the data is stored in memory or on a separate (and permanent) magnetic tape.

2. The most current method is to enter the data directly into the computer through a cathode-ray tube (CRT) or into a microcomputer, and the data is then stored on a disk. This new method is more efficient and more reliable than the previous one.

3. Newer methods being developed will include automatic data entry through interactive data-collection methods. Here, the respondent or the interviewer selects the answer to a question appearing on a video screen. The answer is then automatically recorded by the computer. The main advantage of this method is its high speed and accuracy. The data can be analysed as soon as the questions are answered and there is no error in storing the data.

Summary

Survey administration is a social process that takes into account the relationship and interaction among the interviewer, the questionnaire, and the respondent. The next chapter discusses the first of these components, the questionnaire itself. In this chapter we have examined the other two components, the interviewer and the respondent, and the problems associated with each.

Interviewer problems are often personnel management problems of attracting, holding, and motivating competent employees. Four principal interviewer problems exist: recruiting interviewers, training interviewers, interviewer error, and cheating. The last of these problems, cheating, occurs when interviewers deliberately falsify some aspects of the interviewing process. Cheating can be controlled through proper training, supervision, and such verification checks as use of the FACT method.

Two major types of error stem from respondents: response error and non-response error. The first is a communications problem, in which inaccurate responses are given; the second results from not-at-homes and refusals to co-operate.

Response error is more difficult to detect than non-response error. Both interviewer and respondent, in fact, might be unaware that an error has been made. Usually, response error is caused by semantics or a misunderstanding; occasionally, it is caused by a deliberate false answer from the respondent who wants to mislead the interviewer or avoid answering embarrassing questions.

Both refusals and not-at-homes are increasing, and researchers are becoming more and more concerned about non-response errors. Changing lifestyles have made it more difficult to find people at home and fear of crime has increased the difficulty of getting them to participate in answering questionnaires. Although non-response error can never be eliminated completely, it can be reduced by using advance follow-ups, and, in mail surveys, selective concurrent techniques.

Researchers have developed various ways of treating non-response error, including substitution, weighting, callbacks, and ignoring the problem. Ignoring the problem is the most commonly used approach, although it can cause invalidation of survey results and therefore is the worst possible course of action. Callbacks are usually the best way to increase response rates, although occasionally substitution might be used for objective questions.

Once the data have been collected, they must be edited and coded into a format suitable for numerical processing. Although this might seem like a very straightforward, mechanical step, it often demands much more effort and supervision than one might at first anticipate. Such questionnaire deficiencies as illogical answers, illegible answers, incomplete answers, insufficient answers, and missing answers can cause the researcher a lot of trouble. It should also be realized that even very straightforward coding can be extremely expensive and quite tim-consuming, often using up a major part of the funds available for the project.

All of the coding problems discussed above fall into the basic category of missing data. The researcher generally tries to reduce the amount of missing data by utilizing one of three methods: predicting the individual respondent's probable response, substituting the overall group average or distribution, or randomly inserting a replacement value. A fourth possibility is simply to code the missing data as a blank; this procedure can create problems, however, since most types of numerical analysis treat blanks as zeros, possibly making the results worthless.

The coding process must also take into consideration the type of data that has been collected. Of the four types of data discussed here—nominal, interval, ordinal, and ratio—ratio is the strongest type and nominal the weakest. Although data can be downgraded from strong to weak, weak data cannot be upgraded into strong; hence, special care must be taken not to code nominal data in an improper form.

For Discussion

1. What is meant by social distance between the interviewer and the interviewee? What are the problems associated with social distance? Suggest ways of overcoming the problem of social distance.

2. A verification check reveals that one of your field interviewers has been arbitrarily substituting next-door neighbours when intended respondents are not at home. What is wrong with this procedure? What course of action do you take?

3. a) What is non-response bias? Why is it so important?
   b) What is response error? How can it be minimized?

4. You are conducting a mail survey of homemakers' grocery shopping habits. Develop a plan for ensuring the highest possible response rate.

5. What is the most common type of response error? How would you hold it to a minimum?

6. What are the four methods used by researchers to treat non-response bias? Which is the most commonly used? Why?

7. What factors beyond the control of researchers affect response rate and personal interviews? How can researchers overcome these problems?

8. Since the personal interview usually obtains the highest response rate, this is the most desirable method of communicating by questionnaire. Do you agree or disagree with this statement? Defend your answer.

9. What are the four things that a researcher can do to cope with missing data? Explain. Why is the researcher so anxious to fill in a missing or omitted response, instead of entering it as a blank?

10. What are the four types of data discussed in this chapter? Define them. Give an example of a question with different answer-formatting, causing the same basic question to produce data of different strengths.

Problems

Mini-case: Home Study Institute (Part A)
The Home Study Institute (HSI) is a large correspondence school with its head office in Regina. When it was founded in the 1940s, HSI offered strictly academic subjects that fulfilled the requirements of the surrounding regions for the completion of high school.

The Institute relies heavily on newspaper and radio advertising. Potential students either phone in for more information after hearing radio announcements or send in their names on information coupons clipped from the company's newspaper ads.

Once the name of a prospective student is received, it is given to a district salesperson, who visits the person and sells the course of studies. If the respondent lives in an area outside the range of the sales office, which is the case almost 20% of the time, enrolment is completed through the mail. Students are required to study one course at a time, sending in exams to be corrected after completion of every two or three chapters of the textbook. At the end of their studies, high school diplomas are issued.

After World War II a large percentage of enrolments were war veterans who had dropped out of high school to join the armed forces. At present, 30% of the students are immigrants with a limited knowledge of English or French; 50% are young adults over seventeen who want to complete their high school education in order to get better jobs; and the remainder are middle-aged adults who dropped out of school and now want a chance to finish their educations. The school enrols approximately 23 000 students per year.

In 1971 the Institute introduced several courses that were career-oriented rather than academic. These included *Bookkeeping and Accounting*, *Keyboarding*, *How to Become a Medical Secretary*, *How to Become a Legal Secretary*, *Business English for Secretaries*, and *Business Law*. The new courses were very popular. Within two years the Institute put together a complete business program offering a diploma in Business Administration to high school graduates who completed ten specific courses. Sales increased substantially as this new market area was tapped. Many of the Institute's graduates re-enlisted to take the new program.

In the fall of 1987 the Institute decided to investigate adding a data-processing course to its curriculum. Investment would be high, since HSI would have to purchase or rent computers for its in-house students.

The marketing research firm of R.A. Golden Consultants was contracted to undertake a study to estimate the expected student body. Ray Golden, who worked for five years at a medium-sized research firm before setting up his own company, devised the following plan to determine the market potential for the data-processing course.

Each of the Institute's six sales managers was given a specific number of questionnaires—twelve for each salesperson—to be administered to the next twelve prospective students that each salesperson visited. Salespeople were given three weeks to complete this process, although the Institute knew that some would make twelve calls in one week or less. At the end of the three-week period, salespeople were to sent all of the forms directly to Golden Consultants, who would tabulate the results and report to HSI. No editing was done until the questionnaires reached Golden. Exhibit 7.1 is the survey questionnaire, Exhibit 7.2 is the summary of survey results, and Exhibit 7.3 is the summary of questionnaire responses.

EXHIBIT 7.1
HSI **Survey re a Data-Processing Course**

Please read the following paragraph to your client, and then answer the questions with him or her: "A survey is being conducted to determine your interest in a data-processing course. Thank you for taking the time to complete this questionnaire. All answers will be kept confidential."

1. Name _____
    Address _____
    Please check one:
    Age: under 21_____   30–39_____
          21–29_____   over 40_____
    Sex: Male _____   Female _____
    Marital status: Single _____   Married _____

2. Please indicate present line of work:
    Technical _____   Sales _____   Crafts _____
    Clerical _____   Managerial _____   Other _____
    If other, please describe: _____

3. Has the client ever taken any courses at the Home Study Institute?
    Yes_____   No_____
    If "yes," please indicate which ones:
    Grade 7 _____   Grade 11 _____
    Grade 8 _____   Grade 12 _____
    Grade 9 _____   Business Program _____
    Grade 10 _____
    In what year were the courses completed?_____

4. Please indicate the client's last year of education:
    Grade 7 _____   Grade 11 _____
    Grade 8 _____   Grade 12 _____
    Grade 9 _____   Business Program _____
    Grade 10 _____

5. Is the client interested in data-processing courses? Yes _____ No _____
    If "no," go to question 10. If "yes," please continue.

6. Would the client take the full ten-course program? Yes _____ No _____

7. If "no," how many courses would he or she be willing to take?
    1–2 _____   3–4 _____   5–6 _____   7–8 _____

8. If "yes," what is the maximum price he or she would be willing to pay for the data-processing program?
    $800 _____ $1000 _____ $1200 _____ $1500 _____

9. For those interested in the full ten-course program: Will the client be able to come to the Regina Data Centre to use the computer? Yes _____ No _____ (Approximately five two-hour sessions with a computer will be necessary. They can be arranged at the client's convenience.)

10. For those who answered "no" to question 5, please indicate why the client is not interested in data processing:
    Only wants high school program _____
    Data processing not connected to line of work _____
    Dislikes data processing _____

EXHIBIT 7.2
Summary of Survey Results

Territory	Number of Salespeope	Incomplete Questionnaires	Total Usable Questionnaires	Total Number of Questionnaires Distributed
1	21	198	54	252
2	16	0	192	192
3	18	142	74	216
4	15	125	55	180
5	9	72	36	108
6	13	156	0	156
Totals	92	693	411	1104

Exhibit 7.2 Notes

1. In Territory 2 all forms appear to have been completed in the same handwriting.

2. The sales manager in Territory 6 disagreed with the method of presentation of the survey. Salespeople in that territory were told to give the prospect the form and ask the prospect to return it by mail to the Institute if he or she wanted to help with the survey. It is doubtful that any clients were given the survey form.

3. Many salespeople stopped at question 5. If they did so, results were disregarded.

EXHIBIT 7.3
Summary of Questionnaire Responses
(This material is based on Exhibit 7.2, *Total Usable Questionnaires*)

	%
1. Age: under 21	38
21–29	24
30–39	22
over 40	16
	100
Sex: Male	64
Female	36
	100
Marital Status: Single	32
Married	68
	100

	%
2. Present line of work:	
Technical	27
Clerical	31
Sales	5
Managerial	2
Crafts	16
Other	19
	100

Breakdown of "Other" category:	%
Shipping	2
Driving	3
Armed forces	6
Restaurant work	2
Self-employment	6
	19

3. Has the client ever taken any courses at the	%
Home Study Institute? Yes	4
No	96
	100

The results indicate that 16 people have taken courses
at HSI; years of education completed are as follows:
Grade 9: 5 people
Grade 10: 4 people
Grade 11: 6 people
Grade 12: 1 person
All completed courses between 1961 and 1977.
None has taken the Business Program.

4. Client's last year of education:	
Grade 7	6
Grade 8	16
Grade 9	20
Grade 10	28
Grade 11	24
Grade 12	4
Business Program	0
Other	2
	100

Note: "Other" category: 2% of respondents indicated they have begun university studies and are interested in the Business Program. They also indicated an interest in the data-processing courses.

5. Is the client interested in data-processing courses?   %

      Yes   12
      No   88
                                                            ───
                                                            100
                                                            ───

6. Would the client take the full ten-course program?
      Yes   12
      No   88
                                                            ───
                                                            100
                                                            ───

7. If "no," how many courses would he or she be willing
    to take?
        1–2 courses   51
        3–4 courses   25
        5–6 courses   18
        7–8 courses   6
                                                            ───
                                                            100
                                                            ───

8. If "yes," what is the maximum price he or she
    would be willing to pay for the data-processing program?   %

        $ 800   96
        $1000   4
        $1200   0
        $1500   0
                                                            ───
                                                            100
                                                            ───

    Note: Several salespeople indicated that the client
    would be willing to pay $500–$600 maximum.

9. For those interested in the full ten-course program:
    Will the client be able to come to the Regina
    Data Centre to use the computer?   Yes   95
                                       No   5
                                                            ───
                                                            100
                                                            ───

10. For those who answered "no" to question 5, please
    indicate why the client is not interested in data
    processing:
        Only wants high school program   37
        Data processing not connected to line of work   21
        Dislikes data processing   22
                                                            ───
                                                             80
                                                            ───

Note: Several salespeople filled in other reasons, including "Foreign student—does not
know what data processing is" and "Client is only in Grade 8—would not qualify."

Questions

1. a) What problems do you foresee with the administration of this survey?
   b) Suggest a better method of obtaining the information.

2. a) Suggest ways for making the sample design more efficient.
   b) How would you interpret the data in Exhibits 7.2 and 7.3?

3. Provide a coding scheme for the questionnaire in Exhibit 7.1.

Endnotes

1. Robert Ferber, ed., *Handbook of Marketing Research*. New York: McGraw-Hill, 1974, p. 2–125.
2. Peter B. Case, "How to Catch Interviewer Errors." *Journal of Advertising Research*, 11 (April 1971), pp. 39–43.
3. Ibid., pp. 39–40.
4. Leslie Kanuk and Conrad Berenson, "Mail Surveys and Response Rates: A Literature Review." *Journal of Marketing Research*, 12 (November 1975), pp. 440–53.
5. William C. Dunkleberg and George S. Day, "Nonresponse Bias and Callbacks in Sample Surveys." *Journal of Marketing Research*, 10 (May 1973), pp. 160–68; Ronald E. Turner, "The Package Questionnaire and Nonresponse Bias." *Marketing*, 3. Ed. Michel Laroche. Montreal: Administrative Sciences Association of Canada (ASAC), 1982, pp. 314–22.
6. Dunkleberg and Day, "Nonresponse Bias and Callbacks," pp. 160–68.
7. This section on improving response rates has been adapted from Kanuk and Berenson, "Mail Surveys and Response Rates," p. 450.
8. Jean-Charles Chebat and Jacques Picard, "An Experimental Study of the Effects of Two Non-Monetary Incentives on Response Rates in Mail Questionnaires." *Marketing*, 7. Ed. Thomas E. Muller. ASAC, 1986, pp. 371–77.
9. Kanuk and Berenson, "Mail Surveys and Response Rates," p. 450.
10. Richard Sparkman, Jr., and Meryl A. Cook, "An Experimental Investigation of the Relationship Between Response Rate and Nonresponse Bias in Telephone Surveys of Women." *Marketing*, 7. Ed. Thomas E. Muller. ASAC, 1986, pp. 387–95.
11. Eleanore Singer, "Agreement Between Inaccessible Respondents and Informants." *Public Opinion Quarterly*, 36 (Winter 1972–73), pp. 603–11.
12. C. William Emory, *Business Research Methods*. Homewood, IL: Richard D. Irwin, 1976, p. 276.
13. John R. Dickinson and Eric Kirzner, "Early Survey Respondents May Be Sufficient." *Marketing*, 4. Ed. James D. Forbes. ASAC, 1983, pp. 73–80.
14. Kanuk and Berenson, "Mail Surveys and Response Rates," pp. 450–51.

8 QUESTIONNAIRE CONSTRUCTION

The previous chapter dealt with various problems associated with administering surveys. Now we will discuss in detail the survey questionnaire. A questionnaire is a formal list of questions designed to gather responses from consumers on a given topic. Questionnaires are the major instrument used in obtaining primary data from respondents through the survey approach. As previously stated, a questionnaire can be designed to secure any or all of four types of primary data from consumers: purchase intentions, attitudes and opinions, activities or behaviour, and demographic characteristics.

How often have you been exposed to questionnaires? Probably you have seen many more than you realize. You might be thinking only of mail questionnaires, which often include questions relating to your income or the type of toothpaste you use. Have you ever been stopped by an interviewer in a shopping centre and asked to answer a few questions? If so, you participated in completing a questionnaire. Have you been called on the telephone by someone who said he or she was doing marketing research and asked you to answer a few questions? If so, whether it was legitimate marketing research or a sales promotion effort, you participated in answering a questionnaire.

A questionnaire can be viewed as a method of communicating between interviewer and interviewee. Not all questionnaires are equally successful in securing desired information from respondents. Often clarity is lacking and the respondent fails to understand precisely what the researcher wants to communicate. In other cases, respondents are unwilling to provide necessary information, or they might be influenced by the questioning process. Careful questionnaire structure and sometimes even disguise are needed to help overcome some of these difficulties.

■ Questionnaire Structure and Disguise

Questionnaire studies can be classified by structure and disguise. **Structure** refers to the degree to which the questionnaire is standardized. A structured questionnaire requires respondents to give exact answers and does not, as do unstructured questionnaires, allow respondents to answer freely in their own words. Often a highly structured questionnaire allows respondents to answer only *yes* or *no* to certain questions. Consider the following question:

Which brand of mouthwash do you normally use?
_____ Cepacol   _____ Micrin
_____ Colgate 100   _____ Listerine
_____ Lavoris   _____ Scope

This example illustrates the advantages of a structured questionnaire: ease of administration and of tabulation of data. It also illustrates the main disadvantage of rigid structure: since responses are predetermined, they must embrace all possible alternatives. In the example just presented, if the respondent used no mouthwash or used another brand, there would not have been an appropriate category to check.

Questionnaire **disguise** refers to the degree to which the purpose of the research study is known to the respondent. Undisguised questionnaires make the purpose of the study clear, because the questions are direct. Undisguised questionnaires are much more common then disguised ones, because of the difficulty of administering the latter. Disguised questionnaires usually require highly trained personnel, such as psychologists, to interpret responses correctly, especially if the study is also unstructured.

Questionnaires classified according to structure and disguise fall into four categories: structured-non-disguised, unstructured-non-disguised, unstructured-disguised, and structured-disguised. Let us examine each of these in turn.

Structured-non-disguised

By far the most common type of questionnaire, the structured-non-disguised, is so named because not only are the questions and the allowed responses predetermined, but the purpose of the study is obvious to the respondent from the beginning. The popularity of the structured-non-disguised questionnaire is explained by ease of administration. This questionnaire can be administered by relatively unskilled interviewers, such as university and college students or other part-time or temporary workers, using the telephone, mail, or personal interview approach. Another advantage associated with this type of questionnaire is ease of tabulation and interpretation of responses. Since all replies have been placed in a predetermined category, the questionnaire can be coded so that operators can enter data directly into the computer for analysis.

Two types of questions are found in the structured-non-disguised questionnaire: dichotomous and multiple-choice. A **dichotomous question** allows for only two possible answers. For example, the interviewer might ask, "Do you usually smoke at least one cigar a week?" The responses are either *yes* or *no*; no other answer is possible. Students are usually quite familiar with the dichotomous question, having experienced this format many times on examinations under the guise of true/false questions. **Multiple-choice questions**, also quite familiar to students, permit the respondent to select from several answers the one that is most suitable. The problem with multiple-choice questions is that none of the answers might be entirely appropriate, and the respondent might want to have other choices.

Structured non-disguised questionnaires are most effective when the possible replies are definitely known, clearly understood, and limited in number. Multiple-choice and dichotomous questions work best in securing factual information, such as age, income, and car ownership. They are less, although still somewhat, useful in securing information on buying behaviour, purchase intentions, and motivation. For example, imagine the difficulty in listing all possible vacation places in North America!

Unstructured-non-disguised

Like the structured-non-disguised questionnaire, the unstructured-non-disguised questionnaire makes no attempt to conceal the true objectives of the study from the respondent. What does differ is the structure of the questions themselves: They are usually **open-ended questions**. No dichotomous or multiple-choice questions are used, and the interviewer might not even have a list of formal questions to ask, since the purpose is to get the respondent to talk as freely as possible. Rather than ask a question like "What brand to toothpaste do you normally use?" the researcher is apt to ask, "Why do you use toothpaste?" This is an open-ended question, one that permits the respondents to express themselves freely, without forcing answers into predetermined categories.

The unstructured-non-disguised questionnaire is often associated with in-depth interviewing, where respondents are encouraged to talk at length on the subject being probed. The researcher normally does not have a list of predetermined questions, although a rough outline is usually followed. The time period for an in-depth interview will vary, although one or two hours is not unusual. In-depth interviews can be held individually or in groups. One such type of interview is the focus group interview, which is conducted among small groups of people; the interviewer asks the group as a whole for opinions on a product concept, an advertisement, or a television program. Proponents of the focus group interview claim it is better than individual interviews, where information flows one way, because with focus group interviews, "the group setting causes the opinions of each person to be considered in group discussion. Each individual is exposed to the ideas of others and submits his ideas for the consideration of the group."[1]

Although the focus group usually contains no more than eight to twelve people, the interviews are particularly helpful in developing hypotheses in the planning stage of the marketing research process. Not only do the interviews provide information for developing additional research, but also they are quite useful as a source for new product ideas, advertising themes, and packaging concepts. For example, the Harris Meat Company was experiencing declining sales of luncheon meats and wieners. After conducting some focus group interviews, it became clear that there were some serious packaging problems. In addition, these interviews pointed out some shelf space allocation problems and some pricing problems. The packaging problems also affected the image of the products, as well as the quality of the retail display. Results from these interviews were then used for a quantitative study on packaging, communications, and distribution issues related to these products.[2]

The use of focus groups is widespread in consumer marketing research. Often two to four focus group sessions are used in different parts of the country before going to a full-scale study. For example, it is quite common to use the following four group designs: Vancouver, Toronto, English Montreal, and French Montreal.

However, a word of caution is in order: focus group information is only valid for *exploratory* research, not for *conclusive* research. In other words, focus group results might be helpful in getting a feel for market trends, but it is wrong to assume that there is any statistical validity to the results; the sample sizes are too small. A very common error on the part of many clients is to assume that focus group data are a valid reflection of actual consumer market trends.

Whether individual or group interviews are used, the advantages of the unstructured-non-disguised questionnaire relate to the information that it yields. Usually, a much better quality and a greater quantity of information can be collected from non-structured than from structured interviews. Open-ended questions allow respondents to talk freely and bring out information that would not have surfaced in a more structured questionnaire.

The greatest disadvantages associated with this approach are the high costs involved and the difficulty of tabulating and analysing the responses. Highly skilled marketing researchers must be found to conduct in-depth interviews. Not only are the salaries of these people much higher than those of interviewers administering the typical structured-non-disguised questionnaire, but also the time and expense involved in conducting and analysing the information secured from each interview will be substantially greater. Lengthy personal, not telephone or mail, interviews are required, and the attendant expense often becomes prohibitive. This cost consideration affects all phases of marketing research, and the researcher always faces the problem of a trade-off between expense and the quality of information desired.

Unstructured-disguised

In an earlier chapter it was observed that one recurring problem with direct questions to respondents, especially on sensitive subjects, is the unwillingness of many respondents to provide answers to certain questions. Age, income, and consumption patterns are examples of this problem. When asked, "How many beers did you drink last night?" the respondent might be inclined to answer, "Only one or two," when in fact one or two six-packs were actually consumed. Such problems lead to the usage of the disguised questionnaire, which seeks to obscure the true objectives of the study from the respondent.

Unstructured-disguised questionnaires are particularly important in motivation research, where researchers are exploring the *why* of buyer behaviour. The use of projective techniques, commonly associated with this type of questionnaire, is based on the assumption that people describing a situation will describe it according to their own frames of reference—respondents will project themselves into the situation and thus reveal their own true feelings. For example, in reply to the undisguised question "Will you buy a new car this year?" a respondent might respond very rationally, "No, I won't; my old car runs just fine." However, the researcher might ask, using the projective method, "Do you think your next-door neighbour will buy a new car this year?" The respondent might then answer, "Well, I don't think my neighbour has any business buying a new car, since his present car is adequate and he probably can't afford a new one, but he will probably break down and buy a new car anyway." According to the theory of projective techniques, the respondent has unwittingly projected himself into his neighbour's situation and revealed his own interpretation or probable action in the particular instance described.

The foremost advantage of the unstructured-disguised questionnaire approach is that it is able to secure data that respondents might be unwilling or unable to provide in a more structured format or in an undisguised format. High cost is the main disadvantage of this method. There are other limitations as well: problems in securing highly skilled interviewers, lengthy time requirements for conducting interviews, the difficulty of interpreting responses, and the questionable validity of the extremely small samples on which results are based.

Structured-disguised

Like the unstructured-disguised questionnaire, the structured-disguised questionnaire approach also seeks to conceal the true objectives of the study from respondents. Here again, projective techniques can be used by the researcher. The main difference between this approach and the previous one is that the questions are asked in a more structured format. Asking structured questions in a disguised manner makes a questionnaire fairly easy to administer, but the range of replies is limited by the more rigid format.

Carrying over the projective technique example used earlier, we could give the question a structured-disguised twist by rephrasing it as follows:

What kind of car do you think your neighbour will buy this year?

_____ General Motors	_____ Nissan	_____ Peugot
_____ Ford	_____ Honda	_____ Saab
_____ Chrysler	_____ Toyota	_____ Volvo
_____ American Motors	_____ Mercedes	_____ VW-Audi
_____ Renault	_____ BMW	_____ Other

Of the four methods discussed here for classifying questionnaires by structure and disguise, the unstructured-disguised approach is the one that is least commonly used by marketing researchers. Logically, if a questionnaire is to be disguised, it follows that it should also be unstructured, allowing respondents to provide more and better-quality information. The principal advantage derived from the structured-disguised approach is the ease of administration and interpretation of results.

■ Characteristics of a Good Questionnaire

Constructing a good questionnaire is a difficult task. Questionnaire construction is a process that cannot be completed in an hour or two but is much more likely to require a week of hard work. It is also a task that is never complete: there is no such thing as a "perfect" questionnaire. Questionnaire construction is an art, not an exact science. Even after numerous revisions and extensive pre-testing, a questionnaire will still have some undetected flaws.

The foregoing paragraph is not designed to cause the would-be questionnaire developer to give up in despair before ever attempting the task. Rather, it is designed to instil some caution into a delicate and complicated undertaking, which all too often receives insufficient attention. In constructing and evaluating questionnaires, certain characteristics, found in all professional questionnaires, must be kept in mind. The requirements of a good questionnaire are

- completeness
- conciseness
- clarity
- co-operation of the respondents
- careful construction

Completeness

To be complete the questionnaire must include questions in all subject areas relevant to the project. There is no direct connection between the length of a questionnaire and its completeness. Some questionnaires can be complete with very few questions; others might require several pages of legal-sized paper to cover the research problem adequately. A project designed simply to find out whether consumers would prefer longer business hours for shopping centres will necessitate far fewer questions than one designed to give a comprehensive assessment of ethical standards and practices of professional marketing researchers. The key to completeness is whether a questionnaire adequately covers the objectives of the research problems.

Conciseness

A good questionnaire should be as short as possible, containing only questions relevant to the subject and asking nothing that is not absolutely necessary. The questions themselves should be as short as possible to make them easily understood. The more concise the questionnaire, the less time respondents will need to complete it and the lower the cost of administering it. Unless the information is essential to the completion of the project, the researcher should avoid questions on such sensitive subjects as age and income.

Clarity

Researchers must ensure that questionnaires contain no vague or ambiguous questions. Questions must be designed so they will not be misunderstood.

Consider the question "Do you watch television?" How is the respondent supposed to reply? Should she answer in the affirmative if she has not watched TV in six months? What if she watches only the CBC evening news once every two or three weeks and does not consider herself to be a television watcher? A more clear question is "Do you usually watch at least one hour of television each week?"

Co-operation of the Respondents

Every good questionnaire should include all possible means of ensuring respondent co-operation. Co-operation is important because it increases response rate, thus helping to increase the validity of the survey. With mail questionnaires, a covering letter or advance letter should be sent to explain the objectives of the study and to assure the anonymity of respondents. Offering respondents copies of the results of the questionnaire, tendering small monetary incentives for completed mail questionnaires, and carefully explaining the objectives and purposes of the study are three ways to help increase co-operation. In general, the respondent should be made to feel that it is important to participate by completing the questionnaire.

Careful Construction

Whether the questionnaire is to be administered by mail, telephone, or personal interview, or electronic interaction, it should be constructed in a manner that facilitates tabulation and analysis of the data obtained. It should be a simple matter to process the results by computer. Careful construction of the questionnaire not only can result in better-quality data but also can save money. Careful construction implies, too, that a questionnaire will be pre-tested extensively before it is used in an actual survey.

Now that we have looked at these five characteristics of a good questionnaire, carefully examine Figure 8.1, a questionnaire that appeared in Montreal newspapers after the 1976 Olympics. Questions 1 and 2 are dichotomous and 3 and 4 are open-ended. Do you see anything wrong with this questionnaire? How well does it meet the requirements of a good questionnaire?

■ Format Design of Questionnaires

There is as yet no systematized body of knowledge establishing an exact method of designing questionnaires. However, there are certain established rules and principles to follow in developing a good questionnaire. Before discussing these rules, let us examine the main components of a questionnaire.

Questionnaire Components

The major components of a questionnaire fall into three basic categories: explanation information, basic information, and classification information.

FIGURE 8.1
Questionnaire Used After the 1976 Montreal Olympics

HOW SHOULD THE OLYMPIC STADIUM BE COMPLETED?

1. The combined tower and mobile roof could involve an addi-   yes   no
    tional expenditure of up to $100 million. Should it be completed   ☐   ☐
    according to the original plan of the architect, Taillibert?

2. If the tower were not finished, should the authorities still pro-   yes   no
    ceed to construct another type of roof but at a lesser cost?   ☐   ☐

3. If you agree, what kind of roof would you suggest, an inflatable
    one, a geodesic dome, or what?

4. Within the Stadium, there remains about 200 000 square feet of
    space whose use has yet to be determined. What would you pro-
    pose be done with it?

    Name:

Send us your replies and suggestions **BEFORE MARCH 15, 1977** to:

THE ADVISORY COMMITTEE ON
THE FUTURE OF OLYMPIC INSTALLATIONS
600 Fullum Street, 8th floor, Montreal, Quebec, H2K 2L6

Explanation Information

Explanation information is provided by the researcher to the respondent to explain the purpose of the questionnaire. Explanation information, usually given at the beginning of the questionnaire, is designed to reduce respondent errors and to improve response rates. In the case of mail surveys, this information might take the form of an attached covering letter or directions for answering the questions properly. Explanation information common to most questionnaires includes promises to protect the anonymity of the respondent and assurances that no attempts will be made to sell anything to respondents. Figure 8.2 is an example of explanation information in a questionnaire used to find out what types of products Canadian consumers used and how often they used them. Notice that the explanation information identifies the purpose of the survey, makes an appeal for respondent co-operation, and provides two simple examples to assist the respondent in properly filling out the questionnaire.

Basic Information

The largest and most important part of a questionnaire is the basic information sought by the researcher, the real purpose of the questionnaire. The basic information section might be only a few questions in length or it might be several pages long, depending on the amount of data sought.

The basic information section should contain questions that cover all necessary subjects adequately, but researchers must take pains to avoid asking unnecessary questions and thereby making this section longer than is necessary. Figure 8.3 presents an example of a basic information section in a questionnaire designed to find out what automobiles the respondents own or plan to acquire within the next year. Note the briefness of this part of the questionnaire. Is it too brief? Are all possible alternatives listed? Are too many alternatives listed?

Classification Information

At the end of most questionnaires is a section designed to gather relevant classification information, such as marital status, gender, education, occupation, family income, and family size. Classification information enables researchers to analyse the data obtained, through cross-classification, to determine if there are significant differences among groups of respondents. For example, although we might find that most respondents are negatively oriented toward a new product concept being tested, a certain group of the respondents might be favourably disposed toward the product and this group might be large enough or significant enough to constitute an identifiable and viable target market. Classification information allows the researcher to develop a profile of the consumer most likely to use the product or service in question.

Figure 8.4 shows the classification section used in a survey on consumption habits of Canadians. Information obtained from this part of the questionnaire would allow a company to develop a demographic profile of, for example, consumers who bake bread from scratch (if used in conjunction with Figure 8.2), identify potential target segments among the population who personally do some baking, and devise marketing and communication strategies to increase sales and market share.

FIGURE 8.2
Example of the Explanation Information Section of a Questionnaire

We appreciate the time, courtesy and cooperation you have given us. We value highly the answers you express on this questionnaire. Your name will not be associated with your answers under any circumstances.

Knowledge of the products that are used by you...and thousands of other Canadians...helps Canadian business to produce what you want and need. Your questionnaire, combined with others, will add up to a significant cross-section of the Canadian population.

It is important that you answer ALL questions. If, at any point, you do not know the exact answer, please estimate as best you can.

We have tried to make the questionnaire as easy as possible to answer. All that is required is circling a code to indicate your answer.

FOR EXAMPLE:	If you do not bake, you would circle the code beside NO and follow the arrow to the next section.
BAKING	Do you personnally do any baking?
NO...⓪	
YES...1	

How often do you do the following types of baking?	NEVER	LESS THAN ONCE IN 3 MONTHS	ONCE EVERY 2-3 MONTHS	ONCE A MONTH	2-3 TIMES A MONTH	ONCE A WEEK	MORE THAN ONCE A WEEK
Any Baking From Scratch	0	1	2	3	4	5	6
Baking Bread From Scratch ..	0	1	2	3	4	5	6
Cookies From a Mix	0	1	2	3	4	5	6
Cakes From a Mix	0	1	2	3	4	5	6
Muffins From a Mix	0	1	2	3	4	5	6

ANOTHER
EXAMPLE: If you do bake, you would circle the appropriate code then answer how often.

BAKING   Do you personnally do any baking?

NO...0   YES...①

            ◄

How often do you do the
following types of baking?

	NEVER	LESS THAN ONCE IN 3 MONTHS	ONCE EVERY 2-3 MONTHS	ONCE A MONTH	2-3 TIMES A MONTH	ONCE A WEEK	MORE THAN ONCE A WEEK
Any Baking From Scratch	0	1	2	③	4	5	6
Baking Bread From Scratch ..	⓪	1	2	3	4	5	6
Cookies From a Mix	0	1	2	3	④	5	6
Cakes From a Mix..........	0	1	2	3	4	5	6
Muffins From a Mix	0	①	2	3	4	5	⑥

Source: Print Measurement Bureau

Questionnaire Design Steps

Having examined the principal sections of a questionnaire, we are now in a position to consider some of the rules for questionnaire construction. In designing or constructing an effective questionnaire the researcher has to consider such things as

- what information is needed

- what types of questions will be asked

- questionnaire length

- question wording

- order of questions

- pre-testing the questionnaire

By carefully considering these six design steps (the first five of which are problems to be addressed), the researcher can minimize questionnaire difficulties. However, remember that the flawless questionnaire does not exist: even extensive pre-testing will not remove all of the problems, although they *can* be reduced. Details on each of the questionnaire design steps follow.

FIGURE 8.3

Example of the Basic Information Section of a Questionnaire

This section deals with automobiles that you personally own and/or plan to acquire. Please check the appropriate space.

Now currently own:

It was purchased: New _____   Used _____

Manufacturer:

_____ AMC	_____ Fiat	_____ Peugot	_____ Volvo
_____ BMW	_____ Ford	_____ Renault	_____ Hyundai
_____ Br. Leyland	_____ GM	_____ Saab	_____ Other
_____ Chrysler	_____ Honda	_____ Toyota	
_____ Datsun	_____ Mazda	_____ VW-Audi	

In the next 12 months, plan to acquire or change to:

It will be: New _____   Used _____

Size preferred:

| _____ Sports | _____ Subcompact | _____ Compact | _____ Mid-sized |
| _____ Full-sized | | | |

Manufacturer preferred:

_____ AMC	_____ Fiat	_____ Peugot	_____ Volvo
_____ BMW	_____ Ford	_____ Renault	_____ Hyundai
_____ Br. Leyland	_____ GM	_____ Saab	_____ Other
_____ Chrysler	_____ Honda	_____ Toyota	
_____ Datsun	_____ Mazda	_____ VW-Audi	

FIGURE 8.4
Example of the Classification Information Section of a Questionnaire

DEMOGRAPHICS

1. Are you _____ Male _____ Female

2. Are you _____ single
   _____ married or living together
   _____ separated or divorced
   _____ widowed

3. Please indicate your age bracket
   _____ under 20 years   _____ 40 to 49 years
   _____ 20 to 29 years   _____ 50 to 59 years
   _____ 30 to 39 years   _____ 60 years and over

4. Please indicate your total *family* gross income bracket
   _____ under $10 000   _____ $30 000 to $39 999
   _____ $10 000 to 19 999   _____ $40 000 to $49 999
   _____ $20 000 to 29 999   _____ $50 000 and over

5. Size of your family: _____ 1 _____ 2 _____ 3 _____ 4 _____ 5 or more

6. Do you, or does your family, _____ own your home
   _____ rent

   Is this a _____ detached house
   _____ semi-detached house or a row or townhouse
   _____ an apartment in a duplex or triplex
   _____ an apartment block
   _____ other (specify)

7. Please indicate your highest level of education
   _____ elementary school
   _____ high school
   _____ community college/CEGEP/technical school/diploma
   _____ undergraduate university degree
   _____ graduate university degree

8. What is your occupation? _____

9. What is your employment status? (Circle one number)
   Work full time (30 + hours per week)   1
   Work part-time (less than 30 hours per week)   2
   Retired, Pensioned   3
   Student   4
   Unemployed   5
   Homemaker only   6

THANK YOU AGAIN FOR YOUR HELP

Information Required

The very first thing to be done in designing a questionnaire is to determine just what information is needed. The researcher should sit down and write out a statement of the objectives of the study. A plan must be made if the number of questions is to be kept manageable, because there is always a tendency to add more questions to get more data that might be interesting but is not actually necessary.

If the information requirements of the project are substantial, then use of the telephone might be undesirable and personal interviews or mail questionnaires might be essential. If the information required is not only lengthy but complex, personal interviews might be necessary.

A final item to be considered at this point is whether respondents do not have, or do not want to provide, the required information. For example, in the first case it probably would not be advisable to ask men what brand of laundry detergent is used in their homes, because laundry detergent purchases in Canada are made mainly by women. Also, most respondents would not be able to provide answers to questions about how many litres of milk they drank in the past year or how many bars of soap they used. Some questions might be too sensitive or personal for the respondent to answer truthfully or at all. Some examples are: What is your annual income? Do you fail to declare income to the taxation authorities? Do you cry at movies?

In practice, there might be some means to obtain these types of information. For example, age and income might be asked by providing intervals wide enough to remove the personal element. Indirect or projective questioning could be used to skirt sensitive issues. Finally, assurance of anonymity might elicit more truthful answers.

The researcher should also keep in mind that most people have a fairly short memory span; the average respondent, if asked, "What television program were you watching at 9:00 p.m. last Saturday?" will have difficulty in remembering. Firms involved in surveying television viewing habits often use the telephone to make on-the-spot surveys during certain time periods, rather than waiting and asking the question a week later. When determining what information is required, the researcher should always try to keep the number of questions, and hence the length of the questionnaire, to a minimum.

Types of Questions

At this point the researcher must decide what types of questions will be used in the questionnaire. As discussed earlier in the chapter, there are three basic types: open-ended questions, dichotomous questions, and multiple-choice questions. The open-ended question usually begins with such words as *why*, *how*, or *what*, which are quite useful in getting the respondent to open up. Consider the following open-ended questions:

What brand of vodka do you usually drink? _____

Why do you drink this particular brand? _____

_____

Open-ended questions are safer than multiple-choice questions. For example, if brands of vodka had been listed in a multiple-choice format in the above example the researcher might have omitted certain possibilities. Regarding this problem one author wrote:

> Often the researcher has no way of knowing what the answers to his questions will be, and therefore he cannot list them. What is worse, he may *think* he knows and be wrong, and in that case he may never find out that he *was* wrong.[3]

Unfortunately, the open-ended question presents difficulty in the recording and analysis of responses—a time-consuming, expensive process.

Difficulties in using and administering open-ended questions lead many researchers to favour the simpler approach of using multiple-choice or dichotomous questions in questionnaire construction. Use of such questions is associated particularly with the structured-non-disguised questionnaire format discussed earlier.

Length of Questionnaire

The issue of length in questionnaire construction has two aspects. The first is the length of individual questions. It is advisable to keep each question as short as possible, to minimize respondent confusion or misunderstanding. If the interviewer is asking a long and involved question in a telephone interview, the respondent might forget the first part of the question by the time the last part has been asked. Consider the following example of a too lengthy telephone question:

> Please rank in order of preference the following things you might do on a vacation:
> Watch a movie being made _____
> Live with a foreign family _____
> Hunt big game _____
> Watch a bullfight _____
> Swim in a pool _____
> Fish in the ocean _____
> Backpack _____
> Go to a dog show _____
> Visit relatives _____
> Sail on a lake _____

Obviously, all but the most unusual respondents would have great difficulty in remembering the entire question from start to finish. The only possible way to ask this type of question in its present form is by visual means—in writing.

On the other hand, the researcher should avoid questions that are too brief to be meaningful. Consider, for example, the question

> Do you smoke? Yes _____
> No _____

This question is so brief that it can mean different things to different people. The respondent has no idea of exactly what type of information the researcher is seeking. Does the person who smokes a cigar once a month answer in the affirmative? A better way of asking this question might have been

Do you usually smoke at least one pack of cigarettes each week?   Yes _____

No _____

In this case, the question, although a bit longer, should be clear to the respondent and there is much less chance of misinterpretation.

The second aspect of length, total questionnaire length, is more complicated and controversial. Conventional wisdom holds that questionnaires should be kept as short as possible or respondents will become bored filling them out and response rate will suffer. One authority on mail surveys has written that a "questionnaire containing too many pages of small type will draw very few replies."[4]

There is no clear-cut rule for determining the number of questions to be asked in a survey. In general, it is obvious that one can ask more questions in a personal interview than in a telephone interview, and probably a mail interview would fall between the two. Another consideration is the level of interest of respondents in the subject matter. Surveys of younger people dealing with high-interest subjects such as cars, beer, or jeans would probably elicit more involvement than would surveys dealing with retirement plans. A final consideration on questionnaire length is the appearance of the questionnaire itself. A well-formatted questionnaire, artfully laid out, could be perceived as shorter than one that is poorly formatted and laid out.

Although it might seem logical for lengthy questionnaires to cause lower response rates, this is not the case. Questionnaire length and response rate are independent variables; there is no direct correlation between the two. "It seems logical that response rate would decrease with an increase in questionnaire length, but most of the evidence to date has failed to support this hypothesis. In fact, the opposite result has been found in a number of studies."[5]

If there is no proven direct correlation between questionnaire length and response rate, should the researcher still try to keep a questionnaire as short as possible? The answer is *yes*. Although questionnaire length might not affect response rate, it does affect cost. The longer the questionnaire, the more it costs to administer and to interpret the data obtained. For example, it has been estimated that each question included in the U.S. Bureau of the Census questionnaire "adds approximately $1,000,000 to the cost of the census."[6] Cost considerations prompted the Progressive Conservative government of Brian Mulroney to propose dropping the practice of conducting a census of population every five years. However Canada's population is still counted every five years, while in the United States it is counted every ten years.

In conclusion, the number of questions asked should be related to the amount of information necessary to meet the objectives of the survey as well as to its budget and the nature of the survey and of the subject matter.

Wording of Questions

Of the five design problems covered in this section, the way in which individual questions are formulated presents the researcher with the most difficult task. A major objective of wording is formulation of questions in a way that will elicit the desired information and not biassed responses. Each question must be as neutral as possible.

First, the type and wording of questions are affected by the nature of the survey. For example, in telephone interviewing it is difficult to ask a question that relies on some visual element, such as a scale (e.g., a nine-point like/dislike scale) or a label. Direct questioning on sensitive issues might be difficult in personal interviewing and might require indirect wording (i.e., using projective techniques). In a mail survey, overuse of open-ended questions might discourage respondents from answering.

Second, in wording a specific question, both ambiguous and leading questions must be avoided. Ambiguous questions are those that do not convey a clear meaning to respondents. The "Do you smoke?" question presented earlier was an example of ambiguity. Since questions might seem perfectly clear to the researcher but not to many respondents, extensive pre-testing of questionnaires is needed to clarify potential ambiguities. To avoid ambiguous questions, researchers should avoid such vague words as "sometimes," replacing them with more precise phrases, such as "approximately 50% of the time." Questions should also use simple words that are easily understood by people of any educational or cultural background.

Leading questions might produce biassed answers and are used when the researcher is trying to influence the results of the survey. For example, if interviewers ask, "Do you use *Crest* toothpaste?" there will be a high affirmative response, and such a study will be able to report a more widespread use of *Crest* than will a study asking respondents to name the brand of toothpaste that they use regularly.

Question wording should always avoid identifying the sponsor of the survey, because this identification might bias answers. Questions should be worded in as neutral a manner as possible, never beginning, for example, with such phrases as "Do you think...?" A better way of wording the question in the previous paragraph might have been "What brand of toothpaste do you use?"

Finally, both response rate and quality of information received might be improved in cases where respondents agree to be identified—although "this procedure is likely to bias response patterns."[7]

Order of Questions

The order in which questions are asked is extremely important and should be carefully planned. The objective is to lead the respondent through a simple, logical, and consistent process that avoids bias. Usually, the questionnaire will begin with general, easy-to-answer questions, to induce the respondents to start the process and to reinforce their feeling that this is a simple activity. Once respondents have started answering the questionnaire, it is very likely that they will complete it. Next are the more specific questions and, finally, the personal and open-ended questions are placed toward the end of the questionnaire. In particular, sensitive questions such as age or income should always appear in the classification section, which is usually the last section of the questionnaire.

Question order is particularly important when multiple-choice questions are to be used. Two aspects of question order must be considered here. First, before asking a multiple-choice question, it is often advisable to use a **filter question**. The filter question is designed to reduce respondent bias by filtering out in advance the respondents who belong in none of the appropriate categories. Rather than immediately asking respondents which brand of automobile they own, the filter question would ask, "Do you own an automobile?" This filter question screens out those respondents who, if asked directly which automobile they owned, might be inclined to check one of the categories. Those answering *no* to the filter question are directed to the next section of the questionnaire.

The second aspect of question order in multiple-choice questions involves the order of the choices. It is a phenomenon well known to politicians that respondents have a tendency to check the first category presented. Thus, for example, if a Montreal survey asked,

At which supermarket do you usually shop?
_____ A & P
_____ Steinberg
_____ Metro
_____ Provigo
_____ Other

a disproportionately high number of respondents would check the first item presented, A & P. This problem of **order bias** is eliminated when researchers design questionnaires so that the order of multiple-choice questions is rotated. Thus, only on one-fourth of these questionnaires would A & P appear first. Candidates for public office resolve this problem by drawing lots for first place on the election ballot, a position that often guarantees a substantial number of extra votes.

Order bias can also be present with dichotomous questions. For example, the question "Do you prefer shopping in a shopping centre or downtown?" will result in a disproportionately high number of people answering "a shopping centre." Again, the answer to the problem is rotation. Half the questionnaires should have "downtown" first and the other half should have "shopping centre" first. Otherwise the results might be biassed and misleading.

Pre-testing the Questionnaire

No questionnaire design is ever complete if the questionnaire has not been pre-tested. A pre-test involves trying out the questionnaire under field conditions to eliminate or modify problem areas. This trial run offers the researcher the opportunity to change and clarify the wording of questions and to make final revisions. What might seem clear to the researcher might not be that obvious to respondents; some words or expressions might have different connotations to different social, cultural, or educational groups. Some questions might even appear to be insulting, offensive, or demeaning to some respondents. Therefore, it is critical for a marketing researcher to carefully pre-test a new questionnaire before conducting the survey with the complete sample. Remember that the quality of information obtained through a survey is partly dependent on the quality of the questionnaire itself.

The best pre-tests are done by conducting personal interviews with respondents similar to those to be surveyed in the final study. The number of interviews do not need to be large nor must the sample of respondents be scientifically selected. Usually a dozen interviews with respondents roughly similar to those to be used in the final survey will be sufficient.

What the researcher really wants to know from the pre-test is whether respondents properly understand the questions, so that no communication gaps exist. If confusion emerges, the researcher has the opportunity to change or eliminate the question or questions. Researchers should review whether all five design problems have been adequately resolved in the questionnaire design. The importance of the pre-test is that it represents the researcher's final opportunity to make changes and revisions in the questionnaire before actually sending it into the field for survey research.

If the initial pre-test identifies some serious problems with the questionnaire, these should be modified and the questionnaire pre-tested again, and so on until all major deficiencies have been removed. Then the questionnaire is finalized and pre-coded to facilitate entry into the data bank of the completed questionnaires.

■ Summary

The subject of this chapter has been questionnaire construction. A questionnaire is a formal list of questions designed to gather responses from consumers on a topic being researched. The questionnaire is the main instrument used in obtaining primary data from consumers and represents the principal means of communication between respondent and researcher in survey research.

Questionnaire structure and disguise elements are very important. *Structure* refers to the degree to which the questionnaire is standardized, and *disguise* refers to the degree to which the purpose of the research study is known to the respondent. Questionnaires classified on the basis of structure and disguise are of four types: structured-non-disguised, unstructured-non-disguised, unstructured-disguised, and structured-disguised. The structured-non-disguised questionnaire is the most common because it provides ease of administration, tabulation, and interpretation of the questionnaire and the data obtained. The least commonly employed approach is the unstructured-disguised questionnaire, because of the time, cost, and difficulty involved in interpreting responses.

Three types of questions are normally employed in questionnaires. The first is the open-ended question, which allows respondents to make free responses, without confining answers to any predetermined categories. Second is the multiple-choice question, which allows respondents to check the appropriate categories or answers. Third is the dichotomous question, which permits only two choices, usually *yes* and *no*. The open-ended question offers researchers the best quality and quantity of data but also is most difficult to tabulate and interpret. Multiple-choice and dichotomous questions are easier to tabulate and interpret, but they are criticized for limiting respondent answers and they might not include some of the possible choices.

Questionnaire construction, which should be viewed as an art more than as a science, is a process that is never complete. Requirements of a good questionnaire include completeness, conciseness, clarity, co-operation of the respondents, and careful construction. Every good questionnaire should meet all five of these requirements. Questionnaires can be divided into three parts: explanation information, basic information, and classification information. The explanation information section states the purpose of the questionnaire, makes an appeal for response, and provides information on completing the questionnaire properly. The basic information section represents the real purpose of the questionnaire—data sought by the researcher in the survey. Classification information appears at the end of the questionnaire, and includes personal information on respondents for cross-tabulation purposes.

When designing or constructing a questionnaire the researcher must consider the following five questions: What information is required? What types of questions should be asked? How long should the questionnaire be? How should the questions be worded? In what order should the questions be asked? Careful adherence to these first five steps in questionnaire construction does not guarantee a finished questionnaire; only a rough draft will have emerged when these steps are completed. The questionnaire must then be pre-tested in the field to detect flaws in design or wording. The pre-test process should also be extended to include a trial tabulation of data gathered, because difficulties in coding pre-test data can point the way to improvements in the design of the questionnaire. Only then can the final version of the questionnaire be administered to respondents.

For Discussion

1. Questionnaires can be classified on the basis of structure and disguise. What is meant by these two terms?

2. What are the advantages associated with using an unstructured-disguised questionnaire instead of a structured-non-disguised approach? Compare and contrast these two approaches according to cost, ease of administration and tabulation of data, and quality of data obtained.

3. What is the focus group interview? With what types of questionnaire design is this approach associated?

4. Discuss the relative advantages and disadvantages of each of the following: dichotomous questions, multiple-choice questions, and open-ended questions.

5. The owner/operator of a major gasoline station at a busy urban intersection wants to know more about her customers. Specifically, she wants to know why they purchase gasoline at her station and what improvements in service she can make. Construct a short questionnaire using dichotomous, multiple-choice, and open-ended questions to secure this information.

6. a) Evaluate the questionnaire construction in answer to the previous question for completeness, conciseness, clarity, co-operation of the respon-

dents, and careful construction. How well does it meet all of these requirements of a good questionnaire?

b) Is your service station questionnaire divisible into three parts? Is the basic information section the longest?

7. Although research studies indicate that questionnaire length has no direct bearing on response rate, the questionnaire should still be kept as short as possible. Why?

8. The following five questions might be found on any questionnaire. Evaluate each and discuss why you think it is or is not a good question. Assume that no filter questions are required; judge each question on its own merit.
   a) Are you familiar with the *Journal of Marketing Research*?
   b) Do you believe that public officials should be more responsive to the wishes of their constituents?
   c) Do you prefer Labatt or Molson beer?
   d) What is your annual discretionary income?
   e) Do you normally pay for merchandise using cash or credit cards?

9. What is the purpose of a filter question? Provide an example.

10. a) What is the purpose of a questionnaire pre-test? What size of sample and how much sample control are necessary?
    b) What kind of pre-testing would you recommend for the questionnaire developed in question 5?

Problems

1. **Mini-case: Donny's Pancake Houses Ltd.**
   Donny's Pancake Houses Ltd. is a chain of forty-eight restaurants across Canada, with company headquarters in Toronto. The company was founded in the mid-1960s, when pancake houses became popular in Ontario. Corporate strategy included research into location and potential market. As a result, most of the pancake houses were situated in shopping centres or next to hotels along well-travelled freeways.

   To attract customers, the company frequently ran special promotions with cents-off coupons in local papers and served free coffee several times a week. During the evening, the menu also included hamburgers, steaks, and sandwiches.

   Throughout the first ten years of operation, the company made average earnings. However, in the mid-1970s, increases in the prices of coffee and food, compounded by labour problems, caused the profit picture to darken. Nevertheless, Donny's weathered the storm and profits picked up again. Although the 1980s began well, management noticed a decided decline in business in 1984. Some customers complained about prices and the limited menu. Management was well aware than cheaper breakfasts could be obtained at some of the fast-food outlets that were just breaking into this market. In addition, these franchises were springing up so fast and were so reasonably priced that the owners suspected that they were affecting midday and evening business as well. Obviously, the competition had some benefits that Donny's Pancake Houses Ltd. did not offer.

Prior to 1988, marketing research had been based on only secondary sources and internally generated sales and profit data. Management decided it was time to approach customers directly, to determine their needs and obtain suggestions for improvement.

The vice-president of sales and an assistant developed a questionnaire and decided to conduct a two-day survey on a Saturday and Sunday. Each waitress was instructed to distribute the questionnaire to customers waiting to be served. There was no obligation to answer the questions, because management did not want to inconvenience diners. The survey was conducted simultaneously at the five locations that had shown the most dramatic sales declines in the preceding six months. Exhibit 8.1 shows the questionnaire.

EXHIBIT 8.1
Questionnaire

Donny's Pancake House Ltd.

Hi! We're conducting an attitude survey today to help us bring you better service. Please answer all questions completely and then return this sheet to your waitress.

Information about you:

Name _____

Address _____

Occupation _____

Age _____

Approximate family income _____

1. How often do you and your family eat outside the home?

_____

2. What are your three favourite restaurants in this area?

_____

3. How many times have you eaten at Donny's Pancake Houses?

_____

4. What do you like best about Donny's Pancake Houses?

_____

5. What do you like best about other restaurants?

_____

6. What made you decide to come to Donny's today?

_____

Questions

1. Evaluate the marketing survey techniques devised by the vice- president of sales. How could the plan be improved?

2. Criticize the questionnaire. What kind of bias has been introduced?

2. **Mini-case: Home Study Institute** (Part B)
Reread the Home Study Institute (Part A) mini-case at the end of Chapter 7 and carry out the following assignments.

1. Critically analyse the questionnaire.

2. Rewrite the questionnaire with full instructions for completion.

Endnotes

1. Alfred E. Goldman, "The Group Depth Interview." *Journal of Marketing*, 26 (July 1962), p. 62.
2. Keith K. Cox, James B. Higginbotham, and John Burton, "Applications of Focus Group Interviews in Marketing." *Journal of Marketing*, 40 (January 1976), p. 79.
3. Paul L. Erdos, *Professional Mail Surveys*. New York: McGraw-Hill, 1970, p. 50.
4. Ibid., p. 39.
5. A. Marvin Roscoe, Dorothy Lang, and Jagdish N. Sheth, "Follow-up Methods, Questionnaire Length, and Market Differences in Mail Surveys." *Journal of Marketing*, 39 (April 1975), p. 20.
6. Harper W. Boyd, Jr., Ralph Westfall, and Stanley F. Stasch, *Marketing Research: Text and Cases*. 4th ed. Homewood, IL: Richard D. Irwin, 1977, p. 227.
7. Jean-Charles Chebat and Jacques Picard, "Effects of Personalization and Self Identification of Mailed Questionnaires on Information Quality." *Marketing*, 7. Ed. Thomas E. Muller. Administrative Sciences Association of Canada (ASAC), 1986, p. 384.

9 MEASUREMENT OF MARKETING CONCEPTS

Marketing research would not be possible if concepts of interest to marketers could not be measured. Besides the qualitative questions that are sometimes asked respondents (generally open-ended questions), quantitative responses are often required. For instance, such concepts as sales, number of units consumed, and income seem to lead to straightforward, quantitative answers. However, other concepts might not lend themselves to obvious and straightforward quantification. For example, concepts such as attitude toward marketing stimuli (brands, products, advertisements), perception of brands, personality traits, and consumers' lifestyles are frequently examined in marketing research studies, often requiring elaborate scales for their measurement. In this chapter the basic scaling information that marketing researchers need to know will be briefly discussed. In addition, the scaling techniques that are most frequently used in marketing research will be briefly reviewed in this chapter.

■ Definition of Social Sciences Measurement

Measuring consists of assigning numerals to characteristics of objects/people/states/events, according to pre-specified rules.[1] Several points of this definition might need to be explained. First, in a marketing context objects might be, for instance, brands, products, stores, or shopping centres; people could be consumers, middlemen, or salespeople; events could be purchase occasions or product consumption; states could be the various stages of the product life cycle. Second, measurement applies to characteristics of the objects (or people/states/events), *not* to the objects themselves. A marketing researcher might want to measure how sweet a brand is or how large a package is. In these instances, sweetness and length (two brand *characteristics*) are being measured. Third, assigning numerals is a process by which numerical symbols are attributed to the object (person/state/event) so as to identify as well as possible the level of the characteristic under consideration that is possessed by the object. This symbol might or might not have a quantitative meaning. That is why the word *numeral* instead of the word *number* is used in this definition. The word *number* implies a quantitative meaning and, as will be seen later, some scales have no quantitative content. Fourth, the rule by which a numeral is assigned to the characteristic of the observation is essentially arbitrary. This rule might be devised by the researcher or it might have been devised by other researchers and have reached the status of almost a universal scale in some field of study. Even in such cases, this does not prevent the scale from being essentially a set of arbitrary rules. Of course, this does not mean that any set of rules will do. Some rules might be good, while others might be poor. The importance of devising good rules can be appreciated when one considers the rationale for measuring.

The Rationale for Measurement and Scaling

Through measurement and scaling a researcher tries to translate some real-world phenomenon (for instance, respondents' attitudes toward Brand A and Brand B) into numerals or numbers.[2] The rationale is that numbers can be manipulated, transformed, and analysed through the powerful language of mathematics, in order to reach conclusions. *If* the researcher has properly translated the phenomenon into numbers (through a proper scaling process with good rules), relevant conclusions can be drawn. For instance, once measurements have been obtained, the analyst might be able (through a simple correlation analysis) to identify a significant correlation between the numbers measuring respondents' attitudes toward Brand A and the numbers measuring respondents' attitudes toward Brand B. If these numbers are an adequate representation of respondents' attitudes toward the two brands, the researcher could conclude that respondents with a positive attitude toward Brand A also have a positive attitude toward Brand B, and conversely. Note that without a measurement of attitudes, this conclusion would be very difficult to reach. As mentioned before, this process is efficient only as far as the researcher has been able to secure a good rule that properly translates phenomenon into numbers. The quality of the measurements is essentially assessed through two basic characteristics: the measurement's reliability and validity. These two concepts will be discussed later in this chapter. The rationale for the measurement and scaling process are represented in Figure 9.1.

The Measurement Process

The measurement process typically involves two major sets of stages: definition and task specification.

FIGURE 9.1
The Measurement Process

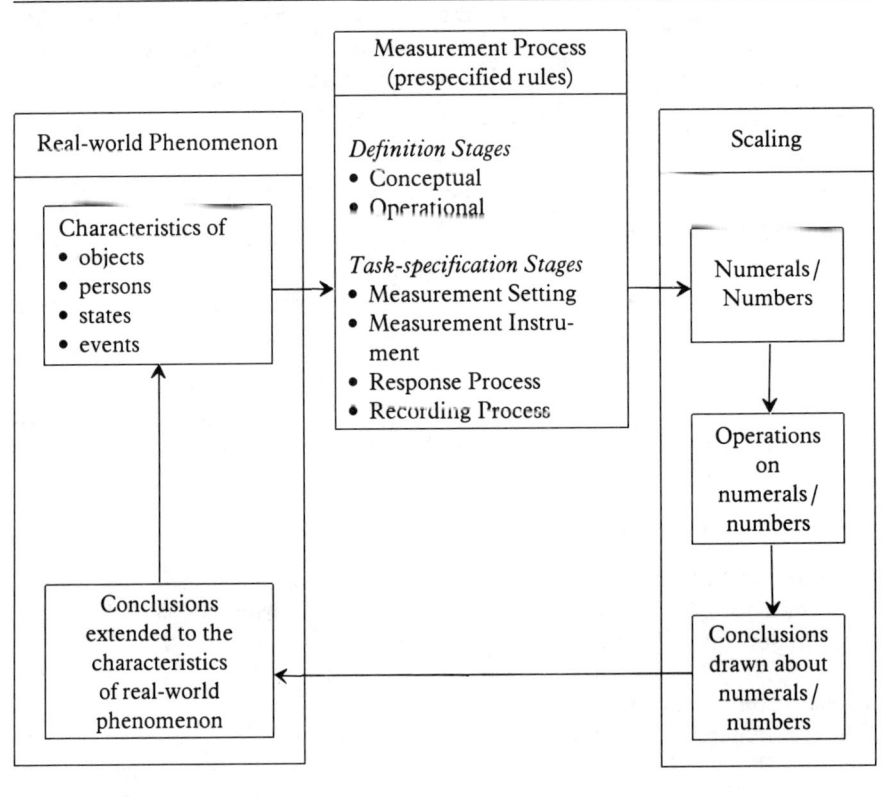

Definition Stages

Conceptual Definition

The natural starting point for the measurement process is a clear and precise definition of the concept to be measured. This definition can use abstract terms and should not be concerned with practical problems and material considerations. For example, let us assume that a researcher needs to measure consumers' preferences for orange juice brands. Conceptually, brand preference could be defined, for instance, as the brand that would be selected by a consumer for his or her own consumption if price and availability were not a factor. Other conceptual definitions could have been selected; the choice would depend on the conceptual definition that best matches the purpose of a study.

Operational Definition

The operational definition of the concept is what the researcher is going to observe or inquire about to assess the extent to which the object/person/state/event possesses the characteristic that has been conceptually defined at the preceding state.[3] The basic fact about operational definitions is that several definitions can be used for measuring a single concept. For instance, in the preceding example, the researcher could operationally define brand preference (conceptually defined as above) as follows.

Observational definition: Brand preference could be measured by the observed brand purchased (all brands being made available to consumers at the same price). In fact, brand preference is inferred from the brand actually selected.

Self-report definition: Brand preference could be reported by the consumers themselves. For instance, interviewers could directly ask consumers to report the brand they would purchase, if all brands were equally priced and available.

Third-party report definition: Alternatively, for convenience purposes, the head of the household could be asked to report the brand that would be selected by the other members of the family (assuming that the household head knows the tastes and preferences of the other family members).

These three possible operational definitions of brand preference are by no means exhaustive. They only illustrate the fact that there are several plausible ways (some more convenient than others) to arrive at a measure of the concept under investigation.

Task-Specification Stages

Once researchers know how to operationalize the concept under investigation, they must specify the various tasks, the measuring instruments, and the conditions under which the measurement will take place.

Measurement Setting

The researcher should specify under which conditions the measurement will take place. Will a questionnaire be self-administered? Will the questions be asked personally by an interviewer? Will the measurement take place at the respondent's home? In a laboratory setting? These are only a few of the questions that the researcher should answer in specifying the conditions under which the measurement will take place.

Measurement Instrument

The measurement instrument must be selected or built up. This could be a single scale (for example, a unidimensional continuum ranging from least preferred to most preferred) or an entire set of scales (a multi-item scale) that must be designed to capture various aspects of a multidimensional construct. In the preceding example, assuming that the researcher has decided to operationalize the concept of brand preference by the self-report approach, he or she might ask the respondent the following question:

Assuming that brands A, B, C, and D are all available at the same price, which one would you prefer?

Response Process

The response process refers to the type of responses that will be requested from the respondents. Sometimes, respondents will be asked to check one box, or to circle a number, or to respond freely to an open-ended question, or any other procedure. In the preceding example, the respondent could be provided with a complete set of possible answers and asked to check the appropriate box:

Brand A	☐
Brand B	☐
Brand C	☐
Brand D	☐
None	☐

Recording Process

The manner in which respondents' answers are going to be recorded often depends on the type of instrument and response process already selected. The recording process could be done by the subject, by the interviewer/observer, or by any mechanical, objective, recording device.

Quality of Scales

Scales vary widely in terms of the quantity of information they contain. Four types of scale are commonly used for measuring marketing concepts: nominal, ordinal, interval, and ratio.

Nominal Scales

Nominal scales (or categorical data) involve the assignment of a numeral to an observation or to an object/person/state/event, for identification purpose only. For example, after completion of a consumer survey, respondents might be numbered from one to ten, according to the order in which the interviews have been recorded, for example, or in any other more or less random order. In such cases the number associated with a specific respondent has no specific meaning, except that it is used as a convenient numerical label that identifies each respondent in the survey. Other examples of nominal scales commonly used in a market survey context are the codes that are associated with specific answers. For example, twenty respondents (identified in Table 9.1 by the letters A to T) might have been asked their preferred hobby from the six categories shown in column 2.

For convenience, each category has been given a code (shown in column 1). Obviously, these codes have no quantitative meaning whatsoever. The assignment of the value zero to subjects E, L, and T has been done simply to help the researcher to process the information. In this case, zero is just a convenient label given to all respondents reporting a preference for watching sporting events. Consequently, nominal scale numerals can be replaced by any new set of distinct numerals. For example, the researcher could have used the numerals shown in column 4 as an alternative coding scheme without changing the amount or the nature of the information contained in the scale in any way.

TABLE 9.1
Example of a Nominal Scale

Code (1)	Category (2)	Observations (3)	Alternative Coding Scheme (4)	Frequency Count (5)	Percentage 6
0	Watching sporting events	E, L, T	63	3	15
1	Participating in sporting events	C, F, I, K, N, P, S	18	7	35
2	Reading	A, M, Q, R	40	4	20
3	Listening to music	G, J	92	2	10
4	Watching television	B, H, O	5	3	15
5	Other	D	0	1	5
	Total			20	100

Mode: 1 (or 18, if alternative coding scheme is used).

As shown in Table 9.1, the most frequent statistics that might be performed on nominal or categorical data are frequency counts of occurrence of observations with the same scale value (i.e., how many fall into each category) and the percentage of observations falling into each category. In addition, such statistics as chi-square or the mode (i.e., the category with the highest frequency) are typically used with nominal scales.

Nominal scales are frequently used in marketing research. For instance, socio-demographic variables such as a respondent's geographic location, type of dwelling, gender, and religion are nominal scaled values. Ownership or consumption of various products and brands are other frequent occurrences.

Ordinal Scales

Ordinal scales involve the ordering of observations (objects/people/states/events) according to the degree to which they possess a given characteristic. At least two types of ordinal scales can be built, depending on whether they require strict ordering or can accommodate weak ordering.

Weak-Order Scales

In weak-order scales (also called ordered categories), ties are allowed and many stimuli can fall into a single category, with no specific order implied within the category. For instance, the left-hand panel of Table 9.2 shows a given respondent's answers to the perceived sweetness of ten orange juice brands (labelled A to J). This respondent has classified the ten brands according to his or her perceived sweetness into four ordered categories, from very low to very high.

According to the data shown in column 3, one can see that this consumer perceives Brands B, C, G, and J as being not as sweet as Brand D, which in turn is not as sweet as Brands A, F, and I, which themselves are not as sweet as Brands E

TABLE 9.2
Example of Ordinal Scales

Rank Order (1)	Category (2)	Brands (3)	Rank Order (4)	Brand (5)	Alternative Rank Order (6)
Weak Ordering			**Strict Ordering**		
			Very Low		
			1	C	2
1	Very Low	B, C, G, J	2	G	15
			3	J	18
2	Rather Low	D	4	B	30
			5	D	40
3	Rather High	A, F, I	6	F	45
			7	I	60
4	Very High	E, H	8	A	100
			9	E	103
			10	H	120
			Very High		

Median: 2.5	Median: 5.5
Quartiles: 1, 2.5, 3	Quartiles: 3, 5.5, 8

and H. However, there is no indication in these data about the relative orders of Brands B, C, G, and J in terms of sweetness. In other words, from a research point of view, these brands must be considered as sharing the same rank (i.e., as ties).

Strict-Order Scales

Obviously, this scale would be still more informative if no ties were allowed in the data, and if the respondent were forced to provide a complete rank order of the ten brands, as shown in the right-hand panel of Table 9.2.

Whether strictly or weakly ordered, ordinal scale values are only *indicative* of an order. Consequently, other numbers could have been used to convey the same information. The only constraint put on these numbers is that they should reflect essentially the same order. For example, the alternative ordering scheme shown in column 6 of Table 9.2 could have been used as well, with no loss of information. Another way to state the same idea is to say that the ordinal scale is defined up to a monotone transformation, in this case a monotonically increasing function (i.e., a function that does not decrease in the relevant range). A monotone function that can transform the first ordering scheme of column 4 of Table 9.2 into the second ordering of column 6 is shown in Figure 9.2.

Ordinal scales can accommodate any order-preserving transformation or statistic. In addition to the statistics that could be performed on nominal scales, one can compute such statistics as the median (i.e., the value at which 50% of the

FIGURE 9.2
**Example of Permissible Monotone Transformation
that Can Be Performed on Ordinal Scales**

Scale 2 (equivalent to Scale 1)

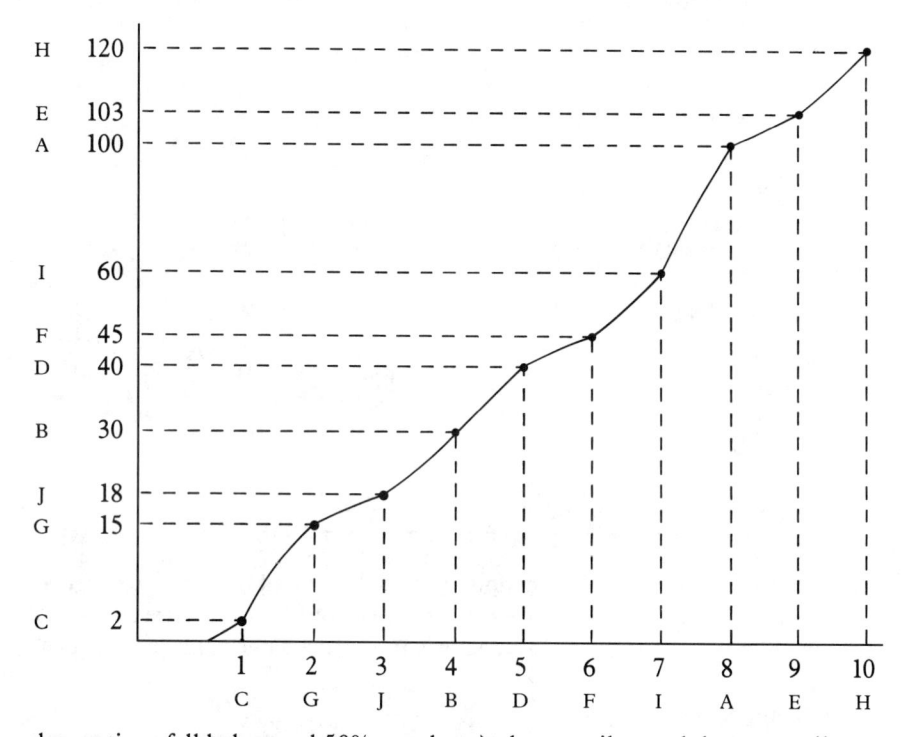

observations fall below and 50% are above), the quartiles, and the percentiles, as well as a large number of non-parametric statistics.[4]

Ordinal scales, and particularly ordered categories, are frequently used in marketing research for measuring such socio-demographic variables as income, age, education level, and social class. Brand preference and attitudes are often measured on strictly ordinal scales.

Interval Scales

Interval scales imply the measurement of objects/people/states/events on a continuum with an *arbitrary* origin, so as to reflect the degree to which they possess a given characteristic. These scales come closer to the common understanding that most people have of a scale. They are commonly used in physics and the experimental and social sciences. For instance, temperature is a typical example of a concept that is measured on interval scales. In interval scales, the zero (as well as the unit) is arbitrarily defined and has no special or universal meaning. For instance, a temperature of zero has no meaning unless one refers to a specific scaling system. If one refers to a Celsius scale, the zero has been arbitrarily defined as being the freezing point of water. Referring to the Fahrenheit temperature scale, the zero point has been defined according to quite different criteria.

The essentially arbitrary nature of the origin of interval scales is the reason why these scales are defined up to a linear transformation of the type $Y = aX + b$, where b corresponds to a change in scale origin, and a corresponds to a change in the scale unit. Thus, in order to transform a set of Celsius-scaled temperatures into Fahrenheit-scaled temperatures, one needs to make the following transformation:

$$F = 32 + 9/5 \, C$$

This is illustrated in Figure 9.3.

Because of the arbitrary nature of the zero of interval scales, certain types of statements cannot be made with this type of data. A simple example can illustrate this point. Figure 9.3 shows the average temperature for January in four cities, A, B, C, and D ($10°C$, $15°C$, $25°C$, and $30°C$, respectively, or alternatively $50°F$, $59°F$, $77°F$, and $86°F$, respectively). Considering the Celsius temperature scale, a careless observer might state that in January, the average temperature in City D is twice as high as that in City B ($30 = 2 \times 15$). Considering the same data but expressed in the Fahrenheit scale, another person would find this statement erroneous ($86 \neq 2 \times 59$). This example illustrates why it would be wrong to make direct comparisons (ratios) of interval scale values. The only permissible statements that might be made with interval data are statements that imply differences

FIGURE 9.3
Relationship Between Two Similar Interval Scales

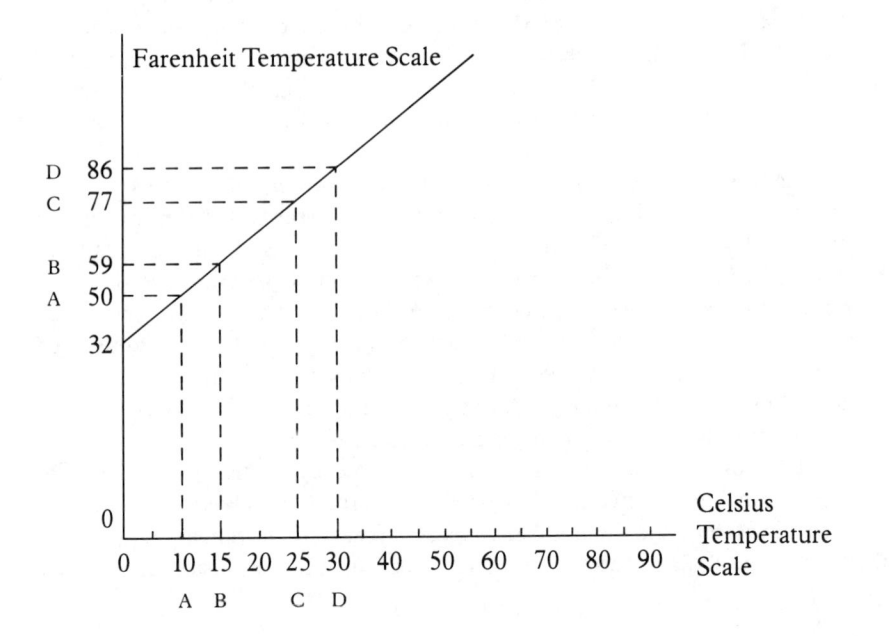

between scale values: the difference between two scale values is insensitive to the scale origin. For example, it would be meaningful to say that the difference in temperatures between Cities c and d is as large as the difference between Cities a and b. As can be easily checked, this statement is true, no matter which scale is used:

Celsius: $15 - 10 = 30 - 25$
Fahrenheit: $59 - 50 = 86 - 77$

In addition to statistics that are permissible with nominal and ordinal data, most usual statistics that involve only additions and/or subtractions of scale values are permissible with interval scales. These statistics include the mean, variance, standard deviation, and the F and t statistics.

Interval scales are frequently used in marketing research for measuring socio-psychological concepts. For instance, consumers' perceptions, attitudes, personality traits, lifestyles, and psychographic data are typically measured on interval scales.

Ratio Scales

Of all the scales, ratio scales contain the most information. They consist of the measurement of objects/people/states/events on a continuum with a *fixed* origin, so as to reflect the degree to which they possess more characteristics. The scale origin has a special meaning—the complete absence of the characteristic. For instance, when a researcher measures consumers' incomes (expressed in dollars), this can be considered as a ratio scale. When a consumer reports an income of zero dollars, this consumer conveys the unequivocable meaning that he or she has absolutely no income.

Ratio scales are defined up to a linear transformation of the type $y = ax$. In other words, the scale origin cannot be changed for the reasons mentioned previously. Only the scale unit remains arbitrary and can be changed by the researcher without altering the information contained in the scale. For instance, respondents' incomes can be expressed in dollars or in cents. This is essentially the same information. The only difference is that all of the scale values must be multiplied by 100 (Income = $100 \times \$$ Income).

Because the origin of ratio scales is fixed, direct comparisons (ratios) of scale values are meaningful. For instance, it would be true to say that Fatima's earnings are twice as large as Max's earnings, regardless of whether their incomes have been measured in dollars, in cents, or any other currency (see Figure 9.4).

In addition to statistics that are permissible with all of the previously discussed types of scale, ratio-scaled data can also accommodate such less frequently used statistics as the harmonic mean, the geometric mean, and the coefficient of variation (the ratio of the standard deviation over the mean). All of these statistics imply multiplication or division by some scale values.

In marketing research, several scales are typically of the ratio type. For example, respondents' income, age (when measured precisely and not through ordered categories), and the number of years of formal education are ratio scales. Certain types of data need to have ratio properties. For instance, attribute

FIGURE 9.4
Examples of Ratio Scales

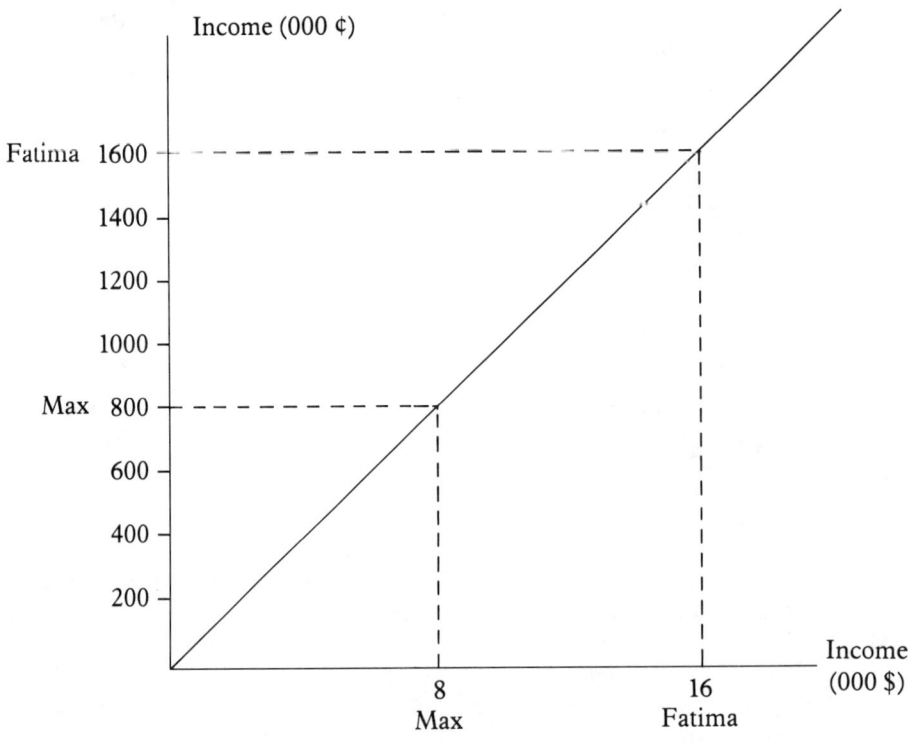

importance weights or attribute saliences need to be ratio-scaled data, because, being weights, they will be typically multiplied by other scale values.

The four main types and basic characteristics of scales are summarized in Table 9.3.

Importance of Scale Quality

As has been discussed, scales are not identical in terms of the amount of information they contain. Nominal scales are the least informative type of scales, followed in increasing order of information content by ordinal, interval, and ratio scales. This hierarchy of scales in terms of their information content can be appreciated by the nature of the transformation to which they can be subjected without altering the amount and the nature of their information. For instance, ratio scales can only accommodate transformation of the type $Y = aX$ because they are so informative that any other type of transformation would distort the information it contains. By contrast, ordinal scales can accommodate a much larger set of transformations (any monotonically increasing transformation will do) because they contain less information that could be distorted by scale transformation.

TABLE 9.3
Main Types and Characteristics of Scales

Scales	Characteristics	Permissible Transformation	Permissible Statistics
Nominal	Assignment of a numeral to an object/person/state/ event for identification purpose only	Can be changed into any new set of distinct numerals	Mode Frequency Percentages Chi-square
Ordinal	Ordering of objects/ people/states/events according to the degree to which they possess a given characteristic • weak ordering (or ordered categories): ties allowed • strict ordering: no ties allowed	Any monotonic (order-preserving) transformation	All above, plus • Median • Quartile • Percentiles • Non-parametric
Interval	Scaling of objects/people/ states/events on a continuum with an arbitrary origin, so as to reflect the degree to which they possess a given characteristic	Any linear transformation of the type $Y = aX + b$	All above, plus • Mean • Variance • F, t
Ratio	Scaling of objects/people/ states/events on a continuum with a fixed origin, so as to reflect the degree to which they possess a given characteristic. The scale origin (zero) means the absence of the characteristic	Any linear transformation of the type $Y = aX$	All above, plus • Harmonic mean • Geometric mean

A researcher's concern for the quality of the measurements of collected data is by no means an academic exercise. As was discussed previously, the type of scale and measurement levels of the data is one of the major criteria for selecting the appropriate data analytic technique or statistic at the data-processing stage. For instance, researchers should understand that if they were to process data *as if* the data were measured at a higher-quality level than the scale actually has, they implicitly assume that the data contain more information than is the case. For instance, if a researcher computes the mean of rank order data, the implicit assumption is that the rank order reflects equal-appearing intervals between consecutive ranks (which, of course, is not accurate). This could lead to a downright false conclusion in the analysis.

The converse, although generally undesirable, is not as serious. For instance, if researchers treated ratio-scaled data as if the data had only ordinal properties, researchers would not be led to draw wrong conclusions. This would be the case, for example, where a researcher transforms ratio income data into a set of ordered categories. However, in such cases researchers would not capitalize on *all* of the information that they have collected. The statistics they would use would not be the most powerful they could have used, and their conclusions are likely to be less precise than those they could have reached, given the data they have collected.

This is the reason why the quality of the scales and the measurement levels of the marketing research data is of major concern to marketing researchers and analysts.

■ Main Types of Scales

Data-collection procedures for scaling depend on the importance of the demand that is made on respondents. For instance, a researcher might assume that respondents can only *compare* stimuli with one another. In this case a respondent might be asked for a series of judgments, such as: Which brand of orange juice is sweeter, A or B? Alternatively, a researcher might assume that respondents can give immediate quantitative values that reflect their judgments. In this case a respondent might be asked to rate Brand A's sweetness on a 10-point scale ranging from 0 (not at all sweet) to 10 (extremely sweet). The values given by the respondent would be assumed to have at least interval properties. The former approach will typically yield ordinal scales. If higher-level scales are needed, the use of a scaling model will be necessary to upgrade the ordinal information to interval or ratio-scaled data.

Main Types of Ordinal Scales

Ordered Category Scales (Weak-Order Scales)

In ordered category scales, respondents are asked to sort the various stimuli into a set of ordered categories according to a specific characteristic. In this case, however, no assumption is being made about the distance that separates the categories. In addition, the respondent might be required to assign a certain number of stimuli to each category, as shown in the following example.

Assign the different brands to the following categories, choosing the one that best reflects your opinion:

not strong at all	not very strong	moderately strong	somewhat strong	very strong

For each respondent, it will be possible to rank-order the various brands in terms of strength, with all brands falling into the same category being considered as ties.

Rank-Order Scales (Strict-Order Scales)

Direct Rank-Order Scales. In the direct rank-order method, respondents are asked to provide a complete rank order (no ties allowed) of a set of stimuli, either according to a specific characteristic or in terms of preference, as illustrated by the following.

Rank these soft drinks in terms of tartness: *Coke, 7-Up, Pepsi.*

The advantage of this method is that it provides the researcher immediately with a complete rank order of the set of stimuli. However, this scale does not provide for a means to check for the respondent's consistency over the various judgments.

Paired-Comparison Scales. The paired-comparison approach is often preferred to the direct rank-order approach because it does provide a means to check for consistency. In the paired-comparison approach, all of the possible pairs of stimuli are formed. Within stimuli $n(n-1)/2$ pairs can be specified. A respondent is shown each pair at a time and is asked to identify which stimulus dominates the other on a specific characteristic. The desirable feature of this approach is that it provides a way to control for the transitivity of a respondent's answers. *Transitivity* in this context means the consistency among the various judgments. For instance, if a respondent says that A is sweeter than B, and that B is sweeter than C, this respondent could be expected to say that A is sweeter than C. In this case, the three judgments would be called transitive. If the respondent said that C is sweeter than A, the three judgments would be intransitive. When asked to compare a large number of pairs of stimuli in a random order, respondents will typically give a certain number of intransitive judgments. Some procedures can be used to build the complete rank order of all of the stimuli to provide the smallest possible number of alterations in the respondent's original judgments.

Main Types of Interval Scales

Rating Scales

Rating scales provide either ordinal or interval data, depending on what the analyst wants to assume about respondent's answers. Although not always warranted, marketing researchers most often assume that interval level data are collected through rating scales. When using rating scales, a marketing researcher needs to make a number of decisions about the type of rating scale to use, whether this should be a comparative or a non-comparative scale, forced vs. non-forced, balanced vs. unbalanced, the number of categories to use, and especially if this should be an even or an odd number.[5] Although these issues have generated extensive debate among researchers, which goes well beyond the scope of this text, the issues will be briefly discussed.[6]

Rating scales can be of the numerical, symbolic, graphic, or verbal type, depending on how the underlying scale continuum is represented. Thus, the underlying continuum can be represented as a series of numbers, by visual symbols, a continuous line (broken down into equal-appearing intervals or not), or by a set of verbal descriptors. Some examples of each type of scale are provided in Figure 9.5.

FIGURE 9.5
Examples of Rating Scales

What is your opinion of Mexico as a vacation site?

1. Numerical scale:

$$-3 \quad -2 \quad -1 \quad 0 \quad 1 \quad 2 \quad 3$$

dislike it
very much

like it
very much

2. Graphical scales:

dislike it
very much

like it
very much

dislike it
very much

like it
very much

3. Pictoral scale:

4. Verbal scale:

dislike it very much	☐
dislike it	☐
indifferent	☐
like it	☐
like it very much	☐

Comparative vs. Non-comparative Rating Scales. Non-comparative scales try to measure a concept without reference to any existing stimulus or present situation. In comparative rating scales, the respondent is asked to respond to a stimulus in comparison with some reference point (for instance, the brand presently used). This reference point is called an *anchor point* (see Figure 9.6).

FIGURE 9.6
Examples of Rating Scale Options

1. Comparative vs. non-comparative rating scales:

    Non-comparative: Overall, how would you rate the taste of Brand A?

    Comparative: Compared to your favourite brand of orange juice, how would
    you rate Brand A?

2. Number of categories:

    • Small vs. Large Numbers:

    small: -2 -1 +1 +2

    large: -5 -4 -3 -2 -1 +1 +2 +3 +4 +5

    • Odd vs. Even Numbers:

    odd: -2 -1 0 +1 +2

    even: -2 -1   +1 +2

3. Forced vs. Non-forced Choice Scales

Forced:		Non-forced:	
like it very much	☐	like it very much	☐
like it	☐	like it	☐
indifferent	☐	indifferent	☐
dislike it	☐	dislike it	☐
strongly dislike it	☐	strongly dislike it	☐
		don't know	☐

4. Balanced vs. Unbalanced

Balanced:		Unbalanced:	
like it very much	☐	like it very much	☐
like it	☐	like it	☐
indifferent	☐	indifferent	☐
dislike it	☐	dislike it	☐
strongly dislike it	☐		

Number of Rating Scale Categories. First, there is the problem of the number of
response choices offered to respondents. The greater the number of points on the
scale (response choices) the greater the precision of the scale—just as a ruler
marked off in thirty-secondths of an inch is more precise than one marked off in
fourths. However, this does not mean that a scale can or should be divided
indefinitely, because there is some question as to how precisely individual
respondents can conceptually divide their opinions. Should the scale, for example, express positive feeling simply as *agree* and *strongly agree*, or can respondents
meaningfully differentiate among *extremely strongly agree, very strongly agree,*
strongly agree, somewhat strongly agree, definitely agree, agree, somewhat agree,

and *only mildly agree*? Then, too, there is the problem of reporting. In the final analysis, most decision makers want an overall summary: how many *for* and how many *against*? Therefore, a large number of response choices on a scale will eventually be collapsed into fewer and more comprehensive categories. This being the case, it makes little sense to incur the extra confusion, coding expense, and tabulating expense inherent in a large number of categories, not to mention the possible bias from improperly collapsing the responses. It makes much more sense to use broader categories from the start.

Second, there is the problem of selecting an odd or even number of categories. The odd-number option implies that there is a neutral point on the scale; should the researcher allow the respondents the luxury of being neutral, or should they be forced to choose one side or the other?

Forced vs. Non-forced Choice Rating Scales. A related problem is for researchers to decide whether they should offer a non-response option (*don't know*) or force the respondent to commit themselves one way or another. Forcing respondents to respond when they actually do not know can create a bias in the answers. On the other hand, providing them with a *don't know* option invites lazy respondents to take advantage of this opportunity.

Balanced vs. Unbalanced Rating Scales. This option refers to whether the scale should or should not include as many positive response categories as negative categories. Here again, selecting an unbalanced scale might produce a bias in the direction that includes the larger number of categories. However, when researchers know in advance that very few answers can be expected on one side of the scale, they might want to reduce the total number of categories by using an unbalanced scale (some examples are shown in Figure 9.6).

The Semantic Differential Scale

One of the most interesting scales, as well as one of the simplest to use, is the semantic differential.[7] In this scale, respondents express their feeling on a given concept according to a set of matched pairs of antonyms, as in the following example.

Strong	___	___	___	___	___	___	___	Weak
Reliable	___	___	___	___	___	___	___	Unreliable
Modern	___	___	___	___	___	___	___	Old-fashioned
Warm	___	___	___	___	___	___	___	Cold
Friendly	___	___	___	___	___	___	___	Unfriendly
Young	___	___	___	___	___	___	___	Old
Masculine	___	___	___	___	___	___	___	Feminine
Dynamic	___	___	___	___	___	___	___	Passive

Despite the seeming inapplicability of some of the adjectives used in the matched pairs, it is amazing how quickly a distinct product or brand image begins to emerge. Consumers really do differentiate between the brands, even on the dimensions that seem nonsensical. In the usual studies that involve use of the semantic differential, at least two brands are tested with the same series of words: the replies for all respondents are averaged for each question and then the averages are plotted as a personality profile, or image analysis, of the two competing brands. As can be seen from the two profiles shown in Figure 9.7, the two brands (General Electric and Private Brand x) are perceived as having very differing profiles. In this example, the General Electric brand would be perceived as more powerful, reliable, and modern than Brand x.

FIGURE 9.7
Image Profiles of Two Brands

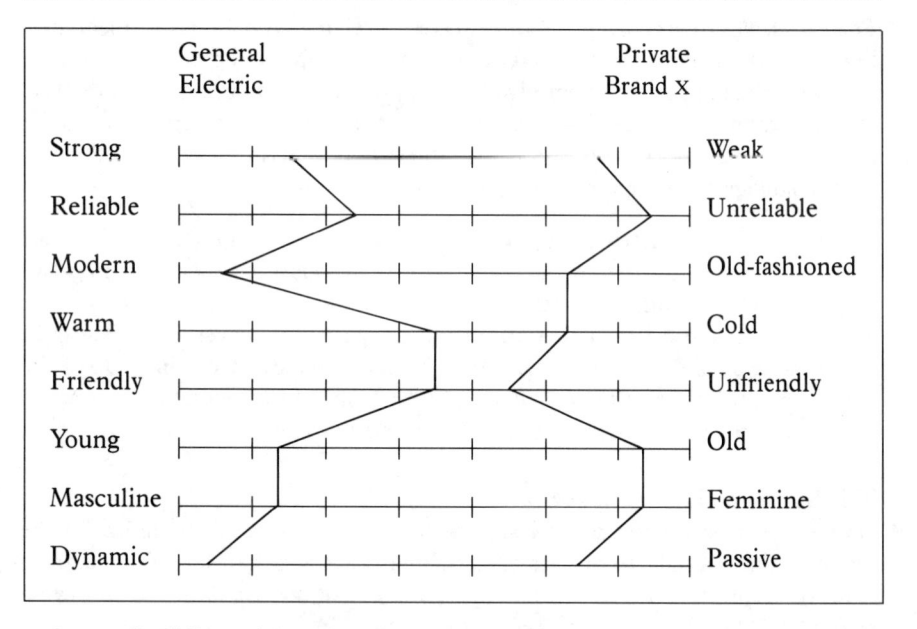

Semantic differential scales generally consist of a range of seven response choices, although such scales with more or fewer than seven positions are often seen. The semantic differential, because of its ease of construction, the simplicity of answering and coding it, the density of information provided (information on a wide variety of dimensions is given in a relatively small amount of space on the questionnaire), and its obvious applicability to marketing and advertising problems, is one of the most popular scales used in marketing.[8]

The Stapel Scale

The Stapel scale can be considered as a simplified version of the semantic differential scale.[9] Originally, the Stapel scale was described as a unipolar, 10-point scale ranging from -5 to +5. Thus, the scale measures a concept in direction and intensity simultaneously. An example of the Stapel scale for measuring the brand images of General Electric and Brand x is shown in Figure 9.8a, and the derived profiles in Figure 9.8b.

FIGURE 9.8
Example of the Stapel Scale

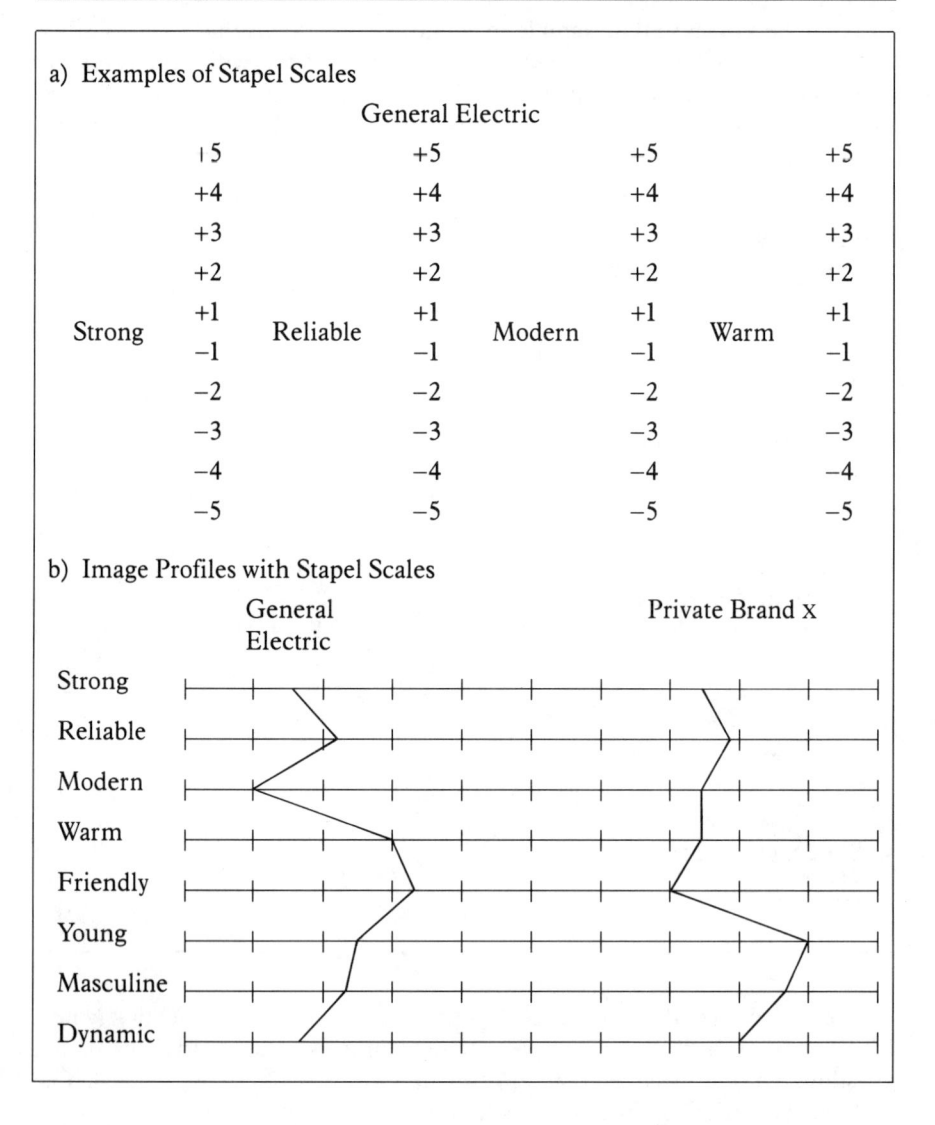

a) Examples of Stapel Scales

General Electric

| Strong | Reliable | Modern | Warm |

b) Image Profiles with Stapel Scales

General Electric   Private Brand x

Strong
Reliable
Modern
Warm
Friendly
Young
Masculine
Dynamic

The advantages of the Stapel scale are that it is easy to administer and it removes the need for the researcher to pre-test the pairs of adjectives to ensure true bipolarity that was necessary with the semantic differential scale. Empirical results suggest that very similar results are obtained when Stapel or semantic differential scales are used.[10]

The Likert Scale (or Summated Scale)

Probably the most common type of attitudinal scale is the Likert scale (named after Rensis Likert).[11] This scale involves a proposition with which the respondent can either agree or disagree. The normative form of the Likert scale offers exactly five choices, ranging from *strongly agree* to *strongly disagree*, with a neutral position in the middle.

As can be shown in the example in Figure 9.9, the items that take a positive attitude are coded +2, +1, 0, -1, and -2 from agree to disagree, while a reverse scale is used for negative attitude statements. The rationale is that a respondent who has a positive attitude toward the concept is likely to agree with the positive items and disagree with the negative ones, and conversely.

FIGURE 9.9
Example of the Likert Scale

	Strongly agree	Agree	Neither agree or disagree	Disagree	Strongly disagree
1. Store X is among the most attractive stores	(+2)	(+1)	(0)	(−1)	(−2)
2. There is little choice offered to the consumer at Store X	(−2)	(−1)	(0)	(+1)	(+2)
3. Salesclerks are not very co-operative at Store X	(−2)	(−1)	(0)	(+1)	(+2)
4. Store X is very conveniently located	(+2)	(+1)	(0)	(−1)	(−2)

The formation of the actual questions to be used in a questionnaire involving a Likert scale is technically a very structured process. Many variations of the questions are postulated, and scores from all of the questions are averaged. The individual questions are then examined to see which discriminated best between those respondents who tended to score high and those who tended to score low on the questions. Only those questions shown to be good discriminators are included in the final questionnaire. Questions are also checked to see if they show a good balance or distribution over the points on the scale.

Although the construction of Likert scales is carefully defined from a technical standpoint, from a practical standpoint virtually any scale that features response choices ranging from *agree* to *disagree* will often be called a Likert scale. Furthermore, scales with greater or fewer than five response choices are often seen and they, too, are usually referred to as Likert scales.

Main Types of Ratio Scales

Some scales are often assumed to yield ratio-scaled data, which are sometimes required by marketing researchers. Attribute importance weights is a case in point. In such cases, the researcher might ask the respondent to provide a judgment implying the ratio of the two stimuli in terms of the relevant characteristic. For example, a respondent might be asked to report how much more expensive Brand A is in comparison with Brand B. If the respondent says 2, for instance, one can deduce $A = 2B$ (or $A/B = 2$). This method is known as *fractionation*. Other more frequently used alternatives are the error choice scale and the constant sum scale.

Error Choice Scale

This scale can be used to detect respondents' attitudes in a slightly more indirect way. In this scale a respondent is given a question and is then asked to pick from a series of answers. The trick is that, in most cases, the respondent will have very little factual information. In other words, the choice will be primarily a function of the respondent's attitude toward the situation and only secondarily a function of true knowledge of the situation. In the following example,

Q. Sear's average net profit margin on sales is

A. 4% 8% 12% 16% 20% 24% 28% 32% 36% 40%

the correct answer is 4%, with the magnitude of the miss being indicative of the strength of the respondents' anti-business feelings.

Constant Sum Scale

In the constant sum technique, a respondent is asked to allocate 100 points (or any other convenient number of points) among the different stimuli to be scaled, to reflect his or her opinion or preferences. For example, a respondent might be asked to allocate 100 points among five attributes for an orange juice, to reflect the importance given to the five attributes when selecting a brand. Note that the allocation of 0 points to an attribute has a unique meaning—no importance whatsoever. The advantage of this method is that it can express a variety of opinion structures. In the preceding example, the three types of answers shown in Table 9.4 lead to different interpretations of the importance weights.

TABLE 9.4
Example of the Constant Sum Scale

Attributes	Attributes Equally Important	Equal-appearing Intervals	One Overriding Attribute
Structure	20	8	0
Thickness	20	14	0
Price	20	20	25
Colour	20	26	0
Natural	20	32	75

■ Validity and Reliability of Measurements

Definitions

At the beginning of this chapter it was stated that researchers try to find good measurement rules that best represent some real-world phenomenon. After having discussed the concepts of measurement and scaling, it might be worthwhile to turn back to the question of what is a "good" scale. Good measurement is a process that yields valid and reliable measures. A scale is said to be valid to the extent that it actually represents what it is supposed to measure. Because scales are artificial constructions, they are often imperfect instruments that include systematic and variable errors. Although some researchers include both types of error in validity,[12] others find it convenient to limit the term *validity* to the degree of systematic error in a measurement. This is the definition that will be used in this text. *Reliability* will refer to the amount of variable errors in a measurement. Consequently, validity will be defined as the extent to which a measurement is free from systematic error; reliability will be defined as the extent to which it is free from variable errors.

Following these definitions, a specific measurement can independently be more or less valid and more or less reliable,[13] as is shown in the four parts of Figure 9.10.

Reliable measurements tend to yield very similar, peakedly distributed values over consecutive measurements of the same concept. Unreliable measurements are likely to be widely dispersed around their mean. With a valid scale, the mean scores over a large number of repeat measures of the same concept will be the true value. With an invalid scale, this mean value will depart more or less from the true value being measured.[14]

Reliability

Among the two broad types of error that affect measurements, reliability errors usually can best be identified and estimated. Estimating reliability can be done in a number of ways that are not mutually exclusive, but that tend to capture various sources of variable errors:[15]

1. *Test-Retest Reliability*: The same measure is applied twice (or several times) on the same observations.

2. *Split Sample Reliability*: A sample is randomly divided into two equal subsamples, and the researcher checks that the variations in each item of interest lies within the range of sampling error.

3. *Alternative-forms Reliability*: Two similar measuring instruments are applied to the same observations to assess whether similar results are obtained.

4. *Interval-comparison Reliability*: The responses to the various items of a multi-item scale are compared.

FIGURE 9.10
Validity and Reliability of Measurements

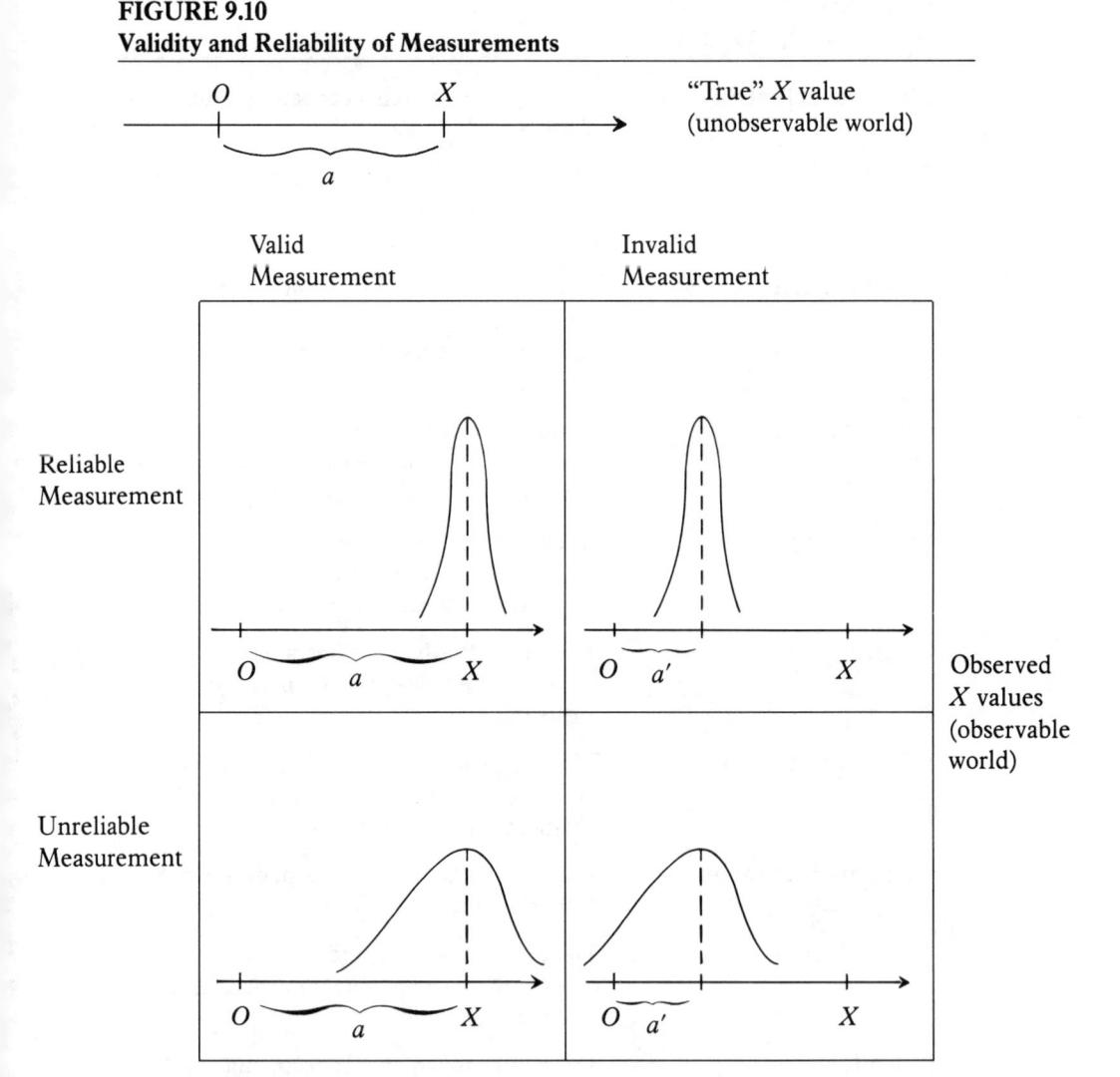

5. *Inter-rater Reliability*: The scores assigned to the same objects/people/ states/events by two or several judges are compared.

Validity

Validity is concerned with the presence of any systematic error in a measurement. There are several types of validity that researchers might want to assess. A list of the most current types of validity assessment is provided in Figure 9.11.[16]

   The field of validity and reliability measurement is well developed and much has been written about it. A more detailed analysis of these concepts is beyond the scope of this textbook, and the interested reader should consult more specialized books.[17]

FIGURE 9.11
Assessing Concept Validity

1. Observational validity	The degree to which a concept is reducible to observations
2. Content validity	The degree to which an operationalization represents the concept about which generalizations are to be made
3. Criterion-related validity	The degree to which the concept under consideration enables one to predict the value of some other concept that constitutes the criterion
• Predictive validity	A subtype of criterion-related validity in which the criterion measured is separated in time from the predictor concept
• Concurrent validity	A subtype of criterion-related validity in which the criterion and the predictor concepts are measured at the same time
4. Construct validity	The extent to which an operationalization measures the concept that it purports to measure
• Convergent validity	The degree to which two attempts to measure the same concept through maximally different methods are convergent
• Discriminant validity	The extent to which a concept differs from other concepts
• Nomological validity	The extent to which predictions based on the concept that an instrument purports to measure are confirmed
5. Systemic validity	The degree to which a concept enables the integration of previously unconnected concepts and/or the generation of a new conceptual system
6. Semantic validity	The degree to which a concept has a uniform semantic usage
7. Control validity	The degree to which a concept is manipulable and capable of influencing other variables of influence

Source: Gerald Zaltman, Christian Pinson, and Reinhard Angelmar, *Metatheory in Consumer Research*. New York: Holt, Rinehart & Winston, 1973, p. 104.

■ Summary

Measurement and scaling are two crucial marketing research activities. Measuring has been defined as assigning numerals to characteristics of objects/people/states/events, according to pre-specified rules. The rationale for scaling has been described as the translation of some real-world phenomenon into the convenient world of numerals and numbers. The measurement process includes two definitional stages: the conceptual (abstract) definition of the concept to be measured and the operational definition (what the researcher needs to observe to obtain the numerical value or the measure). The measurement process is not completely specified until four other aspects are also defined: the measurement setting, the measuring instrument, the response, and the recording processes.

The different levels of scale quality have been defined. Nominal scales involve the use of numerals for identification purpose only. Ordinal scales give only rank-order information. Interval scales come closer to the common understanding that most people have of a scale. In interval scales, the scale origin is arbitrarily defined, while in ratio scales the zero is unique and means the complete absence of the characteristic under investigation.

The main types of scales used in marketing research were briefly described, including the main ordinal scales, ordered categories and strict rank orders. Among the major interval scales, the rating scales, the semantic differential, the Stapel scale, and the Likert scale were discussed. Fractionation and the error choice and constant sum scales were described. Finally, the concept of measurement validity and reliability were briefly discussed.

For Discussion

1. Compare measurement in the social sciences (for instance, attitude measurement) and in the physical sciences (for instance, the measurement of weight or length). Does the measurement process outlined in this text also apply to physical sciences measurement? Be as precise as possible.

2. Contrast the conceptual and the operational definitions in concept measurement. Apply the two definitions to the measurement of the concept of social class.

3. Contrast perceptual and preference scaling.

4. Define and contrast nominal, ordinal, interval, and ratio scales. Give examples of each type, other than those provided in the text.

5. Using examples of ordinal data, show how misleading conclusions could be drawn by assuming interval properties.

6. Using examples of interval scales, show how misleading conclusions could be drawn by assuming ratio properties.

7. Devise four scales by which respondent's income would be measured on
   a) an ordered category scale
   b) a strict rank-order scale
   c) an equal-appearing interval ordered category scale
   d) a ratio scale

   Which of the above scales contains the most information?

8. What are a researcher's main options when deciding to use rating scales? Provide guidelines that would help a researcher to choose among these options.

9. Compare the semantic differential and the Stapel scales.

10. Define and discuss the concepts of scale validity and reliability. Give examples.

Problems

1. As a marketing research assistant, you are requested to measure consumers' attitudes toward fish products in a given market segment. Devise a measuring instrument based on the semantic differential scale, on the Likert scale, and on the Stapel scale.

   Apply each scale to three small groups of consumers coming from the same market segment (defined in terms of age, gender, geographical location, social class). Compare the results. What can you say about each scale validity?

2. The marketing researcher of a manufacturer of pocket radios (Brand x) has investigated the consumer choice process in a specific market segment. She has found that the typical buyer in this segment used the following criteria in the decision process: number of options, weight, warranty, and design. She also found that the importance attached to these criteria are, respectively, 7, 5, 5, and 2. Brand x, as well as the two leading competing brands (A and B) are evaluated by the typical consumer of the market segment as follows:

Brand	Number of Options	Weight	Warranty	Design
X	7	4	2	2
A	5	6	3	3
B	4	4	4	4

a) What conclusions can the researcher draw about consumers' preferences in this market segment?

b) What do you think should be done? Why? How?

3. **Mini-case: The People's Savings Bank**

   Mario Diluca has just been promoted to assistant manager of a branch of the People's Savings Bank (PSB). Diluca has noticed that the branch has been losing customers steadily to neighbouring banks and to other PSB branches in the city. He suspects that the changes are caused by poor service. This is one area that has been sadly neglected by the present manager who, being near retirement age, is content to leave the situation to his successor.

Question

Design a Likert scale attitudinal test to measure service at the People's Savings Bank. Your test should cover such aspects as service, location, hours, interest rates, and so on.

Endnotes

1. S. Stevens, "Mathematics, Measurement, and Psychophysics," in S. Stevens, ed., *Handbook of Experimental Psychology*. New York: Wiley, 1951, p. 1.
2. Fred N. Kerlinger, *Foundations of Behavioral Research*. 2nd ed. New York: Holt, Rinehart, and Winston, 1973, pp. 427–29.
3. Anatol Rapoport, *Operational Philosophy*. San Francisco: International Society for General Semantics, 1953, p. 29.
4. See, for example, Sidney Siegel, *Non-parametric Statistics for the Behavioural Sciences*. New York: McGraw-Hill, 1956.
5. John R. Dickinson, "Order Related Biases in Perception Ratings," *Marketing*, 2. Ed. Robert G. Wyckham. Administrative Sciences Association of Canada (ASAC), pp. 65–72.
6. For an extensive treatment, see J. Guilford, *Fundamental Studies in Psychology and Education*. 3rd ed. New York: McGraw-Hill, 1956.
7. C. Osgood, G. Suci, and P. Tannenbaum, *The Measurement of Meaning*. Urbana, IL: University of Illinois Press, 1957.
8. Cataldo Zuccaro and Thomas Muller, "A Method for Validating Tailormade Semantic Differential," *Marketing*, 3. Ed. Michel Laroche. ASAC, 1982, pp. 332–38.
9. J. Stapel, "Predictive Attitudes," in L. Adler and J. Crespi, *Attitude Research on the Rocks*. Chicago: American Marketing Association, 1968, pp. 96–115.
10. D.I. Hawkins, G. Albaum, and R. Best, "Stapel Scale or Semantic Differential in Marketing Research?" *Journal of Marketing Research*, (August 1974), pp. 318–22.
11. Rensis Likert, "A Technique for the Measurement of Attitudes." *Archives of Psychology*, no. 140, (1932).
12. See Kerlinger, *Foundations of Behavioral Research*.
13. Donald S. Tull and D.I. Hawkins, *Marketing Research, Measurement and Method*. 3rd edition. New York: MacMillan, 1984.
14. Judith Marshall, "An Assessment of the Reliability and Validity of Key Informant Data from Industrial Sales Forces Organization," *Marketing*, 6. Ed. Jean-Charles Chebat. ASAC, 1985, pp. 232–42.
15. Tull and Hawkins, *Marketing Research, Measurement*, p. 231.
16. Gerald Zaltman, Christian Pinson, and Reinhard Angelmar, *Metatheory in Consumer Research*. New York: Holt, Rinehart and Winston, 1973, p. 104.
17. See for instance, Kerlinger, *Foundations of Behavioral Research*.

SAMPLING

To this point we have stressed the qualitative aspects of the marketing research process, not the quantitative. This has been done deliberately, to introduce the general aspects of marketing research without bogging you down in a maze of formulas and complex mathematical symbols. However, some basic understanding of statistics is necessary to the marketing research process. This understanding need not be extensive, because in preparing this text we have ensured that it will be comprehensible to the reader with only a minimal amount of statistical training. We are not trying to turn you into an expert in multivariate techniques—these can be covered in a more advanced course. In this chapter, sampling concepts are discussed.

◼ Basic Sampling Concepts

Each of us is constantly engaged in sampling. We take a few sips of a certain brand of coffee and perhaps become brand-loyal at that moment. We go for our first train ride, the train breaks down, and we decide at that point never again to travel on that railway. We form our impressions of another country from contact with only a very few people from that country. In each case we are sampling although our sampling methodology is hardly scientific and could lead us to incorrect conclusions.

A **sample** is a collection of observations from a parent population or universe. In the case of information, a sample is a portion of the total amount of information that can conceivably be gathered. The *universe* or *population* is the entire collection of items that the researcher wants to study, from which he or she plans to draw conclusions. If every item in a universe is studied, we have a **census**. With large populations, it is usually much too expensive and time-consuming to conduct a census (Statistics Canada's *Census of Population* being a notable exception); such cases necessitate the use of samples, by which certain items from the parent population are studied.

Two kinds of populations exist: finite and infinite. A *finite population* is one containing a finite or fixed number of elements. Examples include the number of *Corvettes* manufactured by General Motors in a week's production, the number of full-time students currently enrolled in Utopia University, and the number of seats in a football stadium.

Finite populations have definable limits; *infinite populations* are without measurable limits of any type and are therefore indeterminate. The number of black-flies in June and the number of illegal immigrants who have come to Canada within the past twenty-five years are examples of infinite populations: they cannot be measured with any degree of precision. Whereas a census might be impractical with a finite population, it would be impossible with an infinite one.

It is often necessary in marketing research studies to make accurate predictions on the basis of samples selected from both finite and infinite populations. Making generalizations about the characteristics of a large population on the basis of a small sample creates many problems. For instance, if we want to forecast accurately the average amount of money that people spend on their summer vacations, we would not use for our sample only amounts spent by university students in Europe. However, it is difficult to determine just *which* vacationers should be included in our sample and *how many* of them should be surveyed.

■ Reasons for Sampling

Since a sample is only a part of a whole, it is not always a reliable indication of the characteristics of the population from which it is drawn. Many researchers have found to their dismay that inferences drawn from samples can be incorrect. There is no certainty that the characteristics of a sample will be the same as those of the universe from which the sample is drawn. Why, then, are samples so widely used by marketing researchers?

The basic idea behind the use of sampling methodology is that a sample can be more quickly, easily, and cheaply secured than a census of every item in a population. This premise is based on the assumption that sample characteristics will accurately represent universe characteristics. If a sample is to represent its population accurately, it must be large enough and must be taken in such a manner that it does not overrepresent some elements in the population while underestimating others.

There are at least six good reasons why a researcher would prefer to use a sample instead of a census: financial constraints, time constraints, universe size, the destructive nature of sampling, the sufficiency of an approximation, and accuracy.

Financial Constraints

Seldom, if ever, in the case of survey research does the research professional have the funds available to do everything he or she would like to do in a given project or to survey each item in the population. Limited funds mean that only a certain number of people can be employed for a limited time period to collect the required information, whether the research is conducted by telephone survey, personal interview, observation, or mail questionnaire. Financial constraints also help to determine sample size by placing a limit on the number of consumers to be surveyed or observations made. Although a nationwide census of all consumers might be desirable in certain cases, financial constraints might limit the geographical size of the area that can be covered.

Time Constraints

Information on which to base marketing decisions is usually needed immediately. Gathering information from the entire population can be an enormously time-consuming process, one that might be totally impractical when market information is needed as soon as possible. For example, in the 1981 *Census of Population*, there was a three-year time lag between the beginning of data collection and the publication of the full results. Seldom can a private organization afford to spend three years conducting a full census in a large universe. Even Statistics Canada must resort to sampling at periodic intervals in order to have current population statistics.

Universe Size

Where the researcher is faced with the task of surveying a large universe, sampling is usually more feasible than taking a complete census. A complete census of the universe might be impossible even when time and money are not the most important considerations. At any given point, some people are out of the country; others are institutionalized in jails or hospitals; still others, such as some miners, sailors, and hunters, are inaccessible. Generally speaking, the larger the population, the greater the likelihood of having to resort to sampling. Where the population is relatively small—for example, manufacturers of steel—a complete census becomes practical. However, with large populations, such as the total number of ultimate consumers of *Coca-Cola*, the researcher is more likely to sample.

Destructive Nature of Sampling

Especially in many quality-control situations—examples would be testing the useful life of light bulbs and fuses, tensile strength of steel bars, resistance to heat of materials—the sampling process is of a destructive nature. Naturally, taking a census is out of the question. What good is it for the sales manager to receive accurate information about the tensile strength of all steel bars produced last week? Even if the results show a very high quality, all of the bars have been tested to the extent that none are left to fill orders from customers. Performing functional tests on every item produced is impossible if it destroys the item. In other cases, such as testing light bulbs to see if they work, although a census might be possible, it is hardly practical.

Similarly, consumers who are interviewed about a problem with a specific brand might be affected by the questioning and change their attitudes as a result.

Thus, a complete census could produce findings that are no longer accurate, since the attitudes of the total population have shifted as a result of the research.

Sufficiency of an Approximation

Quite often an exact description of a characteristic or an exact value of a population parameter is not really necessary for the researcher to make a decision. Sample information will suffice and no census need be taken. It is not necessary for an instructor to know exactly how many students will take a certain course next year in order to decide how many textbooks to order. If too many books are ordered, the book store can return part of the order to the publisher at no cost. Nor is it necessary to know exactly how many loaves of bread are consumed per week to decide what the production level will be, although having fairly precise knowledge might well be desirable.

Accuracy

It is possible for sample results to be more accurate than the results obtained from a census: in a census, there is a greater likelihood of computational errors in the handling and processing of the much greater volume of data obtained. For example, Statistics Canada conducts a sample survey to check the accuracy of its own census. The smaller number of people required to collect sample data can be rigorously trained in the necessary techniques, and survey instruments can be much more complex in a sample than in a census. Finally, statistical controls for achieving greater accuracy are more useful and efficient when the amount of data is small.

◼ Sampling Methodology

Before sampling can commence, the researcher must carefully review the objectives of the study. Then the determination of the sample to be drawn is the result of a five-step process, as illustrated in Figure 10.1: defining the (1) ideal and (2) operational universes, and selecting the (3) sampling frame, (4) sampling method, and (5) sample size.

Ideal Universe

The ideal universe is the set of all sampling units having the information sought by the researcher. For example, if the objective of the survey is to gather the opinions of youths aged eleven to seventeen about designer jeans, the ideal universe would consist of all Canadians aged eleven to seventeen, the number of which can be estimated by using Statistics Canada's census figures or updates of these figures. Of course, locating all of these individuals can be very difficult and/or extremely costly; for example, it would not be practical or economical to send interviewers to very remote areas or even to use telephone or mail surveys to reach individuals in these areas.

FIGURE 10.1
Steps to be Completed to Obtain a Sample

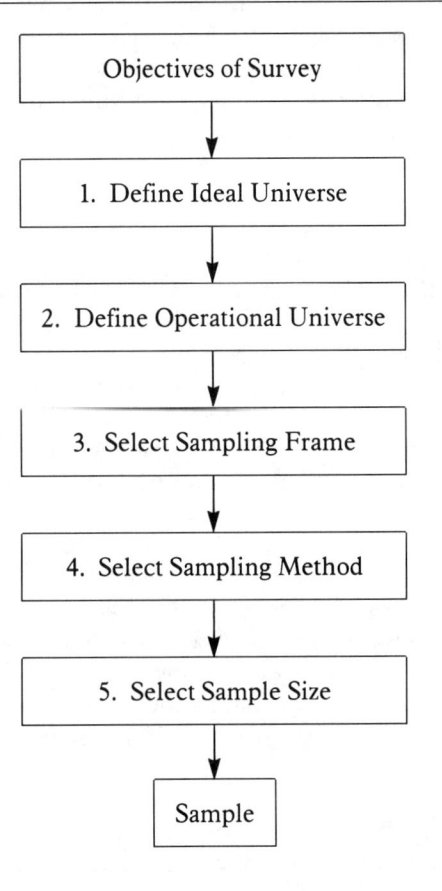

Operational Universe

Because of considerations of cost, time, and availability constraints, an operational universe would have to be defined. The operational universe is the set of all sampling units belonging to the ideal universe that can be reached within specific time and budget constraints. Ideally, the operational universe should be identical to the ideal universe. In practice, this is not the case, and the researcher will have to make some compromises in order to meet budget and time constraints. For example, the designer jeans manufacturer might define the operational universe as Canadians aged eleven to seventeen who, at the time of the survey, live in the twenty-four Canadian census metropolitan areas (CMAs) and who can be reached by telephone.

A comparison of these first two steps allows researchers to determine the types of compromises that were made and whether any systematic bias was possibly introduced into the operational universe. In the previous example, only teen-agers living in the twenty-four largest metropolitan areas (about 56% of the

Canadian population) are included in this definition. Teenagers living outside the CMAs, in smaller cities or towns, or in rural areas, are excluded. In addition, the use of telephone contact might slightly bias the universe: if several telephone numbers reach the same teenager, if the family does not have a telephone because it is too poor, if a telephone number is unlisted, or if a family has just moved and their new telephone number is not in the most recent directory. These types of bias can then be assessed and evaluated. If they are found unacceptable, a new operational universe might have to be defined.

Sampling Frame

The sampling frame is a subset of all acceptable sampling units—units belonging to the operational universe from which the sample will be taken. In the previous example, the sampling frame would be the list of all households in the telephone directories of the CMAs, excluding firms, organizations, and public administrations. A more refined sampling frame would consist of constructing a list of, for example, 100 000 names of teenagers who have agreed to participate in one or two surveys during the next year. This sampling frame would then be used a number of times for several surveys. This method is used by both A.C. Nielsen of Canada and the Bureau of Broadcast Measurement for their television and radio surveys (more details are provided in Chapter 15, "Advertising Research in Canada").

As for the operational universe, the researcher must evaluate the quality of the sampling frame in terms of completeness and accuracy. For example, if the telephone directory is to be used, the researcher should look at such factors as when the directory was last updated and how many families might have moved out of the CMA and how many might have moved in since then. If significant, such factors could further bias the sample and the researcher might have to use a different sampling frame.

Sampling Method

The next step is to determine the sampling method, the specific procedure that will be used to draw the sample from the sampling frame. The sampling method to be used depends on the objective of the study, the quality and cost of the sampling frame, and the cost of collecting information from the sampling units. There are two types of sampling methods: probability and non-probability sampling. In a probability sample, every unit has a known chance of being selected, and the selection is done randomly until the required number of units has been drawn. The simple random sampling method is one example of probability sampling. This method allows the researcher to use statistical techniques to estimate a population parameter and confidence intervals. However, a sampling frame might not be available or suitable for some probability sampling and the researcher might have to resort to non-probability sampling methods. For example, it might be difficult or expensive to reach fishermen by standard methods, so a researcher might decide to interview customers as they enter a store selling fishing equipment. Also, for exploratory research, probability sampling is not necessary since only quantitative information is needed. Sampling methods are fully described later in this chapter.

Sample Size

The next step is to determine the actual size of the sample to be drawn from the sampling frame, using the selected sampling method. The sample size basically depends on the research budget, the desired precision of the results, and the expected rate of non-response. Often, the size of the sample is constrained by the budget allocated to the research project, and therefore the precision is determined by it and by the rate of non-response. Second, the precision of the results increases with the sample size, ignoring the non-response rate for the time being. Thus, if a higher level of precision is needed and/or if a more complex sampling method is used, the sample size will have to be higher. Finally, the original size will have to be adjusted to take into account the expected rate of non-response. For example, if the researcher needs 200 completed questionnaires to achieve a certain precision level, and if the expected rate of non-response by mail is 80%, then 1000 questionnaires will have to be sent out.

After this overview of sampling methodology, we will now examine in more detail the major issues and methods involved in sampling.

■ Sampling Problems

Although sampling has a number of clear advantages over census taking, sampling does present some problems. Three principal problem areas can be identified: the skilled personnel required for administering surveys and interpreting sample data, sampling error, and bias. Certainly researchers must contend with many other problems involved in sampling, but careful attention to each of these will eliminate many potential problems.

Skilled Personnel

For the decision maker to have any faith in sample data, a great deal of the study's time and expense must usually be spent on sampling methodology. Therefore, personnel highly skilled in administering surveys and interpreting sample data must be employed throughout this phase of the research project. People possessing these skills are often difficult to find and expensive to hire. However, if the administering of surveys and interpreting of sample data are left to people with inadequate skills, the reported results might be confusing and misleading.

Sampling Error

No sample is guaranteed to be exactly representative of the universe from which it was drawn. Generally, the larger the sample, the smaller the likelihood that it will differ from the universe but differences, known as **sampling errors**, are sometimes found. A sampling error is the difference between characteristics of the sample and those of the population from which the sample was drawn. Sampling error can occur purely by chance and can be particularly difficult to detect when the characteristics of the total population are unknown in the first place. For example, when political pollsters predict that a candidate will win with 55% of the vote, adding that this prediction is accurate within two percentage points in either direction, nineteen times out of twenty they will be right; the one chance in twenty that they will not be right is caused by sampling error.

Bias

When an error is made in the selection or measurement of respondents, bias is the result. Should the sampling methodology cause one population element to have a systematically higher or lower probability of being selected than other elements in that population, the researcher has induced bias. Bias results from such systematic variance, which does not happen with an accurate sample.

Consider the following case. A sample survey was conducted to find out the average age of students at Utopia University. If the sample had been drawn from students attending evening classes, would bias result? Indeed it would: evening students tend to be older than those attending day classes, so they would not be representative of the full student body.

The most famous example of sample bias (which, incidently, does not have a Canadian equivalent!) occurred in the 1936 U.S. presidential election. In that year the now-extinct *Literary Digest*, a relatively highbrow journal, predicted that Republican candidate Alf Landon would win over Democrat Franklin D. Roosevelt—but Roosevelt won. Sampling error had a negligible impact in this case, since approximately two million voters participated in this sample. What happened?

The *Literary Digest* made the mistake of drawing its sample primarily from the telephone directory. During the height of the depression of the 1930s, many voters could not afford to have a home telephone, and most people in this position were Democrats. Therefore, the sample was biassed toward the more affluent members of society—those who were most likely to vote Republican. Because of bias in sample selection, a tremendous error in forecasting the winner of the 1936 election was made—an error of such magnitude that it is still regularly reported in almost all elementary statistics books.

■ Selecting the Sampling Method

According to the method used to select them, samples can be divided into the two broad categories of probability and non-probability samples. In the case of probability sampling, all items in the universe have known and equal chances, or probabilities, of being selected. With non-probability sampling, sometimes referred to as researcher-controlled sampling, all items in the universe do *not* have known and equal chances of being selected. Figure 10.2 classifies these two basic types of samples and their variations. Let us examine each in greater detail.

Probability Sampling

In probability sampling, also referred to as random sampling, every elementary unit of population has some known element of chance of being selected in the

FIGURE 10.2
Sample Design Classifications

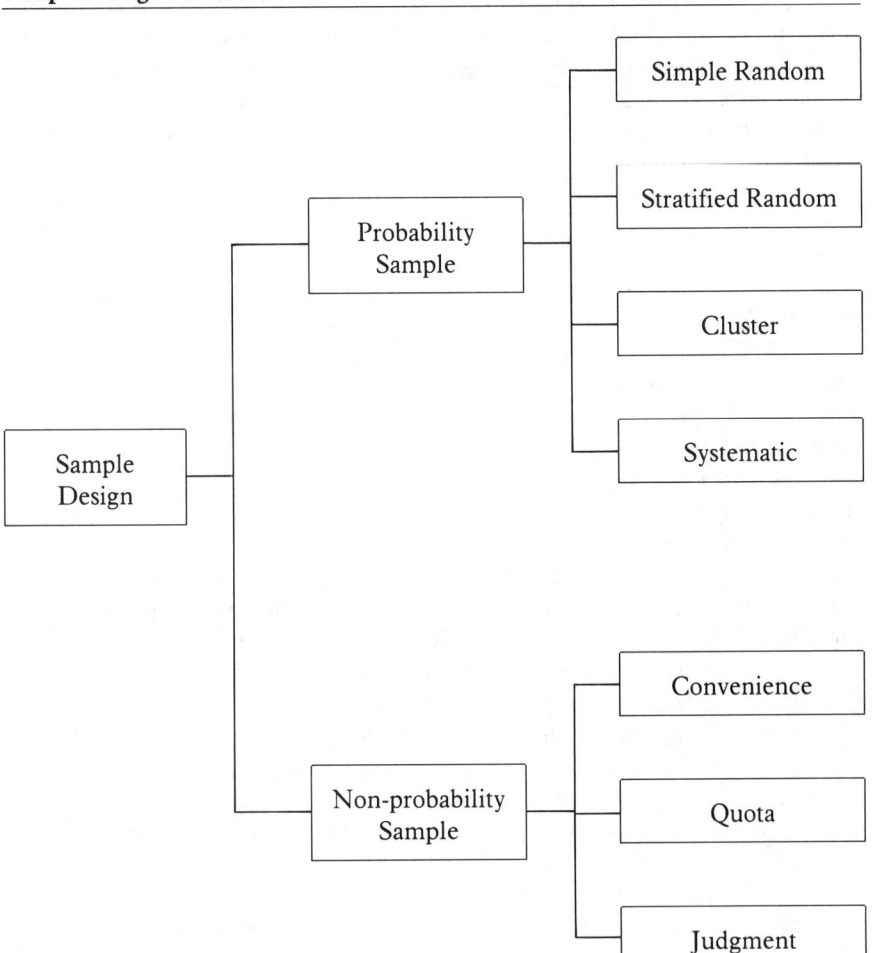

sample. The selection of units is determined purely by chance, using some random device such as a table of random numbers. On this basis, therefore, we could expect different samples to be selected if the procedure were repeated a number of times. There are four main types of probability samples: simple random, stratified random, cluster, and systematic. Although this is not an exhaustive listing of the types of probability samples, these are the four main ones used by researchers.

Simple Random Sampling
The easiest probability sampling concept to grasp is that of simple random sampling. Basically, in a simple random sampling scheme, all units of the population being surveyed have equal probabilities of being selected. An example of the most basic form of a simple random sample would be a lottery draw where

ten thousand tickets valued at one dollar each have been sold to ten thousand different individuals, who have written their names and addresses on the ticket stubs. The ticket stubs are placed in a drum and thoroughly mixed. A blindfolded person then draws ten tickets from the drum and the winners each receive a $1000 prize. In this simple random sample, all ten thousand entrants had known and equal probabilities of being selected—one in one thousand.

Although drawing names from a drum or numbers from a hat constitutes an acceptable and relatively simple method of taking a simple random sample, perhaps the easiest way of taking such a sample is by using a table of random numbers. Tables of random numbers, often known as tables of random digits, consist of rows and columns in which the decimal digits zero through nine appear. These tables of random numbers are generated by a computer so that each decimal digit has the same probability of being selected as all of the others.

Table 10.1 is an example of a partial table of random numbers; a more extensive table of random numbers is provided in Appendix 3, Exhibit E. Although Table 10.1 comprises four-digit random numbers, any combination can be used and the gaps need not appear between the columns, as they do here. Any series of numbers read across, up, or down the table is considered to be random. The only effective restraint is the size of the population being surveyed, which dictates how many digits should be used. A sufficient number of digits must always be selected so that the highest numbered item in the population can be included.

To illustrate the use of such tables, let us assume that a bank has 9999 depositors. The marketing researcher is planning a survey of 100 of the bank's customers to see what they think of the bank's service. A random sample is to be drawn, using a table of random numbers similar to Table 10.1. The researcher could arbitrarily select the numbers in columns 2, 4, 6, and 8, which would give the required random sample of 100. Thus, the first item to be surveyed would be account number 9739, the second would be account number 3769, and so on. If the same number is drawn twice, another number from the table is used to replace the duplicate.

What if the bank had between 10 000 and 100 000 depositors? In this case, the researcher could simply add the last digit of each number in columns 1, 3, 5 and 7 in the table of random numbers, so that the first number selected would have been account number 29 739, the second account number 3769, and so forth. Similar adjustments could be made for a larger or smaller universe.

For example, let us assume that the bank has 6000 depositors instead of 9999. The researcher still selects four-digit numbers, but some of these numbers are greater than 6000; e.g. 9739. The simplest way to deal with this problem is to discard numbers greater than 6000, and to continue drawing four-digit numbers until the sample size of 100 numbers between 0 and 6000 has been reached. An alternative way to deal with this problem is to subtract 6000 from numbers that exceed it; for example, the researcher drawing 9739 would replace that with 3739.

Stratified Random Sampling
Seldom is the researcher faced with a homogeneous population from which to sample; populations in most consumer surveys tend to be heterogeneous. When the population can be divided into distinguishable strata that differ significantly

TABLE 10.1
Partial Table of Random Numbers

Rows	1	2	3	4	5	6	7	8	9	10
					Columns					
	5852	9739	1457	8999	2789	9068	9829	1336	3148	7875
	0440	3769	7864	4029	4494	9829	1339	4910	1303	9161
1	0820	4641	2375	2542	4093	5364	1145	2848	2792	0431
	7114	2842	8554	6881	6377	9427	8216	1193	8042	8449
	6558	9301	9096	0577	8520	5923	4717	0188	8545	8745
	0345	9937	5569	0279	8951	6183	7787	7808	5149	2185
	7430	2074	9427	8422	4082	5629	2971	9456	0649	7981
2	8030	7345	3389	4739	5911	1022	9189	2565	1982	8577
	6272	6718	3849	4715	3156	2823	4174	8733	5600	7702
	4894	9847	5611	4763	8755	3388	5114	3274	6681	3657
	2676	5984	6806	2692	4012	0934	2436	0869	9557	2490
	9305	2074	9378	7670	8284	7431	7361	2912	2251	7395
3	5138	2461	7213	1905	7775	9881	8782	6272	0632	4418
	2452	4200	8674	9202	0812	3986	1143	7343	2264	9072
	8882	3033	8746	7390	8609	1144	2531	6944	8869	1570
	1087	9336	8020	9166	4472	8293	2904	7949	3165	7400
	5666	2841	8134	9588	2915	4116	2802	6917	3993	8764
4	9790	2228	9702	1690	7170	7511	1937	0723	4505	7155
	3250	8860	3294	2684	6572	3415	5750	8726	2647	6596
	5450	3922	0950	0890	6434	2306	2781	1066	3681	2404
	5765	0765	7311	5270	5910	7009	0240	7435	4568	6484
	8408	1939	0599	5347	2160	7376	4696	6969	0787	3838
5	8460	7658	6906	9177	1492	4680	3719	3456	8681	6736
	4198	7244	3849	4819	1008	6781	3388	5253	7041	6712
	9872	4441	6712	9614	2736	5533	9062	2534	0855	7946

from other strata but have considerable internal homogeneity, stratified sampling might give more precise results than simple random sampling. In stratified random sampling, the population is divided into subgroups and a simple random sample is taken from each subgroup, using the procedure detailed for simple random sampling.

Let us examine an oversimplified example. A researcher needs to estimate the average mass of six people gathered in a room. The masses of the six, individually, are 55 kg, 54 kg, 50 kg, 72 kg, 79 kg, and 86 kg. However, an average of the six will not be a very meaningful figure if the first three people are females and the second three are males. By dividing the sample into two strata, male and female, a much more significant figure is obtained for the average mass of each group—53 kg and 79 kg—showing the substantial difference between the groups.

The use of stratified random sampling is desirable from a marketing point of view when we want to engage in market segmentation[1] to develop different products and promotional appeals for different market segments. In such cases it is imperative to have accurate data on identifiable and measurable segments of the market, rather than aggregate population statistics.

Two techniques commonly used for stratifying consumer populations are classifying consumers by age and gender and classifying them by social and economic criteria. Classifying consumers by age and gender is a relatively simple stratification technique, assuming that there are no problems in obtaining these basic demographic data. This procedure can be particularly valid if the researcher, for example, wants to find out what teenage girls think about a new cosmetic product. Drawing a stratified random sample from different social or economic classes is more difficult when sampling is based on income, residence, car-ownership, marital status, or membership in social organizations. For example, in recent years marital status has been a constantly changing phenomenon. There are two conditions under which stratified sampling is not possible:

- There might not be an available frame or list of items in the universe from which the sample might be drawn. For example, if we wanted to interview a sample of farmers in a particular province, it might not be available.

- Even with a frame available, if the units in the universe are widely scattered it might be cheaper to use a large sample of units that lie close to one another than to use a small sample of widely scattered units. For example, it might be cheaper to interview fifty farmers in one county than thirty farmers in thirty different counties.[2]

In such cases the researcher turns to cluster sampling.

Cluster Sampling

Cluster sampling, which involves groups of sample items chosen at random, is best used when stratified sampling is not possible or is too expensive. Cluster sampling is often referred to as a multistage sampling technique; the random selection of primary sampling units can be either a two-stage or a three-stage exercise. For example, the selection of census tracts would be a first stage, the selection of city blocks within the census tract would be a second, and the selection of individual families would be a third. As in this example, much cluster sampling is area sampling, where each cluster comes from a different or separate geographic area. Ideally, each cluster should be selected in such a way that every cluster is heterogeneous, although in practice this often is not possible.

Figure 10.3 illustrates how a two-stage area cluster sample, using census tracts and city blocks, could be taken. Study this simplified example carefully. Can you see how cluster sampling would be easier and cheaper than random sampling? What would be the next step if three-stage sampling were desired?

Researchers are often partial to cluster sampling because it is usually cheaper than simple random sampling from the same population. For example, a national survey using simple random sampling might require data collection from all parts of the country, at considerable expense. By using cluster sampling techniques, the

FIGURE 10.3
Illustration of a Hypothetical Two-Stage Cluster Sample
of Ten Census Tracts with Six Blocks in Each Tract

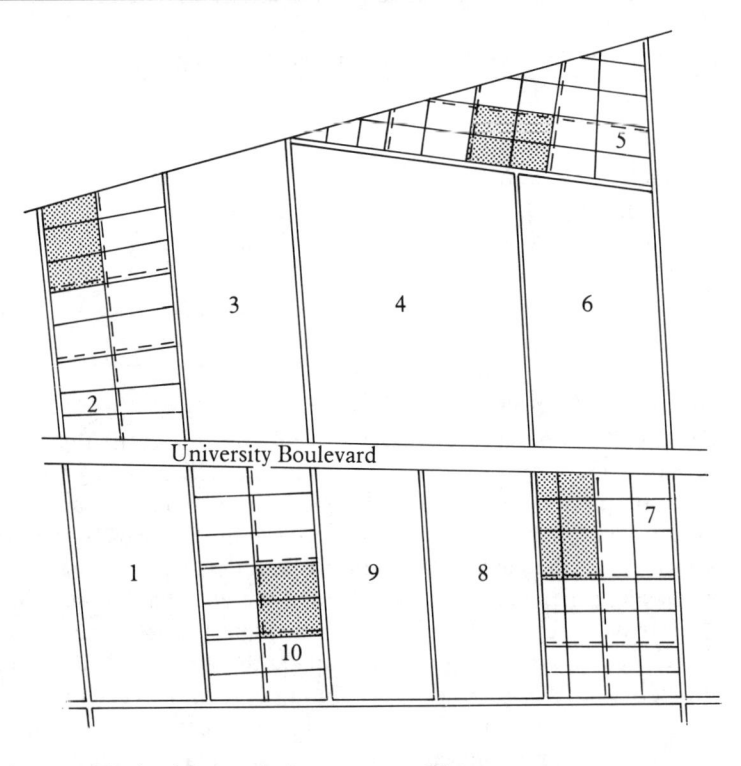

Number of primary units in the population   = 10 census tracts
Number of primary units in the sample   = 4 census tracts (shaded)
Number of items in each primary unit   = 6 blocks
Number of items sampled from each primary unit = 1 block from each tract

researcher is able to limit the travelling required for data collection to only one or
a few areas.[3]

Cluster sample estimates are usually less accurate than the same size of
estimates derived from simple random sampling. For the same budget, however, a
cluster sampling plan might yield more efficient results, because the savings on
travel expenses and time can be devoted to increasing sample size within each
cluster.[4]

In summary, two general advantages of cluster sampling are that it permits
random sampling where a sampling frame is not present and it is often much
cheaper than other probability sampling designs.

Cluster Sampling versus Stratified Sampling
It is sometimes not immediately clear exactly how cluster sampling differs from
stratified sampling, since in both cases population is divided into strata or

subgroups. Table 10.2 provides a concise comparison of these two sampling techniques.

TABLE 10.2
Comparison Between Stratified and Cluster Sampling

Population	Stratified	Cluster
Number of subgroups	Small	Large
Characteristics of subgroups:		
Size of subgroups	Large	Small
Within subgroups	Homogeneous	Heterogeneous
Between subgroups	Heterogeneous	Homogeneous
Selection of subgroups	Non-random	Random

Systematic Sampling

Systematic sampling involves the random selection of the first item and then the selection of a sample item at every nth interval. Many times, systematic sampling is the simplest as well as the most practical way to draw a sample. When used in quality control, perhaps every one-hundredth unit leaving the assembly line is subjected to a detailed quality-control inspection. A table of random numbers can be used to generate the first number and thereby identify the first sampling unit.

Systematic sampling is often utilized when the researcher is using the names listed in a large city telephone directory as the universe. The telephone directory might have 500 pages, with four columns of names on each page. Suppose that a sample of 250 people is to be drawn from this directory. The easiest way to proceed is to select a name from every other page systematically, using a table of random numbers to generate a number for the selection process. Perhaps the first number is 322; the researcher could take the twenty-second name from the third column of every other page to systematically draw a sample of 250 people. In cases where the random number is greater than the number of names on the page, the next random number could be used. Obviously, it would be quite time-consuming to manually count the twenty-two names in each third column, every other page. In this case, the simplest method is to make a ruler with a piece of cardboard and use a black marker to identify the approximate position of the first and twenty-second names on the first column. Then it is a simple matter to use this ruler to pick out all of the other telephone numbers.

Is systematic sampling as valid as simple random sampling? The answer depends on the arrangement of items from which the sample was drawn. In some cases systematic sampling is better than simple random sampling, because the sample is more evenly distributed from the full population.

The main problem in systematic sampling occurs if hidden periodicities[5] are present. Does some systematic variance occur at every interval that has been selected? In our previous example of the telephone directory, hidden periodicities would probably not have occurred. However, what if we had decided to poll systematically the residents of every twelfth house along a street? Probably no systematic variance would occur, but we might find that every twelfth house was on a corner. Houses on corner lots are usually more expensive than those in the middle of the block and usually are occupied by people with higher incomes who might hold opinions and attitudes that are different from those of their less affluent neighbours.

Non-probability Sampling

In the previous section, four main probability sampling designs were discussed: simple random, stratified random, cluster, and systematic. They are called probability samples because all items in the population have equal chances of being selected.

However, in actual practice, probability sampling is not always used. Some investigators are not very scientific in their sampling techniques. In other cases, precise accuracy in sampling might not be necessary. For example, the cost factor of test-marketing a new product on a national scale is such that most new products are test-marketed in only one or a very few cities. These cities are not selected through probability sampling techniques but rather because the researcher thinks they represent "typical" Canadian cities. Consequently, when marketers opt for full-scale national distribution based on sales results in a few test-market cities, this decision is being made on the basis of a non-probability sample. It is not that the large consumer goods manufacturers, such as Canada Packers and Heinz, are unscientific in their research methodology; it is simply that a probability sample is not practical in this instance.

Exactly what is meant by non-probability sampling? Any sampling technique in which the selection of sample items is not determined by chance, but rather by personal convenience, expert judgment, or any type of conscious researcher selection, is called non-probability sampling. Three principal types of non-probability, or non-random, sampling can be identified: convenience, judgment, and quota.

Convenience Sampling

Convenience sampling is so named because it is convenient for the researcher to select the first few sample items quickly, rather than to go through the laborious process of obtaining a probability sample. When approximations will suffice and both time and money are seriously limited, convenience samples are widely used. Selecting sample units from the population solely on the basis of personal convenience to the researcher is widely found in person-on-the-street interviews conducted by television personnel. If it is convenient to do the sampling during a lunch hour, the researcher could draw the sample from a nearby restaurant. Often pre-tests of questionnaires use convenience sampling; in these cases the researcher wants only a trial run of the questionnaire itself.

Convenience sampling is a widespread practice, one in which all of us are participants in one form or another. Since our private convenience samples usually include only our close friends, family members, and people within our social class, we are often surprised when we find that a political candidate whose views are directly opposite to ours and those of nearly all of our friends is elected by a large majority.

Although convenience sampling is not very scientific, its speed and ease ensure its long-term existence as a sampling technique. The important thing to recognize is that projections for the entire population should not be based on a convenience sample, yet it might be a perfectly valid technique in exploratory research, questionnaire pre-testing, and any other case where a representative sample is not considered necessary.

Judgment Sampling

Slightly more scientifically selected than a convenience sample, the judgment sample is determined by the researcher's idea of a representative sample. Judgment samples are selected on the basis of researcher intuition or on some other subjective basis. Therefore, sample representativeness is highly dependent on the good judgment of the researcher and possibly on a lot of luck.

As in the case of convenience samples, judgment samples can be very misleading if they are interpreted as accurate reflections of universe characteristics. Probably the most valid usage of judgment sampling is to obtain expert opinions. Thus, *The Financial Post* might select a sample of twelve of the country's most influential economists to estimate next year's rate of inflation. Certainly the judgment of these experts is much superior to a convenience sample that might arbitrarily be limited to the estimates of the first twelve people found on the street or in a neighbourhood bar. Of course, the problem with expert opinions is first determining who the experts are and then recognizing that expert opinion is not necessarily representative of the general population. Nor will the views espoused by the experts always be well received by the population. U.S. editor, writer, and television show host William F. Buckley, Jr., for example, is alleged to have said, "I'd rather be led by the first 100 people in the phone book than the entire Harvard Law School faculty."

Quota Sampling

The most sophisticated of our three non-probability sampling techniques is quota sampling. In this method, the population is divided into a number of segments and the researcher arbitrarily selects a quota of sample items from each segment or cell. Taking a quota sample is therefore a three-step operation: deciding into how many segments or cells the population will be divided, deciding what percentage of sample items should be in any one cell, and actually selecting the sample items.

Carefully examine Table 10.3, a somewhat simplified illustration of a six-cell quota sample. Here all three steps in drawing a quota sample have been followed. First, the universe was divided on the basis of age and gender, with three cells allocated to age categories and two to gender. Second, the appropriate percentages to be included in each cell (49% male and 51% female, and so forth) were determined. Third was the actual selection of sample items for each cell. For a total sample size of one hundred, accordingly, a field worker would be assigned an interview quota of twelve male subjects aged eighteen to twenty-five—hence the name quota sampling.

How does quota sampling differ from stratified random sampling? In both sampling techniques, a universe is divided up into strata or segments, but there

TABLE 10.3
Illustration of a Six-Cell Quota Sample

Gender	Age			
	18–25 %	26–49 %	50 %	Total %
Male	12	21	16	49
Female	13	21	17	51
Total	25	42	33	100

the similarity ends. In stratified random sampling a random sample is taken within each strata or cell, whereas in quota sampling the researcher arbitrarily selects items from each cell. Look again at Table 10.3; the 12% of male subjects aged eighteen to twenty-five would be chosen at random in a stratified random sample, whereas in a quota sample they would be selected arbitrarily.

Although quota sampling is the most systematic and scientific of the three non-probability sampling techniques, it does not ensure the selection of a representative sample. As with stratified random sampling, difficulty exists in determining the appropriate percentages to be assigned to each cell and in determing in which cell the sample items properly belong. For example, mistakes could be made by researchers in determining respondent age quotas in Table 10.3. Why should 25% of our sample be selected from the eighteen to twenty-five age group? However, the principal drawback of quota sampling is the arbitrary non-random selection of items in each cell by the researcher. This arbitrariness reduces the likelihood of obtaining a representative sample. Still, cost and time constraints sometimes make quota sampling an attractive alternative to stratified sampling.

Determining Sample Size

Normal Distribution and Sample Size

The statistics involved in computing the precision of an estimate (that is, the sampling error) can become quite difficult, and we intend in this text to avoid as many of those statistical complexities as possible. What you should understand is that it is possible to make highly accurate statements about an infinite population based on data collected from a small number of items (random sample) from that population or universe.

At this point we will make use of the normal curve as it relates to the calculation of the sampling error of a percentage estimate. Such an application is easy to understand and we can use it to illustrate the importance of sample size in obtaining precise estimates.

Sample size is of critical importance to the marketing researcher for several reasons. First of all, a look back at the list of factors that have a bearing on the researcher's confidence in a sample will show that only one of those factors—the sample size—is controlled by the researcher. Furthermore, since precision can be increased by increasing the sample size, sampling error can be reduced by whatever amount is desired simply by increasing the size of the sample. Finally, since it is possible to compute the required sample size for any specified level of precision, the researcher can determine the necessary sample size before embarking on a project. Doing so gives a good idea of the task and the costs that lie ahead.

The Central Limit Theorem

The crucial law of sampling statistics is embodied in what is known as the central limit theorem. This most important theorem states that for almost all populations (finite, infinite, and virtually without regard to shape of the distribution), the sampling distribution of the means observed will be approximately normal if the sample size is sufficiently large.

Increases in the precision of estimates derived from sample data can come only with comparatively large increases in sample size. Thus, if you wanted to decrease the magnitude of a given sample error by half, you would have to take a sample four times as large as your original. This relationship is seen in Table 10.4. Because of this relationship, further increases in precision can soon become cost-ineffective.

TABLE 10.4
95% Confidence Level

Size of Sample or Subsample	Approximate Plus-or-Minus Sampling Tolerance for Percentaged Survey Results At or Near						
	5% or 95%	10% or 90%	15% or 85%	20% or 80%	30% or 70%	40% or 60%	50% or 50%
50	7	9	11	12	13	14	15
100	5	6	8	8	10	10	10
200	4	5	5	6	7	7	8
300	3	4	5	5	6	6	6
400	3	3	4	4	5	5	5
500	2	3	4	4	5	5	5
750	2	3	3	3	4	4	4
1000	2	2	3	3	3	3	3
1200	2	2	3	3	3	3	3
1500	2	2	2	3	3	3	3
1600	1	1	2	2	2	2	2

Required Sample Size for Percentage Estimates

The sample size required to achieve a specified level of precision is quite predictable in the case of an estimate of a universe percentage—a sample in which the result of the question will produce a percentage; for example, "What percentage of the voters favour a certain candidate?" Questions involving percentage estimates are quite common in marketing research, and as a result, such tables as Table 10.4 have been developed to show the sampling error (sometimes called the sampling tolerance) that can be expected for various sample sizes. A researcher can tell from the table that, for example, if a survey among a sample of 400 showed that 80% had telephones, it is almost certain that the true percentage is within 4% of 80% (between 76% and 84%). Notice that the precision decreases as the percentage being estimated moves toward 50%. Accordingly, we can say that a sample of 200 has a 95% probability of being within ±8 percentage points when the percentage being estimated is approximately 50%. However, if the percentage being estimated is approximately 10%, a sample of 100 should be 95% sure of being within ±6 percentage points.

Notice also that, as discussed in the section involving the central limit theorem, the sampling tolerances are lowered only as a function of rapidly increasing the sample size. For example, look at the estimate for 15% or 85%: as the sample size goes up in multiples of four from 100 to 400 to 1600, notice that the sampling error drops from 8% to 4% to 2%, or drops by half. Some of the columns might not appear to be following this rule, but that apparent variation is caused only by rounding. Table 10.5 is a slightly condensed version in which the sampling errors have not been rounded; you can see that increases in precision come exactly with large increases in sample size.

TABLE 10.5
95% Confidence Intervals

Sample Size	Sample Error At or Near				
	10%/90%	20%/80%	30%/70%	40%/60%	50%
100	5.88	7.84	8.98	9.60	9.80
400	2.94	3.92	4.49	4.80	4.90
900	1.96	2.61	2.99	3.20	3.26
1600	1.47	1.96	2.24	2.40	2.45

Notice also that these sample estimates begin achieving very respectable precision quite rapidly. As is evident from Table 10.5, even under the worst of conditions (estimating a probability near 50%), by the time the sample size is around one thousand the researcher is 95% confident that the estimate is within three percentage points of the correct answer. Thus, marketing surveys tend to be fairly small in size, involving usually less than a thousand consumers. Critics unskilled in sampling methodology are often sceptical about the small samples involved in marketing, asking, for example, "How can you hope to estimate percentages for a country the size of Canada with a sample of only one thousand?" However, from sampling tolerances we can see that a sample of one thousand is a very strong sample indeed. The size of the population does not figure into these sampling tolerances. As a matter of fact, these tolerances were computed on the basis of a universe population of infinity.

The concepts behind Tables 10.4 and 10.5 can be further clarified by using the following formula in computing the necessary sample size for percentages:

$$Ns = \frac{z^2 p(1-p)}{(AE)^2}$$

where,

Ns is the necessary sample size
p and $(1-p)$ are responses expressed in percentages (**Note**: If percentages are unknown, they can be arbitrarily set at .5 each)
AE is allowable sampling error or desired accuracy between sample percentage and universe percentage
z is the desired confidence interval for the study; it is expressed in standard deviations (see Appendix 3, Exhibit B)

Example: An initial research study found that 50% of respondents preferred Brand x, while the other 50% preferred Brand y. The researcher wants to know at the 95% confidence level that the final results of the sample will be plus or minus 5% of the true universe mean (μ). What is the necessary sample size?

Here, $p = .50$ (50%)
  $1 - p = .50$ (50%)
    $AE = .05$ (5%)
      $z = 2$ (rounded off from $z = 1.96$ in Appendix 3, Exhibit B, which corresponds to area $.475 \times 2 = .95$)

Thus, $Ns = \dfrac{2^2(.5)(.5)}{(.05)^2} = \dfrac{4(.25)}{.0025} = \dfrac{1.00}{.0025} = 400$

Had we been willing to double our allowable error to ±10%, we could have cut our necessary sample size by 75% to 100. (Note that these same data are in Tables 10.4 and 10.5).

$$Ns = \frac{2^2(.5)(.5)}{(.10)^2} = \frac{4(.25)}{.01} = \frac{1.00}{.01} = 100$$

Obviously, the greater the allowable error or sampling error that we are willing to tolerate, the smaller the sample that is necessary. However, the smaller the sample, the less certain we can be that sample data accurately reflect universe data.

Sample Size Determination for General Estimates

In the previous section, the simpler case of the percentage estimate was explained. If the parameter to be estimated is not a proportion, the formula for determining the required sample size becomes

$$Ns = \left(\frac{zS}{AE}\right)^2$$

where,

Ns is the necessary sample size
S is the estimate of the population standard deviation
AE is the allowable sampling error
z is the desired confidence interval expressed in standard deviations
(see Appendix 3, Exhibit B)

In this formula, S is the most difficult to obtain in practice. An estimate of S to be used in determining the sample size can be obtained in one of three ways:

1. It can be estimated from the results of past studies.

2. It can be estimated by conducting a pilot study.

3. Use a rule of thumb and take one-sixth of the expected range of responses.

Example: A researcher would like to estimate the average number of cans of beer purchased weekly by urban males, within a range of error of one can and with a 95% confidence level. The range of purchases is expected to be from 0 to 24 cans. What is the necessary sample size?

Here, $AE = 1$

$z = 2$ (rounded off from 1.96 in Appendix 3, Exhibit B)

$$S = \frac{24}{6} = 4$$

$$Ns = \left(\frac{2 \times 4}{1}\right)^2 = 64$$

Thus the researcher needs a sample size of 64 urban males to estimate the average number of cans of beer purchased per week, within one can, at the 95% confidence level.

Sample Size vs. Representativeness

Of course, the critics concerned about a sample size of one thousand might have a point. A sample of one thousand people from a country as large and as diverse as Canada leaves open the serious question of whether that sample is representative of the population as a whole. Remember, however, that the question of the representativeness of the sample is a function of the specifics of the sample selection and hence is a qualitative problem, a non-sampling error. Although there might be doubts about the representativeness of a sample of one thousand, statistically the sampling error has been quite well controlled.

This distinction between sampling error and non-sampling error brings us to one final point. Another reason why samples in marketing are seldom larger than one thousand is that experienced marketing researchers are always aware that the possibility exists for appreciable amounts of non-sampling error. Marketing researchers generally feel that to try to estimate a percentage much more closely than within two or three percentage points is probably a waste of time and money, since most marketing situations are sufficiently imprecise that the non-sampling error will be at least that great.

■ Summary

This chapter has dealt with sampling concepts. A sample is defined as a subgroup of observations from a larger population or universe (the terms universe or population are used interchangeably to refer to every item of the whole that is being studied). Thus, a sample is only a portion of the total amount of information that can conceivably be gathered. If we have counted all of the items in the universe, we have taken a census, not a sample.

A critical first step in sampling is to define clearly the limits of the population being studied. Depending on the nature of the study being undertaken, we could have a population consisting of all university students in North America, all business students in North America, all business students at Utopia University, all marketing majors at Utopia University, and so forth. Populations might be finite or infinite. A finite population is one containing a fixed number of elements, whereas an infinite population is one without limits of any type. Although it is possible to draw samples from both finite and infinite populations, it is impossible to take a census of an infinite population; only a sample can be drawn from the latter.

Sampling is based on the premise that relatively small numbers of items drawn from a universe will provide an accurate representation of the characteristics of that population. Although this theory does not always hold true in actual practice, we do know that a sample can be more quickly, easily, and cheaply taken than a census. Six main reasons have been identified for sampling instead of census taking: financial constraints, time constraints, universe size, the destructive nature of sampling, the sufficiency of an approximation, and accuracy. Despite these advantages, sampling does present problems. Sampling methodology involves five major stages: definition of an ideal universe and of an operational universe; selection of a sampling frame, sampling method, and sample size. Three main problem areas are identified here: the skilled personnel required for administering surveys and interpreting sample data, sampling error, and bias. Each of these problems, however, is controllable.

Depending on the selection method used, samples are either probability or non-probability. In the case of probability sampling, all items in the universe have known and equal chances, or probabilities, of being selected. In non-probability sampling, all items in the population do not have known and equal chances of being selected. When classifying sample designs, four major types of probability samples can be identified: random, stratified random, cluster, and systematic. Non-probability samples include convenience, judgment, and quota samples. Although probability sampling techniques are generally clearly superior, researchers sometimes find it advantageous to use non-probability sampling when it is not necessary to have a representative sample or when time and cost constraints make probability sampling impractical.

For Discussion

1. A manufacturer of men's clothing has approximately one hundred retail outlets across Canada. The manufacturer needs to begin production of a new line of men's slacks within the next four weeks but thinks it might be a good idea to survey the store managers to get their opinions on how well this new line will sell. In answering each of the following questions, explain your rationale.

   a) Should the manufacturer conduct a census or take a sample of the dealers?
   b) If a sample is taken, should it be probability or non-probability?
   c) If a sample is taken, which type of probability or non-probability sample do you think would be best?
   d) Is the survey even necessary?

2. Explain the difference between a convenience sample and judgment sample. Which is better?

3. Your marketing research instructor has assigned you the task of selecting a probability sample of one hundred students from among the five thousand enrolled at Utopia University. Describe the sampling procedures that you would choose.

4. Describe a research problem that would favour the use of a cluster sample and one that would favour a stratified sample.

5. You are asked to survey at random twenty-five people identified in your local telephone directory. How would you go about selecting this probability sample?

6. A manufacturer of dietetic soft drinks is considering adding a new low-calorie carbonated beverage to her firm's product line, but first she wants to take a survey to find out what potential customers think of this product concept.

   a) What is the manufacturer's relevant population or universe?
   b) How should the sample be selected?
   c) What type of sample should be selected?

7. A radio station wants to find out what local people think about a forthcoming election. The station manager has his disc jockeys request listeners to phone in with their opinions concerning the issues. What are some of the things that might be wrong with this type of sample?

8. Design a two-stage area sample using your own hypothetical data.

9. To measure neighbourhood opinion of a proposed city ordinance, you are instructed to survey the occupants of every fifth house in a residential neighbourhood. Is there anything wrong with this systematically drawn sample?

10. Utopia University is concerned about the attitudes of business people toward the university. In the past, 70% of business people said that their attitudes toward Utopia University were very favourable and that they would hire at least one of its graduating students if they had an available position. The university would like to conduct a new survey and wonders what sample size is needed to obtain an estimate within a 2% error at the 95% confidence level.

Problem

Mini-case: Huron Department Stores
Huron Department Stores, a Fredericton-based firm, has 300 000 users of its credit card throughout Canada. The stores are located mostly in the downtown areas of major cities, with some branches in surrounding suburban shopping centres and a few in outlying areas.

Huron is interested in determining whether the socio-economic characteristics of its card holders have an impact on their spending habits. For example, do upper-income customers use store credit only for major purchases, such as stoves or refrigerators, or also for minor purchases? Is their consumer behaviour the same as that of card holders in lower-income brackets?

Question
What type of sampling should be used to obtain this information—simple random, stratified random, or cluster sampling? Why? Show how each type of sample could be used.

Endnotes

1. For a more detailed treatment of market segmentation, see René Y. Darmon, Michel Laroche, and John V. Petrof, *Marketing in Canada: A Management Perspective*. 3rd ed. Toronto: McGraw-Hill Ryerson, 1989, chapter 7.
2. Charles T. Clark and Lawrence L. Schkade, *Statistical Methods for Business Decisions*. Cincinnati, OH: Southwestern Publishing, 1969, p. 359.
3. John E. Freund and Frank J. Williams, *Elementary Business Statistics*. 2nd ed. Englewood Cliffs, NJ. Prentice-Hall, 1972, p. 419.
4. Donald S. Tull and Del I. Hawkins, *Marketing Research: Meaning, Measurement, and Methods*. 2nd ed. New York: Macmillan, 1980, pp. 390–91.
5. Freund and Williams, *Elementary Business Statistics*, p. 416.

PART 3

DATA ANALYSIS AND REPORT PREPARATION

DATA ANALYSIS: ELEMENTARY STATISTICS

The purpose of this chapter is to introduce the mechanics of data analysis. We will look first at some of the tabulation methods commonly used for the analysis of numerical data. Then, in the second part of the chapter, we will introduce some concepts of univariate statistics.

■ Tabulating the Data

The simple forms of descriptive statistics—percentages, averages, dispersions, and classification tables—are by far the most used and the most useful of all statistical tools. Later in this chapter we will investigate a number of statistical techniques used to analyse averages and percentages, but the fact remains that the averages by themselves, or the percentage breakdowns by themselves, devoid of any further analysis remain the business planner's most useful tools.

Percentages

Surely the most widely used statistic for reporting and summarizing data is the percentage. We are constantly bombarded with reports stating that such and such percentage does this, and so and so percentage does that. Yet despite the disarming simplicity of the percentage, it is sometimes misused, at other times underused, and at still other times overused.

Underuse of the percentage rate: One of the most useful features of the percentage is that it can reduce everything to a common base and thereby allow meaningful comparisons to be made. For instance, suppose that teacher Eezy failed two students last semester, whereas teacher Grimm failed four. Which teacher is the more demanding grader? Actually, the informaton given tells us virtually nothing. We need to know how many students were involved in each case, so that we can determine the *rate* at which students were being failed. If, for instance, we discover that Eezy had five students and Grimm had eighty, we see that Eezy's rate of failures was 2/5 = 0.40 or 40%, whereas Grimm's was 4/80 = 0.05 or 5%.

Yet the percentage is still underused in this regard. The single most valuable thing that can be done for most numerical presentations is conversion of all of the numbers into percentages so that the reader can tell at a glance their relative magnitudes.

A cautionary note on overuse of the percentage as a rate: There is a time, however, when it is best *not* to convert numbers into percentages. This is when the absolute number of entries is very small. For example, suppose a candidate claims that a survey showed that 60% of the voters favour her platform, but then it is discovered that she talked to only five people, three of whom were in favour of her. As this example shows, reporting by percentages can be used to camouflage a small base and make a small sample sound more authoritative. For this reason, many researchers advise against the use of percentages unless a sample of at least fifty is used. Of course, the best way to present data is to provide both the absolute numbers and the derived percentages.

Percentages on a declining base: Another problem with the use of percentages involves interest rates. Suppose that you borrow $100 for a year at 6%, the sum to be paid back with interest in monthly instalments. The loan merchant computes the payments in this way: principal ($100) + interest ($6) = $106/12 = $8.34 per month. The question now is, will you really be paying 6% interest on that loan? The answer is no, because you did not have the use of the entire $100 for the entire year. Since by the end of the year the sum was down to nothing (see Figure 11.1),

FIGURE 11.1
Percentages on a Declining Base

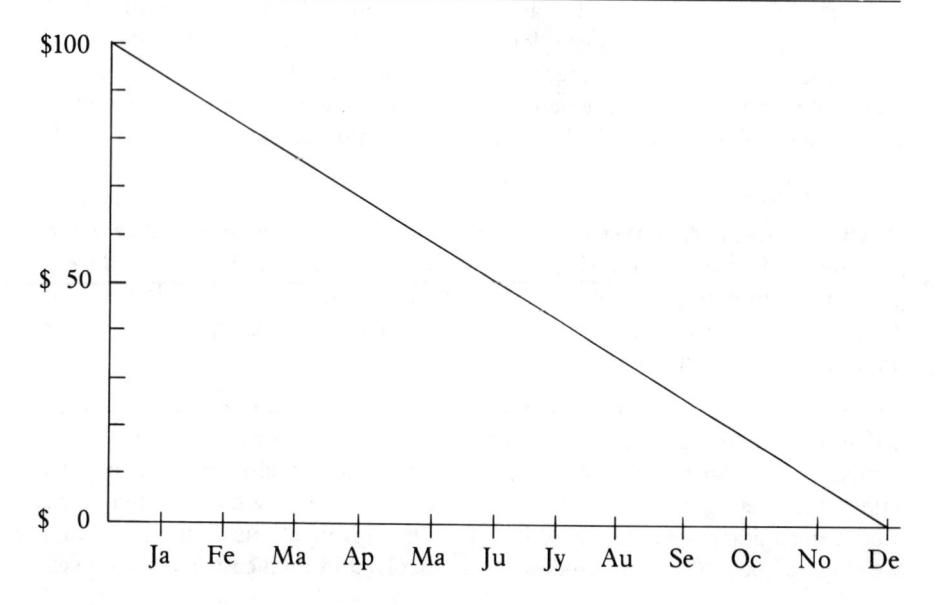

on the average you had the use of only $50, which means that your effective rate of interest was approximately $6/$50 = 0.12 or 12%.

We do not want to get too carried away with these financial formulas and their calculations. Our purpose here is to point out that it is very easy to play all kinds of games with percentages and percentage rates. The reader or user of statistical information expressed in percentage form must be very careful to understand exactly what is being figured, which numbers are being used, and their origin.

Pitfalls of percentage increases and decreases: In the example of interest rates given above, we saw the effect on interest rates of a change in the base. The same effect accompanies percentage increases and decreases. Suppose that you were forced to take a 20% cut in pay. If you were later given a 20% pay raise, would that raise restore your pay to its original amount? The answer is no, because the base would have changed. It would take an increase of 25% to restore the cut of 20%: the reciprocal of 4/5 is 5/4; thus, a reduction of 20%, cutting your pay down to 80% of its original amount, would require an increase of 25% to regain the original figure. Although the mathematics involved here are not terribly sophisticated, it is extremely easy to become careless and make an error. Constant vigilance is required to avoid mistakes.

Averages

Measures of Central Tendency
Three forms of central tendency are commonly used in marketing research: the arithmetic mean, the median, and the mode. Although there are other measures of central tendency, these three cover most marketing usages. The usual order of presentation—mean, median, mode—aside from being alphabetical, also gives the approximate magnitude of usage of each and even indicates their position in a skewed distribution (see Figure 11.2), one which has a more pronounced "tail" on one end. Theoretically speaking, the mode will always occupy the highest point in a skewed distribution, with the mean the farthest out along the tail and the median in between, twice as far from the mode as from the mean. In a symmetric distribution all three will be right in the middle.

FIGURE 11.2
Relative Positions of Median, Mean, and Mode for a Skewed Distribution

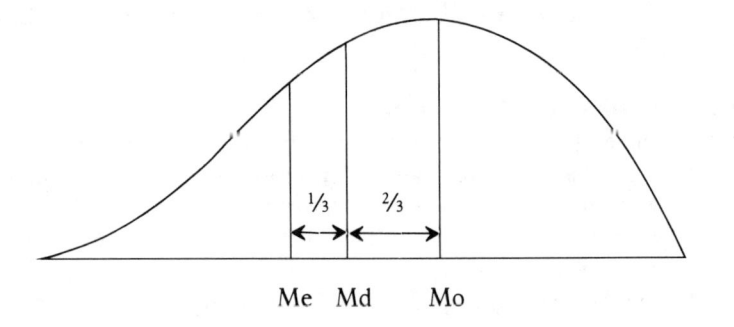

Me Md   Mo

The Mean

The arithmetic mean (abbreviation: Me or μ) or what most people consider to be the average, is the sum of all items divided by the number of items. Of the three measures, the mean is the one most affected by extreme values. It has the form

$$\mu = \text{mean} = \frac{\sum\limits_{i}^{n} x_i}{n}, \text{ where } x_i \text{ is the item number and } n \text{ is the number of items.}$$

No more than a different formulation of the arithmetic mean, the expected value has the form

$$E(\mu) = \sum^{k} x_k p_k, \text{ where } p_k \text{ is the proportion of the value } x_k \text{ occurring and } k \text{ the number of categories.}$$

The expected value is used in many types of marketing analysis. It is sometimes referred to as the *weighted mean*.

The Median

The median (abbreviation: Md) is the middle value of an ordered or arrayed set of numbers (see Figure 11.3). The median is quite popular for population and income studies, since it is not overly affected by extreme values. Each member of the population has one vote in determining where the middle of the group will be, and for this reason the median is sometimes cited as the most democratic measure of central tendency.

FIGURE 11.3
Example of Determination of the Median

Odd Number	*Even Number*
4	4
6	6
7	7 = 6.5
	9

The Mode

The mode (abbreviation: Mo) is the most frequently occurring value of a group of values. It is the least frequently used measure because it is neither a consistent nor a sufficient estimator.

Slanted Statistics and Other Problems

One of the biggest problems with these three measures of central tendency is that they all can qualify as "averages," and yet, as shown in Figure 11.2, they will all be different if the distribution is skewed. Unfortunately, many of the variables of critical concern to marketing researchers have just such skewed distributions (sales, income, travel, consumption, etc.). Because of the different averages involved, there is always the opportunity for "slanting" the statistics in a given direction, and the researcher must be on guard for this slanting. Aside from possible misrepresentations caused by reporting the various averages from a skewed distribution, there are other pitfalls involved with the use of the average.

The Non-existent Average

If the population has some unusual distribution, the average (mean and median, in any case) might be non-existent, or at least of minimal importance (see Figure 11.4). It is like the story of the statistician who has his head in the refrigerator and his feet in the oven. Asked how he was feeling, he replied, "Well, on the average, I feel pretty good." This problem can be critical to marketing strategies because the average frequently obscures significant market segments.

FIGURE 11.4
The Non-existent Average

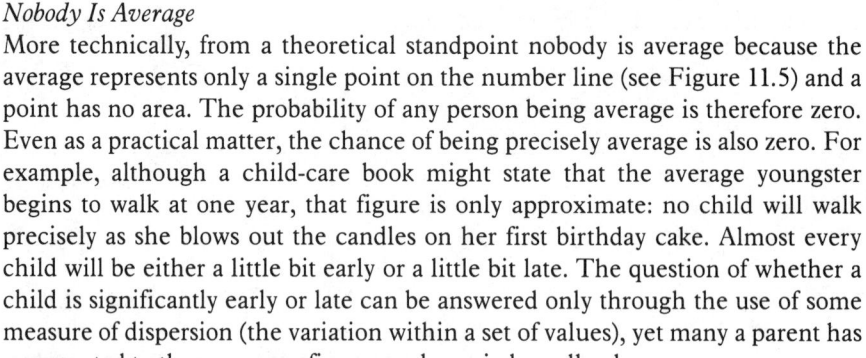

Mean

Nobody Is Average

More technically, from a theoretical standpoint nobody is average because the average represents only a single point on the number line (see Figure 11.5) and a point has no area. The probability of any person being average is therefore zero. Even as a practical matter, the chance of being precisely average is also zero. For example, although a child-care book might state that the average youngster begins to walk at one year, that figure is only approximate: no child will walk precisely as she blows out the candles on her first birthday cake. Almost every child will be either a little bit early or a little bit late. The question of whether a child is significantly early or late can be answered only through the use of some measure of dispersion (the variation within a set of values), yet many a parent has overreacted to these average figures and worried needlessly.

FIGURE 11.5
Nobody Is Actually Average

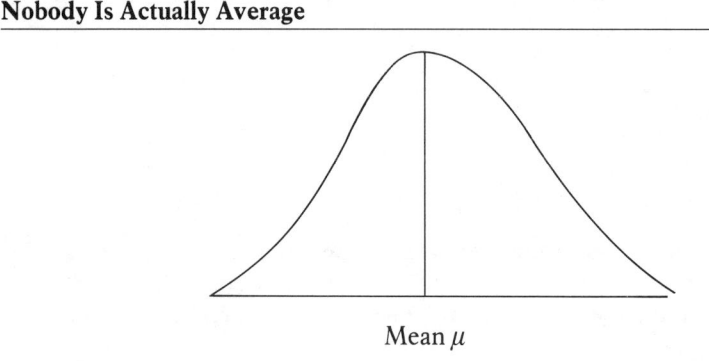

Mean μ

Spurious Precision

Because of the manner in which the average is computed, it is very easy to develop an average that appears much more precise than the data from which it was composed. Consider the following example: $5000 + $3000 + $2000 = $10 000. $10 000/3 = $3333.333 333 333. Thus, the average can be said to be $3333.33, instead of $3300. Although it is always apparent where the increase in decimal places came from, the final answer is overly precise and as such is very misleading. It gives a feeling of exactness and certainty that is unwarranted. This is but another version of the familiar GIGO (Garbage In, Garbage Out) motto—a final answer, like a chain, is no stronger than its weakest link; the final answer can be no more precise than the most imprecise figure used as input. For instance, a study recently reported that fathers spent only 37.1 s per day with their infants under one year of age. Certainly, however, the estimates supplied by the individual fathers were not accurate to the tenth of a second and probably not even to the second. The researcher simply went ahead with the estimates he had, totalled them up, divided by the number of respondents, and then cranked out the quotient to a ridiculous specificity. A more appropriate conclusion would have been that the average time fathers spent with their infants was less than one minute per day.

Sample Problem Involving Measures of Central Tendency

For the following set of numbers (which features an even number of elements), compute the median, the mode, and the arithmetic mean, using the expected value formula.

Initial Data Set	Ordered to Compute Median	Arithmetic Mean	Expected Value
6	1	1	$3/8 \times 1 = 3/8$
5	1 mode = 1	1	
6	1	1	
8	4	4	$1/8 \times 4 = 4/8$
	median = 4.5		
1	5	5	$1/8 \times 5 = 5/8$
1	6	6	$2/8 \times 6 = 12/8$
1	6	6	
4	8	8	$1/8 \times 8 = 8/8$
	$\mu = \Sigma x/n$	$\Sigma x_i = 32$	$E = \Sigma p_k x_k = 32/8 = 4$
	$\mu = 32/8 = 4$		

where $n = 8$ and $k = 4$.

Dispersions

Most of the problems concerning averages that were presented in the last section could have been solved if the exact nature of the distribution had been known. This section will focus primarily on the measures of dispersion, which tell the amount or the magnitude of the spread. Measures that tell something of the shape of the distribution will also be discussed.

Note, however, that the only way to know the exact shape of the distribution is to use a graph showing shape and percentages. Such a picture can convey more important information in a single glance than can be conveyed in pages of numbers—numbers that probably are not going to be read or remembered anyway.

Measures of Dispersion

Range

The crudest measure of spread, the range is often the most useful. It is simply the difference between the highest value and the lowest value.

Interquartile Range

One of the problems with the range is that it can be unduly influenced by an unusually high or low end value. To avoid this problem, the interquartile range is sometimes used. The interquartile range is the range of the middle 50%. To derive it, subtract the value at the end of the third quarter (75%) from the value at the end of the first quarter (25%) (see Figure 11.6).

FIGURE 11.6
Illustration of the Interquartile Range

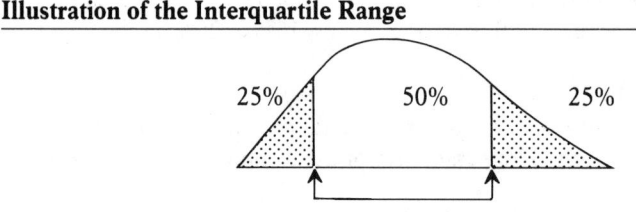

Interquartile Range

Average deviation

Just as its name implies, the average deviation is the average (arithmetic mean) of the deviations of the various items in the group from the mean. The problem of the negative signs is handled by the use of the absolute value: the positive or negative values of the deviations from the mean are ignored and the absolute difference is measured. Without the absolute value, the total of the sum would be zero. The formula for the average deviation is

$$\frac{\sum_{i=1}^{n} |x_i - \mu|}{n}$$

Standard deviation

The standard deviation is just like the average deviation except that, instead of taking the absolute value of the numbers to eliminate the negative signs, the standard deviation takes the square of the deviations of individual values from the arithmetic mean. The magnitude of the numbers is altered by this process, so the result is then brought back into line by taking the square root of the resulting sum. Despite the increased difficulty of computation caused by the squaring process, the standard deviation is generally the preferred measure of dispersion. The reason for this preference is that the standard deviation is one of the parameters of the normal curve (discussed below). The formula for the standard deviation is

$$\sigma = \frac{\text{standard}}{\text{deviation}} = \sqrt{\frac{\sum\limits_{i=1}^{n}(x_i - \mu)^2}{n}}$$

There is an alternate standard deviation formula, which is easier to compute by hand:

$$\sigma = \sqrt{\frac{\sum x^2}{n} - \mu^2}$$

The squared difference before the square root is taken is called the *variance*: its formula is

$$\text{variance} = \frac{\sum\limits_{i=1}^{n}(x_i - \mu)^2}{n}$$

Note that the value of the standard deviation will not be equal to the value of the average deviation; as a rule it will be approximately 15% to 20% larger.

Sample Standard Deviation
In most cases, the calculations are not on the total population, but on a sample taken from that population. The parameters of the sample distribution are then

Sample mean: $\mu = \overline{x}$

Sample standard deviation: $S = \sqrt{\dfrac{\sum\limits_{i=1}^{n}(x_i - \overline{x})^2}{n-1}}$ or $S = \sqrt{\dfrac{n}{n-1}}\,\sigma$

Standard Deviation and Its Relationship to the Normal Curve
As mentioned above, the principal reason for the importance of the standard deviation is that it is one of the parameters of the normal curve (the other parameter being the mean). In practice, this means that if you know the standard deviation and if you know (or assume) that the population is normally distributed, you can determine what percentage of the population falls between selected intervals (as measured in standard deviations). As shown in Figure 11.7, 68% of the population will lie within one standard deviation of the mean (taken from both directions). Since many population characteristics can be assumed to have a normal distribution, the use of the standard deviation in this manner is quite important in marketing research, as in many other disciplines.

Example Involving Measures of Dispersion
Using the same set used in the problem involving measures of central tendency, compute the range, the average deviation, and the standard deviation (here the

FIGURE 11.7
Standard Deviation and the Normal Curve

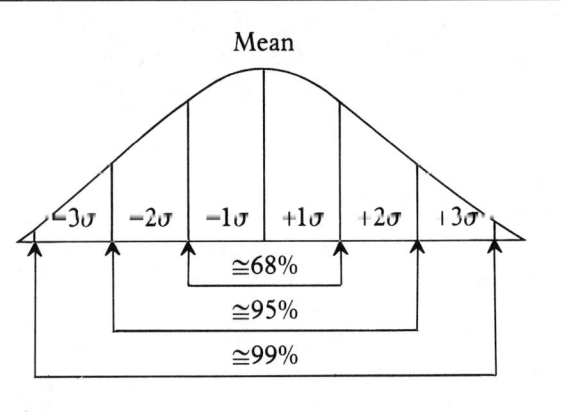

Mean

-3σ -2σ -1σ $+1\sigma$ $+2\sigma$ $+3\sigma$

$\cong 68\%$

$\cong 95\%$

$\cong 99\%$

standard deviation is computed using both formulas; formula (2) is easier to use):

Range: 7 (8 less 1)
Interquartile range: 5 (6 less 1)
Mean: $\mu = 32/8 = 4$

Average Deviation	Standard Deviation	Standard Deviation (alternate formula)
$\|1-4\| = 3$	$(1-4)^2 = 9$	$1^2 = 1$
$\|1-4\| = 3$	$(1-4)^2 = 9$	$1^2 = 1$
$\|1-4\| = 3$	$(1-4)^2 = 9$	$1^2 = 1$
$\|4-4\| = 0$	$(4-4)^2 = 0$	$4^2 = 16$
$\|5-4\| = 1$	$(5-4)^2 = 1$	$5^2 = 25$
$\|6-4\| = 2$	$(6-4)^2 = 4$	$6^2 = 36$
$\|6-4\| = 2$	$(6-4)^2 = 4$	$6^2 = 36$
$\|8-4\| = 4$	$(8-4)^2 = 16$	$8^2 = 64$
$\overline{18}$	$\overline{52}$	$\overline{\sum x^2 = 180}$

$$\text{average deviation} = \frac{\sum |x - \mu|}{n}$$

$$\text{standard deviation (formula 1)} = \sqrt{\frac{\sum (x - \mu)^2}{n}}$$

$$\text{standard deviation (formula 2)} = \sqrt{\frac{\sum x^2}{n} - \mu^2}$$

$$\text{average deviation} = \frac{18}{8}$$

$$\sigma = \sqrt{\frac{52}{8}}$$

$$= \sqrt{\frac{180}{8} - \mu^2}$$

$$\text{average deviation} = 2.25$$

$$\sigma = \sqrt{6.5} = 2.55$$

$$= \sqrt{22.5 - 16}$$

$$\sigma = 2.55$$

$$S = \sqrt{\frac{8}{7}} \sigma = 2.73$$

$$= \sqrt{6.3} = 2.55$$

$$\sigma = 2.55$$

■ Statistical Evaluation of Sample Results

In Chapter 10, two principal sampling problem areas were identified: sampling error and non-sampling error. A brief review of these two terms is advisable, since they and their somewhat unexpected meanings are confusing to many novice researchers.

Sampling error is a *quantitative*, or mathematical, problem. Whenever you take a sample, there is going to be some scatter of the sample results around the universe value that the sample is trying to estimate. Because this is a mathematically defined problem, the amount of sampling error present in a given sample design can be estimated. Furthermore, this error can be controlled by manipulation of the sample size and other aspects of the sample design.

Non-sampling error is a *qualitative* problem. Non-sampling error includes everything that can go wrong in a sample, with the exception of that natural scatter of the sample estimate. Thus, non-sampling error includes selection bias, non-response bias, improper questionnaire design, interviewer bias, and all of the other qualitative problem areas discussed previously in this text. Because non-sampling errors are non-quantitative by definition, there is usually no way to estimate their size.

Survey Errors in Marketing

The total error present in a survey is the total of the sampling and non-sampling errors. Since the non-sampling error cannot be estimated, the only way in which an estimate of the total survey error can be made is by assuming that the non-sampling error is zero. The estimate of sampling error alone then becomes the estimate of total error.

There are many fields of research in which such an assumption is quite valid. For instance, consider the testing of products as they come off a factory production line. The products could be sampled and tested for certain desired characteristics and the non-sampling error would probably be zero: there would be no problem with selection bias, since all of the units would be ready and available for sampling. There also would be no problem with non-response bias, no questionnaire, no subjective interface between interviewer and respondent, problems of wording or order, and so forth. In this case the total error would be the sampling error alone, and that error could easily be calculated.

Usually the marketing researcher has a much more variable situation. In general, marketing involves people, and the processes of measuring and interviewing people bring into play all of the problems noted above. This was what happened in the *Literary Digest* survey in 1936, discussed in Chapter 10. The sampling error alone, which is primarily a function of sample size, should have been 0.08% (0.000 8). The researchers should therefore have been more than 99% sure that their estimate was within 0.1% of being correct. Because their sample estimate said that Landon would get 59.6% of the electoral votes, *statistically* speaking they should have been 99% sure that he would actually get between 59.5% and 59.7% of the votes, a very precise estimate indeed. Of course, this estimate was off, not by one-tenth or two-tenths of a percent, but by tens of percentage points. The reason was the huge non-sampling error.

The potential for non-sampling errors of enormous magnitude in the execution of marketing surveys hangs like the sword of Damocles over the heads of marketing researchers. Since non-sampling error is non-quantitative by definition, it can never be estimated and very often it cannot even be identified. Although marketing analysts frequently give estimates of the probable survey error based on the statistical sampling error, the presence of non-sampling error should always be suspected. Extreme care and vigilance must be taken with the design and execution of the survey in the hope of keeping non-sampling error to an absolute minimum.

Concept of Statistical Confidence Intervals

In dealing with statistical sampling error in a survey, the marketing researcher basically wants to know how much confidence to have in an estimate. One wants to know the probability of an estimate falling within a certain range. For instance, if a survey has produced results showing that 60% of the people favour a certain new product, how confident can one be about those results? How sure can we be that the universe really has approximately 60% favourable responses? (Keep in mind that we are talking about statistical confidence, so that only the sampling error is being considered.) A similar question might arise if two new products were tested, one gaining the favour of 62% of the sample and the other gaining the favour of 58% of the sample. How confident can the researcher be that the observed difference of four percentage points represents a true difference and is not within that normal range of scatter we identify as sampling error?

Probability Levels

Suppose that you had tested a gun and you were of the opinion that the gun was indeed shooting off target. How would you convey that belief to someone else? Well, you might express your opinion in the form of a bet, saying, "I'll bet that gun isn't shooting on target," to which your friend might reply, "Oh, yeah? How *much* do you want to bet?"

If you decide to take him up on the bet, the amount that you bet indicates your confidence—the strength of your belief that you are right; it also gives a measure of the probability with which you are betting. Thus, if you are willing to bet only fifty cents, you are probably not very confident; you feel that the probability of being right is rather low. On the other hand, if you are willing to bet $300 000, you are *very* confident and feel that you have a high probability of being correct.

In marketing, we express belief that there is a difference (note that we never say how *much* difference, only that the difference is not zero) as a probability. The commonly used probability levels are 10%, 5%, and 1%, which represent bets of 90% confidence, 95% confidence, and 99% confidence, respectively.

Probabilities Involved in Confidence Intervals

Where does marketing usually get the probability levels it uses—90%, 95%, and 99%—and how is the level of confidence for a given sample estimate determined? Unfortunately, the answer to these questions can involve some rather tricky mathematics, depending on the precise situation in question. As discussed in the example involving the gun, four distinct factors are involved:

1. *Magnitude of the difference.* For instance, in judging between two brands, the strength of your confidence will depend on the magnitude of the difference between the brands. The larger the difference, the greater confidence you will have in concluding that one brand is better than the other.

2. *Number in the sample (sample size).* The larger the sample, the greater confidence you will have in your results and in your conclusions (other things being equal).

3. *Dispersion of the sample (standard deviation).* Some situations have intrinsically more scatter because of the nature of the phenomenon. The greater the dispersion (the more unstable the population), the less confidence you will have in your results (other things being equal).

4. *Conditions affecting the test (specifics of the sample).* The actual calculation of the degree of confidence varies, depending on the type of data, type of sample, and so forth. Perhaps an example would be appropriate. If you are cooking some meat, the question arises, how *long* should you cook the meat? The answer to that question depends on a variety of factors, including: How big is the piece of meat? How well-cooked do you want it? How hot is the oven? Will the meat be roasted in an open pan or a closed pan? However, the decision on how long to cook the meat also depends on what *type* of meat you have. Each type of meat has its own distribution of cooking times. As with meat, so with samples: there are different types of sample numbers—percentages, averages, frequency distributions, and so forth. And each different type of number has its own particular sampling distribution.

Sampling Distribution

As explained above, the precise determination of the sampling error depends on the shape of the relevant sampling distribution; this aspect of the estimation of the sampling error is what makes that estimation such a complex subject. Unfortunately, the sampling distribution and its corresponding shape change with each change in the sample design. Thus, the sampling error of an estimate from a stratified sample is computed differently from that of an estimate from a cluster sample, because the relevant sampling distributions are different.

However, it is not our intention (and probably not yours either) to become expert at all types of sampling distributions. In this chapter we focus on only three sampling distributions, the normal distribution, the *t*-distribution, and the chi-square distribution.

Common Objective and Procedure of Statistical Testing

All of the statistical testing in this chapter has a common objective, and in it all the tests follow a common format. The objective in each test is to compare the value (often referred to as the statistic) computed from the observed data with a value (often called the parameter) obtained from the theoretical distribution of values. Thus, the actual value (the statistic), which is computed from the observed frequency distributions, is compared with the theoretical value (the parameter) obtained from the tables in the back of the book. In this process, a sample statistic is compared with a population parameter.

For all problems involving any type of statistical test, this book follows a five-step process:

1. The hypothesis is set up—a clear statement of the proposition that is to be statistically tested.

2. Values for the parameters are obtained from the theoretical distribution shown in the tables. These figures tell us within what ranges we can have an "allowable" difference and at what point we have an "excessive" difference.

3. Using the observed data from the problem, the "actual" value of the statistic is computed.

4. Actual is compared with theoretical—statistic versus parameter, or the observed with the expected.

5. On the basis of that comparison, the hypothesis stated at the beginning of the problem is either rejected or accepted.

Statistical Difference Reviewed

Before beginning the discussion of the actual mechanics of various tests, let us review exactly what is meant by "statistically significant difference."

Observed difference is always present. Any time a sample is taken, there will be some variation in the numbers obtained. If the sample is large enough, this observed difference, no matter how small it is, can become a statistically significant difference.

Significant difference is a statistical term. The presence of a significant difference is largely a function of sample size. The idea behind the concept is that a statistically significant difference represents a bet: one is betting at a certain level of probability that the true difference between the observed value (the statistic) and the expected value (the parameter) is not exactly zero.

■ Methods of Univariate Analysis

The most common methods of univariate analysis are the z-test, the t-test and the chi-square test.

The z-test

The z-test is based on the normal distribution and is used with large sample sizes; the population standard deviation is assumed to be known. Otherwise, the t-test should be used, as explained later. The z-test is based on the fact that the following statistic

$$z = \frac{\bar{x} - \mu}{\sigma/\sqrt{n}}$$

has been shown to have a standard normal distribution with a mean of 0 and a standard deviation equal to 1 (see Appendix 3, Exhibit 3).

In using the test the calculated z is compared with the theoretical z_α which corresponds to a chosen level of confidence, α. One could alternatively calculate an interval of confidence μ, such as

$$\mu \pm z_\alpha \frac{\sigma}{\sqrt{n}}$$

In practice, σ is approximated by the sample standard deviation, s.

Example. A supermarket owner wants to know if the average number of visits to his store is or is not equal to 2.

1. The hypotheses to be tested are
   H_0: the average number of visits is 2
   H_1: the average number of visits is not 2

2. At a 95% confidence level (i.e., $\alpha = .05$) the critical value for z is 1.96 (from Appendix 3, Exhibit B).

3. Using a sample of 400 customers, the average number of visits was calculated to be 2.5 and the standard deviation to be $s = 2$. Thus,

$$\frac{s}{\sqrt{n}} = \frac{2}{\sqrt{400}} = .10 \text{ and } z = \frac{2.5 - 2}{.1} = 5$$

4. The calculated value of 5 is greater than the theoretical value of 1.96.

5. **Conclusions:** One must reject the hypothesis that the average number of visits is equal to 2.

An alternate way of looking at the problem is to calculate the 95% confidence interval:

$$2 \pm 1.96\,(.1) \quad \text{or} \quad 1.8 \le \bar{x} \le 2.2$$

This means that for not rejecting the null hypothesis, the calculated average number of visits should be between 1.8 and 2.2. Since it was 2.5, the null hypothesis is rejected.

Alternatively, an interval of confidence can be calculated around the mean as follows:

$$2.5 \pm 1.96\,(.1) \quad \text{or} \quad 2.3 \le \mu \le 2.7$$

This means that the store owner could be 95% confident that the true average number of visits is between 2.3 and 2.7.

The z-test for a proportion. When the researcher is testing a proportion, the mean and standard deviation to be used are

$$\mu = \pi \quad \bar{x} = p$$
$$\sigma = \sqrt{\pi(1 - \pi)}$$

to be used in the formula for z:

$$z = \frac{p - \pi}{\sqrt{\dfrac{\pi(1 - \pi)}{n}}}$$

and for the interval of confidence around π

$$\pi \pm z_\alpha \sqrt{\dfrac{\pi(1 - \pi)}{n}}$$

One-tail z-tests. In the above example, the owner did not know ahead of time if the average number of visits was smaller or greater than 2. When errors on both sides are allowed, the test is said to be two-tailed. Otherwise it is one-tailed. This is explained graphically in Figure 11.8.

FIGURE 11.8
Differences Between Two-Tail and One-Tail z-Test

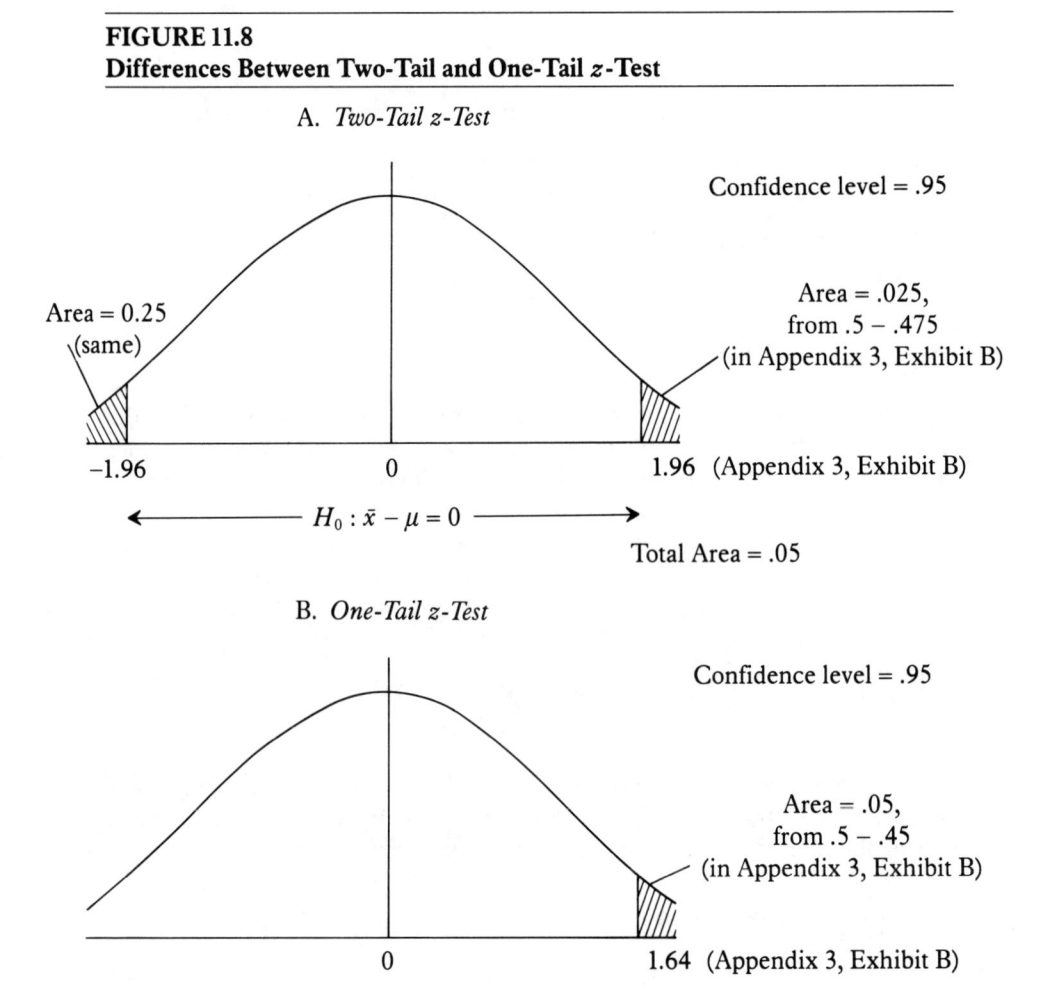

A. *Two-Tail z-Test*

Confidence level = .95

Area = 0.25
(same)

Area = .025,
from .5 − .475
(in Appendix 3, Exhibit B)

−1.96   0   1.96 (Appendix 3, Exhibit B)

$H_0 : \bar{x} - \mu = 0$

Total Area = .05

B. *One-Tail z-Test*

Confidence level = .95

Area = .05,
from .5 − .45
(in Appendix 3, Exhibit B)

0   1.64 (Appendix 3, Exhibit B)

$H_0 : \bar{x} - \mu \leqslant 0$

Let us illustrate the use of a one-tail test for a proportion. In the same survey, the owner asked the customers if they liked the service. He knew that the majority did like it, but not whether it was a clear majority.

1. The hypotheses to be tested are
   H_0: the proportion liking the service is equal to or less than 50%.
   H_1: the proportion is greater than 50%.

2. At a 95% confidence interval (i.e., $\alpha = .05$) the critical value for z is 1.64 (from Appendix 3, Exhibit B)

3. The calculated percentage of customers liking the service is 55%:

$$\pi = .50 \quad \text{and} \quad p = .55$$
$$\sigma = \sqrt{.50(.50)} = .50$$
$$\sqrt{n} = \sqrt{400} = 20$$
$$z = \frac{.55 - .50}{.50/20} = 2$$

4. The calculated value of 2 is greater than the theoretical value of 1.64.

5. **Conclusion:** The null hypothesis is rejected. The owner could be 95% confident that the percentage of customers liking the service is greater than 50%.

The 95% confidence interval is then

$$p \leq 52.5\%$$

The t-test

The t-test is used when the size of the sample is small (less than 30) or when the standard deviation of the population is unknown. The t-distribution resembles the normal distribution, and when n is large the differences between the two are very small.

The t-distribution is contingent on the number of degrees of freedom, which in most cases is $n - 1$. Some t-distributions are illustrated in Appendix 3, Exhibit C. The t-test follows the same procedures as the z-test, as described in the previous paragraphs, that is,

$$t = \frac{\bar{x} - \mu}{s_{\bar{x}}}, \text{with } \gamma = n - 1 \text{ degree of freedom}$$

For example, at the 95% level of confidence, and for a two-tail test with a sample size of 25, the critical $t_{\alpha,\gamma}$ is 2.064 (Appendix 3, Exhibit C). The calculated t, using the values for the example of the average number of visits, is

$$t = \frac{2.5 - 2}{2/\sqrt{25}} = 1.25$$

In this case one cannot reject the null hypothesis.

The Chi-Square Test

The chi-square test is one of the most useful statistical tests, as well as one of the easiest to use. It differs from most of the other statistical tests in that it can work with nominal data. As discussed previously, nominal data are data in which the numbers do not have mathematical properties in the usual sense, but rather can be used only to classify an item into a designated category. Any type of data can be converted into some type of frequency distribution. Data can always be downgraded, and since nominal data is the lowest form, any data can be converted into nominal data. Therefore, unlike other statistical tests, the chi-square test is always appropriate.

The purpose of the chi-square test is to examine mathematically a given frequency distribution to decide mathematically if there is anything unusual about that distribution. In performing this test, the mathematical process will be looking for a *significant difference* between the frequencies that have been observed and those frequencies that were expected.

What Is Chi-Square?

The easiest way to think of chi-square is as a summary of the differences between the observed and the expected distributions (see Figure 11.9).

FIGURE 11.9
Illustration of the Role of the Chi-Square

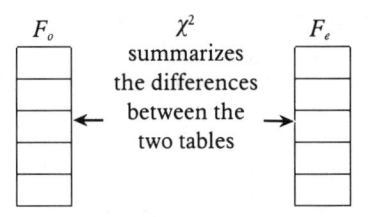

$$F_o \qquad \chi^2 \text{ summarizes the differences between the two tables} \qquad F_e$$

The chi-square distribution is a distribution of the differences (scatter) we would expect even if there was no fundamental difference in the underlying distributions that generated the two tables (Figure 11.10). That is, even if we drew both distributions from the same pile, we would still expect to see some differences between the arrangement of the values in the two tables (Figure 11.11). The distribution of these differences is given by the chi-square tables in Appendix 3, Exhibit A.

FIGURE 11.10
The Chi-Square Distribution

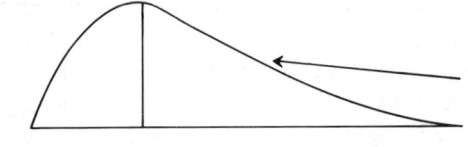

The chi-square distribution represents the distribution of differences that would be expected to result from "normal" scatter.

FIGURE 11.11
Examples of Two Distributions Originating from the Same Source

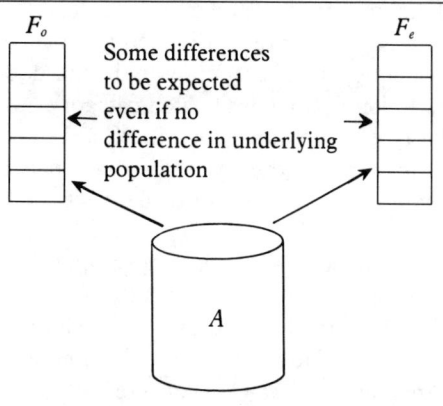

The *chi-square test* looks at the amount of difference (as summarized by the chi-square statistic) that exists between the two tables. If the value of chi-square is low, then it is concluded that the two tables could have come from the same underlying distribution (Figure 11.12).

FIGURE 11.12
What a Small Chi-Square Means

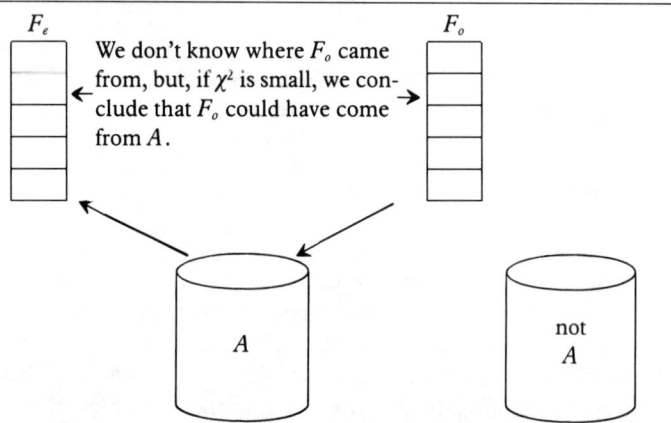

On the other hand, if the difference in the two tables is large, then the conclusion is that the tables must have come from different places; that is, the observed frequency distribution could not have come from the same source that generated the expected frequency distribution (Figure 11.13).

Note that no statement is made concerning the source of the observed table, nor is any statement made about the nature of the population that generated this observed table. The only statement the statistical test will make is that the difference seems so great that the observed distribution must have come from somewhere else. Hence, although the null hypothesis is rejected, the alternative hypothesis states only that the observed frequencies and the expected frequencies are not equal.

FIGURE 11.13
What a Large Chi-Square Means

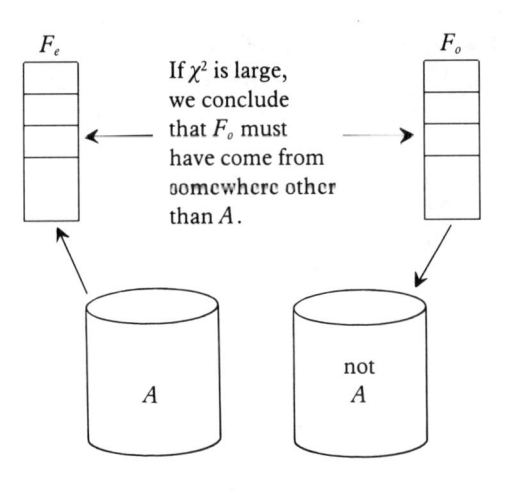

F_e

If χ^2 is large,
we conclude
that F_o must
have come from
somewhere other
than A.

F_o

A

not
A

The Concept behind Cutoff Points

As explained in the discussion of the theoretical chi-square distribution, the values in the chi-square table are computed for the various degrees of freedom under the assumption that there will be *no difference* between the observed and expected distributions. That is to say, the cutoff values of chi-square obtained from the table represent the differences expected from the *normal* scatter of sample estimates, the scatter caused by sampling error. When we choose a 95% cutoff value, we are saying that if there *is* no difference, then 95% of that time the scatter between those two frequency distributions will be less than that cutoff.

Type 1 and Type 2 Errors

Suppose that we compute a given chi-square value and the value is outside the 95% cutoff value. What does that show? Well, the value could be outside the cutoff for one of two reasons:

1. The chi-square in question is one of the 5% expected to fall outside that 95% cutoff (even though the populations are still basically the same).

2. The populations that generated those frequency distributions are not the same. The "true" difference is not zero.

Since hypothesis testing is a mathematical procedure, it tries to play the odds by opting for the second reason. In doing so, it recognizes that 5% of the time an incorrect decision will be made; that is, a difference will have been claimed when in fact there is none. For this reason, another way of speaking of a 95% confidence level is to say that alpha (α)—the symbol used to designate the probability of making that particular type of error—is being set at 5%. Likewise, a 99% confidence interval would require an alpha of 1%, or 0.01. Making the mistake of saying that a difference exists between two populations when there really is none is an example of a type-1 error.

Another type of error is the decision not to reject the idea of a difference, when actually there is some real difference between the populations. This is called a type-2 error, and the probability of making this error is called beta (β).

Example of a Chi-square Test (Goodness-of-Fit Test)

As noted earlier, the chi-square can be used to test any two frequency distributions against each other. Here we will test an observed distribution against an arbitrarily derived expected distribution.

Figure 11.14 shows observed sales over the seasons of the year (frequency observed, F_o) and an assumption of equal sales from each quarter (frequency expected, F_e). If the 120 total sales were divided equally among the four quarters, we would get the expected frequency distribution shown.

FIGURE 11.14
Example of Observed and Expected Frequencies

	F_o		F_e
Winter	30	Winter	30
Spring	25	Spring	30
Summer	25	Summer	30
Fall	40	Fall	30

With these distributions in hand, we can test for significant difference, following the five steps of the common procedure:

1. The hypotheses to be tested are:
    H_0: the seasons are equal ($F_o = F_e$)
    H_1: the seasons are not equal ($F_o \neq F_e$).

2. The theoretical distribution is based on 3 degrees of freedom (d.f. $= 4 - 1$). Therefore, if there is no real difference, just scatter, we can expect an average chi-square value of 3 as a result of our comparison of F_o with F_e. Furthermore, if there is no real difference, only scatter, we can expect to see a value of chi-square as large as 7.81 only 5% of the time and a value of chi-square as large as 11.34 only 1% of the time (see Figure 11.15).

FIGURE 11.15
The Theoretical Distribution and Critical Values

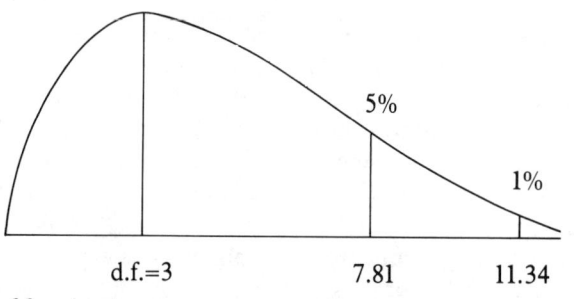

d.f.=3   7.81   11.34

(d.f.: degrees of freedom)

3. The actual value of chi-square (the statistic), which summarizes the amount of difference (or scatter) between the two frequency tables, is computed according to the formula

$$\chi^2 = \Sigma \frac{(F_o - F_e)^2}{F_e}$$

The computation here is

F_o	F_e	$F_o - F_e$	$(F_o - F_e)^2$	$(F_o - F_e)^2/F_e$
30	30	30 − 30	0	$0/30 = 0.00$
25	30	25 − 30	25	$25/30 = 0.83$
25	30	25 − 30	25	$25/30 = 0.83$
40	30	90 − 30	100	$100/30 = 3.33$
				$\overline{4.99 = \chi^2}$

4. Figure 11.16 shows the comparison of the statistic with the parameter, or of the actual value of chi-square, which is 4.99, with the cutoffs from the theoretical distribution.

FIGURE 11.16
The Statistic Versus the Parameter

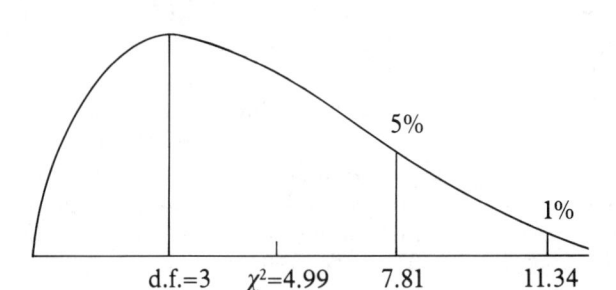

(d.f.: degrees of freedom)

5. **Conclusion:** The actual value of chi-square is inside the theoretical cutoffs. Therefore, we do not reject H_0; we do not declare that there is statistically significant difference among the seasons.

Note that we have not proved that the seasons are equal; we have simply been unable to show that they are not equal. In other words, we have concluded that differences of the magnitude observed in this problem might be attributable simply to random scatter.

Note also that we are always implying rejection or non-rejection at a certain probability level. A chi-square value of 4.99 happens to be significant at the 25% level. Thus, we are 75% sure that we have a significant difference, although we did not obtain the 95% or 99% levels that are considered traditional in most statistical testing.

Rejecting, Accepting, and Not Rejecting

Technically, it is not proper to say that a given chi-square test has shown that there is no difference; we can say only that we have failed to demonstrate that there is a difference. Many students are confused by the fact that *accept* is not the same as *fail to reject*. The reason for this seeming anomaly lies in the nature of the statistical test. The observed distribution is seldom, if ever, truly equal to the theoretical distribution and thus it would be improper to say that two distributions with some actual differences have been *proved* to be equal. Rather, all we can say is that the tables have failed to demonstrate that the distributions are not equal.

Marketing Implications of Non-Rejection

Although non-rejection is really nothing but an inconclusive result, in many actual situations the marketing researcher is not allowed the luxury of "no decision." If two brands are competing and a decision has to be made to cancel one and retain the other, that decision must be made whether the results are statistically significant or not. In such a situation it really might not make much sense to compute the significance at all. In this type of situation, personal judgment might be the bottom line.

Note also that in performing a statistical test and declaring there to be a significant difference, the researcher is pointing out a *statistically* significant difference, a difference tested against the idea of *absolutely zero difference*. As discussed previously, the ability to *prove* this difference is a function of sample size and is a matter of the relative size of the difference. The absolute size of the difference is of no concern, statistically. However, such matters are of great concern to the decision maker. For example, suppose a tire manufacturer developed a tire that, for approximately double the cost, would last five hundred miles longer than the standard tire. The formulas would soon show a significant statistical difference, but the average motorist probably would not perceive any difference and certainly would not be willing to pay twice the price.

In view of the previous discussion of the applicability of statistical tests and the inconclusiveness of non-rejection, you might be wondering about the value of a test like this. Its value is that, by determining the range of normal scatter, the range of sampling error, we are sometimes able to realize that what had previously appeared to be a noteworthy difference between two values actually was completely within the range of normal sampling error. In other words, the differences we observed are really (or possibly) illusionary; they might have been caused simply by the normal scatter expected within all sample estimates.

■ Summary

The purpose of this chapter has been to provide an introduction to the mechanics of data analysis, particularly descriptive statistics (tabulation) and univariate statistics.

Three types of tabulation have been discussed here: percentages, averages, and dispersions. The percentage is the easiest form of summary statistic to use and compute. However, care must be taken, because changes in the base (changes that are often very subtle and can go virtually unnoticed) can cause significant changes in the resulting percentages.

There are three forms of averages—measures of central tendency—that are commonly used in marketing research: the arithmetic mean, the median, and the mode. Although all three classify as measures of central tendency, they will all be different in a skewed distribution; the mean will be the measure farthest out in the tail, the mode will be the point of maximum concentration (the centre of the "hump"), and the median will lie between the other two.

Four measures of dispersion have been discussed: the range, the interquartile range, the average deviation, and the standard deviation. The standard deviation is the preferred measure of dispersion, because it is one of the parameters of the normal curve. With a normally distributed population, use of the standard deviation will permit determination of the percentage of the population that falls between selected intervals. Even without normal distribution of the population, measures of skewedness can be used to determine the shape of a curve.

This chapter has also tried to give some insight into the statistical considerations of sampling. In doing so, the first step was to examine sampling error, or the error that results from the natural scatter of sample estimates about the population value. This sample error contrasts with non-sampling error, or the qualitative error that comes from bias in the way in which the sample is conducted.

Four quantitative factors influence the strength of our confidence in the conclusions we draw from a sample result: the magnitude of the miss, the sample size, the dispersion of the sample values, and the conditions affecting the test. Of these four, only sample size is under the control of the researcher. However, in this case, one factor is enough, because by properly manipulating the sample size, the researcher can achieve any desired level of precision.

Furthermore, it must always be remembered that sampling error is only one type of error that can be encountered in a survey. There is also non-sampling error with which to contend, and whereas the sampling error can be both calculated and controlled, the non-sampling error cannot be. Because the possibility of significant amounts of non-sampling error exists with most marketing surveys, marketing researchers are often relatively unconcerned about obtaining the last decimal places of statistical precision. Most marketing researchers prefer to spend their money on a smaller sample of higher quality rather than on a larger sample of lower quality.

This chapter has also presented three statistical techniques: the z-test, the t-test and the chi-square test. The z-test and t-test are similar in their mechanics and allow the researcher to test whether a mean or a proportion is different (two-tail test) or greater or smaller (one-tail test) than a theoretical value. The t-test is used mostly when the sample size is small or the population standard deviation is unknown. The chi-square technique is very useful in that it is designed to work with nominal data, such as the data in a frequency distribution or classification table. Since any type of data can be downgraded into nominal data, the chi-square is applicable to any type of data. The chi-square test provides a method of determining whether a statistical difference exists between two frequency distributions. In looking for a statistical difference, we are testing whether the difference between the distributions is within that range attributable to "normal" scatter, or whether the difference is so large that we can conclude that there must be some real difference between the distributions. It should be noted, however, that in saying that there is a "real" difference we are not saying how much difference. It is possible to have a statistical difference of such small absolute size that it is of no marketing significance.

For Discussion

1. How can the three measures of central tendency all give different answers if the distribution is skewed?

2. How can measures of central tendency, including the arithmetic mean and the median in particular, often obscure important market segments?

3. Why is the median often referred to as the most democratic measure of central tendency? Why is the standard deviation the preferred measure of dispersion?

4. For the following data set, compute the arithmetic mean, the median, the mode, the expected value, the range, the average deviation, and the standard deviation: data set = 6, 2, 8, 7, 5, 4, 7, 7.

5. Distinguish between sampling error and non-sampling error. Discuss the relationship between sampling and non-sampling error. Is non-sampling error a problem for researchers in all fields?

6. Someone has claimed that a drug has 60% effectiveness, and a sample has been taken to test this claim. In judging whether the sample results support or refute the claim, what four factors would you examine?

7. Of the various factors impinging on the confidence we have in a sample estimate, which one is under the direct control of the researcher?

8. A sample is being made to estimate the percentage of minority students in a certain high school, where it is believed that approximately 20% of the students are from minorities. How many students would have to be sampled to be 95% sure that the estimate is within five percentage points?

9. The Nielsen television ratings survey used to estimate network shares around 30% are currently based on a sample of approximately 1100 homes. The Nielsen researchers are 95% certain that their results are within how many percentage points of the true population percentages? Why would the Nielsen researchers be reluctant to try to get that error down to 1% or less?

10. Two candidates are running for Parliament. One of the candidates takes a poll of two hundred people that shows her to have 51% of the vote, with the other candidate having 46% of the vote and 3% undecided. "I've got the election in the bag!" she crows. 'Even if my opponent gets all 3% of the undecided vote, he still can't catch me!" Does she have the election wrapped up? Discuss.

Problems

1. **Mini-case: Super Drug Mart**

   Super Drug Mart, a large Ontario discount drugstore chain, is planning to enter the Vancouver market. Management would like to estimate the average square metres of selling space of competing drugstores in the area. A stratified sample of these yielded the following data.

Size of Store	Total Number in Vancouver	Total Number in Sample	Mean Size of Stores in Sample (m²)	Standard Deviation of Stores in Sample (m²)
Large	200	6	2000	300
Medium	500	15	1000	200
Small	900	20	200	100

   Question

   What is the average size of discount drugstores in Vanccouver? Find the 95% confidence interval around that size.

2. **Mini-case: Barker Dog Food Company**

   The Barker Dog Food Company has conducted a survey of dog owners to determine if there is a difference between dog food consumed by show dogs and that consumed by all other dogs. The data in Exhibit 11.1 have been obtained.

   EXHIBIT 11.1
   Dog Food Consumption of Show Dogs vs. All Other Dogs

Brand	Number of Dogs Being Fed		
	Show Dogs	All Other Dogs	Total
A	50	270	320
B	30	160	190
C	40	50	90
All other brands	80	320	400
Totals	200	800	1000

   Questions

   1. Calculate the chi-square statistic for this set of data.

   2. How many degrees of freedom are there in this example?

   3. If there is a probability of 0.01 that a value of χ^2 larger than 11.34 will occur as a result of random variations, what can we infer about the data?

3. A certain college expects all of its professors to grade on the following curve: A = 10% B = 20% C = 40% F = 10%. Consider the curious case of Professor X. In a certain class of forty students, he gives the grades shown below. Are his grades within the range of acceptable deviation?

40 Students

	A	B	C	D	E
Observed	7	15	8	6	4

	A	B	C	D	E
Expected	4	8	16	8	4

Suppose that he actually has two classes of forty students and maintains the same distribution shown for the first group over the entire group of eighty students. Use the chi-square to test again for significant difference.

80 Students

	A	B	C	D	E
Observed	14	30	16	12	8

	A	B	C	D	E
Expected	8	16	32	16	8

4. On a certain basketball team the average per-game point totals of the starting five members of the team are: the center = 20 points; one forward = 20 points, the other forward = 10 points, one guard = 25 points, the other guard = 10 points. Test against the hypothesis that all members of the team are contributing equally.

CHAPTER 12

DATA ANALYSIS: INTRODUCTION TO ADVANCED STATISTICS

The previous chapter discussed the elementary statistics that are useful in reducing the data (descriptive statistics), and tests that involve one variable at a time (univariate statistics). When the researcher is interested in testing the relationship between two variables, there are a number of **bivariate** statistics that are useful. These will be described in the first part of this chapter. The second part of this chapter deals with a number of multivariate techniques used to test the relationship among three or more variables.

Diffusion of these techniques to business managers has been encouraged by a better understanding and availability of mainframe computers and microcomputers. The use of computers by marketing researchers is a comparatively recent development. For many years, there was a feeling of mistrust toward marketing research and its tools: marketing research, it was reasoned, was nothing but fancy mumbo jumbo using computers to produce a lot of funny-looking numbers but very little else. Corporate personnel from the president to the salesperson to the janitor did not understand and did not trust researchers or their findings.

But that was thirty years ago. Today most companies are quite comfortable with the use of the computer and with marketing research. They have seen it in operation, they understand it, they know how and why it works and, most importantly, they know that it *does* work. As sophistication grows—and it continues to grow, because each group of new employees is more receptive than the preceding one toward sophisticated research and because of the educational system's increased emphasis on such research—the use of marketing research will continue to grow also. (See Appendix I for a review of the use of microcomputers in marketing research.)

Because the attitudes of managers toward sophisticated research techniques are critical to marketing researchers, this chapter will conclude with a discussion of some of these attitudes.

■ Bivariate Analysis

Bivariate analysis can be used either to test differences between two groups or, more usually, to look at the association between two variables. We will describe five methods of bivariate analysis: the t-test, the z-test, the bivariate chi-square, the analysis of variance, and the regression analysis.

t-test of Difference Between Two Means

In the previous chapter, the t-test was introduced as more appropriate when sample size is small and the population standard deviation is unknown. This is often the case when the researcher is faced with comparing the results obtained from two independent groups or samples. The question raised is whether the *means* of the two groups are identical.

For example, a car manufacturer is interested in finding out if the attitudes toward a new Canadian-made car are different between male and female customers. A survey conducted by the research department found the following results:

	Male	*Female*
Size	$n_1 = 40$	$n_2 = 30$
Mean attitude	$\bar{x}_1 = 6.5$	$\bar{x}_2 = 4.5$
Standard deviation	$s_1 = 2$	$s_2 = 3$

To test the difference between the two means, we follow the five-step common procedure developed in the previous chapter:

1. Hypotheses to be tested:
    H_0: The difference $d = \mu_1 - \mu_2$ is equal to zero, i.e., the two means are equal.
    H_1: The difference d is not equal to zero.

2. The test to be used in the t-test of the difference between the two means:

$$t = \frac{\bar{x}_1 - \bar{x}_2}{s_{\text{diff}}} \qquad \gamma = n_1 + n_2 - 2$$

$$\text{where } s_{\text{diff}} = \sqrt{\frac{(n_1 - 1)s_1^2 + (n_2 - 1)s_2^2}{n_1 + n_2 - 2}\left(\frac{1}{n_1} + \frac{1}{n_2}\right)}$$

With $\gamma = 68$ degrees of freedom, the critical t_α for $\alpha = 0.05$ is approximately 2.00.

3. The actual value of t is

$$t = \frac{6.5 - 4.5}{0.598} = 3.34$$

$$s_{\text{diff}} = \sqrt{\frac{(39)(4) + (29)(3)}{68}\left(\frac{1}{40} + \frac{1}{30}\right)} = 0.598$$

4. The calculated value of 3.34 is greater than the critical value of 2.00.

5. **Conclusion:** One must reject the hypothesis that the two means are equal. Therefore, the car manufacturer can conclude that at the 95% confidence

level, the male group is significantly more favourably disposed toward the new car than is the female group.

One-tail t-test of Differences

As for the univariate case of the previous chapter, it is possible that the researcher has some prior knowledge about the direction of the difference, and might choose to formulate the hypotheses as follows:

H_0: The mean μ_1 is less than or equal to μ_2, i.e., $d \leq 0$.

H_1: The mean μ_1 is greater than μ_2, i.e., $d > 0$.

The procedure is then the same as before, with a new critical value for t_α.

z-test of Difference Between Two Proportions

When the researcher wants to test the difference between two proportions and the sample size is large, the following statistic

$$z = \frac{p_1 - p_2}{s_{diff}}$$

is normally distributed and the standard deviation of the difference is calculated as follows:

$$p = \frac{n_1 p_1 + n_2 p_2}{n_1 + n_2}$$

$$s_{diff} = \sqrt{p(1-p)\frac{n_1 + n_2}{n_1 n_2}}$$

For example, let us assume that the percentage of male and female respondents who indicated that they prefer a Canadian-made car to a foreign-made car is as follows:

	Male	Female
Size	$n_1 = 100$	$n_1 = 60$
Percentage preference	$p_1 = 65\%$	$p_2 = 45\%$

1. Hypotheses to be tested:

   H_0: $\pi_1 = \pi_2$, i.e., the proportions are not significantly different.
   H_1: $\pi_1 \neq \pi_2$, i.e., they are different.

2. For a level of confidence of 95%, the critical z_α is equal to 1.96.

3. The actual value of z is calculated as follows:

$$p = \frac{100(.65) + 60(.45)}{160} = .575$$

$$s_{diff} = \sqrt{(.575)(.425)(.0267)} = .081$$

$$z = \frac{.65 - .45}{.081} = 2.48$$

4. The actual $z = 2.48$ is greater than the critical z of 1.96.

5. **Conclusion**: The null hypothesis must be rejected. Therefore, there are significant differences between male and female potential customers in relation to their preferences for a Canadian-made car over a foreign-made one.

Bivariate Chi-square Test

As seen in the previous chapter, the chi-square test is designed to work with nominal data. In the bivariate case these are in the form of classification tables that show the frequency of occurrence of the various classifications in the breakdown.

As mentioned before, other types of data can be downgraded into nominal data. For instance, suppose you had income figures from two groups, people living in Quebec and people living in Ontario. You could run a statistical test between the arithmetic means of the two groups, or you could take these income figures and break them down into a frequency table like Figure 12.1. The chi-square test could be run on the frequency counts found in that table.

FIGURE 12.1
A Three-by-Two Frequency Table

Income	Ontario	Quebec
Low		
Medium		
High		

Another example might be a comparison of the percentages of people favouring each of two candidates. You could run a statistical test comparing the two percentages, or you could break those "percentage" responses into a frequency table like Figure 12.2. The chi-square test could then be run on the frequency counts found in that table.

FIGURE 12.2
A Two-by-Two Frequency Table

	Candidate A	Candidate B
Votes For		
Votes Against		

Basic Description of Method

In working with the chi-square test, the focus will be on the classifications or, to phrase it another way, the frequency distributions produced by a classification.

The chi-square test provides us with a mathematical way of examining a classification table to see whether the arrangement of values within that table is unusual in some way.

In performing the test, we will be comparing a computed with a theoretical value of chi-square. The theoretical distribution of chi-square is a skewed distribution that varies in shape according to the number of cells in the classification table. More precisely, the chi-square varies in shape according to degrees of freedom, which in the case of the chi-square equal (the number of rows minus one) multiplied by (the number of columns minus one) (see Figure 12.3). Because the shape of the distribution varies with degrees of freedom, we will use the degrees of freedom to guide us to the proper values in the chi-square table. Degrees of freedom also represent the expected value or mean for the chi-square distribution.

FIGURE 12.3
Number of Degrees of Freedom for a Frequency Table

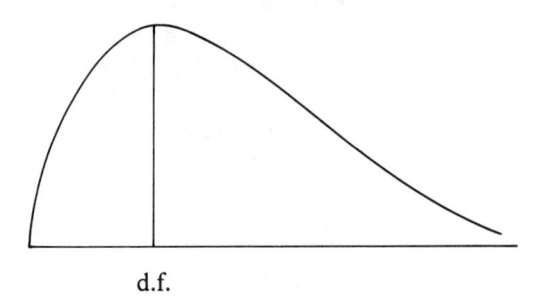

d.f.

d.f. = (number of rows minus 1) (number of columns minus 1)

The chi-square test looks at the distribution by comparing the observed distribution against some expected distribution, to determine if a statistically significant difference is present. These expected distributions take the form of an independence-of-classification test. The purpose of this test is to determine whether the arrangement of values in the classification table is independent of the factors according to which the data were classified.

Let us work through a sample problem to illustrate the use of the degrees of freedom in obtaining the chi-square parameters. The specifics of the solution to the problem will be explained later.

Suppose that we had a classification table like the one in Figure 12.4, which has three rows and four columns. The degrees of freedom in this case would be 6: d.f. $= (3 - 1) \times (4 - 1) = (2) \times (3) = 6$. Therefore, using the tables in Appendix 3, Exhibit A, and using 6 degrees of freedom, we develop a picture of the distribution of chi-square values from a classification table with 6 degrees of freedom.

FIGURE 12.4
A Three-by-Four Classification Table

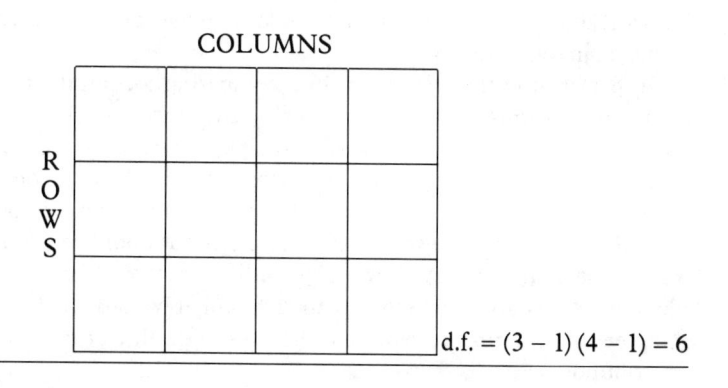

COLUMNS

R
O
W
S

d.f. = (3 − 1) (4 − 1) = 6

Because d.f. = 6, if the numbers classified on the rows had no significant relationship to the numbers classified on the columns, we would nevertheless expect to generate an *average* chi-square of 6. (Note that if there is absolutely no relationship among the numbers in the table, we would expect the value of chi-square to be 6. However, we expect to find some scatter, even among variables with no intrinsic relationship to one another. In this case we expect the average scatter to be 6.)

Furthermore, if there is indeed no significant difference, no relationship (as, by analogy, a gun being on target), then on the basis of the picture developed (Figure 12.5), we would know that only 5% of the time should we get a value of chi-square greater than 12.54, and only 1% of the time should we find a value of chi-square greater than 16.81.

FIGURE 12.5
Example with Six Degrees of Freedom

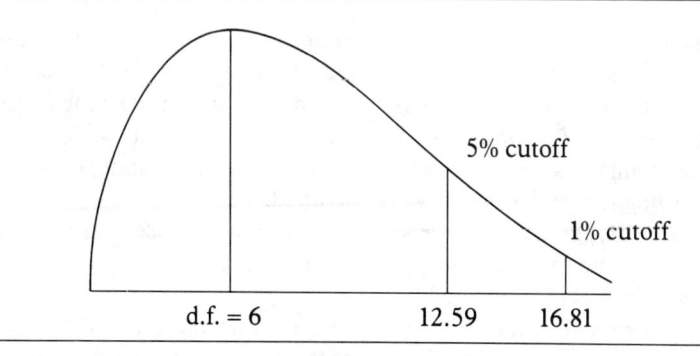

5% cutoff

1% cutoff

d.f. = 6   12.59   16.81

To rephrase, because this chi-square distribution is computed on the assumption that there is no significant relationship (no difference) between the values in the classification table, an actual value of chi-square (the statistic) *outside* that 5% cutoff of 12.59 (the parameter) shows a 95% probability that there is a relationship.

(You might need to reread the preceding sentence several times.) Likewise, if the actual value of chi-square is outside the 1% cutoff of 16.81, then we are 99% sure that there is a relationship. Since this material is probably still quite confusing, we will provide a sample problem.

Example of an Independence-of-Classification Test

The most frequent use of the chi-square test is to perform what is known as an **independence-of-classification test**. The purpose of this test is to see if the arrangements of values within a group of cells is independent of the factors by which they were classified. Thus, in a table in which data are classified by age and gender, the chi-square test will determine whether there appears to be a relationship between age and gender for that set of data. In this test, the expected frequency distribution is not derived arbitrarily, as in the goodness-of-fit test; rather, the expected distribution is derived from the observed distribution, using the row and column totals of the observed distribution.

We will illustrate this process using the classification table in Figure 12.6, which gives a breakdown between gender and test scores. In this test we will be trying to determine whether the males have the higher scores. Although it appears from the table that they do, we want to test that conclusion mathematically. (**Note:** Do not jump to conclusions about an example showing higher scores for males. The example does not say with what those scores are concerned—it might be that the males scored higher on an alcoholic tendency test. The point is that one must always look behind the scenes in analysing numerical data and avoid making assumptions that might prove to be false.)

FIGURE 12.6
Gender and Test Score Classification

	SCORES High	Low	
Gender			
M	14	7	21
F	12	23	35
	26	30	56

To test this table, we will develop the expected distribution from the observed distribution, using the row and column totals or the totals of items shown around the margins of the table in Figure 12.7. Because of this procedure, this method is sometimes called the **method of marginal products**. To compute the expected cell values using the method of marginal products, we will use the formula

$$\text{cell value } (F_e) = \frac{\text{row total} \times \text{column total}}{\text{grand total}}$$

FIGURE 12.7
Frequency-observed Scores

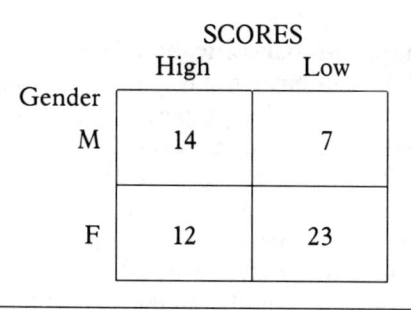

The cell values for the expected table are (Figure 12.8)

$$\text{cell }(1, 1) = \frac{rt \times ct}{gt} = \frac{26 \times 21}{56} = 9.75$$

$$\text{cell }(1, 2) = \frac{rt \times ct}{gt} = \frac{30 \times 21}{56} = 11.25$$

$$\text{cell }(2, 1) = \frac{rt \times ct}{gt} = \frac{26 \times 35}{56} = 16.25$$

$$\text{cell }(2, 2) = \frac{rt \times ct}{gt} = \frac{30 \times 35}{56} = 18.75$$

Notice that we actually did not need to compute all four cell values separately. We needed to find only one of the four cell values and from there we could have found the remaining three by subtracting from the appropriate row and column totals (this process further illustrates what degrees of freedom mean).

FIGURE 12.8
Frequency-expected Scores

	SCORES	
	High	Low
Gender		
M	9.75	11.25
F	16.25	18.75

With F_o and F_e now computed, let us begin the statistical test.

1. The hypotheses are

   H_0: Classifications independent, score not related to sex $(F_o = F_e)$.
   H_1: Classifications not independent, score related to sex $(F_o \neq F_e)$.

FIGURE 12.9
Theoretical Picture

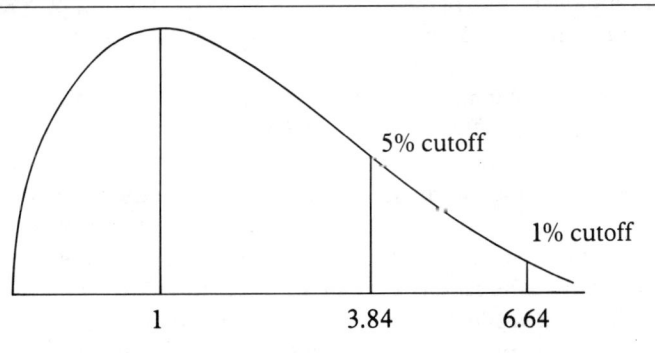

2. The theoretical picture (Figure 12.9): in this case d.f. = 1; if gender and score are not related, we can expect an average scatter of chi-square equal to 1, with a chi-square greater than 3.84 only 5% of the time and a chi-square greater than 6.64 only 1% of the time.

3. The calculations, using the formula

$$\chi^2 = \Sigma \frac{(F_o - F_e)^2}{F_e}$$

are

F_o			F_e		$F_o - F_e$	$(F_o - F_e)^2$	$(F_o - F_e)^2 / F_e$
					14– 9.75	18.0625	1.85
14	7		9.75	11.25	7–11.75	18.0625	1.61
12	23		16.25	18.25	12–16.75	18.0625	1.11
					23–18.75	18.0625	0.96
							$\overline{5.53} = \chi^2$

4. When the statistic is compared with the parameter, the actual value of 5.53 falls between the 5% cutoff and the 1% cutoff (Figure 12.10).

FIGURE 12.10
Statistic vs. Parameter

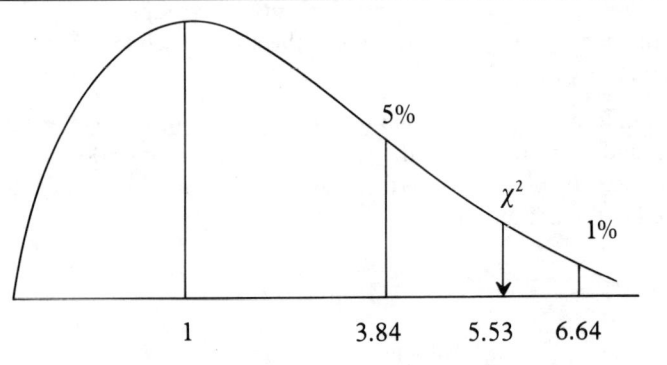

5. **Conclusion:** We are 95% sure that there is a statistically significant difference, although we are not 99% sure. Thus we reject the null hypothesis that the classifications are independent at the 95% level, but do not reject the null hypothesis at the 99% level.

Effect of Sample Size on Chi-Square

Sample size definitely affects the researcher's confidence in sample estimates. Sample size also increases the precision of the confidence that can be given to results of tests involving the chi-square distribution. For example, in Figure 12.11, three chi-square tables are presented. In each case the relative (percentage) breakdown of the items in the tables is the same, although the total number of items in the matrix (the sample size) goes from 12 to 120 to 1200.

Notice that increasing the sample size has increased the precision of the estimate, thus allowing the null hypothesis to be rejected at a higher level of confidence. In the chi-square test, the value of the chi-square statistic increases proportionately with sample size. (**Note:** Although increasing sample size always increases the precision of a test, the relationship is not always linear.)

Analysis of Variance

When the researcher is faced with comparing the means of more than two groups, the t-test is no longer appropriate and the method to be used is called the analysis of variance (ANOVA). In an analysis of variance, the hypotheses to be tested are

$$H_0: \text{All the means are equal.}$$
$$H_1: \text{The means are not equal.}$$

To test these hypotheses, the method uses the F-test and its corresponding distribution (Appendix 3, Exhibit D). The F statistic is a ratio of two variances and it is used to determine if these two variances are equal.

In the analysis of variance, the mean variance within the groups is compared to the variance of the means of the groups (variance between groups). If these two mean variances are equal, F should be around 1, and we could conclude that there is no difference among the means. Thus, the F statistic is

$$F = \frac{\text{mean square between}}{\text{mean square within}} = \frac{MS_{\text{between}}}{MS_{\text{within}}}$$

An F-test has two sets of degrees of freedom:
Numerator: $\gamma_1 = g - 1$, where g is the number of groups
Denominator: $\gamma_1 = n(g - 1)$, where n is the size of each group (all groups must be of equal sizes)

For example, a compact disc manufacturer has obtained the sales data shown in Table 12.1 and wants to know if the three groups are different.

To calculate F, one must partition the total sum of squares into the parts mentioned in the definition of F:

$$SS_{\text{total}} = SS_{\text{within}} + SS_{\text{between}}$$

FIGURE 12.11
Chi-Square Test: Effects of Sample Size

H_0 Classifications are independent, voting patterns are not related to political parties

H_1 Classifications are not independent, voting patterns are related to political parties

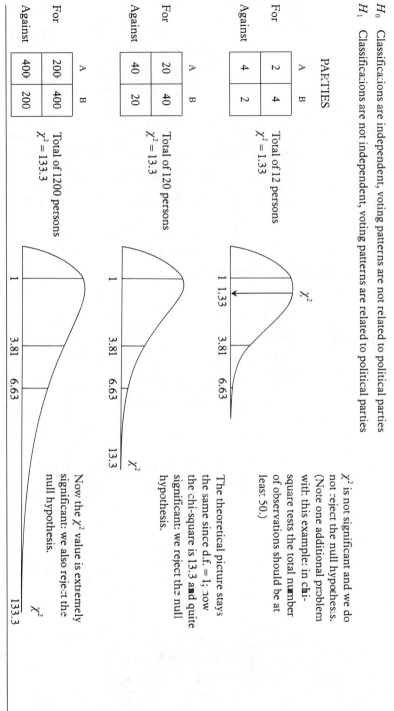

PARTIES

	A	B
For	2	4
Against	4	2

Total of 12 persons
$\chi^2 = 1.33$

	A	B
For	20	40
Against	40	20

Total of 120 persons
$\chi^2 = 13.3$

	A	B
For	200	400
Against	400	200

Total of 1200 persons
$\chi^2 = 133.3$

χ^2 is not significant and we do not reject the null hypothesis. (Note one additional problem with this example: in chi-square test the total number of observations should be at least 50.)

The theoretical picture stays the same since the d.f. = 1; now the chi-square is 13.3 and quite significant: we reject the null hypothesis.

Now the χ^2 value is extremely significant: we also reject the null hypothesis.

TABLE 12.1
Numerical Example for ANOVA Method

Number of compact discs sold last year (in '000s)

	i	Males (15–20)	Females (15–20)	Adults (21–30)
Western Provinces	1	60	45	40
Prairie Provinces	2	90	70	75
Ontario	3	200	190	150
Quebec	4	150	140	100
Atlantic Provinces	5	50	30	30
Mean $\bar{x}_j$		$\bar{x}_1 = 110$	$\bar{x}_2 = 95$	$\bar{x}_3 = 80$
$(\bar{x}_j - \bar{\bar{x}})$		225	0	225

Grand mean $\bar{\bar{x}} = 95$

Calculations of the sum of squares

i	Males (15–20)		Females (15–20)		Adults (21–30)	
	$(x_{i_1} - \bar{x}_1)^2$	$(x_{i_1} - \bar{\bar{x}})^2$	$(x_{i_2} - \bar{x}_2)^2$	$(x_{i_2} - \bar{\bar{x}})^2$	$(x_{i_3} - \bar{x}_3)^2$	$(x_{i_3} - \bar{\bar{x}})^2$
1	2 500	1 225	2 500	2 500	1600	3 025
2	400	25	625	625	25	400
3	8 100	11 025	9 025	9 025	4900	3 025
4	1 600	3 025	2 025	2 025	400	25
5	3 600	2 025	4 225	4 225	2025	3 600
	16 200	17 325	18 400	18 400	8950	10 075

The sum of squares within is the sum of deviations *within* each group, for all groups:

$$SS_{within} = \Sigma(x_{i_1} - \bar{x}_1)^2 + \Sigma(x_{i_2} - \bar{x}_2)^2 + \Sigma(x_{i_3} - \bar{x}_3)^2$$
$$= 16\,200 + 18\,400 + 8950 = 43\,550$$

With $g(n-1) = 12$ degrees of freedom, the mean square within is

$$MS_{within} = 43\,550 \div 12 = 3629$$

The sum of squares between is the sum of deviations of the group means from the grand mean:

$$SS_{between} = 5(\bar{x}_1 - \bar{\bar{x}})^2 + 5(\bar{x}_2 - \bar{\bar{x}})^2 + 5(x_3 - \bar{\bar{x}})^2$$
$$= 5(225) + 5(0) + 5(225) = 2250$$

With $g - 1 = 2$ degrees of freedom, the mean square between is

$$MS_{between} = 2250 \div 2 = 1125$$

Then the F-statistic becomes

$$F = \frac{3629}{1125} = 3.23 \text{ with 12 and 2 degrees of freedom}$$

(Note that by inverting the ratio to have an F greater than one, one also inverts the degrees of freedom.)

Since the critical $F_{12,2}$ at the 95% level of confidence is 19.4, one cannot reject the null hypothesis. It appears that there is no difference among the three groups.

Finally, one can verify that the partitioning of the sum of squares is correct

$$SS_{total} = SS_{within} + SS_{between} = 43\ 550 + 2250 = 45\ 800$$
$$\text{Also: } SS_{total} = \Sigma(x_{i_1} - \bar{\bar{x}})^2 + \Sigma(x_{i_2} - \bar{\bar{x}})^2 + \Sigma(x_{i_3} - \bar{\bar{x}})^2$$
$$\text{(from Table 12.1)}$$
$$SS_{total} = 17\ 325 + 18\ 400 + 10\ 075 = 45\ 800$$

The results from the analysis of variance are usually presented in the form of a summary table, as shown in Table 12.2.

TABLE 12.2
ANOVA Table for the Numerical Example

Source	Sum of Squares	Degrees of Freedom	Mean Square	F-ratio*
Between Groups	2 250	2	1125	
				3.23
Within Groups	43 550	12	3629	
Total	45 890	14		

*By inverting the F, one looks at the F-table with 12 and 2 degrees of freedom.

Simple Linear Regression Analysis

This method is the most widely used in marketing to estimate the relationship between two variables, the dependent variable, and the independent variable. For example, let us assume that, everything else being equal, sales are a function of advertising, and that the relationship is linear within a certain range. The amount spent on advertising has varied in the last few years and the data can be plotted as shown in Figure 12.12.

Simple observation of the data shows that as the advertising budget is increased, the sales during the period also increase. Thus, relationship can be expressed mathematically as

$$\hat{S} = S_0 + aA$$

where S is the estimated sales

S_0 is the sales if the advertising budget is zero

A is the advertising budget

a is the slope of the regression line

The values of S_0 and a are obtained mathematically by minimizing the sum of the squared differences between the predicted ($\hat{S}$) and actual (S) sales values, and

FIGURE 12.12
Simple Linear Regression: Example of the Method
of Least Square

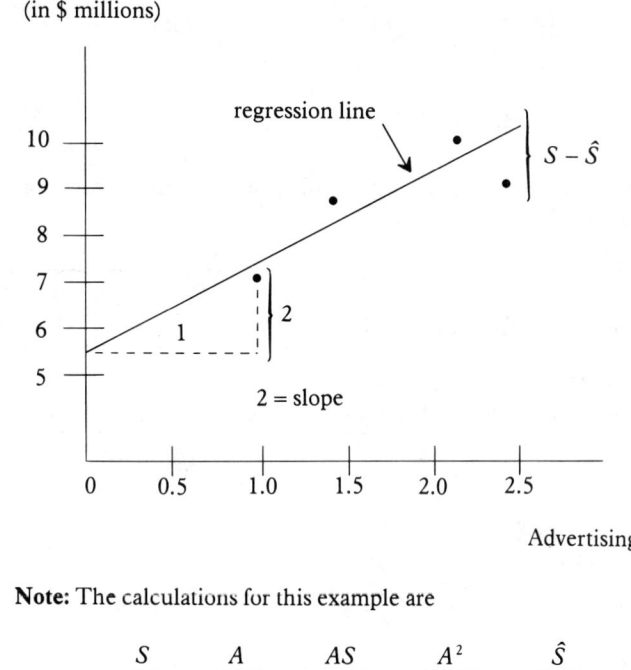

Advertising (in $00 000)

Note: The calculations for this example are

S	A	AS	A^2	$\hat{S}$	$(S - \hat{S})^2$	$(S - \bar{S})^2$
7	1.0	7	1	7.5	0.25	4
9	1.5	13.5	2.25	8.5	0.25	0
10	2.0	20	4	9.5	0.25	1
10	2.5	25	6.25	10.5	0.25	1
Σ 36	7	65.5	13.5	36	1.00	6
Mean 9	1.75					

in doing so one obtains the following:

$$a = \frac{\Sigma AS - n\bar{A}\bar{S}}{\Sigma A^2 - n\bar{A}^2}$$ which is the slope, and

$S_0 = \bar{S} - a\bar{A}$ which is the intercept.

By applying the formulas to the example in Figure 12.12, one finds that

$$a = \frac{65.5 - 4(1.75)(9)}{13.5 - 4(3.06)} = 2$$

$$S_0 = 9 - 2(1.75) = 5.5$$

One could interpret this simple example by saying that if we do not spend anything on advertising, the sales might be at $5.5 million—the result of past efforts—and each $100 000 spent on advertising will most likely bring in $2 million in additional sales.

Most software programs, including advanced calculators, provide these parameters and might also provide the following information:

- The *standard error of estimate*, which is similar to the standard deviation concept:

$$S = \sqrt{\frac{\Sigma(S - \hat{S})^2}{n - 2}} = 0.7$$

With this information one can calculate an interval of confidence for any prediction made by using the formula. For example, at the 95% confidence level, the value of t_{n-2} is 2.92. The prediction for sales arising from an advertising budget of $200 000 are

$$\$5.5 + 2(2) \pm 2.92(0.7) \text{ in millions,}$$
$$\text{or } \$9 \pm \$2.1 \text{ million}$$

Thus, the sales would be predicted at between $6.9 and $11.1 million.

- The *coefficient of determination*, which measures how well the regression line fits the data. More accurately, it is the percentage of total variance that is accounted for in the regression.

$$R^2 = 1 - \frac{\Sigma(S - \hat{S})^2}{\Sigma(S - \overline{S})^2} = 1 - \frac{1}{6} = 0.833$$

This means that 83.3% of the total variance in sales is explained by the variance of the advertising budget.

Multivariate Analysis

Most marketing phenomena are complex and the researcher is often faced with a large amount of variables and some theoretical conceptualizations that involve several variables. For example, attitude is a multidimensional concept, or purchase intention might be a function of attitude, confidence, price, prior experience, etc. Brand image can be evaluated on a large number of dimensions.

To deal with these complexities, marketing researchers have used multivariate techniques and the diffusion of these techniques is being influenced by the better training of researchers, combined with a greater availability of the software necessary to apply these techniques.[1] The revolution brought about by the information age, and the availability and ease of use of microcomputers, is also fueling a better understanding and appreciation of these techniques.

In this last section, we will describe in a non-technical manner some of the most important multivariate techniques. A classification of these techniques is presented in Figure 12.13 and a complete description of these techniques is available in more advanced texts.[2]

FIGURE 12.13
Classification of Multivariate Techniques

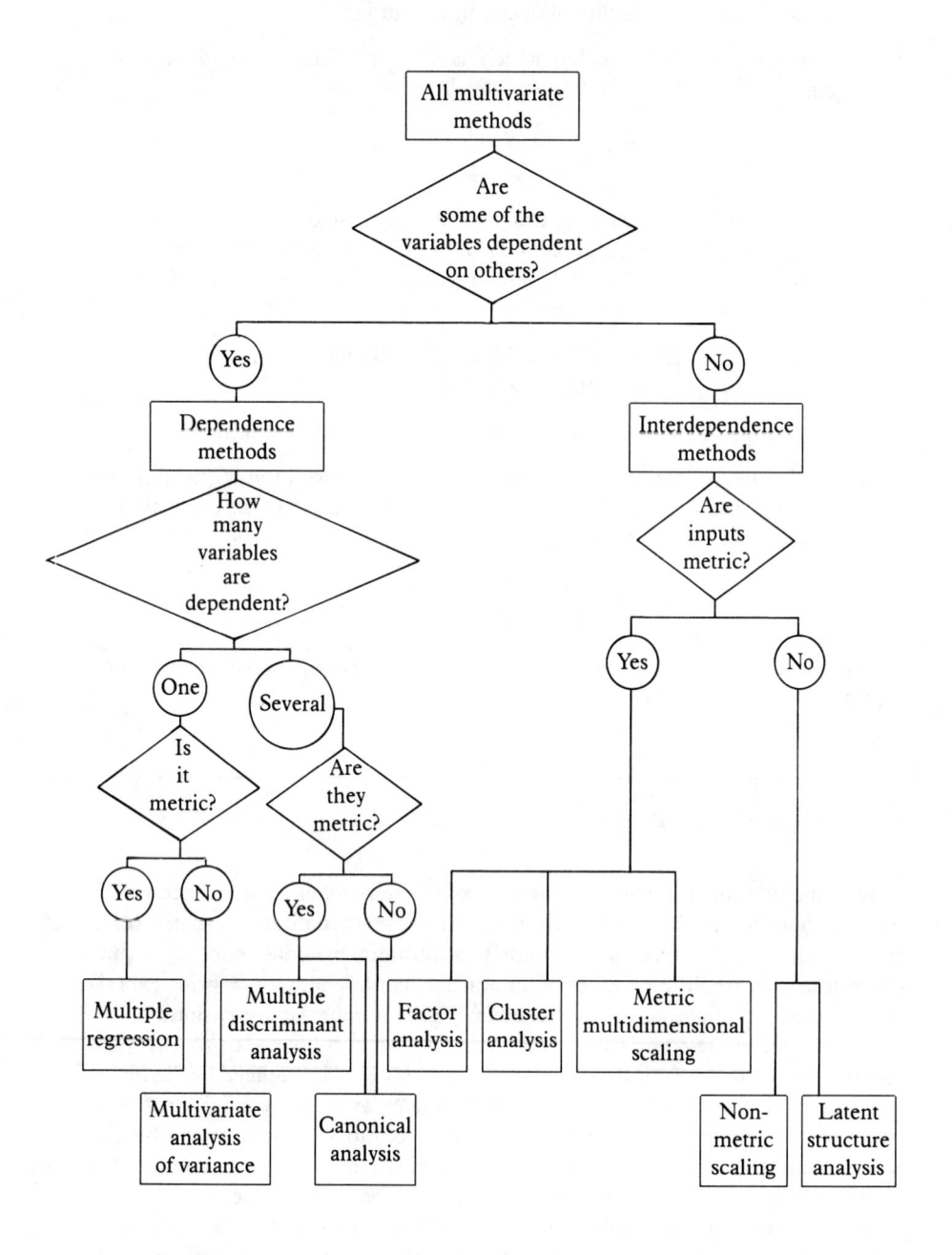

Source: Reprinted by permission from Jagdish N. Sheth, "The Multivariate Revolution in Marketing Research." *Journal of Marketing*, 35 (January 1971), p. 15, published by the American Marketing Association.

Multiple Regression

This is an extension of the simple linear regression method described in the first part of the chapter. Here, the researcher is faced with one dependent variable, Y, and several independent variables, $X_1, \ldots, X_N$. The latter are assumed to explain the behaviour of the former. For example, sales of a brand (V) are assumed to be a linear function of four marketing-mix variables: its price (P), advertising budget allocated to the brand (A), the size of the sales force attached to that brand (S) and the number of retail outlets distributing the brand (R):

$$V = a + b_1P + b_2A + b_3S + b_4R$$

where a is a constant term and b_1, b_2, b_3, b_4 are the coefficients (or weights) of the marketing mix variables.

In constructing such a model, the researcher is attempting to explain the behaviour of sales and to use the estimated parameters in forecasting the sales that would result from a modification of the marketing mix.

In a multiple regression output, the researcher is able to test each coefficient to determine if the corresponding variables provide a significant explanation to the dependent variable. Either a t-test or an F-test might be provided with a significance level. In addition, a coefficient of determination (R^2) indicates the percent total variance that is explained by the independent variables, and an overall test of the regression (of the R^2) is in the form of an F-test. Finally, a standard error of estimate is provided. An example of such output is provided in Table 12.3. In this example, all coefficients are significant at 95% and the independent variables explain 64% of the variance in sales figures.

TABLE 12.3
Hypothetical Multiple Regression Output

Dependent Variable: V

				Sum of		
Multiple R	.8000	ANALYSIS OF VARIANCE	d.f.	Squares	Mean Square	F
R Square	.6400	Regression	4	2000	500	5
STD. DEVIATION 1.250		RESIDUAL	45	4500	100	

Independent Variables	B	Std. Error B	T	Significance
P	−.3500	.1000	−3.5	.001
A	.8000	.3333	2.4	.02
S	.5400	.2000	2.7	.01
R	.3000	.1500	2.0	.05
Constant	1.5000	.1000	15.0	.000

95.0% Confidence Intervals:

P	−.5500,	−.1500
A	.1333,	1.4667
S	.1400,	.9400
R	.0000,	.6000
Constant	1.3000,	1.7000

Limitations

The multiple regression method is very robust but it suffers from some limitations, including:

- If the independent variables are highly correlated, the estimated coefficients might be unstable.

- The method can estimate only linear relations, or relations that can be transformed into linear ones, for example

$$Y = a + b_1x + b_2(x^2)$$

Nevertheless, the method is quite versatile and robust, and some improvements have been made to minimize some of these problems.[3]

Discriminant Analysis

If instead of wanting to explain the behaviour of an interval or ratio-type variable (e.g., sales), the researcher is interested in explaining a nominal and ordinal variable, the method to use is called **discriminant analysis**.[4]

As for multiple regression, the dependent (nominal and ordinal) variable is explained by several independent variables. The principle of discriminant analysis is to find a linear combination of these variables (called the discriminant function) that maximizes the difference between the means of the various groups or categories. The discriminant function also indicates the discriminating power of each independent variable.

For example, a banker wants to establish a procedure to determine whether a loan applicant is a bad risk. On the basis of past data, the best function that discriminates between good- and bad-risk individuals was found to be

$$Z = .5\,E + 1.0\,W + .05\,S$$

where E is the number of years employed full-time; W is the salary of the applicant; and S is the saving rate of the applicant. On the basis of these results, one might surmise that wages and employment records are more important than the saving rate.

This function can, in turn, be used to predict whether future applicants are likely to be good risks for the banker. The quality of the function can be ascertained by looking at the "confusion matrix," constructed by predicting the group membership of the initial sample. A hypothetical example is provided in Table 12.4.

From this table, one can see that the percentage of correctly classified applicants is 85%, which is much better than would be expected by chance (50%). By applying a z-test, one finds that the discriminant function is significantly better than chance at more than a 99.9% confidence level.

Another more complex example was provided in Chapter 2 to explain the construction of the perceptual map shown in Figure 2.7. In this application of multiple discriminant analysis, the groups or categories were the six brands of beer, and the independent variables were the attributes used to evaluate these brands.

TABLE 12.4
Discriminant Analysis: Hypothetical Confusion Matrix

		Predicted		
		Good Risk	Bad Risk	
Actual	Good Risk	45	5	50
	Bad Risk	10	40	50
		55	45	100

Correctly classified: 45% + 40% = 85%

Chance criterion: 50%

Test: $Z = \dfrac{85 - 50}{\sqrt{\dfrac{50 \times 50}{100}}} = \dfrac{35}{5} = 7 > Z_{.0005} = 3.29$

Factor Analysis

The need for factor analysis arises when the researcher is faced with the large number of variables that are related in a complex fashion and attempt to measure some abstract concepts. Thus the principle of factor analysis is to determine a small number of linear combinations of these variables that would explain a large percentage of the total variance. These combinations are called **factors**, and these few factors can in turn be used instead of the large number of original variables. Thus the goal of factor analysis is to *reduce* the large number of original variables into a few factors, while keeping as much information as possible. The simple hypothetical example presented in Table 12.5 illustrates this method, with eight variables being used to evaluate shampoos.

In this table, the factor loadings represent correlations between each variable and each factor. The variables have been regrouped for convenience. The first four variables load heavily on the first factor and the latter could be called the "health motive," since all four seem to relate to that abstract dimension. Similarly, the last four variables deal primarily with the "appearance motive" and load heavily on the second factor, which is then named as such. The first factor explains 40% of the total variance and the second, 30%. Together, the two factors explain 70% of the total information contained in the eight variables; i.e., they are equivalent to 5.6 variables (8 × 70%).

Therefore, by using factor analysis we were able to replace eight variables by only two new variables: health and appearance, while retaining 70% of the original variance.

The number of factors chosen by the researcher depends on the percentage of variance explained by each factor; that is, how much loss of information would the researcher tolerate in order to reduce the number of variables.

TABLE 12.5
Factor Analysis: Hypothetical Example

Variable	Factor Loadings	
	Factor 1: Health	Factor 2: Appearance
1 Makes lots of lather	.9000	−.2000
2 Cleans hair	.8500	.0500
3 Controls dandruff	.9500	−.1000
4 Does not dry out scalp	.7500	.4000
5 Makes hair easy to manage	.2000	.9000
6 Conditions hair	−.0500	.8000
7 Makes hair soft	−.3000	.8500
8 Has a pleasant smell	−.1000	.7500
Explained variance (per factor)	40%	30%
(cumulative)	40%	70%

Cluster Analysis

The purpose of cluster analysis is to regroup individual objects into clusters to maximize the similarities within the clusters and the dissimilarities between the clusters. Depending on the procedure to be used and the definition of similarity, the researcher has a large number of clustering techniques from which to choose.

For example, let us assume that a number of individuals have indicated what their ideal brand of beer would be like on the dimensions of strength and social image. The responses are reported in Figure 12.14 by the letter "x." Looking at the pattern for the preferred types of beer, one can identify four segments, labelled A, B, C, and D depending on the combination of strength and social image. The circles are used simply to indicate the concentrations of points.

A clustering program would identify the four groups A, B, C, and D by giving the list of cluster members. Thus, a cluster is a list of individuals or objects that are close to each other according to some measure of distance (similarity). Also, note that the distance *between* the clusters is as large as it could be, according to some measure of distance (dissimilarity).

In practice, the variables used for clustering are not as obvious and independent as in this example, but the principle is the same and the result can be represented as in the example. This method is quite useful in developing some market segmentation strategies, which is the case in our example.[5]

Multidimensional Scaling

The multidimensional scaling (MDS) technique is useful when the researcher has asked respondents to make some similarity/dissimilarity judgment of objects. This method allows the researcher to reconstruct indirectly the dimensions used by respondents to evaluate the objects.[6]

FIGURE 12.14
Distribution of Brands: Two Major Dimensions

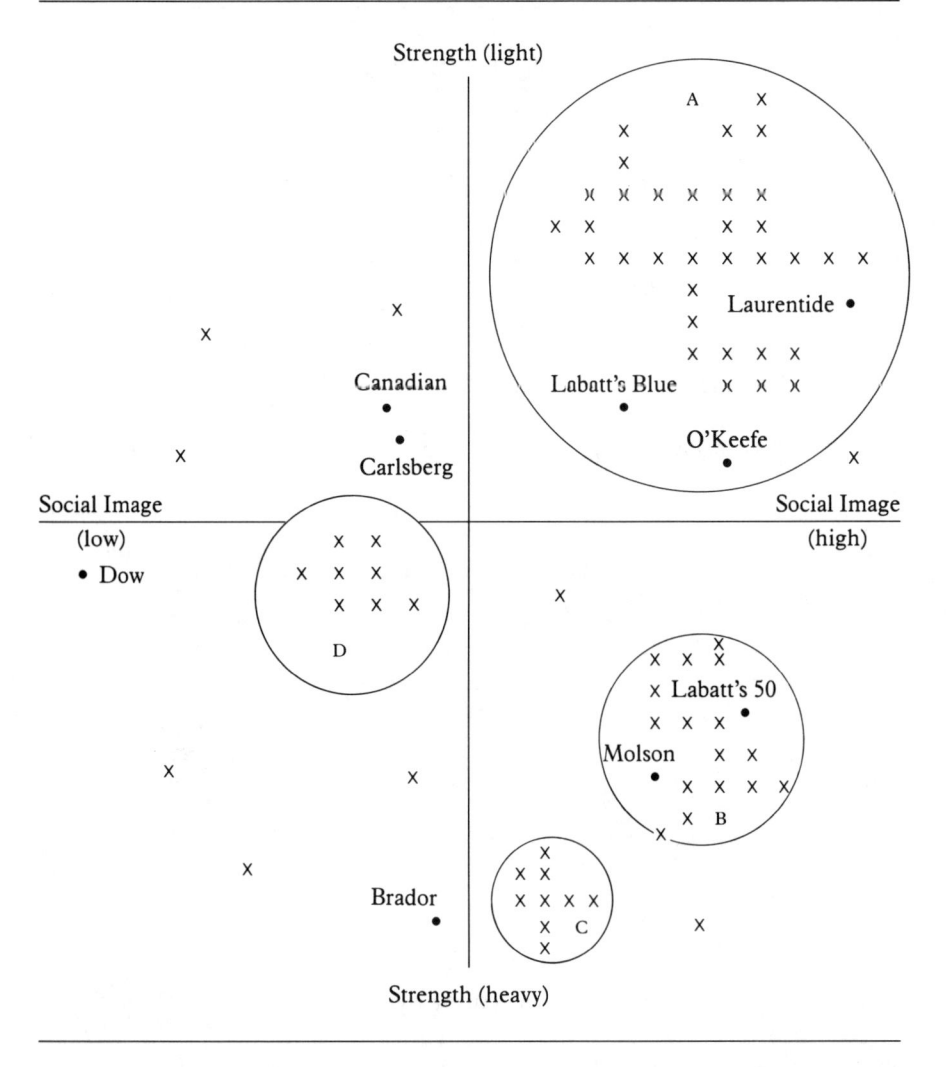

For example, instead of having respondents evaluate thirteen brands of beer on a predetermined set of attributes, they could be asked to indicate how similar brands of beer are to each other. With thirteen brands, the respondent has to evaluate seventy-eight pairs of brands.

By using an MDS technique on similarity data, the researcher can deduce the dimensions used by respondents in evaluating the different pairs. An MDS output will include a mapping like the perceptual map of the brands of beer shown in Figure 12.15. Inspection of the position of the objects can reveal the actual dimensions used by respondents, which in Figure 12.15 are strength and social image or popularity.

FIGURE 12.15
Perceptual Map: Multidimensional Scaling

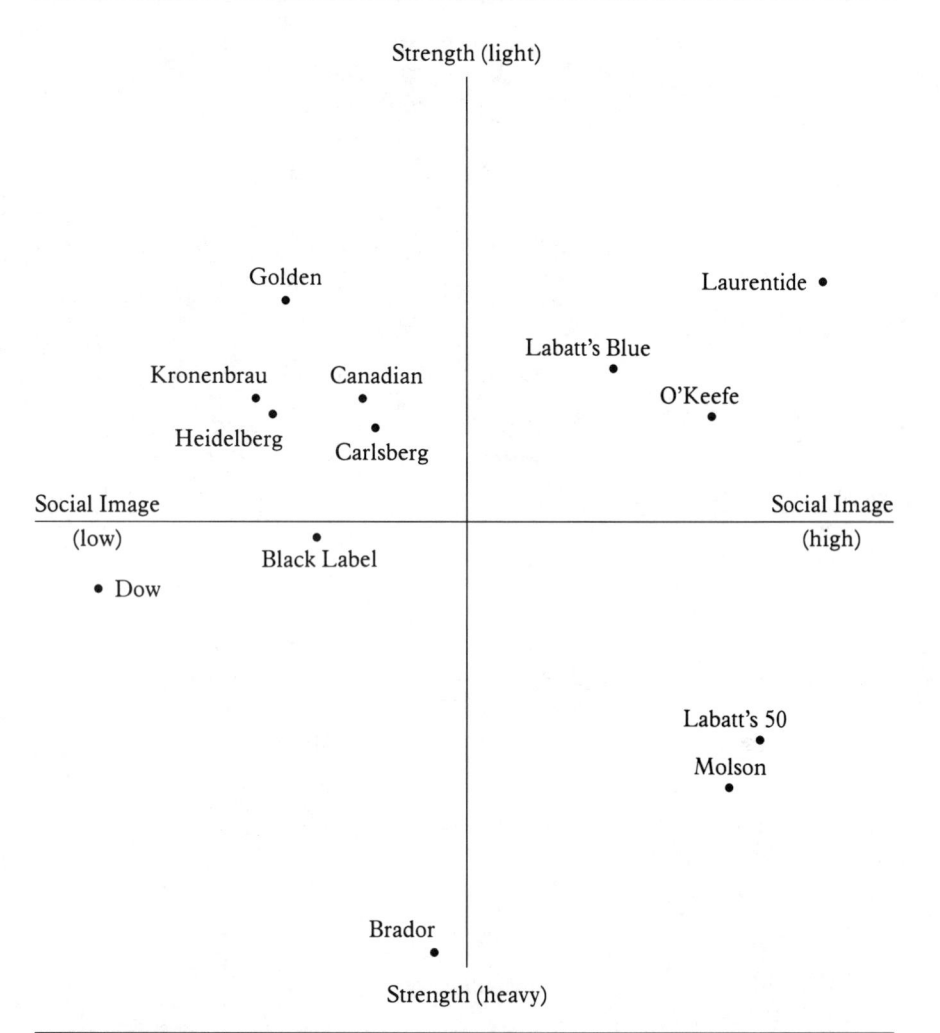

Strength (light)

Golden •

Laurentide •

Labatt's Blue •

Kronenbrau •   Canadian •

O'Keefe •

Heidelberg •   Carlsberg •

Social Image (low)   Social Image (high)

• Black Label

• Dow

Labatt's 50 •
Molson •

Brador •

Strength (heavy)

Source: Courtesy of Jacques E. Brisoux, University of Québec (Trois Rivières)

■ Managers' Attitudes toward More Sophisticated Techniques

In this last section we will review some of the changes that have taken place toward increased sophistication in marketing research. These changes are expected to continue or even intensify with the diffusion of more powerful microcomputers and better software.

More Realistic Goals

One change in the nature of the research effort has been toward a smaller, more definite, more modest analysis. When the computer, along with newly devised mathematical techniques, first came onto the business scene thirty years ago, analysts envisioned these techniques as grand and almost omnipotent. There was talk of total corporate integration and management resource optimization. Entire companies would be cybernetically linked into synergistic systems that would provide for logistical and informational optimization. Well, so much for the jargon of the sixties. The buzzwords flew thick and fast in the early days of the computers and management research, but today both buyers and sellers are more modest in their claims and in their objectives. Technical sophistication continues to grow but the promises are more realistic. Research proceeds more often on a case-by-case basis and researchers, rather than claiming to know everything about everything, have become more specialized, claiming real expertise in only a small section of the overall research spectrum.[7]

Splintering

The changes in research and in the direction of research appear to be but another manifestation of the splintering process that seems to be taking place in many areas of our society. For instance, many magazines were founded and flourished for twenty to thirty years, and then the magazine market splintered. More magazines, and more different magazines, are being sold but the "consensus" magazine no longer exists. Likewise, there is no consensus technique in marketing research. From the mere handful of techniques available just thirty years ago, literally scores of marketing research techniques have been developed.

By the same token, attitudes toward quantitative and technological innovation have also splintered, just as they have done throughout society as a whole. Thirty years ago, most Canadians were solidly behind technology; jets, cars, nuclear power, household gadgets—the more the better. Whereas some Canadians continue to favour technology, a growing group says that technology has gone too far. Likewise, marketing research has seen a division of opinion over the value of mathematical sophistication. In the early days of marketing research, all developments in methodological and computational analysis were hailed as steps of progress for a growing discipline. Today, however, many people question some of the more sophisticated techniques and advocate a simpler treatment. Just as some segments of society are buying microwave ovens and videodisk recorders while other segments strive to live simpler lives, some groups in marketing are pushing mathematical sophistication to mind-boggling lengths while others intentionally are returning to older, more simple forms of analysis.

Reasons for Increased Sophistication

The reasons for the use of increasingly sophisticated techniques are twofold. First, the techniques seem to be providing answers to pressing questions, and secondly—probably more importantly—it is now possible to compute these answers very easily.

In pondering such techniques as multiple discriminant analysis or canonical analysis and the tremendous amount of mathematical sophistication behind them, the first question that enters the mind is "Why?" Why is such an unwieldy piece of mathematics necessary? These various techniques that seem so irrelevant and obscure are actually the mathematical response to some very relevant and obvious questions. In the course of this book (and perhaps in some basic statistics books), you have encountered some of these techniques in their more simple, single-variate forms. Most of the more sophisticated techniques are merely an attempt to answer these same types of questions in their more realistic, multivariate forms. That is, they attempt to answer these questions in the real-world environment, where many independent (predictor) variables have a simultaneous effect on both the dependent (criterion) variable of interest and each other. The following is a review of some of the more common techniques and their objectives (the answers they give, the questions they answer).

- *Regression analysis* is used to describe the nature of a relationship and to make predictions. Simple regression has one predictor variable predicting one criterion variable, whereas multiple regression has two or more independent variables predicting one dependent variable.

- *Correlation analysis* measures the amount of association between variables. Simple correlation measures the association between one variable and another. Multiple correlation measures the association between one variable and a set of others.

- *Canonical analysis* measures the association between two sets of variables, multiple variables associated with multiple variables.

- *Chi-square* looks for significant differences between cell values in a cross-classification table.

- *The z-test* and t-*test* look for significant differences between the averages of two groups.

- *Analysis of variance* looks for significant differences between the averages of two or more groups.

- *Discriminant analysis* attempts to discriminate among members of a group. It identifies which variables are the best discriminators (separators) among the various members of the group.

- *Factor analysis* is a technique that tries to take a large number of variables and break them into a smaller group of factors. The factors might represent the combined "influence" of several discrete variables.

- *Cluster analysis* is a technique that uses the scores of the group members on several variables to break the group into smaller subgroups or clusters (analogous to market segments).

- *Conjoint analysis*, often referred to as *trade-off analysis*, measures the relative importance of the various product benefits or attributes and tries to determine how much of one attribute must be given in exchange for an increase in one of the others.[8]

- *Multidimensional scaling* maps the perceptions of subjects on various items or attributes in multidimensional space. It can show how one brand is perceived in relation to the others.

- *Stochastic techniques* are a fancy name for probabilities. They are generally used to predict brand share or repeat purchasing behaviour, subject to some probability model.

This list of techniques and their uses is meant to be illustrative, not exhaustive. There are more techniques than those listed above and most of the techniques have more uses than the ones listed. As a matter of fact, almost any single technique can be used to answer a variety of questions since most of the techniques have a common source: they all work in some manner with the variation or scatter observed among the variables. Most of them have a common basis in the theory of matrix algebra and are thereby conceptually interrelated.

As the list shows, the questions the techniques answer are the very questions that are of direct relevance to marketers. Techniques, such as a conjoint analysis, that can show which product attributes are viewed as most important and how much of one attribute can be traded against how much of another are of obvious value to a product designer or a promotion strategist.

However, these techniques are extremely difficult to understand conceptually and almost impossible to compute by hand. Hence, even though they have been known to mathematicians for many years, they had for a long time little popularity and even less utilization. Real utilization would wait until the development of the computer and the canned program. With these two items, anybody who could keyboard could use the most sophisticated techniques available, and that is exactly what has happened. With large-scale computers and the canned computer libraries, it is as easy to run sophisticated analyses as it is to run averages and standard deviations. The wide use of these techniques is directly attributable to the simple fact that it is so easy to use them. It is as if you could become a musician by turning on the radio: nowadays, you can become an analyst by calling up a series of computer programs, and with the widespread use of microcomputers, they can be done within minutes in your own office!

Reasons for Decreased Sophistication

Despite the ease with which this sophisticated analysis can be utilized, many researchers decline to take advantage of it—and for some very good reasons, as we will see.

Surely the main reason why some researchers validly shy away from the more advanced techniques is that such techniques are simply too sophisticated: they are too much of a good thing. The problem is that researchers can get so bogged down in minutiae that they miss the important factors, in the old "can't see the forest for the trees" syndrome. To be slightly more specific, the use of extremely complicated techniques is like looking at a picture in a newspaper with a powerful magnifying glass. You want to see more detail, but instead all you can see is dots.

Likewise, when we investigate consumer behaviour, there is a certain level of precision beyond which we cannot carry the analysis. The complex techniques are trying to milk a great deal of precision and certainty from a situation that by its very nature is quite imprecise and very uncertain. Many researchers feel that almost any analysis beyond the most superficial is too much, that the results should be reported in rather vague generalities because, in truth, vague generalizations are about all we really can say about consumers and their behaviour. In fact, despite the efforts of the researchers, sometimes the output of a very sophisticated analysis is nothing more than a loose generality. During one presentation, for example, a very prominent researcher detailed the results of an elaborate cluster analysis that his company had performed on several hundred consumers. Cluster analysis is a natural for marketing research, in that it groups consumers into homogeneous clusters highly analogous to market segments. Researchers can cluster consumers to discover which types of consumers buy which products, what media schedules they prefer, and so forth. At any rate, the researcher's findings showed five distinct clusters. Unfortunately, the clusters were nothing more than five obvious, white, Anglo-Saxon, Protestant stereotypes. The five types were young blue-collar, young white-collar, older blue-collar, older white-collar, and retired limited income. In other words, a tremendous amount of statistical firepower was expended to discover what were already well-known stereotypes.

Another problem along the same lines is that most research is strategic in nature, not operational. That is, the researcher can say that, from the perspective of the research done at that time, it seems that such and such would be a good strategy. However, this approach ignores two very important facts. For one, it does not take into account the dynamic nature of the marketplace. A person who has one opinion this week might have a different opinion next week. Thus, to spend great amounts of time and money to make a sophisticated analysis of consumers at one point in time could be senseless, in that within a few weeks the situation (and all those numbers) will have changed.

Another thing the analysis ignores is the element of execution. In the real world, what counts most is execution, not strategy. For example, suppose that after meticulous research involving a well-executed experimental design, it was determined that the company's products were price-elastic and that a price cut of 10% would increase company profits by 5%. Even assuming that the results of the small experimental survey could in fact be generalized to the entire marketing environment, such a small survey could not account for the possible effects of competition and execution. The firm might discover that a nationwide price cut was immediately matched by all competitors, setting off a price war that drove profits down to almost nothing (the price cuts in the small number of stores used in the experiment were not matched, probably not even noticed). Likewise, the package that looked good in testing could meet with dismal success if competitors run a vigorous advertising campaign or a heavy coupon blitz, or if distribution is spotty and the product is not available on the shelf. In short, the marketplace is full of changes and uncertainties that no amount of research can overcome. As one writer on the subject has sagely advised, "If sophisticated calculations are necessary to justify an investment, don't do it!"[9]

There are yet other reasons why sophisticated analysis is often inadvisable. For one, such analysis is very powerful, and therefore should be used only by those qualified to do so. As in the case of laser brain surgery, just because the technique is wonderful does not mean that everyone should try it; in the wrong hands, or in unskilled hands, the results would be disastrous. In the same manner, many of these newly developed research techniques are actually quite difficult to use properly. Of course, with canned computer programs, anybody can get answers from them, but to use them properly the researcher has to know what he or she is doing. Many assumptions and requirements relating to the way in which the data are collected and entered can affect the results. In addition, the output from many of these more sophisticated techniques requires a great deal of subjective analysis before it can be understood. Used properly the techniques can be excellent diagnostic tools. Unfortunately, the number of people who are truly qualified to use them is still relatively small, and their use by the unqualified can lead to trouble.

Yet another problem with the canned programs and the esoteric forms of analysis they bring is that their use tends to reverse the proper sequence of the research process. In the preferred sequence, research starts with an idea or hypothesis. On the basis of that idea, certain data are gathered and certain analysis is performed. From the results of the analysis, a conclusion is drawn about the original idea.

The existence of these marvelous programs tends to reverse the process by encouraging researchers to perform the analysis first and then think of the hypotheses second. When the analysis was difficult to perform, the researcher would be very selective about which variables to analyse and which techniques to employ. However, it is now just as easy to compute the correlations among forty variables as it is to compute those between two variables. Therefore, the researcher is tempted to use the computer and the canned programs like a gigantic sand-sifter at the beach. The researcher throws in all the data, turns on the programs, and lets the programs find the answers. The problem with this approach is that the results of such analysis are often quite nonsensical. They are fun and sometimes enlightening to look at, but they might not fit into a workable marketing strategy. *If there is a single problem on which most research failures can be blamed, it would be the failure to define the problem and the objectives adequately at the beginning of the research effort*. The existence of canned programs that make formerly exhaustive analysis easy only adds to the temptation to hurry over these first steps and begin the analysis of the data.

Still another problem relates to the implications of the more advanced types of segmentation research. When research first began to be used, marketers were aiming at the mass market. Hence, techniques such as simple averages and percentage breakdowns could be used to develop the best product for the "average" consumer.

As we moved into the sixties, seventies, and eighties, marketing strategy moved from a mass appeal to a more selective appeal. The emphasis today is on market segmentation and on the cultivation of a product variation that more exactly suits the needs and tastes of a smaller target market. Therefore, many of the techniques that have become popular over the last decade are precisely suited to solving the problems inherent in the isolation and identification of target markets. These techniques include cluster analysis, discriminant analysis, multidimensional scaling, and conjoint analysis, to mention just a few examples.

However, as the splintering of the market continues to accelerate, will new and more powerful techniques continue to be developed? Possibly, but maybe not. In the process of continuing to splinter the market in a desire to produce something for everyone, we are elevating the status and the pertinency of mother-in-law research, which gets its name from the assumption that if your mother-in-law likes some product, many other people also would like it. When dealing with a mass market in Canada, even a small percentage of that market might add up to a large number of customers; hence, many variations of a product can be produced. One way to determine those variations is through various types of sophisticated numerical analysis—but an easier and faster way is through mother-in-law research.

A final drawback to the use of sophisticated research is that it could create some legal headaches. For example, if you are using numerical calculations as a basis for making some decision that affects other groups or firms, you must be very sure that those numbers are correct, because if they are not, you could find yourself being sued. (If you did not utilize research techniques at all, but instead relied on judgment, you probably would not be sued for a judgmental error, although you might be sued for having failed to consult such techniques.)

Magazine publishers have taken readership survey companies to court over readership studies showing declines in their magazine readerships. And one really cannot blame the magazines: advertisers are highly influenced by the results of these studies, and a reported decline in readership can easily cost a large-circulation magazine millions of dollars of advertising. That is a great deal of money to lose just because the survey company made a mistake. Along the same lines, one researcher reports having to go to court on more than one occasion to justify the use of a certain statistical test.[10] From the standpoint of the marketing manager operating in the dynamic and competitive marketplace, such distinctions are of no operational importance. If, however, two products are competing on a contract and, on the basis of the tests, one of the products is accepted and one is rejected, an improperly done test might make a world of difference.

As a consequence, some researchers are beginning to shy away from the more involved types of analysis in situations that look touchy, choosing instead to perform very simple analyses with which no one can argue. As mentioned before, the more complicated the technique, the more assumptions that will be involved and the more subjective the interpretation will be. In such situations it is easy to obtain honest differences of opinion (even from trained experts) on the proper method of analysis that should be used.

■ Summary

This chapter has explained in simple, non-technical fashion the bivariate and multivariate methods of analysis. The purpose of bivariate analysis is to test differences between two groups, or more generally to test the association between two variables. The t-test and z-test allow the researcher to determine if two groups have equal means or proportions. The chi-square test, the analysis of variance (ANOVA) and the simple regression analysis are used to determine whether two variables are related.

The purpose of multivariate analysis is to allow the researcher to test more complex relationships among variables. There are a great number of such techniques and only the better known are described in this chapter. Multiple regression and multiple discriminant analysis both have a dependent variable (to be explained) and a series of independent variables. The difference between the two lies in the nature of the dependent variable: interval (and/or ratio) vs. nominal (and/or ordinal). Factor analysis is useful for reducing the number of variables. Cluster analysis allows one to find homogeneous groups of individuals or objects, and multidimensional scaling permits transformation of similarity data into the underlying dimensions used by respondents.

Finally, the attitudes of managers toward more sophisticated techniques were discussed. The research function is growing because management is becoming more sophisticated, developing more trust in research, and is becoming more knowledgeable about its uses.

As in most fields, marketing research is experiencing splintering, with specialization becoming the norm. Like other specialists, marketing researchers are finding themselves knowing more and more about less and less. In addition, there is an increasing polarization: some researchers are advocating the use of numerical techniques of increasing sophistication, while others are arguing against the use of these complicated, analytical techniques.

The impetus for increased numerical sophistication comes from two sources. First, these techniques appear to be the exact mathematical answer to many of the pertinent questions of marketing. Second, and probably more important, the use of these programs has been greatly simplified in recent years by the development of computer program libraries, which eliminate the need for the user to have mathematical or programming ability.

Those arguing for the decreased use of these techniques point to several problems, such as the ability of various techniques to carry the precision of the output past the precision of the input. In addition, many of the techniques are quite sophisticated, and it is easy to misuse and misinterpret the results. Some researchers claim that emphasis on the analysis tends to be overblown, with too much attention given to the methods and not enough to the problem definition. A final argument is the increased danger of legal action concerning the validity and interpretation of a given piece of numerical analysis.

For Discussion

1. Last month, a sample of 80 French Canadians and 120 English Canadians showed that 55% of the French Canadians preferred whisky to gin and that 55% of the English Canadians preferred gin to whisky. Are the two groups different?

2. What is meant by a chi-square goodness-of-fit test? What is meant by a chi-square independence-of-classification test? In the independence-of-classification test, the cell values for the expected frequency distribution are computed by the *method of marginal products*. Why is this method so called?

3. Given the following classification table showing the relationship between classification in school and grades, test for independence of classification.

	A	B	C	D	F
Juniors	6	3	2	3	6
Seniors	2	8	6	3	1

4. An international study of savings revealed the following:

	Canada	Japan	U.S.
Savings per capita (in $000)	3.8	4.7	2.3
Standard deviation	1.7	1.3	1.5
Size	144	125	169

Looking at the nations two by two, what are the differences in savings?

5. The manager of a grocery store wants to see if there is a relationship between the size of the eggs customers buy and the amount of bacon they buy. To determine if there is indeed a relationship, the store owner asks you to monitor one hundred customers and make a chart of the findings. The following shows what you found:

Bacon

		None	.50 kg	1 kg	
E	Small	12	3	0	15
g g s	Medium	12	22	6	40
	Large	6	25	14	45
		30	50	20	100

What do you conclude from these results?

6. Compare multiple regression and discriminant analysis.

7. Explain the role of factor analysis and give three examples that are different from those given in the text.

8. What is the purpose of cluster analysis? Give three different types of applications.

9. Perceptual maps can be obtained from both multiple discriminant analysis and MDS. What is the main difference between the two?

10. "Multivariate methods are much too complicated for most people to use in practice. Only sophisticated research firms and academic researchers can use them." Do you agree with this statement? Justify your answer.

Problems

1. Given the following classification table showing the relationship between age and television watching, test for significant differences in classification (i.e., relationship between age and television watching).

$$F_o$$

		TV Viewing	
		Low	High
Age Groups	20–30	5	10
	30–50	10	10
	50–80	6	9

2. **Mini-Case:** Roland Limited is a fashion retail store that operates in the downtown area of a large Canadian metropolitan area. The owner, Mr. Roland, heard about how marketing research could help him in making better marketing decisions. After long deliberation, he decided to experiment by varying his prices and advertising expenditures for a popular brand of jeans. After ten weeks, he looked at the results and declared that nothing seemed to work: what one learns at school about price and advertising is not practical and that all consumers are irrational.

Week	1	2	3	4	5	6	7	8	9	10
Price ($)	10	11	12	13	14	15	14	13	12	11
Advertising ($)	500	500	1000	1000	1500	1500	1000	1000	1000	1000
Sales (in units)	849	831	863	841	872	851	823	843	860	879

Question
Do you agree with Mr. Roland's assessment of his experiment? Explain.

Endnotes

1. S.B. Ash and J.W. Hanson, "The Use of Research Techniques by Professional Marketing Researchers." *Marketing*, 2. Ed. Robert Wyckham. Administrative Sciences Association of Canada (ASAC), 1981, pp. 11–20.
2. For example, see Donald R. Lehmann, *Market Research and Analysis*, Homewood, IL: Irwin, 1979, Chapters 12, 14, 15, 16 and 17. Also see R.J. Calantone, D. Litvack, and C.D. Schewe, "A Canonical Analysis Approach to the Retail Segment-Media Matching Problem." *Marketing*, 3. Ed. Michel Laroche. ASAC, 1982, pp. 21–30.
3. See, for example, Michel Laroche, "A method of detecting nonlinear effects on cross-sectional survey data." *International Journal of Research in Marketing*, 2 (1985), pp. 61–72.
4. For an example see S. Ahmed and R. DeCamprieu, "Multivariate Search for Energy Conservation Patterns." *Marketing*, 1. Ed. Vernon J. Jones, ASAC, 1980, pp. 1–10.
5. D. Schellinck and J.M. Higgins, "Issues of Validity in Clustering for Market Segmentation." *Marketing*, 1. Ed. V.J. Jones, ASAC, 1980, pp. 331–41.
6. M. Bergier and T. Muller, "Product Positioning in the Fine Arts: An Application of Perceptual Mapping to the Study of Art Prints." *Marketing*, 1. Ed. V.J. Jones, ASAC, 1980, pp. 39–48.
7. Michael Heffring, "Expectations of Marketing Research: The Manager-Researcher Gap." *Marketing*, 1. Ed. Vernon J. Jones, ASAC, 1980, pp. 191–201.
8. For an example of application, see Lorne Bozinoff, "A Conjoint Measurement Approach to Marketing Course Design." *Marketing*, 5. Ed. Sheila Brown, ASAC, 1984, pp. 62–70.
9. Robert Heller, *The Great Executive Dream*. New York: Dell Publishing Co., 1972, p. 345.
10. B. Venkatesh, "Unthinking Data Interpretation Can Destroy Value of Research." *Marketing News*, vol. 11, no. 15 (27 January 1978), p. 9.

CHAPTER 13 THE RESEARCH REPORT

The marketing research process begins with exploratory research and problem definition. The final link in this process is the research report itself—the finished product—which is often the weakest link. This weakness stems from a communications failure, the inability of some researchers to communicate effectively the essence of their findings to an intended audience.

Exactly what is a research report? It is the concise, clear communication of the essential findings of a research study. This communication can be in written, oral or visual (e.g., slides, overhead transparencies) form, or in a combination of all three.

Professional marketing researchers are not the only people confronted with the difficulties of preparing reports. Virtually all people in responsible positions, including those in nearly every phase of business, education, or government, have to prepare research reports of one type or another at regular intervals throughout their careers. Graduation from college or university is no escape from report preparation. In fact, in challenging managerial positions, effective written and oral communications become most important.

It should be clearly recognized that a well-written and well-organized research report is the only truly effective way in which marketing researchers can communicate with top management. Even if all of the steps and procedures in the marketing research process have been well executed up to this point, they are of little use if the research findings cannot be effectively communicated. Before discussing how one prepares a marketing research report, we will examine the principal types of research reports.

◼ Types of Research Reports

Written research reports vary in length, although it is advisable to keep them as short as possible. The short report is more likely than the long report to be read from cover to cover. One variation of the short report is the **executive summary**

report, which can be used to complement a long report. It is, as the name implies, a management summary. As a much shorter version of the final report, the executive summary report presents the main findings, recommendations, and conclusions. Usually omitted are technical sections dealing with research methodology, statistical treatment, and data analyses. The executive summary report can be presented at the beginning of the research report or as a separate document. Usually it is preferable to submit the executive summary at the very beginning of the final research report. This placement allows the reader to gain a quick overview of the full contents of the report without having to read all the material or to look for the final report if the two are not together. If the executive summary report and the final research report are presented as separate reports, one of the two is likely to be misplaced and not read.

A report is a communications vehicle, and therefore must be prepared and presented in a manner that will be favourably received and lead to implementation. A major problem facing researchers is the quantity of data to include in the research report. The answer to this question is determined by the characteristics of the intended audience. These characteristics also determine which of the two main types of reports will be drafted: the technical report or the popular report.

Technical Reports

Normally, technical reports are prepared by research specialists for other marketing research professionals. The technical report assumes that the reader is up to date on the background material relevant to the subject under consideration. Thus, the technical report usually concentrates on detailed research methodology and the findings of the study. Appendixes might be attached to the technical report to present descriptions of the measuring instrument used (for example, a copy of the questionnaire) and computer print-outs (for example, of statistical analyses of variance). Because of its often highly technical nature, the *Journal of Marketing Research* is illustrative of the format for technical reports.

The highly quantitative structure of the technical report is permissible and expected when the audience consists of fellow researchers and others well versed in research jargon. These people, who are usually familiar with current research and theories, are equipped to cope with the technical report. Should the researcher have to present findings to both research specialists and a general audience, a popular report can be drawn up from the technical report and be presented to this latter audience separately. In summary, technical reports should be

- complete
- arranged logically
- impersonal
- accurate
- brief

Popular Reports

A much less complicated instrument than the technical report, the popular report is intended for a more general audience. The popular report is shorter than the technical report, and whereas technical reports might go extensively into research methodology and data analysis techniques used, popular reports concentrate on findings and recommendations.

The popular report usually is prepared for executive decision makers within the organization. Accordingly, it is very important that popular reports be written as clearly and simply as possible without sacrificing any essential information. Extensive methodological details can be omitted, however, since executives are more interested in applying the findings. Although no distortion of facts should enter into the popular report, the report must contain the researcher's conclusions and recommendations. Many researchers might be hesitant to risk stating their opinions, but research reports *should* make positive recommendations. On the other hand, researchers should not be surprised if their recommendations are not implemented.

Sometimes a popular report might begin with an executive summary, a brief report that summarizes the entire report within the scope of one or two pages. It is not expected to be a substitute for the full report, but merely a chance for busy executives to orient themselves quickly without having to read every word of the full report. The executive summary should be designed not only to convey the essential findings and recommendations of the report but also to encourage the reader to follow through and read the full report.

Examine the contrast in writing styles between the technical and popular reports that follow. The example of the technical report is taken from the *Journal of Marketing Research*, an extremely technical journal that is a highly valued publication outlet for research-oriented marketing academicians.

Technical Report Language:

Many if not most of the test-retest correlations presented in the advertising research literature as measures of the reliability of copy testing methodologies are subject to the kinds of ambiguities and limitations noted in the preceding examples. To illustrate, a finding often cited is the test-retest correlations of .67 obtained from an analysis of on-air recall scores for 106 commercials first reported by Clancy and Kweskin and discussed at greater length by Clancy and Ostlund. In describing the data on which this correlation is based, the latter authors note, "The interval between test and retest for each commercial varied from one to eleven weeks." Thus there were numerous and varied opportunities for the different test and retest samples to be affected by nonequivalent sets of influences and therefore it is not surprising to learn, "The average difference between the test and retest score was +6.4 percentage points." Because the variances of the test and retest scores are not reported, the test for their equality suggested heretofore could not be carried out.[1]

Popular Report Language:

Findings from previous research studies in this area are inconsistent and do not give us a clear solution to the problem, because they are not all measuring exactly the same things.

■ Contents of the Research Report

No universally accepted guide establishes the exact contents of marketing research reports. There is no standardized way of presenting either the popular or the technical report. The format of the report depends to a large extent on its nature and the audience for which it is intended. However, there are certain guidelines that can be used to establish the basic contents of any marketing research report. Figure 13.1 is only a suggested guideline and need not be followed exactly in every report.

FIGURE 13.1
Suggested Contents of the Research Report

---

1. TITLE PAGE

2. TABLE OF CONTENTS
   List of Figures
   List of Tables

3. EXECUTIVE SUMMARY
   • Research Objectives
   • Main Findings
   • Conclusions
   • Recommendations

4. INTRODUCTION
   • Background of the Study
   • Research Objectives
   • Justification for the Study

5. RESEARCH METHODOLOGY
   • Research Design
   • Secondary Data
   • Primary Data
   — collection method
   — sampling
   — field work
   — methods of analysis

6. FINDINGS

7. LIMITATIONS

8. CONCLUSIONS AND RECOMMENDATIONS

9. APPENDIXES
   • Questionnaire(s)
   • Selected Tables, Charts, Computer Print-outs
   • Bibliography
   • Other Relevant Material

Title page

The title page is a covering page that should include the title of the report, the name or names of the researchers, for whom the report was prepared, the date of the report, and where it was prepared. If the report is confidential, this restriction and the names of the intended recipients should be clearly identified.

Table of Contents

A table of contents is necessary for all but the shortest of reports. It should list the page numbers of all major sections, subsections, and appendixes (in short reports only the major sections need be identified). In addition, a list of figures and tables showing page numbers sometimes follows the table of contents.

Summary

The summary, often called the executive summary, is usually the most important part of the research report. Many executives do not have the time to read the full report and will read only the summary. Thus, it is very important for the summary to provide the essential information, so that the reader will not miss important details. The summary should provide a description of the objectives of the study, its major findings, and conclusions and recommendations based on those findings. Although the summary should be no longer than one or two pages, it should be able to stand by itself.

It should be noted that not every research report requires a summary. In general, very short reports that can be read in a brief period of time and reports intended for in-depth reading by a select group of executives do not require summaries.

Introduction

This part of the report presents the background and objectives of the research and gives the reader a view of the overall problem and a justification for the study. It is appropriate in the introduction to cite similar studies conducted in the past and to explain how they relate to the present project.

All reports require some introduction. The length of the introduction section is dependent on the reader's familiarity with the subject and the length of the report. Generally speaking, the wider the distribution of the report, the more extensive the introduction required.[2]

Research Methodology

In this section the research design used in conducting the research project should be described. All research reports should contain a description of the research methodology used, but some might give greater attention to this section than do others. Technical reports usually have much more detailed methodological sections than do popular reports.

Included in the research methodology section should be not only a description of the research design but also an explanation of why that particular design was chosen. A discussion of how and why secondary or primary data were used is appropriate. The section should also cover sampling frame, sample size, and confidence intervals obtained in the sample as well as information on field work and methods of analysis. Again, the degree of detail is highly dependent on the background of the audience; in all cases, lengthy, technical charts and graphs are best left for the appendixes.

Findings

The findings constitute the major portion of the report. It is here that the results of the study are presented to the reader. The principal difficulty in presenting findings is deciding which are relevant and should be included and which are irrelevant and should be left out altogether or reserved for a technical appendix— decisions that call for the researcher's good judgment. Every research project generates a mass of findings, most of which are not particularly relevant and therefore should be omitted in the final report.

Limitations

Research professionals recognize there is no such thing as the "perfect" study. Every research report has some qualifications that limit the extent to which the results can be generalized. For example, it would be difficult to apply generalizations from a study of consumer attitudes in the Vancouver area toward purchase of automobile block heating units to a group of similar consumers living in Edmonton.

At the same time, the researcher must not overemphasize the limitations of the report. It is the researcher's job to sell the report, not to undersell it. The limitations section should therefore be balanced to give the reader a clear idea of to what extent the results of the study can be applied to other institutions.

Conclusions and Recommendations

All reports should contain both conclusions and recommendations, which are not the same thing. A conclusion is a deduction based on the findings, whereas a recommendation is a suggested course of action. In other words, the researcher might conclude that there is not a potentially profitable market for a new product and then recommend that the product not be introduced. Unfortunately, this is usually the most neglected segment of the research report. Many people prefer to avoid making unpopular decisions or risky recommendations, preferring instead to let readers draw their own conclusions and make decisions without any recommendations. The argument against making recommendations is that the researcher does not have the full picture and therefore should not be advising higher management. Although recommendations might not be popular and might not be followed, it is still the duty of the research specialist to suggest a specific course of action, unless instructed to the contrary.

Appendixes

Material too detailed or too complex to be placed in the text of the report can be inserted in an appendix, with a reference in the text stating, for example, "A copy of the questionnaire is included in Appendix A." This reference allows the reader to examine the questionnaire at that time or at the end of the report. Also included in the appendixes might be detailed charts, tables, or graphs; relevant computer print-outs; names and addresses of respondents; and any detailed mathematical calculations.

The value of the appendix is that it allows important material to be added without interrupting the text of the report. As a general rule, if there is any question whether material should be included in the report or in the appendix, such material is best reserved for the appendix.

◼ Presenting the Report

Oral Reports

As well as preparing a written report to be read by top management, the marketing researcher might be asked to make an oral presentation to a group of company executives. This oral presentation does not replace, but merely supplements, the written report.

There are several reasons for making oral presentations. First, an oral report allows the researcher a second chance to present the findings of the study, thereby increasing the exposure given to the report and the likelihood of its findings being used. Second, the oral report, like the executive summary report, gives a busy executive a quick view of the research project. Third, the oral presentation is an ideal occasion for executives to ask questions for further clarification and for the researcher to explain points that might not have been evident in the written report.

The importance of preparation for an oral presentation should not be overlooked. If you have only forty-five minutes to explain four months' work, you will need to be efficient in your explanation. The presentation should be rehearsed, several times if necessary, before it is given formally. When making an oral presentation, the researcher should try to make maximum use of visual aids, using an overhead projector, chalkboard, or some other method to graphically present the results. Pictures, graphs, tables, maps, and diagrams are essential visual aids for successful oral presentations and are also important in the written report.

Using Graphs

Any number of different types of graphs can be used by researchers to make effective report presentations. Three of the most important are bar graphs, pie graphs, and line graphs. The value of good graphs is that they add significantly to the audience's ability to understand and follow the report.

Although tables are important aids in graphic presentation, researchers usually prefer graphs, because the latter are usually more easily comprehended by the viewer.

Pie Graphs
Probably the favourite type of graph used by researchers is the pie graph that, like a pie, is a circle divided into slices or sections. It is particularly effective for visually conveying comparative figures on market share or other breakdowns

totaling 100%, because the different sizes of the slices are readily apparent. A pie graph can be used to supplement a table; compare, for example, Table 13.1 and Figure 13.2. Although both the table and the pie graph present the same data, the percentage figures are much more easily and quickly grasped from the pie graph.

TABLE 13.1
Table Showing Full-Time Undergraduate Enrolment at Utopia University in 1990

College	Number	Percentage
Arts	3249	37
Business	2586	30
Science	1154	13
Engineering	915	10
Fine Arts	839	10
Total	8743	100

FIGURE 13.2
Pie Graph Showing Full-Time Undergraduate Enrolment at Utopia University in 1990

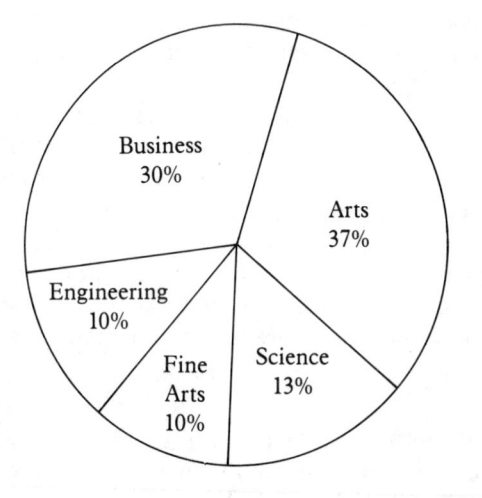

Bar Graphs

The bar graph is another very popular way in which research findings are presented. A bar graph presents the data through a series of bars, either horizontal or vertical, the height or length of which are used to measure some variable. The data presented in Table 13.1 could have been presented using a bar graph, with bars representing student enrolment in each of the five faculties at Utopia University.

However, the bar graph is best and most often used to make comparative representations over time, with changes shown by the length of the bars. Figure 13.3 provides an example of a vertical bar graph that shows changes over time. Notice that this material also could have been presented in a horizontal bar chart; either method is acceptable.

FIGURE 13.3
Bar Graph Showing Growth in Full-Time Student Enrolment at Utopia University for the Period 1980–89

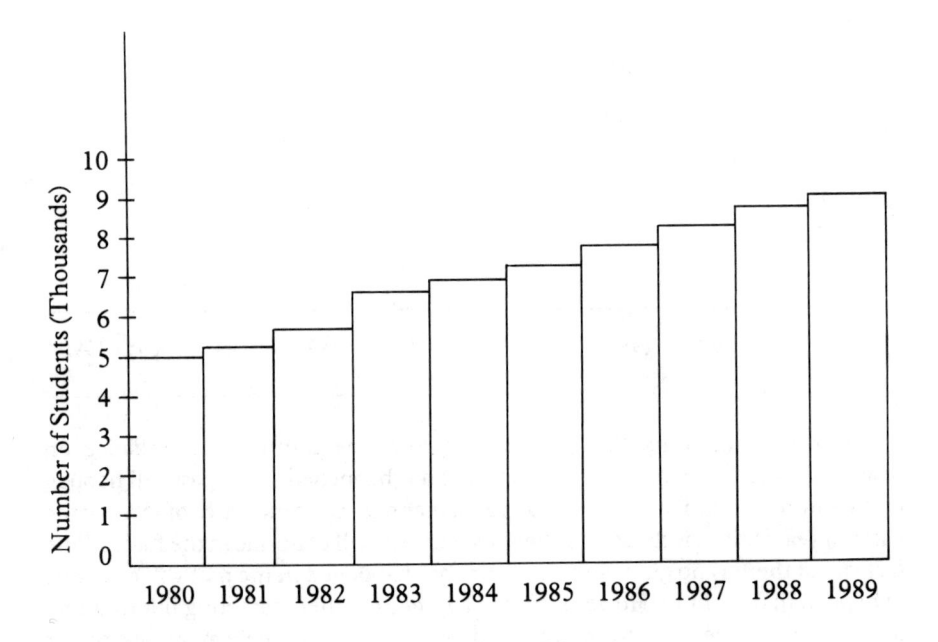

Line Graphs
In addition to pie graphs and bar graphs, research reports often incorporate line graphs. A line graph is a two-dimensional chart that also represents changes or trends over time but is most useful for extrapolations or forecasts. Forecasting is commonly done using the straight line formula $Y_c = a + bX$, which is applied in the sales forecasting section in Chapter 16. Other advantages of a line graph are its ability to compare several series on one chart, to illustrate the movement of the data when the time period is a lengthy one, and to illustrate the trends of a frequency distribution.

Figure 13.4 is an example of a line graph that shows changes over time, incorporating the same data presented in the vertical bar graph in Figure 13.3. It really does not make too much difference which type of graph is used in this instance. However, had we been attempting to forecast changes, perhaps for the years 1991 to 1995, the line graph would have been the better of the two types, because a line can readily be extrapolated to indicate future expected trends.

FIGURE 13.4
Line Graph Showing Growth in Full-Time Student Enrolment
at Utopia University for the Period 1981–90

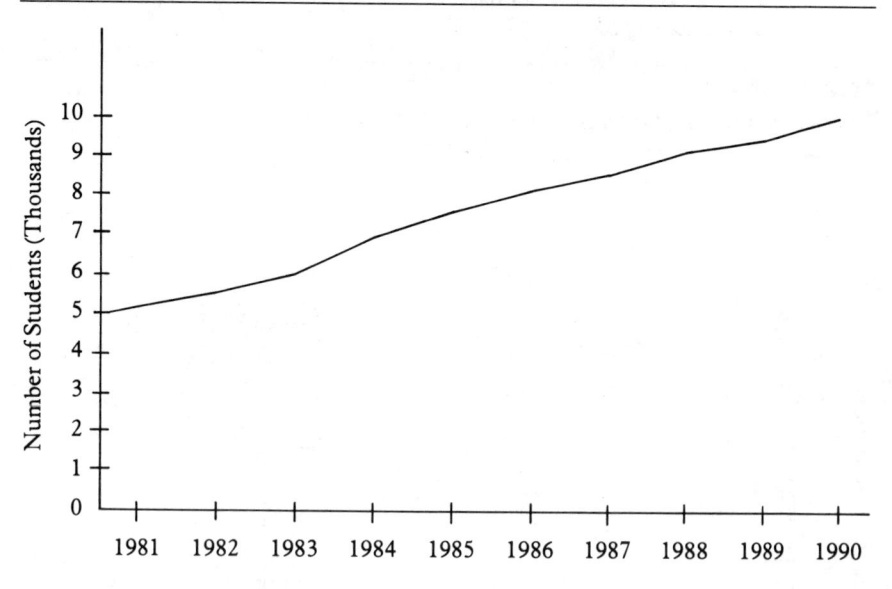

One danger in using line graphs to predict the future is overreliance on historical data. We tend to assume that what has happened in the past will happen in the future: a company that has had regular annual sales increases of 15% for the past ten years might well assume that this increase will continue in the future. The fact is that there is no guarantee that what has happened in the past will continue to happen in the future. However, in the absence of other marketing information, trend forecasts derived from line graph data have an enormous allure for forecasters.

Is the Researcher a Decision Maker?

Earlier in this chapter we noted the importance of including the researcher's recommendations and conclusions in the research report. Despite arguments and tendencies to the contrary, research professionals are obliged to provide management with clear conclusions and recommendations, although their advice will not always be followed. In fact, conflict between executives and research professionals might result from the researcher's suggestions. In explaining the basis for this conflict, one author wrote:

> Executives rise to power either by making correct assumptions about uncertainty or by persuading others that they have done so. Typically, there are few

checks on their judgments. If an executive thinks that others regard him as a good business artist, he can hardly be expected to welcome research which, in effect, challenges both the adequacy and the quality of his skills.[3]

At the beginning of this text we noted that the changing nature of the marketing research function recognizes the increasing importance and complexity of research in most organizations. Although the role of the marketing research specialist is rapidly changing, research directors retain essentially a staff function in most organizations; accordingly, they have limited influence on line managers, who make the key decisions.

In examining the role of researchers as decision makers, a number of policy implications for top executives who work with marketing research personnel could be made:

Top Management Top management would be well advised to recognize the marketing research department as a reservoir of managerial talent. Research revealed little evidence that marketing researchers typically avoid decision responsibility. On the contrary, many researchers were seen to be highly decision oriented. Thus, it would seem reasonable to consider lifting traditional barriers that prevent research personnel from entering line positions that require decision-making skills.

Research Directors Research directors should neither discourage subordinates from assuming decision responsibility nor hold back recommending them for nonresearch positions. Research directors should also provide career paths for researchers who are more interested in research techniques than decision responsibility, even at the risk of losing these "career researchers" to higher-echelon marketing research departments. Otherwise, departmental morale is likely to decline and, in time, the department itself may be perceived by management as a stagnant area in which no talent—research or management—is likely to be found.

Middle Management Middle management must firmly commit itself to developing and maintaining good working relationships with marketing researchers. In this study, researchers were seen to communicate in a manner acceptable to marketing managers and to respect the equality of subjective executive judgment with objective research techniques. Therefore, it seems reasonable to suggest that product, sales, and other marketing managers should reinforce their understanding of the marketing research process. Opportunities for this achievement may be found in more manager-initiated contact with researchers in areas involving line responsibility and in the incorporation of periodic stints in the marketing research department into the management training program.

The effectiveness and efficiency of marketing decisions is largely contingent upon how well the marketing researcher participates in the managerial process. How well he can perform this role depends in part upon the satisfaction he derives from his job and the minimization of friction with managers. As a means of achieving these benefits, companies should consider the enlargement of decision responsibility for the researcher.[4]

■ Evaluating Research Reports

We have stressed from the beginning of this text the need for all managers to have some basic understanding of the marketing research process, regardless of whether they are ever involved in all research activities themselves. We emphasize this point because *all* managers have to make decisions under conditions of uncertainty, and many will require research information in order to reduce that uncertainty.

However, not all research is done in an objective and professional manner. Certainly, research reports vary tremendously in quality, ranging from excellent to worthless. How then is a manager able to judge the quality and hence the dependability of a research report? Several guidelines are available to assist managers in evaluating research reports, such as the following list.

1. **Was the report properly organized?** Did the contents of the report follow the format outlined earlier in this chapter? A poorly organized report does not inspire confidence in the abilities of the author(s).

2. **Has it been well written?** Errors in grammar, spelling, and punctuation are simply not acceptable in a professional report prepared for management. Unfortunately, business executives all too often cite poor writing skills in their assessment of college and university graduates.

3. **What did the executive summary say?** All too often the executive summary becomes a rambling introduction to the report, not the concise summary of key essentials that it should be.

4. **Were the objectives clearly defined?** Surprisingly, a great many reports fail to specify the objectives of the study. This omission could leave the reader uncertain as to what exactly the researcher intended to accomplish. Furthermore, failure to clearly define objectives can cause the focus of the study to shift away from the original goals of the investigation.

5. **Was the methodology justified?** In this case the checklist should include the appropriateness of the sampling frame, sample selection, and sample size, as well as the reliance on qualitative and quantitative information sources. In one study measuring physician interest in a new drug, the entire sample consisted of just eight doctors in a single city.

6. **Has the fieldwork been verified?** Fieldwork should always be verified to detect sloppy interviewing or falsified interviews. One of the most common verification methods is the callback, whereby a supervisor will call back 10% of the people interviewed in order to check the accuracy of the interview data.

7. **Was the report delivered on time?** Few things are more certain to destroy the credibility of a marketing research report, particularly if done by an outside agency, than for the study to arrive after the due date has passed. Marketing research is very dependent on the reputation of the researcher and this reputation necessarily includes adhering to previously established schedules.

8. **Does the research support the findings?** This is one of the most critical checkpoints on our list—the evaluator must carefully evaluate the report to determine if the interpretations are correct. Admittedly, this is not always easy; indeed, it is probably almost always difficult, but erroneous findings can result in companies making costly strategic mistakes.

9. **Were recommendations included?** Unless specified otherwise, recommendations should be included in all research reports. The research report that does not include clear recommendations to management is incomplete and should be rejected.

The foregoing criteria are general and require good judgment to be used in their application. Nevertheless, they can be useful guidelines for the evaluation of research reports.

Summary

The focus of this chapter has been on the research report, the means by which the essential findings of a research study are communicated to the intended audience. The report should be viewed as a communications vehicle, in which the researcher should communicate findings to top management in as complete and concise a manner as possible. Although the report is the end link in the research process, it is often the weakest one because of communications failure resulting from poor preparation and not from any weakness in any of the prior steps.

Depending on the level of the audience to whom the report is addressed, the research report can take either of two forms: technical or popular. The technical report is a detailed report prepared for professionals in the field who are well versed in research methodology and in previous studies. A popular report is geared for a more general audience and gives greater relative importance to findings than to methodology. A combination of the two report styles is appropriate when the audience is a mixture of specialists and generalists. In every case the format of the report is dependent on the characteristics of the audience.

The content of a research report is not standardized. Audience characteristics and the length of the project dictate not only the basic content but also the extent of treatment given to each of the topic areas. Guidelines for writing research reports have been presented in detail. The single largest part of any research report is the findings section, were the results from the research project are reported. Conclusions and recommendations should always be included.

Report presentations are made much more understandable to the audience through graphs and other visual aids. Three major types of graphs are pie graphs, bar graphs, and line graphs. Pie graphs are best for reporting breakdowns that total 100%; line graphs are best for making forecasts into the future. A combination of visual aids will make report presentation much more effective.

To the question of whether the researcher is a decision maker, the answer is *no*— at least not in the classic sense. Marketing researchers fulfil staff functions essentially and cannot make line decisions. For example, the researcher should recommend whether to launch a new product but cannot make the final decision, which remains a line management prerogative. However, all managers need a basic understanding of the research function, even if they are not directly involved in it. Several criteria for the evaluation of research studies, designed to help managers determine which ones they can trust, have been presented in this chapter.

For Discussion

1. You, the researcher, are asked by the sales manager to make a market-share forecast presentation to your company's sales department.
   a) Will you prepare a technical or a popular report? Why?
   b) What type(s) of graphs will you use?
   c) What recommendations might be important?

2. Describe a situation in which each of the following graphs would be most appropriate: (a) bar graph, (b) line graph, and (c) pie graph.

3. For your report to the vice-president of marketing, you have a detailed calculation of sample size and confidence intervals used in a survey of consumer attitudes toward your firm's proposed new product. Where in the report will you place these calculations?

4. Research reports must be both complete and concise. How can a report be both at the same time?

5. When would you use an executive summary, and where in your report would it go?

6. What is the single most important factor in determining the type of research report format to use?

7. How could marketing researchers become more actively involved in the decision-making process?

8. Carefully evaluate and then criticize the guidelines presented in this chapter for evaluating research reports. How would you modify them?

9. What part of the research report format is most often neglected by researchers? Why?

10. What is the purpose of the limitations section in a research report?

Problem

Mini-case: Market-Survey Ltd.
Nien Zhili, vice-president of a medium-sized, multipurpose marketing research agency, was asked by a new client to undertake a market survey of customer

attitudes toward a product that recently had been introduced to the market. The study was to encompass all steps from research design to final report preparation and presentation, including recommendations.

Her careful analysis of the data revealed that the client had made major errors in positioning and promoting the product. She realized that reporting these errors in her report would possibly cause the person who commissioned the study to lose his job.

The report was due in a week, but Zhili was still undecided on the approach to take. There seemed to be no acceptable solution to her dilemma.

Question
How should Zhili write her report?

Endnotes

1. Alvin J. Silk, "Test-Retest Correlations and the Reliability of Copy Testing." *Journal of Marketing Research*, 14 (November 1977), p. 483.
2. Gilbert A. Churchill, Jr., *Marketing Research: Methodological Foundations*. 2nd ed. Hinsdale, IL: Dryden Press, 1979, p. 613.
3. Joseph Newman, "Put Research Into Marketing Decisions." *Harvard Business Review*, 40 (March–April 1962), p. 108.
4. Robert J. Small and Larry J. Rosenberg, "The Marketing Researcher as a Decision Maker: Myth or Reality?" *Journal of Marketing*, 39 (January 1975), p. 7.

PART 4

SELECTED APPLICATIONS

CHAPTER 14 PRODUCT RESEARCH IN CANADA

Product research is the application of research techniques to business problems in the development of new products and the modification of existing products to satisfy consumers and make profits. Like good marketing, good product research always incorporates the marketing concept by combining customer satisfaction with profitable sales.

The dimensions of product research can best be understood by examining the meaning of the word product. A product can be defined as follows:

> The product of a company represents the promise made by the company to satisfy one or more needs (physiological and/or psychological) of the market at a given moment.[1]

From this definition, it should be apparent that product research involves much more than laboratory testing of the physical characteristics of a product. Involved also are a host of intangible attributes, such as price and colour appeal, which must be carefully tested and evaluated by the researcher. Most consumer products are purchased to satisfy customer wants, so the alert firm will promote product benefits rather than just the physical product itself. Product research is an aid in this effort, since the firm will learn what benefits consumers expect to derive from various products and the extent to which these expectations are being satisfied.

■ Importance of Product Research

Successful new products are the lifeblood of a profitable firm. Fickle consumers with ever-changing tastes dictate that corporations provide a steady stream of new products. In complying with consumer demand (or aggravating it, as some critics charge) for new products, marketing-oriented firms are increasingly aware of the growing importance of product research in developing product lines and expanding their product mixes.

A **product line** is a group of products with similar characteristics (thus, DuPont Canada produces a line of paints), whereas a **product mix** describes all of the products produced by a firm (DuPont Canada also produces items such as synthetic fibres, resins, packaging material, etc.), whether the products are related or not. A firm might have several product lines, but it can have only one product mix. Product line and product mix are the same in a case where a firm produces only one product or one group of related products.

Consumer product firms, such as Nabisco, Carnation, Bristol-Myers, Quaker Oats, and Philips, are but a few of the many companies bent on satisfying consumer demands for new products in the marketplace. Increased consumer affluence and faster-changing consumer tastes have enabled these firms to maintain a rapid growth rate in their quest to satisfy what has been called "the consumer's insatiable thirst for new products."

Types of Product Research

Companies operating in Canada are doing all types of product research, as indicated in Table 14.1. In 1984 approximately 59% of all companies were engaged in some form of product research, compared to 4% in 1966, although this figure is considerably lower than that for U.S. companies.[2]

Not surprisingly, competitive product studies and testing of existing product are the categories that generate the largest amount of research. Next comes research on new product modelling and optimization with 48%, indicating the importance of new products for the long-term growth of company sales. Finally, 41% of Canadian companies undertake studies of packaging design characteristics.

TABLE 14.1
Types of Canadian Product Research

Type	% of all companies 1966	% of all companies 1984
New-product modelling/optimization	11	48
Competitive product studies	6	54
Existing-product testing	8	52
Packaging research design characteristics	7	41
Total all-product research	17	59

Source: Adapted from Joyce Chang, David Conway, and George Haines, Jr., "Marketing Research in Canada: A 1985 Update." *Marketing*, 7. Ed. Thomas E. Muller, Administrative Sciences Association of Canada (ASAC), 1986, p. 297.

Reasons for the Importance of New-Product Research

The importance of product research can best be demonstrated by analysing events and conditions that have caused, and are presently causing, product research to assume a position of greater concern to firms. The three main factors are the cost of new products, the new-product failure rate, and the product life-cycle concept.

Cost

The cost of new products continues to soar and is now one of a firm's major expenditures. This is particularly the case for Canadian markets, which have unique characteristics. The small size of Canadian markets creates cost disadvantages for products that are highly sensitive to volume production and sales.[3] Large companies spend millions of dollars every year on research and development of new products: Procter & Gamble alone spends well over $100 million a year on new-product research.

The principal reasons for the high cost of new products include inflation, additional governmental restrictions requiring more research and testing, and the increasing cost of business decisions, stemming from larger operations designed to reach bigger markets to achieve economies of scale in manufacturing and distribution. This increasing cost of new products becomes still greater when considered in light of the new-product failure rate.

Failure Rate

The new-product failure rate is a second major factor contributing to the increased importance of product research. Although estimates concerning the failure rate vary, the overwhelming majority of all new products are failures. The new-product failure rate has been estimated at anywhere from 30% to 90%, depending on how far back the product development process is analysed. Table 14.2 lists the major reasons for new-product failure. Note that the most important one, inadequate market analysis, stems directly from lack of adequate research.

In comparing success rates of new products the definitions used by various sources should be similar. In the percentage of successful products, one must define what "success" (i.e., the number of successful products in the numerator)

TABLE 14.2
Main Reasons for New-Product Failures

Conference Board Study: Consumer & Industrial Markets	Cooper Study: Industrial Markets
1. Inadequate market analysis	1. Technical problems
2. Technical problems	2. Timing too late
3. Poor timing	3. Poor understanding of customer's needs
4. Indistinct image	4. Defensive actions by competitors
5. Improper targeting	5. Poor understanding of market environment
6. Other poor management practices	6. Price competition

Sources: David S. Hopkins, *New Product Winners and Losers*. New York: National Industrial Conference Board, 1980; Robert G. Cooper, "Winning the New Product Game." *Current Topics in Canadian Marketing*. Eds. J.G. Barnes and M.S. Sommers. Toronto: McGraw-Hill Ryerson, 1978, p. 109.

and the stage of research and development considered (i.e., the number of products "considered" in the denominator). If we look at the number of products that were commercialized and if we define a successful product as one that met all of its pre-stated objectives, a recent study by the Conference Board of Canada shows that the new-products failure rate was only *one-third*. In addition, more than 62% of companies indicated that they were satisfied with their success rate and that they expected this rate to increase in the future. It was also found that the median for the numbers of new products was six consumer products and eight industrial products.[4] Finally, the principal cause of failure was found to be a lack of information about the market—an *inadequate information system*. Other reasons given were the occurence of technical problems, particularly in the industrial field, and a bad timing decision in the introduction of the product.[5]

A study conducted among Canadian industrial firms found six major reasons for new-product failure: technical problems; late commercializations; poor understanding of consumer needs; competitive reaction; poor understanding of environmental constraints; and price competition.[6]

A major goal in product research is to reduce the new-product failure rate through extensive research and testing before a product's full-scale introduction to the market.[7] Reduction of this failure rate has been achieved by large consumer goods firms that are engaged in extensive product research, but even these firms have product failures. For example, new-product failures for Heinz (best known for ketchup) include *Great American* soups, *Happy* soups, *Heinz* salad dressings, and *Help* fruit drinks.[8]

Few new-product failures are as spectacular as the failure of the *Edsel* automobile, another victim of poor product research. Properly conducted, product research results in new-product offerings that tend to be more in tune with consumer wants.

Product Life Cycle

The third main factor contributing to the importance of product research is the product life-cycle concept. This concept recognizes that products go through stages of introduction, growth, maturity, and saturation, and then into decline and possible abandonment by manufacturers.

Figure 14.1 shows that the life cycle for a typical product begins with an introductory period where both sales and profits are low. Profits and sales climb during the growth period at a rapid rate. Profits typically peak in the market growth stage, whereas sales might continue climbing into the maturity stages, when profits are actually declining. This seeming paradox of falling profits during a period of rising sales occurs primarily because of intense price competition among manufacturers. At the saturation stage, sales are mostly replacement sales and profits continue to decline. The decline stage might be gradual or abrupt— the product is dropped from the line.

Management of this product life cycle requires product research in forecasting sales and profit curves, timing the introduction of new products, and making decisions to modify or abandon existing products. Product research is necessary if management is to know when to make the product elimination decision. The

FIGURE 14.1
Product Life Cycle for a Typical Product

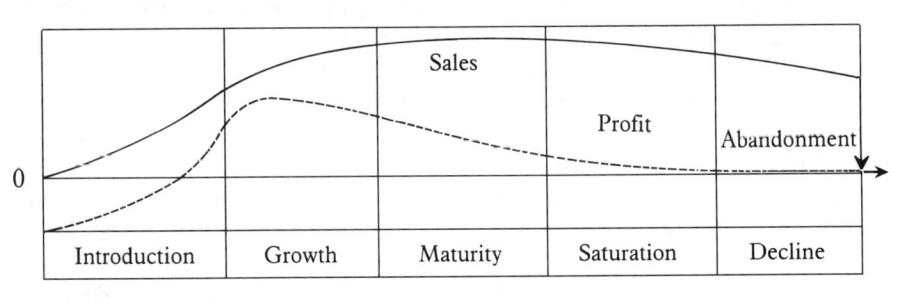

challenge facing new-product research for consumer goods manufacturers is that it is believed that product life cycles are becoming shorter. One study concluded that most new brands will have less than three years of success.[9]

The result of shorter product life cycles is that manufacturers are spending less time in developing new products. One example of this trend is the shampoo industry; a new shampoo appears on the market nearly every three months and competes with all existing brands. This trend places additional pressure on product researchers to compress the time devoted to new-product development.

■ Generation of New-Product Ideas

The marketing manager must generate a great number of ideas for new products because of the high mortality rate of these ideas throughout the search process for new products. For food products, it was found that only 4% of ideas for new products were commercialized.[10] On the average, in a sample of 51 companies operating in different industries, 3.4% of all ideas generated were commercialized and about one-half of these are successes.[11]

This first task should be guided by both the marketing objectives and a knowledge of current consumer needs. It is not necessary at this stage to develop detailed market analysis. The objective is to generate as many ideas as possible and to avoid a bottleneck that could delay the process. For example, a general idea might be to find domestic applications of new developments in electronics, communications, and robotics; e.g., to assist families in the chores of cleaning and/or cooking, or in controlling heating and security systems.

The search for new-product ideas must be systematic, and ideally it should be the responsibility of one specific member or a committee of members belonging to the marketing department of the firm. These ideas might originate from different sources, which can be classified into two categories: ideas suggested to the marketing manager by someone outside the department and ideas developed within the marketing department.

External Sources of Ideas

Among external sources, one finds consumers who, by their communications (letter, telephone, etc.) or by their consumption behaviour sometimes provide some interesting ideas.[12] For example, snacks such as *Bits 'N Bites* by Christie were developed when someone observed that some consumers used a mix of pretzels and cereals to make a salty snack. Another example is *Pressdent*, the idea for which came from an advertising executive who observed his daughter Nathalie, aged 11, trying to insert some toothpaste into an empty container that had a pump.[13] The executive liked the idea of toothpaste in a pump container and went on to develop this product. In addition, letters written to companies by consumers, either praising or complaining about products, sometimes include specific suggestions for improving existing products or introducing new ones. This feedback is so valuable to companies that some innovative ones attempt to generate more of it by creating and promoting "hot-lines," for example, Whirlpool's "Cool-line."

Company sales representatives also regularly receive suggestions when they meet with customers or when they do public demonstrations of their products. In addition, employees often have first-hand knowledge of the products with which they are dealing, and can identify the products' strong and weak points. They often come up with interesting ideas, and firms should tap this creativity by various means such as suggestion boxes and financial rewards such as bonuses, shares, or royalties, or non-financial rewards such as days off or paid vacations.

Other useful sources of new ideas are researchers (e.g., university, government), specialized journals, exhibitions, trade shows, and competitors. For example, the idea for *Grand Pré* came from the International Food Show held in Paris in 1971. *Grand Pré* is fresh milk that has been pasturized at ultra high temperatures and packaged so that it stays fresh for at least three months without refrigeration. Finally there are commercial research bureaus that have personnel trained to find new-product ideas for companies for a fee.

Internal Development of Ideas

Internally, the marketing department might conduct a systematic market analysis for a product category, for example, soap or chocolate bars. At this stage of development of new-product ideas, research techniques, such as product positioning and perceptual mapping, can be very useful. This type of analysis might also be contracted out to consultants.

Internal development consists of determining the general needs of the whole market or a specific segment in a product category, and how the existing brands satisfy these needs. Any gap in the market potentially can accommodate a new product.

For example, several researchers in Canada and the United States have studied the beer market extensively,[14] identifying between 10 and 20 possible beer attributes. Examples of these attributes are mild flavour, low alcoholic content, filling, thirst-quenching, bitter, easy to digest, popular with women, and available in restaurants. In those studies, two major dimensions emerged consistently: a *physical dimension* related to the strength of the beer (low alcoholic content;

sweet, light, mild flavour) and a *social dimension* related to group influence, quality, and price (available in restaurants, expensive, popular, high-quality, imported).

An example of product mapping in the beer market is presented in Figure 14.2. This map was constructed with a sample of approximately 350 regular beer drinkers in the Trois Rivières area of Quebec. The high level of consumption of lighter beers is indicated by the clustering of the lighter brands in the upper part of the map. This is consistent with recent market trends toward lighter beers.[15] This map was constructed before the introduction of light beers and showed very clearly this gap in the market. It also showed that there was room for the introduction of high-image products such as well-known American beers (e.g.,

FIGURE 14.2
Positioning of Thirteen Brands of Beer in the Quebec Market

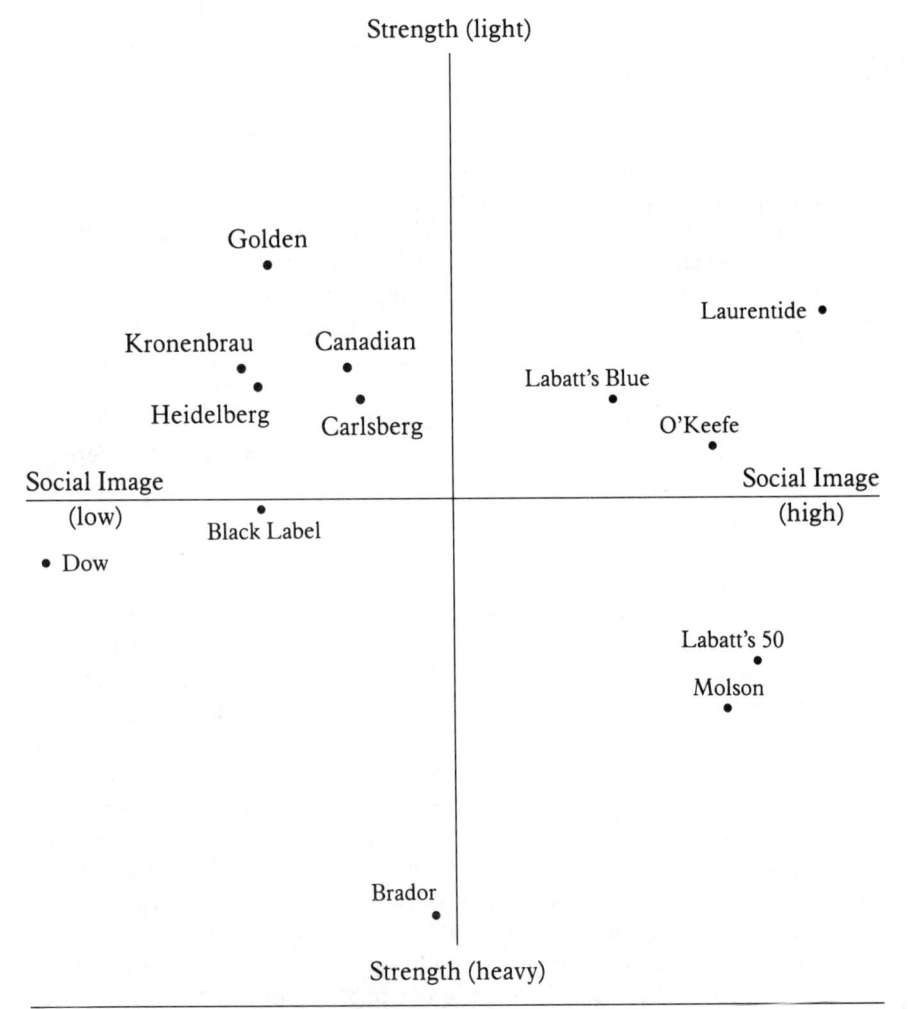

Source: Courtesy of Jacques E. Brisoux, University of Québec (Trois Rivières)

Budweiser, Miller, Coors).[16] *Brador* differentiated itself from the other brands as a heavy premium beer; the lack of competition indicated an opportunity for other premium beers such as *Labatt's Classic*, which was introduced later. *Laurentide* had the strongest social image of all brands. *Molson* and *Labatt's 50* were competing against each other, as were *Laurentide, Labatt's Blue*, and *O'Keefe*. Finally, *Dow* had the lowest social image of all brands, due to problems it had in the past.

Screening of Ideas

Some of the ideas generated by this process can be eliminated because they are not really new, they are not feasible, or because they do not fit the company's image or mission. Any of these reasons would render useless the preliminary evaluation of an idea.[17] In case of doubt, it is often useful to reformulate and then re-evaluate the original idea. Once this stage is completed, the next step is to test these ideas.

■ Product Testing

Product testing is a valuable tool in marketing research. Before launching a new product onto the market, a manufacturer wants to know what consumers think about it. Product testing minimizes the risk in marketing new products, including the risk of a new product failing due to lack of sales and the risk that a new product might require extensive and costly redesigning if it is introduced to the market without first having been adequately tested. By product testing, manufacturers hope to place a stable and acceptable product on the market. Extensive product testing enables them to offer sound warranty policies and to avoid false or misleading claims in the advertising of product benefits.

Figure 14.3 presents an overview of product testing, Fundamentally, there are two main ways in which new products may be tested: technical testing and consumer testing.

Technical Testing

Technical testing is conducted by the manufacturer or by an independent testing laboratory. Technical testing aids the manufacturer in determining how the product compares with competitors' products in composition and performance.

There are basically two phases of technical testing: analysis testing and performance testing. **Analysis testing** reveals the composition of a product—the raw materials used or how it was assembled. **Performance testing** is conducted to find out what a product will do and involves simulating use conditions. For example, extensive performance testing is carried out by North American automobile manufacturers. All new automobile models are tested by professional drivers under almost every imaginable road condition and hazard. The industry desperately wants to avoid expensive product recalls, such as the General Motors recall of nearly five million *Corvairs* to check for safety defects—a move that cost an estimated $50 million and resulted in bad publicity that is still remembered today—more than twenty years after it happened![18]

FIGURE 14.3
Overview of Product Testing

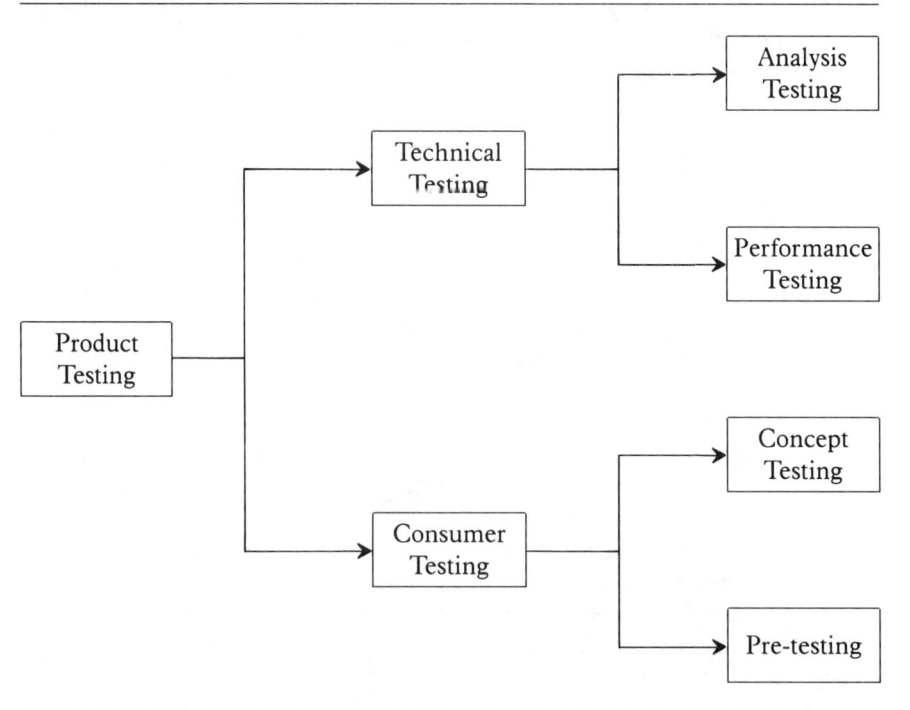

Virtually all major manufacturers are involved in technical testing, as are numerous other organizations. One such organization is the Consumers' Association of Canada (CAC), which publishes the *Canadian Consumer* magazine. (In the United States, a similar organization is Consumers Union, which publishes *Consumer Reports*). Both the CAC and Consumers Union extensively test a wide range of consumer products through analysis and performance tests and then publish the results, much to the concern of manufacturers whose products receive poor ratings. Also, *Good Housekeeping* magazine maintains laboratory facilities for testing advertisers' products. If a product successfully passes the tests, it is then advertised with the *Good Housekeeping* "Seal of Approval." In addition, some branches of the Canadian government are concerned with safety and some conduct product testing (e.g., Consumer and Corporate Affairs Canada, Transport Canada, and Health and Welfare Canada).

The question is often asked whether technical testing should be conducted by the manufacturer or by an independent testing laboratory. Although there are many aspects to the answer, one clear advantage of using an independent testing laboratory is objectivity. Consumers are more likely to believe claims if they have been verified through an independent testing laboratory than if tests have been conducted on the manufacturer's premises and under the manufacturer's supervision. Even so, some manufacturers have been known to distort and misrepresent independent testing data in advertising campaigns. The case of Detroit automakers using Environmental Protection Agency (EPA) data in support of superior gasoline-mileage claims provides an excellent example of abuse of independent testing laboratory data. The objectivity of these independent testing agencies is also subject to question: some, like *Good Housekeeping's* agency, are financially dependent on manufacturers for fees or advertising revenues.

Consumer Testing

Consumer testing is undertaken to determine consumer attitudes toward a new product or product idea. The underlying basis for consumer testing is the expectation that favourable consumer attitudes toward a product or product concept will be translated into sales in the marketplace. The fact that this might not always occur represents the most significant limitation of consumer test data.

Consumer testing usually takes place under controlled conditions that might inadequately represent normal market condition. Testing by consumers is of two main types: concept testing and pre-testing.

Concept Testing

Concept testing represents an attempt to measure consumers' reactions to a new-product concept or idea, to learn what buyers' probable reactions will be before the product's actual development. To measure interest in a product that has not yet been developed, researchers normally use pictures or drawings to help describe the proposed product. Although concept testing has broad applications, its primary utility is as a preliminary screening device for evaluating completely new concepts or product ideas.

Several techniques can be used in concept testing. The most important ones are motivation research, focus group interviews, in-depth interviewing, attitude scaling, projective techniques, and multidimensional scaling.

Motivation research was a popular technique in Canada in the 1950s and 1960s. It was pioneered in the United States by Ernest Dichter, a well-known psychologist. The technique tries to identify consumer motives that might explain specific purchasing behaviour.[19] However, these studies soon showed their limitations and they had virtually disappeared in their original form in the early 1970s. Two main reasons account for this. First, the diagnosis phase that follows the analysis of the mountains of material gathered from in-depth interviews requires a great deal of expertise in psychology. Second, the small sample sizes, sometimes as low as fifty, cast serious doubts on the reliability of these findings. However, today, motivation research is not viewed as the end of the research process, but only as a preliminary step leading to the formulation of research hypotheses about consumer behaviour. Of course, these hypotheses must then be tested through large-scale studies such as surveys on a representative sample of the market.

Focus group interviews use some ten to fifteen individuals who are similar to the target market. The role of the group moderator is to elicit responses from the members in a non-directive manner.[20] Focus group interviews can be used in this context for new concept testing as well as for brand-name selection and brand image and package testing.

In-depth interviews are conducted by a trained interviewer with one individual at a time. The interviewer probes in detail the individual reactions to a new concept, a prototype new product, a new brand name, or a new package. As in the case of motivation research, this method is very expensive and can provide only qualitative information, which is used as a base for further analysis and research.

Attitude scaling and *projective techniques* are methods that tend to be faster and less expensive than some of the ones previously mentioned. Both might use self-administered questionnaires. In attitude scaling questionnaires, the first section describes the new concept, mentions the proposed brand name, or asks the respondents to look at a prototype product or package that is handed out with the questionnaire. Next, the respondents must answer a series of closed or open-ended questions on the product, name, or package.

With *projective techniques*, indirect questioning is used to obtain more accurate answers to sensitive questions. Respondents are asked to assume the identity of another person, such as a neighbour, a character in a drawing (as in the Thematic Apperception Test), or in a verbal statement. The respondent is then asked to write a reaction to this stimulus or to make a statement in answer to a question based on that stimulus.[21]

Multidimensional scaling (described in Chapter 12) is one of the analytical procedures that can be employed in concept-testing data analyses. Figure 14.4 shows an example of this method involving a hypothetical rum manufacturer who wants to measure reaction to some new rum drink mixes.[22] The six rum drink

FIGURE 14.4
Application of Concept Testing for Six New Rum Drink Concepts

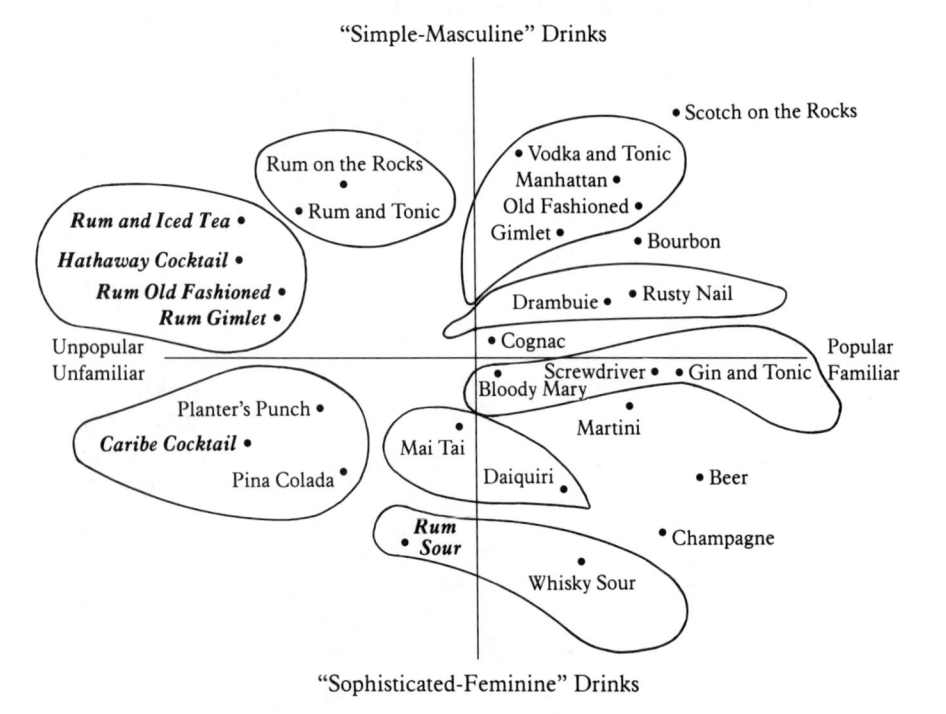

Source: Yoram Wind, "A New Procedure for Concept Evaluation." *Journal of Marketing*, 37 (October 1973), p. 2.

concepts (rum old-fashioned, rum sour, Hathaway Cocktail, Caribe Cocktail, rum and iced tea, and rum gimlet) are described and then tested, along with twenty-two other drinks that are included for control purposes. By analysing this perceptual map of clusters drawn around groupings of drinks, the researcher concluded that a manufacturer interested in a new rum drink concept should promote a rum sour over any of the other five new rum drinks, since it was found that the other five concepts all competed with existing rum drinks, whereas the rum sour competed only with the whisky sour.

Perceptual maps also have been developed for product categories where the number of brands is large and brand differentiation has become difficult. For example, look at the map for the automobile market, as reproduced in Figure 14.5. *Plymouth* is viewed as a practical car with a conservative image, while *Chrysler* is perceived as a more luxurious make. Individual models also can be mapped and the positioning achieved in consumers' perceptions can be compared with the initital marketing objectives of these models. For example, in the study that produced the map in Figure 14.5, the *Chrysler Lancer* and *Commander* models were perceived by consumers as being similar to the Honda *Accord*, which is exactly what the marketing manager had hoped would happen.[23]

Finally, perceptual maps have also found applications in the areas of services and non-profit institutions.[24]

FIGURE 14.5
Perceptual Map of the Automobile Market in 1984

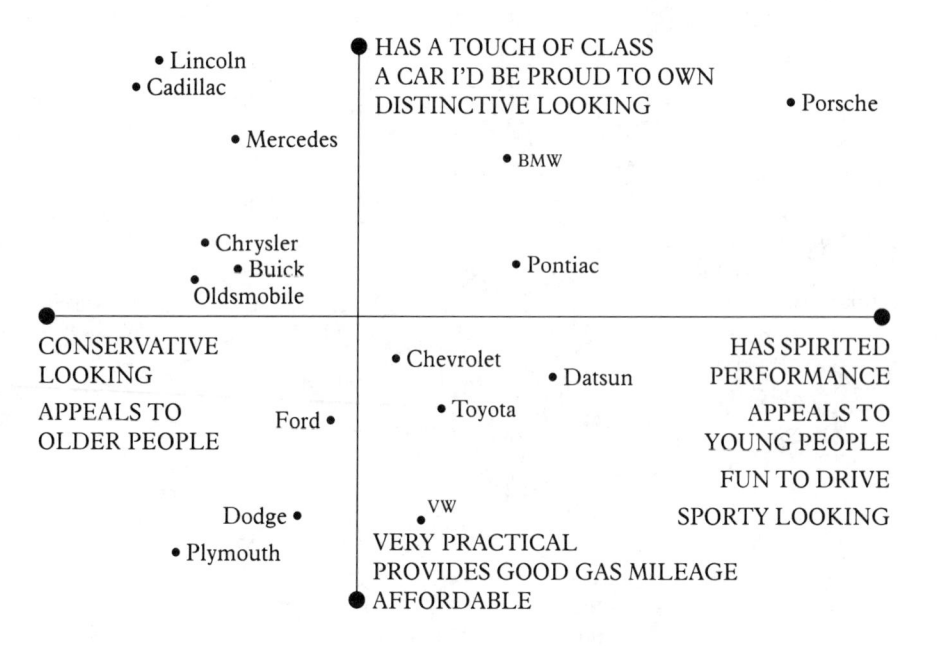

Source: John Koten, "Car Makers Use 'Image' Map as Tool to Position Products," *The Wall Street Journal* (March 22, 1984), p. 33

Pre-testing

If a product idea successfully passes the concept-testing stage, the manufacturer might then choose to begin producing it in limited quantities for pre-testing. **Pre-testing**, the second main form of consumer testing, is done before introducing a product on the market: it is the experimental use of products by a sample of potential consumers.

Pre-testing gives a manufacturer the opportunity to learn consumer reactions to a new product before market introduction. Still, although the time and expense of entering test markets are avoided at this stage, there are problems in consumer pre-testing. Four main problems relate to an appropriate sample, supervision and control, accurate responses, and measurement.

1. *The sample*: Perhaps the major problem encountered is obtaining a sample of prospective consumers that is representative, chosen without bias, and large enough to be statistically significant. Since most firms are unable to overcome this limitation in their pre-testing, the sample is the main problem in evaluating test data.

2. *Supervision and control*: If pre-testing of products takes place in the homes of sample members, there is little opportunity for supervision and control over conditions of use. Another problem in the area of supervision and control concerns the product itself: Should brands, labels, and other distinguishing marks be removed, so that the manufacturer's name or advertising claims cannot influence consumers? If labels are removed, then the question of the realism of the pre-testing process arises, since labels and other distinguishing marks constitute part of the product. However, the labels themselves might bias the results, because knowing the manufacturer's name could distort consumer response.

3. *Accurate responses*: As with all research involving consumer responses, there is the problem of securing accurate replies. If company employees are utilized in pre-testing, will their perceptions of the firm's products be unbiassed? Care must be taken to prevent the use of leading questions that will influence test results. The firm must be willing to spend the necessary funds to hire trained interviewers capable of securing accurate replies from the sample.

4. *Measurement*: The fourth and final main problem faced by researchers in the pre-testing process is one of measurement. Because pre-testing involves the measurement of consumer reactions to a new product, it is necessary to develop accurate methods of measuring these reactions. How does one measure the taste or smell of a food product? What do the words *like* or *dislike* really mean? Can they be translated into *buy* or *would not buy*?

These problems illustrate limitations inherent in the pre-testing process and show why manufacturers of consumer goods normally follow pre-testing with test-marketing, before attempting full-scale distribution of a new product. Despite these limitations, many firms make extensive and successful use of employees for pre-testing new products. Consider the example of Procter & Gamble's pre-testing process, which uses the firm's own employees:

> In the Hair Care Evaluation Center, women have half their hair washed with a new shampoo, and half with their regular brand. Employees sampling a new toothpaste or mouthwash enter a laboratory where they breathe through a hole. A researcher sniffs their breath to judge the product's effectiveness.[25]

■ Use of Panels as a Product-Testing Method

The use of panels in product testing is particularly popular among the larger manufacturers of consumer convenience goods. A panel is a semi-permanent group of people that should be representative of a manufacturer's potential customers, which has the task of evaluating products and product ideas. Panels can be used for concept testing and pre-testing in the product-testing process. However, panel members are not qualified to engage in technical testing of new products, which must be left to people with appropriate expertise.

Different types of panels are used in marketing research, depending on the type of data sought from the panel members. Market Facts of Canada has a consumer mail panels (CPM) division and regularly maintains a list of households to be contacted for mail surveys. Other companies that operate consumer panels are A.C. Nielsen of Canada, International Surveys Limited (ISL), and Dialogue Canada.

Problems in Panel Testing

Panel usage in product research presents several problems. First, panel membership must be representative of prospective customers for the product. Second, the researchers need to establish some degree of control over conditions of use by panel members, to get needed feedback on consumer attitudes toward the product. Third, researchers might need to disguise the identity of the product's manufacturer to eliminate preconceived attitudes about the firm or its products. Fourth, researchers must deal with non-response bias, which occurs if some panel members drop out.

After a new product has been pre-tested by a firm's employees, it might then be sent to a panel for final consumer-use testing before being placed in test markets. At Procter & Gamble, panels constitute another hurdle that must be successfully passed before a product can be test-marketed.[26]

■ Test-Marketing of New Products

A consumer goods firm that has done solid product research will be relatively sure of product success even before going to a test market. Nevertheless, before a new product is distributed nationwide, it is usually tested in one or more cities that demographically represent the full national market. Costs of test-marketing vary with time and the number of cities used, but $250 000 for a two-city test market is typical.

Test-marketing consists of executing the preliminary marketing program developed for the new product in a specific market. If several alternative marketing programs are being compared, there must be at least the same number of test markets. Each one of these test markets should be representative of the overall target market. Under these conditions, the marketing researcher will be able to project the test results into the entire market and revise any analysis already done on the profitability of the new product. Four types of decisions must be made concerning the market test: the marketing program(s) to be tested, the number of cities in which to test them, the length of the test, and the means of controlling the results.

Benefits of Test-Marketing

The decision to test-market a product before a full-scale nationwide push represents a cautious and usually prudent step. Test-marketing assumes that results gathered from the test-market cities can be projected nationwide; this assumption might be questionable, however, since conditions in test markets might differ from those in national markets.

Firms can receive two principal benefits from market testing. The primary benefit is learning more about the product's potential sales. The firm wants to know whether the product's sales potential is large enough to justify full-scale market introduction; if sales are insufficient, the product is considered a failure at this stage and joins the ranks of the might-have-beens.

A secondary benefit derived from test-marketing is the opportunity to pre-test alternative marketing strategies. This procedure can involve using different media and promotional mixes in various test-market cities. The marketing strategy associated with the best sales results in the test markets will then be the one used in the national introduction of the product. Not only does test-marketing provide the benefit of pre-testing promotional strategy, it also allows the firm a final chance to test its product, pricing, and distribution strategies before introduction. A case in point is Procter & Gamble's *Pampers*, which initially failed in test markets because of low sales. Further testing of alternative marketing strategies, mostly pricing, changed the results drastically and eventually the brand became a huge success.[27]

Test Cities

Determining the number of cities to use depends on the objectives and the research budget allocated to the market test. The greater the market test the better the results will be generalized but the higher the costs will be. Thus, the marketing researchers must find an optimum solution to this problem. Finding test cities that are demographically representative of national or even regional markets can be difficult, since no one city perfectly represents an entire nation. In Canada, there is no single city that represents the entire country, unlike Peoria in the United States. Therefore, one must use a combination of cities, and those that are often used are London, Peterborough, Kingston, Sherbrooke, Kitchener-Waterloo, North Bay, St. Catharines, Calgary, Regina, and Sudbury.[28]

The geography of Canada could create severe problems for the marketing researcher wanting to test-market a new product on a region-by-region basis. There are vast differences between the various Canadian regions, which each has its own lifestyle and even its own geographic culture. It is, therefore, extremely risky to test-market a product in, for example, British Columbia before introducing it to other provinces, such as Ontario. Only when the potential benefits of testing alternative marketing strategies—and learning from smaller-scale mistakes—are large enough, would those benefits compensate for the higher risks of an atypical test. An example of this was the introduction of Cadbury's *Thick* chocolate bar first to British Columbia, then to Alberta, and then to Ontario. By the time the product was introduced in Ontario, all of the problems with the name, the packaging, and the advertising had been ironed out, and the product became a huge success.[29] Even in the much larger U.S. market, the following observation has been made regarding test-marketing of new food products:

> People in coastal cities tend to accept nearly all new products quickly. Those who live in the Middle West, however, seem to reject most of them. Thus, it is that Syracuse, New York, which is neither coastal nor Midwestern, is considered to be the ideal test market.[30]

Test Duration

The duration of a market test depends on the nature of the product. One general rule is to take into account the average time between one or several repeat-purchase cycles. Another consideration is the threat of competitors who might find out the test results, and then quickly produce and introduce a comparable product, sometimes beating out the original company.

The length of time that a product might remain in a test market presents a problem to researchers. The longer a product is in a test market, the more time the manufacturer has for ironing out problems before the product is introduced nationally. Sometimes test-market times have been quite lengthy. When General Foods Corporation first brought out its new freeze-dried coffee, *Maxim*, the firm kept *Maxim* in test markets for several years before opting for full market introduction.

However, firms are under increasing pressure to reduce the time that new products are in test markets, for two reasons: shrinking product life cycles and competitive pressures. Shrinking product life cycles, resulting from consumers' never-ending quest for new products, force manufacturers to bring out a constant succession of new products, which intensely compete with one another even though sometimes they are produced by the same manufacturer. A prime example of this multibrand strategy is the heavy-duty detergent industry. In 1975 the detergent market was controlled by three manufacturers—Procter & Gamble, Lever Brothers, and Colgate-Palmolive. These three firms produced twenty-three different detergent brands, all in competition with one another for a total of 94% of the market.[31]

Competitive pressures force manufacturers to limit the length of time a new product can remain in test markets because of the fear that competitors will learn of it and attempt to beat the firm to the market with a similar product. Sometimes, companies prefer to bypass this step rather than take the risk. They take a greater risk by introducing a product that might fail—one that might not have been introduced had a market test been conducted. When Lever Brothers took a year test-marketing its *Mrs. Butterworth's* pancake syrup concept, General Foods, manufacturer of *Log Cabin* syrup, monitored Lever's sales in the test cities. General Foods then managed to introduce buttered syrup nationally at the same time, thus substantially reducing from projected levels the sales of *Mrs. Butterworth's* syrup.

Finally, a last consideration relating to the duration of test-marketing is that of cost, which must be evaluated against the actual benefits of the additional information obtained by the test.

Test-marketing is designed to reduce risk to manufacturers by increasing the certainty that products will be successful in general distribution. However, success in test markets is no guarantee of nationwide product acceptance.

Other Considerations in Test-marketing

First, the raison d'être of the market test is the opportunity for the marketing manager to observe the new product under realistic conditions. The information gained from the market test must be carefully collected and analysed by the researcher. Thus, it is necessary to fully plan the data collection as well as the computer software that will be used to analyse this data. This step is critical in assisting the manager to make the decision whether to market the product on a national scale.

Second, the decision to conduct test-marketing can be affected by the manager's subjective evaluation of the probabilities for success. As mentioned before, these tests are very costly in Canada in relation to the size of the total market to be served.[32] Thus, the marketing manager must make an analysis of the costs and benefits of the test compared to those that would be obtained if no test were conducted.[33]

Finally, it should be mentioned that some computer-based simulations of test-marketing new products exist; the best-known simulation is called ASSESSOR. Such simulations usually involve a series of simulated situations including preferences, measurements, advertising presentations, response to shelf displays, and product usage at home. These provide estimates of consumer evaluations and purchase probability, which are in turn used to predict market shares. This method has been found to be highly accurate and to cost much less than actual test-marketing.[34]

■ Consumer-use Tests

In cases where a manufacturer wants to have consumers evaluate the merits of a product as opposed to the competitors' products under "real" conditions, product researchers utilize consumer-use tests. A consumer-use test enables a manufacturer of consumer products to have the product objectively compared with competing products by consumers under conditions of actual use. Consumer-use tests can be conducted using commercial panels in a laboratory setting, by manufacturers' own employees on company premises, or by independent consumers in their own homes. Consumer-use tests are a form of product testing by consumers but are separate and distinct from concept testing and pre-testing.

To meet the criteria of objectivity, consumer-use tests must be "masked" or "blind." A blind test is one in which all identifying labels or marks are removed from the product to be tested or masked in some way. Not only is the blind test effective in obtaining unbiassed perceptions of relative merits of competing products, it is also an important tool for measuring brand loyalty among customers. Numerous research studies using blind tests have shown that fiercely brand-loyal customers have often been unable to distinguish between their favourite (and supposedly superior) brands and those of competitors. This has been found to be particularly true among brand-loyal beer drinkers, a fact that encourages heavy advertising expenditures among firms in that industry. In establishing a market share for its new *Lite* beer, the Miller Brewing Company used a $10-million advertising blitz campaign. This expenditure amounted to an estimated $6.50 per barrel of beer, as opposed to an industrywide average of $1 per barrel, and was considered a key ingredient in the initial market success of *Miller Lite*.[35] Similarly, heavy advertising spending was a key factor in the successful introduction in Canada of such U.S. beer brands as *Budweiser*, *Miller*, and *Coors*.[36] This raises the issue of advertising effectiveness, which will be examined in the next chapter.

Two basic consumer-use tests are paired-comparison-placement tests and staggered-comparison tests. Both of these are normally blind tests and consumers test the products under conditions of actual use.

Paired-comparison-placement Tests

Also known as side-by-side tests, paired-comparison-placement tests derive their name from the way in which the tests are conducted. Typically, two masked products are placed side by side in front of consumers, who are asked to use and compare the two products and then pick the one preferred. In cases where the manufacturer wants comparisons made among more than two products, comparisons are still made in pairs, in order to establish consumer preferences clearly. If three products, X, Y, and Z were compared all together, instead of in pairs, consumers might give the following preferences:

Product	Consumer Preference
X	48%
Y	32%
Z	20%
Total	100%

Without paired-comparison tests it might be assumed that X is the product most preferred. However, what if the 20% of respondents preferring product Z also preferred product Y over product X? Product Y would then be a 58% to 42% preferential choice over product X. Therefore, it is necessary to run paired-comparison tests, comparing X with Y, X with Z, and Y with Z, in order to obtain completely accurate results.

Staggered-comparison tests

Staggered-comparison tests differ from paired-comparison tests only in their timing. Whereas paired-comparison tests involve simultaneous use of products, staggered-comparison tests require consumers to use the products at different times. Respondents are given two products several days or weeks apart. The respondents might be divided into two groups, with one group given product X first and the other given product Y first, to eliminate any bias resulting from having tried one product first. This also makes the test more realistic, because consumers seldom use two competing products at the same time.

Consumer-use tests have the admirable goal of attempting to create as realistic an atmosphere as possible, but these blind tests do not fully represent actual market conditions and the validity of the research findings is therefore questionable. Still, consumer-use tests are important in obtaining unbiassed information about consumer product preferences and in measuring the basis for brand loyalty.

Despite the most sophisticated new-product research techniques, firms are unable to avoid some market failures among new products. Like marketing research in general, new-product research cannot guarantee marketplace success. However, it is an important aid in making sound decisions, because uncertainty can be reduced and the probability of success can be increased.

■ Summary

Product research is the application of marketing research techniques and the marketing concept to problems in developing new products and modifying existing ones. Approximately 60% of all large consumer goods manufacturing firms conduct some product research. Today, Canadian firms spend more than $3 billion per year on research and development.[37]

In attempting to satisfy consumer desire for new products, firms have expanded product lines and enlarged their product mixes. Understanding and managing the product life cycle is necessary to help reduce product failures.

Product testing involves both technical testing and testing by consumers. Technical testing is conducted to identify the composition of a product (analysis testing) and what it will do (performance testing). Consumer testing measures consumer attitudes toward a new product or product idea. Consumer testing includes concept testing—an attempt to determine consumer attitudes toward a yet undeveloped product—and pre-testing, which involves the experimental use of a new product by a sample of potential customers. Pre-testing presents problems with sample selection, supervision and control, accurate responses, and measurement.

Panels are widely used in product research for testing new products and concepts. A panel is a semi-permanent group of people that should be representative of potential customers, which has the task of evaluating new products or concepts. Despite their wide use, panels are not always ideal testing instruments.

Before a new product is distributed nationwide, it is often placed in test markets that demographically represent the national market. Test-marketing enables the firm to gather information regarding the product's potential sales and allows the pre-testing of alternative marketing strategies. Shrinking product life cycles and competitive pressures have, however, forced many firms to limit their test-marketing efforts.

Manufacturers might want respondents to compare and evaluate competing products in consumer-use tests, where all identifying marks have been removed from the products or masked. These blind or masked tests might be paired-comparison-placement tests, in which the two products are placed side by side and evaluated at the same time, or they might be staggered-comparison tests, in which the two products are evaluated several days or even weeks apart to more closely duplicate actual market conditions. Results indicate little if any difference in the results of these two types of tests.

For Discussion

1. Why should a consumer goods firm engage in product research?

2. What is the relationship between product research and the marketing concept? Can a firm practise the marketing concept without engaging in product research?

3. What do you think is the most important part of product research? Why?

4. Why should product research be concerned with the product life-cycle concept? Is there a connection between the two?

5. Some people say that concept testing is unrealistic. What do you think about the validity of concept testing? What is the purpose of concept testing?

6. Are the firm's own employees the best testers or should professional panels be used? Why?

7. What is test-marketing? Why would a firm want to test-market a product?

8. What effects do shrinking product life cycles have on test-marketing?

9. Develop a product research plan for a new mouthwash. What steps will you follow?

10. Why would it be important to use a blind test if you were trying to determine whether consumers can actually tell the difference between *Coke* (*New* and *Classic*), *Pepsi*, and RC?

Problems

1. **Mini-case: The Darnyi Company**

   The Darnyi Company is a well-known manufacturer of candies, chocolate bars, cookies, and similar food products. Because of thorough marketing research, high quality, and heavy advertising campaigns, the company is rapidly becoming a leader in its field.

   Its newest innovation is *Choco*, instant hot chocolate powder to which only boiling water has to be added. Laboratory and in-home use tests have indicated that *Choco* should be a success. The next step is test-marketing in a medium-sized city. The company has obtained the A.C. Nielsen reports and consumer purchase diary panel data for this city. Nielsen monitors sales at the retail level; the consumer diary panel estimates the number of repeat purchases. The data should enable Darnyi to measure the success of its test market.

   Free samples of *Choco* have been distributed on a random basis to half of the households in the test city. Advertising and promotion are being carried out on a regular basis. A follow-up personal interview is planned for the end of the test period.

   Question

   Design a follow-up questionnaire that would measure the effectiveness of the free sample. Your questionnaire should indicate the extent of awareness, trial, and adoption of *Choco* in households that received the sample, compared with those that did not. In addition, be sure that the questionnaire highlights which market segments were influenced by the free sample (i.e., income group, family size, age, educational background).

2. The research and development department of your company has developed a new digital thermometer that gives an instant reading. This product could be targeted at mothers of young children, who could use this product to ascertain quickly if a child has a fever. The thermometer is unbreakable, unlike the glass variety, and comes with a battery that lasts one year.

   Questions

   1. What method would you use to test this new concept? Prepare all material that you would use in this research.

   2. The research and development department has also indicated that, with proper attachments, this thermometer could also be used as a meat or a candy thermometer. How would you test this additional concept? Again, prepare all of the material that you would use.

Endnotes

1. René Y. Darmon, Michel Laroche, and John V. Petrof, *Marketing in Canada: A Management Perspective*. Toronto: McGraw-Hill Ryerson, 1989, Chapter 8.
2. Joyce Chang, David Conway, and George H. Haines, Jr., "A Comparison of Business Use of Marketing Research in Canada and the United States." *Marketing*, 7. Ed. Thomas E. Muller, Administrative Sciences Association of Canada (ASAC), 1986, p. 284.
3. S.S. Grimly, "Canadian Factors in the Generation and Evaluation of New Products Ideas." *Business Quarterly* (Summer 1974), pp. 32–39.
4. David S. Hopkins, *New Product Winners and Losers*. New York: National Industrial Conference Board, 1980.
5. Ibid.
6. Robert G. Cooper and Blair Little, "Reducing the Risk of Industrial New Product Development." *The Canadian Marketer* (Fall 1974), pp. 7–12; see also, Robert G. Cooper, "Winning the New Product Game," in James G. Barnes and Montrose S. Sommers, *Current Topics in Canadian Marketing*. Toronto: McGraw-Hill Ryerson, 1978, pp. 104–111.
7. Ronald McTavish, "Marketing Research and the Technical Development of New Industrial Products." *Marketing*, 2. Ed. Robert Wyckham, ASAC, 1981, pp. 225–36.
8. *Marketing News*, 10 (19 November 1976).
9. Peter Vanderwicken, "P & G's Secret Ingredient." *Fortune* (July 1974), p. 79.
10. Robert D. Buzzell and Robert E.M. Nourse, *Product Innovation in Food Processing: 1954–1964*. Boston: Harvard Business School, 1967, p. 105.
11. *Management of New Products*. 6th ed. New York: Booz, Allen and Hamilton, Inc., 1965, p. 2.
12. "Helpful Consumers." *The Wall Street Journal* (June 2, 1965), pp. 1–20.
13. "Pressdent," in René Y. Darmon, Michel Laroche, and John V. Petrof, *Le Marketing*. 3rd ed. Montreal: McGraw-Hill Éditeurs, 1986, p. 552.
14. See, for example, Y. Allaire, "The Measurement of Heterogeneous Semantic, Perceptual and Preference Structures." Unpublished doctoral dissertation, MIT, August 1972; R.M. Johnson, "Market Segmentation: A Strategic Management Tool." *Journal of Marketing Research*, 9 (February 1971), pp. 13–18; R.Y. Darmon, "Multiple Joint Space Analysis for Improved Advertising Strategy." *The Canadian Marketer*. Vol. 10, no. 1 (1979), pp. 10–14; J.E. Brisoux, "Le Phénomène des Ensembles Evoqués: Une Etude Empirique des Dimensions Contenu et Taille." Unpublished doctoral dissertation, Université Laval, 1980.
15. Janice C. Simpson, "Light Beers Carve Out Growing Segment of Sales to Calorie-Conscious Drinkers." *The Wall Street Journal* (March 8, 1978).
16. Wayne Grady, "The Budweiser Gamble." *Readings in Canadian Marketing*, U. de Brentani and Michel Laroche, eds. Dubuque, IA: Kendall-Hunt, 1983, pp. 16–21; Lynn R. Helpard, "It Sure Is 'Miller Time' in Canada: Number One in Four Months." *Communiqué*. Montreal: Advertising and Sales Executive Club of Montreal, 1983.

17. Roger A. More, "Correlates of Primary and Secondary Information Acquisition in New Products Market Assessment." *Marketing '77*. Eds. G.H.G. McDougall and R. Drolet, ASAC, 1977, pp. 41–66.

18. George Fisk, "Guidelines for Warranty Service after Sale." *Journal of Marketing*, 34 (October 1973), p. 63.

19. George H. Smith, *Motivation Research in Advertising and Marketing*. New York: McGraw-Hill, 1954; Rena Bartos and Arthur S. Pearson, "The Founding Fathers of Advertising Research: Ernest Dichter: Motive Interpreter." *Journal of Advertising Research* (June 1977), p. 4.

20. Keith J. Cox, James B. Higginbotham, and John Burton, "Applications of Focus Group Interviews in Marketing." *Journal of Marketing* (January 1976), p. 79; Bobby J. Calder, "Focus Groups and the Nature of Qualitative Marketing Research." *Journal of Marketing Research* (August 1977), pp. 353–64.

21. Mason Haire, "Projective Techniques in Marketing Research." *Journal of Marketing* (April 1950), pp. 649–56.

22. Yoram Wind, "A New Procedure for Concept Evaluation," *Journal of Marketing*, 37 (October 1973), p. 2–11.

23. John Koten, "Car Makers Use 'Image' Map as Tool to Position Products." *The Wall Street Journal* (March 22, 1984), p. 33.

24. Michel Bergier and Thomas Muller, "Product Positioning in the Fine Arts: An Application of Perceptual Mapping to the Study of Arts Prints," *Marketing*, 1. Ed. Vernon J. Jones, ASAC, 1980, pp. 39–48.

25. Vanderwicken, "P & G's Secret Ingredient," p. 77.

26. Ibid.

27. Ibid.

28. Joseph N. Fry, "Market Testing in Canada." *The Business Quarterly*. Vol. XXVII, no. 5 (Spring 1962).

29. "Cadbury's Thick Dairy Milk 1979–81 Campaign," in René Y. Darmon and Michel Laroche, *Advertising Management in Canada*. Toronto: John Wiley & Sons Canada Limited, 1984, pp. 524–29.

30. "Food Marketers Spend Billions Persuading Us to Buy Their Products." *The Wall Street Journal* (24 June 1977), p. 24.

31. *Advertising Age* (September–October 1975).

32. B.E. Olson, "The Challenge of New Product Development." *Industrial Canada* (August 1961).

33. William D. Barclay, "Probability Model for Early Prediction of New Product Market Success." *Journal of Marketing* (January 1963), pp. 62–68; Gary A. Mauser, "Comparing Alternative Procedures for Predicting Market Share of New Products." *Marketing*, 3. Ed. Michel Laroche, ASAC, 1982, pp. 155–62.

34. Glen L. Urban, Gerald M. Katz, Thomas F. Hatch, and Alvin J. Silk, "The ASSESSOR Pre Test Market Evaluation System." *Interfaces*, 13 (December 1983), pp. 38–59.

35. "How Miller Won Market Slot for Lite Beer." *Business Week* (13 October 1975), p. 116.

36. Grady, "The Budweiser Gamble"; Helpard, "It Sure Is 'Miller Time' in Canada."

37. Statistics Canada, *Canadian Science Indicators*, 1983, Cat.88-201.

CHAPTER 15 ADVERTISING RESEARCH IN CANADA

Advertising is a multibillion dollar industry in Canada. In 1987 the net advertising revenues from the media alone surpassed the $7-billion mark.[1] Evaluating the effectiveness of spending so much money for advertising is the basic task facing advertising researchers. To help them, researchers have at their disposal many analytical tools, from very simple procedures to very sophisticated decision-support systems.

■ What Is Advertising Research?

Advertising research is one of the most important areas of marketing research, which uses the research techniques and concepts discussed in previous chapters. The American Marketing Association has defined advertising as "any paid form of non-personal presentation and promotion of ideas, goods, or services by an identified sponsor."[2] Advertising research is designed to measure advertising effectiveness and improve advertising efficiency. In this context, *effectiveness* is defined as being how well an advertisement or advertising campaign accomplishes its objectives; *efficiency* is defined as being the manner in which optimum use is made of the advertising budget and media mix in an advertising campaign. Since the fundamental goal in marketing is to sell something (whether an item, a service, or an idea), the ultimate goal in advertising research is to try to measure advertising's impact on sales. Since it is almost impossible to measure advertising's effect on sales directly, most advertising research includes copy and media research. Hence, it is advertising efficiency rather than advertising effectiveness that is most often studied.

■ What Makes Advertising Research Important?

Advertising research has become a subject of increasing importance to business, as total advertising expenditures continue to rise and as techniques for measuring advertising effectiveness continue to improve. The total costs of advertising communications are increasing every year, but an efficient advertising campaign can be a powerful, competitive tool for a firm. Thus, all major aspects of the communications program should be researched by advertisers and/or advertising agencies. These research projects can be conducted on a regular basis (e.g., tracking studies) or on an ad hoc basis to find an answer to a non-recurrent problem.

Therefore, it is very important for an advertiser to know if the money allocated to advertising has been well spent. Only through advertising research can it be determined if efficiency in expenditures and effectiveness in results are being obtained.

■ Four Major Types of Advertising Research

Advertising research investigates and evaluates the four principal aspects of advertising: the target market, the media, the message, and the results of the advertisement, as shown in Figure 15.1.

An advertising message presented on television might appeal to different audiences and produce different results than a similar message carried by another medium. For example, advertising messages for liquor are usually conveyed through magazines and billboards; soap powders are advertised on television and in magazines. Although we will look at each type of research separately, the interrelationship of target, message, media used, and results produced is a focal point that cannot be ignored.

■ Market and Consumer Research

Although market and consumer research is ideally done as a first step in developing the marketing plan, it is often the case that some advertisers do not have a good understanding of the basic determinants of purchase behaviour and a detailed and precise breakdown of the attitudes, behaviours, and distribution of the target market. To answer the first type of information needs, qualitative research methods are typically used, and for the second, more elaborate quantitative methods are used.

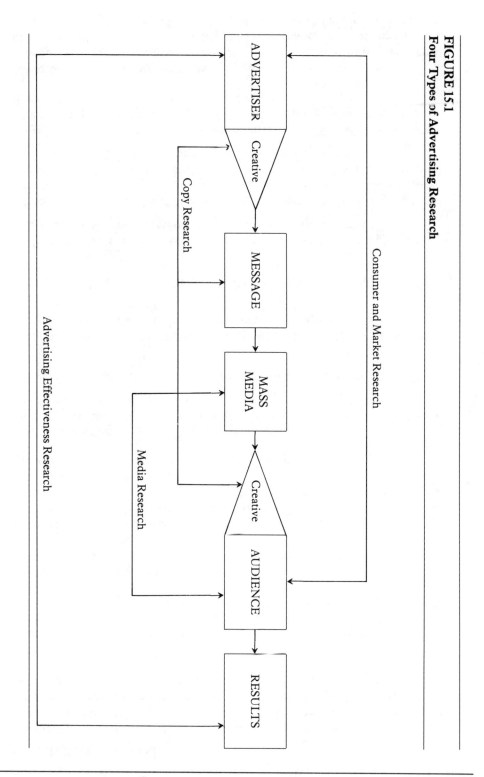

FIGURE 15.1
Four Types of Advertising Research

Qualitative Methods

Qualitative research employs such techniques as motivation research, focus groups, in-depth interviews, attitude scaling, and/or projective techniques. These studies are carried out on very small samples of consumers who are similar to the target market. These types of studies were reviewed in detail in Chapter 14.

Quantitative Methods

There are basically three types of quantitative methods that are used for market and consumer research in the context of developing the advertising plan: customized market surveys, omnibus studies, and advertising monitoring services.

Customized Market Surveys

Customized market surveys have been reviewed in detail throughout this text. They rely on all of the techniques for questionnaire construction, sampling, and survey execution, as well as on the various methods of data analysis. These studies arc essential as input to the development of the marketing plan, which is essential before a detailed advertising plan can be finalized. These types of research are conducted either in-house or by an outside supplier, which can be a research house that is or is not associated with the advertising agency.

Omnibus Studies

Pioneered in Canada in the late 1940s by Canadian Facts, omnibus studies have several interesting characteristics:

- Several thousand interviews can be conducted nationally on a regular basis; for example, every three months.

- The questionnaire is constructed according to the specifications of several clients. For example, one client might contribute two questions, another client four questions, and so on.

- All aspects of the research project including reporting are done by a professional firm.

- All of the clients share the basic costs of the survey and pay a fee according to the number of questions asked and other special services required.

- Each client receives the results based on the questions asked and the target market specified. For example, a manufacturer interested only in the teenaged market would receive the results of the questions asked about that manufacturer's product from the teenaged subgroup of the total sample.

Overall, omnibus studies are reliable, relatively fast, and inexpensive; on the other hand, the advertiser cannot control the sampling methodology and the timing of the survey.

Advertising Monitoring Services

The purpose of advertising monitoring services, mostly done by private companies, is to determine the extent and nature of advertising in the mass media by the firm's competitors. For example, Elliott Research specializes in providing estimates of national advertising spending by company or by brand. Its staff is constantly monitoring advertising in daily newspapers, weekend supplements, consumer magazines, and farm publications, and on radio and television. For each message, the cost is estimated on published rates. These are then computed by brand and company. These results are published on a monthly basis and sent to subscribers.

■ Media Research

In general, media research attempts to measure the media exposure habits of various consumers. Such research might be undertaken by the media themselves or by independent organizations. Typically, the research techniques used for media research are opinion surveys and panels. Many surveys that are conducted in media research tend to use personal interviewing with or without a questionnaire to be mailed later by the respondent. This is because many of these types of questionnaires tend to be lengthy and/or complex.

Research on Print Media

Print media research attempts to provide advertising with three major types of information: circulation and/or readership, audience profile for a medium, and audience profile for a vehicle.

Circulation Studies

The two most important circulation studies are conducted regularly by the Audit Bureau of Circulation (ABC) and the Canadian Circulation Audit Board (CCAB). Both ABC and CCAB are non-profit, tripartite associations of advertisers, advertising agencies, and publishers. ABC audits both daily newspapers and magazines, while CCAB audits only magazines and community newspapers. The objectives of both ABC and CCAB are to issue standardized statements of data reported by a vehicle, to verify the figures shown in the statements, and to disseminate the figures through regularly published reports.

To be eligible for ABC membership, a newspaper or magazine must have at least 70% *paid* circulation. On the other hand, CCAB audits all paid, all controlled (free), or any combination of the two for more than 330 business, trade, professional, and farm publications, consumer magazines, and community newspapers.[3]

NADbank Studies

NADbank stands for Newspaper Audience Databank. This service was developed by the Newspaper Marketing Bureau (established in 1979) as an integrated source of daily newspaper audience information available through on-line computer access. In the latest survey, done in 1986, NADbank was reported to be providing readership data on thirty-two markets, with a sample of 26 000 respondents. In addition to readership information, data on product usage and shopping habits are available to allow cross-classification of these two types of studies;[4] for example, identifying the daily newspaper reading habits of heavy consumers of frozen entrees.

PMB Studies

The Print Measurement Bureau (PMB) is a tripartite, non-profit organization of magazine publishers, advertising agencies, advertisers, and associates, established in 1971 to provide readership data on consumer magazines that they can use to sell advertising space. The first PMB study conducted in 1973 covered twenty consumer magazines. The next two studies were conducted in 1976 and 1979 and each added questions on product usage, general media habits, and psychographics. The third study cost $1.7 million. Starting in 1983, PMB has conducted annual studies with about 6000 interviews, and annual reports combine the data for two years—a sample size of 12 000. Some sixty consumer magazines were included in the PMB 1987 study. These results are made available to advertisers and agencies by subscription. In addition, participating magazines contribute approximately 60% of the total cost of the study.

PMB reports contain data on readership of some sixty consumer magazines, with demographics, duplications of readership, and accumulation of audience; general exposure to radio, outdoor, television, daily and community newspapers, and transit; and qualitative readership data on reading occasions, editorial interest, and so on.

In addition, the PMB 1986 *Product Profile Study* measured purchasing and usage of 811 product categories, covering some twenty product fields as well as fifty-two measures of lifestyle, including psychographics, as shown in Figure 15.2. The data contain usage information of products or services (light, medium, or heavy user), demographics, psychographics, and media habits, covering the sixty magazines plus all other major media for cross-media comparisons. Subscribers receive the standard published information on printed reports or on microfiches. In addition, direct computer access allows cross-classification of product usage with media habits or psychographics.

Some magazines also use the results from these studies to sell advertising space to major advertisers. For example, the *Reader's Digest* advertisement reproduced in Figure 15.3 uses results from the PMB 1987 study to show that its magazine scores the highest interest levels for both men and women adults, as well as for French and English readers.

Customized Studies

Finally, individual vehicles might sometimes, in co-operation with other vehicles, conduct readership studies to develop demographic or psychographic profiles. For example, a survey was recently conducted in Montreal to determine the demographic profile of the readers of the four daily newspapers. Some of the results for two subgroups are shown in Figure 15.4.

Research on Broadcast Media

Broadcast media research attempts to provide advertisers with estimates of radio and television audiences and program ratings, as well as audience composition. The two major syndicated rating services are the Bureau of Broadcasting Measurement (BBM) and A.C. Neilsen of Canada Limited. BBM surveys both radio and television audiences, while Neilsen surveys only television audiences.

FIGURE 15.2
Listing of Contents of PMB Product Profile Questionnaire

Product Profile Section	Contents	Number of Products/ Services
01	MEDIA: Daily newspapers, Radio, TV viewing, Community newspapers	20
02	STORES: How often shop at different store type(s)?	10
03	WOMEN'S PRODUCTS: Cosmetics, Fragrances and Deodorants, Toiletries, Feminine Hygiene, Women's clothing, Hair removal, Hair care	75
04	MEN'S PRODUCTS: Deodorants, Toiletries, Shaving, Hair care, Men's clothing	29
05	PERSONAL CARE PRODUCTS: Personal care, Bar soaps, Remedies, Glasses/Dentures	36
06	FOOD: Food/Shopping, Food, Condiments and Spreads, Cooking and Baking, Snacks/Confectionary	149
07	BEVERAGES: Coffee, Tea, Milk, Soft drinks, Other beverages	34
08	OTHER PACKAGED GOODS: Children's products, Cat food, Dog food, Laundry products, Household products	53
09	LEISURE ACTIVITIES: Participation, Spectator events, Eating out	46
10	AUTO PRODUCTS: Driving, Cars/Vans/Trucks, Motorcycles, Maintenance	26
11	RECREATIONAL EQUIPMENT/FARM:	10
12	HOME/IMPROVEMENTS/PRODUCTS: Home, Improvement/Maintenance, Telephone/Communications, Household durables, Small appliances, Tools and equipment, Television, Radio/Stereo, Home electronics, Cameras, Films, Batteries, Personal goods, Tableware.	106
13	GIFTS: Gift giving, Gift wrap, Greeting cards	20
14	TRAVEL: *Pleasure/Vacation*: Accommodation; Trips to Canada, U.S., Other, Cost	46
15	TRAVEL (cont'd):—*Business Trips*: Transportation; Trips to Canada, U.S., Other. —Class of Air Travel; Language Instruction	35
16	FINANCIAL: Bank services, Loans, Investments, Institutions, Insurance, Credit cards	42
17	MISCELLANEOUS: Mail order clubs, Books and magazines, Lotteries	13
18	BEVERAGE/ALCOHOL: Beer, Liquor, Fortified wine/Vermouth/Aperitifs, Cider, Wines	65
19	TOBACCO PRODUCTS: Cigarettes, Cigars/Cigarillos, Pipe tobacco	16
20	BUSINESS PURCHASING: Office equipment, Computers, etc., Transportation, Financial services	NA
21	PSYCHOGRAPHICS: Likes and dislikes	32
		863
	Of which: Products and Services	811
	Media and Psychographics	52

Source: Courtesy of the Print Measurement Bureau

FIGURE 15.3
Advertisement for *Reader's Digest* and *Sélection* using the results from the PMB 1985 study to show that it ranks first in reader interest among all adults and among French and English Canadians

PMB ASKED:
"How interesting do you find these magazines...?"

Reader's Digest & Sélection, No.1 for reader interest in ~~six~~ seven consecutive PMB studies.

Research shows that the more interest a reader has in a magazine the more interest they will have in your advertising. By using the qualitative data in PMB '87 you can maximize your coverage of high interest readers no matter what target group you may be using.

To make the PMB '87 study an even better planning tool, IMS offers expansion to their existing software to simplify qualitative analysis. With virtually no additional work this expanded program will provide full qualitative comparisons — from average reading minutes, to the number of high interest readers.

Contact IMS or your Reader's Digest Representative for all the details.

Canada's Most Popular Magazines

HERE IS WHAT PMB '87 SAYS:

INTEREST IN MAGAZINE

WOMEN 18+	AVG. INTEREST
ENGLISH	
READER'S DIGEST	8.2
CHATELAINE	7.2
CANADIAN LIVING	7.6
TV GUIDE	7.3
HOMEMAKER'S	6.9
FRENCH	
SÉLECTION	8.2
COUP DE POUCE	7.8
TV HEBDO	7.7
CHÂTELAINE	7.4

MEN 18+	AVG. INTEREST
ENGLISH	
READER'S DIGEST	7.7
MACLEAN'S	7.0
TIME	7.3
TV GUIDE	6.8
FRENCH	
SÉLECTION	7.9
L'ACTUALITÉ	7.3
TV HEBDO	7.5

P.S. *We're still No.1 in audience too!*

Source: Courtesy of Reader's Digest/Sélection

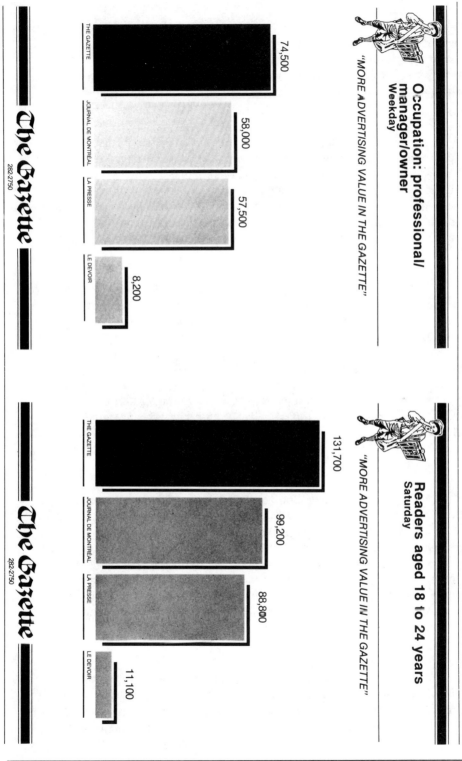

FIGURE 15.4
Sample results from a media audience research study conducted for four Montreal daily newspapers

"MORE ADVERTISING VALUE IN THE GAZETTE"

**Occupation: professional/
manager/owner**
Weekday

THE GAZETTE — 74,500
JOURNAL DE MONTRÉAL — 58,000
LA PRESSE — 57,500
LE DEVOIR — 8,200

"MORE ADVERTISING VALUE IN THE GAZETTE"

Readers aged 18 to 24 years
Saturday

THE GAZETTE — 131,700
JOURNAL DE MONTRÉAL — 99,200
LA PRESSE — 88,800
LE DEVOIR — 11,100

The Gazette
282-2750

The Gazette
282-2750

Source: Courtesy of *The Gazette*, Montreal.

Bureau of Broadcast Measurement

Founded in 1944, BBM is a non-profit, tripartite organization of broadcasters, advertising agencies, and advertisers. Its objective is to survey radio and television audiences and to provide such estimates to its members. Both radio and television surveys use the same basic methodology, as follows.

Sampling

First, the whole of Canada except the Yukon and the Northwest Territories is divided into 370 sampling cells. Within each cell, a sample is randomly drawn from a list of telephone numbers in cities and towns. Each household is then called, using bilingual operators if necessary, to obtain a list of people. The total number of selected households will provide a sampling frame containing enough names for all of the BBM surveys in one year. More than one million names are currently on this list. Each diary sample is then randomly selected from the sampling frame. The method is to select respondents from a random starting point for each of thirteen demographic subgroups in each cell.

Diary

Each respondent in the sample receives a personal diary by mail, with a monetary incentive to gain co-operation. The diary contains a brief questionnaire, or demographic variables, and a daily log to record radio listening or television viewing by quarter-hour, every day for seven consecutive days. When completed, the diary is mailed back to BBM in a prepaid, self-addressed envelope.

A reminder card is dispatched shortly after the diary has been sent to the respondent, to increase the response rate, which runs at approximately 50%. However, the diary method suffers from the limitation of the human element: it assumes that the respondents will faithfully and accurately record their listening or viewing schedule in the diary. Human nature being what it is, this is a questionable assumption to make.

Radio

For radio, the survey is normally conducted during three consecutive weeks and averaged over the three-week period. Diary information is projected to the total population according to age, gender, and language subgroups. The fall survey covers all markets, the spring covers only one—all markets with a minimum of three stations—and the winter and summer ones cover the top nine Canadian census metropolitan areas (CMAs). A sample page of a radio diary is reproduced in Figure 15.5 and a sample page of a BBM Radio Report in Figure 15.6.

Television

Both network and individual television market surveys are regularly conducted. Each network survey is taken over a seven-day period and is issued as a series of fifty-two, one-week reports. On the other hand, each television market survey is taken over two or three weeks and the total number of weeks surveyed for each market is as follows:

FIGURE 15.5
Sample Page from a BBM Radio Diary

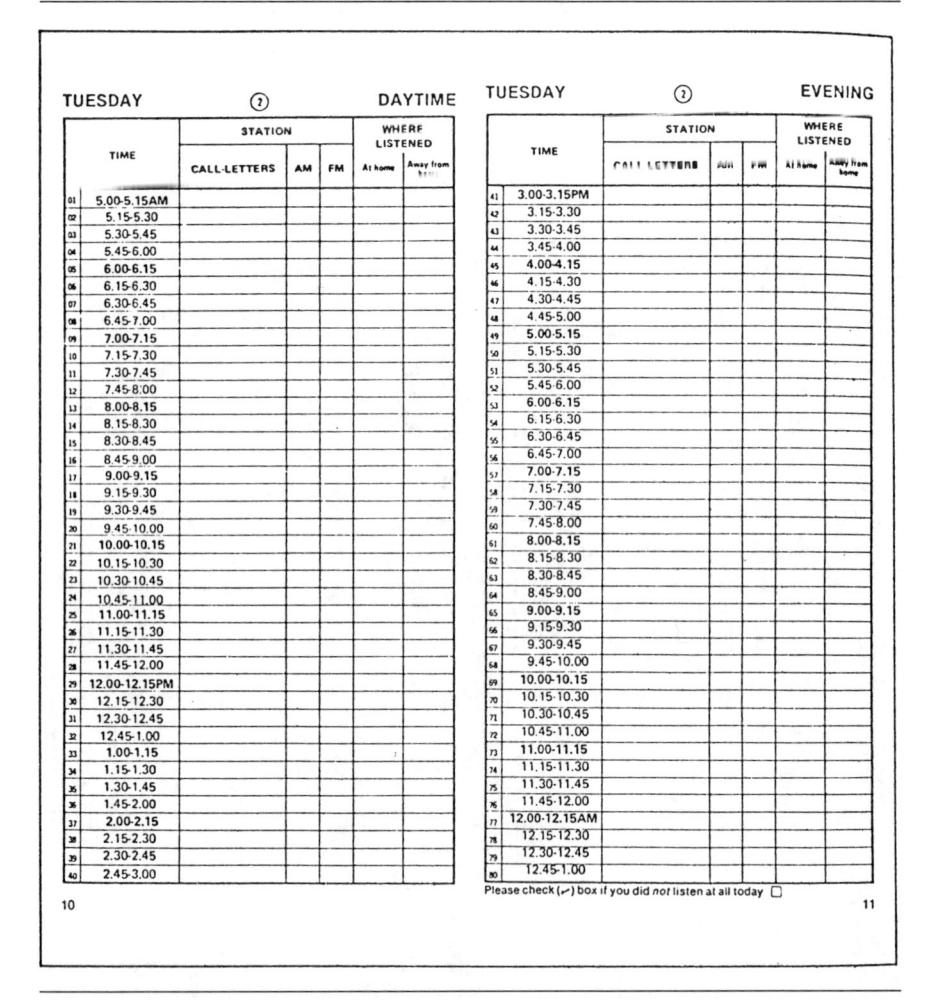

Source: Courtesy of the Bureau of Broadcast Measurement, the industry's rating service

17 weeks: Toronto, Montreal, Vancouver
11 weeks: Halifax, Quebec City, Ottawa, Kitchener, London, Winnipeg,
          Calgary, Edmonton
 9 weeks: Windsor, Hamilton, Victoria
 6 weeks: all other markets

The BBM television diary is similar to the radio diary; a sample page is reproduced in Figure 15.7. Information on cable and pay television is also included in the brief questionnaire. A sample page of BBM television report is reproduced in Figure 15.8.

FIGURE 15.6
Sample Page of BBM Radio Report (CFRB Toronto)

CFRB
TORONTO

SUMMER 1986 ETE

AVERAGE ¼ HOUR AUDIENCE BY HOUR (SAT)   **AUDITOIRE MOYEN DES ¼ D'HEURES PAR HEURE (SAM)**

TIME HEURE	TOTAL 7+ TOUS		ADULTS 18+ ADULTES		WOMEN FEMMES								MEN HOMMES								ADULTS ADULTES			
500 AM	50	–	50	–	40	10	–	–	11	10	–	10	–	–	3	–	–	–	48	48	10	13	38	10
600	341	12	341	12	128	22	–	–	30	22	–	212	39	25	–	73	39	25	–	231	231	42	83	113	118
700	866	41	843	41	474	45	14	7	107	37	7	370	50	14	–	71	50	14	8	14	650	628	76	155	399	229
800	1175	80	1153	80	726	134	46	19	177	115	27	428	50	11	–	104	50	11	6	16	920	909	166	256	584	325
900	1124	70	1092	70	751	166	77	17	226	149	60	342	66	–	–	106	66	–	24	7	979	948	207	298	635	313
1000	970	84	964	84	662	91	13	–	139	91	13	302	44	–	–	95	44	–	6	–	857	851	127	216	570	281
1100	791	91	785	91	522	45	5	–	86	45	5	263	34	–	–	84	34	–	–	5	636	636	74	156	414	222
NOON	431	76	428	73	278	20	–	–	70	20	–	150	17	–	–	56	17	–	3	–	371	368	37	118	227	141
100 PM	410	127	404	127	248	55	11	–	86	55	11	156	43	–	–	81	43	–	6	–	359	353	96	153	211	141
200	328	105	326	105	224	41	2	–	70	41	2	101	24	–	–	49	24	–	3	–	296	293	63	105	204	89
300	238	64	238	64	146	20	–	–	47	20	–	93	22	–	–	33	22	–	–	–	221	221	39	67	130	91
400	294	63	292	63	181	19	2	–	57	19	2	111	16	–	–	28	16	–	2	–	263	263	28	67	164	99
500	427	74	427	74	248	31	2	–	101	37	2	179	17	4	–	30	17	4	–	–	357	357	51	114	224	133
600	493	61	481	61	297	71	19	–	118	71	19	184	33	–	–	62	33	–	12	–	419	407	98	174	278	129
700	242	34	242	34	128	70	9	3	31	18	7	114	20	–	–	41	20	–	–	–	189	189	34	55	122	67
800	240	60	240	60	131	8	2	–	16	8	2	109	29	–	–	40	29	–	–	–	190	190	31	50	117	73
900	284	45	274	45	177	2	2	–	4	2	–	98	14	–	–	24	14	–	–	9	209	199	16	28	116	83
1000	262	32	262	32	183	13	–	–	13	13	–	79	14	–	–	17	14	–	–	–	210	210	27	29	133	78
1100	235	22	235	22	173	25	–	–	29	25	–	62	9	–	–	20	9	–	–	–	208	208	34	48	157	51
MDNT	135	35	135	35	100	15	–	–	15	15	–	35	14	–	–	30	14	–	–	–	129	129	29	39	100	29

AVERAGE ¼ HOUR AUDIENCE BY HOUR (SUN)   **AUDITOIRE MOYEN DES ¼ D'HEURES PAR HEURE (DIM)**

TIME	TOTAL		ADULTS		WOMEN							MEN								ADULTS			
500 AM	28	–	28	–	18	–	–	–	–	–	–	10	–	–	5	–	–	–	28	28	–	5	18	10
600	266	1	266	1	81	21	–	–	24	21	–	185	33	19	–	67	33	19	–	151	151	35	68	67	84
700	564	17	555	17	276	43	13	–	47	43	13	278	53	21	–	71	53	21	–	9	384	375	77	97	216	158
800	1038	44	1038	44	538	82	3	–	107	82	3	499	75	18	–	103	75	18	–	–	714	714	142	193	418	296
900	984	62	984	62	572	62	13	–	110	62	13	412	62	4	–	70	62	4	–	–	736	736	98	149	456	280
1000	818	81	801	70	552	91	13	–	148	91	13	249	59	2	–	63	59	2	6	11	574	557	149	208	379	178
1100	584	56	570	56	402	48	2	–	85	48	2	167	54	–	–	60	54	–	–	14	397	383	80	124	244	139
NOON	460	74	460	74	292	32	–	–	75	32	–	168	25	–	–	28	25	–	–	–	380	380	43	89	243	137
100 PM	326	82	326	82	230	51	21	–	72	51	21	97	45	19	–	45	45	19	–	–	252	252	66	87	176	77
200	182	35	182	35	134	31	7	–	54	31	7	48	13	5	–	13	13	5	–	–	161	161	38	61	124	38
300	214	49	214	49	132	27	2	–	57	27	2	83	24	7	–	24	24	7	–	–	196	196	43	73	126	70
400	138	23	138	23	92	20	4	–	52	20	4	46	5	–	–	5	5	–	–	–	132	132	25	57	87	45
500	200	40	200	40	110	25	2	–	55	25	2	90	5	–	–	7	5	–	–	–	163	163	30	62	102	60
600	252	28	238	28	118	8	5	–	42	8	5	120	10	–	–	15	10	–	–	14	191	177	18	57	97	80
700	132	54	132	54	78	11	11	–	35	11	11	53	13	–	–	17	14	–	–	–	114	114	30	44	67	46
800	120	47	109	37	58	5	5	–	15	5	5	51	15	–	–	29	15	–	–	11	114	103	20	44	52	51
900	242	28	242	28	131	15	4	–	17	15	4	111	7	3	–	44	7	3	–	–	205	205	21	32	123	82
1000	294	25	294	25	129	25	2	–	33	25	2	166	8	3	–	40	8	3	–	–	196	196	33	41	118	78
1100	323	1	323	1	143	11	–	–	20	11	–	180	6	–	–	45	6	–	–	–	206	206	13	31	134	72
MDNT	94		94		72		–	–	2		–	22		–	–	13		–	–	–	94	94		15	72	22

AUDIENCE PROFILE–FULL COVERAGE (WKLY, %)   **PROFIL DE L'AUDITOIRE–RAYONNEMENT (SEM, %)**

	TOTAL 7+ TOUS		WOMEN-FEMMES						MEN-HOMMES							TOTAL 7+ TOUS		WOMEN-FEMMES						MEN-HOMMES					
			18+		18-49		25-54		18+		18-49		25-54				18+		18-49		25-54		18+		18-49		25-54	
	HRS	CUME PORT	HRS	CUME PORT	HRS	CUME PORT	HRS	CUME PORT	HRS	CUME PORT	HRS	CUME PORT	HRS	CUME PORT	HRS	CUME PORT	HRS	CUME PORT	HRS	CUME PORT	HRS	CUME PORT	HRS	CUME PORT	HRS	CUME PORT	HRS	CUME PORT
--TUNED--	797		400		139		163		363		123		157															
AGE																												
7-11	1	3							1	2					WRK STAT													
12-17	1	2							1	3					FULLTIME	36	45	24	33	60	59	53	57	57	64	97	97	96	98
18-24	1	3	1	5	3	15	9	17	1	2	4	7	PARTTIME	5	7	6	8	12	15	13	13	4	5				
25-34	3	6	3	6	13	19	59	60	5	17	9	21	13	16	NOT WRKG	50	42	60	51	23	22	31	26	35	28	3	2	2	1
35-49	16	22	16	21	84	66	32	23	18	26	76	73	50	58	NA	8	6	10	8	5	4	4	3	4	3				
50-54	10	9	8	8					13	11			37	26	OCCUPATN														
55-59	9	10	8	9					12	11					OWNR, MGR	8	10	3	3	18	19	14	17	15	18	26	29	28	29
60+	58	45	65	51					51	43					PROFESNL	5	6	3	4				9		4	10	7	20	23
															CLERICAL	8	9	11	15	18	22	19	23	4	4	10	7	7	8
SEX															SALES	1	2	1	2	4	5	3	5	2	2	3	3	2	2
MASCULIN	40	48	–	–	–	–	–	–	100	100	100	100	100	100	FARMER	2	3							1	1				
FEMININE	60	52	100	100	100	100	100	100							SKILLED	6	6	1	1	1	1	1	1	13	12	15	14	10	13
															UNSKILL	4	5	2	2	10	4	3	3	7	8	12	14	10	13
OFL LANG															NA	55	48	66	59	35	37	44	40	39	33	3	3	4	2
ENG ONLY	95	93	97	95	96	92	97	93	94	94	90	90	93	92	FEM HEAD	47	37	80	77	83	73	87	85						
FR ONLY	–	1	–	–	–	–	–	–	–	–	–	–	–	–	EDUCATN														
BOTH E+F	5	6	3	5	4	8	2	7	5	6	10	10	7	8	NONE	1	1			1									
NA															GRADE	2	2	1	1	3	3	8	5	10	1	–	–	–	–
MOTH TNG															SOMEHIGH	28	23	31	22	6	6	12	8	24	23	18	15	17	17
ENGLISH	83	82	87	86	75	81	80	82	78	78	66	69	72	72	COMPHIGH	26	26	30	30	30	26	38	34	23	24	24	28	21	27
FRENCH	–	1			1	1			1	1	1	1			TECHNCAL	11	12	9	7	16	24	25	20	21	11	14	13	14	11
OTHER	14	14	10	11	20	15	14	14	18	18	33	27	27	24	SOMEUNIV	9	10	9	10	5	13	3	9	11	11			12	12
NA	3	3	2	3	5	4	3	4	3	3	–	1	–	1	COMPUNIV	10	14	6	10	23	25	17	21	3	3	10	33	32	33
SPK MOST															NA	3	3	3	3	2	1	2	1	3	2	1	1	–	1
ENGLISH	90	93	93	93	84	91	88	92	87	93	87	94	91	95	HHLDSIZE														
FRENCH	3	3	3	3	2	4	3	3	3	3	4	3	3	2	1-2 PERS	57	52	65	59	25	24	36	34	49	49	17	19	24	22
OTHER	7	4	3	3	14	5	11	5	11	4	9	3	6	2	3-4 PERS	32	35	25	28	55	50	50	47	42	40	54	56	55	55
NA															5+ PERS	10	14	10	12	20	26	14	19	9	11	28	25	22	23
QUINTILE															NA														
1-LIGHT	1	8	1	6	1	3	1								OWN FM														
2-	8	17	7	19	12	23	10	22	8	16	13	22	9	17	•IN HOME	85	90	87	91	93	95	93	95	89	94	97	97	96	97
3-MEDIUM	17	25	13	20	19	27	23	32	29	31	24	34	21	21	•IN CAR	46	49	41	53	65	70	59	66	54	66	69	78	63	74
4-	27	26	25	29	31	30	26	27	31	24	30	22	27	23	EITHER	87	92	89	93	96	98	95	97	85	92	95	97	97	98
5-HEAVY	46	24	54	27	35	13	45	18	36	22	22	22	35	25															

Source: Courtesy of the Bureau of Broadcast Measurement, the industry's rating service

FIGURE 15.7
Two Sample Pages of BBM Television Diary

24 **TUESDAY DAYTIME**

6A

	TIME	TV SET ON	TV SET OFF	NAME OF PROGRAM	STATION CALL LETTERS	CHANNEL NUMBER		1	2	3	4	5	6	7	8
01	**6.00-6.14AM**						01								
02	6.15-6.29						02								
03	6.30-6.44						03								
04	6.45-6.59						04								
05	**7.00-7.14**						05								
06	7.15-7.29						06								
07	7.30-7.44						07								
08	7.45-7.59						08								
09	**8.00-8.14**						09								
10	8.15-8.29						10								
11	8.30-8.44						11								
12	8.45-8.59						12								
13	**9.00-9.14**						13								
14	9.15-9.29						14								
15	9.30-9.44						15								
16	9.45-9.59						16								
17	**10.00-10.14**						17								
18	10.15-10.29						18								
19	10.30-10.44						19								
20	10.45-10.59						20								

								1	2	3	4	5	6	7	8
21	**11.00-11.14**						21								
22	11.15-11.29						22								
23	11.30-11.44						23								
24	11.45-11.59						24								
25	**12.00-12.14PM**						25								
26	12.15-12.29						26								
27	12.30-12.44						27								
28	12.45-12.59						28								
29	**1.00-1.14**						29								
30	1.15-1.29						30								
31	1.30-1.44						31								
32	1.45-1.59						32								
33	**2.00-2.14**						33								
34	2.15-2.29						34								
35	2.30-2.44						35								
36	2.45-2.59						36								
37	**3.00-3.14**						37								
38	3.15-3.29						38								
39	3.30-3.44						39								
40	3.45-3.59						40								

25 **DON'T FORGET TO GIVE US YOUR COMMENTS ON TV—ON PAGE 35.**

26 **TUESDAY EVENING**

6B

	TIME	TV SET ON	TV SET OFF	NAME OF PROGRAM	STATION CALL LETTERS	CHANNEL NUMBER		1	2	3	4	5	6	7	8
41	**4.00-4.14PM**						41								
42	4.15-4.29						42								
43	4.30-4.44						43								
44	4.45-4.59						44								
45	**5.00-5.14**						45								
46	5.15-5.29						46								
47	5.30-5.44						47								
48	5.45-5.59						48								
49	**6.00-6.14**						49								
50	6.15-6.29						50								
51	6.30-6.44						51								
52	6.45-6.59						52								
53	**7.00-7.14**						53								
54	7.15-7.29						54								
55	7.30-7.44						55								
56	7.45-7.59						56								
57	**8.00-8.14**						57								
58	8.15-8.29						58								
59	8.30-8.44						59								
60	8.45-8.59						60								

								1	2	3	4	5	6	7	8
61	**9.00-9.14**						61								
62	9.15-9.29						62								
63	9.30-9.44						63								
64	9.45-9.59						64								
65	**10.00-10.14**						65								
66	10.15-10.29						66								
67	10.30-10.44						67								
68	10.45-10.59						68								
69	**11.00-11.14**						69								
70	11.15-11.29						70								
71	11.30-11.44						71								
72	11.45-11.59						72								
73	**12.00-12.14AM**						73								
74	12.15-12.29						74								
75	12.30-12.44						75								
76	12.45-12.59						76								
77	**1.00-1.14**						77								
78	1.15-1.29						78								
79	1.30-1.44						79								
80	1.45-1.59						80								

☐ **Please check (✓) here if this set not used today.**

27 **PLEASE CHECK THAT THE QUESTIONS ON PAGE 32–34 ARE ANSWERED FOR EACH PERSON.**

Source: Courtesy of the Bureau of Broadcast Measurement, the industry's rating service

FIGURE 15.8
Sample Page of BBM Television Report (Montreal—All Stations)

MONTREAL — BBM FALL 1985 AUTOMNE — TUESDAY 4:00 PM – 2:00 AM MARDI — 19

CENTRAL MARKET % / % MARCHE CENTRAL (RTG COTE / SHR PART; RATINGS / COTES)

TIME PERIODS / PERIODES HORAIRES — STATION	PROGRAM/EMISSION	WKS / SEM	TOTAL 2+ TOUS RTG	TOTAL 2+ TOUS SHR	AD 18+ AD	WOMEN FEMMES 18+	WOMEN 18/49	WOMEN 25/54	MEN HOMMES 18+	MEN 18/49	MEN 25/54	12/17	2/11
730- 800 PM	(CONT.)												
WVNY	BENNY HILL	2	4	10	4	4	3	4	5	4	4	2	3
CBFT	AGENT FAIT BONHE	3	11	26	11	13	11	14	9	7	8	15	7
CBMT	GOLDEN GIRLS	3	4	10	5	6	5	4	3	2	2	2	1
CFCF	NEW WILDERNESS	3	4	10	5	5	4	5	5	4	6	2	1
CFTM	DEUX FONT/PAIRE	3	13	30	12	13	14	14	11	12	10	17	13
CIVM	DEFI: SURVIVRE	3	1	3	1	1	2	2	1	2	2	1	1
WCAX	PRICE IS RIGHT	3	2	5	2	2	1	1	2	-	-	1	2
WPTZ	MASH	3	1	3	2	2	1	1	2	1	2	2	-
WVNY	BENNY HILL	3	3	7	4	3	2	2	4	3	2	1	2
800- 830 PM	ALL STNS	123	43	100	46	50	43	48	41	36	39	38	30
CBFT	M. LE MINISTRE	123	15	35	17	22	17	21	11	9	11	13	7
CBMT	FIFTH ESTATE	123	4	9	5	5	3	3	4	3	4	-	-
CFCF	VARIOUS	123	6	13	6	5	4	5	7	7	7	4	6
	A.TEAM	23	7	16	7	7	6	6	8	8	8	6	8
CFTM	DIVERS	123	8	19	8	8	9	9	8	8	8	10	8
	DEUX FONT/PAIRE	23	9	20	8	9	11	10	7	8	8	12	10
CIVM	ARRIMAGE	123	1	1	1	1	1	1	1	1	1	1	-
WCAX	VARIOUS	123	2	4	2	1	2	1	2	2	2	2	2
WPTZ	VARIOUS	123	2	4	2	2	2	2	2	1	1	2	1
	A.TEAM	23	-	1	-	-	-	-	-	-	-	-	1
WVNY	VARIOUS	123	3	8	3	3	3	3	3	3	2	4	4
	WHO'S THE BOSS	23	5	11	5	5	5	5	5	4	3	7	6
OTHERS		123	3	7	3	4	3	3	3	3	3	2	2
CBFT	M. LE MINISTRE	1	16	39	18	24	19	21	12	10	12	13	6
CBMT	FIFTH ESTATE	1	5	13	6	6	4	4	6	5	6	1	1
CFCF	WORLD SERIES	1	3	7	3	2	2	2	5	5	4	1	2
CFTM	SERIE MONDIALE	1	7	17	8	5	5	5	10	8	9	4	4
CIVM	ARRIMAGE	1	-	1	-	-	1	1	-	-	1	-	-
WCAX	HOMETOWN	1	3	7	2	2	2	1	3	3	3	5	5
WPTZ	A-TEAM	1	4	10	4	4	4	5	4	4	3	7	3
WVNY	WORLD SERIES	1	-	-	-	-	-	-	-	-	-	-	-
CBFT	M. LE MINISTRE	2	14	33	15	21	17	21	9	8	9	13	11
CBMT	FIFTH ESTATE	2	3	7	4	4	1	2	3	1	3	-	-
CFCF	A.TEAM	2	8	18	8	8	5	5	9	8	8	5	7
CFTM	DEUX FONT/PAIRE	2	8	18	7	7	8	9	6	6	7	13	9
CIVM	ARRIMAGE	2	1	1	1	1	2	2	-	1	1	1	-
WCAX	SP:DINOSAUR	2	1	3	2	1	2	2	2	2	3	1	-
WPTZ	A.TEAM	2	-	-	-	-	-	-	-	-	-	-	-
WVNY	WHO'S THE BOSS	2	5	11	5	5	6	6	5	4	4	5	4
CBFT	M. LE MINISTRE	3	15	33	17	21	15	19	13	9	10	13	4
CBMT	FIFTH ESTATE	3	3	6	4	4	3	3	3	3	2	-	-
CFCF	A.TEAM	3	7	15	6	6	6	6	7	7	8	6	8
CFTM	DEUX FONT/PAIRE	3	10	22	10	11	13	12	9	9	8	12	11
CIVM	ARRIMAGE	3	1	2	1	1	1	2	1	1	1	1	-
WCAX	NORTH BEACH &RAW	3	1	2	1	1	1	1	1	-	1	-	-
WPTZ	A.TEAM	3	1	1	-	-	1	1	-	1	1	-	1
WVNY	WHO'S THE BOSS	3	5	12	5	5	4	4	5	4	2	8	7
830- 900 PM	ALL STNS	123	43	100	46	51	44	49	42	35	39	37	23
CBFT	AMOUR DE QUARTIE	123	10	24	11	15	12	14	8	5	7	10	4
CBMT	FIFTH ESTATE	123	4	9	5	5	3	3	4	3	3	-	-
CFCF	VARIOUS	123	6	14	6	5	5	5	7	8	7	4	5
	A.TEAM	23	7	17	8	7	6	6	8	9	9	6	7
CFTM	DIVERS	123	12	29	14	15	13	15	12	10	12	11	6
	CHIEN ET LOUP	23	14	33	16	18	17	19	12	10	12	14	7
CIVM	VISAGE	123	1	3	1	2	2	3	1	1	2	1	-
WCAX	VARIOUS	123	2	4	1	1	2	1	2	2	2	2	2
WPTZ	VARIOUS	123	2	4	2	2	2	2	1	1	1	2	1
	A.TEAM	23	-	1	-	-	-	-	-	-	-	-	1
WVNY	VARIOUS	123	3	6	2	2	2	2	2	2	2	5	2
	GROWING PAINS	23	4	9	4	4	3	4	3	3	2	7	4
OTHERS		123	3	7	4	4	3	3	3	3	4	2	1
CBFT	AMOUR DE QUARTIE	1	14	34	16	21	17	21	10	8	10	11	4
CBMT	FIFTH ESTATE	1	5	13	6	6	3	4	7	5	6	1	1
CFCF	WORLD SERIES	1	3	8	4	3	2	3	5	5	5	1	2
CFTM	SERIE MONDIALE	1	9	21	10	8	7	8	12	9	12	5	3
CIVM	VISAGE	1	1	2	1	2	1	1	1	1	1	-	-
WCAX	HOMETOWN	1	3	6	2	2	2	1	3	3	3	5	5
WPTZ	A-TEAM	1	4	10	4	4	5	5	4	3	3	6	3

EXTENDED MARKET % / % MARCHE ETENDU (RTG COTE / SHR PART; RATINGS / COTES)

STATION	PROGRAM/EMISSION	TOTAL 2+ TOUS RTG	TOTAL 2+ TOUS SHR	ADULTS ADULTES 18+	ADULTS 18/34	ADULTS 18/49	ADULTS 25/54	WOMEN FEMMES 18+	WOMEN 18/34	WOMEN 18/49	WOMEN 25/54	MEN HOMMES 18+	MEN 18/34	MEN 18/49	MEN 25/54	12/17	2/11
730- 800 PM	(CONT.)																
WVNY	BENNY HILL	4	9	4	3	4	4	4	4	3	4	5	3	4	5	2	2
CBFT	AGENT FAIT BONHE	12	27	13	9	10	12	15	11	12	15	10	8	9	9	13	7
CBMT	GOLDEN GIRLS	4	8	4	5	4	3	5	6	5	3	3	3	2	2	2	1
CFCF	NEW WILDERNESS	4	9	5	3	4	5	5	3	4	5	4	3	4	5	2	1
CFTM	DEUX FONT/PAIRE	14	33	14	14	15	14	15	15	16	15	12	13	13	12	21	15
CIVM	DEFI: SURVIVRE	1	3	1	2	2	2	1	1	2	2	1	2	2	2	1	1
WCAX	PRICE IS RIGHT	2	5	2	-	1	1	2	1	1	1	2	-	-	1	1	2
WPTZ	MASH	1	3	1	1	1	1	1	2	1	1	1	1	1	2	1	-
WVNY	BENNY HILL	3	7	3	3	2	2	3	2	2	1	4	4	3	2	1	1
800- 830 PM	ALL STNS	44	100	47	38	41	45	51	42	44	49	43	35	38	41	38	31
CBFT	M. LE MINISTRE	16	36	18	11	13	16	23	14	17	21	12	8	9	11	12	8
CBMT	FIFTH ESTATE	4	8	4	3	3	3	5	3	3	3	4	3	3	4	-	1
CFCF	VARIOUS	6	12	6	5	5	5	5	4	4	4	6	6	6	6	5	5
	A.TEAM	7	15	7	7	6	6	6	6	5	5	7	7	7	7	6	7
CFTM	DIVERS	9	21	9	9	10	10	9	9	10	9	10	9	9	10	11	9
	DEUX FONT/PAIRE	10	22	9	11	11	10	10	12	12	11	9	9	10	10	14	11
CIVM	ARRIMAGE	1	1	1	-	1	1	1	-	1	1	-	-	1	1	1	-
WCAX	VARIOUS	2	4	2	2	2	2	1	2	2	1	2	2	2	2	2	2
WPTZ	VARIOUS	1	3	1	2	1	1	1	2	1	2	1	2	1	1	2	1
	A.TEAM	-	1	-	-	-	-	-	-	-	-	-	-	-	-	-	1
WVNY	VARIOUS	3	7	3	3	3	3	3	3	3	3	3	3	3	2	4	3
	WHO'S THE BOSS	5	10	5	5	4	4	5	5	5	5	4	5	4	3	6	5
OTHERS		3	7	4	3	3	3	4	4	3	3	3	3	3	4	1	2
CBFT	M. LE MINISTRE	17	40	19	13	15	18	24	16	19	22	13	10	11	13	11	8
CBMT	FIFTH ESTATE	5	13	7	5	5	5	6	5	4	5	7	5	5	6	1	2
CFCF	WORLD SERIES	3	7	3	2	3	3	2	1	2	2	5	3	4	4	2	1
CFTM	SERIE MONDIALE	8	18	8	6	7	8	6	4	6	6	11	7	9	10	5	4
CIVM	ARRIMAGE	-	1	-	-	-	1	-	-	1	1	-	-	-	1	-	-
WCAX	HOMETOWN	3	6	2	4	3	2	2	3	2	2	3	4	3	3	4	5
WPTZ	A-TEAM	4	9	4	5	3	3	4	5	4	4	4	5	3	3	6	3
WVNY	WORLD SERIES	-	-	-	-	-	-	-	-	-	-	-	-	-	-	-	-
CBFT	M. LE MINISTRE	15	35	16	10	13	15	22	13	18	22	10	6	8	9	13	11
CBMT	FIFTH ESTATE	3	6	4	1	1	2	4	-	1	2	3	1	1	2	-	-
CFCF	A.TEAM	7	17	8	6	7	6	7	5	5	5	8	8	8	7	6	6
CFTM	DEUX FONT/PAIRE	8	18	7	7	8	9	7	9	8	9	7	6	7	8	13	10
CIVM	ARRIMAGE	1	1	1	-	1	1	1	-	1	2	-	-	1	1	1	-
WCAX	SP:DINOSAUR	1	3	1	1	2	2	1	1	1	1	2	2	2	3	1	-
WPTZ	A.TEAM	-	-	-	-	-	-	-	-	-	-	-	-	-	-	-	-
WVNY	WHO'S THE BOSS	5	11	5	6	5	5	5	6	5	6	5	5	5	4	4	4
CBFT	M. LE MINISTRE	16	33	18	10	12	15	22	13	14	19	14	7	9	10	12	4
CBMT	FIFTH ESTATE	3	6	3	3	2	2	4	3	2	2	3	2	2	2	-	-
CFCF	A.TEAM	6	14	6	7	6	7	6	7	6	6	7	6	6	7	6	8
CFTM	DEUX FONT/PAIRE	12	26	12	14	14	12	12	14	15	13	11	13	12	11	15	13
CIVM	ARRIMAGE	1	2	1	1	1	1	1	1	1	1	1	1	1	1	1	-
WCAX	NORTH BEACH &RAW	1	2	1	1	1	1	1	2	2	1	1	1	-	1	1	-
WPTZ	A.TEAM	1	1	1	-	1	1	-	-	1	1	1	-	1	1	-	1
WVNY	WHO'S THE BOSS	5	10	4	4	4	3	4	3	4	4	4	5	4	2	8	6
830- 900 PM	ALL STNS	44	100	48	37	41	45	52	40	45	50	43	34	37	41	37	23
CBFT	AMOUR DE QUARTIE	11	25	12	7	9	11	15	9	12	14	8	5	6	7	9	5
CBMT	FIFTH ESTATE	4	8	4	3	3	3	5	3	3	3	4	3	3	3	-	1
CFCF	VARIOUS	6	13	6	6	6	6	5	5	5	5	7	7	7	7	5	5
	A.TEAM	7	16	7	8	7	7	6	7	6	6	8	9	9	8	6	7
CFTM	DIVERS	14	32	15	11	13	15	16	12	15	16	14	9	12	13	13	6
	CHIEN ET LOUP	16	37	18	13	15	17	20	17	19	20	15	10	12	14	16	8
CIVM	VISAGE	1	3	1	1	1	2	2	1	2	2	1	1	1	1	1	-
WCAX	VARIOUS	2	4	2	2	2	2	1	2	2	1	2	2	2	2	2	2
WPTZ	VARIOUS	1	3	1	2	1	1	2	2	2	2	1	1	1	1	2	1
	A.TEAM	-	1	-	-	-	-	-	-	-	-	-	-	-	-	-	1
WVNY	VARIOUS	2	5	2	2	2	2	2	2	2	2	2	2	2	2	4	2
	GROWING PAINS	4	8	3	3	3	3	3	3	3	3	3	3	3	3	6	3
OTHERS		3	7	4	3	3	4	4	3	3	4	3	3	3	4	2	1
CBFT	AMOUR DE QUARTIE	15	35	17	11	13	16	22	12	17	21	12	9	9	11	10	6
CBMT	FIFTH ESTATE	6	13	7	5	5	5	6	4	4	4	7	5	5	6	1	2
CFCF	WORLD SERIES	3	8	4	3	4	4	3	2	2	3	5	4	5	5	2	1
CFTM	SERIE MONDIALE	9	21	10	6	9	10	8	4	7	8	13	8	10	12	6	3
CIVM	VISAGE	1	2	1	-	1	1	2	-	1	1	-	-	1	1	-	-
WCAX	HOMETOWN	3	6	2	4	3	2	2	4	3	2	3	4	3	3	5	4
WPTZ	A-TEAM	4	9	4	5	4	3	4	5	4	5	3	4	3	2	6	3

FULL COVERAGE AUDIENCES (000) / AUDITOIRES DANS RAYONNEMENT (000) — ¼ HOUR AVERAGES / MOYENNES PAR ¼ D'HEURE

STATION	PROGRAM/EMISSION	TOTAL 2+ TOUS	ADULTS ADULTES 18+	ADULTS 18/49	ADULTS 25/54	WOMEN FEMMES 18+	WOMEN 18/34	WOMEN 18/49	WOMEN 25/54	MEN HOMMES 18+	MEN 18/34	MEN 18/49	MEN 25/54	12/17	2/11
730- 800 PM	(CONT.)														
WVNY	BENNY HILL	129	112	69	67	49	19	29	30	63	17	41	37	6	10
CBFT	AGENT FAIT BONHE	465	393	209	208	237	62	118	126	156	53	91	82	32	40
CBMT	GOLDEN GIRLS	140	128	69	47	84	36	47	31	44	18	22	16	6	7
CFCF	NEW WILDERNESS	153	142	78	83	70	14	36	40	72	20	42	43	4	8
CFTM	DEUX FONT/PAIRE	572	434	322	270	243	100	174	150	191	84	147	121	62	77
CIVM	DEFI: SURVIVRE	52	46	25	26	28	7	13	12	18	8	13	14	3	4
WCAX	PRICE IS RIGHT	80	67	13	15	41	6	10	11	26	-	4	4	3	10
WPTZ	MASH	51	46	29	21	27	14	17	8	19	8	12	12	5	-
WVNY	BENNY HILL	107	99	43	28	41	9	16	10	58	22	27	17	2	6
800- 830 PM	ALL STNS														
CBFT	M. LE MINISTRE	611	538	269	273	356	83	173	180	182	49	96	93	35	39
CBMT	FIFTH ESTATE	130	126	51	55	68	16	24	26	58	14	27	28	1	3
CFCF	VARIOUS	205	166	102	88	76	25	42	39	90	34	60	50	14	25
	A.TEAM	250	197	123	105	94	34	53	48	103	42	69	58	19	34
CFTM	DIVERS	395	309	219	191	152	63	110	95	157	60	109	97	35	52
	DEUX FONT/PAIRE	432	321	248	210	173	81	134	112	148	66	115	97	46	66
CIVM	ARRIMAGE	19	16	15	15	10	2	9	9	6	1	5	6	2	2
WCAX	VARIOUS	66	50	39	35	21	12	18	13	29	13	21	22	7	9
WPTZ	VARIOUS	71	53	36	30	28	12	19	17	25	11	17	13	10	9
	A.TEAM	26	21	15	11	10	3	7	5	11	3	8	6	2	3
WVNY	VARIOUS	103	80	53	42	43	18	28	25	37	17	26	17	9	14
	WHO'S THE BOSS	154	119	79	62	64	27	41	37	55	24	38	25	14	21
OTHERS															
CBFT	M. LE MINISTRE	645	567	303	301	380	95	192	192	187	61	111	109	34	45
CBMT	FIFTH ESTATE	186	177	82	86	89	26	38	40	88	24	44	46	2	8
CFCF	WORLD SERIES	114	103	61	54	39	7	20	20	63	19	41	33	5	7
CFTM	SERIE MONDIALE	321	283	160	155	110	27	63	59	173	49	98	95	14	24
CIVM	ARRIMAGE	12	10	8	10	6	-	6	6	4	-	2	4	-	2
WCAX	HOMETOWN	105	68	58	47	28	17	23	14	39	24	35	33	16	22
WPTZ	A-TEAM	162	116	77	68	63	30	43	40	54	26	35	28	25	21
WVNY	WORLD SERIES	2	2	2	2	-	-	-	-	2	2	2	2	-	-
CBFT	M. LE MINISTRE	593	502	272	267	343	78	184	186	159	36	87	81	40	51
CBMT	FIFTH ESTATE	99	99	26	38	59	4	14	19	40	7	13	19	-	-
CFCF	A.TEAM	265	217	129	102	104	26	50	46	113	48	79	57	19	29
CFTM	DEUX FONT/PAIRE	371	268	194	179	142	69	105	93	127	47	89	86	41	61
CIVM	ARRIMAGE	20	16	16	16	12	2	12	12	4	-	4	4	2	2
WCAX	SP:DINOSAUR	57	48	40	40	18	11	17	15	30	10	22	25	3	5
WPTZ	A.TEAM	28	23	15	9	13	4	7	3	10	2	8	6	4	1
WVNY	WHO'S THE BOSS	150	124	85	73	66	33	46	42	58	24	39	31	10	16
CBFT	M. LE MINISTRE	595	544	232	250	344	75	143	161	200	49	89	88	31	20
CBMT	FIFTH ESTATE	104	102	45	40	56	18	22	20	46	10	24	20	-	1
CFCF	A.TEAM	235	178	117	109	84	42	57	50	93	35	60	59	19	38
CFTM	DEUX FONT/PAIRE	494	374	303	240	204	94	163	132	170	85	140	108	50	70
CIVM	ARRIMAGE	26	22	19	19	12	5	10	10	10	4	9	9	3	2
WCAX	NORTH BEACH &RAW	36	34	19	18	17	8	13	10	17	3	5	7	2	1
WPTZ	A.TEAM	24	19	16	13	7	3	7	7	12	4	8	6	-	5
WVNY	WHO'S THE BOSS	158	115	73	51	62	21	37	33	52	24	36	18	18	25
830- 900 PM	ALL STNS														
CBFT	AMOUR DE QUARTIE	409	357	187	192	233	53	122	126	124	34	64	66	25	26
CBMT	FIFTH ESTATE	127	123	50	53	68	16	24	27	55	15	26	26	1	3
CFCF	VARIOUS	212	176	116	96	79	29	46	40	97	43	70	55	14	23
	A.TEAM	251	202	138	110	93	39	58	49	109	53	80	61	18	31
CFTM	DIVERS	589	510	304	286	282	87	168	156	228	66	137	131	40	38
	CHIEN ET LOUP	699	599	363	337	356	117	212	196	243	73	151	142	52	48
CIVM	VISAGE	39	36	25	29	24	4	16	19	12	4	9	10	2	2
WCAX	VARIOUS	64	48	38	33	21	14	19	13	27	12	19	19	7	9
WPTZ	VARIOUS	73	55	38	31	30	12	21	18	25	10	17	13	9	9
	A.TEAM	29	24	17	12	12	4	8	6	12	4	9	6	2	3
WVNY	VARIOUS	78	60	35	33	31	11	17	18	29	11	18	14	10	9
	GROWING PAINS	116	88	51	48	46	16	25	27	42	15	27	20	15	13
OTHERS															
CBFT	AMOUR DE QUARTIE	579	512	272	289	340	76	175	191	173	55	97	99	30	36
CBMT	FIFTH ESTATE	188	177	80	80	88	24	35	36	89	27	45	43	3	8
CFCF	WORLD SERIES	136	124	73	66	50	10	23	23	74	23	51	43	5	7
CFTM	SERIE MONDIALE	368	333	186	184	135	27	78	75	198	52	108	109	16	19
CIVM	VISAGE	32	30	14	19	23	2	8	13	8	2	6	6	-	2
WCAX	HOMETOWN	102	67	61	48	28	20	27	17	39	22	34	31	15	21
WPTZ	A-TEAM	162	118	81	68	67	29	48	43	51	24	33	25	24	21

SONDAGES BBM SURVEYS (CANADA)

Source: Courtesy of the Bureau of Broadcast Measurement, the industry's rating service

A.C. Nielsen of Canada Limited

A.C. Nielsen of Canada is a privately owned company that provides television audience estimates, program ratings, and special services. It issues two types of reports.

The *Nielsen Television Index (NTI) Network Reports* cover all network audiences and programs for fifty-two weeks per year. These reports are issued weekly; a sample page is shown in Figure 15.9.

The *Nielsen Broadcast Index (NBI) Local Market Reports* measure station and program audiences per quarter-hour in each of Canada's forty-two designated market areas. The number of weeks surveyed varies from six to twenty-one, depending on the size of the market. A sample page is shown in Figure 15.10.

The sampling methodology of A.C. Nielsen is also a two-step process but it is different from that of BBM. First, some areas are defined as measurement cells. Next, the sampling frame is constructed from telephone directories, and a sample of households (not individuals, as for BBM) is selected, with the possibility of including one household that has participated in one or two past surveys and has agreed to participate again. The sample must contain less than half of such respondents. Each selected household receives a diary, along with some monetary incentive. *All* individuals in the household must participate by recording the station call letters, channel number, and the name of the program watched. When completed, the diary is mailed back to A.C. Nielsen. A reminder card is also sent to increase the response rate. As in the case of BBM, the response rate is approximately 50%. A sample page of a Neilsen diary is reproduced in Figure 15.11.

People Meters

People meters, a new system of electronic audience measurement, are presently under study by BBM. When the system becomes fully operational in Canada, advertisers will have information on who watched the commercials and will be able to correlate this information with purchases after viewing. This device consists of a computer attached to television sets that records when the television set is on and to what channel and program the set is tuned. With additional equipment, the meter can correlate the audience data with product usage, and the system can later be augmented to include additional viewer input through a small typewriter-type device.[5]

Introduced successfully in the United Kingdom several years ago, the system was tested in Boston in November 1985. The test revealed that

- measurement through people meters was as accurate as direct measure of television use

- pushbutton accuracy is between 91% and 93%

- long-term panel members do not differ from short-term members: no long-term fatigue or boredom was detected

- the dropout rate was about 2% per month[6]

This new technology will probably replace the diary method, at least in major markets, and the challenge facing researchers is to find efficient methods to deal with the enormous amounts of data generated by it.[7]

FIGURE 15.9

Sample Data from Nielsen NTI Report for CBC Network

NIELSEN WEEK/SEMAINE
SEPT 01 SEPT, 1986

CBC FULL

DAY AND TIME TV LISTINGS –
AVERAGE 1/4 HOUR AUDIENCE

NIELSEN 49

COPYRIGHT 1985 A.C. Nielsen Company of Canada Limited

Source: Courtesy of A. C. Nielsen of Canada Limited

FIGURE 15.10

Sample Data from Nielsen NBI Report for Toronto/Hamilton Designated Market Area

NBI TIME PERIOD/SECTION DES PERIODES HORAIRES NBI
DESIGNATED MARKET AREA/MARCHE DESIGNE — MONTREAL

STATION TOTAL AUDIENCES (000) / AUDITOIRES DE ZONE DE RAYONNEMENT (OOD) — AUGUST/AOUT 1986

TIME/HEURE	STATION	WEEKS/SEMAINES	PROGRAM/EMISSION
FRIDAY 8.30PM–9.30PM			
	CBFT	1	JOURNALST TRIP
	CBMT	1	JOURNALST TRIP
	CFCF	23	COPNA TH GAMES
	CFCF	1	MURDER-WROTE
	CFCF	23	CFCF FOOTBALL
	CFTM	1	KNIGHT RIDER
	CFTM	23	CFL FOOTBALL
	CIVM		HIST-AUTR. MOND
	CKAC		STATION SOLEIL
	WPTZ	12	MISTRL'S DGHTRS
	WPTM	12	TALE TE ZONE-CBS
	WPTM		APL BELVEDERE
	WVNY	3	A-TEAM NBC
	WVNY	12	KNIGHT RDR-NBC
	WVNY	3	APL BELVEDERE
		3	NFL PRE-SEASON
			HUT & PVT
9.00PM			
	CBFT	1	JOURNALST TRIP
	CBMT	1	RETURN TO EDEN
	CFCF		CFCF FOOTBALL
	CFCF	23	CFL FOOTBALL
	CFTM		CINEMA-VEN
	CFTM	1	CINEMA
	CIVM	23	CBS FRI-MOV
	CKAC		MISTRL'S DGHTRS
	WPTZ		CAVIDOS
	WPTM	2	CITY
	WVNY	1	NFL PRE-SEASON
	WVNY	2	MIAMI VICE-NBC
		3	ROADIES
			NFL PRE-SEASON
			HUT & PVT

Column groupings in the report body (left to right):

- METRO AGGLO — HHLDS % FOYERS %
- MULTI-WEEK AVERAGES / MOYENNES MULTI-HEBDO (RTG SHR, AUG AUG OCT PAR)
- HH % FOYERS — WEEKLY RATINGS / COTES HEBDO (RTG SHARE/PART, WK SEM, YR SEM)
- DEMOGRAPHIC RATINGS % / COTES DEMOGRAPHIQUES %
  - VIEWERS TOTAL TELESP.
  - WOMEN / FEMMES
  - MEN / HOMMES
- VIEWERS TOTAL TELESP. (HH FOY., 2+, 18+, 18-49, 25-54, TO-TAL)
- WOMEN / FEMMES (18-34, 18-49, 25-54, WKG TRA, TO-TAL)
- MEN / HOMMES (18-34, 18-49, 25-54, TO-TAL)
- TEENS / ADOL (BOYS, GIRLS/FILLES)
- CHD / ENF (2-11)
- LOH / MM (TO-TAL)

FIGURE 15.11
Nielsen Television Viewing Diary: Instructions and Sample Page

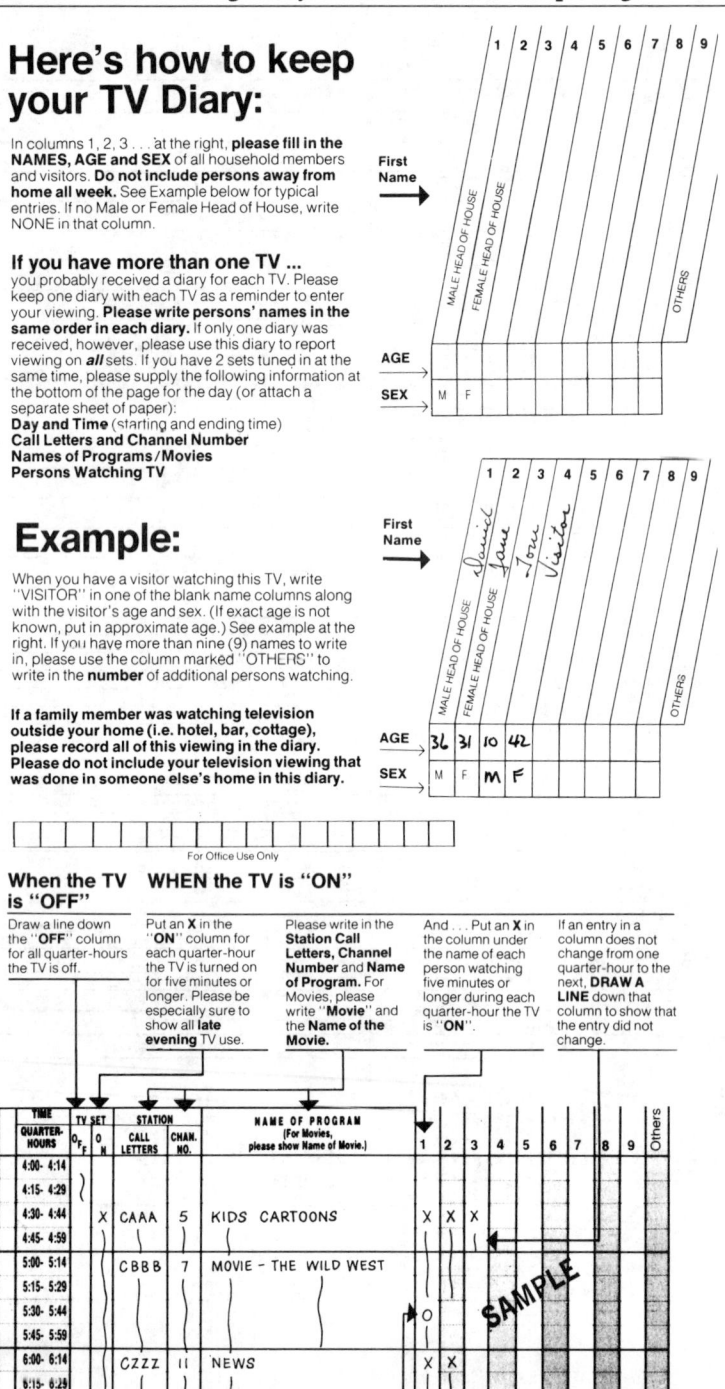

Here's how to keep your TV Diary:

In columns 1, 2, 3 ... at the right, **please fill in the NAMES, AGE and SEX** of all household members and visitors. **Do not include persons away from home all week.** See Example below for typical entries. If no Male or Female Head of House, write NONE in that column.

If you have more than one TV ...
you probably received a diary for each TV. Please keep one diary with each TV as a reminder to enter your viewing. **Please write persons' names in the same order in each diary.** If only one diary was received, however, please use this diary to report viewing on **all** sets. If you have 2 sets tuned in at the same time, please supply the following information at the bottom of the page for the day (or attach a separate sheet of paper):
Day and Time (starting and ending time)
Call Letters and Channel Number
Names of Programs/Movies
Persons Watching TV

Example:

When you have a visitor watching this TV, write ''VISITOR'' in one of the blank name columns along with the visitor's age and sex. (If exact age is not known, put in approximate age.) See example at the right. If you have more than nine (9) names to write in, please use the column marked ''OTHERS'' to write in the **number** of additional persons watching.

If a family member was watching television outside your home (i.e. hotel, bar, cottage), please record all of this viewing in the diary. Please do not include your television viewing that was done in someone else's home in this diary.

When the TV is "OFF"
Draw a line down the ''OFF'' column for all quarter-hours the TV is off.

WHEN the TV is "ON"
Put an **X** in the ''ON'' column for each quarter-hour the TV is turned on for five minutes or longer. Please be especially sure to show all **late evening** TV use.

Please write in the **Station Call Letters, Channel Number** and **Name of Program.** For Movies, please write ''**Movie**'' and the **Name of the Movie.**

And ... Put an **X** in the column under the name of each person watching five minutes or longer during each quarter-hour the TV is ''**ON**''.

If an entry in a column does not change from one quarter-hour to the next, **DRAW A LINE** down that column to show that the entry did not change.

If the TV is ''ON'' but **NO ONE IS WATCHING**, fill in the Station and program information, and put a ''**0**'' in the first person column.

FIGURE 15.11 (continued)

See EXAMPLE in front of diary for method of drawing lines down columns to show that entries remain the same.

MONDAY

4:00 P.M.

	TIME QUARTER-HOURS	TV SET OFF	TV SET ON	STATION CALL LETTERS	STATION CHAN. NO.	NAME OF PROGRAM (For Movies, please show Name of Movie.)	1	2	3	4	5	6	7	8	9	Others
41	4:00- 4:14															
42	4:15- 4:29															
43	4:30- 4:44															
44	4:45- 4:59															
45	5:00- 5:14															
46	5:15- 5:29															
47	5:30- 5:44															
48	5:45- 5:59															
49	6:00- 6:14															
50	6:15- 6:29															
51	6:30- 6:44															
52	6:45- 6:59															
53	7:00- 7:14															
54	7:15- 7:29															
55	7:30- 7:44															
56	7:45- 7:59															
57	8:00- 8:14															
58	8:15- 8:29															
59	8:30- 8:44															
60	8:45- 8:59						1	2	3	4	5	6	7	8	9	Other

EVENING

2:00 A.M.

61	9:00- 9:14															
62	9:15- 9:29															
63	9:30- 9:44															
64	9:45- 9:59															
65	10:00-10:14															
66	10:15-10:29															
67	10:30-10:44															
68	10:45-10:59															
69	11:00-11:14															
70	11:15-11:29															
71	11:30-11:44															
72	11:45-11:59															
73	12:00-12:14															
74	12:15-12:29															
75	12:30-12:44															
76	12:45-12:59															
77	1:00- 1:14															
78	1:15- 1:29															
79	1:30- 1:44															
80	1:45- 1:59						1	2	3	4	5	6	7	8	9	Other

IF ANY VIEWING BE-TWEEN 2:00 A.M. AND 6:00 A.M., PLEASE GIVE DETAILS HERE.

Source: Courtesy of A. C. Nielsen of Canada Limited

Evaluation of Broadcast Media Measuring Techniques

None of the techniques used in measuring broadcast media audiences is without significant flaws or limitations. As a result, measurements derived from these techniques, such as the Nielsen or BBM ratings, will undoubtedly continue to be subject to criticism from both experts and laymen. Criticism is to be expected, especially in light of the life-and-death power that these ratings exercise over radio or television programs.

Despite these limitations, measurements of broadcast media audiences are necessary because program sponsors must have some idea whether their messages are reaching the people they want to reach and whether the money they are paying the media is being well spent. However, none of these media-measuring techniques evaluates the relative efficiency of the various types of media. Left unanswered is the question of whether television or magazines constitute the most efficient medium for relaying advertising messages. Answers to this type of question can be determined only through a case-by-case approach, taking into account a number of factors such as cost, product, target audience, and type of message.

◼ Copy Research

Copy research is concerned with all aspects of the message; it should be called creative research, since it often involves creative planning and execution. Copy research attempts to answer such questions as: Is the message completely understood by the consumers? Does it attract favourable attention? Is the theme used in the message correctly remembered by consumers?

The researcher might want to evaluate an advertisement *before* it is run (pre-testing) or *after* it has been run (post-testing). In some cases it might be desirable to both pre-test and post-test the advertisement to evaluate the testing procedures being used.

Pre-testing the Advertisement

Pre-testing is used more commonly than post-testing, because it is much more important to measure advertising effectiveness *before* an advertisement has been run than after.[8] Therefore, pre-testing should be viewed as a means of saving money, whereas post-testing is often devoted to finding out what went wrong. Many of the techniques used in pre-testing can also be used in post-testing, and vice versa. Two of the most common pre-testing techniques are consumer jury tests and laboratory tests.

Consumer Jury Tests

Consumer jury tests are a useful method for evaluating an advertisement's effectiveness before it is run. A "jury" composed of hypothetical customers is asked to evaluate an advertisement. The number of prospective customers on the jury might range from a dozen to several hundred. The test can take a number of forms. Jurors might evaluate one advertisement or many; they might view advertisements individually or collectively; and the evaluation process might take place at home or under controlled conditions.

One variation used on consumer jury tests is the mock magazine or newspaper, also called the portfolio test. This method allows firms to have new advertisements tested and compared with advertisements for competing products.

Both television commercials and print advertisements can be evaluated through the use of consumer jury testing methods. In either case, the normal method is to have jurors look at several advertisements to determine which receives the best rating The two main procedures for evaluation are order of merit and paired comparisons.

Order of merit involves having each respondent rank several advertisements in order of preference. It is usually inadvisable to ask respondents to rank more than six advertisements at once, since the average consumer can rarely work with more than six with any degree of accuracy.

The **paired-comparison method** is particularly advantageous when the researcher wants to have jurors evaluate more than six advertisements. In this method, respondents compare two advertisements at a time, so that only two are being considered at any one time. Each advertisement is compared with every other advertisement in the group. The winner in each comparison is noted on a score card, and at the end, the number of times that each ad won is totalled.

A major advantage of the paired-comparison method over the order-of-merit method is that it enables the researcher to obtain advertisement ratings of greater consistency and accuracy. It also allows the evaluation of a larger number of advertisements; however, this advantage can disappear if the number of advertisements to be evaluated becomes too large. The number of advertisements being evaluated should not exceed ten; otherwise, the procedure becomes too tedious. Use of the following formula for paired-comparison combinations

$$\frac{n(n-1)}{2}$$

when n equals the number of advertisements being evaluated, permits calculation of the number of comparisons to be made. For example, in a case where respondents were asked to rank eight advertisements using the paired-comparison method, a total of twenty-eight comparisons would be involved:

$$\frac{n(n-1)}{2} = \frac{8(8-1)}{2} = \frac{8(7)}{2} = \frac{56}{2} = 28$$

Three major types of consumer jury tests are used in Canada: focus groups, mall tests, and theatre tests.

Focus groups can be used at any level of creative development, such as the concept stage, using some of the standard projective techniques already reviewed,[9] or with rough sketches or storyboards, or with finished advertisements or commercials. The moderator questions participants to determine their reactions to the messages, how much they remember after exposure, whether they liked the messages, and so on.[10]

It is often advisable to run more than one focus group either to minimize some chance event, to test different executions of the same strategy, or even to test different creative strategies. In the last two cases, each group is exposed to a different version and the qualitative results are compared.

Mall tests (also called *ad hoc commercial testing*) are conducted when respondents are intercepted in shopping malls and plazas that have been chosen according to certain demographic characteristics. Respondents are asked to participate in viewing a program, with commercials, and responding to certain questions. Although, there are some drawbacks to this method, it is relatively inexpensive, can use larger samples than focus groups, and can provide quick answers to a copy problem.

For example, the *Dadson Compare Test* is a mall test that uses two groups for testing a commercial: a test group and a control group. A series of questions on attitudes toward and intention to buy the brand are asked of members of the control group, who do not see the commercial. The test group is shown the commercial and then is asked the same questions. Differences between the responses of the two groups are measured, analysed, and reported to the client.

Theatre tests are conducted with a larger number of respondents who have been selected according to demographic characteristics and who have agreed to go to a theatre at a particular time to preview a television program. The prearranged time could be during a lunch hour on weekdays, in the evening, or on the weekend. The television program shown contains the test commercial(s). After the program is viewed, the respondents are given a questionnaire to answer that is designed to assess the effects of the test commercial(s).

For example, the *Clucas method* is a theatre test that can be used for both rough and finished commercials. It uses one hundred respondents who, after they have seen a twenty-five minute program, are asked to recall each test commercial as precisely as possible. In this manner, the test analyses how a commercial is experienced and to what extent it achieves the advertiser's communication objectives.

Evaluation of Consumer Jury Tests
Although jury tests are useful and have a wide application, certain fundamental difficulties are inherent in their usage, including the following.

1. *Sample selection problems*: It is difficult to obtain a jury that accurately reflects the market. For example, focus groups are often too small and the bias might be large. Also, mall tests could be biassed because of the type of neighbourhoods in which the malls are situated or the type of people that they attract.

2. *Measurement criteria problems*: On what basis is the advertisement being evaluated? What is the definition of *effective* in this case? Does *effective* mean that respondents like the ad best, find it most believable, or think it is the most entertaining one? All of these tests can measure only the verbal communications elements of the message, because of the nature of the data collection.

3. *Respondent control problems*: Unless respondents evaluate advertisements under controlled conditions, there is no guarantee that the evaluation process is being done properly. When group evaluations take place, some respondents might influence others.

4. *Artificial nature of the test*: The most serious weakness of the consumer jury test is that it tends to be unrealistic. Since it is only a test, the conditions are not what they would be in the actual marketplace. Jurors' answers are only hypothetical.

Despite these weaknesses, the jury test remains popular. This method allows the researcher to obtain an evaluation in a relatively brief period of time and at a much lower cost than if the advertisement had been run through the mass media.

Laboratory Tests

As a method of pre-testing advertisements, respondents' physiological reactions to advertisements can be measured in the laboratory through the use of mechanical devices. Five principal measuring devices utilized in such testing are: the eye camera, the perceptoscope, the psychogalvanometer, the tachistoscope, and eye-blink cameras.

Eye Camera

The eye camera,[11] or oculometer as it is also known, was first developed about 1890, but it was not used in advertising research until 1938, when results of its use were reported by *Look* magazine. In an eye camera test, the respondent views an advertisement while the camera records how long and on what area of the advertisement the reader's attention is focussed. More specifically, it measures and traces the exact point of focus of the eye. The eye does not see an entire magazine page or television screen at once. An any given instant, the eye is actually focussing on a very tiny section of only a few square centimetres. The purpose of the eye camera is to trace the movement of the eye as it travels over a page or screen. To what parts does the eye first move? The headline? The picture? Are there parts of the ad that seem to attract virtually no attention? These and other such questions can be answered with the eye camera.

Although the eye camera has the advantage of accurately measuring on what part of the advertisement the respondent's eye focusses, it does not measure interest in the advertisement. It is an instrument of questionable usefulness, despite its objectivity.

Perceptoscope

A pupilmetric device,[12] the perceptoscope attempts to measure respondent arousal or interest in a particular advertisement. This instrument records changes in the pupil size of the respondent's eye. The principle involved is that pupil dilation indicates interest, while pupil contraction indicates lack of interest in what is being viewed. Although the perceptoscope is an instrument of great potential for measuring respondent interest in advertisements, it does not directly measure advertising effectiveness.

Psychogalvanometer

The psychogalvanometer or galvanometer,[13] is another mechanical device used for pre-testing advertisements under laboratory conditions. This instrument, similar to a lie detector, has been used by psychologists to measure respondent reactions and emotions. These are recorded by measuring, through electronic impulses, perspiration changes in the palm of the hand. Presumably, an increase in perspiration indicates a reaction to a given advertisement. However, left unanswered is the question of whether a favourable or an unfavourable reaction is being recorded. In addition to the fact that the reading of the galvanic responses requires no small amount of subjective interpretation, there is the larger problem of the applicability and validity of such an obviously artificial viewing situation. Probably all commercials could have fairly strong impacts if the advertisers were able to strap the viewers into chairs wired with all types of electronic equipment and then force them to watch each commercial intently. The measurement of galvanic skin responses is a controversial technique in advertising research, useful mainly for advertisements of a sensitive nature.

Tachistoscope

Another research technique involving the eye is the tachistoscope, a machine that can flash images at extremely high rates of speed—so fast, in fact, that in some cases the eye does not consciously see anything. The tachistoscope is most commonly used in marketing to measure the impact of various creative efforts. Subjects are shown these ads at extremely high speeds and then asked questions concerning each of them.

How, you might ask, can respondents comment meaningfully on an ad that they hardly even saw? The answer is that, although the image went by so fast that their conscious minds could not assimilate it, the image was still taken in by their subconscious minds, through what is called subliminal or subthreshold effects. The subconscious mind might not recognize the ad for what it actually is, containing a name brand and an illustration and some copy, but will probably perceive it as an entire image or pattern, as a Gestalt or conceptual whole. If the ad is loaded with hidden meanings—sexual images, death images, happy images, and so forth—these meanings will penetrate the subconscious and be revealed in subsequent testing. Advertisements are also tested on quality dimensions: some combinations of colours and designs register better than do others. Finally, ads are tested for recognition, to determine which can be most quickly recognized as containing a specific product and which are most easily identified with a particular brand. It is very startling to see the way in which the use of the tachistoscope can reveal significant differences between relatively similar-looking advertisements.

Eye-blink Cameras

These cameras measure the respondent's rate of eye-blinking. According to researchers, a person normally blinks approximately thirty times per minute. As people's tension increases, their eye-blink rates decrease. By monitoring eye-blinking, researchers can identify commercials that are more interesting to the viewer. Note, however, that interpretation of results is quite subjective. As with the psychogalvanometer and the perceptoscope, the increased interest might be good or bad: mechanical measurements of interest will increase with either anger or happiness. Then, too, there is the ever-present problem that no clear relationship connects interest and sales. The presence of a beautiful or scantily clad young woman in an advertisement usually will increase the interest level among males for that ad (which explains why many ads feature a beautiful, provocatively dressed, young woman). What is debatable is whether the presence of the young woman helps to sell the product. Since an ad has to be seen before it has any chance for effectiveness, some advertisers continue to utilize these sexist themes. However, it is entirely probable that their use might actually be dysfunctional, in that it alienates an ever-growing group of people.

Other laboratory techniques still in their infancy and being developed are the use of electroencephalographs (EEGs),[14] computer analysis of voice pitch,[15] and the Facial Action Coding System (FACS), which relates emotions to muscle movements in the respondent's face.

These laboratory testing devices remain instruments of limited utility to the advertising researcher. However, with proper use by qualified experts, such devices can play a worthwhile role as aids in the pre-testing process.

Post-testing the Advertisement

If advertising pre-testing was an established science of great precision, there would be little need for the post-testing of advertisements. Unfortunately, pre-testing is primarily a screening device that, it is hoped, will enable the researcher to eliminate the least effective advertisements.

Post-testing is designed not only to measure effectiveness (or lack of effectiveness) of advertisements after they have already been run, but to find out the reasons why an advertisement was effective or ineffective.

Since it is generally assumed that one significant and measurable factor is respondent memory of an advertisement, post-testing techniques are often concerned with measuring what (if anything) the respondent remembers about the advertisement. Three standard techniques used in post-testing are recognition tests, recall tests, and the split-run method.

Recognition Tests

Recognition tests, also known as readership tests, are designed to find out which advertisements respondents have read.[16] The best-known and most widely used recognition tests are the *Starch Advertisement Readership Ratings*, which have been conducted by the Daniel Starch organization since 1923 in the United States and since 1949 in Canada.

First, a particular issue of a magazine is tested after a suitable waiting period has passed to give subscribers the opportunity to read and look through it: two days for a daily publication or three weeks for a monthly one. A minimum of one hundred readers per gender are sampled according to the geographic and demographic distribution of the audience.

The interview is conducted by a trained interviewer. A copy of the test issue is coded according to the list of advertisements to be tested and according to the starting point of the interview. Each interviewer is assigned a different starting point to minimize the order effect. To minimize boredom, no more than ninety items are tested with each respondent. The interviewer follows the same procedure with each respondent who meets the quota requirements, who has read or looked through the particular issue of the publication, and who agrees to co-operate. Starting from the assigned page in the publication, the interviewer turns the pages and asks a series of questions about each advertisement that are related to seeing and reading certain parts: the headline, the illustration, the brand name, the signature, and the copy blocks. For each advertisement, the respondent is coded as follows:

- Ad as a whole: a *noted* reader if the respondent has previously seen this advertisement; an *associated* reader if the respondent also saw or read some part of the advertisement that clearly indicated the brand or the advertiser; a *read most* reader if the respondent read half or more of the written material in the advertisement

- Copy blocks: a *read some* reader if the respondent read some of the copy

- Headline, slogan, signature, or illustration: The appropriate item is checked if the respondent saw the illustration or the signature, or read the headline or the slogan.

After all advertisements have been tested, the interviewer completes the interview after asking some basic demographic data for cross-tabulation purposes. Next, the results are tabulated and a report is sent to all subscribers. The Starch readership report contains three items.

- an issue of the magazine with labels on parts of the tested advertisements that indicate the percentage of some group of readers (e.g., male adults) in each of the above categories (a sample page of a labelled advertisement is provided in Figure 15.12)

- a summary report providing readership figures for all tested advertisements, arranged according to the product category and ad size. Also included in the report are the ad rank in the issue according to the numbers of readers and readership indexes based on the issue median.

- adnorm data reports containing figures for two years of the publication. These are used to compare results with a norm for an advertisement that is similar in size and colour.

Interpretation of these codes is as follows: the *noted* score could relate to attention paid to the ad itself; the *associated* score could relate to recognition of the brand name; the *read most* score could relate to interest or involvement in the message. The pattern among this set of numbers for this advertisement and for competitive ones might help to identify some copy or layout problems.[17]

Recognition tests have the advantage of simplicity and have proved to be a valid measurement of reader interest and awareness of advertisements. On the other

FIGURE 15.12
Sample Page of Labelled Advertisement in a Starch Report

Note that the results are given for male readers; also, the illustration, headline, slogan, and signature were tested.

Source: Courtesy of Starch INRA Hooper

hand, there is no proven direct positive correlation between recognition of advertisements and sales of the product advertised. Additionally, researchers must cope with respondents' claims to have seen more advertisements than they could have seen, which necessitate the insertion of dummy advertisements in order to cross-check reader claims.

Recall Tests

Recall tests, like recognition tests, measure market penetration of advertisements. The respondent is asked to recall or remember an advertisement. The recall test differs from the recognition test in that the respondent in the recall test is not shown the advertisement in advance.

There are three main types of recall tests: *unaided recall*, in which the respondent is given no help whatsoever by the interviewer; *aided recall*, in which the respondent is given cues; and the *triple associated test*, in which the interviewer measures the respondent's recall in associating product, brand name, and copy theme. The triple associated test is useful when the researcher wants to find out if an advertising campaign is successful in promoting consumer awareness of a product through the brand name and copy theme. Thus, respondents could be asked, "What gasoline (product) advertises that it will put a tiger in your tank (copy theme)?" If the reply is "*Exxon*," then the association with the brand name has been successful.

Recall tests effectively tell how successful an ad has been in penetrating the respondent's memory. The scores "reflect the advertiser's ability to register the sponsor's name, and to deliver a meaningful message to the consumer."[18] However, a high recall score does not necessarily mean that consumers will buy the product; it means that consumers remember the advertisement.

One such method is the Day-after Recall (DAR) test, often used for television commercials. It uses 150 randomly selected respondents who were watching television on the day that the commercial was first aired. Results are compared to some norms and reported quickly to the advertiser. Only one exposure is tested and only verbal reactions are measured.

Split-run Method

Recall and readership (or recognition) tests are normally used in post-testing advertisements. However, they might sometimes be used in pre-testing split-runs, where two variations of an advertisement are inserted into two otherwise identical press runs of a magazine. Since this technique involves varying only the advertisement, the researcher has a controlled experiment in which the effectiveness of advertisements A and B can be measured. Even in split-run tests, this technique has limited application. In describing the problem, Martin Mayer has written:

> The comparative ratings of the two ads on all three tests (aided, unaided recall, and readership) will guide the agency in deciding which advertisements to run, but the test is most useful in deciding technical questions—such as, shall we use one big picture of a cake made with Betty Crocker mix or two small pictures of two goodies made with two different kinds of mix?[19]

■ Advertising Effectiveness Research

Measuring the effectiveness of advertising is an awesome task that might frustrate the three most interested parties:

- advertisers, who want to know if the money they are spending is producing worthwhile results

- advertising agencies, who must prove to advertisers that their creative efforts can produce desired results

- advertising media, each of which wants to demonstrate that its medium is the most effective vehicle for carrying the advertiser's message to prospective customers

Despite the complementary and conflicting interests present among these three parties, all have a stake in accurate advertising research. Unfortunately, though, thorough research in advertising effectiveness is a staggering chore because of three main factors: the problematic effect of advertising on sales, time and cost considerations, and vulnerability of research methodology and interpretation.

First, and most important, is the problem of isolating and measuring the effect that advertising has in producing sales. In a laboratory experiment, one factor can be allowed to vary while all other variables are held constant. This procedure is not possible in the business world where advertising operates: the business world is not a laboratory, and many factors operating at the same time might account for sales, only one of which is advertising. For example, do soft drink sales rise in the summer because of extra advertising or because of the hot weather?

Time and cost factors present a second problem in advertising research. Good advertising research is both expensive and time-consuming. It cannot be done on a shoestring budget, and problems are bound to arise when top executives want quick answers concerning the anticipated effectiveness of a proposed advertising campaign. As a result, advertisements are sometimes rushed through the pre-testing and are introduced to the market without proper screening.

Third, there also are some weaknesses in research methodology and in interpreting results. Researchers themselves exhibit considerable disagreement over the validity of the different methods of measuring audience reaction. Research methods are subject to abuse and the results are subject to misinterpretation and misrepresentation.

Facing the researcher are such questions as: Is aided recall or unaided recall best? Are consumer jury tests realistic? Should people who casually leaf through magazines in a doctor's office be included in the total audience for that publication? Are the readership figures themselves accurate?

Overcoming these difficulties in advertising research is a matter of legitimate concern to the advertising researcher, although considerable progress has been made in this direction in recent years. However, until more rapid strides have been made, advertising research will remain a highly inexact process, and researchers will continue to be confounded in attempting to perform the central task of measuring the effectiveness of advertising.

■ Summary

Advertising research is designed to measure the effectiveness and improve the efficiency of advertising. To accomplish these tasks, the researcher evaluates the market, the media, the message, and the results of the advertisement.

Because of the rapid growth in total advertising expenditures and improved research techniques, advertising research has acquired a position of increasing importance: advertisers want to know if their advertising dollars have been well spent. Still, advertising research faces three main problems: isolating and measuring the effect of advertising on sales, overcoming time and cost constraints, and curtailing abuses and weaknesses in advertising research methodology. The result is that most advertising research concentrates on measuring advertising effectiveness through copy testing and media research.

Market or consumer research can be either qualitative or quantitative. Media research measures audiences and exposure patterns to the various media. Media information is available from many sources, such as syndicated services like Starch, BBM, and Nielsen, media or industry associations, or through customized studies. Despite the existence of these and other techniques, media research remains an extremely controversial and inexact function.

Copy research is used to learn if the message has been properly coded by the creative director and properly decoded by the target audience. In evaluating the copy, or message, of an advertisement, two main testing methods are used: pre-testing and post-testing. Pre-testing—testing an advertisement *before* it has been run—might involve the use of projective techniques, in-depth interviews, consumer jury tests, and laboratory techniques. Post-testing—testing advertising copy *after* it has been run—involves the use of recall, such as DAR tests and recognition, or readership tests such as those conducted by Starch. The split-run technique allows comparison of two different advertising messages in two otherwise identical press runs of a magazine.

Finally, the problems in determining the effectiveness of the whole campaign were discussed.

For Discussion

1. Is it possible to measure the effect of advertising on a firm's sales? Why or why not?

2. "Research is the last thing I want to include in my advertising budget." Do you agree? Comment on this statement.

3. Do you think consumer awareness of, or interest in, an advertisement is a reliable measurement of the effectiveness of that advertisement? Explain your answer.

4. What are three laboratory techniques used for pre-testing advertisements? Are they realistic?

5. What is the difference between pre-testing and post-testing advertisements? Which is better?

6. Explain what each of the ad-as-a-whole Starch scores measures, and compare them. How would you use them? Which one would you use most often?

7. What type of recall test question might be asked in the following manner: "What cigarette advertises that it 'tastes good like a cigarette should'?"

8. What is the purpose of media research? Elaborate on your answer.

9. Evaluate the research methodology of the Neilsen and BBM services for television media research, particularly their sampling procedures.

10. What is the total audience concept in media research? How does it differ from circulation?

11. Discuss the strengths and weaknesses of the Day-after Recall method for copy testing.

Problems

1. **Mini-case: Fisher Cigarettes** (Part A)
   Fisher cigarettes, one of several brands made by the Dominion Tobacco Company, have experienced a 3% drop in market share over the past two years. *Fisher* cigarettes are made from a special blend of dark tobacco that give them a taste similar to European cigarettes. Parker Manzi, the advertising agency that handles all of Dominion Tobacco's advertising, uses the motto "A Strong Cigarette for a Strong Taste" when describing *Fisher*.

   The cigarette's image has remained unchanged for the past twenty-two years, and Dominion Tobacco executives generally believe that *Fisher* smokers are extremely brand-loyal. Until now, market-share statistics seemed to support this conclusion. In a recent effort to improve a deteriorating sales situation, Dominion's brand manager asked permission to switch advertising agencies. He decided to go with Boyle & Borg (B & B), a firm that had turned around sales of another sinking brand of cigarettes a few years before.

   B & B wanted to conduct a research investigation to determine people's image of *Fisher* cigarettes. The former agency had used a backdrop of a fishing village, with a fisherman docking his boat and lighting up a *Fisher* afterward. Other ads focussed on a ship's captain sitting alone in his cabin smoking a *Fisher*. Most of the newspaper and outdoor advertising showed only the *Fisher* logo (a fisherman) and the motto.

   The first part of the B & B investigation included sentence completion, which was judged to be the easiest way in which to determine the cigarette's image. The results of the survey were as follows:

1. "The fisherman in the *Fisher* commercial is a good example of the type of man who..."

lives in a small town	12%
enjoys smoking	10
is lazy	6
is tough	12
smokes *Fisher*	11
is hardworking	24
drinks a lot	15
is a loner	5
has no education	1
is poor	4
	100%

2. "A fishing village is the type of place..."

I would like to visit	19%
that is picturesque	12
I would like to live in	4
that is quiet	23
I would not want to live in	11
that is dying out	3
that is boring	7
that is poor	9
where fishermen live	8
that is on the ocean	4
	100%

3. "*Fisher* has a _____ tar and nicotine count."

high	74%
average	26
	100%

(Responses varied, but most fell into these two categories. None said "low." Some said "acceptable." Several respondents indicated that they "couldn't care less about tar and nicotine content.")

4. "People who smoke *Fisher* smoke them because..."

they like the strong taste	41%
they like them	24
they taste good	18
other cigarettes are too mild	10
they want to be different	5
no one will ask for one	2
	100%

5. "The type of person most likely to smoke *Fisher*..."

is an individualist	23%
likes strong cigarettes	34
is strong	13
lives in the country	12
works in a factory	8
smokes too much	4
is a man, not a woman	6
	100%

6. "The type of person who smokes *Fisher* has a(n) _____ income."

high	5%
average	35
low	41
steady	19
	100%

7. "The type of person who smokes *Fisher* works..."

in an office	24%
in a factory	27
at manual labour	13
as an artist	21
is unemployed	8
outdoors	5
hard	2
	100%

8. "The type of person who smokes *Fisher* feels that sports are..."

fun to watch	28%
good exercise	22
unnecessary	38
something other people do	12
	100%

9. "People who smoke *Fisher* are most likely to engage in _____ sports."

no	55%
dangerous	5
team	12
active	4
outdoor	3
individual	19
miscellaneous	2
	100%

(Miscellaneous sports named that did not fit the categories above were chess, flying, fishing, boxing.)

10. "People who smoke *Fisher* are _____ sociable."

not very	71%
very	29
	100%

Questions

1. Interpret the findings of this sentence completion test.

2. Suggest other methods of obtaining the same information. Which is the best method? What problems would B & B have with the method used?

3. Set up a semantic differential scale comparing *Fisher* to any other brand of cigarettes.

2. **Mini-case: Fisher Cigarettes** (Part B)
   Boyle & Borg (B & B), a large advertising firm, recently acquired the account of Dominion Tobacco Company's *Fisher* cigarettes. The brand lost 3% of its market share during the past two years, probably because of poor advertising. (See Part A of this case for more information.)
   The team of copywriters at B & B that is working on the new ad image for *Fisher* has developed two sets of ads. Each set consists of four ads that, if successful, can be built on in the future. The ads will be run in general-interest magazines such as *Time* and *Macleans*, as well as in more specialized magazines such as *Camping Canada*, *Canadian Yachting*, and *Outdoor Canada*. Extensive newspaper campaigns in major cities are also anticipated.

Question

Should the firm use pre-testing or post-testing of the ads? Discuss the various methods involved in each. Which method would you recommend that B & B try?

3. MOVAN is a moving company in your area. To increase awareness of its name during the peak moving season, MOVAN is planning to advertise on radio during next May and June. You have been asked to develop a research program to evaluate the effects of this campaign. Write a research proposal, including the choice of the survey method, the sampling methodology, and the questionnaire that you will use.

4. You have been asked to develop a procedure for testing the various components of a print advertisement: the illustration, the headline, and the text (copy blocks). Write a complete research proposal, giving the technique you would use and a sample of the complete questionnaire(s) you would be using.

Endnotes

1. Canadian Media Directors' Council, *Media Digest 1988/89*, p. 15.
2. Ralph S. Alexander and The Committee on Definitions, *Marketing Definitions*. Chicago, IL: American Marketing Association, 1963.
3. Canadian Media Directors' Council, *Media Digest 1986/87*, p. 77.
4. Ibid; see the NADbank special section in *Marketing* (September 29, 1986).
5. Colin Wright, "People Meters; Numbers crunched while you wait." *Marketing* (October 28, 1985), pp. 11–14; Peter Swain, "The road toward people meters." Ibid., pp. 13–16.
6. "Tests show that accuracy of AGB People Meters high in Boston area." *Marketing News* (March 14, 1986), p. 9.
7. "Will smaller shops drown in a flood of new data?" *Marketing*, (October 28, 1985) pp. 17–19; "For the advertiser, a bridge between two sets of information." Ibid, p. 18.
8. Mark Lowell, "Pretests Taking the Lead." *Creativity* (Spring 1980), pp. 27–28.
9. Mason Haire, "Projective Techniques in Marketing Research." *Journal of Marketing* (April 1950), pp. 649–56.
10. Keith J. Cox, James B. Higginbotham, and John Burton, "Applications of Focus Group Interviews in Marketing." *Journal of Marketing* (January 1976), p. 79; Bobby J. Calder, "Focus Groups and the Nature of Qualitative Marketing Research." *Journal of Marketing Research* (August 1977), pp. 353-64.
11. Norman H. Mackworth, "A Stand Camera for Line-of-Sight Recording." *Perception and Psychophysics* (March 1967), pp. 119–27.
12. Roger D. Blackwell, James S. Hensel, and Brian Sternthal, "Pupil Dilation: What Does It Measure?" *Journal of Advertising Research*, vol. 10, no. 4 (1970), pp. 15–18.
13. "Psychogalvanometer Testing Most Productive." *Marketing News* (June 16, 1978), p. 11.
14. Herbert E. Krugman, "Brain Wave Measures of Media Involvement." *Journal of Advertising Research*, vol. 11, no.1 (1971), pp. 3–9.
15. "Voice Analysis May Give Insights into Consumer Advertising Attitudes." *Product Marketing* (April 1977), pp. 14–17.
16. For outdoor posters, Starch uses a *Port-A-Scope*, which shows a poster with varying thresholds levels, from one to five seconds. The respondent is questioned after each of the three exposures.
17. Robert G. Blunden, T.K. Clarke, and Eileen MacDougall, "A Single Method for Predicting Starch Scores by Micro-Computer." *Marketing*, 5. Ed. Sheila Brown, Administrative Sciences Association of Canada (ASAC), (1984), pp. 41–52; Karen Blotnicky, "The Effects of Informative Ad Strategies on Starch Measures of Ad Effectiveness for Men and Women." *Marketing*, 8. Ed. Ronald E. Turner, ASAC, 1987, pp. 38–47.
18. William D. Wells, "Recognition, Recall, and Rating Scales." *Journal of Advertising Research*, vol. 4, no. 3 (September 1964), p. 8.
19. Martin Mayer, *Madison Avenue, U.S.A.* New York: Harper and Row, 1958, p. 279.

16 SALES AND DISTRIBUTION RESEARCH

Among other factors, a company relies on the success of its sales force for its existence. Every operating aspect of the company is determined by the nature and level of the company's sales, including procurement, purchasing, production, warehousing, shipping, personnel, and accounting. That is why sales forecasting and sales control are major tasks often carried out by the marketing research department.

■ Demand Measurement and Forecasting

Sales Forecasting: A Major Activity

Although the job of sales estimation and sales forecasting might sound mundane in comparison with other topics such as consumer surveys for new-product development or consumer motivation, the job of estimating sales potential and developing sales forecasts is one of the most critical tasks that the marketing research department is required to handle. In fact, no marketing planning can be effective without sound sales forecasting. For instance, budgeting for raw materials and other components of production, finished-goods inventory, total personal selling and advertising expenditures, and all other major elements of the business operation depend on it. The basic sales forecast, therefore, is used to establish objectives relating to individual products, customers, and geographic territories.

In some firms, sales estimation represents virtually the entire effort of the marketing research department. Furthermore, it is a job that becomes more important with each passing year: as shipping costs, warehousing costs, and distribution costs continue to climb, the accuracy of the sales forecast (which is used to schedule production) becomes more critical. These forecasts are made even more critical by the decentralized nature of most modern businesses. No longer is it a simple matter of the proprietor individually deciding to start, stop, speed up, or slow down production to the pace of the market. All of these planning decisions must now be made in a decentralized environment, which involves the co-ordinated effort of many departments that are often scattered over several different areas of the country.

In addition, the larger scale of production also entails a longer lead time and implies that the forecast must remain valid for a longer period of time if the investment is to be recovered. Because of the tremendous importance of these sales estimates to the entire corporate operation, they are often quite sophisticated and great care and expense is lavished on their preparation. However, the casual corporate observer is usually unaware of the intensity of this effort: much of it is conducted in virtual secrecy, since these forecasts would be of almost equal value to a competitor.

Principal Types of Forecasts

In terms of the time period covered, there are three principal types of forecasts: short range, intermediate, and long range. The short-range forecast is considered to cover a period of one year or less; the intermediate forecast one to five years; and the long-range forecast, more than five years. The farther into the future that one attempts to see, the more difficult the forecast becomes. The long-range forecast projects potentials that are based on various broad assumptions. If the assumptions are inaccurate, there is usually time for adjustment through periodic revisions. The most difficult forecast is the intermediate, because it involves prediction of the turning points of the economic cycle. Short-range forecasts must consider the influence of seasonal factors in predictions of monthly or quarterly sales figures.

Forecasting Market Demand

Sales As a Result of Marketing Activities

If all of the resources involved in the marketing program could be quantified and summarized by one single number, we would call that number the level of marketing activities. This number would account for such factors as the product quality index, packaging costs, distribution and promotion expenditures, and opportunity costs of a price below or above competitive levels, as well as all other marketing expenses attached to the marketing of a given product. This level of marketing activity is designated by the symbol A in Figure 16.1a. Following the basic principles of economic theory, one can expect sales to increase as one puts more resources into the marketing program, and consequently, sales are likely to be an increasing function of marketing activities.

At low levels of marketing activities, sales might increase at an increasing or at a decreasing rate. For instance, Figure 16.1a shows the case where sales stay at the zero level when no marketing activity takes place during a certain period of time. When the level of marketing activities is low, sales start increasing slowly (up to A_1). Only after marketing activities overpass A_1 do sales start increasing at an increasing rate (up to level A_2). This sales function is typical of new-product sales responses to marketing activities.

FIGURE 16.1
Sales Response Functions to the Marketing Effort

a) New Product

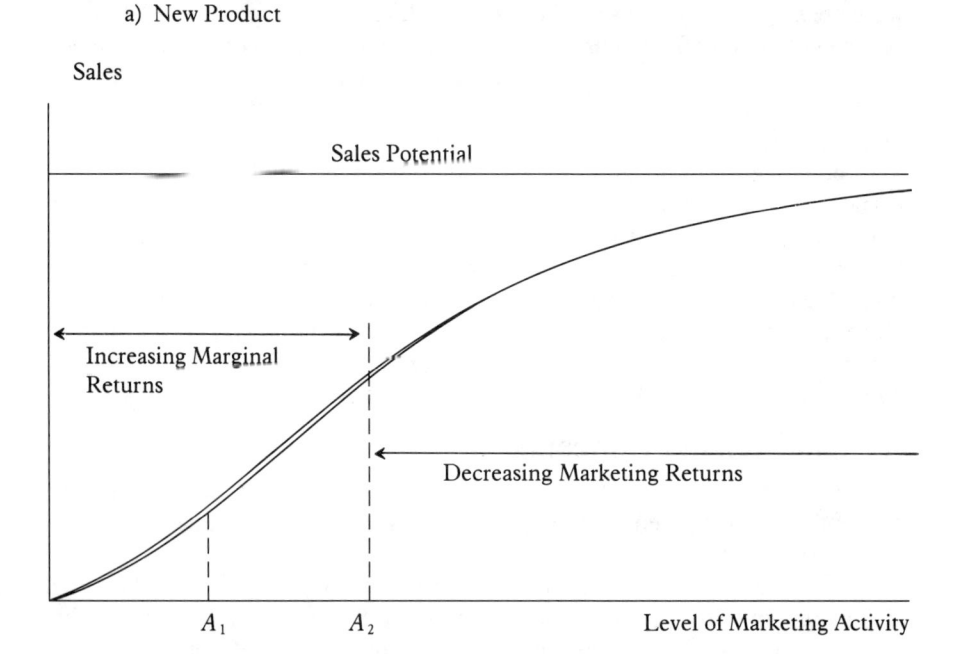

b) Existing Product

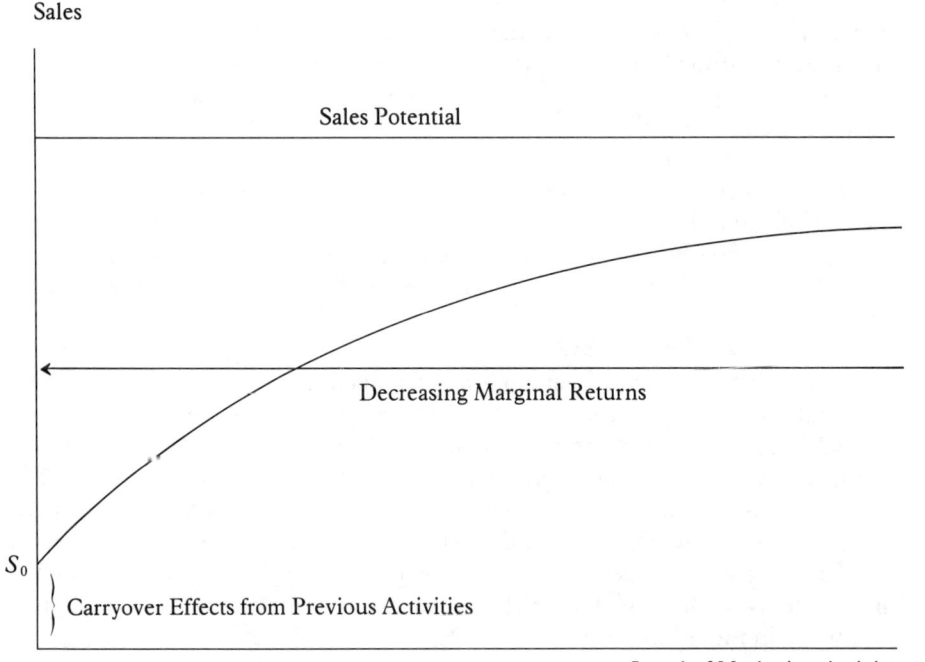

Figure 16.1b shows the sales response function of an established product. The curve intercepts the sales axis at S_0, which indicates that even if no marketing activity takes place during the current period, the effect of marketing activities from previous months can still be felt and result in a certain sales level. This is the result of carryover effects: current marketing activities have not only an immediate effect but also can be felt in subsequent months. Advertising and other marketing expenditures are known to have some lasting effects that give them the characteristics of an investment.[1]

In both Figure 16.1a and 16.1b, after the marketing activities have reached a certain level, additional spending results in still more sales, but the curves will always eventually increase at a decreasing rate.[2] This is the well-known economic theory principle of decreasing marginal returns. If marketing activities were increased up to a very large amount, sales could not overpass a maximum value. Once a market is saturated, it should be clear on intuitive grounds that no additional marketing effort is likely to induce people to buy more than they need. This maximum value is the company's *sales potential*.

Demand-related Concepts

People involved in market demand forecasting need a good grasp on such basic concepts as market potential, sales potential, and market and company's demand and sales forecasts.

Market potential is the maximum sales level that could possibly be achieved, if all of the firms in a given industry would make sufficiently large marketing expenses so as to saturate the market. Consequently, market potential can be thought of as an upper limit for industry sales, which typically will never be achieved.

Sales potential is a similar concept, but at the firm's level rather than the industry level. Sales potential is the maximum in sales that could possibly be achieved by a firm if it increased its marketing activities considerably. Generally, of course, sales potential for any given firm in an industry is substantially smaller than the market potential.

Market demand for a specific product or service is the function that links sales to the various levels of marketing activity necessary to generate those sales. The market demand function applies to the given product class in a specific market.

Company's demand function is a very similar concept, but instead of applying to a whole industry, it is applicable to the demand function of the products of a specific firm.

Sales forecasts comprise a given point of the demand function—the level of sales that will be achieved *given* a certain level of marketing activities. This definition has implications for the sales forecasting process. To establish sales forecasts, one should first specify what marketing resources and what marketing program will be used, and from there establish the probable sales outcome. As will be seen later, several often-used forecasting procedures imply the reverse order: the forecasted sales level is determined first and the marketing resources necessary to achieve the forecast are then determined. These procedures go against the logic of the market demand function. The relationships among these different concepts are illustrated in Figure 16.2.

FIGURE 16.2

Relationships among Market Potential, Sales Potential, Market Demand, and Sales Forecasts

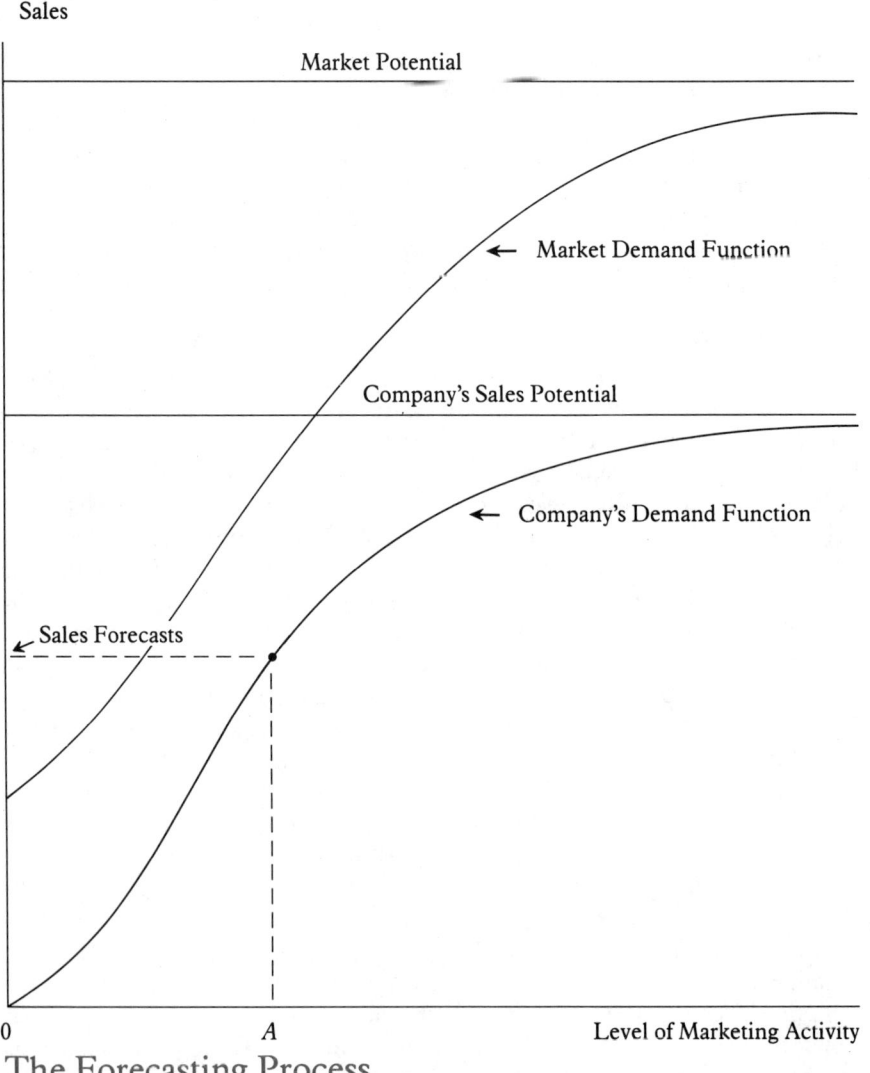

The Forecasting Process

Sales forecasting is often a pyramidal process. It generally starts with an estimate of the total market potential. Then the firm's sales potential is derived and finally, given some specification of the contemplated marketing expenditures, the company's sales forecasts are determined. In the following paragraphs, we will consider the three major levels at which forecasts are made: the market potential, the firm's sales potential (taking competition into account), and the company's sales forecasts for existing and new products.

Estimating Market Potential

Factors Affecting Market Potential

The estimation of the sales potential of an area is dependent on many factors, some obvious and some not so obvious. Obvious factors would include population size and population density and the income of the area, both total and per capita. Even in locales with the same per capita income, differences in the distribution of those incomes might make a tremendous difference in the buying habits of the two regions (see, for example, Figure 16.3).

Regional needs and preferences also might have a significant effect. For example, even if the income and population of an area in Quebec and an area in British Columbia were the same, the area in Quebec would have more sales potential for heavy winter outerwear than would the Vancouver area. Although this is a blatantly obvious example, the fact remains that each area of the country has its own preferences and its own specific demand schedule for each product.

Buying Power Index

Because of the importance of population, income, and previous buying habits, and because of the ready accessibility of figures for these categories, they are often used as guidelines to the market potential of various areas. One of the better-known adaptations of such figures is the "Buying Power Index" published by *Sales and Marketing Management in Canada* magazine. In this index, each section of the country is rated in comparison with the Canadian average. The values of population, income, and past year's retail sales are figured into a formula that weights the income factor as 50%, the retail sales factor as 30%, and the population factor as 20%. Without going into the mechanics of exactly how these figures are obtained and utilized, it should be clear that there is no such thing as a truly objective estimate. Every estimate is prepared according to certain assumptions—assumptions that might be quite reasonable but are nevertheless subjective in nature. In the "Buying Power Index," the assignment of the weights of 50%, 30%, and 20% is a subjective decision; if the assignment of the weights is changed, so are the values of the index computed. A firm that sells a very expensive product might want the income factor rated at 90%, whereas a firm selling some inexpensive commodity product, such as soap or potatoes, might want the population factor rated at 90%.

In addition, such general estimators, although useful, do not allow for the dynamics of the market. They do not make allowance for changing market conditions, such as those observed in the home insulation business: previous demand schedules for insulation have gone out the window and insulation producers have gone to double and triple shifts to keep pace with the still-growing demand. Nor do these general estimators anticipate changes in the overall level of economic activity, such as a nationwide recession. Most significantly, they fail to differentiate between overall retail demand for all products as opposed to specific demand for individual products. As noted previously, the demand for each product varies markedly among regions.

Although we are about to discuss various methods by which sales estimates and forecasts can be made, it is important at this juncture to realize the subjective

FIGURE 16.3

Sales Forecasting for Two Areas with the Same Average per Capita Income

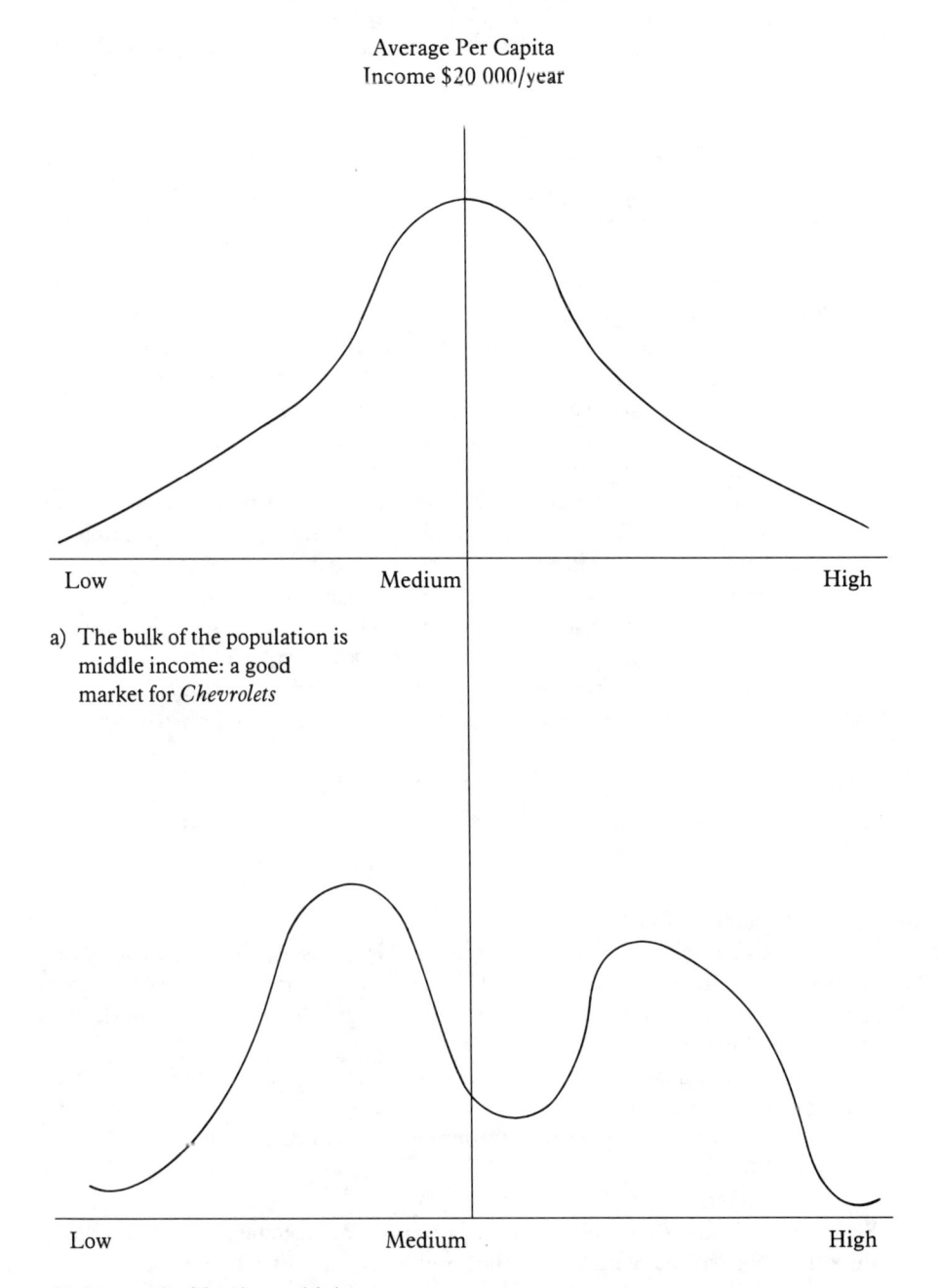

Average Per Capita
Income $20 000/year

Low　　　　　　　Medium　　　　　　　　　High

a) The bulk of the population is
   middle income: a good
   market for *Chevrolets*

Low　　　　　　　Medium　　　　　　　　　High

b) Income is either low or high:
   a good market for *Cadillacs*
   and bicycles

nature of such forecasting. As we have just seen, estimates of sales potential vary with a host of factors, some objective, some subjective, some quantitative, and some qualitative. Thus, any sales estimate must examine not only quantitative aspects, such as the number of people, their income, and their product and brand preferences as shown by previous spending habits, but also less quantitative factors, such as general economic forecasts, consumer trends, and demographic shifts.

Estimating Sales Potential

After a company's market potential has been estimated, the company's sales potential can be derived by accounting for the competitive strength in the market. To derive the company's sales potential, the analyst must attempt to gauge the strength of the company's own competitive stance, as well that of the competition, for the upcoming year. Aside from being difficult and sometimes impossible to measure, the competitive efforts of both the individual firm and the competitors can be quite volatile. Although market-share positions usually tend toward stability over time, they can fluctuate rapidly, especially during periods of transition, such as the entry of new competitors into the market, old competitors dropping out, or new management teams. Unfortunately for the modern-day forecaster, all of these situations are happening with ever-increasing frequency. New firms—especially international and foreign competitors—are entering the market as never before. Old firms are dropping out as managements become more finance-conscious and prune lagging divisions from the corporate trees. And there is more management shake-up as the trend toward diversification through merger and acquisition continues. Every time a large firm acquires a subsidiary, there will be inevitable changes in the competitive posture of that firm. All of these aspects make the art of forecasting at least one part luck for each part skill.

Forecasting Sales of Existing Products

Most sales forecasting methods for existing products can be classified as qualitative or quantitative.

Qualitative Methods

These methods rely essentially on opinions (or guesses). Although sometimes highly subjective, these sources should not be ignored as a source of forecasting input. In a rapidly changing environment, they are often the best guide (and sometimes the only guide) to future events.

The five main qualitative methods are based on the opinions of salespeople, management's opinions, experts' opinions (the Delphi process), middlemen's opinions, or customers' intentions (through the survey technique).

Salespeople's Opinions
Sales representatives are often requested to supply management with estimates of the sales that will be achieved in the months ahead. These forecasts are then carefully revised by management and aggregated to constitute a basis for the company's sales forecasts. This method is frequently used in industrial marketing,

where salespeople have only a few large customers and are in the best position to assess their future sales.[3]

Talking to the sales force can be advantageous in several ways. First, because the salespeople are closer to the ultimate customers, they usually have a better feel for the market. Studies comparing estimates of manufacturers and wholesalers and of manufacturers and retailers show that retailers tend to do better than wholesalers, and wholesalers tend to predict more accurately than do manufacturers. This finding implies that the closer one is to the ultimate consumers, the better one's forecasting will be. Another advantage of sales force estimates is that, by making the salespeople feel like a part of the management team, these estimates often improve relations between management and the sales staff.

Dealing with the sales force can have drawbacks, however. One of the most serious problems involves the question of sales quotas. Often the sales forecast becomes the basis for the sales quota, which in turn will be used to monitor the salespeople's selling efforts and ultimately to determine their commissions and bonuses. Thus, salespeople might be motivated to underestimate the sales potential of their areas significantly in hopes of being given low quotas that, when exceeded, will provide them with healthy bonuses.

Another drawback to the use of the sales force in producing these estimates is that the time spent on such management duties subtracts from the time they can devote to the actual selling.

Management's Opinion

The second qualitative method of forecasting consists of polling various key administrators concerning their sales estimates for the coming year. These forecasts generally tend to be inflated due to the enthusiasm of most administrators and their positive attitudes toward their company's future performance.

Experts' Opinions (the Delphi Process)

In this method (also called the jury of executive opinion) managers, executives, and other decision makers in the company are asked for their predictions of the future (this method could just as well be called "executive estimates"). An extended version of this basic technique is known as the Delphi process (after the oracle of Apollo at Delphi). In the Delphi technique, developed in the 1950s by the Rand Corporation in the United States, estimates are first obtained from all executives. These estimates are averaged, distributions are computed, and then the averages are returned to the executives, who re-estimate the events with the advantage of the collective wisdom expressed by the group. These new estimates are averaged and the process begins again. This process is shown in Figure 16.4.

Of course, what will happen is obvious—all of those people with extreme predictions will quickly become embarrassed and pull their estimates back into line with the group average. This is one reason why so many economic forecasts are both dull and wrong. People do not like to stick their necks out, to go out on a limb by themselves; it is much safer to go with the group. One of the sad things about corporate and government life is that it is better to be wrong with a group than to be correct by oneself. Then, too, a large consensus tends to have a bandwagon effect, which creates a self-fulfilling prophecy. If "everyone" is

FIGURE 16.4
The Delphi Process

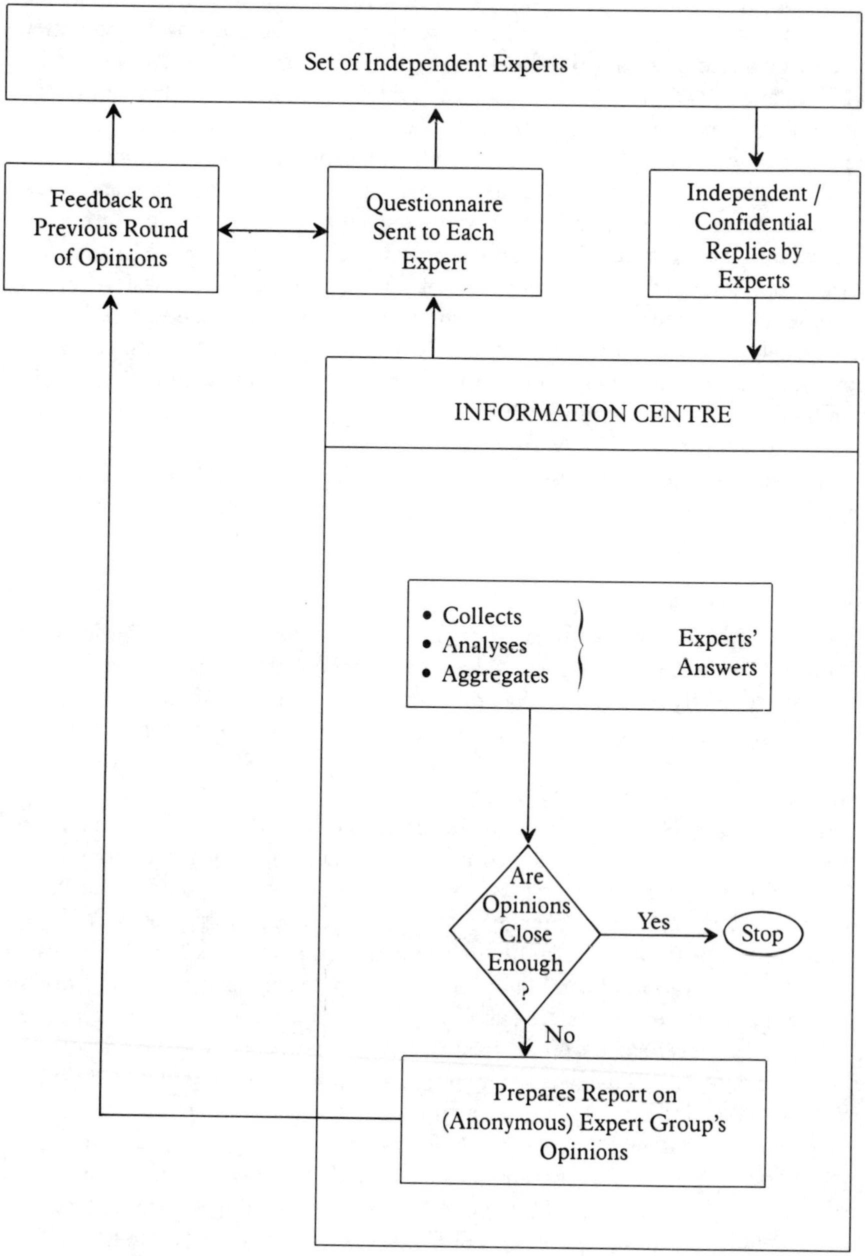

Set of Independent Experts

Feedback on
Previous Round
of Opinions

Questionnaire
Sent to Each
Expert

Independent /
Confidential
Replies by
Experts

INFORMATION CENTRE

- Collects
- Analyses   } Experts'
- Aggregates   } Answers

Are
Opinions
Close
Enough
?

Yes → Stop

No

Prepares Report on
(Anonymous) Expert Group's
Opinions

predicting a slight decline in the economy and business people believe those predictions and act on them, then business people will begin to pursue more conservative policies, to "batten down the hatches." These conservative policies (deferring capital investment, reducing inventories, and so forth) will then result in the very slowdown that was predicted. This is one reason why government forecasts are always optimistic: for capital reasons, the government is constantly in the position of trying to boost public and corporate confidence, so that business, bankers, and consumers will continue to enlarge their operations through more expansive policies.

Authors Kaynak and Macauley applied the Delphi technique to forecast the future trends of tourism in Nova Scotia. Commenting on the usefulness of the technique, the two authors state:

> The cost effectiveness of this technique was clearly demonstrated by the fact that it took only two rounds of measurement and refinement until a considerable degree of convergence emerged toward the midrange of the distribution and the total group response reached a "consensus."[4]

Middlemen's Opinions
Another simple way to forecast sales is to ask middlemen to predict sales for the periods to come. This procedure can lead to accurate results, especially when it is supplemented and combined with other forecasting approaches.

Consumers' Intentions
This method is also called the survey method. In this case, a representative sample of consumers taken from a specific market is questioned about the quantities of a certain product that they intend to buy during a future period of time. These interviews can be carried out personally, by mail, or by telephone. This method has proven useful, particularly for forecasting sales of industrial products and consumer durables.

Quantitative Methods
Quantitative methods for sales forecasting include the use of consumption coefficients, business indicators, regression analysis, and time-series analyses.

Consumption Coefficients
Using consumption coefficients, the analyst tries to identify all of the factors that influence sales in a specific industry. For example, let us assume that a Quebec manufacturer has identified population size as an important consumption explanatory variable. Let us also assume that this manufacturer has also noticed that per capita consumption has increased over the past few years at a constant rate of 0.5 units per year. If the present consumption rate is 4 units per capita, it can be easily forecasted that in five years the consumption rate will reach: $8 + (0.5 \times 5) = 10.5$ units per capita. If demographic projections for the same period show a total population increase in the province to seven million inhabitants, industry sales in a five-year period will reach $7\ 000\ 000 \times 10.5 = 73\ 500\ 000$ units. If the company projects a market share of 10% in five years, the forecasted sales would be $7\ 350\ 000$ units.

Business Indicators

The government, as well as many private sources, collects great volumes of data on literally thousands of facets of economic activity, things such as volume of production, lineage of help-wanted advertising, unemployment figures, inventory backlogs, building permits, and so on. Over time, some of these facets have revealed unique and distinctive relationships to the overall economy. These relationships take a variety of forms. Sometimes the individual activity will tend to precede the movement of the overall economy and can therefore be used as a *leading indicator*. At other times the individual facet tends to move behind the overall economy, thus forming a *lagging indicator*. Leading indicators are the most desired, and the government publishes regular reports on them. The U.S. Commerce Department even compiles an index of nine such factors: stock prices, consumer instalment debt, average work week, new durable-goods orders, plant and equipment orders, ratio of price-to-unit labour costs, industrial material prices, building permits, and initial claims for unemployment insurance. By studying these various indexes, firms can often anticipate changes in market activity.

Regression Analysis

Through the use of the least square criterion, regression analysis finds a mathematical relationship between sales and a number of economic variables or internal variables. Generally, but not always, the relationship is linear. One example of such a relationship was provided by Kristian Palda in a now-classical study on advertising effectiveness. Using the regression technique on the sales data of the Lydia Pinkham Company, a manufacturer of a vegetable compound, he found that the sales level during one period was a function of the advertising expenditures of the company, the sales of the previous period, and personal disposable income.[5] Thus, regression analysis provides a measure of variation in the dependent variable (sales) following a given change in the independent variables (such as disposable income or advertising expenditures).

Some independent variables are under a company's control (such as advertising) and are generally more easily forecasted than are sales. Other variables (such as disposable income) are also easy to forecast, because they tend to follow rather stable trends. Consequently, management can easily predict sales by using the forecasted values of the independent variables in the regression equation. As was seen earlier, this method provides a measure of the accuracy of the estimates (standard error of estimate) and a measure of the extent of the relationship between dependent and independent variables (coefficient of determination).

Time-Series Analysis

The basic rationale of time-series analysis is that certain economic activities are said to vary with time, which has the same effect mathematically as saying that the change in economic activity is caused by the change in time (see Figure 16.5). Although things do, of course, change over time, it must be remembered it is not time itself that is causing the changes. Thus, time-series efforts are almost invariably doomed to results that fall short of the success envisioned by the

FIGURE 16.5
Example of a Time-Series

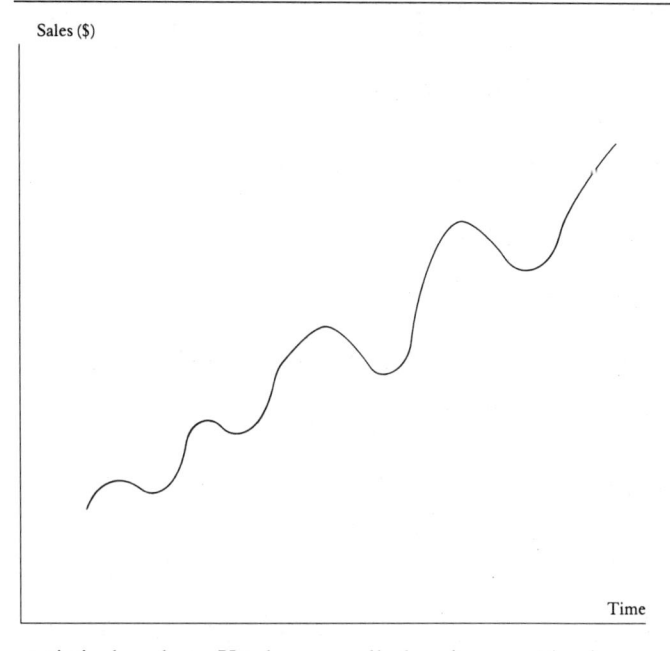

Sales ($)

Time

statistical analysts. Yet, because all planning must be done over time, the study of time-series remains a lively topic.[6]

Time-Series Extrapolation by Scatter Diagram. The easiest, fastest, and sometimes most meaningful way to extrapolate time-series data is through use of a scatter diagram. As illustrated in Figure 16.6, a scatter diagram is only a rough plot of the relevant data through which the researcher has sketched a curve that summarizes the data. Although this method lacks precision and objectivity, it compensates for those shortcomings by being inexpensive to perform and simple to understand. In addition, because users can adjust the curve to conform with their subjective evaluation of the situation, there are instances in which the simple scatter diagram can quite accurately predict the future. A mathematically derived straight line regression produces the graph in Figure 16.7. However, it seems obvious that the last two time periods represent a vastly different operating situation, and hence, the prediction from this graph would seem improbable. The prediction given by the scatter diagram in Figure 16.8 seems much more probable.

Time-Series Extrapolation by Short-cut Formula. A simple formula for predicting next year's sales uses the percentage of sales increase or decrease of this year compared to last year:

$$\text{next year's sales} = (\text{this year's sales}) \times \left(\frac{\text{this year's sales}}{\text{last year's sales}}\right)$$

FIGURE 16.6
Scatter Diagram of Sales vs. Time

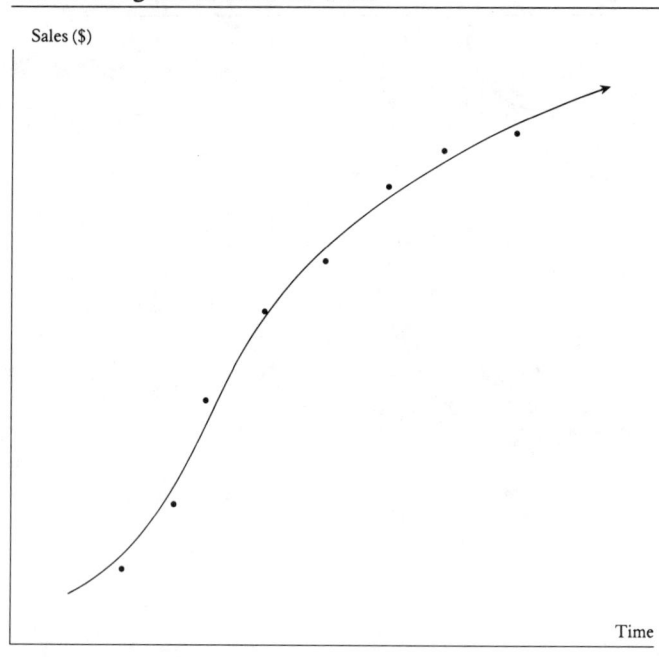

Sales ($)

Time

FIGURE 16.7
Example of Inappropriate Regression (Straight) Line for Describing Time-Series Data

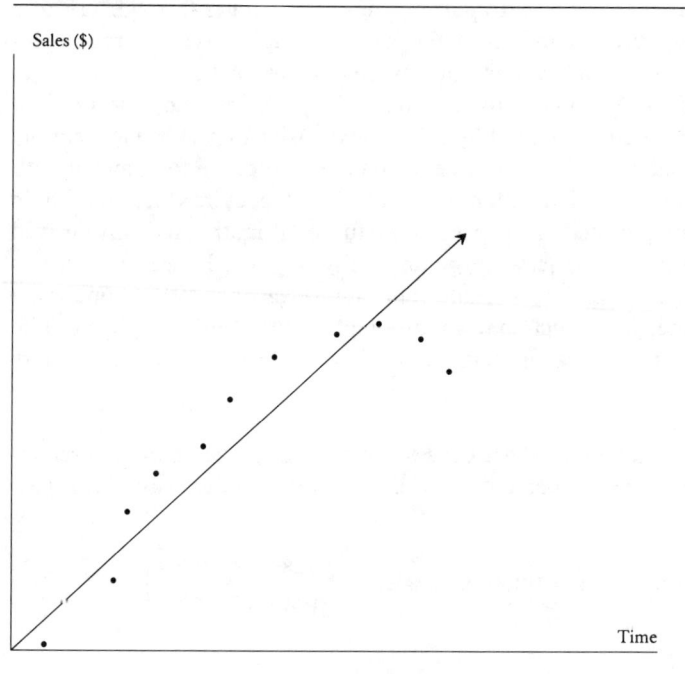

Sales ($)

Time

FIGURE 16.8
Comparable Analysis Using a Curvi-Linear Relationship

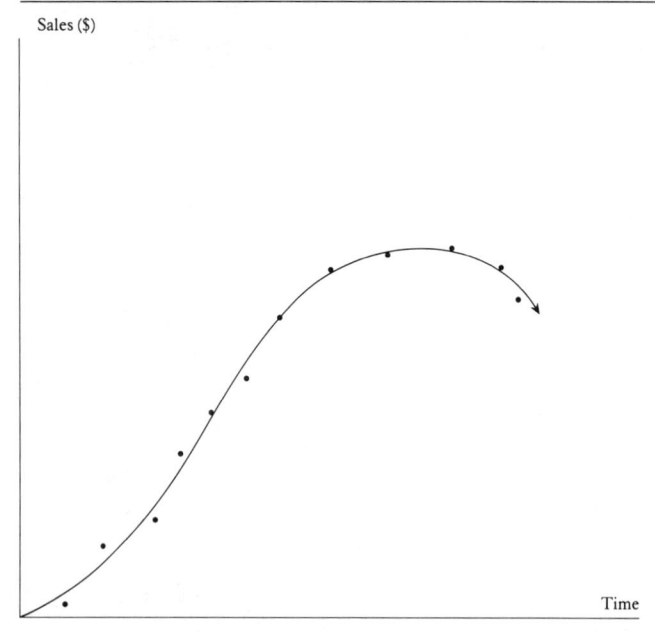

Sales ($)

Time

Thus, if sales this year were $8 million and last year were $6 million, the prediction of sales for next year would be

$$\text{next year's sales} = \$8 \text{ million} \times (8/6) = \$10.67 \text{ million}$$

Although this method is easy to use and simple to understand, it does have two drawbacks that should be mentioned. First of all, it takes only two time periods into account, this year and last year. If there is anything unusual about either of those two periods, estimates made from this method will be highly suspect. A second problem is that this formula assumes that the increase or decrease for next year will be of exactly the same magnitude as the increase or decrease this year. In the real world, such constant (logarithmic) changes are very hard to sustain for any length of time.

Time-Series Extrapolation by Linear Regression. If data are plotted in the manner discussed in the scatter diagram section, with time along the x-axis and sales along the y-axis, then time-series analysis becomes a regression problem with time as the independent variable. To perform this regression analysis, we will utilize a technique known as simple, least-squares, linear regression. In other words, we will compute a regression equation that incorporates only *one* independent variable—time—as a predictor of one dependent variable—sales—and that graphs as a straight line (linear regression). Furthermore, this line will be computed in such a way that the sum of the squares of the vertical deviations from the various data points to the line will be a minimum (least squares).

The ultimate result of least-squares analysis is the formation of the equation

$$S_t = S_0 + bt$$

where t and S_t are the variables and S_0 and b are the regression coefficients (see Figure 16.9).

FIGURE 16.9
Trend Analysis in Time-Series Data

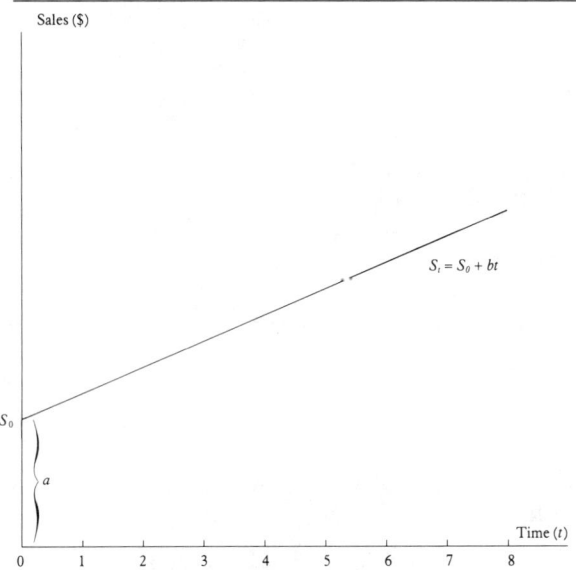

b = the slope, the rate of increase or decrease
S_0 = the S intercept, the value of S when $t = 0$ (or the point where the line crosses the S-axis)

$$S_0 = \frac{\Sigma S_t}{n}, \quad b = \frac{\Sigma t S_t}{\Sigma t^2}$$

where n is the number of time periods under consideration. We are trying to use time-series regression analysis to estimate the probable sales for 1989. Taking the relevant information from the graph, we can compute the formula $S_t = S_0 + bt$ in the following examples.

Example 1: Forecast sales for 1989 using the least-squares method
(even number of years)

Years (t')	Sales (S_t)	$t^\star$	t^2	tS_t
1984	97	−3	9	−291
1985	99	−1	1	− 99
1986	100	+1	1	+100
1987	101	+3	9	+303
Totals	397		20	+ 13

$$S_0 = \frac{\Sigma S_t}{n} = \frac{397}{4} = 99.25$$

$$b = \frac{\Sigma t S_t}{\Sigma t^2} = \frac{13}{20} = .65$$

$S_7 = S_0 + bt$

$S_7 = 99.25 + (.65)(7) = 103.80$

Thus, the sales forecast for 1989 is 103.80.

*Note: For computational convenience, the sum of t should always be 0. In an even number of years, it is computed as $-1, -3, -5$, etc. With an odd number of years, the middle year is 0 and we number $-1, -2$, etc. The value of t in our equation $S_t = S_0 + bt$ is the year for which we are forecasting. In the previous example, it is 7 for 1989 sales. The number of years is n.

Example 2: Forecast sales for 1989 using the least-squares method
(odd number of years)

Years (t')	Sales (S_t)	t	t^2	tS_t
1983	94	-2	4	-188
1984	97	-1	1	- 97
1985	99	0	0	0
1986	100	+1	1	+100
1987	101	+2	4	+202
Totals	491		10	+ 17

Again, using our formulas from the previous example:

$$S_0 = \frac{\Sigma S_t}{n} = \frac{491}{5} = 98.2$$

$$b = \frac{\Sigma t S_t}{\Sigma t^2} = \frac{17}{10} = 1.7$$

$S_4 = S_0 + bt$

$S_4 = 98.2 + (1.7)(4) = 105$

Thus, our sales forecast for 1989 is 105 (see Figure 16.10). Note again that the value for t is 4, the number of years we are forecasting for away from the midpoint.

It is important to note that although least-squares linear regression is extremely popular in sales forecasting, it suffers from one fundamental weakness: the method assumes that the future is a function of the past. In our examples of forecasting for 1989, the method showed that sales would increase as they had through the years 1983–87. This might not be the case. For example, during the 1960s when university enrolments were growing, universities responded by

FIGURE 16.10
Data for Time-Series Regression Analysis

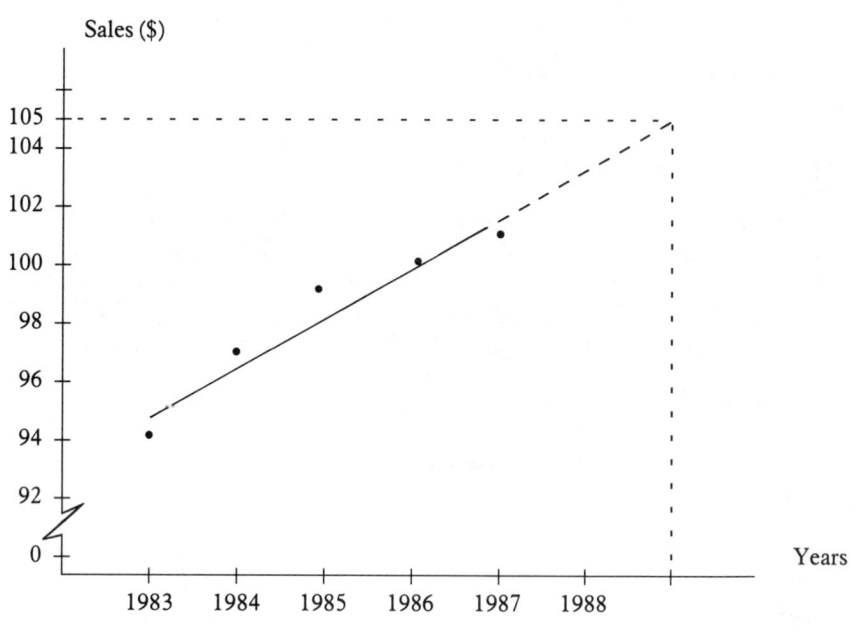

rapidly increasing physical facilities and number of faculty members. Today many universities have regretted their optimism.

Components of Time-Series. Researchers have also noted that variation of data over time might be a function of several different factors, all of which seem to be varying over time. These factors, usually referred to as the *four components of time-series*, are trend, cyclical, seasonal, and erratic variation. The following explains and illustrates these four components in order of duration, from the longest to the shortest.

Trend is the long-term rise or fall in the data. In working the time-series problems, we computed the trend equation, $S_t = S_0 + bt$. Trend answers the question, "When examined as a whole, is the variable of interest rising or falling?" In analysing time-series data, trend is usually viewed as representing time periods of from ten to twenty years. For example, automobile manufacturers in the United States discontinued the production of convertibles because the sales *trend* had been downward for many years.

The most important component of the time-series data is the *cyclical* fluctuation associated with the basic health of the economy, or more simply, the business cycle. Usually from two to ten years in duration, the business cycle is the focus of constant study. However, despite intensive effort, mathematical attempts to plot and predict the cycle over time usually do not work well, because the cyclical variations are caused not by time but rather by political and scientific activity at home and abroad. For example, because of the energy crisis and the subsequent recession, automobile sales were down in the period 1974–76. With the upturn in the economy, however, automobile sales went up in 1977–87.

Much of the variation in time-related data shows regular periodic patterns and might be *seasonal*. Seasonal variation includes both changes dictated by the seasons of the year (such things as Christmas, summer, travel, and cold-weather heating) and changes of shorter duration (such as bigger grocery bills at the first of the month when many people receive their pay cheque, movie attendance on weekends, etc.). For example, the automobile industry usually experiences a flurry of activity during late summer and early fall, when the models from the previous season are sold off and those for the new season are brought in. Noting this annual sales spurt, manufacturers of other products, such as washers and refrigerators, have tried to introduce the model-year concept to their products, although with only limited success.

Erratic variation is very short-term fluctuation that is totally unpredictable. For example, car sales in Niagara were no doubt far below normal for the month of January 1987 for the simple reason that, because of a blizzard that occurred then, no one could get out to shop for cars.

To summarize, trend, seasonal variation, cyclical variation, and an erratic component influence time-series and can be represented by the equation

$$X = T \cdot S \cdot C \cdot E \cdot \text{ or } T + S + C + E$$

where X represents the series resulting from the combined forces.

Forecasting Sales of New Products

For new products, the firm generally does not have a previous track record to use as a basis for sales estimates. In such cases, two methods are typically used: surveys of consumers' intentions and test-marketing.

Consumer Intentions
Surveys of consumer intentions test consumers' responsiveness to a product. Sometimes just the product concept is tested; at other times, samples of the product are produced and distributed to a sample of consumers (often the consumer mail panels). On the basis of the response of these consumers, management decides whether to push ahead with the project, to rework the product, or to drop it completely. The major disadvantage with this method is that it involves a rather artificial marketing environment. To say to consumers, "Would you like to buy a pair of heavy-duty kitchen scissors for $2.49?" is much different from fighting to gain market distribution and then persuading these shoppers actually to select the product from competing items on the shelf and to pay for it themselves.

Test-Marketing
To obtain a measure of how the product would fare in the more exacting light of the real-world marketplace, complete with apathetic consumers, reluctant middlemen, and hostile competitors, the next step is usually test-marketing. In this case, one or more cities are selected for market testing of the product. Sales are carefully monitored, especially the rate of repeat sales, since the novelty of the product along with the introductory specials will bring in a number of one-time-only trial users. With a few notable exceptions (such as vasectomies and coffins),

the key to the success of most products lies in repeat business. By graphing the relationship between introductory and repeat purchases, as shown in Figure 16.11, the firm can ascertain within two or three purchase cycles whether the product is going to be a success.[7]

FIGURE 16.11
Relationship Between Trial and Repeat Purchases

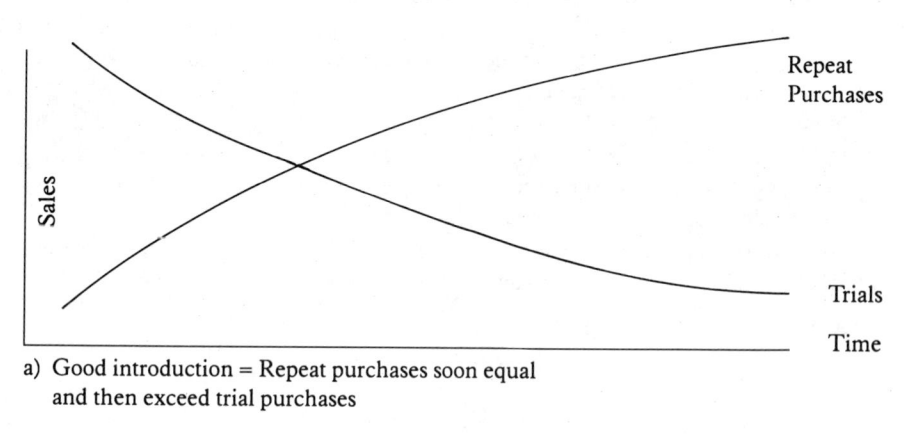

a) Good introduction = Repeat purchases soon equal
   and then exceed trial purchases

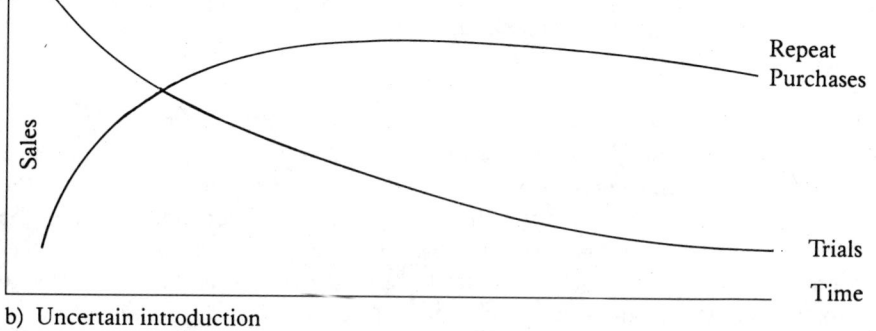

b) Uncertain introduction

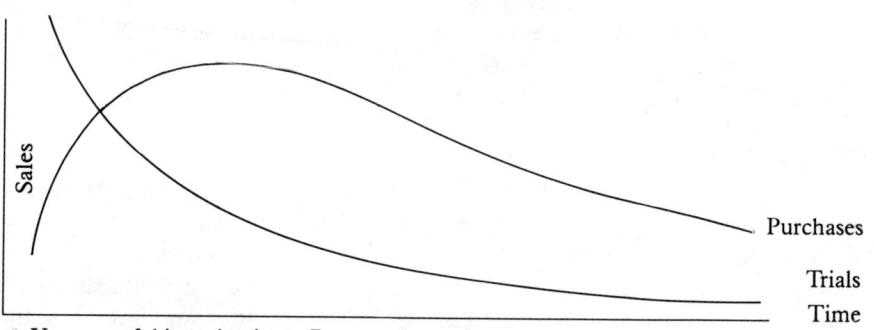

c) Unsuccessful introduction = Repeat sales turn
    downward soon after introduction

■ Other Types of Sales and Distribution Research

Besides demand measurement and forecasting, other important sales and distribution research include such activities as designing and assigning sales territories, carrying out sales analysis and distribution and location analysis. These activities are not the only types of sales force and distribution research, but they are examples of the most frequently conducted research studies in this area.

Designing and Assigning Sales Territories

As noted earlier, one of the main applications of sales estimates and forecasts is development of sales quotas and assignment of sales territories. Hence, one of the main activities of many marketing research departments is assisting in the development of these sales territories. Obviously, the objective of the assignment of the territories is to equalize the load among salespeople while providing sales goals and quotas that are fair to both the company and the individual salesperson. Although this might seem like a simple task, it should be realized that, once again, there are a host of interconnected factors, all of which must be considered. The following factors illustrate their diversity, but it should be realized that this list is only illustrative and not exhaustive.

Dollar Sales Volume

The most obvious breakdown of sales territories is by dollar sales volume. A company wants its salespeople to operate in areas of approximately equal sales potential, so that commissions resulting from sales will be roughly equal. However, in addition to total dollar volume, care must also be taken to balance the number of sales. It would be highly inequitable to give one salesperson two huge accounts from which a handsome income could be earned with only two calls per week, while another salesperson might have to call on two hundred small accounts to make the same salary.

Geography

Another factor to be considered is geography. The ideal is to create contiguous territories of approximately equal size. Discrepancy in size frequently creates friction between the "rural" sales force and the "urban" sales force. The rural salesperson calling on small accounts in scattered towns might spend the majority of selling time driving between accounts and might be on the road virtually every night of the week. On the other hand, the urban salesperson, in addition to having the advantage of concentrated territories, might be home for supper every night. Many people have the idea that corporate selling involves a great deal of travelling. Of course, some selling positions do involve travel away from home, but much business selling is done in concentrated territories within a few minutes' driving time of each other.

The Product Line

In some firms, the emphasis is on assigning territories by product. One salesperson will have exclusive responsibility for only one of the product lines that the company makes, and if the customer wants a different product from the same company, a different salesperson will be called in. IBM, for example, has some salespeople that sell nothing but typewriters, others that sell nothing but small business computers, and others that sell nothing but large computers. The advantage of this method is that the salesperson becomes quite knowledgeable within the area of specialty.

The Customer

In yet other firms, the assignment of selling responsibility will be done on the basis of customers, and the salesperson will have selling responsibility for every product in the company catalogue. The advantage of this system is that the salesperson develops greater rapport through the intensity of this type of association with the customer. The company might also save on selling expenses, in that only one salesperson, rather than several, will call on the customer.

The Competition

Still other factors that must be considered are the nature of the competition, the market potential, and the sales potential. The competitive strategy of the firm will have a bearing on how the territories are staffed and assigned. If the market and sales potential are believed to be high, a very intensive selling effort could be chosen, with each salesperson having only a small number of accounts. On the other hand, if the potential is considered to be low, the selling effort could be minimized.

The purpose of reviewing these factors has been to illustrate the complexity of the problem of the assignment of selling territories. To divide the territories by a single factor, such as total sales dollar or total travelling time, would be relatively simple. However, to divide the territories by total sales dollar while simultaneously dividing them by travel time, by the number of accounts, by product line, and by customer, can become an enormous task for the research department. And since the efforts and the pay of the sales force are dependent on the equity of these divisions, any inequities, real or imaginary, are sure to be speedily brought to the attention of supervisors. As with so many types of business analysis, the mathematics of the analysis are not terribly sophisticated. However, the lack in mathematical sophistication is more than offset by the complexity caused by the multitude of factors impinging on the situation and by the importance of these factors: business decisions are not made lightly, because frighteningly large amounts of money are often at stake.

Sales Analysis

One vital element of any good sales management program will be a comprehensive program of sales analysis. Sales analysis involves identification of who bought how much of what for how much, where, when, and who sold it. In sales analysis, the company tries to break its sales down by customer (What are the demographics of the customers?), by product (What items are the best sellers? The worst?), by quantity (Who are the big customers?), by price (How sensitive is the product to price competition and price-related dealing?), by area (Where is the corporate strength concentrated?), and by salesperson (Who are the best performers and why? The worst performers and why?).

At the heart of a marketing control system there must be a measuring system that produces regular reports on how well the company is doing in relation to its established objectives.[8] Marketing information and research are important func tions of the fulfilment of this task. Chapter 7 showed that marketing information systems are becoming more sophisticated and capable of supplying management with up-to-date measurements of performance for a company's various depart-ments.

The impetus to install a management information system comes from the nature of product distributions existing in most markets. The pattern for most companies is a very skewed sales distribution: some customers buy a great deal and others very little; likewise, some products sell very well and others sell very poorly. In fact, many marketing books summarize this relationship in what is known as the "20–80 rule," which says that for most products, approximately 20% of the customers will provide 80% of the sales and profits. Given this kind of distribution, it is imperative that management isolate and identify these top performers. These, whether they be products, customers, territories, or salespeo-ple, represent the heart of any company's business, and their health and cultiva-tion should be the primary focus of management concern.

A second objective of sales analysis is to evaluate sales patterns over time. For example, if sales in a particular product line have been decreasing unexpectedly, it might be discovered that new competitive lines have been successfully placed on the market. Most of the time, however, analysis of performance uncovers only problem areas and marketing managers must turn to other sources for answers. Frequently, the nature of the problem provides some indication of the procedures that should be followed to obtain a solution.

Distribution Analysis

One piece of sales information that is required by the company is not available from the sales invoices—the profit of the sales. Although the selling price will be prominently displayed, the profit, especially the true profit, is much harder to determine.

Use of the term *true profit* underscores the fact that the real profit that a firm makes on a sale is not the simple difference between buying price and selling price, the product markup. The true profit is the amount of profit after *all* of the costs have been taken from the selling price. These include not only the cost of the merchandise (the buying price or cost of goods), but also the costs of selling, handling, shipping, warehousing, returns, and adjustments, as well as allocation for corporate overhead. In short, everything involved in selling the product to the customer is included. The usual name for determination of true profits is *distribution analysis*.[9]

Because of the tremendous difficulty of performing it, distribution analysis has been underutilized as a management tool. However, as companies have become larger and as more sophisticated mathematical techniques and computational tools have become available, an increasing number of firms have turned to distribution analysis in an effort to improve the efficiency of their operations. For example, distribution analysis might show that many of the products carried in the product line are simply not making any money.[10] They are indeed being sold at prices above their costs of production, but when the entire distribution costs are added, the items are actually losing money.[11] In a classic case, the Nicholson File Company dropped 90% of its product line and achieved an increase in both sales and profits!

Of course, distribution analysis does not work for all firms. It works best when the direct costs of production represent a large percentage of the selling price. Conversely, as the percentage of indirect costs (overhead) becomes larger, distribution analysis becomes progressively more difficult to perform. For industries and products in which indirect costs are extremely high, such as transportation or heavy industry, distribution analysis might be virtually impossible. For instance, how would you figure the profit margin on a single airline ticket? Some of the costs are direct, such as the fuel, the food, the pilots, and so forth, but how do you allocate the cost of the airport? The obvious answer is to take the total value of these various indirect costs (or joint costs, or overhead costs) and divide the figure by the total number of passengers that the airport is expected to handle. The only problem here is that this approach leaves unanswered the question of the number of passengers expected. The price of a given airline seat is based not on the costs associated with that passenger, but rather on the basis of an estimate of all of the passengers that are expected. High indirect costs are the reason why many industries, such as transportation, steel, chemicals, and so forth, will sometimes sell at very low margins: they are willing to take any business, as long as it helps to pay for the overhead.

Location Analysis

To this point, this chapter has been written from the viewpoint of a manufacturer attempting to estimate the sales of a given product. A conceptually similar, although mechanically different, situation is faced by the retailer who attempts to estimate the probable sales for a given retail location. The estimation of such sales has given rise to a slightly different type of forecasting known as *location analysis*.

Location analysis is a hybrid of marketing and real estate that concerns itself with the investigation of various sites (both present and future) and with a determination of the probable profitabilities of those locations. Accordingly, a site investigation will include not only such marketing factors as population density, traffic counts, and zoning restrictions, but also real estate factors such as site availability and cost.

As always, there are also a host of qualitative factors to consider. One such factor would be the competition. Someone opening a Chinese restaurant in a town of fifty thousand would not want to be located next door to another Chinese restaurant; the town is too small to support two restaurants so close together. And yet that is just what happened once, when two Chinese restaurants (there were two others in town already) opened within a block of each other. Of course, this duplication was probably not deliberate; very likely when the two owners signed leases they were unaware that the other was moving into the next block. Perhaps this situation illustrates a case of insufficient market research: had the owners of the restaurants been more thorough in their investigations, they might have avoided this problem.

In other cases, however, a business will welcome its competitors because they strengthen the trading area.[12] When the first shopping malls were built, they usually contained only one large department store, because the department stores were wary of sharing their business with competitors. However, over time, the department stores realized from experience that malls could draw many more customers if several department stores were located in each. Thus, shopping malls being constructed today usually feature at least two, and sometimes three or more, large department stores.

Another factor to be considered is the traffic count. Generally, a high traffic count is considered good, but there are cases in which the traffic is so heavy that customers have difficulty reaching the business. Then, too, traffic poses a parking problem. Stores that require quick access and parking within close proximity, such as grocery stores, drug stores, and liquor stores, are therefore usually located in shopping centres, whereas stores that are more suited to browsing, such as fashion and craft shops, are located in either shopping malls or downtown shopping districts.

Subjective evaluations must also be made of the neighbourhood and the relationship between its image and the image that the store is trying to present. Furthermore, it must be remembered that the establishment of a store is usually a proposition of at least twenty years, and accordingly, expectations of the direction and character of neighbourhood change must be considered.

■ Summary

This chapter has reviewed some of the major problems and techniques in sales estimation and sales forecasting. The responsibility for these estimates is usually assigned to the marketing research department and often constitutes the bulk of its effort. Sales estimation is an area of great importance to the firm because of the tremendous number of operating plans directly determined by the level of the estimates. Furthermore, the calculation of these estimates continues to grow both in importance and in difficulty, as the scope of business activities widens and the pace of business life accelerates.

Techniques for the development of sales forecasts are qualitative techniques and quantitative extrapolation. Qualitative techniques, which are essentially opinions, are often provided by company executives and the company sales force. The use of market surveys usually begins with consumer concept testing and might continue through full-scale market tests.

Quantitative extrapolation involves the use of previous sales data for the forecast of future sales. The use of scatter diagrams, short-cut formulas, and linear regression time-series analysis, as well as the use of seasonal and cyclical indicators, have been discussed as methods of producing estimates through objective extrapolation.

The assignment of sales territories is a critical subject. Setting sales quotas is a very delicate and sensitive issue to the sales staff, and many factors, both quantitative and qualitative, must be taken into account.

Sales analysis involves study of the sales records to determine what product is sold, where, when, to whom, at what price, by whom, and in what quantities. The objective of sales analysis is to isolate and identify those areas of corporate strength that can be emphasized and those areas of corporate weakness that can be either improved or discarded.

Distribution analysis is an extension of sales analysis, in which the objective is to determine the profitability of a given sale. This task is a very difficult one, in which all of the costs involved in the manufacture, sale, distribution, and servicing of an account are computed to find the true profit represented in the sale. Although never easy, distribution analysis becomes progressively more difficult as the proportion of indirect costs involved in the selling of an item increases.

Location analysis represents an extension of the concepts of sales forecasting from a single product to a retail location. Location analysis is a hybrid between marketing analysis and real estate, because both the sales potential and the real estate costs must be considered.

For Discussion

1. Why is sales estimation becoming more important to both the individual firm and the economy?

2. Despite new sophisticated tools and techniques, sales estimation and forecasting are becoming progressively more difficult. Why?

3. What are the major techniques of sales forecasting discussed in this chapter?

4. Why is the use of the sales force to produce a sales forecast sometimes risky?

5. Contrast the problems associated with estimating market potential, sales potential, and sales forecasts.

6. What is the major assumption in objective extrapolation? What dangers are present in that assumption? Discuss that assumption in relation to the estimate of 1988 sales produced for the mini-case study, problem 2, which follows these questions.

7. What are the components of time-series? Discuss.

8. Discuss, compare, and contrast distribution analysis and sales analysis. Under what industry and product conditions is distribution analysis particularly difficult?

9. What are the leading indicators? Discuss their use.

10. What is the difference between location analysis and sales analysis? What is the difference between location analysis and real estate? Under what conditions can a location be not as good as it seems to be?

Problems

1. **Mini-case: Home Study Institute** (Part C)

   Question
   Reread the Home Study Institute (Part A) mini-case at the end of Chapter 7. Then prepare a research plan that could be used by Ray Golden for estimating market potential and market demand for the data-processing course.

2. Given the following sales data; find the estimate for sales in 1988 by the technique of least-squares regression.

Year	Sales
1984	$3000
1985	$4000
1986	$6000
1987	$6000

3. The company's monthly sales for past years are shown in the following table.
   a) Compute a seasonal index for each month. What type of product would display such a seasonal pattern?
   b) The sales forecasts for 1988 are $22 000 000. Forecast monthly sales for 1988.

Month	Sales 1985 ($000)	Sales 1986 ($000)	Sales 1987 ($000)
January	100	130	160
February	80	110	150
March	110	140	170
April	130	135	180
May	150	160	220
June	180	200	240
July	210	250	280
August	150	170	200
September	140	150	190
October	110	130	150
November	115	145	155
December	120	150	160

Endnotes

1. See Joel Dean, "Does Advertising Belong in the Capital Budget?" *Journal of Marketing*, 30 (October 1966), pp. 15–21.
2. These carryover effects were first observed in an advertising context by Hubert Zielske and Kristian Palda. See Hubert A. Zielske, "The Remembering and Forgetting of Advertising." *Journal of Marketing*, 23 (January 1959), pp. 239–43; Kristian S. Palda, *The Measurement of Cumulative Advertising Effect*. Englewood Cliffs, NJ: Prentice-Hall, 1964.
3. "Sales Forecasting and Practices." *Experience in Marketing Management*, 25. New York: The Conference Board, 1970.
4. Erdener Kaynak and James R. Macauley, "Use of the Delphi Technique for the Prediction of Future Tourism Trends in Nova Scotia." *Marketing*, 5. Ed. S. Brown. Administrative Sciences Association of Canada (ASAC), 1984, pp. 172–81.
5. Kristian S. Palda, *The Management of Cumulative Advertising Effects*. Englewood Cliffs, NJ: Prentice-Hall, Inc., 1964.
6. The field of time-series is well developed and many excellent textbooks are available. See, for instance, Robert G. Brown, *Smoothing, Forecasting and Predictions of Discrete Time Series*. Englewood Cliffs, NJ: Prentice-Hall 1963.
7. Scott J. Armstrong, *Forecasting: From the Crystal Ball to the Computer*. New York: John Wiley & Sons, 1976.
8. S. Sharma and D.D. Achabal, "STEMCOM: An Analytical Model for Marketing Control." *Journal of Marketing*, 46 (Spring 1982), pp. 104–13.
9. Alfred R. Oxenfeld, "The Marketing Audit as a Total Evaluation Program." *Analyzing and Improving Marketing Performance: Marketing Audits in Theory and Practice*. New York: American Management Association, 1959, 26.
10. Philip Kotler, *Marketing Management: Analysis, Planning and Control*. 3rd edition. Englewood Cliffs, NJ: Prentice-Hall, 1972, p. 779.
11. Abe Shuchman, "The Marketing Audit: Its Nature, Purposes and Problems." *Analyzing and Improving Marketing Performance*. Report no. 32. New York: American Management Association, 1959, pp. 16–17.
12. Hiro Matsusaki, "The Estimation of Retail Trading Areas by Using a Probabilistic Gravity Model: An Evaluation from a Cross-Cultural Perspective." *Marketing*, 1. Ed. V.J. Jones. ASAC, 1980, pp. 248–50.

APPENDIXES

1 MICROCOMPUTERS IN MARKETING RESEARCH[1]

by Jerry A. Rosenblatt

Most large corporations use large mainframe computers to handle their financial and accounting functions (such as payroll cheques and cost controls). Mainframe computers are intended for large-scale problems and can be used by many individuals at the same time.

Microcomputers are relatively new and fundamentally different from their predecessors. One of the major distinctions is that desktop personal computers are intended for use by one person or by a relatively small group of individuals. Now individuals in corporations can have hands-on access to significant computing power—some desktop personal computers have more power than large mini- or mainframe computers. In addition, microcomputers are available at a fraction of the cost of mini- or mainframe computers.

Some of the other major advantages are that virtually no programming skills are required, and yet the user can perform very complex tasks (such as sophisticated data manipulation and analysis, graphics generation, and word processing). Until only a few years ago, these functions could be executed only on large mainframe computers.

This appendix discusses some of the issues that should be considered when marketing research managers are considering the use of microcomputers in their departments.

■ Equipment

Hardware Requirements

The standard hardware configuration for most desktop personal computers is

- 640 RAM (random access memory)
- one floppy disk drives (either 5¼-inch or 3½-inch format)

- one 20-megabyte hard disk (sometimes referred to as a fixed disk)

- monitor (monochrome is recommended for word processing; graphics screen is required for any type of on-screen graphics capabilities)

- variety of I/O (input/output) devices (parallel and serial ports or other connector-types for printers/plotters, modems, and other monitors)

- printer (either a letter-quality printer dedicated to word processing, such as a laser printer, or some type of dot-matrix printer with graphics capabilities for producing pie graphs/bar graphs, etc., and near-letter-quality word-processing features)

Compatibility

Compatibility is one of the most important criteria that a marketing research manager should consider. In industry, IBM-PC/XT/AT compatibility has become the norm, due to the tremendous number of software manufacturers producing products for MS DOS (MicroSoft-Disk Operating System) based systems. However, the notion of compatibility must be extended beyond this. It is essential for marketing researchers to be compatible with the rest of the people in their companies and with other individuals with whom they must interact. Compatibility of software, hardware, and people is a major consideration.

Convenience

Immediate, desktop convenience is the major benefit gained with the use of microcomputers. Department personnel no longer have to rely on the corporation mainframe computer or the mainframe computer operators. Analysis of sales data and report generation (both graphics and word processing) can be done right at a person's desk. For sceptics who still perceive microcomputers to be toys, it is interesting to note that the new generation of microcomputers, such as the 80286, 80386 (running at 10, 12, 16, or 25 MHz), is as fast as, and in some cases, faster than, many minicomputers.

■ Data Analysis

Spreadsheet/Database Packages

A number of completely integrated spreadsheet/database packages are available that can provide the marketing research manager with all of the tools necessary to increase productivity and enable easier decision making. As far as integrated packages are concerned, my favourite is SMART. For spreadsheets with some database I prefer LOTUS 1-2-3 (at least the Release 2 version) and SUPERCALC. All of these packages have exhaustive spreadsheet applications, with some database capabilities. The SMART system is a completely integrated spreadsheet, database, word processor, and graphics generator, which can process slides, printer hard copies, 35-mm photos, etc.

In general, when one wants to use the spreadsheet format, there are three main environments in which one can work:

- the worksheet environment, to calculate numbers, test assumptions, and analyse results. The great advantage of a spreadsheet is the possibility for analysing "what if" scenarios

- the graphics environment, to draw numeric data (either on the screen, printer, plotter, 35-mm slide, etc.) for the purpose of illustrating and analysing trends

- the database environment, to organize and manage information such as names, addresses, customers, sales territories, regions, etc.

The great advantage of integrated software such as SMART or LOTUS 1-2-3 (Release 2) is that each of the independent functions can be used separately or in conjunction with each other. For example, one could enter information into the database, move it to the worksheet and calculate the latest information on the numeric data, construct meaningful "what if" scenarios with the data, and then graph the information in any one of a number of different graphic forms, (such as pie graphs, bar graphs, line graphs, etc.). With completely integrated software such as SMART, one could even generate the written report with the SMART word-processing module. However, with other, more powerful word-processing packages on the market and the recent introduction of desktop publishing, word processing using integrated packages has been less than state of the art.

Forecasting is another form of data analysis that is entirely feasible using spreadsheets or databases, and a number of software packages have been designed specifically for forecasting. Many of these packages offer up to ten or twelve methods for forecasting (including Box-Jenkins, exponential smoothing, etc.). If one is a good forecaster and is familiar with the functional form and environmental assumptions of the model, any integrated spreadsheet could be utilized to generate similar forecasts, with graphical output. For the inexperienced forecaster, any of the major forecasting packages that are currently commercially available would be sufficient.

Statistical Analysis

My personal preferences for statistical analysis packages are SPSS/PC+ and SYSTAT. Both are relatively complete statistical analysis packages that can be used by novice marketing researchers and by experienced multivariate data crunchers.

SPSS/PC+ is the microcomputer version of the well-known mainframe version SPSSX. The complete system is distributed as three products: SPSS/PC+ Basic System; SPSS/PC+ Advanced Statistics; and SPSS/PC+ Tables. The base system would probably be sufficient for most marketing researchers because this package includes virtually all of the univariate statistics, including frequencies, cross-tabs, *t*-tests, ANOVA, correlation, regression, non-parametric analysis, etc., that are used in professional marketing research.

The Advanced Statistics module contains all of the multivariate statistical analyses that more advanced marketing researchers would want. This package contains an exceptionally good range of multivariate data analysis techniques and is definitely not recommended for the novice.

The Tables module is one that is highly recommended for two reasons. First, it allows the user to prepare presentation-level tables (see Table A1.1 for an example of the type and quality of table that can be produced directly by the SPSS/PC+ Tables program). In other words, you can format a variety of types of tables and print them directly as output from your analysis. This eliminates the need to have your tables keyboarded, saving time and eliminating extra work and the possibility of errors in the keyboarded tables. Another feature of the Tables module (which the manufacturer should have included in the Basic System) are the multiple variable response analyses. This technique, commonly used in marketing research, involves some very cumbersome methodology if one does not have the Tables module.

If one is familiar with any SPSS mainframe version, converting to SPSS/PC+ is quite easy and most enjoyable. The program can be run entirely interactively or entirely in batch mode, which affords the researcher complete flexibility. There is an excellent on-line help feature, as well as an extremely powerful full-screen text editor. The text editor allows one to edit program files from within the SPSS/PC+ system if an error is detected when running a program. It is a simple task to edit the line with the error and rerun the program from that point. This is a very handy feature.

It is impossible to highlight all of the excellent features of SPSS/PC+ here. It should suffice to say that if one is searching for a complete statistical package, you really need not look any further. One further note, if you are at all familiar with the mainframe version of the SPSS documentation, you will appreciate the micro-version documentation. It is extremely detailed and gives very good examples of how the programs can be utilized.

If there is one disadvantage of SPSS/PC+, it is that it requires a hard disk (minimum of 10 mg) and 384K RAM. If one wants to use the Tables module or some of the Advanced Statistics, 448K RAM is required. It is highly recommended that, if you should decide to use SPSS/PC+, you obtain a system with a 20-mg hard disk and 640K RAM. In addition, an 8087 math co-processor speeds up most statistical procedures significantly. One last item, the cost of SPSS/PC+, while reasonable for most professional marketing researchers, is currently approximately $1400.00 for the complete system.

SYSTAT, marketed and supported by Systat Inc., is another excellent alternative statistical package. It can perform all of the standard and more advanced statistical procedures that anyone (either novice or experienced) would need. It possesses many of the features of SPSS/PC+, including interactive or batch-processing mode, on-line editor (although not nearly as powerful as SPSS/PC+), on-line help, etc. SYSTAT, however, has two major advantages when compared with SPSS/PC+: it can be run on a two-floppy disk system, and it requires only 256K RAM. This, combined with its considerably lower price tag (currently about $495) is a big advantage.

However, one caution is necessary. Disk space is extremely important for SYSTAT. The size of the problem you can construct is dependent on the amount of disk space available. Thus, if you are analysing a data set with 75 variables and 2000 cases, you had better have a hard disk. While there is technically no limit on the number of cases, the limitation is the amount of disk space that you have.

TABLE A1.1
Sample Output Table Produced by SPSS/PC+ Tables Program

Question #3: How important is type of package in helping you to determine which brand to buy?

Importance	Total	Region					Income			Monthly Expenditure		
		ATL	QUE	ONT	PRA	BC	< 20K	20–39K	> 40K	<$2	$2–7	>$7
Total	1232 (100%)	110 (100%)	325 (100%)	506 (100%)	166 (100%)	125 (100%)	244 (100%)	384 (100%)	523 (100%)	381 (100%)	466 (100%)	165 (100%)
1-Unimportant	256 (20.8%)	22 (20.0%)	92 (28.3%)	95 (18.8%)	25 (15.1%)	22 (17.6%)	49 (20.1%)	87 (22.7%)	101 (19.3%)	8€ (22.6%)	83 (17.8%)	33 (20.0%)
2	70 (5.7%)	6 (5.5%)	11 (3.4%)	37 (7.3%)	10 (6.0%)	6 (4.8%)	14 (5.7%)	24 (6.3%)	29 (5.5%)	20 (5.2%)	26 (5.6%)	11 (6.7%)
3	62 (5.0%)	8 (7.3%)	17 (5.2%)	27 (5.3%)	7 (4.2%)	3 (2.4%)	13 (5.3%)	18 (4.7%)	28 (5.4%)	17 (4.5%)	25 (5.4%)	7 (4.2%)
4	290 (23.5%)	31 (28.2%)	66 (20.3%)	116 (22.9%)	44 (26.5%)	33 (26.4%)	53 (21.7%)	93 (24.2%)	129 (24.7%)	97 (25.5%)	100 (21.5%)	43 (26.1%)
5	230 (18.7%)	27 (24.5%)	47 (14.5%)	92 (18.2%)	35 (21.1%)	29 (23.2%)	46 (18.9%)	66 (17.2%)	107 (20.5%)	86 (22.6%)	89 (19.1%)	24 (14.5%)
6	163 (13.2%)	11 (10.0%)	33 (10.2%)	81 (16.0%)	23 (13.9%)	15 (12.0%)	32 (13.1%)	52 (13.5%)	69 (13.2%)	48 (12.6%)	75 (16.1%)	16 (9.7%)
7-Important	137 (11.1%)	5 (4.5%)	51 (15.7%)	49 (9.7%)	17 (10.2%)	15 (12.0%)	30 (12.3%)	36 (9.4%)	56 (10.7%)	24 (6.3%)	59 (12.7%)	26 (15.8%)
No Response	24 (1.9%)	—	8 (2.5%)	9 (1.8%)	5 (3.0%)	2 (1.6%)	7 (2.9%)	8 (2.1%)	4 (.8%)	3 (.8%)	9 (1.9%)	5 (3.0%)
Mean	4.0	3.8	3.8	4.0	4.2	4.2	4.1	3.9	4.0	3.8	4.2	4.0
S.D.	2.0	1.8	2.2	2.0	1.8	1.9	2.0	2.0	1.9	1.9	2.0	2.1
Valid(n)	1208	110	317	497	161	123	237	376	519	378	457	160

Values Range From: 1 = Very Unimportant to 7 = Very Important

NOTE: This table was created by the SPSS/PC+ Tables program and printed with an HP LASERJET.

A nasty characteristic of SYSTAT is the manner in which it displays its error messages. Should you encounter a disk space error message, you will be hard pressed to decipher the hex code format, and to worsen the experience, it ends the SYSTAT run and boots you back into DOS. However, at least at the time of writing, the man who wrote the programs is available for telephone consultation. I know this for a fact because I have called him and spoken to him. He knows his software very well. Aside from these rather technical issues, SYSTAT is a very professional and usable statistical analysis package.

Professional Cross-tabulation

Cross-tabulation is the major technique used in bivariate data analysis. It organizes data by groups, categories, or classes, which facilitates comparisons. Usually cross-tab programs generate a joint frequency distribution on two or more sets of variables. Many of the marketing research industry's most successful mainframe cross-tabulation programs are now available on microcomputer (IBM-PC/AT version). For example, UNCLE, which is one of the most powerful cross-tab programs, has the following features:

- a powerful report generator

- row, column, job, and session titles are available; most titles can be up to 999 characters

- options include titling, automatic dating and pagination, table numbers, display cell frequencies, vertical and horizontal percentages, and horizontal or vertical rank numbers in cells

- printing can be suppressed if cell counts are less than a specified n or between-specified values are encountered

- there are virtually unlimited report and data manipulation options

- "select if's," etc., are possible for respondent selection and screening

- a relatively full range of univariate statistics, including chi-square, means, medians, standard deviation and error, t-test

- the system accepts unlimited numbers of rows, titles, respondents, and data cards per respondent

These are but a few of the excellent features offered in the UNCLE system. The major drawbacks of UNCLE are the cost (roughly $4000 U.S.) and its appetite for memory (requires a 640K RAM system).

Management Science (Modelling)

More sophisticated applications in the area of marketing research involve marketing modelling or, as it has recently been called, marketing science. Using microcomputers, it is now possible to develop advertising models, consumer and industrial response functions, marketing effectiveness studies, salesperson and territory allocation models, advertising budgeting models, etc.[2]

■ Data Collection

CATI

Computer assisted telephone interviewing (CATI) has been around for a number of years. However, with the availability of microcomputers and easy telephone communication through modems, CATI is now available to more users. Some of the major advantages of this research technique are

- easy and automatic random respondent selection

- random rotation of either entire or partial sets of questions

- random rotation of possible answers

- automatic complex looping and branching (easy control of difficult skip patterns)

- automatically controlled callbacks

- up-to-the-minute tabulations of sample disposition

- up-to-the-minute tabulations of study findings

- reduced interviewing time

- less interviewer bias (as we currently understand it)

- fewer data entry errors and fewer data verification procedures

Interactive Data Collection

Some of the major problems associated with data collection are the artificiality of laboratory-type situations; the low response rates suffered by mail surveys; the obtrusiveness of, and sometimes the questionable results from, mall interviews; and the shallowness or limited nature of telephone interviewing.[3] The employment of a computer-based interactive approach can help solve some of these problems.

A quantitative questionnaire that consumers answer on a personal computer (or CRT attached to a local area network) can be utilized in a mall setting, giving researchers instant results. If quotas concerning the sample are required, the computer can immediately screen oversampling of specific segments. One of the greatest advantages of on-site computer interviewing is the immediacy with which results can be obtained. The Chevrolet Division of General Motors Corporation used to hire field interviewers to ask passersby about the new products it unveiled at auto shows. After the show, the interviewers, often unexperienced, would all bring their hundreds of completed forms to the central office, where the data would be coded, keyboarded, and processed. Two months later, the auto show results were available.[4] The problem was that the time delay would make it almost impossible for the automaker to implement the findings. Now IBM personal computers are used at the car shows to sample the opinions of the attendees. Results are available to management the next day. This is a great technological and practical advance.

The major advantages of on-site computer interviewing are

- quota controls

- alleviation of problems of
  —shortages of interviewers
  —interviewer training
  —interviewer bias

- complete data sets (no missing data)

- avoidance of illogical skip patterns, such as when a consumer responds *do not own a Brand X television*, and then proceeds to answer questions about his or her Brand X television

- data is immediately available for analysis (it does not have to be coded and entered, which reduces potential sources of error)

- easier response to sensitive questions (it is possible that consumers might respond more easily to sensitive questions with a CRT than with an individual)

Some disadvantages of on-site computer interviewing include

- people's fears, because this is a new technology

- open-ended questions cause a problem because consumers have to key in their answers, and not everyone is able to do this (some possible solutions include tape records or voice-activation devices)

The major current uses of on-site interactive interviewing are shopping mall surveys (replacing the traditional intercept) and trade shows, where there is high traffic and a more knowledgeable respondent.

Currently, certain marketing research firms are considering the use of small personal computers to interview professionals in their offices. The use of computers might reduce the potential for interview refusals. Pharmaceutical manufacturers are considering equipping their "detail men" with personal computers to enable them to present extremely professional-looking slide shows and graphical computer presentations. One of the additional advantages of this technology is consistency in the messages that are presented.

Data Manipulation

For those who analyse their own data, the ability to edit, view, clean, and transform the database is essential. This process is significantly easier on a microcomputer, as compared with the relatively outdated editors that are available on most mainframe computers. Personal Editor II (by IBM) is an example of a program that allows the user to easily clean data files. The ability to block off columns and to search for and replace strings within columns (as opposed to rows) is one of the most appreciated features. In addition, a compiler is available for microcomputers for virtually all languages that one would want to use to transform data files. For example, FORTRAN, C, APL, COBOL, PASCAL, and, of course, BASIC are just some of the compilers available for microcomputers.

■ Data Presentation

One of the most enjoyable features of the microcomputer revolution is the ability to develop graphics at one's desk. Programs such as ENERgraphics, 35-mm Express, and Harvard Graphics, as well as most integrated spreadsheets such as LOTUS 1-2-3 (Release 2) and the SMART system, all have the capability of developing tremendous graphic output. It is a relatively simple and quite inexpensive task to develop all types of business graphics. Not only can these graphics be seen on the screen, but also one can easily make paper copies on dot-matrix or laser printers, or plotters, or develop 35-mm slides or instant Polaroid pictures with equipment such as the Polaroid Palette. This instant desktop capability is a real advantage for the marketing researcher, who no longer has to wait one or two weeks for the return of graphic presentations from an outside graphics supplier. And the cost! For example, the average cost of having a 35-mm slide made is currently between $35 and $50. Once the equipment has been purchased (for around $2500), the cost of producing one Polaroid 35-mm slide is less than a dollar. This would amount to a significant saving in a very short period of time. Some examples of the type of graphs that can be generated relatively simply and quickly at the managing researcher's desk are illustrated in Figures A1.1 through A1.4.

Endnotes

1. Any software or hardware that is mentioned in this section is referred to for the purpose of providing examples of the type of software that is either currently available or will be available in the near future. These products are mentioned because the author has had experience (in most cases, positive) with them. This does not imply that other similar products are inferior, or that the publisher of this book or the other authors endorse these products.
2. For example, the Scientific Press has software specifically designed to help the marketing researcher develop the different models that are described in detail in Gary L. Lilien and Philip Kotler, *Marketing Decision-Making: A Model-Building Approach.* New York: Harper and Row, 1983.
3. For an interesting discussion of these issues, see Nancy Church, "Computer Interactive Data Collection Methodology: A Review and Preliminary Observations." *Marketing*, Proceedings of the 1985 ASAC Conference; and D. Rosen and R. Olshavsky, "Interactive Data Collection: Implications for Laboratory Research." Ed. J. Lindquist, *Proceedings of the Eighth Annual Conference of the Academy of Marketing Science*, 1984, pp. 82–86.
4. See Bernie Whalen, "On-Site Computer Interviewing Yields Research Data Instantly." *Marketing News*, vol. 18, no. 23, (Nov. 9, 1984).

FIGURE A1.1
Three-Dimensional Bar Graph

PHARMACEUTICAL MARKETING RESEARCH

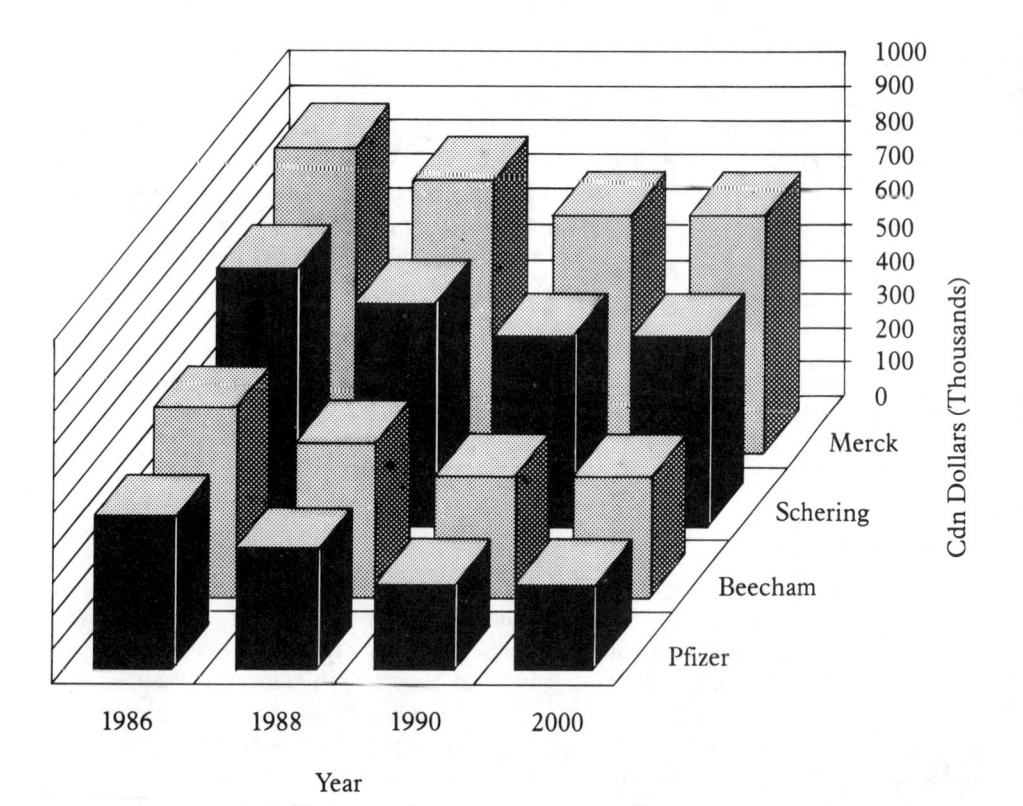

Note: This bar graph was created using ENERgraphics and the HP 7470A Plotter. The amount of time taken to input the data is less than two minutes; it takes approximately three to five minutes to plot the graph on paper or on an acetate.

FIGURE A1.2
Horizontal Bar Graph

PHARMACEUTICAL MARKETING RESEARCH

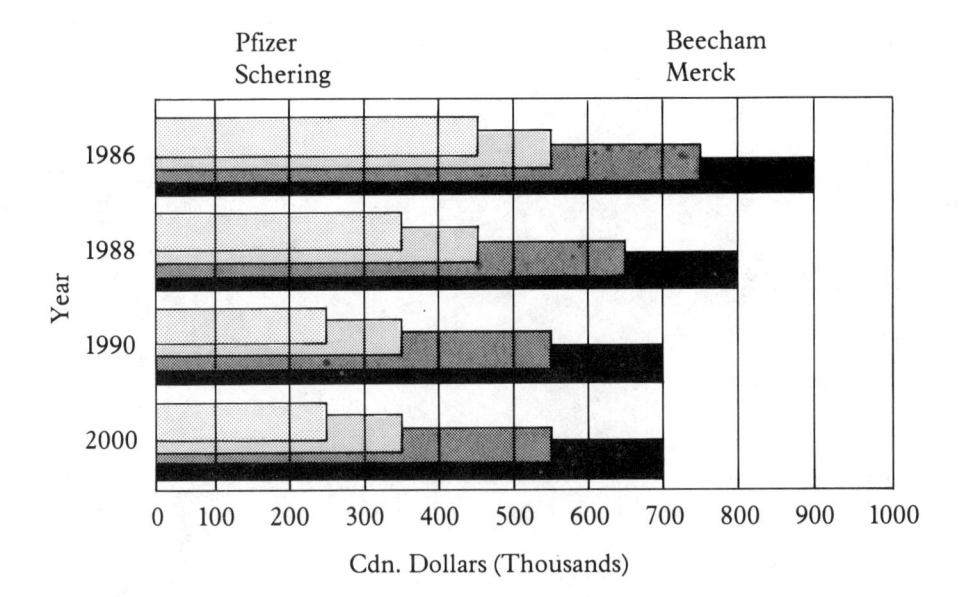

Note: This bar graph was created using ENERgraphics and the HP 7470A Plotter. The amount of time taken to input the data is less than two minutes; it takes approximately three to five minutes to plot the graph on paper or on an acetate.

FIGURE A1.3
Smoothed Line Graph

PHARMACEUTICAL MARKETING RESEARCH

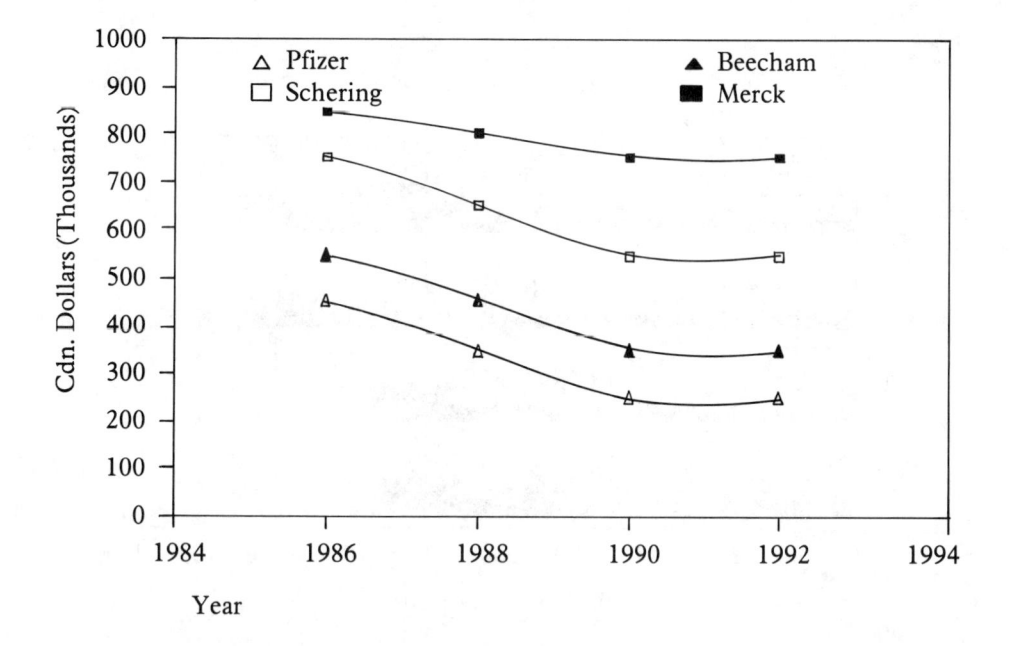

Note: This line graph was created using ENERgraphics and the HP 7470A Plotter. The amount of time taken to input the data is less than two minutes; it takes approximately three to five minutes to plot the graph on paper or on an acetate.

FIGURE A1.4
Reduced Graphs, All Placed On One Sheet

PHARMACEUTICAL MARKETING RESEARCH

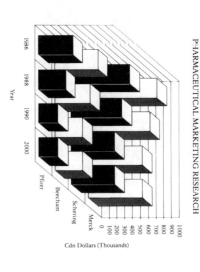

PHARMACEUTICAL MARKETING RESEARCH

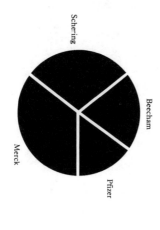

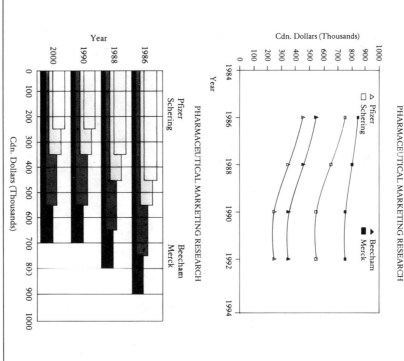

PHARMACEUTICAL MARKETING RESEARCH

PHARMACEUTICAL MARKETING RESEARCH

Note: Each graph was created using ENERgraphics and the HP 7470A Plotter. The amount of time taken to input the data is less than two minutes per chart; it takes approximately three to five minutes to plot each graph on paper or on an acetate.

ETHICAL ISSUES IN MARKETING RESEARCH IN CANADA

Marketing research is concerned with obtaining information relevant to the solving of marketing problems. In doing so, survey firms or research departments deal with clients, competitors, and respondents, as indicated in Figure A2.1. Some potential for abuse is present in each area of interaction, raising concern among practitioners and regulatory bodies as to what is ethical: What kind of *right* conduct is expected from professionals?

FIGURE A2.1
Major Areas of Ethical Responsibilities of a Survey Firm

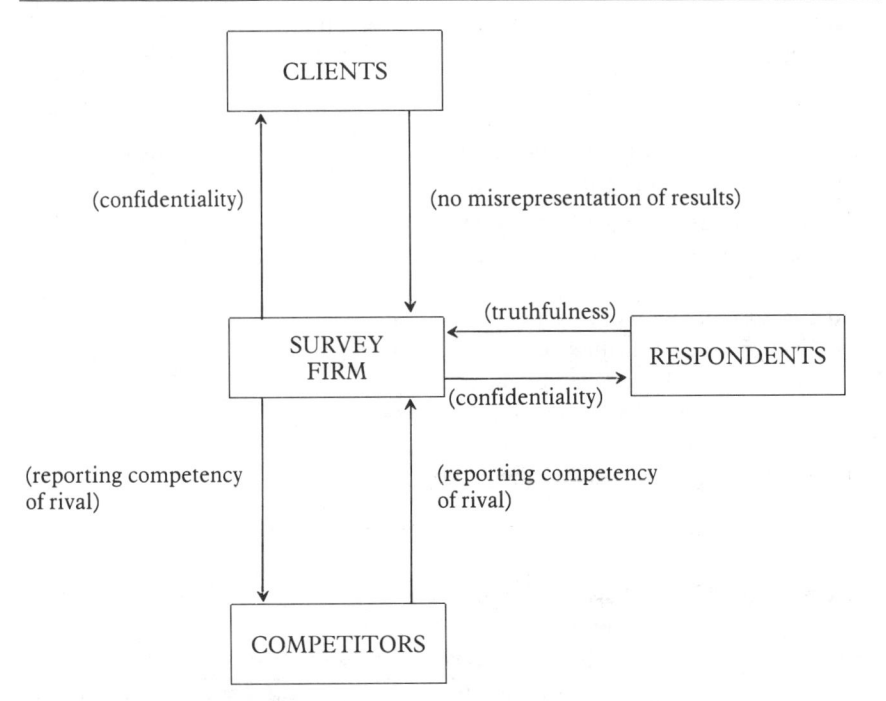

To answer this question, some associations have published guidelines about what constitutes an ethical research practice, sometimes with some enforcement provisions. At the end of this appendix the *Rules of Conduct and Good Practice* of the Professional Marketing Research Society (PMRS) and the *Abridged Standards* of the Canadian Association of Marketing Research Organizations (CAMRO) have been reproduced. A comparative analysis of the codes of ethics of the three major associations of interest to Canadian researchers[1] is provided in Table A2.1. This table shows that none of the three codes is complete. However, the four elements common to all of these associations are research integrity and competence; full, open disclosure of methods; confidentiality to clients; and confidentiality to respondents.

TABLE A2.1
Abstracts of Codes of Ethics of the Three Major Research Associations

Relationships and Ethical Elements	AMA	PMRS	CAMRO
Research Group to Clients			
Research integrity, competence	X	X	X
Full, open disclosure of methods	X	X	X
Validation of work		X	X
Confidentiality	X	X	X
Revealing fact that study is syndicated or omnibus		X	
Research Group to Respondents			
Fairness, protection of rights (no harm, harassment, invasion of privacy, loss of dignity)		X	X
Confidentiality (identity, individual response)	X	X	X
No audio or visual recording without awareness			X
Openness, honesty, no misrepresentation	X	X	
Client to Research Group			
Revealing of presence of competition for project		X	X
Where competitive, client preliminary reaction to proposal			X
No misrepresentation of results	X		
No dissemination of results outside client group without research group approval		X	X
Revealing of full background and problem of study to research group			X
Study design elements remain the property of research group	X	X	

Key:
AMA: American Marketing Association
PMRS: Professional Marketing Research Society
CAMRO: Canadian Association of Marketing Research Organizations

Source: Adapted from R.W. Crosby and A.B. Blankenship, "Some Ethical Considerations Between Buyers and Sellers of Research." *PMRS Journal* (November 1982), p. 3.

■ Attitudes and Behaviour of Commercial Marketing Research Executives in Canada

A recent study shed some light on the reported behaviour of research executives in Canada.[2] Some of the major findings of this study are summarized below.

Ethical Issues Involving Client-initiated Practices

Seven research practices were related to the protection of individual researchers and research organizations from the abuses of others, particularly clients. The perceptions of the frequency of client-initiated abuses are summarized in Table A2.2. Although most of these practices are dealt with in the ethical codes, high estimates were attached to the perceived frequency of occurrence of most. In four out of the seven practices, more than 71% of the subjects perceived that these practices occurred at least occasionally. The most frequently perceived client-initiated abuse was "having researchers bid on projects they really have no chance of securing, for purely technical compliance with a company's purchasing policy of obtaining competitive bids for proposed studies." Of the subjects surveyed, 85% perceived that this situation occurred at least occasionally; 38% perceived that it occurred fairly often, and 14% perceived that it occurred very often.

TABLE A2.2
Perceptions of Frequency of Client-initiated Abuse

Survey Question	Never (%)	Rarely (%)	Occasionally (%)	Fairly often (%)	Very often (%)	Regularly (%)
How frequently or infrequently are research proposals solicited from several firms, only to have the best features of each combined into the one actually performed by the low bidder or by an in-house research department?	0	29	53	12	6	0
How frequently or infrequently are researchers asked to bid on projects they really have no chance of securing, but are asked to do so for purely technical compliance with a company's purchasing policy of obtaining competitive bids for proposed studies?	0	15	32	38	14	1

TABLE A2.2 (continued)
Perceptions of Frequency of Client-initiated Abuse

Survey Question	Never (%)	Rarely (%)	Occasionally (%)	Fairly often (%)	Very often (%)	Regularly (%)
How frequently or infrequently do clients approach research organizations on a full proposal basis when there is no reasonable probability that the project under consideration will actually be commissioned?	0	45	40	13	1	1
How frequently or infrequently is a phony marketing research approach used in order to help sell products door to door or over the telephone?	7	22	38	15	9	9
How frequently or infrequently are research proposals solicited from several firms, where the client's sole purpose is to generate ideas, with no intention of accepting any of them?	6	53	26	6	8	1
How frequently or infrequently are research proposals evaluated solely on their merit, unless other criteria (size and/or special capabilities of the research firm) are made known in advance?	4	14	29	27	26	0
How frequently or infrequently do clients knowingly portray research findings in a biased or distorted fashion when publishing them?	0	39	46	8	7	0

Unethical Research Practices Involving Respondents

Several ethical issues involve the protection of respondents from abuses by the individual researcher or research organization. These results are presented in Table A2.3. From this table it is evident that, for every practice, the number of

TABLE A2.3
Unethical Research Practices Involving Protection of Respondents

Research Practice	Approved of the practice (%)	Agreed it is a common industry practice (%)	Actually confronted with the practice (%)
Using one-way observation mirrors or hidden TV cameras without the prior consent of those being observed.	7	20	29
Using hidden coding systems to identify individuals responding to a mail survey that purports, or appears, to call for anonymous responses.	20	33	46
Using concealed tape recorders to record face-to-face personal interviews (or phone conversations) without the prior consent of those being interviewed.	5	19	32
Misleading prospective respondents as to the approximate duration of an interview in order to secure their co-operation and minimize overall refusal rates.	32	72	76
Complying with a client's request to hand over the original data collection forms used in a study, including the names and addresses of respondents, even though respondents had been led to believe that their anonymity would be protected.	8	31	63
Promising respondents a report of the completed results of the study in which they participated but not following through.	0	20	29
Not forewarning respondents of the possibility that follow-up contacts for further research or verification purposes will be made.	37	56	56

subjects who agreed that it was a common industry practice was larger than the number of subjects who approved of the practice.

Only one research practice was disapproved of by 100% of the subjects. That practice was "promising respondents a report of the completed results of the study in which they participated, but not following through." This practice was also perceived to be less common in industry practice than several of the other items: only 20% agreed that it was a common industry practice.

The practice of which most subjects (37%) approved was "not forewarning respondents of the possibility that follow-up contacts for further research or verification purposes will be made." This was followed closely (32% approved) by the approval of "misleading prospective respondents as to the approximate duration of an interview in order to secure their co-operation and minimize overall refusal rates." These two practices, which involved deception of respondents, were also perceived by the largest number of subjects to be common industry practices; 56% agreed with the former and 72% agreed with the latter.

As shown in Table A2.3, the number of subjects who had been confronted with the decision of whether or not to engage in an unethical practice ranged from 29% to 76% across the various items. Of the subjects, 76% were confronted with the practice of misleading prospective respondents as to the approximate length of an interview; 56% were confronted with not forewarning respondents of the possibility of follow-up contacts; and 63% were confronted with complying with a client's request to hand over data, including the name and address of the respondents, even though respondents had been led to believe that their anonymity would be protected. The frequency of actual engagement in the unethical practice by those who had been confronted with making a decision is presented in Table A2.4.

The practice that was most frequently confronted (by 76% of subjects) and that was also most frequently followed was misleading prospective respondents as to the approximate length of the interview. Many of the 32 subjects (86% of those who had been confronted with the decision) who had actually engaged in this practice qualified their participation in the practice in the following ways:

- But not by more than five minutes or so.

- People usually are not in as much of a hurry as they think, especially if the questions are interesting.

- Rarely, and only because it is often the case that once involved in the survey, the respondents enjoy the interview and the time passes quickly.

- Respondents were misled unintentionally. We found that our questionnaire time depended too much on the speed of the respondent. Usually our questionnaires were too long.

The research practices in which least participation was shown for subjects who had been confronted with the decision were using one-way observation mirrors or hidden television cameras without prior consent (29%); using concealed tape recorders without prior consent (29%); complying with a client's request to hand over original data (26%); and promising respondents a report of the completed results but not following through (38%).

TABLE A2.4
Unethical Research Practices Involving Protection
of Respondents: Frequency of Actual Behaviour

Survey Question	Never (%)	Rarely (%)	Occa-sionally (%)	Often (%)	Fairly Often (%)	Very Regularly (%)
Using one-way observation mirrors or hidden TV cameras without the prior consent of those being observed.	71	19	5	0	0	5
Using hidden coding systems to identify individuals responding to a mail survey that purports, or appears, to call for anonymous responses.	50	15	23	6	3	3
Using concealed tape recorders to record face-to-face personal interviews (or phone conversations) without the prior consent of those being interviewed.	71	13	13	0	3	0
Misleading prospective respondents as to the approximate duration of an interview to secure their co-operation and to minimize overall refusal rates.	14	30	40	14	2	0
Complying with a client's request to hand over the original data collection forms used in a study, including the names and addresses of respondents, even though respondents had been led to believe that their anonymity would be protected.	75	15	10	0	0	0
Promising respondents a report of the completed results of the study in which they participated, but not following through.	62	28	5	0	0	5
Not forewarning respondents of the possibility that follow-up contacts for further research or verification purposes will be made.	24	24	23	17	5	7

■ The Bottom Line

The discrepancy between personal approval and perception of common industry practice implies that individuals perceive themselves to have higher ethical standards than their colleagues in the field of marketing research. Ethical behaviour obviously involves personal convictions about the morality of a particular practice.

The curbing of client-initiated abuse is a difficult matter, primarily because clients are not necessarily bound by the same ethical code as is the marketing researcher. Several people have suggested that such abuse could be curbed somewhat by researchers requesting payment for the preparation of research proposals.[3] Despite the fact that both CAMRO and PMRS standards have provisions for levying such a fee, the majority of researchers sampled have not instituted this business practice because they are afraid that they might lose business to researchers who do not charge a fee for this.

The finding that researchers approve *more* of unethical practices involving the protection of respondents than they do of unethical practices involving clients is not only disturbing but of great practical significance.

Although the frequency of actual engagement in unethical practices involving deception or invasion of respondents' rights was small, it nevertheless warrants attention. Protecting the rights of respondents is a major concern of both CAMRO and PMRS and specific provisions are provided for this purpose, because possibly even one ethical transgression could damage the reputation of the marketing research industry in general.

Endnotes

1. R.W. Crosby and A.B. Blankenship, "Some Ethical Considerations Between Buyers and Sellers of Research." *PMRS Journal* (November 1982), pp. 1–8.
2. Michel Laroche, K.L. McGown, and Joyce Rainville, "How Ethical Are Professional Marketing Researchers?" *Business Forum* (Winter 1986) pp. 20–25.)
3. R. Bezilla and J.B. Haynes, "Ethics in Marketing Research." *Business Horizons* (April 1976), 19, pp. 83–86.

PROFESSIONAL MARKETING RESEARCH SOCIETY

■ Rules of Conduct and Good Practice (1984)

■ Introduction

This document is currently divided into two chapters: Chapter A—For The General Professional Marketing Research Society Membership and Chapter B— For The Qualitative Research Division Membership. Within each chapter are a number of sections and each section may include two types of statements:

1. *Rules of Conduct* are considered mandatory; their violation could result in disciplinary action on the part of the Society as per the Constitution.

2. *Good Practice* guidelines represent an *ideal* toward which members should strive.

In the reading of this document, and for all purposes thereof, all references to and use of the masculine gender shall be deemed to be references to and use of the feminine gender where appropriate in the course of the affairs of the Society.

The acceptance of marketing and social "research"* as a reliable source of information and, hence, its growth as a profession, depends upon the confidence of the business community and the public in the integrity of those professionally engaged in this type of work.

Membership in the Professional Marketing Research Society (P.M.R.S.) implies acceptance of—Chapter A Rules of Conduct and Good Practice, and membership in the Qualitative Research Division implies acceptance of both Chapter A and B. *Members of the Society undertake to refrain from any activity likely to impair confidence in marketing research in general and to comply with whatever general professional practices may be laid down from time to time by the Society.*

■ A) For the General P.M.R.S. Membership

I. The Responsibility of the Members to the Public

Most marketing research depends on the co-operation of "respondents"* either in their personal or in their business capacity. Marketing researchers, therefore, have a direct responsibility to ensure that respondents are in no way embarrassed or

*See Appendix for definitions.

hindered in other ways as a result of any "interview"*. The purpose of interviewing respondents shall be limited to the finding out of information or observation of reactions relevant to the research problem at hand. Every possible attempt should be made by members to ensure a continuing climate of goodwill, responsibility and trust. A meticulous standard of good manners with respondents should be maintained and everything should be done to leave respondents positively disposed to marketing research.

Rules of Conduct

1.1　Interviewing may not be used as a disguise for selling or developing sales leads, nor for deliberately influencing the opinions of those interviewed.

1.2　Any statement or assurance given to a respondent in order to obtain co-operation shall be factually correct and honoured.

1.3　No procedure or technique shall be used in which the respondent is put in such a position that they cannot exercise their right to withdraw or refuse to answer at *any stage* during or after the interview. Any request of the respondent to terminate the interview must be granted and, if he so requests, any information already given must be deleted.

1.4　The interviewer should explain to all respondents at the commencement of the interview, when applicable, the presence and purpose of any 1-way mirror or audio/visual monitoring equipment.

1.5　The identity of individual respondents shall not be revealed by the "practitioner"* to the "client"* or anyone other than persons belonging to the organization of the practitioner concerned (either by supplying lists of individual respondents or by passing on answers to questions linked to the names of the individual respondents even when the client has supplied the original list of potential respondents) and members are entitled to give respondents such an assurance.

Exceptions to the aforesaid rule may be made in the following instances:

i) if the consent of respondents has been obtained before revealing their names to the client,

ii) if disclosure of these names is essential for the data processing, for verification of the original research, or to carry out further research. In such instances, however, the practitioner responsible for the original interview must insist that all the Rules of Conduct in this document are observed by all parties involved, via appropriate instructions in writing.

1.6　Interviewers must carry with them identification from the organization they represent for all face-to-face interviewing. Interviewers must identify themselves by name and organization in an introductory statement on *all* interviews. If requested by the respondent, the interviewer should provide the name, address and/or telephone number of the organization they

*See Appendix for definitions.

represent. This information should be clearly indicated on any question-naire handed out to respondents.

1.7   No respondent should be pressured into testing products which he does not want to try. Product information such as ingredient lists and instructions including the name, address and/or telephone number of the practitioner should be available where possible.

1.8   Before children under the age of 12 are *interviewed*, or asked to complete a questionnaire, the permission of a parent, guardian, or other person respon-sible for them, such as a teacher, shall be obtained. In obtaining this permission the interviewer shall allow the responsible person to see or hear the questions which will be asked or, if this is not practical, shall describe the nature of the *interview* in sufficient detail to enable a reasonable person to reach an informed decision, e.g. not only should the subject matter of the *interview* be described, but any sensitive, embarrassing or complex ques-tions should also be brought to the attention of the responsible person.

1.9   If computerized telephone interviewing techniques (e.g. collecting data or conducting an interview via taped message with no human interviewer) are employed, the type of machinery that automatically disconnects or "frees the line" when the respondent hangs up the phone, must be used.

Good Practice

1.10   A potential respondent who has initially refused to take part in a study should not be contacted for the same study on more than one subsequent occasion in person or by telephone. Any second call should be conducted by a specially trained interviewer or (field) supervisor (i.e. *not* the original interviewer).

1.11   It should be recognized that when communicating with any member of the public it is important that the materials used are appropriate in terms of content and wording to that particular public.

1.12   "Overly-long questionnaires"* should be avoided at all costs. If the respond-ent asks, interviewers should indicate to the respondent a reasonably accurate estimate of the duration of the interview. When appropriate interviewers should make appointments for interviews in advance when interviewing representatives of companies or other organizations.

1.13   The practitioner should inform the local authorities (e.g. police, security, etc.) before carrying out interviews under circumstances or about topics which might make the public suspicious or cause them to report the interviewer's activities.

1.14   If a respondent is interviewed as part of a study, the practitioner should not deliberately seek an additional interview with this specific respondent unless re-interviewing is required by the study's design or unless the

*See Appendix for definitions.

respondent's permission was obtained during the initial interview (and each subsequent interview).

1.15   Incentives should be avoided where possible for quantitative studies. Even when incentives are used, they should be offered as a small token of appreciation (e.g. lottery tickets and small gift items).

1.16   When interviewing 12 to 15 year old respondents discretion should be used when addressing sensitive subject matter or information (e.g. delete "household income" question, etc.)

II. The Responsibility of Clients to Practitioners

Rules of Conduct

2.1   In some instances potential clients ask for competitive bids from two or more practitioners, and when properly done, such practice is completely within the Rules of Conduct. However, certain conditions are essential to meet the standards of proper practice. These include:

i) Whenever a client asks more than one practitioner for a "proposal"* or "cost estimate"*, this fact and the number of proposals or cost estimates being requested must be communicated to the practitioners concerned. For any study, *the practitioner is then entitled to indicate in advance that he will request payment for the cost of preparing such a proposal or cost estimate.*

ii) During and following the proposal or cost estimate process, both the client and the practitioner must respect the confidentiality of each party's technical input or ideas. Specifically, in a competitive situation, no unique technique or idea included in a practitioner's proposal may be used by the prospective client in conjunction with another practitioner unless an appropriate payment has been made. (See 2.1 i) above.) Additionally, in a competitive situation, all unaccepted proposals in whole or in part remain exclusively the property of the originating practitioner unless an appropriate charge has been made. (See 2.1 i) above.) Conversely, no unique technique or idea included in a prospective client's specifications during the proposal or cost estimate process may be offered to other prospective clients by the practitioner without the originating client's approval.

2.2   Reports provided by a practitioner are the property of the client and are normally for the use within the client company or associated companies (including the client's agents). If a wider circulation of the results of the study, either in whole or in part is intended, the following minimum standards of disclosure should be adhered to in order that there will be an adequate basis for judging the reliability and validity of the results reported:

i) The client should ensure that dissemination of the study findings will not give rise to misleading interpretations and that the study findings will not be quoted out of their normal context.

*See Appendix for definitions.

ii) If a practitioner's name is to be used he must be consulted prior to dissemination of findings and is entitled to refuse permission for its name to be used in connection with the study until the practitioner has approved the exact form and contents of the dissemination.

iii) For all reports of survey findings the client has released to the public, the client must be prepared to release the following details on request: sponsorship of the survey; dates of interviewing; methods of obtaining the interviews (in-home, telephone or mail); population that was sampled; size of sample; size and description of the sub-sample, if the survey report relies primarily on less than the total sample; exact wording of questions upon which the release is based, an indication of what allowance should be made for sampling error; and the percentage upon which conclusions are based.

2.3   Unless otherwise agreed and provided that the practitioner has followed the stipulated procedures and all reasonable precautions have been taken, the client is responsible for any damages sought by the public as a result of using any product or material supplied by the client. Additionally, when testing products or materials, proper usage instructions will be provided by the client and any cautions necessary for normal sale, must be highlighted (e.g. possible allergic reactions) and a listing of ingredients will be made available by the client where it is appropriate.

Good Practice

2.4   Clients have a responsibility to provide practitioners with enough information about a project for the latter to do a professional job. Specifically, clients should provide insight, preferably in writing, into the following areas:

i) A statement of the research problem or, if unable to define the research problem, a perspective on the problem in terms of its general background.

ii) A statement of the type of decision(s) that is likely to be influenced by the research results or the uses to which the research results will be applied.

iii) A broad indication of the budget available.

2.5   When requesting proposals some indication should be provided as to how the successful proposal will be determined. Factors which might be used to determine the organization selected could include:

i) Innovative approaches to solving the problem under review.

ii) Ability to provide the necessary information gathering and analysis resources—personnel, facilities, equipment, etc

iii) Relevant experience of the research firm.

iv) Background/experience of individuals to be assigned to the work.

v) Recognition of the limitations of the research.

vi) Cost.

2.6　Clients should provide a prompt notification to all proposers once a selection has been made on a proposal or cost estimate.

2.7　Clients should only request a reasonable number of competitive proposals or cost estimates (e.g. 2 to 4) on any given project.

2.8　Clients should not assume that the contingency cost range included in some research proposals or cost estimates (e.g. +/– X%) may be applied to changes in the research specifications. Changes in specifications may be justification for revising the original estimate.

III.　The Responsibility of Practitioners to Clients

Rules of Conduct

3.1　Research specifications, such as background, objectives and technical approaches or ideas, provided by a client or potential client remain the property of the client and contents may not be revealed to third parties without the client's permission. (See Section 2.1)

3.2　Unless authorized by the client, the practitioner will not reveal to respondents, interviewers or any other person not directly concerned with the study, the identity of the client, including the fact that he had undertaken or considered undertaking research in a particular area, confidential material relating to the study or the results of any study commissioned exclusively for that client.

3.3　If any aspect of a project is to be sub-contracted to another practitioner, the originating practitioner is obliged to inform the client before committing to the project.

3.4　When the same project is carried out on behalf of more than one client or two or more projects are combined in one interview, the practitioner is obliged to inform each client concerned that another client exists and to inform each client of the *generic* subjects addressed by the other client's project before the client commits to the project.

3.5　"Primary"* and "secondary"* "records"* are the property of the practitioner. The practitioner is entitled to destroy primary records 1 year from the end of the fieldwork (providing secondary records are adequate to enable reconstruction of the results) and to destroy secondary records 2 years from the end of the fieldwork without reference to the client. The preferred method of destruction is shredding on premises. If the client wishes exceptions to this, he must make special arrangements with the practitioner. The practitioner must provide reasonable access for the client on non-syndicated studies, to the completed questionnaires or data forms, cards/tapes provided the client bears the reasonable cost of preparing any duplicates or masking individual identity.

*See Appendix for definitions.

3.6   Unless otherwise specifically made clear that this practice will not be followed, the practitioner will automatically "verify"* or "monitor"* a minimum of 10% of each interviewer's completed interviews.

The practitioner will inform the client, prior to commencement of the study, the proposed nature of the verification* or monitoring* including the proportion of each interviewer's interviews to be covered. Upon request from the client, the practitioner is obliged to disclose the results of the verification. If verification of an interviewer's completed interviews suggests problems, verification must be done until there is firm evidence of either valid or invalid work. If the interviews appear to be invalid, 100% of the interviewer's interviews must be either rejected or replaced. In this case, the practitioner is obliged to inform the client immediately of these problems with verification.

3.7   For each survey, a practitioner will provide the following information, where applicable, to the client (either in a report or in supporting documentation if a formal report is not being prepared):

i) Copy of questionnaire, interviewers' instructions and visual exhibits.

ii) The name of organization for which the study was conducted and name of organization conducting it, including sub-contractors.

iii) The specific objectives of the study.

iv) The dates on or between which the fieldwork was done and the time periods of interviewing.

v) The universe covered (intended and actual) including details of the sampling method and selection procedures.

vi) The size and nature of the sample and details of any weighting methods used.

vii) The contact record based on the last attempt to obtain an interview, with the exception of mall surveys and quota samples where it is not appropriate.

viii) The method of recruitment when prior recruitment of respondents is undertaken.

ix) The method of field briefing sessions.

x) Weighted and unweighted bases for all conventional tables, clearly distinguishing between the two.

xi) A statement of response rates, how they were calculated, and a discussion of possible bias due to non-response.

xii) The method by which the information was collected e.g. mall intercept, telephone, etc.

*See Appendix for definitions.

xiii) The details of any incentives provided to respondents.

xiv) Sources of desk research.

xv) An adequate description of verification or monitoring procedures and results of the same.

xvi) The detail of any special statistical methods used in the analysis of the results.

3.8   The practitioner will limit the information supplied to prospective clients regarding their experience, capacities and organization to a factual and objective description.

3.9   When changes are made to the specifications of a study by either the practitioner or the client, the practitioner should inform the client of any fee changes at the time the specifications are revised.

3.10 A practitioner will conduct a study in the manner agreed upon. However, if it becomes apparent in the course of a study that changes in the plans should be made, the practitioner is obliged to make his views (including cost estimates) known to the client immediately.

3.11 A practitioner is obliged to allow clients to verify that work performed meets all contracted specifications and to examine and be present at all operations of the practitioner's organization relevant to the execution of the study.

Good Practice

3.12 The practitioner should make known any current involvement in the same general subject area before accepting a project. However, exclusive use of a practitioner over a given time period may be established only by special arrangements between client and practitioner.

3.13 When reporting findings of a study in either written or oral form, the practitioner should make a clear distinction between the objective results and their own opinions and recommendations.

3.14 The practitioner should provide to the client in the report, or a supporting document to fieldwork, tables, etc., in addition to the items listed in 3.7.

i) A discussion of any aspects of the research which may bias the results.

ii) An assessment of the reliability of the sources used in desk research.

iii) The name(s) of the individual(s) responsible for the study and report.

iv) A list of sampling points used in the study (upon request).

3.15 The practitioner will assist the client in the design and execution of effective and efficient studies. If the practitioner questions whether a study design will provide the necessary information, the practitioner should make his own reservations known.

3.16 During and following the proposal or cost estimate process, cost quotations may be made public without the practitioner's permission, as long as an individual quotation cannot be associated with a given practitioner.

3.17 A practitioner will not use the names of clients in promotional material without the express permission of the client.

IV. General Rules of Practice for Members

Rules of Conduct

4.1 Members shall not try to turn to account or to use the fact of their membership in P.M.R.S. as evidence of particular professional competence, except insofar as membership implies the member subscribes to the Rules of Conduct and Good Practice.

Unless authorized by the executive, members, when talking to the "press" or media representatives, should request that their membership in P.M.R.S. not be included in any subsequent articles or media reports to avoid their personal views or options being confused with those of P.M.R.S.

4.2 Members recognize that marketing and social research is more an art than a science. It therefore follows that what is practical, sound and useful to clients is frequently more a matter of judgment than of definite rules and regulations.

It is because such judgment follows from experience within the field that members of the Society believe they have a responsibility to their respective clients and management to point out the limitations of marketing research as appropriate.

Members of the Society will do everything possible to extend and maximize the use of marketing and social research. They will also discourage research which, in their best judgment, is considered inadequate, inappropriate or subject to providing misleading information for the problem at hand.

4.3 Members commissioning market or social research work with a practitioner known not to be bound by these Rules of Conduct and Good Practice, shall ensure that the practitioner is familiar with its content and agrees in writing to abide by them.

Good Practice

4.4 When considering interviews with small populations that are likely to be of interest to other researchers, members should be especially careful to minimize the total number of interviews conducted to avoid "over research- ing" such populations. For the same reason, members interested in such populations should attempt to undertake syndicated research projects within those populations.

■ B) For the Qualitative Research Division Membership

V. Responsibility to the Public

Rules of Conduct

5.1   Any statement or assurance given to a respondent in order to obtain co-operation shall be factually correct and honoured.

5.2   The respondent shall be allowed to remain anonymous or, in special circumstances where this is not possible, the respondent should be informed, when being recruited, that his responses may not be anonymous.

5.3   Qualitative interviews must not be used for selling or developing sales leads and, for this reason, surnames and/or addresses and telephone numbers may not be supplied to the client. The interview itself should not be used by the client to deliberately try to influence the opinions of those interviewed.

5.4   Most marketing research depends upon the co-operation of respondents. All persons involved in a qualitative research project, therefore, have a direct responsibility to ensure that respondents or potential respondents are not embarassed in any way.

5.5   Members must not harass, badger, grill or belittle any member of the public either while trying to recruit for or during the conducting of any qualitative study. Clearly, behaviour cannot be precisely defined but sincere and consistent efforts to show respect to the respondents are, nevertheless, a mandatory requirement of the Society's Rules of Conduct and Good Practice.

5.6   The respondent's right to withdraw, or to refuse to co-operate at any stage, shall be respected.

5.7   The *moderator* must explain to all respondents at the commencement of the interview (group or individual in-depth), where appropriate,

i) the presence and purpose of the 1-way mirror;

ii) the presence and purpose of the video-camera;

iii) the presence and purpose of the tape recorder;

iv) the confidentiality of the respondents' names and addresses.

Good Practice

In conjunction with the above Rules of Conduct:

5.8   The *client* has a particular responsibility to ensure that the moderator does not (or is not asked to) exceed "acceptable" limits or "harassment" of respondents. The client has an equal responsibility for their own attitude and behaviour (and that of other persons present at the invitation of the client), not only in front of the respondent but also when watching the interview in a separate location. In addition, if exposed to the respondent, the client should be careful not to introduce unsuitable bias by their reactions or comments.

5.9 It is the responsibility of the recruiter to ensure that the respondent is properly qualified for inclusion in the study. Recruiters also have a responsibility to explain to participants in the study exactly what is expected of them: for example, the importance of punctuality, the likely full length of the interview period, the date, time and exact location (with details of parking, nearest public transit stop, etc.), whether they will be asked to taste food or beverages, the payment (and any associated terms), whether or not smoking will be allowed during the group. It is a good idea if this information is confirmed in writing or through a follow-up, reminder telephone call.

5.10 The moderator has a responsibility to keep the session within the time limits specified to respondents on the occasion of their recruitment.

The moderator also has the responsibility of ensuring that all respondents have an equal opportunity to participate in the discussion. If the offensive language or behavior of one respondent inhibits other respondents from fully participating, the moderator may have to ask the offending participant to leave.

5.11 No respondent should be pressured into taste testing any products which he does not want to try. Ingredient lists should be available if requested.

5.12 The issue of payment to participants who arrive too late to be included in the discussion should be clarified by recruiter, moderator and/or client prior to commencement of the study. Since the fault is often not solely that of the respondent, it is suggested that some payment should always be made. (How much and who actually picks up that cost is a matter for negotiation between parties involved; it is suggested that at least half the promised amount be paid.)

VI. Other Responsibilities of the Recruiter

Rules of Conduct

6.1 The following Rules of Conduct are assumed to be *in operation* for any qualitative research undertaken by: members of QRD, unless changes to any or all of the Rules have *been discussed and agreed to by all parties involved in the research study*.

i) All respondents must meet usage/trial/ownership standards including type of brand, frequency of use/trial or other time limits specified for the study.

ii) All respondents must meet demographic specifications for the study, including marital status, age, sex, income, occupation, household composition, etc.

iii) No respondents (nor anyone in their immediate families or households) may *work* in an occupation that has anything to do with the topic area (whether wholesale, retail, sales, service or consultant) nor in advertising, marketing, marketing research, public relations or the media (radio, television, newspaper, etc.) nor *may respondents themselves ever have worked in such occupations.*

iv) No respondent may be recruited who has attended, *in the past five years*, a focus group discussion or in-depth interview on the *same general topic* as defined by the moderator.

v) No respondents should be recruited who *know each other* for the same study, unless they are in *different groups, or interviews, that are scheduled back-to-back.*

vi) No respondent may be recruited who has attended a group discussion or in-depth interview *within the past year*.

vii) No respondent may be recruited who has attended *five or more* focus groups or in-depth interviews ever, *unless he/she has not attended a group discussion/in-depth interview in the past five years.*

viii) At least *one half* of the respondents recruited for each group/study involving in-depth interviews must never have attended a group discussion or in-depth interview before.

ix) All respondents must have been living in the specified market area for at least the past two years.

x) All respondents must be able to speak and read in the language of the group or study being conducted.

Good Practice

6.2   Before accepting a project, it is important that the recruiter clearly understands the moderator's (or client's) specifications; the recruiter has a responsibility to query any points of confusion and to highlight potential problems.

Once accepted, instructions should be followed explicitly. No changes to the agreed upon questionnaire should be made without prior approval from the moderator or client. Any information given to respondents (for example, the topic, whether there will be taste testing, etc.) must have been approved beforehand.

If problems in recruiting arise, the moderator (or client) should be advised immediately.

6.3   Recruiters have a responsibility to make every effort to ensure that all recruited respondents comply with specifications detailed for the project and that they turn up at the correct place, at the right time, being fully aware of what is expected of them. Confirmatory/reminder re-screening should, where possible, be conducted by someone other than the original recruiter.

Screening questionnaires used in the recruitment should be made available to the moderator in advance of the research sessions.

VII. Other Responsibilities of the Moderator

A) To the Recruiter

Rules of Conduct

7.1 To protect the respondents, persons recruited for a specific study should be used by the moderator only for that study and not be recalled to participate in another qualitative study without permission of the initial recruiter.

Good Practice

7.2 The moderator should clearly define (preferably in writing) the complete specifications for the study to the recruiter (e.g. specific usage/trial/owner-ship standards; demographic specifications, etc.) as well as what, if anything, the respondent can be told about the topic, or session, in advance. In addition the moderator should obtain confirmation that the recruiter will follow the accepted Recruiting Guidelines of the Qualitative Research Division.

B) To the Client

Rules of Conduct

7.3 When responsible for recruiting, the moderator must obtain agreement from the client regarding recruitment specifications, supervise the recruiting for the study and ensure that recruitment goals are met (or provide an explanation when they are not met).

7.4 *Unless otherwise agreed*, the client can assume that the moderator will listen to taped interviews, or work from "transcripts", when preparing the analysis.

7.5 Each report should include a standard statement emphasizing the non-projectability of the results. Specifically, reports should not include precise percentaged results unless it is made clear at that point in the report, that the result applied only to those respondents and is not necessarily true of the population at large; proportions may be used (e.g. one-third).

7.6 Each report should also contain a copy of the recruiting questionnaire and details of respondent qualifications together with a copy of the discussion outline, and, if possible, any materials used as stimuli during the interview.

7.7 All material relating to clients must remain confidential to persons wholly or substantially employed by the moderator, unless otherwise authorized by the client.

Unless authorized to do so by the client, the moderator should not reveal to recruiters or respondents nor any other person not directly concerned with the work of the study, the name of the client commissioning the study.

Good Practice

7.8   The moderator must ensure that the client understands the non-projectabil-ity of qualitative research to the population at large before embarking upon the project.

7.9   The moderator has responsibility to ensure that he has a clear understand-ing of the problem and the reasons why the research is being undertaken. A discussion outline should be provided for perusal by the client well in advance of the first session.

However, flexibility should be demonstrated when moderating the sessions in order to pursue areas which emerge as possibly meaningful but have not been included in the preliminary discussion outline.

The moderator should check with the client before dismissing the group to ensure no areas of special concern have been missed.

7.10   The moderator must remain objective and observe rigorous neutrality (except when playing the devil's advocate) while conducting the group session and when preparing the report/analysis.

VIII.   Other Responsibilities of the Client

Note: In some circumstances, the client may directly arrange for the recruiting. In such circumstances, the "client" is required to assume the responsibilities to the recruiter outlined in Sections 3.1 and 3.2.

Good Practice

8.1   *One* person at the *client* company should take responsibility for final liaison with the moderator.

8.2   The moderator should be given every opportunity to understand the prob-lems to be researched and should be included as early as possible in the planning stages of the project.

8.3   An outline of the research objectives and the immediate use to which the qualitative research learning will be put should be provided, in writing, for the moderator. This briefing document should be approved by *all* members of the client team before being given to the moderator.

It is helpful if key members of the client team (e.g. product managers, agency personnel as well as marketing research personnel) can be available for follow-up discussion of this briefing. Examples of all stimuli to be used (e.g. product, advertising, packaging, etc.) should ideally be available for review well in advance of the first interviewing sessions.

Specifications regarding the screening criteria should be agreed upon and, preferably, confirmed in writing.

8.4   Response to the moderator's suggested "discussion outline" should be provided as quickly as possible, to allow time for further discussion. The client should ensure that all issues currently under evaluation are included in the discussion outline.

8.5 The client has a responsibility, in agreeing to the proposed cost of the study, to ensure that the moderator understands:

i) whether a written analysis is required, and by what date

ii) whether the client expects to be given tape recordings of the proceedings

iii) whether the client requires transcripts of proceedings

iv) whether simultaneous translation is required for groups in a language other than English.

v) how many copies of the report/presentations of the results, etc., are required.

8.6 The client with resposibility for the study (See 8.1 above) should, wherever possible, watch all qualitative research sessions. Where this is impossible, the client should attend the first session so that the moderator can obtain clarification of any unexpected issues.

Clients watching qualitative research sessions should do so with appropriate seriousness and decorum.

APPENDIX

■ DEFINITIONS

1. "Research" refers to any examination or collection of information.

2. The term "respondent" refers to any individual, organization or group of persons to whom the practitioner approaches, either directly or indirectly, to collect information.

3. The term "interview" refers to any form of contact intended to generate information from a respondent (see #2 above).

4. The term "client" shall be understood to include any individual, organization, institution, department or division—including any belonging to the same organization as the practitioner—which is responsible for commissioning a research project.

5. The term "practitioner" shall be understood to include any individual, organization, department or division, including any belonging to the same organization as the "client" (see #4 above), which is responsible for or acts as a consultant on all or part of a research project.

6. An "overly-long questionnaire" may vary in length of time depending on variables such as subject matter, the number of open ended questions and the frequency of use of complex scales. As a general guideline, the following are generally considered "overly-long":

A personal interview in-home	over 60 minutes
A telephone interview	over 30 minutes
A mall-intercept interview	over 30 minutes

7. The term "proposal" refers to a practitioner submission that requires his recommendations as to technique, sampling or other design facets as well as a cost estimate.

8. The term "cost estimate" refers to a practitioner's submission that provides a cost estimate based on specifications provided by the client.

9. The term "primary records" refers to the most comprehensive record of information on which a research project is based e.g. completed questionnaires, taped recordings of interviews, etc.

10. The term "secondary records" is any record of information on which a research project is based apart from primary records (see #9 above) e.g. computer input, coding and editing instructions, etc.

11. The term "records" refers to both primary and secondary records collectively (see #9 and #10 above).

12. The term "verify" refers to the process of re-contacting an original respondent to confirm that the interview was in fact done and that selected aspects of the interview were carried out in the manner prescribed by the questionnaire and instructions.

13. The term "monitor" refers to the process of a supervisor listening to an interviewer interview a respondent.

ABRIDGED CAMRO STANDARDS

The following constitute standards by which all CAMRO members are bound:

■ Validation

a. Where No On Site Supervision Is Provided
   A minimum of 10% of each interviewer's work must be validated.

b. Where On Site Supervision Is Provided
   A minimum of 10% of all interviews conducted must be directly monitored.
   In the case of either a. or b., evidence of such validation must be kept on file for
   a minimum of 6 months.

c. Non-Validation
   In the event of non-validation of an interviewer's work, 100% of that interviewer's work must be either rejected or replaced.

d. Full Disclosure
   The method of validation, the proportions of work validated, and the responsibility for validations must be fully described in the report.

■ The Report

The report must include:

1. A full description of the sample, sample design, and its execution.

2. The results of the last attempt to make contact with each potential respondent,
   with the exception of those mall surveys and quota samples where it is not
   appropriate.

3. A copy of the questionnaire used.

4. Copies/descriptions of any exhibits used during the conduct of the interview.

5. Descriptions of any secondary source data used.

On request, the supplier must provide the client with the following:

1. When, how, and by whom, fieldwork was conducted.

2. Who tabulated the data.

3. Who processed the data.

Validation and report procedures must always be followed by a CAMRO member
unless explicitly agreed upon with the client. In the event of such agreement, a
failure to comply with CAMRO standards must be clearly stated in the report.

■ Interview I.D.

Personal Interviews–interviewers must carry company I.D. with expiry date. Telephone Interviews–research company must be identified at the start of the interview.

■ Audio/Visual Recording of Interviews

1. Not permitted without the knowledge of respondents.

2. If a one-way mirror is used in a group discussion, the participants must be made aware of this and the possibility that there may be viewers.

■ Confidentiality

1. The confidentiality of the respondent must be assured.

2. Except in the case of syndicated studies, the client is assured that his project is held in complete confidence by the research agency.

3. Market survey reports are normally for use within the client's own organization. If a wider circulation of the whole, or any part, of the report is required, the market research agency is entitled to be consulted and to approve the exact form of publication. Furthermore, if the client divulges the whole, or any part, of the report without prior authorization, the agency is then entitled to answer all bona fide enquiries about the survey they have conducted.

■ Storage and Disposal of Research Materials

The research organization shall be entitled to destroy original questionnaires 12 months after the end of field work, and other data forms (such as punched cards or tape) 24 months after the end of the field work without reference to the client. If the client wishes exceptions to this, he/she must make special arrangements with the research organization.

STATISTICAL TABLES

EXHIBIT A
Chi-square Distribution

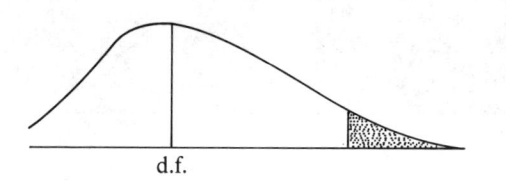

d.f.

The table below shows the shaded area.

DEGREES OF FREEDOM (d.f.)	CHI-SQUARE VALUES			
	PROBABILITY (P)			
	.10	.05	.02	.01
1	2.706	3.841	5.412	6.635
2	4.605	5.991	7.824	9.210
3	6.251	7.815	9.837	11.345
4	7.779	9.488	11.668	13.277
5	9.236	11.070	13.388	15.086
6	10.645	12.592	15.033	16.812
7	12.017	14.067	16.622	18.475
8	13.362	15.507	18.168	20.090
9	14.684	16.919	19.679	21.666
10	15.987	18.307	21.161	23.209
11	17.275	19.675	22.618	24.725
12	18.549	21.026	24.054	26.217
13	19.812	22.362	25.472	27.688
14	21.064	23.685	26.873	29.141
15	22.307	24.996	28.259	30.578
16	23.542	26.296	29.633	32.000
17	24.769	27.587	30.995	33.409
18	25.989	28.869	32.346	34.805
19	27.204	30.144	33.687	36.191
20	28.412	31.410	35.020	37.566
21	29.615	32.671	36.343	38.932
22	30.813	33.924	37.659	40.289
23	32.007	35.172	38.968	41.638
24	33.196	36.415	40.270	42.980
25	34.382	37.652	41.566	44.314
26	35.563	38.885	42.856	45.642
27	36.741	40.113	44.140	46.963
28	37.916	41.337	45.419	48.278
29	39.087	42.557	46.693	49.588
30	40.256	43.773	47.962	50.892

Source: Biometrika, 32 (1941), pp. 187–91. By permission of the Biometrika Trustees.

EXHIBIT B
Areas Under the Standard Normal Curve*

*Percentage figures are obtained by doubling
the entry. Example: If z is 1.96, double .475
for the 95% confidence level.

0   Z

z	0.00	0.01	0.02	0.03	0.04	0.05	0.06	0.07	0.08	0.09
0.0	0.0000	0.0040	0.0080	0.0120	0.0160	0.0199	0.0239	0.0279	0.0319	0.0359
0.1	.0398	.0438	.0478	.0517	.0557	.0596	.0636	.0675	.0714	.0753
0.2	.0793	.0832	.0871	.0910	.0948	.0987	.1026	.1064	.1103	.1141
0.3	.1179	.1217	.1255	.1293	.1331	.1368	.1406	.1443	.1480	.1517
0.4	.1554	.1591	.1628	.1664	.1700	.1736	.1772	.1808	.1844	.1879
0.5	.1915	.1950	.1985	.2019	.2054	.2088	.2123	.2157	.2190	.2224
0.6	.2257	.2291	.2324	.2357	.2389	.2422	.2454	.2486	.2517	.2549
0.7	.2580	.2611	.2642	.2673	.2704	.2734	.2764	.2794	.2823	.2852
0.8	.2881	.2910	.2939	.2967	.2995	.3023	.3051	.3078	.3106	.3133
0.9	.3159	.3186	.3212	.3238	.3264	.3289	.3315	.3340	.3365	.3389
1.0	.3413	.3438	.3461	.3485	.3508	.3531	.3554	.3577	.3599	.3621
1.1	.3643	.3665	.3686	.3708	.3729	.3749	.3770	.3790	.3810	.3830
1.2	.3849	.3869	.3888	.3907	.3925	.3944	.3962	.3980	.3997	.4015
1.3	.4032	.4049	.4066	.4082	.4099	.4115	.4131	.4147	.4162	.4177
1.4	.4192	.4207	.4222	.4236	.4251	.4265	.4279	.4292	.4306	.4319
1.5	.4332	.4345	.4357	.4370	.4382	.4394	.4406	.4418	.4429	.4441
1.6	.4452	.4463	.4474	.4484	.4495	.4505	.4515	.4525	.4535	.4545
1.7	.4554	.4564	.4573	.4582	.4591	.4599	.4608	.4616	.4625	.4633
1.8	.4641	.4649	.4656	.4664	.4671	.4678	.4686	.4693	.4699	.4706
1.9	.4713	.4719	.4726	.4732	.4738	.4744	.4750	.4756	.4761	.4767
2.0	.4772	.4778	.4783	.4788	.4793	.4798	.4803	.4808	.4812	.4817
2.1	.4821	.4826	.4830	.4834	.4838	.4842	.4846	.4850	.4854	.4857
2.2	.4861	.4864	.4868	.4871	.4875	.4878	.4881	.4884	.4887	.4890
2.3	.4893	.4896	.4898	.4901	.4904	.4906	.4909	.4911	.4913	.4916
2.4	.4918	.4920	.4922	.4925	.4927	.4929	.4931	.4932	.4934	.4936
2.5	.4938	.4940	.4941	.4943	.4945	.4946	.4948	.4949	.4951	.4952
2.6	.4953	.4955	.4956	.4957	.4959	.4960	.4961	.4962	.4963	.4964
2.7	.4965	.4966	.4967	.4968	.4969	.4970	.4971	.4972	.4973	.4974
2.8	.4974	.4975	.4976	.4977	.4977	.4978	.4979	.4979	.4980	.4981
2.9	.4981	.4982	.4982	.4983	.4984	.4984	.4985	.4985	.4986	.4986
3.0	.4987	.4987	.4987	.4988	.4988	.4989	.4989	.4989	.4990	.4990
3.1	.4990	.4991	.4991	.4991	.4992	.4992	.4992	.4992	.4993	.4993
3.2	.4993	.4993	.4994	.4994	.4994	.4994	.4994	.4995	.4995	.4995
3.3	.4995	.4995	.4995	.4996	.4996	.4996	.4996	.4996	.4996	.4997
3.4	.4997	.4997	.4997	.4997	.4997	.4997	.4997	.4997	.4997	.4998
3.6	.4998	.4998	.4999	.4999	.4999	.4999	.4999	.4999	.4999	.4999
3.9	.5000									

Source: Reprinted by permission from *Statistical Methods* by George W. Snedecor and
William G. Cochran, 7th ed., Ames, IA: Iowa State University Press, 1980.

EXHIBIT C
t-Distribution

$\dfrac{\alpha}{2}$ $\dfrac{\alpha}{2}$

Two-tail area (α)		.20	.10	.05	02	.01
d.f.	1	3.078	6.314	12.706	31.821	63.657
	2	1.886	2.920	4.303	6.965	9.925
	3	1.638	2.353	3.182	4.541	5.841
	4	1.533	2.132	2.776	3.747	4.604
	5	1.476	2.015	2.571	3.365	4.032
	6	1.440	1.943	2.447	3.143	3.707
	7	1.415	1.895	2.365	2.998	3.499
	8	1.397	1.860	2.306	2.896	3.355
	9	1.383	1.833	2.262	2.821	3.250
	10	1.372	1.812	2.228	2.764	3.169
	11	1.363	1.796	2.201	2.718	3.106
	12	1.356	1.782	2.179	2.681	3.055
	13	1.350	1.771	2.160	2.650	3.012
	14	1.345	1.761	2.145	2.624	2.977
	15	1.341	1.753	2.131	2.602	2.947
	16	1.337	1.746	2.120	2.583	2.921
	17	1.333	1.740	2.110	2.567	2.898
	18	1.330	1.734	2.101	2.552	2.878
	19	1.328	1.729	2.093	2.539	2.861
	20	1.325	1.725	2.086	2.528	2.845
	21	1.323	1.721	2.080	2.518	2.831
	22	1.321	1.717	2.074	2.508	2.819
	23	1.319	1.714	2.069	2.500	2.807
	24	1.318	1.711	2.064	2.492	2.797
	25	1.316	1.708	2.060	2.485	2.787
	26	1.315	1.706	2.056	2.479	2.779
	27	1.314	1.703	2.052	2.473	2.771
	28	1.313	1.701	2.048	2.467	2.763
	29	1.311	1.699	2.045	2.462	2.756
	30	1.310	1.697	2.042	2.457	2.750
	40	1.303	1.684	2.021	2.423	2.704
	60	1.296	1.671	2.000	2.390	2.660
	120	1.289	1.658	1.980	2.358	2.617
	α	1.282	1.645	1.960	2.326	2.576

Source: R. A. Fisher and F. Yates, *Statistical Tables for Biological, Agricultural and Medical Research.* London, England: Longman Group, Table III. Reproduced by permiccion.

EXHIBIT D
F-Distribution

V_2 = Degrees of Freedom Within Groups

$\alpha = .05$

V_1 = Degrees of Freedom Between Groups

	1	2	3	4	5	6	7	8	9	10	12	15
1	161.4	199.5	215.7	224.6	230.2	234.0	236.8	238.9	240.5	241.9	243.9	245.9
2	18.51	19.00	19.16	19.25	19.30	19.33	19.35	19.37	19.38	19.40	19.41	19.43
3	10.13	9.55	9.28	9.12	9.01	8.94	8.89	8.85	8.81	8.79	8.74	8.70
4	7.71	6.94	6.59	6.39	6.26	6.16	6.09	6.04	6.00	5.96	5.91	5.86
5	6.61	5.79	5.41	5.19	5.05	4.95	4.88	4.82	4.77	4.74	4.68	4.62
6	5.99	5.14	4.76	4.53	4.39	4.28	4.21	4.15	4.10	4.06	4.00	3.94
7	5.59	4.74	4.35	4.12	3.97	3.87	3.79	3.73	3.68	3.64	3.57	3.51
8	5.32	4.46	4.07	3.84	3.69	3.58	3.50	3.44	3.39	3.35	3.28	3.22
9	5.12	4.26	3.86	3.63	3.48	3.37	3.29	3.23	3.18	3.14	3.07	3.01
10	4.96	4.10	3.71	3.48	3.33	3.22	3.14	3.07	3.02	2.98	2.91	2.85
11	4.84	3.98	3.59	3.36	3.20	3.09	3.01	2.95	2.90	2.85	2.79	2.72
12	4.75	3.89	3.49	3.26	3.11	3.00	2.91	2.85	2.80	2.75	2.69	2.62
13	4.67	3.81	3.41	3.18	3.03	2.92	2.83	2.77	2.71	2.67	2.60	2.53
14	4.60	3.74	3.34	3.11	2.96	2.85	2.76	2.70	2.65	2.60	2.53	2.46

Continued on next page

V_2 = Degrees of Freedom Within Groups

V_1 = Degrees of Freedom Between Groups

	1	2	3	4	5	6	7	8	9	10	12	15
15	4.54	3.68	3.29	3.06	2.90	2.79	2.71	2.64	2.59	2.54	2.48	2.40
16	4.49	3.63	3.24	3.01	2.85	2.74	2.66	2.59	2.54	2.49	2.42	2.35
17	4.45	3.59	3.20	2.96	2.81	2.70	2.61	2.55	2.49	2.45	2.38	2.31
18	4.41	3.55	3.16	2.93	2.77	2.66	2.58	2.51	2.46	2.41	2.34	2.27
19	4.38	3.52	3.13	2.90	2.74	2.63	2.54	2.48	2.42	2.38	2.31	2.23
20	4.35	3.49	3.10	2.87	2.71	2.60	2.51	2.45	2.39	2.35	2.28	2.20
21	4.32	3.47	3.07	2.84	2.68	2.57	2.49	2.42	2.37	2.32	2.25	2.18
22	4.30	3.44	3.05	2.82	2.66	2.55	2.46	2.40	2.34	2.30	2.23	2.15
23	4.28	3.42	3.03	2.80	2.64	2.53	2.44	2.37	2.32	2.27	2.20	2.13
24	4.26	3.40	3.01	2.78	2.62	2.51	2.42	2.36	2.30	2.25	2.18	2.11
25	4.24	3.39	2.99	2.76	2.60	2.49	2.40	2.34	2.28	2.24	2.16	2.09
26	4.23	3.37	2.98	2.74	2.59	2.47	2.39	2.32	2.27	2.22	2.15	2.07
27	4.21	3.35	2.96	2.73	2.57	2.46	2.37	2.31	2.25	2.20	2.13	2.06
28	4.20	3.34	2.95	2.71	2.56	2.45	2.36	2.29	2.24	2.19	2.12	2.04
29	4.18	3.33	2.93	2.70	2.55	2.43	2.35	2.28	2.22	2.18	2.10	2.03
30	4.17	3.32	2.92	2.69	2.53	2.42	2.33	2.27	2.21	2.16	2.09	2.01
40	4.08	3.23	2.84	2.61	2.45	2.34	2.25	2.18	2.12	2.08	2.00	1.92
60	4.00	3.15	2.76	2.53	2.37	2.25	2.17	2.10	2.04	1.99	1.92	1.84
120	3.92	3.07	2.68	2.45	2.29	2.17	2.09	2.02	1.96	1.91	1.83	1.75
∞	3.84	3.00	2.60	2.37	2.21	2.10	2.01	1.94	1.88	1.83	1.75	1.67

V₁ = Degrees of Freedom Between Groups

α = .01

V₂ = Degrees of Freedom Within Groups	1	2	3	4	5	6	7	8	9	10	12	15
1	4052	4999.5	5403	5625	5764	5859	5928	5982	6022	6056	6105	6157
2	98.50	99.00	99.17	99.25	99.30	99.33	99.36	99.37	99.39	99.40	99.42	99.43
3	34.12	30.82	29.46	28.71	28.24	27.91	27.67	27.49	27.35	27.23	27.05	26.87
4	21.20	18.00	16.69	15.98	15.52	15.21	14.98	14.80	14.66	14.55	14.37	14.20
5	16.26	13.27	12.06	11.39	10.97	10.67	10.46	10.29	10.16	10.05	9.89	9.72
6	13.75	10.92	9.78	9.15	8.75	8.47	8.26	8.10	7.98	7.87	7.72	7.56
7	12.25	9.55	8.45	7.85	7.46	7.19	6.99	6.84	6.72	6.62	6.47	6.31
8	11.26	8.65	7.59	7.01	6.63	6.37	6.18	6.03	5.91	5.81	5.67	5.52
9	10.56	8.02	6.99	6.42	6.06	5.80	5.61	5.47	5.35	5.26	5.11	4.96
10	10.04	7.56	6.55	5.99	5.64	5.39	5.20	5.06	4.94	4.85	4.71	4.56
11	9.65	7.21	6.22	5.67	5.32	5.07	4.89	4.74	4.63	4.54	4.40	4.25
12	9.33	6.93	5.95	5.41	5.06	4.82	4.64	4.50	4.39	4.30	4.16	4.01
13	9.07	6.70	5.74	5.21	4.86	4.62	4.44	4.30	4.19	4.10	3.96	3.82
14	8.86	6.51	5.56	5.04	4.69	4.46	4.28	4.14	4.03	3.94	3.80	3.66
15	8.68	6.36	5.42	4.89	4.56	4.32	4.14	4.00	3.89	3.80	3.67	3.52
16	8.53	6.23	5.29	4.77	4.44	4.20	4.03	3.89	3.78	3.69	3.55	3.41
17	8.40	6.11	5.18	4.67	4.34	4.10	3.93	3.79	3.68	3.59	3.46	3.31
18	8.29	6.01	5.09	4.58	4.25	4.01	3.84	3.71	3.60	3.51	3.37	3.23
19	8.18	5.93	5.01	4.50	4.17	3.94	3.77	3.63	3.52	3.43	3.30	3.15

Continued on next page

Exhibit D continued

V₁ = Degrees of Freedom Between Groups

V₂ = Degrees of Freedom Within Groups	1	2	3	4	5	6	7	8	9	10	12	15
20	8.10	5.85	4.94	4.43	4.10	3.87	3.70	3.56	3.46	3.37	3.23	3.09
21	8.02	5.78	4.87	4.37	4.04	3.81	3.64	3.51	3.40	3.31	3.17	3.03
22	7.95	5.72	4.82	4.31	3.99	3.76	3.59	3.45	3.35	3.26	3.12	2.98
23	7.88	5.66	4.76	4.26	3.94	3.71	3.54	3.41	3.30	3.21	3.07	2.93
24	7.82	5.61	4.72	4.22	3.90	3.67	3.50	3.36	3.26	3.17	3.03	2.89
25	7.77	5.57	4.68	4.18	3.85	3.63	3.46	3.32	3.22	3.13	2.99	2.85
26	7.72	5.53	4.64	4.14	3.82	3.59	3.42	3.29	3.18	3.09	2.96	2.81
27	7.68	5.49	4.60	4.11	3.78	3.56	3.39	3.26	3.15	3.06	2.93	2.78
28	7.64	5.45	4.57	4.07	3.75	3.53	3.36	3.23	3.12	3.03	2.90	2.75
29	7.60	5.42	4.54	4.04	3.73	3.50	3.33	3.20	3.09	3.00	2.87	2.73
30	7.56	5.39	4.51	4.02	3.70	3.47	3.30	3.17	3.07	2.98	2.84	2.70
40	7.31	5.18	4.31	3.83	3.51	3.29	3.12	2.99	2.89	2.80	2.66	2.52
60	7.08	4.98	4.13	3.65	3.34	3.12	2.95	2.82	2.72	2.63	2.50	2.35
120	6.85	4.79	3.95	3.48	3.17	2.96	2.79	2.66	2.56	2.47	2.34	2.19
∞	6.63	4.61	3.78	3.32	3.02	2.80	2.64	2.51	2.41	2.32	2.18	2.04

Source: *Biometrika*, 33 (1943), pp. 72–88. By permission of the Biometrika Trustees.

EXHIBIT E Table of Random Numbers

49247	86161	39665	07642	82510	05142	29779	78284	49613	78059
14537	67342	43019	58647	62375	34485	15155	71344	17330	56304
23278	17916	43274	41386	60709	43007	74870	59634	27826	15880
64717	04117	31951	36419	43437	29325	37161	74701	27515	26832
26763	77539	35411	03525	92335	77480	23169	44641	38202	79443
13543	02008	67206	92136	13164	91382	44794	40309	89437	55900
90830	19471	49841	07676	04022	46793	06601	71951	32297	05342
73312	72642	19307	40996	55535	6078	85232	10841	63898	46210
03348	15094	78330	02479	02368	79372	77140	09051	94062	50386
91310	28918	95858	32861	40482	40281	62468	64111	90656	81837
94390	87875	74118	41338	68749	95125	42232	67329	43431	90882
41815	09913	91111	13032	38778	34917	66416	34106	62274	63401
50222	64057	95081	92939	78864	39811	73793	00839	93186	21525
07772	69782	84817	08418	39206	14419	10551	11832	20611	39221
06265	78969	98329	50734	01814	88935	95866	04626	33536	09212
98068	03532	16355	36259	37501	74580	12075	97459	79209	58582
26718	86935	01361	34346	20663	18291	34368	12553	48627	10849
53690	62562	63124	70007	57664	41684	30771	58016	11177	19068
90319	80880	86384	14087	20431	38026	64323	18995	70717	81751
50485	37028	93309	53839	71247	18470	66960	05119	75119	29088
11363	91479	68259	59812	41275	65118	22925	20692	11221	62541
26866	03114	95241	35622	63067	99767	53623	56851	53857	85544
20536	90545	79192	48657	52126	09961	28603	91649	72907	90465
75899	63319	52743	23558	15608	49089	48424	32966	22027	20687
09600	09198	17034	78646	04959	92237	66182	14194	73665	17599
03985	25593	54991	29602	44277	10983	57464	93459	40050	96359
94752	47444	33575	78080	75399	31543	20491	04181	88253	38853
43789	38797	24531	98985	87911	39385	16455	47868	48264	49642
03124	98417	70412	74476	33457	83122	78514	11300	68931	68475
13959	85567	56353	64626	69669	19117	89275	39294	16478	61819
64957	86587	16738	83468	83536	01068	78923	25834	05492	74330
59221	54716	71479	35122	06666	07998	55727	04467	97981	57769
95233	87652	61470	12733	88273	76819	70794	86935	09729	88615
67644	16683	99041	61690	77416	18003	72410	86383	96835	91406
68690	79225	71625	04859	50011	98882	71933	94552	32095	48784
20478	62525	98481	10511	98528	88951	75130	22239	57977	34546
83557	07315	81820	51138	43900	49072	36493	40352	77397	84647
50106	44769	22064	04943	79304	23440	05667	45032	07122	87887
08611	20434	47615	68550	90670	17948	00551	68995	22452	70189
14078	26664	90599	70403	44291	88886	52363	44399	98895	99946
58775	95672	28974	77707	26967	81569	81356	16411	08935	60588
15704	16371	65841	38968	08756	21519	14924	51467	59967	00638
26043	68366	37371	54661	41287	10260	52004	90992	73520	42621
94834	02497	09060	31510	11761	14032	05177	82248	16444	74515
15434	87504	40004	39532	16039	69272	62712	58679	58027	00254

■ Author Index

■ Subject Index